15.000

Nuevo
DICCIONARIO
REVISADO
Appleton-Cuyás
ESPAÑOL-INGLÉS
INGLÉS-ESPAÑOL

The New REVISED
Appleton-Cuyás
SPANISH-ENGLISH
ENGLISH-SPANISH
DICTIONARY

...to
...re

Second Edition

 Prentice Hall General Reference
15 Columbus Circle
New York, NY 10023

A Prentice Hall Book

Library of Congress Cataloging-in-Publication Data

Cuyás, Arturo
   The new revised Appleton-Cuyás dictionary.
   ISBN 0-13-472820-3
     1. Spanish language—Dictionaries—English.
2. English language—Dictionaries—Spanish.   I. Title.
PC4640.C8 1982 463'.21 81-15816
                    AACR2

Manufactured in the United States of America

15   16   17   18   19   20

CONTENTS

PART I
SPANISH-ENGLISH

PARTE II
INGLÉS-ESPAÑOL

PREFACE

Few prefatory remarks are necessary in presenting *The New Appleton-Cuyás Dictionary*. It is an offspring of *Appleton's Spanish-English English-Spanish Dictionary* by Arturo Cuyás, a work whose reputation is solidly established in both the English- and Spanish-speaking worlds. It is based on the Fourth Edition of that work, as revised and enlarged by Dr. Lewis E. Brett and Miss Helen S. Eaton. The same exacting scientific standards that characterized the work of Don Arturo Cuyás and Dr. Brett and Miss Eaton have been followed in the long, detailed and careful compilation of the present dictionary.

The New Appleton-Cuyás Dictionary is intended for those general students of Spanish or English whose needs do not warrant the acquisition of as exhaustive a dictionary as the large Cuyás. It is also designed for college students, translators, businessmen, travelers, social workers, and others who, although they may already own the parent Cuyás, also require a smaller book that can be carried around for ready consultation on the spot. The main objective in the preparation of this portable dictionary has been to offer, concisely and effectively, as much matter from the parent dictionary as is compatible with the aims and size of the new work. Within its scope, this dictionary answers the basic expressional needs in every capital field of human endeavor and covers all levels of accepted usage in both tongues. We believe that because of efficient condensation of definitions and thrifty use of space, *The New Appleton-Cuyás* offers a greater number of principal and subsidiary terms than any other dictionary of similar size.

In the selection of lexical matter judicious use has been made of all frequency counts and lists of words and idioms available in both languages. Terms and expressions of high oral and written incidence that appear in the parent work have been included in the present dictionary. New, up-to-date words and phrases have been added. The criterion for selection of entries has been the standard, educated use in both languages. For standard usage of Spanish on the American continents, the dictionaries of Santamaría and Malaret were duly consulted, among other sources of reference. In the Spanish vocabulary, the western hemisphere currency of word and idiom has been properly indicated, thus: (Am.) for general continental usage, and (Mex.), (Arg.), etc., for those of only regional validity.

We call the attention of the reader to the following special, useful features, seldom encountered together in portable dictionaries: lists of cardinal, ordinal, and fractional numbers; complete tables of irregular verbs; clear and simple keys to speech sounds; tables of weights and measures; thermometer equivalences; abbreviations in common usage; and lists of proper and geographical names.

We were indeed fortunate to have as direct collaborators in this endeavor Professor Alberto Andino, formerly of the University of Las Villas, Cuba, Dr. Fernando Figueredo, formerly a distinguished member of the Cuban Bar Association, and Mr. Bernard Witlieb, a lexicographer who holds an A.M. degree from New York University; and none the less fortunate in having at all moments the wise and experienced counsel in editorial matters of Miss Catherine B. Avery, of the staff of Appleton-Century-Crofts.

E.G.D.

New York University
New York

ADVICE TO THE USER

1. *Arrangement.* In order to save space and make our dictionary richer in entries, we have grouped together families of words closely related in origin and meaning or in spelling, whenever this arrangement did not interfere with alphabetical order. For further saving of space, the common parts of words of the same family have been omitted. The omitted part is always referred to the head entry of the group. All main entries are in boldface type. Idioms and expressions within entries are italicized and alphabetized by the first word. In definitions, semicolons are used to separate different areas of meaning; commas for synonyms within areas. The user must be aware that the Spanish alphabet is different from its English counterpart: ch, ll, and ñ are independent letters; therefore, all words or syllables beginning with ch, ll, or ñ come after c, l, and n, respectively—thus, **fecha** follows **fecundo**, **ella** follows **eludir** and **añadido** follows **anzuelo**.

2. *Gender of Nouns.* In the Spanish-English section the gender of Spanish nouns is indicated as follows: *m.* for nouns that are exclusively masculine (ex., **hombre, banco, buey, sofá, amor**), *f.* for nouns that are only feminine (ex., **mujer, casa, fe, libertad, costumbre**), *mf.* for those which have a masculine and a feminine meaning without change in form (ex., **artista, amante, testigo**), and *n.* for those which have a masculine form ending in *o* and a corresponding feminine form ending in *a* (ex., **obrero, abogado**), in which case only the masculine form is entered. Nouns having a gender inflexion different from the above are listed separately for the masculine and feminine (ex., **actor, actriz**).

3. *Diminutives.* Diminutives are entered only when they have special meanings or when they have become nouns in their own right (ex., **aherita, cucharilla, ventanilla, portezuela**).

4. *Verbs.* All irregular verbs are identified by the abbreviations *vti., vii., vri.,* and *vsi.* The numbers and letters in brackets next to the abbreviations refer to the *Table of Irregular Verbs* on page iii.

5. *Adverbs.* All Spanish adverbs of manner are formed by adding *-mente* to the feminine singular form of the corresponding adjective (ex., **rápido: rápida, rápidamente**). Only those Spanish adverbs not conforming to the above or whose meaning does not correspond to their English cognates are entered.

6. *Abbreviations.* All abbreviations used to indicate limitations of range, geographic or otherwise (ex., *Mex.*, Mexico; *aer.*, aeronautics; *med.*, medicine), are fully identified in the list of *Abbreviations used in Part II* on page xxxi.

7. *Pronunciation.* Spanish being a quasi-phonetic language, the transcription of each individual word has been considered unnecessary. A clear, simple explanation of approximate English equivalents of Spanish phonemes is given on page v.

8. *Accentuation.* Words ending in a vowel, *n*, or *s* are stressed in the next to the last syllable (ex., **casa, comen, puertas.**) Words ending in a consonant other than *n* or *s* are stressed in the last syllable (ex., **comprar, atroz, paste!**). Stresses that do not follow these two rules are indicated by a written acute accent (ex., **árbol, acción, rápido.**)

SPANISH PRONUNCIATION

I. Vowels

Approximate English Equivalents

a About midway between the *a* in *father* and the *a* in *cat*.

e About midway between the *a* in *hate* and the *e* in *bet*.

i Very like the *i* in *machine* or the *ee* in *teeth*.

o Somewhat similar to the *o* in *note* or the *o* in *or*.

Approximate English Equivalents

u Very close to the *oo* in *moon* or the *u* in *rule*. It is always silent after *q* and also after *g*, unless marked with dieresis (ex., *vergüenza*).

y It is a vowel when standing alone or at the end of a word, and as such it is pronounced as *i* above.

II. Consonants

b As in English but slightly softer at the beginning of a word or when preceded by *m* or *n*. Between vowels or preceded by a vowel and followed by *l* or *r* it is pronounced without the lips coming into complete contact.

c Before *e* or *i* it has the sound of the *th* of *think* in the Castilian speech of Spain. In the popular speech of many parts of Spain and in all Spanish America it is pronounced like the English *s* in *say*. Before *a*, *o* and *u* and at the end of a syllable or a word it is always like the English *k* in *key*.

ch It is considered a single letter and always pronounced like the *ch* in *church*.

d Similar to English *d* in *dance*. Between vowels or at the end of a word it has the sound of the English *th* in *mother*.

f As English *f*.

g Before *a*, *o* and *u* or preceding a consonant it is like the *g* in *go*. Before *e* and *i* it sounds like the *ch* in the Scottish word *loch*.

h Always silent.

j Like *g* above before *e* or *i*.

l As English *l*.

ll Treated like a single letter. Sounds very close to the *lli* in *million* or in *brilliant* in the Castilian speech of Spain. In many parts of Spain and in most of Spanish America it is pronounced like the *y* in *yet*.

m As English *m*.

n As English *n* but before *b* or *v* it is sounded like an *m*.

ñ It sounds very similar to the *ny* in *canyon* or the *ni* in *onion*.

p As in English but somewhat softer.

q Occurs only in the combinations *que*, *qui* in which the *u* is silent. It has the sound of the English *k* in *key*.

r At the beginning of a word or preceded by *l*, *n*, or *s* it is strongly rolled. Otherwise it is pronounced with a single touch of the tongue.

rr It is treated as a single letter, and it is strongly trilled.

s Like the English *s* in *see*.

t Similar to the English *t* but less explosive.

v Same as *b* above.

x Sounds like *ks* or *gs* when placed between vowels. When followed by a consonant it is pronounced as the English *s* in *same*.

y (See Vowels above.) Preceding a vowel it is similar to the English *y* in *year*.

z In Castile it is pronounced like the *th* of *thick*. In many parts of Spain and in all Spanish America it sounds like the English *s* in *case*.

SYNOPSIS OF SPANISH GRAMMAR

I. GENERAL REMARKS

The Spanish alphabet consists of 28 separate symbols, compared to the 26 letters of the English alphabet. Ch, ll, and ñ are distinct symbols and occupy separate places in the alphabet, following c, l and n respectively. The w of the English alphabet is not a part of the Spanish alphabet. Rr, though considered a separate symbol, does not occupy a separate place in the Spanish alphabet. The double consonants in Spanish are cc and nn. Each letter or symbol has a fixed pronunciation that is, under clearly defined rules, invariable. There is no gliding or blending of sounds, as in English, nor do changes occur in the pronunciations of the same letters when they appear in different words, as is so often the case in English. (See pp. v-xvi SPANISH PRONUNCIATION, for a description of the pronunciation of individual Spanish letters and combinations of letters.) The differences between the Spanish of Spain and that of other Spanish-speaking countries consist in minor variations of pronunciation and in additions to the vocabulary that arise from geographical location and ethnic background.

A written accent over a vowel indicates that the syllable containing the vowel is accented, as: lápiz (*pencil*), biología (*biology*), automóvil (*automobile*), termómetro (*thermometer*), condición (*condition*). When a syllable is added to a word that has no written accent, as in forming certain plurals, a written accent may be added to show retention of the original stress, as: germen, gérmenes; virgen, vírgenes. Words without a written accent and ending in a vowel, -n or -s, have the accent on the next to the last syllable. Accordingly, certain words that add a syllable in the plural or in forming the feminine, drop the written accent, as: condición, condiciones; japonés, japonesa. All other words are accented on the last syllable.

There are three genders in Spanish: masculine, feminine and neuter.

Capital letters are used in Spanish as in English, with the following exceptions:

a) the subject pronouns yo, usted and ustedes are not capitalized except at the beginning of a sentence, or when usted and ustedes are abbreviated, as they usually are. Vd. and Vds. are commonly used abbreviations for usted and ustedes respectively.

b) names of months and days of the week are masculine and are not capitalized;

El sábado, 17 de julio *Saturday, July 17*

Only sábado (*Saturday*) and domingo (*Sunday*) of the days of the week have plural forms;

c) adjectives formed from proper nouns are not capitalized, even when used as nouns, as: los españoles (*the Spaniards*);

d) titles spelled out (señor, señora, señorita, don, doña) are not capitalized except when they begin a sentence. When these titles are abbreviated, they are capitalized (Sr., Sra., Srta., D., Da.);

e) book and film titles are not capitalized except for the first word and proper names;

La verdad sospechosa
El capitán veneno

Punctuation in Spanish is much the same as in English, except that the Spanish add an inverted question mark and an inverted exclamation point before a question and an exclamation respectively.

¿Qué cosa quiere? *What does he want?*
¡Fuego! *Fire!*

II. PARTS OF SPEECH

A. Articles

1. The indefinite articles in Spanish are un, una, unos and unas. They agree in gender and number with the nouns and are generally repeated before each noun.

un libro (masculine)	*a book*
un ojo (masculine)	*an eye*
una pluma (feminine)	*a pen*
una manzana (feminine)	*an apple*
unos muchachos (masculine)	*some boys*
unas pinturas (feminine)	*some paintings*
Tengo un coche, una casa y una televisión	*I have a car, house and television*

It is not necessary to use the indefinite article in the following cases:

a) when denoting a quantity, as: otro (*another*), medio (*half*), cien, ciento (*a, one hundred*), and mil (*a, one thousand*);

Hay cien soldados aquí	*There are a hundred soldiers here*
Necesito otro lápiz	*I need another pencil*

b) when a predicate noun is unmodified;

Juan es médico	*John is a doctor*

c) when the meaning of one is obvious;

Lleva abrigo	*He is wearing a coat*

2. The definite articles in Spanish are el, los, la, las and the neuter form lo. Every Spanish noun has its corresponding article. The article appears in conjunction with the noun in most cases and agrees with it in gender and number.

el libro (masculine)	*the book*
la pluma (feminine)	*the pen*
los muchachos (masculine)	*the boys*
las pinturas (feminine)	*the paintings*
lo útil (neuter)	*the useful*
Los libros, los lápices y la pluma están en la mesa	*The books, pencils and pen are on the desk*
El señor Martínez está enfermo	*Mr. Martin is ill*
Vende los huevos a veinte centavos la docena	*He sells eggs at twenty cents a dozen*
Va a la iglesia los domingos	*He goes to church on Sundays*
El año que viene	*Next year*
Es la una	*It is one o'clock*

The definite article is not generally used with **mediodía** (*noon*) and **media-noche** (*midnight*).

Es medianoche	*It is midnight*

The definite article **el** replaces **la** before feminine nouns beginning with stressed **a** or **ha**.

El agua está fría	*The water is cold*

El following the preposition **a** contracts to **al**.

Juan va al taller	*John is going to the shop*

El following the preposition **de** contracts to **del**.

Él lleva el abrigo del padre	*He is wearing his father's coat*

The neuter form **lo** is used with an adjective to form a noun.

Lo importante es estudiar mucho	*The important thing is to study a great deal*

The definite article is not used:
a) with **don** and **doña**;

Doña María está aquí	*Madam Mary is here*

b) when speaking directly to a person;

¿Cómo está Vd., señor Martínez?	*How are you, Mr. Martin?*

c) when the noun is preceded by a possessive or demonstrative pronoun or adjective;

Este libro es negro	*This book is black*

d) before a numeral in a title.

Carlos Quinto	*Charles the Fifth*

B. Nouns

1. Spanish nouns are masculine or feminine or have one form for both genders; there are no neuter nouns. Nouns ending in -o are usually masculine. Nouns ending in -dad, -ción and -sión are feminine. Nouns ending in -a, -ie, -ud and -umbre are usually feminine. The gender is indicated in the vocabulary of this dictionary.

2. The plural of Spanish nouns is generally formed by adding -s to the singular of those that end in an unaccented vowel, and -es to those that end in an accented vowel or a consonant. Those ending in -z change the -z to -c and add -es. Some nouns (generally those ending in -s in the singular) have the same form for both the singular and the plural.

SINGULAR		PLURAL	
la casa	*house*	las casas	*houses*
la decisión	*decision*	las decisiones	*decisions*
la dificultad	*difficulty*	las dificultades	*difficulties*
el libro	*book*	los libros	*books*
la raíz	*root*	las raíces	*roots*
el lápiz	*pencil*	los lápices	*pencils*
el paraguas	*umbrella*	los paraguas	*umbrellas*

The masculine plural is used to indicate both masculine and feminine when both genders are included collectively.

Mis primos	*My cousins*
Mis hermanos	*My brothers and sisters*

C. Adjectives

1. Adjectives agree in gender and number with the nouns they modify and generally, but not necessarily, follow the noun. Those that end in -o are generally masculine; those that end in -a are generally feminine. An adjective ending in -o changes -o to -a to form the feminine and adds an -s to form the plural.

la casa roja	*the red house*
el libro rojo	*the red book*
las casas rojas	*the red houses*
los libros rojos	*the red books*

Some adjectives have only one ending and are both masculine and feminine.

una situación artificial	*an artificial situation*
un satélite artificial	*an artificial satellite*
un pintor modernista	*a modernistic painter*
las tendencias modernistas	*modernistic tendencies*

Some adjectives lose their masculine singular ending when preceding the noun they modify.

el buen hombre	*the good man*
el primer piso	*the first floor*
un mal paso	*a false step*

2. *Comparison of adjectives.* The comparative and superlative degrees of adjectives in Spanish are formed by placing más (*more*) or menos (*less*), for the comparative degree, and el más (*most*) or el menos (*least*), for the superlative degree, before the positive form of the adjective.

POSITIVE		COMPARATIVE		SUPERLATIVE	
bonito	*pretty*	más bonito	*prettier*	el más bonito	*prettiest*
feliz	*happy*	más feliz	*happier*	el más feliz	*happiest*
listo	*clever*	menos listo	*less clever*	el menos listo	*least clever*

Comparisons employing que (*than*) as a conjunction are expressed by más (or menos) . . . que.

Hablo más despacio que él   *I speak slower than he*
Este libro es menos interesante que   *This book is less interesting than that one* ése

Comparisons employing tan (*as*) are expressed by tan . . . como.
Mi casa es tan grande como la   *My house is as big as yours* tuya

In Spanish there is an absolute superlative which is formed by placing muy (*very*) before the adjective, or by adding the endings -ísimo or -érrimo to the positive degree of the adjective. These endings are not equivalent to the -est of English superlatives. They have an intensive force and are translated by *very* or *extremely* followed by the adjective.

POSITIVE		COMPARATIVE	
hermoso	*beautiful*	más hermoso	*more beautiful*
difícil	*difficult*	más difícil	*more difficult*
célebre	*famous*	más célebre	*more famous*

SUPERLATIVE		ABSOLUTE SUPERLATIVE	
el más hermoso	*most beautiful*	muy hermoso	*very beautiful*
		hermosísimo	*extremely beautiful*
el más difícil	*most difficult*	muy difícil	*very difficult*
		dificilísimo	*extremely difficult*
el más célebre	*most famous*	celebérrimo	*extremely famous*

The comparison of some adjectives is irregular.

POSITIVE		COMPARATIVE		SUPERLATIVE	
bueno	*good*	mejor	*better*	el mejor	*best*
grande	*big, great*	más grande	*bigger, greater*	el más grande	*biggest, greatest*
		mayor	*greater, older*	el mayor	*greatest, oldest*
malo	*bad*	peor	*worse*	el peor	*worst*
pequeño	*small*	más pequeño	*smaller*	el más pequeño	*smallest*
		menor	*smaller, younger*	el menor	*smallest, youngest*

3. *Possessive adjectives.* Like all adjectives in Spanish, the possessive adjectives agree in number and gender with the nouns they modify. The Spanish possessive adjectives are:

SINGULAR		PLURAL
mi	*my*	mis
tu	*your*	tus
su	*his, her, your, its*	sus
nuestro	*our*	nuestros
vuestro	*your*	vuestros
su	*their, your*	sus

D. Adverbs. As in English, Spanish adverbs modify a verb, an adjective or another adverb. Many adverbs are formed by adding -mente to the feminine singular form of the adjective.

ADJECTIVE		ADVERB	
clara	*clear*	claramente	*clearly*
rápida	*rapid*	rápidamente	*rapidly*

The comparative and superlative degrees of adverbs are formed in the same manner as the comparative and superlative degrees of adjectives, but the superlative degree of adverbs is seldom used.

POSITIVE		COMPARATIVE		SUPERLATIVE	
claramente	*clearly*	más claramente	*more clearly*	el más claramente	*most clearly*
rápidamente	*rapidly*	más rápidamente	*more rapidly*	el más rápidamente	*most rapidly*

The comparison of some adverbs is irregular.

POSITIVE		COMPARATIVE		SUPERLATIVE	
bien	*well*	mejor	*better*	mejor	*best*
mal	*bad*	peor	*worse*	peor	*worst*
mucho	*much*	más	*more*	más	*most*
poco	*little*	menos	*less*	menos	*least*

E. Pronouns

1. *Personal pronouns.* Personal pronouns serve as subjects, direct objects of a verb, indirect objects of a verb, and possessives. In Spanish, the verb ending indicates the subject. It is therefore unnecessary to use a subject pronoun with the verb, unless clarity or emphasis is desired. *It*, when used as a subject, is never translated. The third person, usted, **Vd.** and ustedes, **Vds.**, (*you*), is generally used when addressing persons. The second person singular or plural (the *you* of English) is the familiar form in Spanish and is limited in use. The following table lists personal pronouns used as the subject and as the direct object of a verb.

SUBJECT			DIRECT OBJECT	
1st person	yo	*I*	me	*me*
2nd person	tú	*you*	te	*you*
3rd person	él	*he*	lo	*him*
	ella	*she*	la	*her*
	usted, Vd.	*you*	lo, la	*him, her*
	ello	*it* (seldom used)	lo	*it*

PLURAL

1st person	nosotros	*we*	nos	*us*
2nd person	vosotros	*you*	os	*you*
3rd person	ellos	*they*	los	*them*
	ellas	*they*	las	*them*
	ustedes, Vds.	*you*	los, las	*them*

Direct object pronouns follow, and are attached to, an infinitive, a present participle, or a verb in the affirmative command.

Él quiere traerlo después	*He wants to bring it later*
Estoy buscándola	*I am looking for her*
Hágalo ahora	*Do it now*

In other cases, they are placed before the verb.

Nos llamaron ayer	*They called us yesterday*

Indirect object pronouns are placed in the same order in a sentence as direct object pronouns. The indirect object pronouns are:

	SINGULAR		PLURAL	
1st person	me	*to me*	nos	*to us*
2nd person	te	*to you*	os, vos	*to you*
3rd person	le, se	*to him, her, you*	les	*to them, you*

Se as a 3rd person indirect object pronoun should not be confused with the reflexive se. Since le and se mean *to him, to her* or *to you*, it may be necessary in a sentence to add a clarifying phrase, a él, a ella, or a Vd. Possessive pronouns agree in gender and number with the object possessed. They are as follows:

SINGULAR		PLURAL	
el mío	*mine*	los míos	
la mía	*mine*	las mías	
el tuyo	*yours*	los tuyos	
la tuya	*yours*	las tuyas	
el suyo	*his*	los suyos	
la suya	*hers*	las suyas	
el nuestro	*ours*	los nuestros	
la nuestra	*ours*	las nuestras	
el vuestro	*yours*	los vuestros	
la vuestra	*yours*	las vuestras	
el suyo	*theirs*	los suyos	
la suya	*theirs*	las suyas	

Éste es mi libro y ése es el suyo *This is my book and that one is yours*
(de Vd.)

2. *Relative pronouns.* Relative pronouns refer to nouns or pronouns that are antecedents in a sentence, and may be the subject or the object of a verb. The most common relative pronouns are:

que	*which, that, who, whom, when*
cual	*which, as, such as*
quien	*who whom, whoever, whomever, which, whichever*
cuyo	*whose, of which, of whom, whereof*

Que and cual are used without distinction as to gender. Que refers to persons or things and may be the subject or the object of a verb; it has no plural.

El hombre que vino a comer	*The man who came to dinner*
El hombre que vimos es mi hermano	*The man whom we saw is my brother*

The prepositons **a**, **de** and **en** are used with **que** when referring to things.

El cine delante del que . . .	*The movie in front of which . . .*

Lo que and lo cual are used when referring to a clause or an idea.

No comió esta mañana, lo que me sorprendió	*He didn't eat this morning, which surprised me*

The following are interchangeable forms; the article indicates gender.

el que	*who, whom, which*	el cual
la que		la cual
los que		los cuales
las que		las cuales

Quien is both masculine and feminine. In both its singular (**quien**) and plural (**quienes**) forms, it may serve as the object of a preposition.

La muchacha con quien fue al cine está aquí	*The girl with whom he went to the movies is here*

Quien is sometimes used in the singular with a plural antecedent. Cuyo has masculine (**cuyo**), feminine (**cuya**) and plural (**cuyos**, **cuyas**) forms, and agrees in gender and number with its antecedent.

3. *Demonstrative pronouns.* Demonstrative pronouns specify particular persons or objects and indicate their relative distance from the speaker or from the person addressed. Demonstrative pronouns become demonstrative adjectives when preceding a noun and are written without an accent.

DEMONSTRATIVE PRONOUNS			DEMONSTRATIVE ADJECTIVES	
SINGULAR	PLURAL		SINGULAR	PLURAL
éste (m.)	éstos	*this, these*, near speaker	este	estos
ésta (f.)	éstas		esta	estas
esto (neut.)				
ése (m.)	ésos	*that, those,*	ese	esos
ésa (f.)	ésas	near person	esa	esas
eso (neut.)		addressed		
aquél (m.)	aquéllos	*that, those,* away	aquel	aquellos
aquélla (f.)	aquéllas	from speaker	aquella	aquellas
aquello (neut.)		and addressee		

The neuter forms, **esto**, **eso** and **aquello** carry no accent and are used to refer to some general idea or to an object not yet identified.

tal	tales	*such, such a one, such things*
tanto	tantos	*that*

Tal and tanto are adjectives as well as pronouns and carry no accent as either.

4. *Indefinite Pronouns.* Indefinite pronouns have the same function in Spanish as in English. They are:

alguien	*somebody, someone*
nadie	*nobody, no one, none*
cualquiera	*any one*
quienquiera	*whoever*
algo	*some*
nada	*nothing*

Alguien, nadie, algo and **nada** have the same form for the masculine and feminine. They have no plural forms. Other parts of speech may also act as indefinite pronouns, among these are the interrogatives **cuál** (*which*) and **quién** (*who*), the demonstrative pronoun **tal** (*such a*), and the adjectives **alguno** (*some*), **ninguno** (*none*), **todo** (*all*), **mucho** (*many*), **demasiado** (*too much, too many*), **bastante** (*sufficient, enough*), **harto** (*sufficient*), and **poco** (*few*).

F. Interrogatives. Interrogatives in Spanish always carry an accent. Some common interrogatives are.

¿qué?	*what? which?*	¿cuándo?	*when?*
¿quién?	*who? whom?*	¿cómo?	*how?*
¿de quién?	*whose?*	¿dónde?	*where?*
¿cuál	*which one?*	¿adónde?	*to where?*
¿cuánto?	*how much?*	¿por qué?	*why?*

Quién, cuál and **cuánto** have the plural forms **quiénes, cuáles** and **cuántos,** and are used as pronouns. The other interrogatives have no plural form. **Qué** may be used as an adjective or a pronoun and may refer to either persons or things.

G. Verbs. Verbs in Spanish are regular, radical-changing, orthographic-changing, and irregular in their conjugations. The following remarks describe some of the more important characteristics of verbs and their conjugations. A table of model conjugations of regular, radical-changing, orthographic-changing and irregular verbs at the end of this section.

1. Many verbs require a preposition before an infinitive. Some of the most common are:

a) those that require the preposition **a;**

acertar	*to manage, succeed*	enviar	*to send*
acostumbrarse	*to accustom oneself, get used to*	invitar	*to invite*
acudir	*to come to, resort to*	ir	*to go*
aprender	*to learn*	llegar	*to arrive*
apresurarse	*to hasten*	negarse	*to refuse*
atreverse	*to dare*	obligar	*to compel*
ayudar	*to help*	pasar	*to pass, go by*
bajar	*to come down*	persuadir	*to persuade*
comenzar	*to begin*	ponerse	*to start*
correr	*to run*	proceder	*to proceed*
disponerse	*to prepare*	subir	*to go up*
echar(se	*to start*	tornar	*to return, turn*
empezar	*to begin*	venir	*to come*
enseñar	*to teach*	volar	*to fly*
entrar	*to enter*	volver	*to return, do again*

b) those that require the preposition **de;**

acabar	*to finish, conclude*	dejar	*to discontinue, leave*
acordarse	*to remember*	encargarse	*to undertake, take on oneself*
alegrarse	*to be glad*	extrañarse	*to be surprised*
avergonzarse	*to be ashamed*	gozar	*to enjoy*
cesar	*to cease*	olvidarse	*to forget*
concluir	*to conclude, finish*	tratar	*to try*

Acabar de is also used to mean *to have just.*

Acabo de llegar a Nueva York   *I have just come to New York*

c) those that require the preposition **en;**

acordar	*to agree*	pensar	*to think*
complacerse	*to take pleasure*	persistir	*to persist*
consentir	*to consent*	quedar	*to agree, decide*
empeñarse	*to persist, insist*	tardar	*to be slow, delay*
insistir	*to insist*	vacilar	*to hesitate*

d) those that require the preposition **con.**

contar	*to count on, rely*
soñar	*to dream*

2. The infinitive of the verb is sometimes used as a noun, and often takes **el** in this case.

El estudiar es difícil   *Studying is difficult*

The infinitive follows most common verbs (**poder, saber, desear, esperar,** etc.) without a preposition, but some verbs require a preposition before the infinitive, see above.

3. The present participle (gerund) is formed by adding **-ando** to the stem of verbs whose infinitives end in **-ar**, and **-iendo** to the stem of verbs whose infinitives end in **-er** and **-ir.**

INFINITIVE		PRESENT PARTICIPLE
hablar	*to speak*	hablando
comer	*to eat*	comiendo
vivir	*to live*	viviendo

Some verbs having an irregular form of the present participle are:

INFINITIVE	PRESENT PARTICIPLE	INFINITIVE	PRESENT PARTICIPLE
caer	cayendo	oír	oyendo
corregir	corrigiendo	pedir	pidiendo
creer	creyendo	poder	pudiendo
decir	diciendo	seguir	siguiendo
divertirse	divirtiéndose	sentir	sintiendo
dormir	durmiendo	servir	sirviendo
ir	yendo	traer	trayendo
leer	leyendo	venir	viniendo

The present participle is used with some tense of **estar** to form a progressive tense.

Estoy hablando   *I am speaking*

4. The past participle is formed by adding **-ado** to the stem of verbs whose infinitives end in **-ar**, and **-ido** to the stem of verbs whose infinitives end in **-er** and **-ir.**

INFINITIVE	PAST PARTICIPLE
hablar	hablado
comer	comido
vivir	vivido

Some verbs having an irregular form of the past participle are:

INFINITIVE	PAST PARTICIPLE	INFINITIVE	PAST PARTICIPLE
abrir	abierto	poner	puesto
cubrir	cubierto	proveer	provisto
decir	dicho	pudrir	podrido
escribir	escrito	romper	roto
freír	frito	soltar	suelto
hacer	hecho	ver	visto
imprimir	impreso	volver	vuelto
morir	muerto		

The past participles of compounds of the above verbs, as **entreabrir, descubrir, describir,** etc., are also irregular.

5. There are three regular conjugations in Spanish.

a) The first conjugation includes the verbs ending in **-ar** in the infinitive.

INFINITIVE		PRESENT PARTICIPLE	PAST PARTICIPLE
hablar	*to speak*	hablando	hablado
estudiar	*to study*	estudiando	estudiado
caminar	*to walk*	caminando	caminado

b) The second conjugation includes the verbs ending in -er in the infinitive

INFINITIVE		PRESENT PARTICIPLE	PAST PARTICIPLE
comer	*to eat*	comiendo	comido
entender	*to understand*	entendiendo	entendido
beber	*to drink*	bebiendo	bebido

c) The third conjugation includes the verbs ending in -ir in the infinitive.

INFINITIVE		PRESENT PARTICIPLE	PAST PARTICIPLE
vivir	*to live*	viviendo	vivido
partir	*to depart*	partiendo	partido
subir	*to go up*	subiendo	subido

6. *Tenses of the indicative mood.*

a) *Present Tense.* The present tense is used to express action in the present, habitual or customary action, or a general truth.

Juan trabaja en el jardín *John works in the garden*

It is formed by dropping the infinitive endings and adding personal endings. Verbs of the first regular conjugation add -o, -as, -a, -amos, -áis, -an; verbs of the second regular conjugation add -o, -es, -e, -emos, -éis, -en; verbs of the third regular conjugation add -o, -es, -e, -imos, -ís, -en.

b) *Imperfect Tense.* The imperfect tense is used to describe the past, a continuing action in the past, or what was habitual or customary in the past.

La ventana estaba abierta *The window was open*
Caminaba por la calle *I was walking down the street*
Jugábamos cuando estábamos de *We played when we were on vacation*
vacaciones

It is formed by dropping the infinitive endings and adding personal endings. Verbs of the first regular conjugation add -aba, -abas, -aba, -ábamos, -abais, -aban; verbs of the second and third regular conjugations add -ía, -ías, -ía, -íamos, -íais, -ían. Ir, ser and ver (and its compounds) are irregularly conjugated in the imperfect tense, see the Verb Table.

c) *Preterit (Past) Tense.* The preterit tense is used to express an action completed in the past and to form the passive voice in the past.

Concha cerró la puerta *Concha closed the door*
América fue descubierta por Colón *America was discovered by Columbus*

It is formed by dropping the infinitive endings and adding personal endings. Verbs of the first regular conjugation add -é, -aste, -ó, -amos, -asteis, -aron; verbs of the second and third regular conjugations add -í, -iste, -ió, -imos, -isteis, -ieron.

d) *Future Tense.* The future tense is used as in English. In addition, it expresses probability or conjecture in the present; its use corresponds exactly to that of the conditional in the past.

Él trabajará mañana *He will work tomorrow*
¿Qué hora será? *I wonder what time it is*
Serán las tres *It is probably three o'clock*

It is formed by dropping the infinitive endings and adding the same personal endings in all three conjugations, -é, -ás, -á, -emos, -éis, -án. The future endings are the same for all verbs, whether regular or irregular.

7. *Conditional Mood.* The conditional mood is used as in English. It also expresses probability in the past. Its use corresponds exactly to that of the future tense.

Si fuera Vd. lo compraría *If I were you, I would buy it*
Serían las siete *It was probably seven o'clock*

It is formed by adding the personal endings of the imperfect tense of the second and third conjugations to the infinitive, -ía, -ías, -ía, -íamos, -íais, -ían.

8. *Subjunctive mood and tenses.* The subjunctive mood expresses wish, obligation, or a condition improbable or contrary to fact.

a) The tense of the subjunctive in a subordinate clause is determined by the tense of the verb in the main clause. When the verb in the main clause is in the present or in the future tense, the verb in the subordinate clause will be in the present subjunctive. When the verb in the main clause is in the preterit, imperfect or conditional, the verb in the subordinate clause will be in the imperfect subjunctive.

b) When futurity is implied, the subjunctive is required following such adverbs, or adverbial locutions, of time as:

cuando	*when*
después que	*after*
hasta que	*until*
luego que	*as soon as*
mientras que	*while*
antes (de) que	*before* (always followed by the subjunctive)
Lo veré cuando él venga	*I shall see him when he comes*

c) The subjunctive is required following such conjunctive locutions as:

a menos que	*unless*
antes (de) que	*before*
para que	*in order that*
como si	*as if, as though*
con tal que	*provided that, as long as*
sin que	*without*
Me habló como si fuera mi padre	*He spoke to me as though he were my father*
Lo haré con tal que me ayude	*I shall do it provided you help me*

d) The subjunctive is used in noun clauses introduced by **que** (*that*) when the following conditions exist at the same time:

1. the sentence contains two clauses;
2. the subject in the subordinate clause differs from the subject of the main clause;
3. when a verb of emotion or feeling, command, request, permission, prohibition, approval, advice, necessity, cause, denial, doubt, or an impersonal locution in the main clause, affects the subject and/or the verb of the subordinate clause.

Me alegro de que ellos se vayan	*I am glad that they are going*
Ellos temían que no llegásemos a tiempo	*They feared that we would not arrive on time*
Dígale a Pedro que me ayude	*Tell Peter to help me*
No creo que él diga la verdad	*I don't believe he is telling the truth*
Es posible que le escribamos	*It is possible that we will write to him*

e) *Present Subjunctive.* In addition to its uses in subordinate clauses, the present subjunctive expresses a command.

No sea Vd. tonto	*Don't you be silly*
Escriban Vds. la lección	*Write the lesson*

It is formed by dropping the infinitive endings and adding personal endings. Verbs of the first regular conjugation add -e, -es, -e, -emos, -éis, -en; verbs of the second and third regular conjugations add -a, -as, -a, -amos, -áis, -an.

f) *Imperfect Subjunctive.* The imperfect subjunctive is formed by dropping the ending -ron of the third person plural of the preterit and adding personal endings. There are two sets of endings that are usually interchangeable, but the form in -ra is the more commonly used in modern Spanish. The two sets of endings are the same for all three conjugations. They are: -ra, -ras, -ra, -ramos, -rais, -ran and -se, -ses, -se, -semos, -seis, -sen. The imperfect subjunctive is rarely used by itself, but it may appear in such simple sentences as:

Quisiera verlo	I should like to see him
Debiera Vd. ir	You should go
¿Pudiera Vd. decírmelo?	Would you be able to tell it to me?

g) *Future Subjunctive.* The future subjunctive is formed by dropping the infinitive endings and adding personal endings. Verbs of the first regular conjugation add -are, -ares, -are, -áremos, -areis, -aren; verbs of the second and third conjugations add -iere, -ieres, -iere, -iéremos, -iereis, -ieren.

9. *Imperative Mood.* The imperative mood expresses a command. There is one tense only, the present. The forms of the imperative mood are the second person singular and plural (familiar form) and they are formed by dropping the infinitive ending and adding -a and -ad respectively in the first conjugation, -e and -ed in the second conjugation, and -e and -id in the third conjugation.

10. *Compound Tenses.* The compound tenses express a completed action. There is a corresponding compound tense for each of the simple tenses. They are formed with the auxiliary verb **haber** (regularly conjugated) and the uninflected past participle of the verb.

PERFECT INDICATIVE

	SINGULAR	PLURAL
1st person	he amado	hemos amado
2nd person	has amado	habéis amado
3rd person	he amado	han amando

PLUPERFECT INDICATIVE

1st person	había amado
2nd person	habías amado
	etc.

PRETERIT ANTERIOR INDICATIVE

1st person	hube amado
2nd person	hubiste amado
	etc.

FUTURE PERFECT INDICATIVE

1st person	habré amado
2nd person	habrás amado
	etc.

CONDITIONAL PERFECT

1st person	habría amado
2nd person	habrías amado
	etc.

PERFECT SUBJUNCTIVE

1st person	haya amado
2nd person	hayas amado
	etc.

PLUPERFECT SUBJUNCTIVE

1st person	hubiera amado
2nd person	hubieras amado
	etc.

FUTURE PERFECT SUBJUNCTIVE

1st person	hubiere amado
2nd person	hubieres amado
	etc.

11. *The Passive Voice.* The passive voice is formed with the auxiliary verb **ser** (*to be*) and an inflected past participle; it is seldom used in Spanish. It should be noted that not all constructions employing ser and a past participle are passive, for some past participles have an active meaning in certain constructions. The same can be said of the verb ser when used with the past participle of an intransitive verb.

Los libros fueron escritos por Cervantes   *The books were written by Cervantes*

La niña está acompañada por su madre   *The girl is accompanied by her mother*

12. *Radical-changing Verbs.* In these verbs a change occurs in the radical when the tonic accent (voice stress) falls on the radical vowel -e or -o. Radical-changing verbs are divided into three classes.

a) To the first class belong those verbs ending in -ar and -er whose radical vowels -e or -o change to -ie and -ue respectively when the radical receives the stress. The changes occur in all of the singular and in the third person plural of the present indicative, in the present subjunctive, and in the imperative singular. See acertar and volver in the Verb Table.

b) To the second class belong those verbs ending in -ir whose radical vowels -e or -o change to -ie and -ue respectively when the radical receives the stress. The changes occur as in the verbs of the first class. They also change -e to -i and -o to -u in the first and second persons plural of the present subjunctive, in the third person singular and plural of the preterit, in all of the imperfect subjunctive, and in the present participle. See sentir and dormir in the Verb Table.

c) To the third class also belong those verbs ending in -ir whose radical vowel -e changes to -i when the radical receives the stress. The change occurs in all of the singular and in the third person plural of the present indicative, in all of the present subjunctive, in the third person singular and plural of the preterit, in all of the imperfect subjunctive, in the imperative singular, and in the present participle. See pedir in the Verb Table. Other verbs of this class are those ending in -eír. See reír in the Verb Table.

Note. Most common verbs that have -e or -o in the radical are radical-changing verbs.

13. *Orthographic-changing Verbs.* Orthographic-changing verbs are those which undergo a change in spelling in order to maintain the sound of the final consonant before the infinitive ending.

a) Verbs ending in -car change to -c to -qu before an -e. See embarcar in the Verb Table.

b) Verbs ending in -gar change the -g to -gu before an -e. See amargar in the Verb Table.

c) Verbs ending in -zar change the -z to -c before an -e. See alcanzar in the Verb Table.

d) Verbs ending in -guar change the -gu to -gü before an -e. See averiguar in the Verb Table.

e) Verbs ending in -cer or -cir preceded by a consonant change the -c to -z before -a and -o. See mecer and zurcir in the Verb Table.

f) Verbs ending in -cer or -cir preceded by a vowel change the -c to -zc before -a and -o. See agradecer and conducir in the Verb Table. Some notable exceptions to this rule are: cocer and its compounds, and mecer, in which the -c changes to -z, and hacer and decir, which are highly irregular. See the Verb Table.

g) Verbs ending in -ger or -gir change the -g to -j before -a and -o. See recoger in the Verb Table.

h) Verbs ending in -guir change the -gu to -g before -a and -o. See distinguir in the Verb Table.

i) Verbs ending in -quir change the -qu to -c before -a and -o. See delinquir in the Verb Table.

j) Verbs ending in -eer change the -i of the ending to -y. See leer in the Verb Table.

k) Verbs ending in -uir (except those ending in -guir and -quir) insert -y before -a, -e and -o, and replace an unstressed -i between vowels with -y. See construir in the Verb Table.

14. Reflexive Verbs. Reflexive verbs are used more frequently in Spanish than in English. Verbs that are intransitive in English are often reflexive in Spanish. Some Spanish verbs are always reflexive. Others may be reflexive or not, depending on the use. Reflexive verbs always occur in conjunction with a reflexive pronoun.

PRESENT INDICATIVE

	SINGULAR	PLURAL
1st person	yo me lavo	nosotros nos lavamos
2nd person	tú te lavas	vosotros os (vos) laváis
3rd person	él se lava	ellos se lavan

Lavar is an example of a verb that may be reflexive or not. In the sample conjugation above, it is reflexive, in the sense of *to wash oneself*. It can also be used transitively and without the reflexive pronoun.

When the subject of a reflexive verb is two or more persons or things, and the action of the verb falls upon the plural subject, the verb is used with a reciprocal meaning.

Las muchachas se visitan	*The girls visit each other*
José, Pedro y Juan se escriben	*Joseph, Peter and John write each other*

15. Impersonal Verbs. These verbs are used only in the infinitive and in the third person singular. They are generally used in a causative sense, their subject being implied but not stated. The verbs haber and hacer, when used impersonally, mean *there is* or *there are*. Some impersonal verbs are used transitively but only in a metaphorical sense. The pronoun se and the active form of the verb is also used to form some impersonal constructions.

Llueve hoy	*It is raining today*
Nieva	*It is snowing*
Hay polvo	*It is dusty*
Se prohibe fumar	*It is forbidden to smoke*

Some typical impersonal verbs are.

alborear	*to dawn*	helar	*to freeze*
amanecer	*to dawn*	llover	*to rain*
anochecer	*to grow dark*	lloviznar	*to drizzle*
diluviar	*to rain heavily*	nevar	*to snow*
escarchar	*to frost*	relampaguear	*to lighten*
granizar	*to hail*	tronar	*to thunder*

16. Defective Verbs. These are verbs that lack some tenses and persons. They must not be confused with some verbs that, while not being truly defective, are seldom used in some of their persons. Defective verbs are sometimes used in a metaphorical sense. Some typical defective verbs are:

abolir	*to abolish*
agredir	*to assault*
aguerrir	*to accustom to war*
arrecirse	*to become stiff with cold*
atañer	*to concern*
aterirse	*to become stiff with cold*
balbucir	*to stammer*
concernir	*to concern*
despavorir	*to be aghast*
embaír	*to deceive*
empedernir	*to harden*
garantir	*to guarantee*
manir	*to keep meat until it becomes gamey*
soler	*to be in the habit of*
transgredir	*to transgress*
usucapir	*to usucapt*

17. *Ser and Estar.* Each of these verbs means *to be,* but they are not interchangeable. Ser denotes a permanent state or condition.

La casa es blanca — *The house is white*

Estar denotes a temporary state or condition.

La puerta está abierta — *The door is open*

18. *Negation.* In Spanish, the negative no always precedes the verb.

No quiero ir — *I don't want to go*
No la veo — *I don't see her*

H. Prepositions. Some common prepositions are:

a	*at, to, for*	hacia	*towards*
antes, ante	*before*	hasta	*until*
con	*with*	para	*for, to*
contra	*against*	por	*by, for, through*
de	*of, from*	según	*according*
desde	*from*	sin	*without*
en	*in, on, at*	sobre	*on, upon*
entre	*between, among*	tras, detrás	*behind*

I. Conjunctions. Some common conjunctions are:

que	*that*	perque, que	*because*
también	*also*	pues, pues que	*since*
además	*moreover*	por	*by, for*
y, e	*and*	por tanto	*therefore*
ni	*neither, nor*	por cuanto	*whereas*
o, u, ya	*or, either, whether*	para que	*that*
sea que	*whether*	a fin de	*in order that*
tampoco	*neither*	si	*if*
mas, pero	*but*	sino	*but*
aun, cuando, aun cuando	*even*	con tal que	*provided*
aunque	*although, though*		
a menos de, a menos que	*unless*	como, así como	*as*
pues, puesto que	*since*	así	*so*

E is used instead of **y** when the following word begins with **i** or **hi.** U is employed instead of **o** when the word immediately following begins with **o** or **ho.**

IRREGULAR VERBS

KEY FOR THE IDENTIFICATION OF TENSES AND PARTS OF SPANISH VERBS

A	Present Indicative.	F	Conditional.
B	Present Subjunctive.	G	Imperfect Subjunctive.
C	Imperfect Indicative.	H	Imperative.*
D	Preterite Indicative.	I	Past Participle.
E	Future Indicative.	J	Gerund.

* For all positive and negative imperative forms with *usted*, *ustedes*, and *nosotros* and for the negative forms with *tú* and *vosotros* the present subjunctive is used.

Reflexive and reciprocal verbs attach the object pronouns (me, te, se, nos, os, se) at the end of the infinitive (*peinarse; amarse*), the positive imperative (*péinate; péinese; amaos*), and the gerund (*peinándose; amándose*). In all the tenses of the indicative and the subjunctive these pronouns are detached and placed before the verb (me *peino*, te *peinas*, se *peina*, nos *peinamos*, os *peináis*, se *peinan*; nos *amamos*, os *amáis*, se *aman*, etc.).

SPANISH IRREGULAR AND ORTHOGRAPHIC CHANGING VERBS

1) A number placed next to the entry indicates that the irregular verb follows the pattern of conjugation of the model given under that number in Part I below. (Example: **pensar** [1], behaves like the model **acertar** —changes e to ie—in the same tenses A, B, H.)
2) A letter placed next to the entry indicates that the orthographic changing verb follows the spelling irregularities of the model verb given under that letter in Part II below. (Example: **aplazar** [a], behaves like the model **alcanzar**.)
3) A number and a letter placed next to the entry indicate that the verb belongs to both of the above categories. (Example: **almorzar** [12-a], behaves like both **contar** and **alcanzar**.)
Only the irregular forms are given.

I. IRREGULAR VERBS

No.	Verb	Irregular Tenses (See Key)	
1	acertar	A	acierto, aciertas, acierta; aciertan.
		B	acierte, aciertes, acierte; acierten.
		H	acierta, acierte; acierten.
2	adquirir	A	adquiero, adquieres, adquiere; adquieren.
		B	adquiera, adquieras, adquiera; adquieran.
		H	adquiere, adquiera; adquieran.
3	agradecer	A	agradezco.
		B	agradezca, agradezcas, agradezca; agradezcamos, agradezcáis, agradezcan.
		H	agradezca; agradezcamos, agradezcan.
4	andar	D	anduve, anduviste, anduvo; anduvimos, anduvisteis, anduvieron.
		G	anduviera or anduviese, anduvieras or anduvieses, anduviera or anduviese; anduviéramos or anduviésemos, anduvierais or anduvieseis, anduvieran or anduviesen.
5	asir	A	asgo.
		B	asga, asgas, asga; asgamos, asgáis, asgan.
6	bendecir	A	bendigo, bendices, bendice; bendicen.
		B	bendiga, bendigas, bendiga; bendigamos, bendigáis, bendigan.
		D	bendije, bendijiste, bendijo; bendijimos, bendijisteis, bendijeron.

No.	Verb	Irregular Tenses (See Key)	
		G	bendijera or bendijese, bendijeras or bendijeses, bendijera or bendijese; bendijéramos or bendijésemos, bendijerais or bendijeseis, bendijeran or bendijesen.
		H	bendice, bendiga; bendigamos, bendigan.
		I	bendito (also the regular: bendecido).
		J	bendiciendo.
7	caber	A	quepo.
		B	quepa, quepas, quepa; quepamos, quepáis, quepan.
		D	cupe, cupiste, cupo; cupimos, cupisteis cupieron.
		E	cabré, cabrás, cabrá; cabremos, cabréis, cabrán.
		F	cabría, cabrías, cabría; cabríamos, cabríais, cabrían.
		G	cupiera or cupiese, cupieras or cupieses, cupiera or cupiese; cupiéramos or cupiésemos, cupierais or cupieseis, cupieran or cupiesen.
		H	quepa, quepamos, quepan.
8	caer	A	caigo.
		B	caiga, caigas, caiga; caigamos, caigáis, caigan.
		H	caiga; caigamos, caigan.
9	ceñir	A	ciño, ciñes, ciñe; ciñen.
		B	ciña, ciñas, ciña; ciñamos, ciñáis, ciñan.
		D	ciñó; ciñeron.
		G	ciñera or ciñese, ciñeras or ciñeses, ciñera or ciñese; ciñéramos or ciñésemos, ciñerais or ciñeseis, ciñeran or ciñesen.
		H	ciñe, ciña; ciñamos, ciñan.
		J	ciñendo.
10	cerner, cernir	A	cierno, ciernes, cierne; cernimos, cernís, ciernen.
		B	cierna, ciernas, cierna; ciernan.
		E	cerniré, cernirás, cernirá; cerniremos, cerniréis, cernirán.
		F	cerniría, cernirías, cerniría; cerniríamos, cerniríais, cernirían.
		H	cierne, cierna; ciernan.
11	conducir	A	conduzco.
		B	conduzca, conduzcas, conduzca; conduzcamos, conduzcáis, conduzcan.
		D	conduje, condujiste, condujo; condujimos, condujisteis, condujeron.
		G	condujera or condujese, condujeras or condujeses, condujera or condujese; condujéramos or condujésemos, condujerais or condujeseis, condujeran or condujesen.
		H	conduzca; conduzcamos, conduzcan.
12	contar	A	cuento, cuentas, cuenta; cuentan.
		B	cuente, cuentes, cuente; cuenten.
		H	cuenta, cuente; cuenten.
13	dar	A	doy.
		D	di, diste, dio; dimos, disteis, dieron.
		G	diera or diese, dieras or dieses, diera or diese; diéramos or diésemos, dierais or dieseis, dieran or diesen.

No.	Verb	Irregular Tenses (See Key)	
14	decir	A	digo, dices, dice; dicen.
		B	diga, digas, diga; digamos, digáis, digan.
		D	dije, dijiste, dijo; dijimos, dijisteis, dijeron.
		E	diré, dirás, dirá; diremos, diréis, dirán.
		F	diría, dirías, diría; diríamos, diríais, dirían.
		G	dijera or dijese, dijeras or dijeses, dijera or dijese; dijéramos or dijésemos, dijerais or dijeseis, dijeran or dijesen.
		H	di, diga; digamos, digan.
		I	dicho.
		J	diciendo.
15	desosar	A	deshueso, deshuesas, deshuesa; deshuesan.
		B	deshuese, deshueses, deshuese; deshuesen.
		H	deshuesa, deshuese; deshuesen.
16	discernir	A	discierno, disciernes, discierne; disciernen.
		B	discierna, disciernas, discierna; disciernan.
		H	discierne, discierna; disciernan.
17	dormir	A	duermo, duermes, duermo; duermen.
		B	duerma, duermas, duerma; durmamos, durmáis, duerman.
		D	durmió; durmieron.
		G	durmiera or durmiese, durmieras or durmieses, durmiera or durmiese; durmiéramos or durmiésemos, durmierais or durmieseis, durmieran or durmiesen.
		H	duerme, duerma; durmamos, duerman.
		J	durmiendo.
18	entender	A	entiendo, entiendes, entiende; entienden.
		B	entienda, entiendas, entienda; entiendan.
		H	entiende, entienda; entiendan.
19	erguir	A	yergo, yergues, yergue; yerguen.
		B	yerga, yergas, yerga; irgamos, irgáis, yergan.
		D	irguió; irguieron.
		G	irguiera or irguiese, irguieras or irguieses, irguiera or irguiese; irguiéramos or irguiésemos, irguierais or irguieseis, irguieran or irguiesen.
		H	yergue, yerga; irgamos, yergan.
		J	irguiendo.
20	estar	A	estoy, estás, está; están.
		B	esté, estés, esté; estén.
		D	estuve, estuviste, estuvo; estuvimos, estuvisteis, estuvieron.
		G	estuviera or estuviese, estuvieras or estuvieses, estuviera or estuviese; estuviéramos or estuviésemos, estuvierais or estuvieseis, estuvieran or estuviesen.
		H	está, esté; estén.
21	haber	A	he, has, ha or hay (impersonal form); hemos or habemos, han.
		B	haya, hayas, haya; hayamos, hayáis, hayan.
		D	hube, hubiste, hubo; hubimos, hubisteis, hubieron.
		E	habré, habrás, habrá; habremos, habréis, habrán.
		F	habría, habrías, habría; habríamos, habríais, habrían.
		G	hubiera or hubiese, hubieras or hubieses, hubiera or hubiese; hubiéramos or hubiésemos, hubierais or hubieseis, hubieran or hubiesen.
		H	he, haya; hayamos, hayan.

No.	Verb	Irregular Tenses (See Key)	
22	hacer	A	hago.
		B	haga, hagas, haga; hagamos, hagáis, hagan.
		D	hice, hiciste, hizo; hicimos, hicisteis, hicieron.
		E	haré, harás, hará; haremos, haréis, harán.
		F	haría, harías, haría; haríamos, haríais, harían.
		G	hiciera or hiciese, hicieras or hicieses, hiciera or hiciese; hiciéramos or hiciésemos, hicierais or hicieseis, hicieran or hiciesen.
		H	haz, haga; hagamos, hagan.
		I	hecho.
23	huir	A	huyo, huyes, huye; huyen.
		B	huya, huyas, huya; huyamos, huyáis, huyan.
		H	huye, huya; huyamos, huyan.
24	ir	A	voy, vas, va; vamos, vais, van.
		B	vaya, vayas, vaya; vayamos, vayáis, vayan.
		C	iba, ibas, iba; íbamos, ibais, iban.
		D	fui, fuiste, fue; fuimos, fuisteis, fueron.
		G	fuera or fuese, fueras or fueses, fuera or fuese; fuéramos or fuésemos, fuerais or fueseis, fueran or fuesen.
		J	yendo.
25	jugar	A	juego, juegas, juega; juegan.
		B	juegue, juegues, juegue; jueguen.
		H	juega, juegue; jueguen.
26	mover	A	muevo, mueves, mueve; mueven.
		B	mueva, muevas, mueva; muevan.
		H	mueve, mueva; muevan.
27	mullir	D	mulló; mulleron.
		G	mullera or mullese, mulleras or mulleses, mullera or mullese; mulléramos or mullésemos, mullerais or mulleseis, mulleran or mullesen.
		J	mullendo.
28	oir	A	oigo, oyes, oye; oyen.
		B	oiga, oigas, oiga; oigamos, oigáis, oigan.
		H	oye, oiga; oigamos, oigan.
28'	oler	A-B-H	It is conjugated in the same way that No. 26 (mover) but with an "h" before diphthong "ue": huelo, hueles, etc.
29	pedir	A	pido, pides, pide; piden.
		B	pida, pidas, pida; pidamos, pidáis, pidan.
		D	pidió; pidieron.
		G	pidiera or pidiese, pidieras or pidieses, pidiera or pidiese; pidiéramos or pidiésemos, pidierais or pidieseis, pidieran or pidiesen.
		H	pide, pida; pidamos, pidan.
		J	pidiendo.
30	placer	A	plazco.
		B	plazca, plazcas, plazca (or plegue or plega); placamos, placáis, plazcan.
		D	plugo (or plació); pluguieron (or placieron).
		G	pluguiera or pluguiese (or placiera or placiese).
		H	plazca; plazcamos, plazcan.

No.	Verb	Irregular Tenses (See Key)	
31	poder	A	puedo, puedes, puede; pueden.
		B	pueda, puedas, pueda; puedan.
		D	pude, pudiste, pudo; pudimos, pudisteis, pudieron.
		E	podré, podrás, podrá; podremos, podréis, podrán.
		F	podría, podrías, podría, podríamos, podríais, podrían.
		G	pudiera or pudiese, pudieras or pudieses, pudiera or pudiese; pudiéramos or pudiésemos, pudierais or pudieseis, pudieran or pudiesen.
		H	puede, pueda; puedan.
		J	pudiendo.
32	poner	A	pongo.
		B	ponga, pongas, ponga; pongamos, pongáis, pongan.
		D	puse, pusiste, puso; pusimos, pusisteis, pusieron.
		E	pondré, pondrás, pondrá; pondremos, pondréis, pondrán.
		F	pondría, pondrías, pondría; pondríamos, pondríais, pondrían.
		G	pusiera or pusiese, pusieras or pusieses, pusiera or pusiese; pusiéramos or pusiésemos, pusieseis, pusieran or pusiesen.
		H	pon, ponga; pongamos, pongan.
		I	puesto.
33	pudrir or podrir	I	podrido. (When the infinitive used is "podrir," the verb is conjugated as "pudrir," which only is irregular in its p.p.)
34	querer	A	quiero, quieres, quiere; quieren.
		B	quiera, quieras, quiera; quieran.
		D	quise, quisiste, quiso; quisimos, quisisteis, quisieron.
		E	querré, querrás, querrá; querremos, querréis, querrán.
		F	querría, querrías, querría; querríamos, querríais, querrían.
		G	quisiera or quisiese, quisieras or quisieses, quisiera or quisiese; quisiéramos or quisiésemos, quisierais or quisieseis, quisieran or quisiesen.
		H	quiere, quiera; quieran.
35	reir	A	río, ríes, ríe; ríen.
		B	ría, rías, ría; riamos, riáis, rían.
		D	río; rieron.
		G	riera or riese, rieras or rieses, riera or riese; riéramos or riésemos, rierais or rieseis, rieran or riesen.
		H	ríe, ría; riamos, rían.
		J	riendo.
36	roer	A	It is a regular form but it can be conjugated "roigo" and "royo" in the first person singular.
		B	It is a regular form too but it can be conjugated "roiga" and "roya," etc.
37	saber	A	sé.
		B	sepa, sepas, sepa; sepamos, sepáis, sepan.
		D	supe, supiste, supo; supimos, supisteis, supieron.
		E	sabré, sabrás, sabrá; sabremos, sabréis, sabrán.
		F	sabría, sabrías, sabría; sabríamos, sabríais, sabrían.
		–	

No.	Verb	Irregular Tenses (See Key)	
		G	supiera or supiese, supieras or supieses, supiera or supiese; supiéramos or supiésemos, supierais or supieseis, supieran or supiesen.
		H	sepa; sepamos, sepan.
38	salir	A	salgo.
		B	salga, salgas, salga; salgamos, salgáis, salgan.
		E	saldré, saldrás, saldrá; saldremos, saldréis, saldrán.
		F	saldría, saldrías, saldría; saldríamos, saldríais, saldrían.
		G	sal, salga; salgamos, salgan.
39	sentir	A	siento, sientes, siente; sienten.
		B	sienta, sientas, sienta; sintamos, sintáis, sientan.
		D	sintió; sintieron.
		G	sintiera or sintiese, sintieras or sintieses, sintiera or sintiese; sintiéramos or sintiésemos, sintierais or sintieseis, sintieran or sintiesen.
		H	siente, sienta; sintamos, sientan.
		J	sintiendo.
40	ser	A	soy, eres, es; somos, sois, son.
		B	sea, seas, sea; seamos, seáis, sean.
		C	era, eras, era; éramos, erais, eran.
		D	fui, fuiste, fue; fuimos, fuisteis, fueron.
		G	fuera or fuese, fueras or fueses, fuera or fuese; fuéramos or fuésemos, fuerais or fueseis, fueran or fuesen.
		H	sea; seamos, sean.
41	tañer	D	tañó; tañeron.
		G	tañera or tañese, tañeras or tañeses, tañera or tañese; tañéramos or tañésemos, tañerais or tañeseis, tañeran or tañesen.
		J	tañendo.
42	tener	A	tengo, tienes, tiene; tienen.
		B	tenga, tengas, tenga; tengamos, tengáis, tengan.
		D	tuve, tuviste, tuvo; tuvimos, tuvisteis, tuvieron.
		E	tendré, tendrás, tendrá; tendremos, tendréis, tendrán.
		F	tendría, tendrías, tendría; tendríamos, tendríais, tendrían.
		G	tuviera or tuviese, tuvieras or tuvieses, tuviera or tuviese; tuviéramos or tuviésemos, tuvierais or tuvieseis, tuvieran or tuviesen.
		H	ten, tenga; tengamos, tengan.
43	traer	A	traigo.
		B	traiga, traigas, traiga; traigamos, traigáis, traigan.
		D	traje, trajiste, trajo; trajimos, trajisteis, trajeron.
		G	trajera or trajese, trajeras or trajeses, trajera or trajese; trajéramos or trajésemos, trajerais or trajeseis, trajeran or trajesen.
		H	traiga; traigamos, traigan.
44	valer	A	valgo.
		B	valga, valgas, valga; valgamos, valgáis, valgan.
		E	valdré, valdrás, valdrá; valdremos, valdréis, valdrán.
		F	valdría, valdrías, valdría; valdríamos, valdríais, valdrían.
		H	val(e), valga; valgamos, valgan.

No.	Verb	Irregular Tenses (See Key)	
45	venir	A	vengo, vienes, viene; vienen.
		B	venga, vengas, venga; vengamos, vengáis, vengan.
		D	vine, viniste, vino; vinimos, vinisteis, vinieron.
		E	vendré, vendrás, vendrá; vendremos, vendréis, vendrán.
		F	vendría, vendrías, vendría; vendríamos, vendríais, vendrían.
		G	viniera or viniese, vinieras or vinieses, viniera or viniese; viniéramos or viniésemos, vinierais or vinieseis, vinieran or viniesen.
		H	ven, venga; vengamos, vengan.
		J	viniendo.
46	ver	A	veo.
		B	vea, veas, vea; veamos, veáis, vean.
		C	veía, veías, veía; veíamos, veíais, veían.
		H	vea; veamos, vean.
		I	visto.
47	volver	A	vuelvo, vuelves, vuelve; vuelven.
		B	vuelva, vuelvas, vuelva; vuelvan.
		H	vuelve, vuelva; vuelvan.
		I	vuelto.
48	yacer	A	yazco (or yazgo or yago).
		B	yazca (yazga, yaga), yazcas (yazgas, yagas), yazca (yazga, yaga); yazcamos (yazgamos, yagamos), yazcáis (yazgáis, yagáis), yazcan (yazgan, yagan).
		H	yace (or yaz), yazca (yazga, yaga); yazcamos (yazgamos, yagamos), yazcan (yazgan, yagan).

No. 49 Verbs with Irregular Participles

Verbs	Regular Participle	Irregular Participle
abrir	—	abierto
absolver	—	absuelto
absorber	absorbido	absorto
abstraer	abstraído	abstracto
adscribir	—	adscrito
afligir	afligido	aflicto
circunscribir	—	circunscrito
cubrir	—	cubierto
descubrir	—	descubierto
despertar	despertado	despierto
devolver	—	devuelto
disponer	—	dispuesto
elegir	elegido	electo
encubrir	—	encubierto
enjugar	enjugado	enjuto
entreabrir	—	entreabierto
entrever	—	entrevisto
escribir	—	escrito
excluir	excluido	excluso
eximir	eximido	exento
expresar	expresado	expreso
extender	extendido	extenso
extinguir	extinguido	extinto
freír	freído	frito
fijar	fijado	fijo
hartar	hartado	harto
imponer	—	impuesto
imprimir	imprimido	impreso
incluir	incluido	incluso
inscribir	—	inscrito

Verbs	Regular Participle	Irregular Participle
insertar	insertado	inserto
interponer	—	interpuesto
invertir	invertido	inverso
maldecir	maldecido	maldito
matar	matado	muerto
morir	—	muerto
nacer	nacido	nato
poner	—	puesto
posponer	—	pospuesto
predecir	—	predicho
predisponer	—	predispuesto
prender	prendido	preso
prescribir	—	prescrito
presumir	presumido	presunto
presuponer	—	presupuesto
pretender	pretendido	pretenso
prever	—	previsto
propender	propendido	propenso
proponer	—	propuesto
proscribir	—	proscrito
prostituir	prostituído	prostituto
proveer	proveído	provisto
reabrir	—	reabierto
reelegir	reelegido	reelecto
rehacer	—	rehecho
reimprimir	—	reimpreso
reponer	—	repuesto
resolver	—	resuelto
romper	—	roto
sobreponer	—	sobrepuesto
sofreir	sofreído	sofrito
sujetar	sujetado	sujeto
superponer	—	superpuesto
suponer	—	supuesto
surgir	surgido	surto
suscribir	—	suscrito
suspender	suspendido	suspenso
sustituir	sustituído	sustituto
transcribir	—	transcripto
tra(n)sponer	—	tra(n)spuesto
truncar	truncado	trunco
yuxtaponer	—	yuxtapuesto

No. 50   Defective Verbs or Verbs Which Have Some Especial Characteristics

Verbs	
abolir	Only tenses having endings with "i" are used; abolió, abolía, aboliré, etc.
acaecer	Used only in the infinitive and in the third person of all tenses.
acontecer	See *Acaecer.*
agredir	See *Abolir.*
atañer	Used only in the third person of all tenses, especially "atañe," "atañen."
aterirse	See *Abolir.*
balbucir	Persons of this verb which do not have the ending "i" are conjugated in the same way as the regular verb "balbucear."
concernir	Only the gerund (concerniendo) and the third person of all tenses are used, especially: concierne, conciernes; concernía, concernían; concierna, conciernan.
granizar	See *Acaecer.*
preterir	See *Abolir.*
soler	Used only in the present and imperfect indicative. The participle "solido" is used only in the present perfect tense.
transgredir	See *Abolir.*

II. ORTHOGRAPHIC CHANGING VERBS

Verbs marked with letter		
a	"z" changes to "c" before "e" and "i," and "c" changes to "z" before "a," "o," "u."	alcanzar; alcance, alcancemos, etc. mecer: mezo, mezas, etc. zurcir: zurza, zurzo, etc.

b	1) Verbs ending -gar: "g" changes to "gu" before "e," "i."	1) amargar: amargue, amarguen, etc.
	2) Verbs ending -guar: "gu" changes to "gü" before "e," "i."	2) averiguar: averigüe, averigüemos, etc.
	3) The group "gu" changes to "g" before "a," "o."	3) distinguir: distingo, distingamos, etc.
c	"g" changes to "j" before "a," "o."	recoger: recojo; recojas, etc.
d	"qu" changes to "c" before "a," "o." "c" changes to "qu" before "e," "i."	delinquir: delinco; delinca, etc. embarcar: embarque, embarquemos, etc.
e	verbs ending -aer, -eer, -uir: tonic "i" of verb ending changes to "y" in the gerund and in the third person of tenses "D" and "G."	caer: cayó; cayera or cayese; cayendo. construir: construyó; construyera or construyese; construyendo. leer: leyó; leyera or leyese; leyendo.

ABBREVIATIONS USED IN PART I

a.	adjective.	
abbr.	abbreviation.	
adv.	adverb.	
(aer.)	aeronautics.	
(agr.)	agriculture.	
(alg.)	algebra.	
(Am.)	Spanish America(n).	
(anat.)	anatomy.	
(app.)	applied.	
(arch.)	architecture.	
(Arg.)	Argentina.	
(arith.)	arithmetic.	
art.	article.	
(artil.)	artillery.	
(astr.)	astronomy; astrology.	
aug.	augmentative.	
(bib.)	Biblical.	
(biol.)	biology.	
(bot.)	botany.	
(carp.)	carpentry.	
(chem.)	chemistry.	
(coll.)	colloquial.	
(collect.)	collectively.	
(com.)	commerce.	
comp.	comparative.	
conj.	conjunction.	
(contempt.)	contemptuous.	
contr.	contraction.	
(cook.)	cooking.	
defect.	defective.	
dim.	diminutive.	
(eccl.)	ecclesiastic.	
(econ.)	economics.	
(elec.)	electricity.	
(eng.)	engineering.	
(esp.)	especially.	
f.	feminine; feminine noun.	
(fam.)	familiar.	
(fig.)	figurative(ly).	
(fort.)	fortifications.	
fut.	future.	
(gen.)	generally.	
(geog.)	geography.	
(geol.)	geology.	
(geom.)	geometry.	
ger.	gerund.	
(gram.)	grammar.	
(herald.)	heraldry.	
(hist.)	history.	
(hort.)	horticulture.	
(humor.)	humorous.	
(hydraul.)	hydraulics.	
(ichth.)	ichthyology.	
imp.	imperfect.	
imper.	imperative.	
impers.	impersonal.	
ind.	indicative.	
inf.	infinitive.	
interj.	interjection.	
interrog.	interrogative.	
(jewel.)	jewelry.	
(lit.)	literally.	
m.	masculine; masculine noun.	

(mason.)	masonry.	
(math.)	mathematics.	
(mech.)	mechanics.	
(med.)	medicine.	
(metal.)	metallurgy.	
(Mex.)	Mexico.	
mf.	noun (not inflected to show gender).	
(mil.)	military.	
(min.)	mining, mineralogy.	
(mus.)	music.	
n.	noun (inflected, usually *-o* to *-a*, to show gender).	
(naut.)	nautical.	
(neol.)	neologism.	
neut.	neuter.	
nom.	nominative case.	
(opt.)	optics.	
(ornith.)	ornithology.	
pers.	person; personal.	
(pert.)	pertaining (to).	
(pharm.)	pharmaceutical.	
(philos.)	philosophy.	
(phot.)	photography.	
(phys.)	physics.	
(physiol.)	physiology.	
pl.	plural.	
(poet.)	poetry.	
(pol.)	politics.	
poss.	possessive.	
pp.	past participle.	
prep.	preposition.	
pret.	preterit.	
(print.)	printing.	
pron.	pronoun.	
(ref.)	referring (to).	
refl.	reflexive.	
rel.	relative (pronoun).	
(rhet.)	rhetoric.	
(RR.)	railroad.	
(S.A.)	South America(n).	
(sew.)	sewing.	
sing.	singular.	
(Sp.)	Spain, Spanish.	
subj.	subject; subjunctive.	
super.	superlative.	
(surg.)	surgery.	
(tech.)	technology.	
(tel.)	telegraph(y); telephone.	
(theat.)	theater.	
V.	see.	
va.	auxiliary verb.	
vai.	irregular auxiliary verb.	
vi.	intransitive verb.	
vii.	irregular intransitive verb.	
vr.	reflexive verb.	
vri.	irregular reflexive verb.	
vt.	transitive verb.	
vti.	irregular transitive verb.	
(vulg.)	vulgar, low.	
(zool.)	zoology.	

TABLES OF WEIGHTS
AND MEASURES

Metric Weights
(Unidades Métricas de Peso)
1 gramo (g.) = .03527 ounces (oz.)
1 kilogramo (kg.) = 1.000 gramos =
2.2046 pounds (lb.)
1 quintal métrico = 100 kg. = 220.55
pounds
1 tonelada métrica = 10 quintales =
2,205 pounds

Metric Liquid and Dry Measures
(Unidades métricas de capacidad)
1 litro (l.) = 1 decímetro cúbico (dm.)
= .908 qt. U.S. dry measure = 1.0567
qt. U.S. liquid measure
1 decálitro (dl.) = 10 litros = 9.08 U.S.
qt. dry measure = 2.64 gal. U.S. liquid measure = 2.837 bushels
1 hectólitro (hl.) = 100 l. = 26.417 gal.
1 kilólitro (kl.) = 1.000 l. = 28.337
bushels = 264.17 gal.

Metric Linear Measures
(Unidades métricas de longitud)
1 milímetro (mm.) = .039 inches (in.)
1 centímetro (cm.) = 10 mm. = .393
inches
1 decímetro (dm.) = 10 cm. = 3.94
inches
1 metro (m.) = 10 dm. = 3.28 feet (ft.)
1 kilómetro (km.) = 1,000 m. = 3,280
feet, approx. 5/8 of a mile

Old Weights Still Encountered
(Unidades antiguas todavía en uso)
1 libra = 16 onzas = 0,460 kg. = 1.014
lb.
1 arroba = 25 libras = 11,51 kg. = 25.-
36 lb.
1 quintal = 4 arrobas = 46,09 kg. =
101.43 lb.
1 tonelada = 20 quintales = 922 kg.
= 2,028 lb.

Old Measures Still Encountered
(Unidades antiguas todavía en uso)
1 cuartillo = 0,005 l. = 1.05 qt.
1 celemín = 4 cuartillos

Old Measures Still Encountered
(Unidades antiguas todavía en uso)
1 pulgada = 2,3 cm. = .92 inches
1 pie = 12 pulgadas
1 vara = 3 pies
1 legua = 6,666 varas = 5,572 km.

Metric Square Measures   (Unidades métricas de superficie)
1 centiárea = 1 metro cuadrado (m.²) = 1.196 square yards (sq. yd.)
1 área = 100 metros cuadrados = 119.6 square yards
1 hectárea = 1.000 metros cuadrados = 2.471 acres

THERMOMETER

0 centigrade (freezing point) = 32 Fahrenheit
100 centigrade (boiling point) = 212 Fahrenheit

To reduce degrees centigrade to degrees Fahrenheit multiply by 9/5 and
add 32.

A

a, *prep.* to; in; at; according to; by; for; of; on; toward.—*a beneficio de,* for the benefit of.—*a caballo,* on horseback.—*a la derecha,* at the right.—*a máquina,* by machine. —*a mi gusto,* according to my taste. —*a oscuras,* in the dark.—*a tiempo,* on time.—*al anochecer,* toward the evening.—*di el libro a Pedro,* I gave the book to Peter.

abacería, *f.* grocery.—**abacero,** *n.* grocer.

abad, *m.* abbot.—**abadía,** *f.* abbey.

abajo, *adv.* under, underneath, below, down.—*a. de,* beneath.—*boca a.,* face down.—*de arriba a a.,* from top to bottom.—*venirse a.,* to fall.

abalanzar, *vti.* [a] to balance; to hurl, impel.—*vri.* to rush on or upon; to venture on.

abalorio, *m.* glass bead; bead work.

abandonado, *a.* negligent; slovenly.— **abandonar,** *vt.* to abandon, desert; to give up.—*vi.* to despair; to give oneself up to; to be neglectful.— **abandono,** *m.* abandon; neglect; despondency.

abanicar, *vti.* [d] to fan.—**abanico,** *m.* fan.

abaratar, *vt.* to cheapen; to abate.— *vr.* to fall in price.

abarcar, [d] *vti.* to clasp, embrace, contain; to comprise.

abarrotar, *vt.* to stew; to overstock. —**abarrotero,** *n.* (Am.) retail grocer.—**abarrotes,** *m. pl.* (Am.) groceries; goods; foodstuffs.

abastecedor, *n.* caterer, provider, purveyor, supplier.—**abastecer,** *vti.* [3] to purvey; to supply.—**abastecimiento,** *m.* providing; supply; provisions, supplies.—**abasto,** *m.* supply of provisions; (fig.) abundance.—*dar a.,* to be sufficient (for); to provide, furnish.

abatido, *a.* dejected, crestfallen; abject; lowered.—**abatimiento,** *m.* depression, low spirits.—**abatir,** *vt.* to throw down; to knock (bring, shoot) down; to humble, abase; to discourage; to lower, strike (a flag). —*vr.* to become disheartened; to swoop down.

abdicación, *f.* abdication.—**abdicar,** *vti.* [d] to abdicate.

abdomen, *m.* abdomen.—**abdominal,** *a.* abdominal.

abducción, *f.* (logic & anat.) abduction.

abecé, *m.* a-b-c, alphabet; rudiments.—**abecedario,** *m.* alphabet; primer; rudiments.

abedul, *m.* birch.

abeja, *f.* bee.—**abejón,** *m.* drone.— **abejorro,** *m.* bumblebee.

aberración, *f.* aberration; error; mania.

abertura, *f.* aperture, opening; cleft, crevice, slit; gap.

abeto, *m.* spruce; fir; hemlock.

abierto, *pp.* of ABRIR.—*a.* open, clear; frank, sincere; full-blown.

abigarrado, *a.* variegated, motley.

abismado, *a.* dejected; overwhelmed; absorbed in meditation.—**abismal,** *a.* abysmal.—**abismar,** *vt.* to depress; to overwhelm.—*vr.* to be immersed (in thought, grief, etc.).— **abismo,** *m.* abyss; chasm; precipice.

abjuración, *f.* abjuration.—**abjurar,** *vt.* to abjure, forswear, retract under oath.

ablandamiento, *m.* softening, mollification.—**ablandar,** *vt. & vi.* to soften; to loosen; to mitigate.—*vr.* to soften, relent, mellow.

abobado, *a.* silly, stultified; openmouthed.

abochornar, *vt.* to overheat; to shame; to embarrass.—*vr.* to blush; to become embarrassed.

abofetear, *vt.* to slap.

abogacía, *f.* law, legal profession.— **abogado,** *n.* lawyer, advocate; mediator.—**abogar,** *vii.* [b] to advocate, plead (as a lawyer); to intercede.

abolengo, *m.* ancestry, lineage; inheritance.

abolición, *f.* abolition, extinction.— **abolir,** *vti.* [50] to abolish; to revoke, repeal.

abolladura, *f.* denting; embossing; bump; bulge.—**abollar,** *vt.* to emboss; to dent; to batter; to crumple.

abominable, *a.* abominable, detestable.—**abominación,** *f.* abomination, execration.—**abominar,** *vt.* to abominate, abhor.

abonado, *n.* subscriber; commuter.— *a.* reliable, apt, inclined; (agr.) rich (soil).—**abonar,** *vt.* (com.) to credit with; to pay; to guarantee, indorse, answer for; (agr.) to manure.— *vr.* to subscribe; to buy a season or commutation ticket.—**abono,** *m.* surety; assurance; payment; subscription; indorsement; fertilizer; installment.

abordaje, *m.* the act of boarding a ship.—**abordar,** *vt.* (naut.) to ram, collide with, board (a ship); to broach (a subject), enter upon (a matter); to accost, approach (a person).

aborrecer, *vti.* [3] to hate, abhor.— **aborrecible,** *a.* hateful; abhorrent. —**aborrecimiento,** *m.* abhorrence, hatred.

abortar, *vi.* to miscarry, abort; to fail; (med.) to have a miscarriage; to have an abortion.—**abortivo,** *a.* abortive, producing abortion.— **aborto,** *m.* miscarriage, abortion; monstrosity.

abotagarse, abotargarse, *vri.* [b] to swell; to bloat.

abotonar, *vt.* to button.—*vi.* to bud. —*vr.* to button up.

abrasador, *a.* burning, extremely hot. —**abrasar,** *vt.* to burn; to parch, scorch; to dry up.—*vr.* (en or de) to burn (with); to boil (with) (any violent passion); to burn up, down.

abrasivo, *m. & a.* abrasive.

abrazadera, *f.* clasp, clamp, cleat.— **abrazar,** *vti.* [a] to embrace, hug; to clamp, cleat; to contain; to adopt (a religion, etc.).—**abrazo,** *m.* hug, embrace.

abrelatas, *m. sing.* can opener.

abreviación, *f.* abbreviation; abridgment; shortening; hastening.—**abreviar,** *vt.* to hasten; to abridge, abbreviate.—**abreviatura,** *f.* abbreviation (of word); contraction.—*en a.,* in abbreviation.

abridor, *m.* opener; nectarine.—*a. de latas,* can opener.

abrigar, *vti.* [b] to shelter, shield; to cover; to keep warm; to cherish.— *vri.* to take shelter; to cover oneself; to put on a wrap.—**abrigo,** *m.* overcoat; shelter, protection; wrap; aid, support; cover.—*al a. de,* sheltered from, shielded by.

abril, *m.* April.

abrillantar, *vt.* to polish, shine; to brighten; to add splendor.

abrir, *vti.* [49] to open, unlock, unfasten, uncover; to cut open; to dig.—*a. paso,* to make way, to clear the way.—*vii.* to open; to clear (of weather).—*vri.* to open, expand; to crack.

abrochar, *vt.* to clasp, button, fasten.

abrojo, *m.* (bot.) thistle thorn, prickle.—*pl.* hidden reefs.

abrumador, *a.* overwhelming, crushing; wearisome.—**abrumar,** *vt.* to crush, overwhelm, oppress; to annoy.—*vr.* to become foggy.

abrupto, *a.* abrupt; craggy; rugged.

absceso, *m.* abscess.

absolución, *f.* absolution; pardon, acquittal.

absolutismo, *m.* despotism, absolutism.—**absoluto,** *a.* absolute, unconditional; despotic.—*en a.,* unqualifiedly; absolutely; (in negative

sentences) at all.—*lo a.,* the absolute.

absolutorio, *a.* absolutory, absolving. —**absolver,** *vti.* [47-49] to absolve; to acquit.

absorber, *vti.* [49] to absorb; to imbibe.—**absorción,** *f.* absorption.— **absorto,** *pp. i.* of ABSORBER.—*a.* amazed; absorbed in thought.

abstemio, *a.* abstemious.—*n.* teetotaler.

abstenerse, *vri.* [42] to abstain, forbear.—**abstinencia,** *f.* abstinence, temperance; fasting.

abstracción, *f.* abstraction; concentration.—**abstracto,** *pp. i.* de ABSTRAER.—*a. & m.* abstract.—**abstraer,** *vti.* [43-49] to abstract.—**abstraído,** *a.* retired; absent-minded.

absuelto, *pp.* of ABSOLVER.—*a.* acquitted, absolved.

absurdo, *a.* absurd, nonsensical.—*m.* absurdity, nonsense.

abuchear, *vt.* to boo, hoot.—**abucheo,** *m.* booing, hooting.

abuela, *f.* grandmother.—**abuelo,** *m.* grandfather; elderly man; ancestor.

abultar, *vt.* to bulge.—*vi.* to be bulky or large.

abundamiento, *m.* abundance.—*a mayor a.,* furthermore; with greater reason.—**abundancia,** *f.* abundance, plenty.—**abundante,** *a.* abundant, plentiful, teeming.—**abundar,** *vi.* to abound.

aburrido, *a.* bored; tiresome, boresome.—**aburrimiento,** *m.* weariness, annoyance.—**aburrir,** *vt.* to vex; to tire, bore.—*vr.* to grow tired; to be bored.

abusar, *vi.* to exceed, go too far; to take undue advantage.—*a. de,* to abuse, use wrongly; to betray (a confidence); to take undue advantage of; to impose upon.—**abusivo,** *a.* abusive.—**abuso,** *m.* misuse, abuse.

abyección, *f.* abjection, abjectness; degradation.—**abyecto,** *a.* abject, servile, slavish.

acá, *adv.* here; hither.—*¿de cuándo a.?* since when?—*por a.,* here, hereabouts; this way.

acabado, *a.* perfect, faultless; wasted; dilapidated.—*m.* (art) finish.— **acabamiento,** *m.* completion, end; physical decline.—**acabar,** *vt. & vi.* to finish; to complete; to end.— *a. con,* to finish, destroy.—*a. de* (foll. by *inf.*), to have just (foll. by *pp.*).—*a. por,* to end by, to . . . finally.—*vr.* to be finished; to end, be over; to grow feeble or wasted; *acabársele a uno (el dinero, la* *paciencia, etc.*) to run out of (money, patience, etc.).

academia, *f.* academy; literary, scientific or artistic society; university. —**académico** *a. & n.* academic; academician

acaecer, *vii.* [3-50] to happen, come to pass.—**acaecimiento**, *m.* event.

acalorado, *a.* heated, excited, angry. —*n.* (fig.) hothead.—**acaloramiento**, *m.* ardor, heat, excitement.—**acalorar**, *vt.* to heat, inflame, excite. —*vr.* to grow warm; to get overheated; to get excited.

acallar, *vt.* to quiet, hush; to mitigate.

acampar, *vt., vi. & vr.* to encamp.

acanalado, *a.* striated, fluted, corrugated, grooved.—**acanalar**, *vt.* to make a channel in; to flute, corrugate, groove.

acantilado, *m.* cliff; escarpment.—*a.* steep, sheer.

acantonar, *vt.* to quarter (troops).

acaparador, *n.* monopolizer.—**acaparar**, *vt.* to monopolize; to corner, control (the market); to buy up, hoard.

acariciar, *vt.* to fondle, caress; to cherish.

acarrear, *vt.* to carry, cart, transport.—*vr.* to bring upon oneself.—**acarreo**, *m.* carrying, transportation; cartage.

acaso, *m.* chance, accident.—*adv.* perhaps; by chance, by accident.—*por si a.*, just in case.

acatamiento, *m.* obeisance, respect, homage.—**acatar**, *vt.* to obey; to accept; to respect.

acatarrarse, *vr.* to catch cold.

acaudalado, *a.* rich, opulent.

acaudillar, *vt.* to command, lead.

acceder, *vi.* to accede, agree, consent. —**accesible**, *a.* accessible, approachable; attainable.—**acceso**, *m.* access; entrance; admittance; (med.) access, fit, attack.—**accesorio**, *a.* accessory; secondary.—*pl.* spare parts; accessories.

accidentado, *a.* seized with a fit; rugged, uneven (ground).—**accidentarse**, *vr.* to have a fit or stroke. —**accidente**, *m.* accident; chance; sudden fit; (gram.) inflection.—*por a.*, accidentally, by chance.

acción, *f.* action; feat; lawsuit; battle; (lit.) plot; (com.) stock, share. —*a. de gracias*, thanksgiving.—**accionar**, *vi.* to gesticulate.—*vt.* (mech.) to operate, move.—**accionista**, *mf.* stockholder, shareholder.

acechanza, *f.* waylaying; snare, trap. —**acechar**, *vt.* to lie in ambush for; to spy on.—**acecho**, *m.* waylaying,

lying in ambush.—*al a.* or *en a.*, in wait, in ambush.

acedía, *f.* acidity, heartburn, sourness; roughness; asperity of address.

aceitar, *vt.* to oil; to rub with oil. —**aceite**, *m.* oil; essential oil.—*a. de ricino*, castor oil.—**aceitera**, *f.* oil cruet; oil can.—**aceitoso**, *a.* oily. —**aceituna**, *f.* olive.—**aceitunado**, *a.* olive-colored.

aceleración, *f.* acceleration; haste. —**acelerador**, *a.* accelerating.—*m.* accelerator.—**acelerar**, *vt.* to accelerate; to hasten, hurry, rush. —*vr.* to move fast; to make haste.

acémila, *f.* pack animal.

acendrado, *a.* purified, refined; unspotted, stainless.—**acendrar**, *vt.* to purify or refine; to free from stain or blemish.

acento, *m.* accent, stress; way of speaking; written accent.—**acentuación**, *f.* accentuation.—**acentuar**, *vt.* to accentuate; to emphasize; to write accents.

aceptable, *a.* acceptable, admissible. —**aceptación**, *f.* acceptation; acceptance, approval, applause.—**aceptar**, *vt.* to accept, admit; (com.) to honor.

acera, *f.* sidewalk; row of houses on either side of a street.

acerado, *a.* steely; strong; hard; sharp.

acerbo, *a.* tart; harsh, cruel; poignant.

acerca de, *prep.* about, with regard to.—**acercamiento**, *m.* approximation, approach, rapprochement. —**acercar**, *vti.* [d] to bring or place near or nearer.—*vri.* to draw near, come, approach.

acerico, *m.* pincushion.

acero, *m.* steel; sword; courage.

acérrimo, *a. super.* very strong (taste, odor); very harsh; very vigorous; very stanch or stalwart.

acertado, *a.* fit, proper; wise.—**acertar**, *vti.* [1] to hit the mark; to do the right thing; to guess, be right. —*vii.* to guess right.—*a. con*, to find, come upon.—**acertijo**, *m.* riddle.

aciago, *a.* unfortunate, sad; fateful.

acíbar, *m.* aloes; bitterness; displeasure.

acicalar, *vt.* to embellish.—*vr.* to dress in style; (coll.) to doll up.

acicate, *m.* inducement; goad.

acidez, *f.* acidity, tartness.—**ácido**, *m.* acid.—*a.* acid; sour; harsh.

acierto, *m.* good judgment; accuracy; rightness; skill; good aim; good guess.

aclamación, *f.* acclamation.—**aclamar,** *vt.* to shout, applaud, acclaim.

aclaración, *f.* explanation.—**aclarar,** *vt.* to make clear; to explain; to thin; to rinse.—*vi.* to clear up; to recover brightness.

aclimatar, *vt.* to acclimatize.—*vr.* to get acclimatized.

acobardar, *vt.* to intimidate, frighten. —*vr.* to become frightened, intimidated.

acogedor, *a.* welcoming, kindly.— **acoger,** *vti.* [c] to receive; (fig.) to harbor, shelter.—*vri.* to take refuge. —**acogida,** *f.*, **acogimiento,** *m.* reception; place of meeting; refuge; shelter.—*tener buena (mala) a.,* to be well (unfavorably) received.

acogotar, *vt.* to grab by the neck; to strangle.

acojinar, *vt.* to quilt; (mech.) to cushion.

acolchado, *a.* quilted.—*m.* (hydraul. eng.) mattress.—**acolchar, acolchonar,** *vt.* to quilt.

acólito, *m.* altar boy, acolyte; assistant.

acometedor, *n.* aggressor; enterprising person.—*a.* aggressive; enterprising.—**acometer,** *vt.* to attack, rush on, (coll.) go for; to undertake. —**acometida,** *f.*, **acometimiento,** *m.* ttack, assault; branch or outlet (in a sewer).

acomodado, *a.* convenient, fit; wealthy; fond of comfort; reasonable.—**acomodador,** *n.* usher (*f.* usherette) in a theater.—**acomodar,** *vt.* to arrange; to accommodate; to set to rights; to place; to reconcile; to furnish, supply; to take in, lodge.—*vi.* to fit; to suit.—*vr.* to condescend; to adapt oneself; to put up with; to settle.—**acomodaticio,** *a.* compliant, accommodating.—**acomodo,** *m.* employment, situation; arrangement; lodgings.

acompañamiento, *m.* accompaniment; retinue; attendance.—**acompañante,** *mf.* chaperon; companion; (mus.) accompanist.—*a.* accompanying.— **acompañar,** *vt.* to accompany; to attend, escort; to enclose (in letters).

acompasado, *a.* measured; rhythmical; slow.

acondicionado, *a.* of a (good, bad) disposition; in (good, bad) condition; of (good, bad) qualit·.—*aire a.,* air-conditioned.—**acondicionar,** *vt.* to condition; to prepare, arrange.

acongojar, *vt.* to afflict, grieve.—*vr.* to become anguished; to grieve.

aconsejable, *a.* advisable.—**aconsejar,** *vt.* to advise, counsel.—*vr.* (con) to consult (with).

acontecer, *vii.* [3-50] to happen, come about.—**acontecimiento,** *m.* event, happening.

acopio, *m.* gathering; storing; assortment; collection; supply; stock.

acoplamiento, *m.* coupling; joint; scarfing.—**acoplar,** *vt.* to couple, join, connect; to hitch, yoke; to scarf (timber); to reconcile; to pair; to mate (animals).—*vr.* to settle a difference, come to an agreement; to mate (of animals).

acoquinar, *vt.* to cow, intimidate. —*vr.* to be cowed.

acorazado, *m.* armored ship, ironclad. —*a.* ironclad; (elec.) shell.—**acorazar,** *vti.* [a] to armor.

acordar, *vti.* [12] to resolve; to agree upon; to remind; to tune, harmonize.—*vii.* to agree.—*vri.* (de) to remember, recollect.—*si mal no me acuerdo,* if I remember rightly. —**acorde,** *a.* agreed; in tune; in accord.—*m.* chord; harmony of sounds and colors.—**acordeón,** *m.* accordion.

acordonar, *vt.* to lace; to mill (a coin); to cord; to cordon or rope off.

acorralar, *vt.* to corral; to surround; to corner.

acortar, *vt.* to shorten, lessen, reduce; to obstruct.—*a. la marcha,* to slow down.—*vr.* to shrivel, contract; to be bashful; to fall back.

acosamiento, acoso, *m.* relentless persecution.—**acosar,** *vt.* to pursue relentlessly; to vex, harass.

acostado, *a.* reclining, lying down; in bed.—**acostar,** *vti.* [12] to lay down; to put to bed.—*vri.* to lie down; to go to bed.

acostumbrado, *a.* habitual, customary; used to, accustomed.—**acostumbrar,** *vt.* to accustom, train.— *vi.* to be accustomed, to be in the habit of.—*vr.* to get used to, become accustomed to.

acotación, *f.* stage direction (in a play); marginal note; elevation marked on a map.—**acotamiento,** *m.* enclosure, reservation; boundary mark.—**acotar,** *vt.* to set boundary marks on; to mark out; to annotate; to select.

acre, *a.* sour; acrimonious; tart; mordant.—*m.* acre (square measure).

acrecentamiento, *m.* increase.—**acrecentar,** *vti.* [1] to increase; to improve.

acreditado, *a.* reputable.—**acreditar,** *vt.* to assure, affirm; to verify, prove; (com.) to recommend, answer for, guarantee; to accredit, authorize.—vr. to establish one's reputation.

acreedor, a. meritorious, deserving. —n. creditor.—a. hipotecario, mortgagee.

acribillar, vt. to perforate; to riddle; to cover with wounds.

acrisolado, a. honest, virtuous, upright.

acrobacia, f. stunt.—**acróbata,** mf. acrobat.

acta, f. document; minutes; certificate.—levantar a., to draw up the minutes; to note, set down.

actitud, f. attitude; position, posture.

activar, vt. to make active; to expedite, hasten.—**actividad,** f. activity, energy.—en a., in operation. —**activo,** a. active.—m. (com.) assets.

acto, m. act, action, deed; public function.—a. seguido, immediately after.—en el a., at once.—**actor,** m. player, actor.—parte actora, plaintiff.—**actriz,** f. actress.—**actuación,** f. actuation; action; part played. —pl. (law) proceedings.

actual, a. present, of the present time.—**actualidad,** f. present time. —en la a., nowadays.—pl. current affairs; newsreel.

actuar, vi. to act; to perform judicial acts.—vt. to put in action, actuate.

actuario, n. actuary.

acuarela, f. water color (painting).

acuario, m. aquarium.

acuartelamiento, m. quartering or billeting (of troops); quarters.— **acuartelar,** vt. to quarter, billet.

acuático, a. aquatic.—**acuatizar,** vii. [a] (aer.) to alight on the water.

acuchillar, vt. to cut, hack; to slash, cut open; to knife.

acudir, vi. to go; to come; to attend; to respond (to a call); to go or come to the rescue; to resort; to have recourse.

acueducto, m. aqueduct; water-supply line.

acuerdo, m. resolution; determination; opinion; report; advice; remembrance; accord; agreement, convention, pact; harmony.—de a., in agreement; of the same opinion; in accordance.

acumulación, f. accumulation; gathering.—**acumulador,** n. accumulator. —m. battery.—**acumular,** vt. to accumulate, gather, pile up.—**acumulativo,** a. cumulative; joint.

acuñación, f. coining, minting; wedging.—**acuñar,** vt. to coin, mint; to wedge.

acuoso, a. watery.

acurrucarse, vri. [d] to huddle up.

acusación, f. accusation.—**acusado,** n. & a. defendant, accused.—**acusador,** n. acuser; prosecutor.—**acusar,** vt. to accuse; to prosecute; to indict; to acknowledge (receipt).—vr. (de) to confess (to).—acuse, m. acknowledgment (of receipt).

acústica, f. acoustics.

achacar, vti. [d] to impute.—**achacoso,** a. sickly, ailing.—**achaque,** m. indisposition; minor chronic ailment; excuse, pretext; motive; subject, matter.

achatar, vt. to flatten, squash.

achicar, vti. [d] to diminish, lessen; to shorten; to humble, belittle; to bail, drain.—vri. to humble oneself; to be cowed.

achicharrar, vt. & vr. to burn to a crisp.

adagio, m. adagio; proverb, maxim.

adán, m. (fig.) slovenly man.

adaptabilidad, f. versatility.—**adaptable,** a. adaptable; versatile.—**adaptación,** f. adaptation.—**adaptar,** vt. to adapt, fit.—vr. to adapt oneself.

adecuación, f. fitness; adequateness. —**adecuado,** a. adequate, suitable, proper.—**adecuar,** vt. to fit; to adapt.

adefesio, m. (coll.) nonsense, absurdity; blunder; queer person; ridiculous attire.

adelantado, a anticipated; advanced; far ahead; proficient; precocious; bold, forward; (of a clock) fast; early (fruits, plants).—por a., in advance.—**adelantamiento,** m. advance; progress; improvement; increase; anticipation; promotion.— **adelantar,** vt. & vi. to progress, advance; to grow; to keep on; to anticipate; to pay beforehand; to improve; to go fast; (of a clock) to gain.—vr. to take the lead; to come forward.—a. a, to surpass, outdo.—**adelante,** adv. ahead; farther on; forward.—de a., ahead, in the front; forward, head (as a.).—de aquí en a., de hoy en a., or en a., henceforth, from now on, in the future.—llevar a., to go ahead with, carry on.—más a., farther on. —salir a., to come through, come out well or ahead.—interj. forward! go on!—**adelanto,** m. advance, progress; improvement; (com.) advance payment.

adelfa, f. rosebay.

adelgazamiento, m. slimming; thinness.—**adelgazar,** vti. [a] to make slender; to thin out; to lessen.—vri. to become thin or slim.

ademán, *m.* gesture; attitude.—*pl.* manners.

además, *adv.* moreover, furthermore, besides.—*a. de,* besides.

adentro, *adv.* within, inside.—*mar a.,* out to sea.—*tierra a.,* inland.—*interj.* come in! let's go in!—*m. pl.* innermost thoughts.

adepto, *a.* adept; initiated.—*n.* follower, partisan.

aderezamiento, *m.* embellishment; dressing.—**aderezar,** *vti.* [a] to dress, embellish, adorn; to prepare; to cook, season; to size (cloth).—**aderezo,** *m.* dressing; adorning; arrangements, preparation; finery; set of jewelry; trappings.

adeudado, *a.* indebted; in debt.—**adeudar,** *vt.* to owe; (com.) to be subject to duty; to charge, debit.—*vr.* to run into debt.

adherencia, *f.* adhesion; adherence.—**adherir,** *vti.* [39] & *vri.* to adhere; to stick.—**adhesión,** *f.* adhesion; attachment; following.—**adhesivo,** *a.* adhesive.

adición, *f.* addition; remark or note added to a text.—**adicional,** *a.* additional.—**adicionar,** *vt.* to add to; to extend.

adicto, *n.* & *a.* follower; addict; addicted, devoted.

adiestramiento, *m.* training; practice; drill.—**adiestrar,** *vt.* to instruct, train.—*vr.* to practice, train.

adinerado, *a.* rich, wealthy.

¡adiós!, *interj* good-bye!—*m.* good-bye, farewell.

aditamento, *m.* addition, adjunct.

adivinación, *f.* divination, foretelling.—**adivinanza,** *f.* riddle.—**adivinar,** *vt.* to guess; to divine; to solve (a riddle).—**adivino,** *n.* diviner; fortuneteller; soothsayer.

adjetivo, *n.* & *a.* adjective.

adjuntar, *vt.* to enclose, send enclosed or with something else.—**adjunto,** *a.* adjoined; enclosed, attached; adjunct.—*n.* assistant.

administración, *f.* administration, management; board (of directors); central office.—*a. de correos,* post-office station.—**administrador,** *n.* administrator; manager; director; trustee.—*a. de aduanas,* collector of customs.—*a. de correos,* postmaster.—**administrar,** *vt.* to administer, govern.—**administrativo,** *a.* administrative.

admirable, *a.* admirable, excellent.—**admiración,** *f.* admiration; wonder.—*punto de a.,* exclamation point (!).—**admirador,** *n.* admirer.—**admirar,** *vt.* to admire.—*vr.* (de) to be surprised, amazed at.

admisible, *a* admissible.—**admisión,** *f.* admission, acceptance.—**admitir,** *vt.* to receive· to admit; to let in; to accept.

adobar, *vt.* to dress, prepare or cook (food); to pickle (meat, fish); to tan (hides).

adobo, *m* dressing for seasoning or pickling (meat, fish)· mending, repairing.

adocenado, *a.* common, ordinary, vulgar.

adoctrinar, *vt.* to instruct, indoctrinate.

adolecer, *vii.* [3] (de) (fig.) to suffer from.

adolescencia, *f.* adolescence; teen-age.—**adolescente,** *mf.* & *a.* adolescent; teen-age(r).

adonde, *adv.* (*interr.* **¿adónde?**) where; (where to?).—**adondequiera,** *adv.* wherever.

adopción, *f.* adoption.—**adoptar,** *vt.* to adopt; to embrace (an opinion).—**adoptivo,** *a.* adoptive, adopted.

adoquín, *m.* cobblestone; (coll.) blockhead.—**adoquinado,** *m.* & *a.* pavement; paved.—**adoquinar,** *vt.* to pave.

adorable, *a.* adorable.—**adoración,** *f.* adoration, worship.—**adorar,** *vt.* to adore, worship.

adormecedor, *a.* soporific.—**adormecer,** *vti.* [3] to cause drowsiness or sleep; to lull to sleep; to calm.—*vri.* to fall asleep; to grow numb.—**adormecimiento,** *m.* drowsiness; sleepiness; numbness.—**adormilado,** *a.* drowsy.

adornar, *vt.* to adorn, embellish, ornament; to furnish, garnish.—**adorno,** *m.* adornment, ornament; trimming.

adquirir, *vti.* [2] to acquire, obtain, get.—**adquisición,** *f.* acquisition; purchase.—**adquisitivo,** *a.—poder a.,* purchasing power.

adrede, *adv.* purposely, intentionally.

adrenalina, *f.* adrenaline.

adscribir, *vti.* [49] to inscribe; to add as an employee.—**adscrito,** *pp.* of ADSCRIBIR.—*a.* written after.

aduana, *f.* custom house.—**aduanero,** *n.* custom house officer; revenue officer.—*a.* custom house, customs.

adueñarse, *vr.* to take possession.

adulación, *f.* flattery, adulation.—**adulador,** *n.* flatterer, adulator.—**adular,** *vt.* & *vi.* to flatter, adulate.—**adulón,** *n.* & *a.* toady, cringer; cringing.

adulteración, *f.* adulteration.—**adulterar,** *vt.* to adulterate; to corrupt; to sophisticate; to tamper with.

—**adulterio,** *m.* adultery.—**adúltero,** *n.* adulterer, adulteress.

adulto, *n.* & *a.* adult.

adusto, *a.* austere, stern; sullen.

advenedizo, *n.* newcomer; outsider; upstart.—*a.* strange; extraneous; newly arrived.—**advenimiento,** *m.* advent, coming.

adventicio, *a.* accidental.

adverbial, *a.* adverbial.—**adverbio,** *m.* adverb.

adversario, *m.* opponent, adversary; enemy.—**adversidad,** *f.* adversity, misfortune.—**adverso,** *a.* adverse; unfavorable; untoward.

advertencia, *f.* advice; warning; notice; foreword.—**advertido,** *a.* forewarned; wise.—**advertir,** *vti.* [39] to take notice of; to advise; to give notice or warning; to point out.

adyacente, *a.* adjacent.

aéreo, *a.* aerial; airy; aeronautical; air.—*por correo a.*, by air mail.—*fuerza a.*, air force.—**aerodinámica,** *f.* aerodynamics.—*a.* streamline(d).—**aeródromo,** *m.* military airport.—**aeromoza,** *f.* (airplane) stewardess.—**aeronauta,** *mf.* aeronaut.—**aeronáutica,** *f.* aeronautics.—**aeronave,** *f.* airship, dirigible.—**aeroplano,** *m.* airplane, aircraft.—**aeropuerto,** *m.* airport.

afabilidad, *f.* affability, friendliness.—**afable,** *a.* affable, kind, friendly.

afamado, *a.* celebrated, noted, famous.

afán, *m.* anxiety, solicitude, eagerness.—**afanarse,** *vr.* to act or work eagerly or anxiously; to toil.—**afanoso,** *a.* solicitous; laborious, painstaking; hard, difficult.

afear, *vt.* to deform, deface; to make ugly or faulty; to impair; to decry, censure.

afectación, *f.* sophistication; affectation.—**afectado,** *a.* affected; moved; sophisticated; stuffy.—**afectar,** *vt.* to affect, concern; to move; to affect, feign, put on.—**afectividad,** *f.* affection.—**afectivo,** *a.* affective; easily moved.—**afecto,** *m.* affection, love, fondness.—*a.* affectionate; (a) fond (of), inclined (to).—**afectuoso,** *a.* affectionate.

afeitado, *m.* shave, shaving.—**afeitar,** *vt.* to shave.—*vr.* to shave (oneself).—**afeite,** *m.* rouge, cosmetic, paint; make-up.

afelpado, *a.* velvety.

afeminado, *a.* & *m.* effeminate (man).—**afeminamiento,** *m.*, **afeminación,** *f.* effeminacy.

aferrado, *a.* headstrong, obstinate.—**aferramiento,** *m.* grasping, seizing;

attachment; obstinacy.—**aferrar,** *vt.* to grasp, grip, seize; to moor, anchor.—*vr.* to persist obstinately, to cling.

afianzamiento, *m.* bail; support; fastening, securing.—**afianzar,** *vti.* [a] to prop up; to fasten, secure.—*vri.* to steady oneself, make oneself firm.

afición, *f.* fondness; taste, inclination; affection.—*tomar a. a*, to become fond of.—**aficionado,** *n.* & *a.* amateur; (sports) fan.—*a. a*, fond of.—**aficionar,** *vt.* to inspire affection, fondness or liking.—*vr.* **(a) to** fancy; to become fond of.

afijo, *a.* affixal.—*m.* affix.

afilado, *a.* sharp, keen.—**afilador,** *m.* sharpener.—**afilar,** *vt.* to sharpen, whet, grind.

afiliar, *vt.* **(a)** to affiliate (with).—*vr.* **(a)** to join, affiliate oneself (with).

afín, *a.* akin, kindred; related.

afinación, *f.* finishing touch, refining; tuning.—**afinador,** *n.* finisher; piano tuner; tuning key.—**afinamiento,** *m.* refinement.—**afinar,** *vt.* to perfect; to refine; to tune.—*vr.* to become polished.

afinidad, *f.* affinity; resemblance; analogy.

afirmación, *f.* affirmation.—**afirmar,** *vt.* to affirm, assert; to make fast, secure, fasten.—*vr.* to hold fast; **to** steady oneself or make oneself firm; to maintain firmly.—**afirmativo,** *a.* affirmative.

aflicción, *f.* affliction, sorrow, grief.—**aflictivo,** *a.* afflictive, distressing.—**afligir,** *vti.* [49-c] to afflict, grieve.—*vri.* to grieve, languish, become despondent.

aflojamiento, *m.* relaxation; loosening, slackening.—**aflojar,** *vt.* to loosen, slacken, relax, let loose.—*vi.* to grow weak; to abate.—*vr.* to weaken; to grow cool in fervor or zeal; to lose courage.

afluencia, *f.* flowing; influx.—**afluente,** *m.* affluent, tributary.—**afluir,** *vii.* [23-e] **(a)** to congregate, assemble (in); to flow (into).

afonía, *f.* laryngitis.

afortunado, *a.* lucky, fortunate.

afrenta, *f.* affront, outrage; disgrace.—**afrentar,** *vt.* to affront; to insult.—*vr.* to be ashamed; to blush.—**afrentoso,** *a.* ignominious.

africano, *n.* & *a.* African.

afrontar, *vt.* to confront; to face.

afta, *f.* (med.) thrush.

afuera, *adv.* out; outside; in public.—*interj.* out! clear the way! one side!—*f. pl.* suburbs, outskirts.

agachar, vt. to lower, bow down.—vr. to stoop, squat, cower.—a. las orejas, (coll.) to humble oneself; to bend the knee.

agalla, f. gill; tonsil.—pl. (coll.) courage.—tener a. (coll.) to have guts; (Am.) to be greedy; to be shrewd.

agarrada, f. tussle.—**agarradero,** n. holder, handle.—**agarrado,** a. (coll.) stingy, close-fisted.—**agarrar,** vt. to grasp, seize; (coll.) to obtain; to catch; to come upon.—vr. to clinch, grapple, hold on to.

agarrotar, vt. to tie firmly; to execute; to strangle.

agasajar, vt. to receive and treat kindly; to regale; to entertain.—**agasajo,** m. friendly treatment, consideration, regard.

agazaparse vr. to hide by crouching or squatting; to huddle up.

agencia, f. agency; commission; agent's bureau, office.—**agenciar,** vt. to solicit, promote, negotiate.—**agente,** m. agent; broker; promoter; policeman.

ágil, a. nimble, fast, light.—**agilidad,** f. agility, nimbleness.

agitación, f. agitation; excitement.—**agitador,** n. agitator, rouser.—a. agitating, stirring.—**agitar,** vt. to agitate; to stir, shake up; to ruffle.—vr. to flutter; to become excited.

agobiar, vt. to weigh down; to overwhelm; to oppress.—vr. to bow; to crouch.—**agobio,** m. bending down; oppression, burden.

agonía, f. agony; death struggle; violent pain; anxious desire.—**agonizante,** a. & mf. dying; dying person.—**agonizar,** vii. [a] to be dying, in the throes of death.

agostar, vt. to scorch, wither.—vr. to become parched; to dry up, wilt.—**agosto,** m. August.—hacer su a., to take the opportunity to feather one's nest.

agotamiento, m. draining; exhaustion.—**agotar,** vt. to drain; to exhaust, use up.—vr. to become exhausted; to give out; to wear oneself out; to be out of print.

agraciado, a. graceful, gracious.—n. grantee.—**agraciar,** vt. to adorn, embellish; to favor; to grace; to grant.

agradable, a. agreeable; pleasing, pleasant.—**agradar,** vi. to be pleasing; to please.

agradecer, vti. [3] to thank for; to be grateful for.—**agradecido,** a. thankful.—**agradecimiento,** m. gratefulness, gratitude.

agrado, m. affability, agreeableness;

pleasure; liking.—ser del a. de uno, to like someone.

agrandamiento, m. enlargement.—**agrandar,** vt. to enlarge; to increase; to let out (dress).

agrario, a. agrarian.

agravar, vt. to aggravate; to make worse, more serious.—vr. to get worse, more serious.

agraviar, vt. to wrong, offend, insult.—vr. to take offense.—**agravio,** m. offense, insult, affront.

agraz, a. unripe.—m. unripe grape; (coll.) displeasure.

agredir, vti. [50] to attack, assault.

agregado, m. aggregate; assistant; attaché.—**agregar,** vti. [b] to add, join; to collect, gather; to aggregate.

agresión, f. aggression.—**agresivo,** a. aggressive, offensive.—**agresor,** n. aggressor, assaulter.

agreste, a. rustic, wild; rude, uncouth.

agriar, vt. to make sour or tart; to irritate, exasperate.—vr. to sour, turn acid.

agrícola, a. agricultural.—**agricultor,** n. farmer, agriculturist.—**agricultura,** f. agriculture, farming.

agridulce, a. bittersweet.

agrietarse, vr. to crack; to chap (skin).

agrimensor, m. land surveyor.—**agrimensura,** f. land surveying.

agrio, a. sour, acrid; rude.

agrupación, f. cluster; crowd; group; gathering.—**agrupar,** vt. to group; to cluster.—vr. to crowd together; to form groups.

agua, f. water; liquid; rain; slope of a roof.—pl. luster of diamonds; clouds (in silk, etc.); gloss (in feathers, stones).—a. abajo, downstream.—a. arriba, upstream.—a. bendita, holy water.—a. dulce, fresh water.—a. nieve, sleet.—estar con el a. hasta el cuello, to be in a fix, in difficulties.—estar entre dos aguas, to be undecided, be on the fence.—hacer aguas, to urinate.—¡hombre al a.! man overboard!—**aguacate,** m. avocado, alligator pear.—**aguacero,** m. heavy rain.—**aguachirle,** m. inferior wine.—**aguada,** f. watering station; drinking water source.—**aguado,** a. watery, watered.—**aguafuerte,** m. etching.—**aguafiestas,** mf. spoilsport.—**aguamarina,** f. aquamarine.

aguantar, vt. to bear, endure; to resist; to maintain; to hold.—vr. to forbear.—**aguante,** m. strength, resistance; patience, endurance.

aguar, vt. [b] to dilute with water; to mar (pleasure).—vr. to be spoiled, ruined; to become thin (appl. to liquids), get watery; (Am.) to back down, be intimidated.

aguardar, *vt.* to wait for, await; to expect.

aguardentoso, *a.* mixed with hard liquor; harsh (voice).—**aguardiente,** *m.* brandy, firewater.

aguarrás, *m.* turpentine.

aguazal, *m.* marsh, fen.

agudeza, *f.* sharpness; fineness; wit, witticism; repartee.—**agudo,** *a.* sharp, acute; keen-edged; shrill, screechy; witty, clever, sparkling.

agüero, *m.* omen.

aguerrido, *a.* battle-tested, veteran.

aguijón, *m.* sting (of insect); prick; spur, goad.—**aguijonazo,** *m.* thrust with a goad.—**aguijonear,** *vt.* to prick, goad; to push, urge.

águila, *f.* eagle.—**aguileño,** *a.* aquiline. —**aguilucho,** *m.* eaglet.

aguinaldo, *m.* Christmas bonus or gratuity.

aguja, *f.* needle; hatpin; spire, steeple; bodkin; obelisk; hornfish; needle shell; hand (of a clock); magnetic compass; (R.R.) switch rail; spindle.—**agujerear,** *vt.* to pierce, perforate.—**agujero,** *m.* hole; dugout.—**agujeta,** *f.* little needle.— *pl.* charley horse, pain from over-exercise.

agusanarse, *vr.* to become worm-eaten, putrid.

aguzador, *n.* sharpener.—*a.* sharpening.—**aguzar,** *vti.* [a] to whet, sharpen; to urge, excite.—*a. las orejas,* to prick up one's ears.

aherrojar, *vt.* to chain, put in irons.

ahí, *adv.* there; yonder.—*de a.,* hence. —*por a.,* somewhere around here; that way; over there; more or less.

ahijado, *n.* godchild; protégé.

ahinco, *m.* earnestness, eagerness, ardor.

ahito, *a.* gorged, sated; stuffed; full; replete; disgusted, bored.—*m.* indigestion; satiety.

ahogado, *a.* drowned; close, unventilated; suffocated.—*estar* or *verse a.,* to be overwhelmed or swamped.—*n.* suffocated or drowned person.—**ahogar,** *vti.* [b] to drown; to choke, throttle, smother; to oppress; to quench, extinguish.—*vri.* to drown; to be suffocated.—**ahogo,** *m.* oppression, tightness (of the chest, etc.); suffocation; pain.

ahondar, *vt.* to deepen; to dig; to go deep into.—*vi.* to go deep, penetrate; to progress in knowledge.

ahora, *adv.* now.—*a. bien,* now, now then.—*a. mismo,* right now, just now; at once.—*hasta a.,* so far;

hitherto, until now.—*por a.,* for the present.

ahorcado, *n. & a.* hanged (person). —**ahorcar,** *vti.* [d] to hang (execute by hanging).—*vri.* to hang, be hanged; to hang oneself.

ahorita, *adv.* (Am.) just now.—*a. mismo,* this very minute, just now; at once.

ahormar, *vt.* to fit, shape, adjust; to last, break in (shoes); to bring to reason.

ahorrar, *vt.* to save, economize; to spare; to avoid.—**ahorrativo,** *a.* thrifty, frugal.—**ahorro,** *m.* economy.—*pl.* savings.—*caja de ahorros,* savings bank.

ahuecar, *vti.* [d] to make hollow, scoop out; to loosen.—*a. la voz,* to speak in a deep, solemn tone.—*vri.* to become hollow; to swell, put on airs.

ahumado, *a.* smoky; smoked.—**ahumar,** *vt.* to smoke; to cure in smoke. —*vi.* to fume; to emit smoke.—*vr.* to be blackened by smoke.

ahuyentar, *vt.* to put to flight; to drive away.

aindiado, *a.* half-breed, mestizo-looking.

airado, *a.* angry, wrathful.

aire, *m.* air; atmosphere; wind; air, appearance; carriage, gait; tune.—*al a. libre,* outdoors.—*de buen,* or *mal a.,* in a good, or a bad humor.—*en el a.,* in suspense, in the air.—*tomar el a.,* to take a walk.—**airear,** *vt.* to air; to ventilate; to aerate.—*vr.* to take the air; to cool oneself.—**airoso,** *a.* airy, windy; graceful, gracious; successful.

aislado, *a.* isolated; insulated.—**aislador,** *m.* isolator; insulator.—*a.* isolating; insulating.—**aislamiento,** *m.* isolation; insulation; insulating material.—**aislar,** *vt.* to isolate; to insulate.—*vr.* to become isolated; to seclude oneself.

ajar, *vt. & vr.* to crumple; to wilt, wither.

ajedrecista, *n.* chess player.—**ajedrez,** *m.* chess.

ajeno, *a.* another's; alien, foreign; unaware, ignorant; oblivious.

ajetrearse, *vr.* to tire oneself out; to bustle about.—**ajetreo,** *m.* bustle; fatigue; agitation.

ají, *m.* (Am.) green pepper.

ajo, *m.* garlic; swear word.—*echar ajos (y cebollas),* to swear, curse.

ajuar, *m.* trousseau; household furniture.

ajustado, *a.* agreed upon; tight; fitted.—**ajustar,** *vt.* to adjust; to adapt, fit; to regulate; to agree about, concert; to tighten; to engage, hire.—*vr.* to settle; to conform; to be engaged or hired.—*ajuste, m.* adjustment; fitting; agreement; engagement; settlement. —*pl.* couplings.

ajusticiar, *vt.* to execute, put to death.

al, (*contr.* of **a & el**) to the; on, at; about.—*le di la carta al criado,* I gave the letter to the servant.—*al llegar,* on arrival.—*al amanecer,* at daybreak.—*estoy al partir,* I am about to leave.

ala, *f.* wing; row; wing (of a building); brim (of a hat); leaf (of a door, table).—*cortar las alas a uno,* to clip one's wings.—*dar alas,* to embolden, encourage.

alabanza, *f.* praise.—**alabar,** *vt.* to praise, commend.—*vr.* to boast.

alabastro, *m.* alabaster.

alabear, *vt.* & *vr.* to warp.

alacena, *f.* cupboard; closet; cabinet.

alacrán, *m.* scorpion.

alado, *a.* winged.

alambicado, *a.* pedantic, affected; rarified.—**alambicamiento,** *m.* distillation; pedantry, affectation.—**alambicar,** *vti.* [d] to distill; to use affected language.—**alambique,** *m.* still.

alambrada, *f.* wire fence; wire defenses.—**alambrado,** *m.* wire cover; electric wiring.—**alambrar,** *vt.* to fence with wire.—**alambre,** *m.* wire. —*a. de puas,* barbed wire.—**alambrera,** *f.* wire netting; wire screen.

alameda, *f.* alameda, public walk shaded with trees; poplar grove.—**álamo,** *m.* poplar.

alarde, *m.* ostentation, boasting, bluff. —*hacer a.,* to boast; to show off.—**alardear,** *m.* to boast.

alargar, *vti.* [b] to lengthen; to extend; to stretch out; to protract, prolong.—*vri.* to be prolonged; to drag; to become longer; to enlarge.

alarido, *m.* howl, outcry, shout, scream, screech.

alarma, *f.* alarm.—**alarmante,** *a.* alarming.—**alarmar,** *vt.* to alarm.—*vr.* to become alarmed.—**alarmista,** *n.* alarmist.

alazán, *a.* sorrel-colored (of horses). —*m.* a horse of that color.

alba, *f.* dawn; alb.—*al a.,* or *al rayar el a.,* at daybreak.

albacea, *mf.* (law) executor, executrix.

albanés, *n.* & *a.* Albanian.

albanil, *m.* mason, bricklayer.—**albañilería,** *f.* masonry (occupation or work).

albarda, *f.* packsaddle.

albaricoque, *m.* apricot.

albayalde, *m.* white lead.

albedrío, *m.* will; free will; impulsiveness.

alberca, *f.* pond, reservoir; (Am.) swimming pool.

albergar, *vti.* [b] to lodge, shelter, harbor; to take in (lodgers).—*vr.* to lodge; to find shelter or lodging.—**albergue,** *m.* lodging; shelter; (animal) den.

albóndiga, *f.* meat ball.

albor, *m.* dawn; whiteness; beginning. —**alborear,** *vi.* to dawn.

albornoz, *m.* hooded cloak; bathrobe.

alborotador, *n.* agitator, rioter.—*a.* rowdy.—**alborotar,** *vt.* to disturb, agitate.—*vi.* to create an uproar; to act noisily.—*vr.* to become excited; to fuss; to riot.—**alboroto,** *m.* excitement; disturbance; tumult; hubbub, fuss.

alborozar, *vti.* [a] to gladden, exhilarate.—*vri.* to rejoice.—**alborozo,** *m.* merriment, gaiety, joy.

albur, *m.* risk, chance.—*correr un a.,* to venture, chance, risk.

alcachofa, *f.* artichoke.

alcahueta, *f.* bawd, procuress, gobetween.—**alcahuete,** *m.* procurer; abettor; gossip.—**alcahuetear,** *vt.* & *vi.* to aid, abet; to pander.

alcaide, *m.* warden; jailer.

alcalde, *m.* mayor.—**alcaldesa,** *f.* mayoress; wife of the mayor.—**alcaldía,** *f.* mayor's office; city hall.

álcali, *m.* alkali.—**alcalino,** *a.* alkaline.

alcance, *m.* reach; overtaking; pursuit; arm's length; range (of fire arms, etc.); deficit; scope.—*pl.* mental powers; ability.—*al a. de,* within reach of.—*a largo a.,* long term.—*dar a.,* to catch up with.

alcancía, *f.* piggy bank; money box.

alcanfor, *m.* camphor.—**alcanforado,** *a.* camphoric.

alcantarilla, *f.* sewer; drain.—**alcantarillado,** *m.* sewerage system.—*a.* provided with sewers.—**alcantarillar,** *vt.* to make or install sewers.

alcanzado, *a.* needy; in debt.—**alcanzar,** *vti.* [a] to reach; to overtake, come up to; to obtain, attain.—*a. a uno algo,* to hand, pass something to someone.

alcaparra, *f.* caper.

alcatraz, *m.* pelican.

alcayata, *f.* spike; wall hook.

alcázar, *m.* castle, fortress.

alce, *m.* elk; moose.

alcoba, *f.* alcove; bedroom.

alcohol, *m.* alcohol.—**alcohólico,** *a.* alcoholic.

alcornoque, *m.* cork tree; (coll.) blockhead.

alcurnia, *f.* lineage.

aldaba, *f.* knocker (of a door); latch; handle (door, furniture).—*tener buena a.*, or *buenas aldabas,* to have powerful friends.—**aldabonazo,** *m.* knocking.

aldea, *f.* village, hamlet.—**aldeano,** *n.* villager, peasant.—*a.* rustic, unpolished.

aleación, *f.* alloy; alloying.

alebrestarse, *vr.* (Am.) to cut capers; to become frightened or excited.

aleccionador, *a.* instructive.—**aleccionamiento,** *m.* instruction, coaching.—**aleccionar,** *vt.* to teach, instruct, coach.

aledaño, *a.* bounding, bordering.—*m.* boundary, border.

alegación, *f.* allegation, argument.—**alegar,** *vti.* [b] to allege, affirm; to quote; to adduce; to argue.—**alegato,** *m.* allegation; (law) summing-up.

alegrar, *vt.* to make merry, exhilarate; to enliven; to brighten.—*vr.* (de) to rejoice (at); to be glad (of or to); to be happy; to get tipsy.—**alegre,** *a.* merry, joyful; lively; cheerful; funny; gay; bright (of colors); optimistic; tipsy.—*a. de cascos,* featherbrained.—**alegría,** *f.* mirth, merriment; gaiety; rejoicing, joy.—**alegrón,** *m.* (coll.) sudden, unexpected joy; a flash.

alejamiento, *m.* removal to a distance; receding; retiring; withdrawal.—**alejar,** *vt.* to remove to a distance; to move away; to separate; to estrange.—*vr.* to recede; to withdraw or move away.

alelarse, *vr.* to become stupefied.

alelí, *m.* = ALHELÍ.

alemán, *n.* & *a.* German.

alentador, *a.* encouraging, cheering.—**alentar,** *vii.* [1] to breathe.—*vti.* to encourage, cheer; to inspire.

alergia, *f.* allergy.—**alérgico,** *a.* allergic.

alero, *m.* eaves, overhang; splashboard of a carriage.

alerta, *m.* alarm, alert.—*a.* watchful, vigilant, alert.—*interj.* look out! watch out!—**alertar,** *vt.* to render vigilant; to put on guard.

aleta, *f.* fin; (mech.) leaf of a hinge; blade (of a propeller); fender (of a car).

aletargar, *vti.* [b] to cause drowsiness.—*vri.* to become drowsy, sluggish.

aletazo, *m.* blow with the wing; flapping.—**aletear,** *vi.* to flutter (wings or fins).—**aleteo,** *m.* fluttering (of wings or fins).

alevosía, *f.* perfidy, treachery.—**alevoso,** *a.* treacherous.

alfabético, *a.* alphabetical.—**alfabeto,** *m.* alphabet.

alfarería, *f.* pottery; potter's art.—**alfarero,** *n.* potter.

alféizar, *m.* window sill or embrasure.

alfeñique, *m.* sugar paste; weakling.

alférez, *m.* ensign; second lieutenant.

alfil, *m.* bishop (in chess).

alfiler, *m.* pin; scarfpin; brooch.—*a. de seguridad,* safety pin.—*pegar* or *prender con alfileres,* to do in a slipshod way.—**alfilerazo,** *m.* pinprick.—**alfiletero,** *m.* pincase, needle case; pincushion.

alfombra, *f.* carpet.—**alfombrar,** *vt.* to carpet.

alforja, *f.* saddlebag.

alforza, *f.* pleat, tuck; (coll.) scar.

alga, *f.* seaweed.

algarabía, *f.* jargon; din, hubbub.

algarroba, *f.* carob.—**algarrobo,** *m.* locust tree; carob tree.

algazara, *f.* din, clamor.

álgebra, *f.* algebra.—**algebraico,** *a.* algebraic.

algo, *pron.* something.—*adv.* somewhat, a little.—*a. es a.,* every little bit counts.

algodón, *m.* cotton; cotton plant.—*a. en rama,* raw cotton.—**algodonal,** *m.* cotton plantation.—**algodonero,** *a.* pertaining to cotton.—*m.* cotton plant; cotton dealer.

alguacil, *m.* constable; bailiff; mayor; sheriff.

alguien, *pron.* somebody, someone.

algún, alguno, *a.* some, any.—*alguna que otra vez,* sometimes, once in a while.—**alguno,** *pron.* somebody, someone.—*a. que otro,* a few, some.—*pl.* some, some people.

alhaja, *f.* jewel, gem; valuable object.

alharaca, *f.* clamor, fuss, ado.

alhelí, *m.* (bot.) wallflower.

alhucema, *f.* lavender.

aliado, *n.* & *a.* ally, allied.—**alianza,** *f.* alliance; agreement; wedding ring.—**aliarse,** *vr.* to become allied; to form an alliance.

alicaído, *a.* drooping, weak; dejected, crestfallen.

alicates, *m. pl.* pliers.

aliciente, *m.* attraction, inducement.

alienado, *a.* insane.—**alienista,** *mf.* alienist.

aliento, *m.* breath, wind; breathing; encouragement; bravery.—*dar a.,* to encourage.

aligeramiento, *m.* alleviation, lightening.—**aligerar,** *vt.* to lighten; to alleviate; to hasten; to shorten.

alimaña, *f.* destructive animal.

alimentación, *m.* feeding; food, nourishment.—**alimentar,** *vt.* to feed, nourish; to nurture; to encourage;

to foster. —**alimenticio,** *a.* nourishing; nutritious.—**alimento,** *m.* food, nourishment.—*pl.* allowance; alimony; board.

alineación, *f.* alignment.—**alinear,** *vt.* to align; to line up; to put into line.—*vr.* to fall in line; to form a line.

aliñar, *vt.* to dress or season (food); to adorn.—**aliño,** *m.* dressing or seasoning; ornament, decoration; cleanliness.

alisar, *vt.* to plane, smooth; to polish, burnish.

alisios, *m. pl.* trade winds.

alistamiento, *m.* enrollment; conscription, levy.—**alistar,** *vt. & vr.* to enlist, enroll; to get or make ready.

aliviar, *vt.* to alleviate, relieve, soothe; to lighten; to reprieve.—**alivio,** *m.* alleviation, easement, mitigation, relief; reprieve.

aljibe, *m.* cistern; reservoir, pool; water tank.

alma, *f.* soul; human being; inhabitant; essence, core; bore of a gun. —*a. de cántaro,* fool.—*a. de Dios,* kind-hearted person; harmless creature.—*a. en pena,* ghost.—*a. mía, mi a.,* my dearest; my love.

almacén, *m.* store, shop; warehouse, repository; storage house, depot; grocery store; dockyard.—*pl.* department store.—**almacenaje,** *m.* storage.—**almacenar,** *vt.* to store; to lay up, hoard; to put in storage. —**almacenista,** *m.* wholesaler; department store or warehouse owner.

almanaque, *m.* almanac, calendar.

almeja, *f.* clam.

almena, *f.* battlement.

almendra, *f.* almond.—**almendrado,** *a.* almond-shaped.—*m.* macaroon.—**almendro,** *m.* almond tree.

almíbar, *m.* syrup.—**almibarado,** *a.* syrupy, sugary; flattering.

almidón, *m.* starch.—**almidonado,** *a.* starched; stiff; straightlaced, stuffy. —**almidonar,** *vt.* to starch.

almirantazgo, *m.* admiralty.—**almirante,** *m.* admiral.

almirez, *m.* brass mortar.

almizcle, *m.* musk.—**almizclero,** *a.* musk.

almohada, *f.* pillow; bolster.—*consultar con la a.,* to sleep on the matter. —**almohadilla,** *f.* pincushion; pad; small pillow.—**almohadón,** *m.* cushion.

almorranas, *f. pl.* hemorrhoids, piles.

almorzar, *vii.* [12-a] to lunch.—*vti.* to have for lunch.—**almuerzo,** *m.* lunch.

alocado, *a.* half-witted; wild; reckless.

alojamiento, *m.* lodging; quartering of soldiers.—**alojar,** *vt.* to lodge; to quarter (troops).—*vr.* to take lodgings; to lodge; to room, put up at.

alondra, *f.* lark.

alpargata, *f.* hemp sandal.

alpinismo, *m.* mountain climbing.—**alpinista,** *mf.* mountain climber.

alpiste, *m.* birdseed.

alquilar, *vt.* to let, rent; to hire; to fee.—*vr.* to serve for wages; to hire out.—**alquiler,** *m.* wages; rent, rental; the act of hiring or letting.

alquitrán, *m.* tar, pitch; (naut.) stuff made of pitch, grease, etc.—**alquitranado,** *a.* tarry.

alrededor, *adv.* around.—*a. de,* about, around, (coll.) approximately.—**alrededores,** *m. pl.* environs, outskirts.

alta, *f.* (med.) discharge (from hospital); (mil.) certificate of enlistment. —*darse de a.,* to be admitted (in a profession, social club), to become a member.

altanería, *f.* haughtiness, insolence.—**altanero,** *a.* haughty, arrogant, insolent.

altar, *m.* altar.

altavoz, *m.* loudspeaker.

altea, *f.* marshmallow.

alterable, *a.* alterable, changeable.—**alteración,** *f.* alteration; strong emotion; tumult; commotion.—**alterado,** *a.* disturbed, agitated.—**alterar,** *vt.* to alter, change, transform; to disturb, stir up.—*vr.* to become altered, disturbed, agitated; to become angry.

altercado, *m.* altercation, quarrel, wrangle.—**altercar,** *vti.* [d] to dispute, altercate; to quarrel, wrangle.

alternador, *m.* (elec.) alternator.—**alternar,** *vt., vi. & vr.* to alternate.—**alternativa,** *f.* alternative, choice; service by turn.—**alternativo,** *a.* alternate, alternating.—*corriente alterna,* alternating current.

alteza, *f.* Highness (title); loftiness.

altibajos, *m. pl.* unevenness of ground; ups and downs, vicissitudes.

altiplanicie, *f.,* **altiplano,** *m.* plateau, tableland.

altisonante, *a.* high-sounding, pompous.

altitud, *f.* height; altitude.

altivez, *f.* haughtiness, arrogance, insolence; pride.—**altivo,** *a.* haughty, proud; overbearing, arrogant.

alto, *a.* high; elevated; tall; eminent; lofty; loud.—*altas horas,* the small hours.—*altos hornos,* blast furnaces.

—*de lo a.*, from above.—*m.* height, elevation; hill; top; story, floor; summit, mountain top, crest; top floor; heap, pile; (mil.) halt; place or time of rest.—*hacer a.*, to halt. —*pasar por a.*, to overlook, forget.— *adv.* high, high up; loud, loudly; (voice) high.—*interj.* (mil. command) halt!—**altoparlante,** *m.* v. ALTAVOZ.—**altozano,** *m.* hillock, knoll; height.—**altura,** *f.* height, altitude; tallness, stature; summit, top; (naut.) the latitude; altitude; level, standard.—*estar a la a. de*, to be equal to.—*pl.* the heavens, Heaven. —*a estas alturas*, at this moment.

alucinación, *f.* hallucination.—**alucinar,** *vt.* & *vr.* to dazzle, fascinate, delude.

alud, *m.* avalanche.

aludido, *a.* referred, aforementioned. —**aludir,** *vi.* to allude, refer.

alumbrado, *m.* illumination, lighting. —*a.* lit, lighted; tipsy.—**alumbramiento,** *m.* childbirth; lighting.— **alumbrar,** *vt.* to light; to illuminate, light up; to enlighten.—*vi.* to give, or shed light; to give birth.— *vr.* to get tipsy.

aluminio, *m.* aluminum.

alumno, *n.* pupil, student.

alusión, *f.* allusion, reference, hint.— **alusivo,** *a.* allusive, hinting.

alza, *f.* rise (in price).—**alzada,** *f.* height (of horse); (law) appeal.— **alzado,** *a.* & *n.* (of) a lump sum; revolted, insurgent.—**alzamiento,** *m.* lifting, raising; insurrection.—**alzar,** *vti.* [a] to raise; to lift; to pick up; (eccl.) to elevate the host.—*a. cabeza,* to recover from a calamity or a disease.—*a. velas,* to sail away; to move.—*vri.* to revolt; to rise; (law) to appeal.—*alzarse con,* to run off with something, steal something.

allá, *adv.* there; thither, over there. —*a. en mi niñez,* in the old times of my childhood.—*a. por el año de 1900,* about 1900.—*a. veremos,* we shall see.—*a. voy,* I am coming.—*el más a.,* the beyond.—*más a.,* farther. —*muy a.,* much beyond, far beyond.

allanamiento, *m.* leveling; smoothing; acceptance of a judicial finding; breaking into, trespassing.— **allanar,** *vt.* to level, smooth; to flatten; to remove or overcome (difficulties); to pacify, subdue; to break into (a house).—*vr.* to abide (by), acquiesce.

allegado, *a.* near, related.—*n.* relative; ally.—**allegar,** *vti.* [b] to reap; to collect; to solicit, procure.—*vri.* to come near, approach; to adhere to.

allende, *adv.* beyond, over, on the other side.—*a. el mar,* overseas.

allí, *adv.* there, in that place; thereto. —*por a.,* that way; through there; thereabouts.

ama, *f.* mistress of the house; landlady; (woman) owner.—*a. de llaves,* housekeeper.

amabilidad, *f.* amiability, affability; kindness.—**amable,** *a.* amiable, affable; kind.

amaestrar, *vt.* to instruct, train, coach.

amagar, *vti.* [b] to threaten; to hint. —*vii.* to threaten; to be impending; to feign.—**amago,** *m.* threat; hint; indication, sign.

amalgama, *f.* amalgam.—**amalgamar,** *vt.* to amalgamate.

amamantar, *vt.* to nurse, suckle.

amanecer, *vii.* [3] to dawn.—*m.* dawn, daybreak.—*al a.,* at dawn, at daybreak.

amanerado, *a.* full of mannerisms.— **amanerarse,** *vr.* to adopt mannerisms; to become affected.

amansamiento, *m.* taming; breaking (horses).—**amansar,** *vt.* to tame, domesticate; to break (a horse); to pacify, soothe.—*vr.* to calm down; to become subdued.

amante, *mf.* & *a.* lover; mistress; loving.

amanuense, *m.* clerk; scribe.

amañar, *vt.* to do cleverly.—*vr.* to be handy; to manage things cleverly.

amapola, *f.* poppy.

amar, *vt.* to love.

amarar, *vi.* to set down on water.

amargar, *vti.* [b] to make bitter.— *vri.* to become bitter.—**amargo,** *a.* bitter.—*m.* bitterness; bitters; (Am.) maté tea.—**amargor,** *m.,* **amargura,** *f.* bitterness.

amarillear, *vi.* to show a yellow tinge. —**amarillento,** *a.* yellowish.—**amarillez,** *f.* yellowness.—**amarillo,** *a.* & *n.* yellow.

amarra, *f.* cable; rope.—**amarradero,** *m.* hitching post; tying or fastening place; moor'ng berth.—**amarrar,** *vt.* to tie, fasten; to lash, moor.— **amarre,** *m.* tying; mooring; mooring line or cable.

amartillar, *vt.* to hammer; to cock (a gun).

amasar, *vt.* to knead; to mash; to amass, accumulate.—**amasijo,** *m.* dough; (act of) kneading; paste, mixture; medley, hodgepodge.

amatista, *f.* amethyst.

amatorio, *a.* amatory.

amazona, *f.* Amazon; horsewoman.— **amazónico,** *a.* Amazonian.

ambages, *m. pl.* circumlocutions;

maze; beating around the bush.— *sin a.*, in plain language.

ámbar, *m.* amber.—**ambarino,** *a.* amberlike.

ambición, *f.* ambition; aspiration.—**ambicionar,** *vt.* to seek eagerly; to aspire to; to covet.—**ambicioso,** *a.* ambitious, aspiring; covetous, greedy.

ambiente, *m.* atmosphere, air; environment.

ambigüedad, *f.* ambiguity.—**ambiguo,** *a.* ambiguous, uncertain, doubtful.

ámbito, *m.* bounds, area; scope.

ambos, *a.* both.

ambulancia, *f.* ambulance; field hospital.—**ambulante,** *a.* walking; shifting; roving, wandering; moving.

amedrentar, *vt.* to scare, frighten, intimidate.

amén, *m.* amen, so be it.—*a. de*, besides; aside from.

amenaza, *f.* threat, menace.—**amenazador,** *a.* threatening, menacing.—**amenazar,** *vti.* [a] to threaten, menace; to be impending.

amenguar, *vti.* [b] to diminish; to defame.

amenidad, *f.* amenity.—**amenizar,** *vti.* [a] to render pleasant or agreeable.—**ameno,** *a.* pleasant, agreeable; readable.

americano, *a.* & *n.* American.

ametralladora, *f.* machine gun, tommy gun.—**ametrallar,** *vt.* to shell; to machine-gun.

amianto, *m.* asbestos.

amiga, *f.* female friend; mistress.—**amigable,** *a.* friendly; fit, affable.

amígdala, *f.* tonsil.—**amigdalitis,** *f.* tonsilitis.

amigo, *m.* friend.—*ser a. de*, to be a friend of; to have a taste for.—**amigote,** *m.* pal, chum.

amilanamiento, *m.* abject fear; terror.—**amilanar,** *vt.* to frighten; to cow.—*vr.* to become terrified; to cower, quail; to flag.

aminorar, *vt.* to lessen; to enfeeble.

amistad, *f.* friendship, friendliness.—*pl.* friends.—*hacer a.*, or *amistades*, to become acquainted; to make friends.—*hacer las amistades*, to make up, become reconciled.—**amistoso,** *a.* friendly, amicable.

amnistía, *f.* amnesty.—**amnistiar,** *vt.* to pardon, grant amnesty.

amo, *m.* master; owner; boss.

amodorrado, *a.* drowsy, sleepy.—**amodorrarse,** *vr.* to become drowsy.

amohinarse, *vr.* to sulk.

amolador, *n.* & *a.* grinder, sharpener, whetter; grinding, sharpening, whetting.—**amoladura,** *f.* whetting,

grinding.—**amolar,** *vti.* [12] to grind, sharpen, hone.

amoldar, *vt.* to mold, shape; to adjust; to adapt.—*vr* to conform, adapt oneself.

amonestación, *f.* admonition, warning.—*pl.* banns.—*correr las amonestaciones*, to publish the banns.—**amonestar,** *vt.* to admonish, warn, advise; to publish the banns.

amoníaco, *m.* ammonia.

amontonamiento, *m.* heaping; piling; crowding.—**amontonar,** *vt.* & *vr.* to heap up, pile up; to crowd.

amor, *m.* love; the object of love.—*pl.* love affairs.—*a. propio*, self-respect, self-esteem.—*con* or *de mil amores*, with all one's heart, with the greatest pleasure.

amoratado, *a.* livid, bluish.—**amoratarse,** *vr.* to grow or become purplish.

amordazar, *vti.* [a] to gag, muzzle.

amorío, *m.* love affair; love making.—**amoroso,** *a.* affectionate, loving; tender.

amortajar, *vt.* to shroud (a corpse).

amortiguación, *f.*, **amortiguamiento,** *m.* softening, mitigation, lessening.—**amortiguador,** *m.* shock absorber; muffler.—**amortiguar,** *vti.* [b] to lessen; to muffle; to deafen (a sound); to soften; to absorb (shocks).

amortización, *f.* amortization.—**amortizar,** *vti.* [a] to amortize; to pay on account; to redeem (debt, etc.).

amoscarse, *vri.* [d] to get peeved, annoyed.

amotinado, *a.* mutinous, riotous.—*n.* mutineer.—**amotinamiento,** *m.* mutiny.—**amotinar,** *vt.* & *vr.* to excite to rebellion or riot; to mutiny, rebel.

amovible, *a.* removable.

amparar, *vt.* to shelter; to protect, help.—*vr.* to enjoy protection; to defend oneself; to seek shelter.—**amparo,** *m.* aid; protection; shelter.

amperaje, *m.* amperage.—**amperímetro,** *m.* amperimeter.—**amperio,** *m.* ampere.

ampliación, *f.* enlargement.—**ampliador,** *n.* amplifier.—*a.* amplifying.—**ampliar,** *vt.* to amplify; to enlarge; to magnify.—**amplificador,** *a.* amplifying.—*n.* amplifier, loudspeaker.—**amplificar,** *vti.* [d] = AMPLIAR.—**amplio,** *a.* ample, roomy, extensive, large.—**amplitud,** *f.* largeness, fullness; amplitude; extent.

ampolla, *f.* blister; decanter; water bubble; bulb.—**ampollar,** *vt.* to blister; to make hollow.—*vr.* to ɔubble up.—**ampolleta,** *f.* small vial; sandglass.

ampulosidad, *f.* verbosity.—**ampuloso,** *a.* pompous, bombastic.

amputación, *f.* amputation.—**amputar,** *vt.* to amputate.

amueblar, *vt.* to furnish (a room, a house, etc.).

anacrónico, *a.* anachronistic.—**anacronismo,** *m.* anachronism.

ánade, *n.* duck; goose.

analfabetismo, *m.* illiteracy.—**analfabeto,** *a.* & *n.* illiterate (person).

análisis, *mf.* analysis.—**analista,** *mf.* analyst.—**analítico,** *a.* analytical.—**analizador,** *m.* analyzer.—**analizar,** *vti.* [a] to analyze.

analogía, *f.* analogy; resemblance.—**analógico, análogo,** *a.* analogous, similar.

anaquel, *m.* shelf.—**anaquelería,** *f.* shelving, case of shelves.

anaranjado, *a.* orange-colored.—*n.* orange (color).

anarquía, *f.* anarchy.—**anárquico,** *a.* anarchical.—**anarquismo,** *m.* anarchism.—**anarquista,** *n.* & *a.* anarchist(ic).

anatema, *m.* anathema, excommunication.—**anatematizar,** *vti.* [a] to anathematize.

anatomía, *f.* anatomy; dissection.—**anatómico,** *a.* anatomical.

anca, *f.* haunch, croup (animals); rump; hip.

ancestral, *a.* ancestral.

ancianidad, *f.* old age.—**anciano,** *n.* & *a.* aged; old (man, woman).

ancla, áncora, *f.* anchor.—*echar anclas,* to anchor.—*levar anclas,* to weigh anchor.—**anclar,** *vi.* to anchor.

ancho, *a.* broad, wide—*m.* width, breadth.—*a sus anchas,* with absolute freedom.

anchoa, anchova, *f.* anchovy.

anchura, *f.* width, breadth.—**anchuroso,** *a.* vast, spacious, extensive.

andada, *f.* walk, track, trail.—*pl.* footprints.—*volver a las andadas,* to go back to one's old tricks.—**andadura,** *f.* gait; amble (of horses).

andaluz, *n.* & *a.* Andalusian.

andamiada, *f.,* **andamiaje,** *m.* scaffolding.—**andamio,** *m.* scaffold.

andanada, *f.* broadside; grandstand for spectators; reproof; tirade.

andante, *a.* walking.—**andanza,** *f.* occurrence, event.—*pl.* rambles, wanderings.—**andar,** *vii.* [4] to walk, go; (watch, machine, etc.) to run, work, move, go; to act, behave; to elapse, pass; to be; to get along, be going.—*¡anda!* move on! get up! go ahead!—*a. en,* to be attending to,

or engaged in; to be going on, be near; to ride in (a carriage, automobile, etc.).—*andarse con rodeos,* or *por las ramas,* to beat around the bush.—*a todo a.,* at full speed.—**andariego,** *a.* restless, roving; fast walker, runner.—**andarín,** *m.* professional walker, runner.

andas, *f. pl.* stretcher; litter; bier.

andén, *m.* sidewalk by a road, wharf or bridge; platform (of a RR. station).

andino, *a.* & *n.* Andean, of the Andes.

andrajo, *m.* rag, tatter; despicable person.—**andrajoso,** *a.* ragged, in tatters.

andurriales, *m. pl.* byroads, lonely places.

anécdota, *f.* anecdote.—**anecdótico,** *a.* anecdotal.

anegado, *a.* overflowed; wet, soaked.—**anegar,** *vt.* to inundate, flood; to submerge; to flush; to drown, sink.—*vr.* to become wet or soaked; to be flooded.

anejo, *a.* = ANEXÓ.

anemia, *f.* anemia.—**anémico,** *a.* anemic.

anestesia, *f.* anesthesia.—**anestesiar,** *vt.* to anesthetize.—**anestésico,** *m.* & *a.* anesthetic.

anexar, *vt.* to annex.—**anexión,** *f.* annexation.—**anexo,** *a.* annexed, joined.

anfibio, *n.* amphibian.—*a.* amphibious.

anfiteatro, *m.* amphitheater; balcony of a theater.

anfitrión, *m.* host (at a banquet).

angarillas, *f. pl.* handbarrow; panniers; cruet stands.

ángel, *m.* angel.—**angélico,** *a.* angelic(al).

angina, *f.* angina.

angostar, *vt.* & *vr.* to narrow; to become narrow, contract.—**angosto,** *a.* narrow.—**angostura,** *f.* narrowness; narrows (in a river, etc.).

anguila, *f.* eel.

angular, *a.* angular.—*piedra a.,* cornerstone.—**ángulo,** *m.* angle.

angustia, *f.* anguish, grief, sorrow.—**angustiar,** *vt.* to cause anguish, distress.—**angustioso,** *a.* full of, or causing, anguish.

anhelante, *a.* eager, yearning, longing.—**anhelar,** *vi.* to desire anxiously, long for, covet.—**anhelo,** *m.* strong desire; longing; panting.—**anheloso,** *a.* anxious, panting.

anidar, *vi.* to nest; to nestle; to dwell; to shelter.—*vr.* to nest; to settle (in a place).

anilina, *f.* aniline.

anilla, *f.* ring; curtain ring; hoop.—**anillado,** *a.* in the form of a ring, annulated.—anillo, *m.* finger ring; small hoop.

ánima, *f.* soul; bore of a gun.—animación, *f.* animation, liveliness.—animado, *a.* lively, animated.—animador, *n.* one who animates or enlivens, master of ceremonies.—animadversión, *f.* animadversion; enmity.

animal, *m.* animal; dunce, blockhead.—*a.* animal; stupid, brutish.

animar, *vt.* to animate, give life; to encourage.—*vr.* to become lively; to cheer up.—ánimo, *m.* spirit, soul; courage.—animosidad, *f.* animosity; courage.—animoso, *a.* brave, spirited.

aniñado, *a.* childish.—aniñarse, *vr.* to become childish.

aniquilamiento, *m.* destruction, annihilation.—aniquilar, *vt.* to annihilate, wipe out.

anís, *m.* anise, anisette; licorice.

aniversario, *m.* anniversary.—*a.* annual, yearly.

ano, *m.* anus.

anoche, *adv.* last night.—anochecer, *vii.* [3] to grow dark (at the approach of night).—*m.* nightfall, dusk.—anochecida, *f.* nightfall.

anodino, *n.* & *a.* anodyne; insignificant.

anonadamiento, *m.* annihilation; crushing.—anonadar, *vt.* to annihilate; to crush, overwhelm.

anónimo, *a.* anonymous, nameless.—*m.* anonymous letter.

anormal, *a.* abnormal.—anormalidad, *f.* abnormality.

anotación, *f.* annotation; note; entry.—anotar, *vt.* to write down; to annotate; to enter (in register).

ansia, *f.* anxiety; eagerness; anguish.—*pl.* pangs.—ansiar, *vt.* to desire anxiously.—ansiedad, *f.* anxiety; worry.—ansioso, *a.* anxious; eager.

antagónico, *a.* antagonistic.—antagonismo, *m.* antagonism.—antagonista, *mf.* antagonist; opponent.

antaño, *adv.* yesteryear; yore.

antártico, *a.* antarctic.

ante, *prep.* before; in the presence of.—*a. todo,* above all.—*m.* elk; buffalo; buffalo skin.

anteanoche, *adv.* night before last.

anteayer, *adv.* day before yesterday.

antebrazo, *m.* forearm.

antecámara, *f.* antechamber; lobby.

antecedente, *a.* & *m.* antecedent.—antecesor, *n.* predecessor, forefather.

antedatar, *vt.* to antedate.

antedicho, *a.* aforesaid.

antelación, *f.* precedence in order of time.

antemano, *a.* beforehand.—*de a.,* beforehand.

antena, *f.* antenna; aerial (of radio); feeler.

antenoche, *adv.* = ANTEANOCHE.

anteojo, *m.* spyglass; small telescope.—*pl.* eyeglasses, spectacles; binoculars; opera glasses.

antepasado, *a.* (of time) passed.—*año a.,* year before last.—*n.* ancestor.

antepecho, *m.* railing; window sill.

anteponer, *vti.* [32] to prefer; to place before.

anterior, *a.* previous; earlier; former; above, preceding.—anterioridad, *f.* priority.—*con a.* beforehand.

antes, *adv.* before; formerly; first; rather.—*a. bien,* on the contrary; rather.

antesala, *f.* anteroom, waiting room.—*hacer a.,* to be kept waiting.

antiaéreo, *a.* antiaircraft.

antibiótico, *m.* & *a.* antibiotic.

anticipación, *f.* anticipation; foretaste.—anticipado, *a.* early, ahead of time.—*por a.,* in advance.—anticipar, *vt.* to anticipate (in the sense of "to do, cause to happen," etc., before the regular time); to advance (money, payment); to lend.—*vr.* to anticipate, act first; to happen earlier than the expected time.—anticipo, *m.* advance; advance payment; (law) retainer.

anticomunista, *mf.* & *a.* anticommunist.

anticongelante, *m.* & *a.* antifreeze.

anticuado, *a.* antiquated, obsolete.—anticuario, *n.* & *a.* antiquarian.

anticuerpo, *m.* antibody.

antideslizante, *m.* & *a.* antiskid.

antidetonante, *m.* & *a.* antiknock.

antídoto, *m.* antidote.

antier, *adv.* (Am.) v. ANTEAYER.

antifaz, *m.* veil that covers the face; mask.

antigualla, *f.* object of remote antiquity; outmoded custom or object.—antigüedad, *f.* antiquity; ancient times; antique.—antiguo, *a.* antique; ancient, old.—*a la a.,* after the manner of the ancients, in an old-fashioned manner.—*de a.,* since old times.—*los antiguos,* the ancients.

antihigiénico, *a.* unsanitary.

antílope, *m.* antelope.

antillano, *n.* & *a.* West Indian.

antimonio, *m.* antimony.

antinomia, *f.* antinomy; contradiction; paradox.

antipatía, *f.* antipathy; dislike, aversion.—antipático, *a.* uncongenial, disagreeable.

antipatriótico, *a.* unpatriotic.

antípoda, *a.* antipodal.—*m. pl.* antipodes.

antisemita, *mf.* & *a.* anti-Semite.

antiséptico, *n.* & *a.* antiseptic.

antojadizo, antojado, *a.* capricious, whimsical, fanciful.—**antojarse,** *vr.* to arouse a fancy; to cause a capricious desire.—*se me antojó,* I took a fancy to.—**antojo,** *m.* whim, fancy; birth mark.—*a su a.,* as one pleases; arbitrarily.

antología, *f.* anthology.

antorcha, *f.* torch.

antracita, *f.* anthracite.

antropología, *f.* anthropology.

anual, *a.* annual, yearly.—**anuario,** *m.* yearbook; trade or professional directory.

anudar, *vt.* to knot; to tie, unite.

anuencia, *f.* compliance, consent.

anulación, *f.* annulment, voiding, nullification; abatement.—**anular,** *vt.* to annul, make void; to cancel, quash.—*a.* ring-shaped.—*dedo a.,* ring finger.

anunciador, *n.* & *a.* announcer, announcing; advertiser, advertising.—**anunciante,** *n.* announcer; advertiser.—**anunciar,** *vt.* to announce; to advertise; to foretell.—**anuncio,** *m.* announcement; notice; advertisement.

anzuelo, *m.* fishhook; lure.

añadido, *m.* hair switch.—*a.* annexed. —**añadidura,** *f.* addition, increase; extra, over.—*por a.,* in addition, to make matters worse.—**añadir,** *vt.* to add, join.

añagaza, *f.* allurement, enticement; trick.

añejo, *a.* old; of old vintage; stale.

añicos, *m. pl.* shreds, fragments.—*hacer a.,* to shatter.

añil, *m.* indigo; indigo blue.—**añilar,** *vt.* to blue (clothes).

año, *m.* year.—*al a.,* by the year; after a year.—*a. bisiesto,* leap year. *a. económico,* or *fiscal,* fiscal year. —*a. escolar,* school year.—*a. nuevo,* New Year.—*tener 10 años,* to be 10 years old.—**añoso,** *a.* old, aged.

añoranza, *f.* longing; yearning.—**añorar,** *vi.* to long for; to yearn for, be homesick for; to reminisce.

apabullar, *vt.* to flatten, crush.

apacentar, *vti.* [1] to graze, pasture; (fig.) to nourish.

apacible, *a.* gentle, placid, calm.

apaciguamiento, *m.* pacification, appeasement.—**apaciguar,** *vti.* [b] to appease, pacify.

apachurrar, *vt.* to crush, flatten.

apadrinar, *vt.* to sponsor; to favor; to protect; to be godfather at a christening; to be best man at a wedding; to act as a second in a duel.

apagar, *vti.* [b] to put out, extinguish; to turn off; to soften; to deaden.—*vri.* to become extinguished, die out; to go out.—**apagón,** *m.* blackout.

apaisado, *a.* more wide than high.

apalabrar, *vt.* to make an arrangement; to come to an agreement; to speak about, discuss; to engage.

apalancar, *vti.* [d] to lever.

apalear, *vt.* to beat up, thrash; to cane; to horsewhip.

apañar, *vt.* to grasp, seize; to carry away; to pilfer; to patch, mend; to contrive, manage.

aparador, *m.* sideboard, cupboard; show window.

aparato, *m.* apparatus; appliance; pomp, show; system.—**aparatoso,** *a.* pompous, showy.

aparcería, *f.* (agricultural) partnership.—**aparcero,** *n.* (agricultural) partner.

aparear, *vt.* to match, mate; to pair.

aparecer, *vii.* & *vri.* [3] to appear, show up, turn up.—**aparecido,** *n.* ghost, specter.

aparejado, *a.* fit; ready; equipped.—**aparejar,** *vt.* to prepare; to saddle or harness; to rig; to equip.—*vr.* to get ready; to equip oneself.—**aparejo,** *m.* preparation; harness, gear; packsaddle; tackle; rigging.—*pl.* equipment, trappings.

aparentar, *vt.* to feign, pretend.—**aparente,** *a.* apparent.

aparición, *f.* apparition; appearance (coming in sight); ghost.

apariencia, *f.* appearance, aspect; probability; semblance.

apartadero, *m.* (RR.) siding.

apartado, *a.* distant; aloof; remote; different.—*m.* compartment; P.O. letter box; paragraph, section.—**apartamento,** *m.* apartment.—**apartamiento,** *m.* separation; retirement; aloofness; secluded place; (Am.) apartment.—**apartar,** *vt.* to set apart; to separate, divide; to dissuade; to remove; to sort.—*vr.* to withdraw; to hold off; to desist; to retire; to separate.—**aparte,** *m.* paragraph; (theat.) aside.—*adv.* separately; aside.

apasionado, *a.* passionate; impassioned; partial.—*n.* admirer.—**apasionamiento,** *m.* passion; partiality. —**apasionar,** *vt.* to rouse, excite, thrill; to fill with passion.—*vr.* to become impassioned, passionately fond; to fall passionately in love.

apatía, *f.* apathy, indolence.—**apático,** *a.* apathetic, indolent.

apeadero, *m.* (RR.) secondary station; landing.—**apear,** *vt.* to dismount, cause to alight; to bring down; to dissuade.—*vr.* to alight, get off.

apechugar, *vti.* [b] to push with the chest.—*a. con,* to put up with something courageously; to accept.

apedrear, *vt.* to stone.

apegarse, *vri.* [b] to become attached to; to become fond of.—**apego,** *m.* attachment, fondness.

apelable, *a.* appealable.—**apelación,** *f.* appeal; remedy, help.—**apelar,** *vt.* & *vi.* to appeal; to have recourse to.—**apelativo,** *m.* apellation.

apelotonar, *vt.* & *vr.* to form into balls; to pile up.

apellidado, *a.* named (last name), by the name of.—**apellidar,** *vt.* to call by name (last name).—*vr.* to be called (have the last name of).—**apellido,** *m.* family name, last name.

apenar, *vt.* & *vr.* to cause pain, sorrow; to grieve; (Am.) to cause embarrassment, shame.

apenas, *adv.* scarcely, hardly; no sooner than; as soon as.

apéndice, *m.* appendix.—**apendicitis,** *f.* appendicitis.

apercibimiento, *m.* readiness; warning; summons.—**apercibir,** *vt.* to provide; to prepare; to warn, advise; to summon.—*vr.* (a) to get ready (to).—*a. de,* to notice.

apergaminado, *a.* like parchment; dried up.

aperitivo, *m.* aperitif; appetizer.

apero, *m.* farm implement; tool.—*pl.* equipment (for an activity).

apertura, *f.* (act of) opening or beginning.

apesadumbrar, *vt.* & *vi.* to grieve; to make (become) sad, grief-stricken.

apestado, *a.* & *n.* pestered, annoyed; satiated.—**apestar,** *vt.* to infect with the plague; to corrupt, turn putrid; to annoy, bother; to sicken, nauseate.—*vi.* to stink.—**apestoso,** *a.* stinking, sickening; offensive; boring.

apetecer, *vti.* [3] to hunger for; to like; to desire.—*vii.* to be desirable, appetizing.—**apetecible,** *a.* desirable; appetizing.—**apetencia,** *f.* appetite, hunger; desire.—**apetito,** *m.* appetence.—**apetitoso,** *a.* appetizing, inviting, palatable.

apiadarse, *vr.* (de) to pity, take pity (on).

ápice, *m.* apex, summit, top, pinnacle.

apilar, *vt.* to heap, pile up.

apiñado, *a.* crowded, close together.—**apiñamiento,** *m.* pressing together; crowding, congestion.—**apiñar,** *vt.* & *vr.* to press together, crowd.

apio, *m.* celery.

apisonamiento, *m.* tamping.—**apisonar,** *vt.* to tamp; to roll.

aplacar, *vti.* [d] to appease, pacify, placate.

aplanamiento, *m.* leveling, flattening; dejection.—**aplanar,** *vt.* to make level, even; to flatten; to terrify or astonish.—*vr.* to tumble down; to dismay; to get depressed.

aplastante, *a.* crushing, overpowering.—**aplastar,** *vt.* to smash, crush, squash; to confound.—*vr.* to flatten; to collapse.

aplaudir, *vt.* to applaud, clap; to approve; to praise.—**aplause,** *m.* applause; clapping; approbation.

aplazamiento, *m.* postponement; adjournment.—**aplazar,** *vti.* [a] to postpone; to adjourn; to procrastinate.

aplicable, *a.* applicable, suitable, fitting.—**aplicación,** *f.* studiousness; diligence.—**aplicado,** *a.* applied, studious; industrious.—**aplicar,** *vti.* [d] to apply; to put on; to clap; to attribute or impute; to adjudge.—*vri.* to apply oneself; to devote oneself diligently.

aplomado, *a.* calm, grave; serious; plumbed, vertical.—**aplomar,** *vt.* to make straight or vertical, to plumb.—*vi.* to plumb, be vertical.—**aplomo,** *m.* self-assurance, aplomb; verticalness.

apocado, *a.* pusillanimous, timid; irresolute.—**apocar,** *vti.* [d] to lessen; to belittle.—*vri.* to humble, belittle oneself.

apodar, *vt.* to nickname.

apoderado, *n.* proxy; attorney.—**apoderar,** *vt.* to empower; to grant power of attorney to.—*apoderarse de,* to take possession of, seize.

apodo, *m.* nickname.

apogeo, *m.* apogee; height (of fame, etc.).

apolillarse, *vr.* to be moth-eaten, worm-eaten.

apolítico, *a.* non-political.

apología, *f.* apologia, defense, praise.

apoltronarse, *vr.* to grow lazy; to loiter.

aporreado, *a.* cudgeled; miserable, dragged out.—**aporrear,** *vt.* to beat, cudgel, maul; to pester.—*vr.* to overwork, to become overtired.—**aporreo,** *m.* beating, cudgeling; pestering.

aportación, *f.,* **aporte,** *m.* contribution.—**aportar,** *vi.* to contribute; to make port; to arrive.

aposentar, *vt.* to lodge.—*vr.* to take lodgings.—**aposento,** *m.* room or apartment.

aposta, *adv.* on purpose.

apostar, *vti.* [12] to bet; to post, station.—*a. a que,* to bet that.—*apostárselas a,* or *con,* to compete with.

apostasía, *f.* apostasy.—**apóstata,** *mf.* & *a.* apostate.

apóstol, *m.* apostle.—**apostolado,** *m.* apostleship.—**apostólico,** *a.* apostolic.

apostrofar, *vt.* to apostrophize.—**apóstrofe,** *f.* apostrophe.—**apóstrofo,** *m.* apostrophe (').

apostura, *f.* natural elegance, graceful bearing.

apoyar, *vt.* to rest, lean, support; to back, defend; to aid; to abet.—*vi.* (en or sobre) to rest (on).—*vr.* (en) to rest (on); to lean (on or against); to be supported (by); to be based (on).—**apoyo,** *m.* prop, stay; support; protection, aid; backing.

apreciable, *a.* appreciable, noticeable; worthy of esteem; nice, fine; valuable.—**apreciación,** *f.* estimation, valuation; appreciation.—**apreciar,** *vt.* to appreciate, price, value; to esteem.—**aprecio,** *m.* esteem, high regard; appraisement, valuation.

aprehender, *vt.* to apprehend, arrest, seize.—**aprehensión,** *f.* seizure, capture; apprehension; fear.—**aprehensor,** *n.* captor.

apremiante, *a.* urgent, pressing.—**apremiar,** *vt.* to press, urge; to compel, oblige.—**apremio,** *m.* pressure, constraint; judicial compulsion.

aprender, *vt.* & *vi.* to learn.—**aprendiz,** *n.* apprentice.—**aprendizaje,** *m.* apprenticeship.

aprensión, *f.* apprehension; scruple; fear; distrust, suspicion.—**aprensivo,** *a.* apprehensive, fearing.

apresar, *vt.* to seize, grasp; to capture; to imprison.

aprestar, *vt.* to prepare, make ready; to aid.—*vr.* to get ready.

apresurado, *a.* hasty, quick.—**apresuramiento,** *m.* hastiness, quickness.—**apresurar,** *vt.* to hurry, hasten.—*vr.* to make haste, hurry up.

apretar, *vti.* [1] to tighten; to press down, compress; to clench (teeth, fist); to grip (hand in greeting); to squeeze; to urge.—*vii.* to pinch (of shoes, etc.); to be tight (of clothes).—**apretón,** *m.* sudden pressure; struggle, conflict; squeeze;

short run, spurt.—*a. de manos,* handshake.—**apretujar,** *vt.* (coll.) to squeeze tightly.—**aprieto,** *m.* jam, crush; stringency, difficulty, quandary; cramp; tight spot.

aprisa, *adv.* quickly, hurriedly, promptly; fast.

aprisionar, *vt.* to imprison; to tie, handcuff.

aprobación, *f.* approval, approbation; consent.—**aprobar,** *vti.* [12] to approve; to pass (in an examination).

aprontar, *vt.* to prepare quickly; to make ready; to expedite.

apropiación, *f.* appropriation; giving or taking possession; confiscation; adaptation.—**apropiado,** *a.* appropriate, proper, fitting.—**apropiar,** *vt.* to adapt; to fit.—*apropiarse de,* to take illegal possession of.

aprovechable, *a.* available, fit to be used.—**aprovechado,** *a.* saving, thrifty, studious.—*n.* go-getter.—**aprovechamiento,** *m.* utilization, use; exploitation; profit, benefit; progress, diligence.—**aprovechar,** *vt.* to utilize, make good use of; to profit.—*vi.* to be useful, profitable or beneficial; to avail; to progress, get ahead.—*aprovecharse de,* to take advantage of, make the most of.

aprovisionar, *vt.* to supply.

aproximación, *f.* approximation, approach.—**aproximado,** *a.* approximate; nearly correct.—**aproximar,** *vt.* to place or bring near; to approximate.—*vr.* to get near, approach.

aptitud, *f.* aptitude, natural ability.—*pl.* qualifications.—**apto,** *a,* apt, capable, competent.

apuesta, *f.* bet, wager.

apuesto, *a.* elegant, stylish, spruce.

apuntación, *f.* note; memorandum; musical notation.—**apuntador,** *n.* one who takes or keeps notes; (theat.) prompter.

apuntalar, *vt.* to prop; to shore up.

apuntar, *vt.* to aim, level; to point out, mark; to note, make a note of; to hint; to sketch; (theat.) to prompt.—*vi.* to begin to appear.—**apunte,** *m.* annotation, memorandum; rough sketch.

apuñalar, *vt.* to stab.

apurado, *a.* worried; needy; exhausted; difficult; in haste.—**apurar,** *vt.* to drain to the last drop; to exhaust (a subject); to press, hurry; to worry, annoy.—*vr.* to hurry up; to get worried.—**apuro,** *m.* need, want; worry; plight, predicament, quandary; rush, hurry.

aquejar, *vt.* to grieve, afflict, ail.

aquel (*fem.* **aquella**), *a.* that (over there).—*pl.* those (yonder).—**aquél** (*fem.* **aquélla**), *pron.* that one; the former; those.—**aquello**, *pron. neut.* that, that thing, that matter.

aquí, *adv.* here; hither.—*de a. en adelante*, from now on, hereafter.—*hasta a.*, up till now.—*por a.*, this way, through here.

aquiescencia, *f.* (law) acquiescence, consent.

aquietar, *vt.* to quiet; to pacify.—*vr.* to become calm; to quiet down.

aquilatar, *vt.* to examine closely; to assay.

ara, *f.* altar.

árabe, *mf.* Arab.—*a.* Arabian; Arabic.—**arábigo**, *a.* Arabian, Arabic.

arado, *m.* plow; (Am.) piece of cultivated land.

aragonés, *n. & a.* Aragonese.

arancel, *m.* tariff.—*a. de aduanas*, customs, duty.—**arancelario**, *a.* pertaining to tariff.

arandela, *f.* (mech.) washer; pan of a candlestick; sconce.

araña, *f.* spider; chandelier.

arañar, *vt.* to scratch.—**arañazo**, *m.* scratch.

arar, *vt.* to plow.

arbitraje, *m.* arbitration.—**arbitrar**, *vt.* to arbitrate; to umpire; to act unhampered; to contrive.—**arbitrariedad**, *f.* arbitrariness; arbitrary act.—**arbitrario**, *a.* arbitrary; arbitral.—**arbitrio**, *m.* free will; means; arbitration; bond; compromise; discretion, judgment.—**árbitro**, *m.* arbitrator, arbiter, umpire, referee.

árbol, *m.* tree; mast; upright post; axle or shaft; arbor; spindle; drill.—*a. genealógico*, family tree.—**arbolado**, *a.* wooded; masted.—*m.* woodland.—**arboleda**, *f.* grove.—**arbusto**, *m.* shrub.

arca, *f.* ark; chest; coffer.

arcada, *f.* arcade; row of arches.—*pl.* retching.

arcángel, *m.* archangel.

arcano, *a.* occult.—*m.* deep secret.

arce, *m.* maple, maple tree.

arcilla, *f.* clay.

arco, *m.* arc; arch; bow.—*a. iris*, rainbow.

arcón, *m.* large chest; bin, bunker.

archimillonario, *a. & n.* multimillionaire.

archipiélago, *m.* archipelago.

archivar, *vt.* to file; to deposit in archives.—**archivero**, *n.* archivist; file-case, file-drawers.—**archivo**, *m.* archives; file; public records.

arder, *vi.* to burn; to rage (of war, etc.); to be consumed.—*a. en rescoldo*, to smolder.

ardid, *m.* trick, scheme, stratagem.

ardiente, *a.* ardent, burning; passionate, fervent.

ardilla, *f.* squirrel.

ardor, *m.* ardor; hotness, heat; dash, valor.—**ardoroso**, *a.* ardent; fiery, vigorous.

arduo, *a.* arduous.

área, *f.* area; square decameter (See Table).

arena, *f.* sand, grit; arena.—**arenal**, *m.* sandy ground; desert.—**arenero**, *m.* sand dealer; sandbox.

arenga, *f.* harangue, speech.—**arengar**, *vii.* [b] to harangue, deliver a speech.

arenque, *m.* herring.

arete, *m.* eardrop, earring.

argamasa, *f.* mortar.

argelino, *a. & n.* Algerian.

argentado, *a.* silvered, silver-plated.—**argentar**, *vt.* to plate or adorn with silver; to polish like silver.—**argentino**, *a. & n.* Argentinian.—*a.* silvery.

argolla, *f.* ring; staple; hoop.

argucia, *f.* trick, scheme; cunning.

argüir, *vii. & vti.* [23-e] to argue.—**argumentación**, *f.* argumentation; reasoning.—**argumentar**, *vi.* to argue, dispute.—**argumento**, *m.* argument; summary; plot (of a play, etc.).

aridez, *f.* drought; barrenness, aridity.—**árido**, *a.* arid, dry, barren.—*pl.* dry articles, esp. grains and vegetables.

ariete, *m.* battering ram.

ario, *n. & a.* Aryan.

arisco, *a.* churlish, cross, unsociable; shy.

arista, *f.* sharp edge or angle.

aristocracia, *f.* aristocracy.—**aristócrata**, *mf. & a.* aristocrat.

aritmética, *f.* arithmetic.—**aritmético**, *a.* arithmetical.—*m.* arithmetician

arma, *f.* weapon, arm; technical division of military forces; means, power, reason.—*pl.* armed forces; military profession.—**armada**, *f.* navy; fleet; squadron.—**armador**, *m.* outfitter, ship owner; adjuster, fitter, assembler; jacket.—**armadura**, *f.* armor; framework, shell of a building; setting, fitting; truss; framing, mounting; trestle; reinforcement (of concrete); armature (of a dynamo, etc.).—**armamento**, *m.* armament, accoutrements.—**armar**, *vt.* to arm; to man; to bind; to assemble, mount; to adjust, set, frame; to reinforce (concrete); to form, prepare; to start, cause; (naut.) to equip, fit out, put in commission.—*vr.* to prepare oneself; to arm oneself.

armario, *m.* wardrobe; clothes closet; cabinet; bookcase.

armatoste, *m.* hulk; unwieldy machine; cumbersome piece of furniture; fat, clumsy fellow.

armazón, *f.* framework, skeleton, frame; hulk (of a ship).

armería, *f.* armory, arsenal; gunsmith trade or shop.—**armero,** *m.* armorer, gunsmith; keeper of arms.

armiño, *m.* ermine.

armisticio, *m.* armistice.

armonía, *f.* harmony.—**armónico,** *a.* harmonious.—**armonio,** *m.* harmonium, reed organ.—**armonioso,** *a.* harmonious.—**armonización,** *f.* harmonization.—**armonizar,** *vti. & vii.* [a] to harmonize.

arnés, *m.* harness; coat of mail.

aro, *m.* hoop, rim; staple; earring; wedding band; arum.—*entrar por el a.,* to be forced to yield.

aroma, *m.* aroma; perfume, fragrance. —**aromático,** *a.* aromatic, fragrant. —**aromatizar,** *vti.* [a] to perfume.

arpa, *f.* harp.

arpía, *f.* shrew, harpy; fiend.

arpillera, *f.* sackcloth, burlap.

arpón, *m.* harpoon.—**arponear,** *vt.* to harpoon.—**arponero,** *n.* harpooner.

arquear, *vt.* to arch; to beat (wool); to gauge (ships).—*vr.* to arch, become arched.—**arqueo,** *m.* arching; bending; checking of effects in a safe; balance (in accounting); (naut.) tonnage.

arquería, *f.* series of arches; arcade; archery.—**arquero,** *n.* treasurer, cashier; archer; bowmaker.

arquetipo, *m.* archetype.

arquitecto, *m.* architect.—**arquitectónico,** *a.* architectural.—**arquitectura,** *f.* architecture.

arrabal, *m.* outlying district.—*pl.* outskirts, slums.—**arrabalero,** *a.* ill-bred.

arracimarse, *vr.* to cluster.

arraigado, *a.* inveterate, fixed.—**arraigar,** *vii.* [b] to take root.—*vri.* to settle, establish oneself; to take root.—**arraigo,** *m.* settling in a place; the act of taking root.

arrancada, *f.* sudden departure; violent sally.—**arrancado,** *a.* (Am.) broke, poor, penniless.—**arrancar,** *vti.* [d] to root out, extirpate; to pull out, tear off.—*vii.* to start.—**arranque,** *m.* extirpation; impulse (of passion, charity, love, etc.); sudden start, sudden impulse; starter.

arrasar, *vt.* to level, raze, demolish. —*vi.* to clear up (of sky).

arrastrado, *a.* miserable, wretched; dragging out (of life, etc.); knavish; contemptible.—*n.* downcast one.—**arrastrar,** *vt.* to drag; to drag down, degrade; to pull along; to haul; to attract; to influence, persuade.—*vi.* to drag, touch the floor or ground; to play a trump (in cards). —*vr.* to crawl, creep, drag along.—**arrastre,** *m.* dragging; haulage.

arrayán, *m.* myrtle.

¡**arre!** *interj.* gee, get up!—**arrear,** *vt.* to drive (horses, etc.).

arrebatado, *a.* rash, impetuous; sudden, violent.—**arrebatador,** *a.* ravishing.—**arrebatar,** *vt.* to carry off; to snatch; to attract, hold (the attention, etc.); to enrapture, captivate.—*vr.* to be carried away by passion.—**arrebatiña,** *f.* struggle, scuffle, free-for-all.—**arrebato,** *m.* sudden attack; rapture; surprise.

arrebol, *m.* redness; rouge; red sky or clouds.—**arrebolar,** *vr.* to redden.

arrebujar, *vt.* to jumble together; to huddle, bundle.—*vr.* to wrap oneself up.

arreciar, *vt. & vi.* to increase in strength or intensity.

arrecife, *m.* reef.

arrechucho, *m.* fit of anger; sudden and passing indisposition.

arredrar, *vt.* to scare, intimidate.—*vr.* to be or become afraid; to be intimidated.

arreglar, *vt.* to arrange; to adjust, settle; to regulate.—*vr.* to tidy oneself up; to turn out right; to settle differences, come to an agreement; to compromise.—**arreglo,** *m.* disposition, arrangement; adjustment; repair; (com.) agreement; compromise, settlement.—*con a. a,* according to; in accordance with.

arrellanarse, *vr.* to sit at ease, make oneself comfortable.

arremangar, *vti.* [b] to tuck up, turn up, roll up (the sleeves, etc.).—*vri.* to roll up one's sleeves.

arremeter, *vt.* to assail, attack.—**arremetida,** *f.* attack, assault.

arremolinarse, *vr.* to whirl; to crowd together; to mill around.

arrendador, *n.* hirer; tenant.—**arrendar,** *vti.* [1] to rent, let, lease, hire.—**arrendatario,** *n.* lessee, tenant.

arreo, *m.* ornament, decoration.—*pl.* harness, trappings, accessories.—*adv.* successively, uninterruptedly.

arrepentido, *a.* remorseful, repentant. —**arrepentimiento,** *m.* repentance. —**arrepentirse,** *vri.* [39] to repent, regret.

arrestado, *a.* bold, audacious.—**arrestar,** *vt.* to arrest, imprison.—*vr.* (Am.) to dare.—**arresto,** *m.* imprisonment, arrest; spirit, enterprise.

arriar, *vt.* to lower, strike (a flag, etc.).

arriba, *adv.* up, above, high; upstairs; upwards; overhead.—*a. de,* above; higher up.—*cuesta a.,* uphill. —*de a. a abajo,* from top to bottom; up and down.—*para a.,* upwards.—*por a.,* at, or from, the top. —*por a. de,* above, over.—*interj.* up!—**arribada,** *f.* arrival (of a ship).—**arribar,** *vi.* to put into port; to reach; to recover; to prosper by dubious means.—**arribo,** *m.* = ARRIBADA.

arriendo, *m.* renting; lease; rent.

arriero, *m.* muleteer.

arriesgar, *vti.* [b] to risk, hazard, jeopardize.—*vri.* to venture; to dare; to run a risk.

arrimar, *vt.* to place near; to stow; to put beside or against; to put by; to give up.—*vr.* to go near (to); to seek the protection (of); to join.—**arrimo,** *m.* putting near, beside or against; support, protection.

arrinconar, *vt.* to corner; to put away, lay aside; to pigeonhole; to neglect, forsake.—*vr.* to live secluded; to retire.

arriscado, *a.* bold, rash; brisk, spirited; craggy.

arroba, *f.* weight of twenty-five pounds.

arrobador, *a.* enchanting, entrancing. —**arrobamiento, arrobo,** *m.* rapture, bliss; ravishment; trance.—**arrobarse,** *vr.* to be enraptured, entranced.

arrocero, *m.* rice planter or dealer.— *a.* pertaining to rice.

arrodillar, *vt.* to make kneel down.— *vr.* to kneel down.

arrogancia, *f.* arrogance; stately carriage.—**arrogante,** *a.* arrogant; spirited.

arrogar, *vti.* [b] to arrogate; to adopt.—*vri.* to usurp; to assume (power or rights).

arrojado, *a.* rash, dashing, fearless.— **arrojar,** *vt.* to throw, fling; to cast out; to vomit; to emit; to bring forth; to dismiss, drive out.—*vr.* to launch, throw oneself forward; to venture.—**arrojo,** *m.* fearlessness, dash, boldness.

arrollador, *a.* rolling; violent, sweeping.—**arrollar,** *vt.* to roll up; to carry off, sweep away; to trample, run over; to defeat, destroy.

arropar, *vt.* to cover, wrap.—*vr.* to wrap oneself, bundle up.

arrostrar, *vt.* to defy, face.

arroyo, *m.* small stream, brook; gutter.—**arroyuelo,** *m.* rivulet, rill.

arroz, *m.* rice.—**arrozal,** *m.* rice field.

arruga, *f.* wrinkle, crease.—**arrugar,** *vti.* [b] to wrinkle; to crease, crumple.—*vri.* to become wrinkled, creased or crumpled; (Am.) to become intimidated.

arruinar, *vt.* to demolish, ruin, destroy.—*vr.* to become ruined.

arrullador, *a.* lulling, soothing.— **arrullar,** *vt.* to lull; to bill and coo.—**arrullo,** *m.* billing and cooing; lullaby.

arrumaco, *m.* caress, fondling.

arrumbar, *vt.* to put away as useless; to silence; to remove from a trust; (naut.) to determine the direction.—*vi.* to take bearings.

arsenal, *m.* shipyard, navy yard; arsenal.

arsenical, *a.* (chem.) arsenical.

arte, *m.* art; skill, craft; trade, profession; artifice, device; intrigue.— *bellas artes,* fine arts.—**artefacto,** *m.* manufacture, handiwork, contrivance, appliance, device.

arteria, *f.* artery; trunk or main line; main highway.

artería, *f.* cunning, trick, artfulness. —**artero,** *a.* cunning, artful.

artesa, *f.* trough.

artesanía, *f.* workmanship, artisanship.—**artesano,** *n.* artisan; craftsman; mechanic.

artesiano, *a.* artesian.

artesonado, *a.* paneled (ceiling).

ártico, *a.* arctic.

articulación, *m.* articulation, joint.— **articulado,** *a.* jointed; articulate.— **articular,** *vt.* to unite, join; to articulate.—*a.* articular.—**artículo,** *m.* article.—*a. de fondo,* leading article (newspaper).

artífice, *mf.* artisan, craftsman.—**artificial,** *a.* artificial; sophisticated.— **artificio,** *m.* workmanship, craft; artifice; cunning; trick, ruse; contrivance, device.—**artificioso,** *a.* skillful, ingenious; artful, cunning.

artillar, *vt.* to mount (cannon).— **artillería,** *f.* artillery, gunnery.— **artillero,** *m.* artilleryman, gunner.

artimaña, *f.* trap, snare, stratagem.

artista, *a.* & *mf.* artist.—**artístico,** *a.* artistic.

arveja, *f.* (Am.) green pea.

arzobispado, *m.* archbishopric.—**arzobispo,** *m.* archbishop.

as, *m.* ace.

asa, *f.* handle.

asado, *m.* & *a.* roast.—**asador,** *m.* spit (rod); roaster.—**asadura,** entrails.

asalariado, *a.* working for a salary or wages; serving for hire.—*n.* salaried person, wage earner; hireling.—**asalariar,** *vt.* to fix a salary for; to hire.

asaltante, *mf.* assailant, assaulter; highwayman.—**asaltar,** *vt.* to assault, storm, assail; to surprise.—**asalto,** *m.* assault; attack.

asamblea, *f.* assembly; legislature; meeting.—**asambleísta,** *mf.* assemblyman.

asar, *vt.* to roast.—*vr.* to be roasting; to be very hot.

asaz, *adv.* enough; greatly, very.

asbesto, *m.* asbestos.

ascendencia, *f.* lineage.—**ascendente,** *a.* ascendant, ascending.—**ascender,** *vii.* [18] to ascend, climb; to be promoted.—*vti.* to promote.—**ascendiente,** *mf.* ancestor.—*m.* influence.—**ascensión,** *f.* ascension.—**ascenso,** *m.* promotion; ascent.—**ascensor,** *m.* elevator.

asceta, *m.* ascetic, hermit.—**asceticismo, ascetismo,** *m.* asceticism.

asco, *m.* nausea, disgust, loathing; despicable thing.—*darle a uno a.,* to make one sick.—*estar hecho un a.,* to be very dirty.—*hacer ascos,* to turn up one's nose.

ascua, *f.* red-hot coal, ember.—*estar en ascuas,* to be on tenterhooks.

aseado, *a.* clean, neat.—**asear,** *vt.* to clean; to adorn, embellish.—*vr.* to clean oneself up.—**aseo,** *m.* cleanliness, neatness, tidiness.

asechanza, asechar, asecho, = ACECHANZA, ACECHAR, ACECHO.

asediar, *vt.* to besiege, blockade.—**asedio,** *m.* siege, blockade.

asegurado, *n.* & *a.* insured (person).—**asegurador,** *n.* & *a.* insurer; insuring.—**asegurar,** *vt.* to assure; to secure, fasten; to affirm; to insure.—*vr.* to make sure; to hold fast; to be insured, take out insurance.

asemejar, *vt.* to liken, compare.—*vr.* (a) to look like, resemble.

asentaderas, *f. pl.* buttocks.—**asentador,** *m.* razor strop.—**asentar,** *vti.* [1] to place, seat; to adjust; to arrange, settle; to enter (an account, etc.); to hone.—*vii.* to fit, settle.—*vri.* to establish oneself, settle.

asentimiento, *m.* assent.—**asentir,** *vii.* [39] to agree, to assent.

aseo, *m.* cleanliness, cleanness, tidiness.

asepsia, *f.* asepsis.—**aséptico,** *a.* aseptic.

asequible, *a.* attainable, obtainable, available.

aserción, *f.* assertion, affirmation.

aserradero, *m.* sawmill; sawpit; sawhorse.—**aserrar,** *vti.* [1] to saw.—**aserrín,** *m.* sawdust.

asesinar, *vt.* to murder; to assassinate.—**asesinato,** *m.* murder, assassination.—**asesino,** *n.* & *a.* murderer(ess), assassin.

asesor, *n.* consultant, adviser.—**asesorar,** *vt.* to give legal advice.—*vr.* to take advice.—**asesoría,** *f.* office, pay and fees of a consultant.

aserto, *m.* assertion, affirmation.

asestar, *vt.* to point, aim; to level.—*a. un golpe,* to deal a blow.

aseveración, *f.* asseveration, assertion.—**aseverar,** *vt.* to asseverate, affirm, assert.

asfaltar, *vt.* to asphalt.—**asfalto,** *m.* asphalt.

asfixia, *f.* asphyxia.—**asfixiante,** *a.* asphyxiating.—**asfixiar,** *vt.* to asphyxiate, suffocate.—*vr.* to be asphyxiated.

así, *adv.* so, thus, in this manner, like this; therefore.—*a. a.,* so-so, middling.—*a. como,* as soon as, just as.—*a. como a.,* just like that, without rhyme or reason.—*a. no más,* so so, just so.—*a. que,* so that.—*a. y todo,* and yet; just the same.

asiático, *n.* & *a.* Asian, Asiatic.

asidero, *m.* hold; handle; occasion, pretext.

asiduidad, *f.* assiduity, perseverance.—**asiduo,** *a.* assiduous, persevering.

asiento, *m.* seat; site; solidity; settling; bottom; sediment; treaty, contract; entry; registry; stability, permanence; list, roll.

asignación, *f.* assignment; allocation of money.—**asignar,** *vt.* to assign; to appoint; to ascribe.—**asignatura,** *f.* subject (in school curriculum).

asilar, *vt.* to shelter; to place in an asylum.—**asilo,** *m.* asylum; refuge; shelter; private hospital, nursing home.

asimilable, *a.* assimilable.—**asimilación,** *f.* assimilation.—**asimilar,** *vt.* to assimilate.

asimismo, *adv.* likewise, in like manner.

asir, *vti.* [5] & *vii.* to grasp or seize; to hold; to take root.—*vri.* (de) to take hold (of); to avail oneself of.

asistencia, *f.* attendance, presence; assistance, aid.—**asistente,** *mf.* assistant, helper; military orderly.—**asistir,** *vi.* to attend, be present (at).—*vt.* to tend; to attend; to take care of; to assist, help, serve; to accompany.

asma, *f.* asthma.—**asmático,** *a.* asthmatic.

asno, *m.* donkey, ass.

asociación, *f.* association; fellowship; union.—**asociado,** *n.* & *a.* associate(d).—**asociar,** *vt.* to associate. —*vr.* to associate; to form a partnership; to join.

asolar, *vti.* [12] to raze, devastate, lay waste.

asolear, *vt.* to sun.—*vr.* to be sunburned; to bask in the sun.

asomar, *vi.* to begin to appear.—*vt.* to show, put out (as, one's head out the window).—*vr.* to show oneself at (window, etc.).

asombradizo, *a.* timid, shy.—**asombrar,** *vt.* to astonish, amaze; to frighten.—*vr.* to wonder, be astonished (at).—**asombro,** *m.* amazement or astonishment; dread, fear.—**asombroso,** *a.* astonishing, marvelous.

asomo, *m.* indication, sign; conjecture, suspicion.—**ni por** *a.,* not even remotely.

asonada, *f.* attack of a mob, mobbing; riotous crowd.

aspa, *f.* vane of a windmill; reel; cross stud.—**aspaviento,** *m.* exaggerated wonder or fear; fuss.

aspecto, *m.* aspect, look, appearance.

aspereza, *f.* asperity; roughness; severity; harshness, rough place.— **áspero,** *a.* rough; harsh; uneven; gruff.—**asperón,** *m.* scourer.

aspillera, *f.* loophole; embrasure.

aspiración, *f.* aspiration; ambition; breathing in.—**aspirador,** *m.* vacuum cleaner.—**aspirante,** *mf.* candidate, applicant.—**bomba** *a.,* suction pump. —**aspirar,** *vt.* to inhale; to aspire; to covet; to aspirate; to suck.—*vi.* to aspire; to draw, breathe in, inhale.

aspirina, *f.* aspirin.

asquear, *vt.* to disgust, nauseate, sicken.—**asquerosidad,** *f.* filthiness, baseness.—**asqueroso,** *a.* filthy, loathsome, squalid; vile, revolting.

asta, *f.* horn; antler; mast, pole, flagstaff; lance.

asterisco, *m.* asterisk.

astilla, *f.* chip, splinter.—**astillar,** *vt.* to splinter.—*vr.* to break into splinters.—**astillero,** *m.* shipyard, dockyard.

astro, *m.* star; planet; heavenly body.—**astrología,** *f.* astrology.— **astrólogo,** *n.* astrologer.—**astronauta,** *mf.* astronaut.—**astronomía,** *f.* astronomy.—**astronómico,** *a.* astronomic.—**astrónomo,** *n.* astronomer.

astucia, *f.* astuteness, cunning, slyness.

astur, asturiano, *n.* & *a.* Asturian.

astuto, *a.* astute, cunning, sly, crafty, sneaky.

asueto, *m.* recess, vacation, holiday; leisure.

asumir, *vt.* to assume, take upon oneself (command, responsibilities, etc.); to raise, elevate.

asunto, *m.* topic, theme, subject, matter; affair, business.

asustadizo, *a.* scary, easily frightened. —**asustar,** *vt.* to frighten, scare.— *vr.* to be frightened.

atacar, *vti.* [d] to attack; to button; to fit; to ram (gun); to corner.

atadijo, *m.* ill-shaped parcel.—**atado,** *m.* bundle, parcel.—*a.* faint-hearted, good-for-nothing; fastened, tied.— **atadura,** *f.* fastening, binding; knot.

atajar, *vt.* to intercept; to interrupt; to take a short cut.—**atajo,** *m.* short cut; interception.

atalaya, *f.* watchtower; height.—*m.* guard; lookout.

atañer, *vii.* [50] to relate, affect; to belong, pertain, concern.

ataque, *m.* attack; offensive works; fit, seizure; wrangle.

atar, *vt.* to tie, fasten, bind; to lace; to deprive of motion.

atarantado, *a.* astonished; dizzy.— **atarantar,** *vt.* to astound, dumbfound.—*vr.* to be or become dumbfounded.

atardecer, *m.* late afternoon.—*vii.* [3] to draw towards evening.

atareado, *a.* busy, overworked.— **atarear,** *vt.* to overwork, load with. —*vr.* to be exceedingly busy.

atascadero, *m.* muddy place; obstruction.—**atascar,** *vti.* [d] to stop up; to jam, obstruct.—*vri.* to get stuck; to stick; to jam, become obstructed; to stall.

ataúd, *m.* coffin, casket.

ataviar, *vt.* to adorn; to deck out, trim.—*vr.* to dress up.—**atavío,** *m.* dress; finery, gear.

ateísmo, *m.* atheism.

atemorizar, *vti.* [a] to scare, frighten.

atemperar, *vt.* to temper, soften; to accommodate.

atención, *f.* attention; civility; kindness.—*pl.* affairs, business.—**atender,** *vii.* [18] to attend, be attentive; to pay attention.—*vti.* to take care of; to show courtesy to; to wait on.

atenerse (a), *vri.* [42] to follow, adhere to; to abide (by), stick (to).

atentado, *m.* offense, violation, transgression; crime.—**atentar,** *vt.* to attempt, try.

atento, *a.* attentive; polite, courteous.

ateo, *n.* & *a.* atheist(ic).

aterciopelado, *a.* velvety.

aterido, *a.* stiff with cold.—**aterirse,** *vri.* [50] to become stiff with cold.

aterrador, *a.* frightful, terrifying, dreadful.—**aterrar,** *vt.* to terrify; to awe; to appall.—*vr.* to be filled with terror, to be awed or appalled.

aterrizaje, *m.* landing.—**aterrizar,** *vii.* [a] to land.

aterrorizar, *vti.* [a] to frighten, terrify, terrorize.—*vri.* to be terrified.

atesorar, *vt.* to treasure; to hoard, accumulate.

atestación, *f.* testimonial.—**atestado,** *m.* attestation.—**atestar,** *vt.* to attest, witness; to cram, stuff.

atestiguar, *vti.* [b] to depose, witness, attest; to give evidence.

atiborrar, *vt.* to stuff.—*vr.* to stuff oneself.

ático, *a.* Attic; elegant.

atildamiento, *m.* meticulousness in dress or style.—**atildarse,** *vr.* to dress up.

atinar, *vi.* to hit the mark; to guess right; to say or do the right thing. —*a. con,* to find, hit upon.

atisbar, *vt.* to watch, pry; to scrutinize.—**atisbo,** *m.* sign, indication; glimpse, peek.

atizador, *m.* poker.—**atizar,** *vti.* [a] to poke (the fire); to snuff or trim (a candle, etc.); to rouse, stir.—*a. un golpe,* to deliver a blow.

atizonarse, *vr.* (of plants) to become mildewed.

atlántico, *n.* & *a.* Atlantic.

atlas, *m.* atlas.

atleta, *mf.* athlete.—**atlético,** *a.* athletic.—**atletismo,** *m.* athletics.

atmósfera, *f.* atmosphere.—**atmosférico,** *a.* atmospheric.

atol(e), *m.* (Am.) non-alcoholic cornflour drink.

atolondrado, *a.* hare-brained, thoughtless, giddy, careless.—**atolondramiento,** *m.* thoughtlessness, bewilderment.—**atolondrar,** *vt.* to confound, stun.—*vr.* to become confused, stunned.

atolladero, *m.* morass, quagmire, bog. —**atollarse,** *vr.* to be bogged, to stick in the mud; to be in a quandary.

atómico, *a.* atomic.—**átomo,** *m.* atom.

atónito, *a.* astonished, amazed, aghast.

atontado, *a.* foolish, stupid.—**atontamiento,** *m.* stupefaction, stunning. —**atontar,** *vt.* to stun, stupefy; to confound, confuse.—*vr.* to become stupid, dull, stunned.

atorar, *vt.* (Am.) to obstruct; to jam, choke, clog.—*vr.* to stick in the mire; to fit the bore closely; to choke; to stuff oneself.

atormentador, *n.* torturer, tormentor. —**atormentar,** *vt.* to torment, torture; to afflict.

atornillar, *vt.* to screw; to turn a screw.

atosigar, *vti.* [b] to harass, press.

atrabancar, *vti.* [d] to huddle; to perform in a hurry.

atrabiliario, *a.* ill-tempered; unpredictable.

atracar, *vti.* [d] to dock, moor; to come alongside; to cram; to hold up, rob.—*vri.* to overeat, stuff oneself with food.—**atraco,** *m.* holdup, robbery.—**atracón,** *m.* overeating.— *darse un a.,* to gorge, stuff oneself.

atracción, *f.* attraction.—**atractivo,** *a.* attractive.—**atraer,** *vti.* [43] to attract; to allure.

atragantarse, *vr.* to choke; to gobble up food.

atrancar, *vti.* [d] to bar, bolt (a door); to obstruct.—*vri.* to lock oneself in; to become crammed, obstructed.

atrapar, *vt.* to catch, grab; to trap; to overtake; to deceive.

atrás, *adv.* back; aback; backward, behind; past; ago.—**atrasado,** *a.* late; behind time; backward.— **atrasar,** *vt.* to retard, delay; to set, put back (timepiece).—*vi.* (of timepiece) to lose or be slow.—*vr.* to remain, be left or fall behind; to lose time; to be late.—**atraso,** *m.* lateness; tardiness; delay; backwardness.—*pl.* arrears.

atravesar, *vti.* [1] to place across; to go through; to cross; to pierce.— *vr.* to lie across, be in the way; to break in, interrupt, intrude (in); to meddle; to have an encounter or fight (with).

atrayente, *a.* attractive.

atreverse, *vr.* to dare; to venture.— *a. con,* to be insolent to.—**atrevido,** *a.* bold, fearless; forward, insolent. —**atrevimiento,** *m.* boldness, audacity, insolence.

atribución, *f.* attribution; attribute; power, authority.—**atribuir,** *vti.* [23-e] to attribute, ascribe, impute. —*vri.* to take to or on oneself.

atribular, *vt.* to grieve, afflict, distress.—*vr.* to be or become grieved or distressed.

atributo, *m.* attribute, quality.

atrición, *f.* contrition; attrition.

atril, *m.* music stand; lectern; book stand.

atrincheramiento, *m.* entrenchment; trenches.—**atrincherar,** *vt. & vr.* to entrench; to mound.

atrio, *m.* court; portico; entrance hall.

atrocidad, *f.* atrocity.

atronador, *a.* thundering, stunning.— **atronar,** *vti.* [12] to deafen, stun; to stupefy, bewilder.

atropellamiento, *m.* confusion.—**atropellar,** *vt.* to trample under foot; to knock down; to run over, hit, injure; to push through; to outrage.—*vr.* to move or act hastily or recklessly; to rush.—**atropello,** *m.* trampling, running over; injuring, abuse, outrage.

atroz, *a.* atrocious; huge, vast, enormous.

atuendo, *m.* dress, garb, attire.

atún, *m.* tunny fish; stupid person.

aturdido, *a.* hare-brained, giddy.— **aturdimiento,** *m.* bewilderment; confusion.—**aturdir,** *vt.* to bewilder, daze; to rattle; to stun.—*vr.* to become bewildered.

aturrullar, *vt.* to confound, bewilder.

atusar, *vt.* to trim; to comb and smooth (the hair).—*vr.* to smooth one's hair, mustache, beard.

audacia, *f.* audacity, boldness.—**audaz,** *a.* bold, fearless, audacious.

audiencia, *f.* audience, hearing; provincial court.—**auditivo,** *a.* auditory. —**auditor,** *n.* judge.—**auditorio,** *m.* audience, assembly of listeners.

auge, *m.* apogee; culmination; summit.—*ir en a.,* to be on the increase.

aula, *f.* classroom; lecture room.

aullar, *vi.* to howl; to yell, cry.— **aullido, aúllo,** *m.* howl.

aumentar, *vt. & vr.* to augment, increase, enlarge, magnify.—**aumentativo,** *a.* increasing; (gram.) augmentative.—**aumento,** *m.* increase, augmentation, etc.

aún (aun), *adv. & conj.* even.— *adv.* yet, still; as yet.—*a. cuando,* even though.

aunar, *vt.* to unite, join; to combine; to unify.—*vr.* to be united or confederated.

aunque, *conj.* (al)though, notwithstanding, even if.

¡aúpa!, *interj.* up!

aura, *f.* gentle breeze; applause, acclamation; (Am.) buzzard.

aureola, *f.* aureola, halo.

aureomicina, *f.* aureomycin.

auricular, *a.* auricular.—*m.* telephone receiver; earphone.

auscultar, *vt.* to sound (with stethoscope).

ausencia, *f.* absence.—**ausentarse,** *vr.*

to absent oneself.—**ausente,** *a.* absent.

auspiciar, *vt.* to sponsor; to promote. —*auspiciado por,* under the auspices of, sponsored by.—**auspicios,** *m. pl.* auspices, sponsorship; presage; omens.

austeridad, *f.* austerity.—**austero,** *a.* austere.

australiano, *n. & a.* Australian.

austríaco, *n. & a.* Austrian.

autenticar, *vti.* [d] to authenticate; to attest.—**autenticidad,** *f.* authenticity.—**auténtico,** *a.* authentic, genuine.

auto, *m.* automobile; judicial decree or sentence; edict.—*pl.* (law) records of a case.

autobús, *m.* bus.—**autocamión,** *m.* truck.

autocracia, *f.* autocracy.—**autócrata,** *mf.* autocrat.

autóctono, *a.* aboriginal, native.

autógrafo, *m.* autograph.

autómata, *m.* robot, automaton.— **automático,** *a.* automatic.

automóvil, *m.* automobile.—**automovilismo,** *m.* motoring.—**automovilista,** *n.* devotee of motoring.—*a.* automotive.

autonomía, *f.* autonomy; home rule; self-determination.

autopsia, *f.* autopsy.

autor, *m.* author.—**autora,** *f.* authoress.—**autoridad,** *f.* authority.— **autoritario,** *a.* authoritarian; authoritative; overbearing.—**autorización,** *f.* authorization.—**autorizar,** *vti.* [a] to authorize, empower; to legalize; to prove by quotation; to approve, exalt.

aval, *m.* guarantee; indorsement.

auxiliar, *vt.* to aid, help, assist; to attend.—*a.* auxiliary, assisting.—*mf.* helper, assistant.—**auxilio,** *m.* aid, assistance, help.

avalar, *vt.* to vouch for.

avalorar, *vt.* to estimate, value, appraise.

avaluar, *vt.* to estimate, assess, appraise.—**avalúo,** *m.* valuation, appraisal.

avance, *m.* advance; improvement; attack.—**avanzada, avanzadilla,** *f.* (mil.) outpost; advance guard.— **avanzar,** *vii.* [a] to advance, progress; to improve.—*vti.* to advance, push forward.

avaricia, *f.* avarice.—**avaricioso, avariento,** *a.* avaricious, miserly.— **avaro,** *n.* miser.—*a.* avaricious, miserly.

avasallador, *a.* overwhelming, dominating.—**avasallar,** *vt.* to subject, dominate, enslave, subdue.

ave, *f.* fowl; bird.—*a. de corral,* poultry.

avecindarse, *vr.* to settle, become a resident; to establish oneself.

avejentar, *vt. & vr.* to age.

avellana, *f.* hazelnut.—**avellanado,** *a.* nutbrown; wrinkled.—**avellano,** *m.* hazelnut tree.

avemaría, *f.* Hail Mary; rosary bead. —¡Ave María!, *interj.* Good Heavens!

avena, *f.* oats.

avenencia, *f.* agreement.

avenida, *f.* avenue; way of access; flood.—**avenido,** *a.*—*bien* or *mal avenidos,* on good or bad terms.— **avenirse,** *vri.* [45] to settle differences; to agree; to compromise.

aventajar, *vt.* to advance, improve; to surpass; to prefer.—*vr.* to excel, exceed; to advance, rise.

aventar, *vti.* [1] to fan, blow; to winnow.—*vii.* to breathe hard.—*vri.* to be inflated or puffed up; to escape, run away.

aventura, *f.* adventure; contingency, chance, event, risk.—**aventurar,** *vi.* to venture, hazard, risk.—*vr.* to run the risk of.—**aventurero,** *n.* adventurer.—*a.* adventurous; undisciplined.

avergonzar, *vti.* [12-a-b] to shame. —*vr.* to be ashamed.

averiguación, *f.* investigation.—**averiguar,** *vti.* [b] to inquire, investigate, ascertain, find out.

avería, *f.* damage; mischief; misfortune.—**averiar,** *vt.* to damage.— *vr.* to be damaged; to spoil (foods).

aversión, *f.* aversion, dislike.

avestruz, *f.* ostrich.

avezado, *a.* accustomed; trained; practiced.

aviación, *f* aviation.—**aviador,** *n.* aviator.—*f.* aviatrix.

aviar, *vt.* to equip; to lend, advance money to; to supply; to prepare; to go, get on the way.

avidez, *f.* covetousness, avidity.— **ávido,** *a.* (de) avid, eager, anxious.

aviejarse, *vr.* to age, grow old.

avieso, *a.* perverse; mischievous; crooked, irregular.

avinagrado, *a.* sour, acrimonious.— **avinagrar,** *vt.* to sour, acidulate.— *vr.* to become sour.

avío, *m.* preparation, provision; money advanced.—*pl.* gear, utensils; paraphernalia.

avión, *m.* airplane.—*a. de caza,* pursuit plane.—*a. de chorro,* jet plane.

avisado, *a.* cautious, sagacious, clearsighted.—**avisar,** *vt.* to inform, announce, give notice of; to warn, advise.—**aviso,** *m.* information, notice; advertisement; advice, warning.

avispa, *f.* wasp.—**avispado,** *a.* lively, brisk, clever.—**avisparse,** *vr.* to be on the alert; to fret.—**avispero,** *m.* nest of wasps; carbuncle.

avistar, *vt.* to sight at a distance. —*vr.* to have an interview, meet.

avituallar, *vt.* to provide food.

avivar, *vt.* to quicken, enliven; to encourage; to revive.—*vr.* to revive; to cheer up.

avizor, *a.* alert, watchful.—**avizorar,** *vt.* to watch; to keep a sharp lookout.

axila, *f.* armpit.

axioma, *m.* axiom; maxim.

ay, *m.* moan, lament.—*interj.* ouch!; alas!

aya, *f.* governess, instructress.—**ayo,** *m.* tutor or guardian; teacher.

ayer, *adv.* yesterday.

ayuda, *f.* help, aid.—**ayudante,** *mf.* assistant; helper; adjutant.—**ayudar,** *vt.* to aid, help, assist.

ayunar, *vi.* to fast.—**ayuno,** *m.* fast, abstinence.—*a.* (de) uninformed (of); ignorant (of); unaware (of). —*estar en ayunas,* to fast; to be uninformed.—*quedarse en ayunas,* not to catch on; to miss the point.

ayuntamiento, *m.* municipal government; town hall; sexual intercourse.

azabache, *m.* jet (stone).

azada, *f.* hoe.—**azadón,** *m.* hoe, spud.

azafata, *f.* stewardess, air hostess.

azafrán, *m.* saffron.

azahar, *m.* orange or lemon blossom.

azar, *m.* hazard, chance; disaster; accident.—*al a.,* at random.—*correr (ese* or *el) a.,* to take (that) chance, run the risk.—**azaroso,** *a.* unlucky; hazardous.

ázoe, *m.* nitrogen.

azogar, *vti.* [b] to silver with mercury.—**azogue,** *m.* mercury, quicksilver.

azoramiento, *m.* embarrassment, uneasiness.—**azorar,** *vt.* to disturb, startle; to confound, embarrass; to bewilder.—*vr.* to become embarrassed, uneasy, or startled.

azotaina, *f.* drubbing, flogging, spanking.—**azotar,** *vt.* to whip, lash; to thrash.—**azotazo,** *m.* lash.—**azote,** *m.* whip; scourge; stroke, blow.

azotea, *f.* flat roof.

azteca, *mf. & a.* Aztec.

azúcar, *m.* sugar.—**azucarado,** *a.* sugary; affectedly sweet or affable.— **azucarar,** *vt.* to sugar; to sweeten; to coat or ice with sugar.—**azucarera,** *f.* sugar bowl.—**azucarero,** *m.* sugar master; sugar bowl; sugar producer or dealer.—*a.* sugar.

azucena, *f.* white lily.

azufre, *m.* sulfur; brimstone.

azul, *a.* & *m.* blue.—*a. celeste,* sky blue.—*a. marino,* navy blue.—azulado, *a.* bluish.

azulejado, *a.* tiled.—azulejo, *m.* glazed tile; little bluebird.

azur, *a.* azure.

azuzar. *vti.* [a] to urge, set (dogs) on; to incite, goad.

B

baba, *f.* drivel, spittle, saliva; slime.—babear, *vi.* to drivel; to slaver.—babero, *m.* bib, feeder.

Babia, *f.*—*estar en B.,* to be woolgathering.—babieca, *m.* ignorant, stupid fellow.

babor, *m.* (naut.) port, portside.—*de b. a estribor,* athwart ship.

babosa, *f.* (zool.) slug.—babosear, *vi.* = BABEAR.—baboso, *a.* driveling, slavering; silly; overaffectionate.

babucha, *f.* slipper.

bacalao, *m.* cod.

bacía, *f.* metal basin; shaving dish.

bacilo, *m.* bacillus.

bacín, *m.* high chamber pot; stupid man.

bacteria, *f.* bacterium.—bacteriano, *a.* bacterial.—bacteriología, *f.* bacteriology.—bacteriológico, *a.* bacteriological.—bacteriólogo, *n.* bacteriologist.

báculo, *m.* walking stick, staff; support, aid.—*b. pastoral,* bishop's crosier.

bache, *m.* deep hole, pothole, rut (in the road).

bachiller, *n.* bachelor (degree); babbler, prater.—bachillerato, *m.* baccalaureate, B.A. degree.

badajo, *m.* clapper of a bell.

badana, *f.* dressed sheepskin.

badulaque, *a.* foolish; good-for-nothing.—*m.* fool.

bagaje, *m.* beast of burden; baggage of an army.—*pl.* equipment of an army on the march.

bagatela, *f.* trifle.

bahía, *f.* bay, harbor.

bailable, *a.* (of music) composed for dancing.—*m.* ballet.—bailador, *n.* dancer.—bailar, *vi.* to dance, spin.—*b. al son que le toquen,* to adapt oneself to circumstances.—*b. como un trompo,* to dance well.—bailarín, *n.* dancer; ballet dancer.—baile, *m.* dance, ballet; ball.—*b. de etiqueta,* formal dance.—*b. de máscaras,* masquerade.—*b. de trajes,* fancy-dress ball.—bailotear, *vi.* (coll.) to dance clumsily, frequently.—bailoteo, *m.* awkward dancing.

baja, *f.* fall in price; (mil.) casualty; vacancy.—*dar de b.,* to drop (a person from a list, etc.).—*darse de b.,* to drop out, resign from.—bajada, *f.* descent; slope.—bajamar, *f.* low water, low tide.—bajar, *vi.* to descend; to fall; to come or go down; to drop, lessen, diminish.—*vt.* to lower, reduce; to bring or take down, let down.—*vr.* to bend over, stoop; to crouch, grovel; to alight; to get out (of a vehicle); to get down; to bow down.

bajeza, *f.* meanness; vile act or remark; low action.

bajío, *m.* shoal, sand bank; (Am.) low land.

bajo, *a.* low, shallow; short; abject; base; common; (of color) dull; (of sound) deep, low; coarse, vulgar; downcast.—*por lo b.,* on the sly; in an undertone.—*adv.* softly, in a low voice.—*prep.* under.—*m.* bass (voice, singer, instrument); ground floor; sand bank.—*pl.* underskirts; trousers' cuffs.

bala, *f.* bullet, shot, ball; bale.—*b. perdida,* stray bullet; (fig.) a good-for-nothing.

balada, *f.* ballad.

baladí, *a.* trivial, frivolous; trashy.

baladronada, *f.* boast, bravado.

balance, *m.* oscillation, rolling, rocking, swinging; balance; balance sheet; (Cuba) rocking chair; (aer.) rolling.—balancear, *vt.* to balance; to put into equilibrium.—*vi.* & *vr.* to roll, rock, swing; to waver.—balanceo, *m.* rocking, rolling; wobbling.—balancín, *m.* splinter bar, swing bar; (mec.) walking beam; oscillating beam.

balandro, *n.* sloop.

balanza, *f.* scales; balance.

balar, *vi.* to bleat.

balastar, *vt.* to ballast.—balasto, *m.* (RR.) ballast.

balazo, *m.* shot, bullet wound.

balbucear, *vi.,* balbucir, *vii.* [11] to hesitate in speech, stammer.—balbuceo, *m.* stammer, babble.—balbuciente, *a.* stammering, stuttering.

balcón, *m.* balcony; porch.

baldar, *vt.* to cripple.

balde, *m.* bucket, pail.—*de b.,* gratis; free.—*en b.,* in vain, with no result.—baldear, *vt.* to wash (floors, decks).—baldeo, *m.* washing (floors, decks).

baldío, *a.* untilled, uncultivated; barren.—*m.* wasteland.

baldón, *m.* affront, insult.

baldosa, *f.* paving tile; slab; flat paving stone.—baldosado, *m.* tile pavement.

balear, *a.* & *mf.* Balearic; person

of or from the Balearic Islands.—
vt. (Am.) to shoot (wound or kill).

balido, *m.* bleating, bleat.

balín, *m.* small bullet.—*pl.* buckshot.

baliza, *f.* buoy.—**balizar**, *vti.* [a] to
mark with buoys.

balneario, *a.* pertaining to baths.—*m.*
bathing resort; watering place.

balompié, *m.* football.—**balón**, *m.*
football; (auto) balloon tire.—*b. de
gas*, gas bag.—**baloncesto**, *m.* basketball. Also BASKETBOL.

balsa, *f.* raft; pool, pond.

bálsamo, *m.* balsam, balm; (fig.)
balm.—**balsámico**, *a.* balsamic,
balmy.

baluarte, *m.* bastion; bulwark; defense.

balumba, *f.* bulk, heap; jumble.

ballena, *f.* whale; whalebone.—**balle-
nato**, *m.* young whale.—**ballenera**,
f. whaleboat.—**ballenero**, *a.* whal-
ing, whale.—*n.* whaler, whale fisherman.

ballesta, *f.* crossbow.

bambalina, *f.* fly (in theatrical
scenery).

bambolear, *vi. & vr.* to swing, sway.
—**bamboleo**, *m.* swinging, swaying.

bambolla, *f.* (coll.) boast, sham.—
bambollero, *n. & a.* boaster; boasting.

banana, *f.*, **banano**, *m.* banana.

banca, *f.* bench; stand; (com.) banking.—**bancario**, *a.* banking; financial.—**bancarrota**, *f.* bankruptcy;
failure.

bancaza, *f.* bedplate.

banco, *m.* bench; settee; pew;
(mech.) bed, table; pedestal;
school of fish, shoal; (com.) bank.—
b. de ahorros, savings bank.—*b.*, or
cámara de compensaciones, clearing
house.

banda, *f.* band; ribbon; sash; scarf;
band, gang; covey; edge; side of
a ship; cushion (of a billiard table).
—**bandada**, *f.* covey; flock of birds.
—**bandazo**, *m.* (of ship) violent roll
to side.—**bandear**, *vi.* to band.—*vr.*
to conduct for oneself.

bandeja, *f.* tray; salver.

bandera, *f.* flag, banner; colors.—*b.
de popa*, ensign.—**bandería**, *f.* band,
faction.—**banderilla**, *f.* baiting dart
(bullfight).—*poner a uno una b.*,
to taunt or provoke one.—**banderín**,
m. camp colors; flag; railway signal; recruiting post.—**banderola**, *f.*
streamer; pennant; signal flag.

bandidaje, *m.* banditry; gang.—**ban-
dido**, *m.* bandit, robber.

bando, *m.* proclamation, edict; faction, party.

bandolera, *f.* woman bandit; bando-

leer, shoulder belt.—**bandolerismo**,
m. banditry.—**bandolero**, *m.* highwayman, robber.

bandullo, *m.* (coll.) belly; guts.

banquero, *m.* banker.

banqueta, *f.* backless bench; stool;
footstool; (Mex.) sidewalk.

banquete, *m.* banquet.—**banquetear**,
vt., vi. & vr. to banquet, feast.

banquillo, *m.* little stool.—*b. de los
acusados*, defendant's seat.—**ban-
quito**, *m.* stool, footstool.

bañadera, *f.* (Am.) bathtub.—**bañar**,
vt. to bathe, wash, lave; to wet,
water; to dip; to coat, apply a
coating or layer to, plate.—*vr.* to
take a bath.—**bañera**, *f.* bathtub.—
bañista, *mf.* bather.—**baño**, *m.*
bath; bathing; bathtub; bath-
room; coat, coating (of paint, etc.);
(chem.) bath.—*b. María*, double
boiler.—*pl.* bathhouse; spa.

baqueano, *n. & a.* = BAQUIANO.

baqueta, *f.* ramrod.—*pl.* drumsticks.—
a la b., harshly, despotically.

baquiano, *n.* (Am.) guide.—*a.* skillful,
expert.

bar, *m.* bar (for drinks); saloon,
tavern.

baraja, *f.* pack of cards; game of
cards.—**barajar**, *vt.* to shuffle (the
cards); to jumble together.

baranda, *f.* railing; banister.—**baran-
dilla**, *f.* balustrade, railing.

barata, *f.* (fam.) barter, exchange;
(Am.) bargain sale.—**baratear**, *vt.*
to sell cheap; to haggle.—**baratijas**,
f. pl. trifles, trinkets.—**baratillero**,
n. peddler; seller of secondhand
goods or articles.—**baratillo**, *m.*
secondhand shop; remnant sale;
bargain counter.—**barato**, *a.* cheap;
low (priced), reasonable.—*adv.*
cheaply.—*m.* bargain sale, bargain
counter.—*cobrar el b.*, to sell protection by compulsion.—**baratura**,
f. cheapness.

baraúnda, *f.* noise, hurly-burly, confusion.

barba, *f.* chin; beard; whiskers;
wattle.—*pl.* beard, whiskers; fibers;
rough edges of paper.—*b. corrida* or
cerrada, thick beard.—*b. de ballena*,
whalebone.—*en sus barbas*, to his
face.—*tener pocas barbas*, to be
young or inexperienced.

barbacoa, *f.* (Am.) barbecue; barbecued meat.

barbaridad, *f.* barbarity; atrocity;
cruelty; rudeness; (Am.) excess (in
anything); nonsense; blunder.—
barbarie, *f.* fierceness; cruelty; barbarity; lack of culture.—**barbarismo**,
m. barbarism; barbarousness.—**bar-
barizar**, *vti.* [a] to barbarize.—*vii.*

to make wild statements.—**bárbaro,**
a. barbarous, uncivilized; bar-
barian; rude, unpolished.—*n.* bar-
barian.

barbechar, *vt.* to plow for seeding;
to fallow.—**barbecho,** *m.* fallow.

barbería, *f.* barber's shop.—**barbero,**
m. barber.—**barbilla,** *f.* point of
the chin.—**barboquejo,** *m.* chin
strap; hat guard.

barbotar, *vt. & vi.* to mumble.

barbudo, *a.* having a long or thick
beard.

barca, *f.* boat, barge, bark.—*b. chata,*
ferryboat.—**barcaza,** *f.* (naut.)
barge.

barco, *m.* boat, vessel, ship.

bardo, *m.* bard, poet.

barítono, *m.* baritone.

barloventear, *vi.* to ply to windward;
to beat about.—**barlovento,** *m.*
windward.

barniz, *m.* varnish.—**barnizar,** *vti.*
[a] to varnish.

barométrico, *a.* barometric.—**baró-
metro,** *m.* barometer.

barquero, *m.* bargeman, boatman,
ferryman.—**barquichuelo,** *m.* small
barge or boat.—**barquilla,** *f.* little
boat; car, basket (of a dirigible).

barquillo, *m.* thin rolled wafer.

barra, *f.* (mech., eng.) bar, beam,
rod, crowbar; stripe; sand bar;
stick (cosmetics); shaft of a carriage; (Arg.) gang (of boys);
(naut.) spar; thill; railing in a
court room; (Am.) fans (at a
game); (theat.) claque.

barrabasada, *f.* serious mischief;
reckless, harmful action.

barraca, *f.* barrack, cabin, hut.—
barracón, *m.* big cabin.

barranca, *f.,* **barrancal, barranco,** *m.*
deep hollow; cliff; gorge, ravine;
precipice; great difficulty, obstacle.

barredura, *f.* sweeping.—*pl.* sweepings, chaff.

barreminas, *m.* minesweeper (ship).

barrena, *f.* drill; auger; gimlet;
(aer.) spin; spinning dive.—*b. de
gusano,* wimble; rock drill.—*b.
grande,* borer, auger.—**barrenado,** *a.*
bored, drilled.—*m.* boring, drilling.
—**barrenador,** *m.* auger or borer.—
barrenar, *vt.* to drill, bore; to foil;
to infringe (a law).—*b. una roca,*
or *mina,* to blast a rock or a mine.

barrendero, *n.* sweeper, dustman
(woman).

barrenillo, *m.* insect that bores into
trees; (Am. coll.) worries.—**barreno,**
m. large borer, drill or auger; bored
hole, blast hole.

barreña, *f.,* **barreño,** *m.* earthenware
basin.

barrer, *vt.* to sweep; (naut.) to rake.
—*al b.,* (com.) on an average.

barrera, *f.* barricade, barrier, parapet; turnpike, tollgate; clay pit.

barriada, *f.* district, quarter, neighborhood.

barrica, *f.* cask, keg.

barricada, *f.* barricade.

barrido, *m.* sweeping.

barriga, *f.* belly; pregnancy.—**barri-
gón, barrigudo,** *a.* big-bellied,
paunchy.

barril, *m.* barrel; keg.

barrio, *m.* district, ward, quarter;
suburb.—*barrios bajos,* slums.—*el
otro b.,* the other world; eternity.

barro, *m.* mud; clay; earthenware.—
pl. pimples on the face.

barrote, *m.* short and thick iron bar;
round rung (of a ladder).

barruntar, *vt.* to conjecture, guess.—
barrunto, *m.* conjecture; presentiment; guess; hint; indication, sign.

bártulos, *m. pl.* household goods;
tools.

barullo, *m.* confusion, disorder.

basamento, *m.* (arch.) base and
pedestal.—**basar,** *vt.* to support,
give a base to; to base; (surv.) to
refer (operation, etc.) to a base
line.—*vr.* (en) to base one's opinion
(on).

basca, *f.* nausea; squeamishness.

base, *f.* base, basis; (mil., chem.,
alg., geom.) base.- **básico,** *a.* basic.

basílica, *f.* basilica, privileged church.

basilisco, *m.* basilisk (animal, cannon).—*estar hecho un b.,* to be
furious.

basketbol, basquetbol, *m.* basketball.—
basketbolista, *mf.* basketball player.

¡basta!, stop! that will do!

bastante, *a.* sufficient, enough.—*adv.*
enough; rather, fairly, pretty.

bastar, *vi.* to suffice; to be enough.

bastardilla, *f.* italics (type).—*a.*
italic.—**bastardo,** *n.* illegitimate son,
bastard.—*a.* degenerate; false.

bastidor, *m.* frame; easel; embroidery
frame; stretcher for canvas; wing
of stage scenery; window sash.—
entre bastidores, behind the scenes.

bastilla, *f.* hem.

bastión, *m.* bulwark, bastion.

basto, *m.* packsaddle; pack; (cards)
ace of clubs.—*pl.* clubs (cards).—*a.*
coarse, rude; homespun.

bastón, *m.* cane, walking stick; gad;
baton.- **bastonazo,** *m.* blow with a
walking stick.

basura, *f.* sweepings, litter, rubbish;
garbage, refuse.—**basurero,** *m.* dung-
hill, garbage dump; garbage man;
street cleaner; scavenger.

bata, *f.* house coat; smock; wrap; dressing gown; lounging robe.

batacazo, *m.* violent, noisy fall; thud.

batahola, *f.* bustle, hubbub, uproar.

batalla, *f.* battle, struggle.—*b. campal,* pitched battle.—**batallador,** *n.* & *a.* battler; battling; fighter; fighting.—**batallar,** *vi.* to battle, fight, struggle.—**batallón,** *m.* battalion.

batán, *m.* fulling mill.—**batanear,** *vt.* (coll.) to beat, strike.

batata, *f.* sweet potato.

bate, *m.* (Am.) baseball bat.

batea, *f.* tray; foot tub; flat-bottomed boat.

bateador, *n.* (Am.) batter.—**batear,** *vt.* & *vi.* to bat.

batería, *f.* battery; (mus.) percussion instruments; (Am. baseball) battery.—*b. de cocina,* kitchen utensils.

batey, *m.* (Cuba) center square in a sugar mill.

batiburrillo, *m.* = BATURRILLO.

batida, *f.* hunting party.—**batido,** *a.* beaten, trodden (as roads).—*m.* batter of flour, eggs, etc.—**batidor,** *m.* beater; scout; ranger; leather beater; stirring rod.—**batiente,** *m.* jamb (of a door); leaf (of a door).

batintín, *m.* (Am.) gong.

batir, *vt.* to beat, pound; to defeat; to strike; to demolish; to flap; to stir; to reconnoiter.—*b. el record,* to beat, or break the record.—*b. palmas,* to clap the hands.—*vr.* to fight; to duel.

baturrillo, *m.* hodgepodge; confusion.

batuta, *f.* conductor's wand; baton.—*llevar la b.,* to lead; to preside.

baúl, *m.* trunk, chest.

bautismal, *a.* baptismal.—**bautismo,** *m.* baptism, christening.—**bautista,** *mf.* baptizer; Baptist.—**bautizar,** *vti.* [a] to baptize, christen; to nickname.—**bautizo,** *m.* baptism; christening party.

baya, *f.* berry, any small globular fruit.

bayeta, *f.* baize, thick flannel.

bayo, *a.* bay, cream-colored.—*m.* bay horse.

bayoneta, *f.* bayonet.—**bayonetazo,** *m.* bayonet thrust or wound.

baza, *f.* trick (at cards).—*meter b.,* to meddle, intrude, butt in.—*no dejar meter b.,* not to let one put in a single word.

bazar, *m.* bazaar, market place; department store; fair.

bazo, *m.* spleen; milt.

bazofia, *f.* scraps; garbage; waste meat; refuse.

beatería, *f.* affected piety, sanctimoniousness; bigotry.—**beatitud,** *f.* be-

atitude, blessedness, holiness.—**beato,** *a.* blessed; beatified; devout; sanctimonious, overpious.—*n.* pious person; overpious, prudish person.

bebé, *m.* baby; doll.

bebedero, *m.* drinking place or trough; spout.—**bebedor,** *n.* tippler, toper.—**beber,** *vt.* & *vi.* to drink; to swallow; to pledge, toast.—*b. como una esponja,* to drink like a fish.—**bebida,** *f.* drink, beverage; potion.—**bebido,** *a.* drunk; intoxicated.

beca, *f.* scholarship; fellowship; academic sash.—**becario,** *n.* scholarship or fellowship holder.

becerro, *m.* yearling calf; calfskin.

becuadro, *m.* (mus.) natural (tone).

bedel, *m.* beadle, warden; usher (at school, etc.).

beduíno, *n.* & *a.* Bedouin; uncivil.

befa, *f.* jeer, scoffing.

befo, *a.* = BELFO.

beisbol, *m.* baseball (game).—**beisbolero,** *n.* beisbolista, *mf.* baseball player.

bejuco, *m.* rattan.

beldad, *f.* beauty.

belén, *m.* Christmas creche; confusion; bedlam.

belfo, *a.* having a thick lower lip.—*m.* lip of an animal.

belga, *mf.* & *a.* Belgian.

bélico, *a.* warlike.—**belicoso,** *a.* warlike, bellicose; quarrelsome.

beligerancia, *f.* belligerency.—**beligerante,** *mf.* & *a.* belligerent.

bellaco, *a.* artful, sly, cunning, roguish.—*m.* rogue, villain, knave.—**bellaquear,** *vi.* to cheat, swindle; to play knavish, roguish tricks.—**bellaquería,** *f.* knavery, roguery, cunning; vile act or expression.

belleza, *f.* beauty.—**bello,** *a.* beautiful, fair.

bellota, *f.* acorn.

bembo, *n.* & *a.* thick-lipped.—*n.* thick lip, esp. Negro's lip.—**bembón,** *a.* (of persons) thick-lipped.

bemol, *m.* (mus.) flat.—*tener bemoles,* (coll.) to be very difficult, a tough job.

bencina, *f.* benzine.

bendecir, *vti.* [6] to bless.—**bendición,** *f.* blessing, benediction.—**bendito,** *pp. i.* of BENDECIR.—*a.* blessed, sainted; simple-minded.

benefactor, *n.* benefactor.

beneficencia, *f.* beneficence, charity; department of public welfare.—**beneficiar,** *vt.* to benefit; to cultivate, develop, exploit; to purchase.—*vr.* to profit.—**beneficiario,** *n.* beneficiary.—**beneficio,** *m.* benefit; profits; favor, benefaction.—*b. bruto,* gross profit.—*b. neto,* clear profit.—**beneficioso, a.** beneficial, profitable.—**benéfico, a.** beneficent, charitable.

benemérito, a. meritorious, worthy.

beneplácito, m. approval, consent.

benevolencia, f. benevolence, kindness.—**benévolo, a.** benevolent, kind.

benignidad, f. benignity, kindness; mildness.—**benigno, a.** benign, kind; mild.

beodo, a. drunk.—**n.** drunkard.

berbiquí, m. drill brace; wimble.

berenjena, f. eggplant.—**berenjenal, m.** bed of eggplants.—*meterse en un b.,* to get into a mess.

bergante, m. brazen-faced villain, rascal.

bermejizo, a. crimson, reddish.—**bermejo, a.** bright reddish.

bermellón, bermillón, m. vermilion.

berrear, vi. to cry like a goat, bellow.—**berrido, m.** bellowing.

berrinche, m. tantrum; rage, temper.

berro, m. watercress.

berza, f. cabbage.

besar, vt. to kiss.—**beso, m.** kiss.

bestia, f. beast, quadruped; (fig.) dunce, idiot; ill-bred fellow.—*b. de carga,* beast of burden.—**bestial, a.** bestial, brutal.—**bestialidad, f.** brutality; stupid notion.

besugo, m. sea bream; red gilthead.

besuquear, vt. & vi. to kiss repeatedly; to spoon.—**besuqueo, m.** (coll.) spooning.

betabel, f. (Mex.) beet.

betún, m. bitumen, pitch; shoeblacking; coarse wax.—**betunar, vt.** to pitch, tar.

biberón, m. nursing bottle.

Biblia, f. Bible.—**bíblico, a.** Biblical.—**biblioteca, f.** library.—**bibliotecario, n.** librarian.

bicarbonato, m. bicarbonate.

bicicleta, f. bicycle.

bichero, m. boat hook.

bicho, m. bug, insect; grub; any animal (gen. small); ridiculous fellow; (Cuba) clever fellow.

bidé, bidel, m. bidet.

biela, f. connecting rod; crank.

bien, m. good, supreme goodness; benefit; righteousness; object of love.—*en b. de,* for the sake, good, or benefit of.—*pl.* property; possessions; estate.—*bienes de fortuna,* worldly possessions.—*bienes gananciales,* matrimonial common property.—*bienes inmuebles,* real estate.—*bienes muebles,* goods and chattels.—*hombre de b.,* honest man.—*adv.* well; all right; right; very; happily; perfectly.—*b. que,* although.—*encontrar,* or *hallar b.,* approve.—*más b.,* rather.—*o b.,* or

else; otherwise.—*si b.,* while, though, —*y b.,* well, now then.

bienaventurado, a. blessed; fortunate. —**bienaventuranza, f.** beatitude; bliss; well-being.—*pl.* beatitudes.— **bienestar, m.** comfort; well-being. —**bienhechor, n.** benefactor.—**bienvenida, f.** welcome; safe arrival.— **bienvenido, a.** welcome.

biftec, m. beefsteak.

bifurcación, f. a forking or branching out.—**bifurcarse, vri.** [d] to branch off, fork; to divide into two branches.

bigamia, f. bigamy.—**bígamo, a. & n.** bigamous; bigamist.

bigornia, f. anvil.

bigote, m. mustache.—**bigotudo, a.** having a heavy mustache.

bilingüe, a. bilingual.

bilioso, a. bilious.—**bilis, f.** bile.

billar, m. billiards.—**billarista, mf.** billiard player.

billete, m. bill, bank note; note, brief letter; ticket.—*b. de ida y vuelta,* round-trip ticket.—**billetera, f.** wallet.

billón, m. billion.

bimensual, a. occurring twice a month. —**bimestral, bimestre, a.** bimonthly. —**bimestre, m.** a period of two months.

binóculos, m. pl. opera glasses; binoculars.

biografía, f. biography.—**biográfico, a.** biographical.—**biógrafo, n.** biographer.

biología, f. biology.—**biólogo, n.** biologist.

biombo, m. folding screen.

bioquímica, f. biochemistry.—**bioquímico, a.** biochemical.—**n.** biochemist.

birlar, vt. to snatch away; to rob, pilfer; to kill or knock down at one blow.

birlibirloque, m.—*por arte de b.,* by magic.

birmano, n. & a. Burmese.

birreta, f., birrete, m. biretta; academic cap.

bisabuela, f. great-grandmother.— **bisabuelo, m.** great-grandfather.

bisagra, f. hinge.

bisbisar, vi. to mutter.—**bisbiseo, m.** muttering.

bisel, m. bevel, bevel edge.—**biselado, m.** beveling.—**biselar, vt.** to bevel.

bisiesto, a.—*año b.,* leap year.

bisnieta, bisnieto = BIZNIETA, BIZNIETO.

bisojo, a. cross-eyed.

bisoño, n. & a. novice; inexperienced.

bisturí, m. surgical knife.

bizarría, *f.* bravery; magnanimity.— **bizarro,** *a.* brave; gallant; generous.

bizco, *a.* cross-eyed.

bizcocho, *m.* biscuit; sponge cake.

biznieta, *f.* great-granddaughter.— **biznieto,** *m.* great-grandson.

blanco, *a.* white.—*n.* white person.— *m.* white (color); aim, goal.—*dar en el b.,* to hit the mark.—*de punta en b.,* cap-a-pie; in full regalia.— *quedarse en b.,* to be frustrated, disappointed.—**blancura,** *f.* whiteness.—**blancuzco,** *a.* whitish.

blandir, *vt.* to brandish, flourish, swing.

blandengue, *a.* bland, exceedingly kind.—**blando,** *a.* soft, pliant; smooth; bland; pusillanimous; gentle, kind.—**blanducho, blandujo,** *a.* flabby.—**blandura,** *f.* softness; delicacy; gentleness.

blanqueador, *m.* blancher, whitewasher; bleacher.—**blanqueadura,** *f.,* **blanqueamiento, blanqueo,** *m.* whitening, bleaching, whitewashing. —**blanquear,** *vt.* to whiten; to whitewash; to bleach.—*vi.* to show white; to begin to turn white.— **blanquecino,** *a.* whitish.—**blanquillo,** *m.* (Mex.) egg.

blasfemar, *vi.* to blaspheme.—**blasfemia,** *f.* blasphemy.—**blasfemo,** *n. & a.* blasphemer; blasphemous.

blasón, *m.* coat of arms; honor, glory. —**blasonar,** *vi.* to boast, brag.

bledo, *m.* wild amaranth.—*no me importa un b.,* I don't care a straw.

blindado, *n. & a.* iron-clad.—**blindaje,** *m.* blindage; armor.—**blindar,** *vt.* to armor; to protect with blindage.

bloque, *m.* block; coalition.—**bloqueador,** *n. & a.* blockader; blocking.—**bloquear,** *vt.* to blockade; to block, freeze (funds).—**bloqueo,** *m.* blockade.

blusa, *f.* blouse.

boardilla, *f.* = BUHARDILLA.

boato, *m.* ostentation, pomp.

bobina, *f.* bobbin; coil.

bobada, bobería, *f.* foolish speech or action.—**bobalicón,** *n.* blockhead, simpleton.—**bobear,** *vi.* to act or talk foolishly; fritter away (time). —**bobo,** *a.* foolish, simple.—*n.* fool, booby.

boca, *f.* mouth; entrance; opening.— *a b. de jarro,* at close range.—*andar de b. en b.,* to be the talk of the town.—*b. abajo,* prone, face downwards.—*b. arriba,* supine, on one's back.—*b. de agua,* hydrant.—*b. del estómago,* pit of the stomach.—*b. de riego,* hydrant.—*no decir esta b.*

es mía, to be mum.—**bocacalle,** *f.* opening of a street or street intersection.—**bocadillo,** *m.* mid-morning luncheon or small luncheon; sandwich, roll.—**bocado,** *m.* mouthful, morsel, bite; bit (of a bridle).— **bocamanga,** *f.* part of a sleeve near the wrist.—**bocanada,** *f.* mouthful (of liquor); puff (of smoke).

boceto, *m.* sketch.

bocina, *f.* horn; trumpet; speaking tube; megaphone.

bocio, *m.* goiter.

bocón, *n.* braggart; wide-mouthed person.

bocha, *f.* bowl, ball for playing at bowls or bowling.

bochinche, *m.* tumult, hubbub.

bochorno, *m.* embarrassment; sultry weather.—**bochornoso,** *a.* embarrassing; shameful; sultry; humiliating.

boda, *f.* wedding, nuptials.

bodega, *f.* wine vault or cellar; winery; retail grocery; storeroom, warehouse; hold (of ship).—**bodegón,** *m.* tavern; still life.—**bodeguero,** *m.* keeper of a wine vault; liquor dealer; grocer.

bodoque, *m.* pellet; wad; lump; dunce, idiot.

bofe, *m.* lung; (Am. coll.) snap, easy job.—*echar los bofes,* to toil; to pant, be out of breath.

bofetada, *f.* **bofetón,** *m.* slap in the face, buffet.

boga, *f.* rowing.—*en b.,* vogue, popularity.—**bogar,** *vii.* [b] to row.

bogavante, *m.* large lobster; stroke oar.

bohardilla, *f.* = BUHARDILLA.

bohemio, *n. & a.* Bohemian; Czech; gypsy; bohemian (life or person).

bohío, *m.* Indian hut, hovel, cabin.

boicot, *m.* boycott.—**boicoteador,** *n. & a.* boycotter; boycotting.—**boicotear,** *vt. & vi.* to boycott.— **boicoteo,** *m.* boycott(ing).

boina, *f.* beret.

boj, *m.* box tree, boxwood.

bola, *f.* ball; marble; globe; falsehood, fib; (Mex.) shoe blacking; (Mex.) tumult, riot.—**bolazo,** *m.* blow with a ball; fib, lie.—**boleada,** *f.* (Mex.) shoeshine.—**boleador,** *m.* bowler; (Mex.) bootblack.—**bolear,** *vi.* to bowl; to boast; to lie, fib.— **boleo,** *m.* bowling.—**bolera,** *f.* bowling alley.—**bolero,** *m.* bolero; (Mex.) bootblack.

boleta, *f.* ballot; pass; pay order; certificate; lodging billet.—**boletería,** *f.* box, or ticket, office.—**boletín,** *m.* bulletin; ticket.—**boleto,** *m.* ticket.

boliche, *m.* bowl, bowling alley; saloon; gambling joint; small stove.

bolígrafo, *m.* ball-point pen.
boliviano, *n.* & *a.* Bolivian.
bolo, *m.* (bowling) a ninepin; dunce.
—*pl.* bowls, bowling.
bolsa, *f.* purse; pouch, bag, satchel; stock exchange; exchange center.—**bolsillo**, *m.* pocket; purse.—*rascarse el b.*, to spend much money.—**bolsista**, *m.* stockbroker; speculator.—**bolso**, *m.* moneybag; purse.
bollo, *m.* small loaf or roll, muffin, bun; lump; tuft; dent; swelling; fritter.
bomba, *f.* pump; bomb; fire engine; skyrocket; high hat.—*a prueba de b.*, bomb proof, indestructible.—*b. neumática*, air pump.—*fruta b.*, papaya.—**bombardear**, *vt.* to bombard; to bomb.—**bombardeo**, *m.* bombardment.—**bombardero**, *m.* bomber (airplane); bombardier.—**bombazo**, *m.* explosion; bomb hit; bad news.—**bombear**, *vt.* to pump.—**bombeo**, *m.* pumping; curving, bulging.—**bombero**, *m.* fireman.—**bombilla**, *f.* small tube for drinking maté; electric light bulb.
bombo, *m.* large drum; bass drum; pomp, ostentation.—*dar b.* to flatter, praise excessively.—*a.* dazed, stunned; stupid; lukewarm; slightly rotten.
bombón, *m.* chocolate, bonbon, sweet.—**bonbonera**, *f.* box for bonbons.
bonachón, *a.* good-natured, kind; innocent.
bonanza, *f.* fair weather; prosperity.
bondad, *f.* goodness; kindness.—*tener la b. (de)*, please.—**bondadoso**, *a.* kind, kind-hearted.
bonete, *m.* bonnet, college cap; skullcap; secular clergyman; bonnet of a fortress; preserve jar; second stomach of ruminants.
bonhomía, *f.* honesty, kindliness.
boniato, *m.* sweet potato.
bonificación, *f.* discount; allowance; bonus.—**bonificar**, *vti.* [d] to discount (the price of something).
bonitamente, *adv.* brazenly; craftily; neatly.—**bonito**, *a.* pretty.—*m.* bonito, striped tunny.
boñiga, *f.* cow dung; castings.
boqueada, *f.* gasp, gasping.—**boquear**, *vi.* to gape, gasp; to breathe one's last; to end.—**boquera**, *f.* crack in the corner of the mouth.—**boquete**, *m.* gap, narrow entrance.—**boquiabierto**, *a.* astonished; open-mouthed.—**boquilla**, *f.* cigar or cigarette holder; mouthpiece of a wind instrument; small mouth.
borbotar, *vi.* to gush out; to boil or bubble fiercely; to spurt.—**borbollón, borbotón**, *m.* bubbling, gush-

ing up of water.—*a borbotones*, impetuously.
borceguí, *m.* high laced shoe; half-boot.
bordado, *m.* embroidery; embroidering.—*a.* embroidered.—**bordador**, *n.* embroiderer.—**bordadura**, *f.* embroidery.—**bordar**, *vt.* to embroider.
borde, *m.* border, edge, rim, brim; flange.—*al b. de*, on the verge of.—**bordear**, *vt.* to skirt, go along the edge of; to approach, get near.
bordo, *m.* board, the side of a ship.—*a b.*, on board, aboard.
bordón, *m.* walking staff; bass-string of guitar.
borinqueño, *n.* & *a.* Porto Rican.
borla, *f.* tassel, tuft; powder puff; doctorate.—*tomar la b.*, to graduate.
borra, *f.* sediment, waste; yearling ewe; coarse wool.
borrachera, *f.* drunkenness; madness, great folly.—**borrachín, borrachón**, *m.* drunkard; sot.—**borracho**, *n.* drunkard.—*a.* drunk.
borrador, *m.* eraser; rough draft.—**borradura**, *f.* erasure, striking out, deletion.—**borrar**, *vt.* to erase, rub out, cross out, blot out; to obliterate.
borrasca, *f.* storm; hazard, danger.—**borrascoso**, *a.* stormy.
borrego, *n.* yearling sheep; simpleton, blockhead.
borricada, *f.* drove of donkeys; stupid word or action.—**borrico**, *m.* donkey; blockhead.
borrón, *m.* blot; blur; rough draft; stigma.—**borroso**, *a.* full of dregs; blurred, indistinct.
boscaje, *m.* cluster of trees; thicket.
bosque, *m.* woods, forest.
bosquejar, *vt.* to sketch, outline; to plan; to make a rough model of.—**bosquejo**, *m.* sketch; rough outline.
bostezar, *vii.* [a] to yawn, gape.—**bostezo**, *m.* yawn, yawning.
bota, *f.* boot; small leather wine bag.—*ponerse las botas*, to hit the jackpot.
botadura, *f.* launching (of a ship).
botánica, *f.* botany.—**botánico**, *a.* botanical.—*n.* botanist.
botar, *vt.* to cast, pitch, throw; to throw out (of a job), fire; to launch; to misspend; to throw away.—*vi.* & *vr.* (of unbroken horse) to jump and kick, caper; to bound; to rebound.—**botarate**, *m.* spendthrift; madcap, thoughtless person.
botavara, *f.* (mar.) gaff; boat hook.
bote, *m.* leap, bound, bounce; rearing of a horse; can or jar; rowing

boat.—*de b. en b.*, crowded, crammed.

botella, *f.* bottle.—**botellón,** *m.* demijohn.

botica, *f.* drug store.—**boticario,** *n.* apothecary, druggist.

botija, *f.* earthen round, short-necked jug; fat person.

botillería, *f.* ice-cream parlor.—**botillero,** *n.* one who prepares or sells ice cream and refreshments.

botín, *m.* booty, spoils of war; spats; bootee.—**botina,** *f.* woman's boot.—**botinería,** *f.* shoe shop or factory.

botiquín, *m.* medicine chest; first-aid kit; (Am.) wine shop.

botón, *m.* button; knob; sprout, bud, blossom.—**botonadura,** *f.* set of buttons.—**botones,** *m. sing.* bellboy.

bóveda, *f.* arch; vault; vault for the dead.

boxeador, *n.* boxer, pugilist.—**boxear,** *vi.* to box.—**boxeo,** *m.* boxing.

boya, *f.* buoy.

boyada, *f.* herd of oxen.

boyante, *a.* buoyant, floating; prosperous.—**boyar,** *vi.* to buoy; to float.

boyero, *m.* ox driver.

bozal, *m.* muzzle (for dogs, etc.).—*a.* of pure breed, unmixed; newly immigrating; inexperienced; simple, half-witted; coarse; wild.

bozo, *m.* down (on face); mustache; area around the lips.

braceada, *f.* violent stretching out of the arms.—**bracear,** *vi.* to move or swing the arms.—**braceo,** *m.* repeated swinging of the arms.—**bracero,** *m.* day laborer.—*de b.*, or *de bracete*, arm in arm.

bragas, *f. sing. & pl.* breeches; child's diaper; hoisting rope.—**braguero,** *m.* truss, bandage for a rupture.—**bragueta,** *f.* fly of trousers.

bramante, *a.* roaring.—*m.* twine, packthread.—**bramar,** *vi.* to roar, groan, bellow.—**bramido,** *m.* roar, bellow.

brasa, *f.* ember; red-hot coal or wood.—*estar en brasas*, to be on tenterhooks.—**brasero,** *m.* brazier; fire pan.

brasileño, brasilero, *n. & a.* Brazilian.

bravata, *f.* bravado, boast; bluster, threat.—**braveza, bravura,** *f.* bravery; courage; anger.—**bravío,** *a.* ferocious, wild.—**bravo,** *a.* brave; angry; wild, fierce.—**bravucón,** *m. & a.* bully; boaster; boasting.

braza, *f.* fathom (measure).—**brazada,** *f.* stroke (swimming, rowing); uplifting of the arms; armful.—**brazado,** *m.* armful.—**brazal,** *m.* armband; bracer; armlet.—**brazalete,**

m. bracelet.—**brazo,** *m.* arm (of the body, a chair, etc.); branch, bough; strength, power.—*pl.* workmen, hands.—*a b. partido*, hand to hand, with all one's strength.—*del b.*, by the arm; arm in arm.

brea, *f.* pitch, tar.

brebaje, *m.* beverage, potion.

brécol, *m.* broccoli.—**brecolera,** *f.* flowering broccoli.

brecha, *f.* breach, opening, gap.

brega, *f.* struggle; fight.—*andar a*, or *en, la b.*, to work hard.—**bregar,** *vii.* [b] to contend, struggle; to overwork.

breña, *f.*, **breñal, breñar,** *m.* craggy and brambled ground.—**breñoso,** *a.* craggy and brambled.

brete, *m.* fetter, shackle; difficulty.—*en un b.*, in a difficult situation, hard pressed to do it.

bretón, *n. & a.* Breton.

breva, *f.* early fruit of a fig tree; choice cigar; advantage, profit.

breve, *a.* brief, short.—*en b.* shortly, in a little while.—**brevedad,** *f.* brevity, briefness.—**breviario,** *m.* breviary; epitome.

brezal, *m.* moor, heath.—**brezo,** *m.* (bot.) heath, heather.

bribón, *n.* vagrant, rogue.—**bribonada,** *f.* knavery, petty villainy.—**bribonear,** *vi.* to loiter about, idle.—**bribonería,** *f.* rascality; vagrancy.

brida, *f.* bridle, rein.

brigada, *f.* brigade; group of people doing a task together; sub-lieutenant.—**brigadier,** *m.* brigadier general.

brillante, *a.* brilliant, bright; shining, sparkling.—*m.* brilliant, diamond.—**brillantez,** *f.* dazzle, brilliance.—**brillo,** *m.* shine, brightness, luster, sparkle.—**brillar,** *vi.* to shine, sparkle, glitter; excel.

brincar, *vii.* [d] to leap, jump, caper, skip.—**brinco,** *m.* leap, jump, hop, caper.

brindar, *vt.* to toast, drink the health; to offer.—**brindis,** *m.* drinking the health of another; toast.

brío, *m.* vigor, enterprise, courage.—**brioso,** *a.* vigorous, courageous, spirited.

brisa, *f.* breeze.

británico, *a. & n.* British; Britisher.

britano, *n. & a.* Briton; British.

brizna, *f.* fragment; splinter or chip; string (of beans, etc.); shred.

broca, *f.* reel, bobbin; drill bit.

brocado, *m.* (gold or silver) brocade.

brocal, *m.* curbstone of a well.

bróculi, *m.* broccoli.

brocha, *f.* painter's or shaving brush.—*de b. gorda*, crude, badly done.—

brochada, *f.,* **brochazo,** *m.* stroke of the brush.

broche, *m.* clasp; hook and eye; fastener; brooch.

broma, *f.* joke, jest; gaiety, fun; prank.—**bromear,** *vi.* to joke, jest, make fun.—**bromista,** *mf.* joker; wag.—*a.* joking, waggish, prankish.

bronca, *f.* quarrel, wrangle; dispute.

bronce, *m.* bronze.—**bronceado,** *a.* bronzed; bronze-colored.—*m.* bronzing.—**broncear,** *vt.* to bronze; to adorn with brass.

bronco, *a.* rough, unpolished; morose; rude; hard; abrupt; hoarse; wild (of horse).

bronconeumonía, *f.* bronchopneumonia.—**broncopulmonía,** *f.* bronchial pneumonia.

bronquedad, *f.* harshness; brittleness.

bronquial, *a.* bronchial.—**bronquio,** *m.* bronchus.—**bronquitis,** *f.* bronchitis.

broquel, *m.* shield, buckler; support, protection.

brotar, *vi.* to bud, germinate, shoot forth; to gush, rush out; to break out; to issue, appear.—**brote,** *m.* germination of vines; bud of trees; shoot; outbreak (of a disease).

broza, *f.* rotted branches, leaves, etc. on the ground; rubbish, chaff; undergrowth, brushwood.

bruces, *n. pl.*—*caer de b.,* to fall flat on one's face.—*de b.,* forward; face downward; on one's stomach.

bruja, *f.* witch.—**brujería,** *f.* witchcraft, sorcery.—**brujo,** *m.* sorcerer, conjurer; wizard.

brújula, *f.* magnetic needle; compass.

bruma, *f.* mist, fog.—**brumoso,** *a.* foggy, misty.

bruno, *m. & a.* dark brown, blackish.

bruñir, *vti.* [27] to polish, burnish.

brusco, *a.* blunt, rude, brusk; abrupt, sudden.

brusquedad, *f.* bluntness, rudeness; bruskness; abruptness.

brutal, *a.* brutal, brutish.—*m.* animal (quadruped).—**brutalidad,** *f.* brutality; brutishness, unkindness; brutal or stupid action.—**bruto,** *a.* brutish; crude (of oil, etc.); gross (profits, etc.); unpolished.—*en b.,* in a rough state, in the rough.—*m.* beast, brute; blockhead.

bruza, *f.* horse brush; stove brush; scrubbing brush; printer's brush.

bu, *m.* bugaboo.—*hacer el b.,* to scare, frighten.

bubón, *m.* bubo.—**bubónico,** *a.* bubonic.

búcaro, *m.* flower vase.

bucear, *vi.* to dive, plunge.—**buceo,** *m.* diving; searching under water.

bucle, *m.* ringlet, curl, lock of hair.

buchada, *f.* mouthful.—**buche,** *m.* belly; (coll.) bosom; mouthful (of liquids); double chin; (Am.) goiter.

budismo, *m.* Buddhism.—**budista,** *mf. & a.* Buddhist.

buen(o), *a.* good; kind; suited, fit; appropriate; well, in good health; in good condition.—*buenos días,* good morning, good day.—*buenas noches,* good evening.—*buenas tardes,* good afternoon.—*de buenas a primeras,* unexpectedly.—*adv.* all right; that is enough.—**buenamente,** *adv.* freely, spontaneously.—**buenaventura,** *f.* good luck; fortune (as told by a fortune teller).

buey, *m.* ox, bullock.

bufanda, *f.* scarf, muffler.

bufar, *vi.* to puff and blow with anger; to snort.

bufete, *m.* desk or writing table; lawyer's office or clientele.

bufido, *m.* snort, bellow, roar.

bufo, *a. & n.* comic; farcical, clownish; crude.

bufón, *m.* buffoon; jester.—*a.* funny, comical.—**bufonada,** *f.* buffoonery; jest.

buhardilla, *f.* garret; skylight.

buho, *m.* owl.

buhonero, *m.* peddler, hawker.

buitre, *m.* vulture.

bujía, *f.* spark plug; candlestick; candle; candle power.

bula, *f.* papal bull; (eccl.) dispensation.

bulbo, *m.* bulb (plants).

búlgaro, *n. & a.* Bulgarian.

bulto, *m.* bulk, volume, size; bundle, package; lump, swelling; indistinct shape or form.—*escurrir, huir,* or *sacar el b.,* to sneak out; to dodge.

bulla, *f.* chatter, noise, shouting; noisy crowd.—**bullanga,** *f.* noise, tumult.—**bullanguero,** *a.* fond of noisy merriment.—**bullicio,** *m.* noise, bustle.—**bullicioso,** *a.* boisterous riotous; merry and noisy.

bullir, *vii.* [27] to boil, bubble up; to swarm, teem; to bustle; to stir, move about.

buñuelo, *m.* fritter, bun; anything poorly done or spoiled; failure.

buque, *m.* vessel, ship; steamer.

burbuja, *f.* bubble.—**burbujear,** *vi.* to bubble.—**burbujeo,** *m.* bubbling.

burdel, *m.* brothel.

burdo, *a.* coarse, rough; ordinary, common.

buril, *m.* chisel; graver.—**burilar,** *vt.* to engrave.

burla, *f.* scoffing, mockery, taunt; gibe; jest, fun; trick, deception.—**burlador,** *n.* seducer; jester.—**burlar,** *vt.* to ridicule, mock, scoff;

to abuse; to deceive; to evade.—*vr.*
(de) to mock, laugh (at), make
fun (of).—**burlesco,** *a.* burlesque,
ludicrous.—**burlón,** *a.* bantering,
waggish, mocking.—*n.* scoffer; joker;
teaser.

buró, *m.* bureau; writing desk.—
burocracia, *f.* bureaucracy.—**buro-
crático,** *a.* bureaucratic.—**burocra-
tismo,** *m.* red tape.

burrada, *f.* stupid action or saying.—
burro, *n.* ass, donkey; windlass.
—*a.* stupid.

bursátil, *a.* relating to the stock exchange.

busca, *f.* search; pursuit.—**busca-
pleitos,** *mf.* trouble maker.—**buscar,**
vti. [d] to seek, search for.—*vri.*
to bring upon oneself.—**buscavidas,**
mf. busybody; hustler; thrifty
person.

busilis, *m.* (coll.) difficulty, difficult
point, snag.

búsqueda, *f.* search.

busto, *m.* bust, bosom.

butaca, *f.* armchair; easy-chair;
(theater) orchestra seat.

butifarra, *f.* sausage.

buzo, *m.* diver.

buzón, *m.* letter drop; letter box.

C

cabal, *a.* just, complete; perfect,
thorough; full; faultless.—*estar en
sus cabales,* to be in one's right
mind.

cábala, *f.* premonition; cabal, intrigue.

cabalgadura, *f.* riding horse or mule.
—**cabalgar,** *vii.* [b] to ride on
horseback.

caballa, *f.* horse mackerel.

caballeresco, *a.* knightly, chivalrous;
gentlemanly.—**caballería,** *f.* riding
animal; cavalry; horsemanship;
mount; horse; knighthood; chivalry; (Am.) land measure (about
33½ acres).—**caballeriza,** *f.* stable.
—**caballerizo,** *m.* head groom of a
stable.—**caballero,** *m.* knight; cava-
lier; gentleman.—*c. de industria,* defrauder, swindler.—**caballerosidad,**
f. chivalry, quality of a gentleman;
nobleness.—**caballeroso,** *a.* noble,
generous; gentlemanly.—**caballete,**
m. ridge of a roof; sawhorse;
trestle; easel; gallows of a printing press.—**caballista,** *m.* horseman;
expert in horses.—**caballo,** *m.* horse;
(cards) the queen; (chess) the
knight.—*a mata c.,* at breakneck
speed.—*c. de batalla,* favorite idea.

cabaña, *f.* cabin, hut; hovel.

cabaret, *m.* cabaret, nightclub.

cabecear, *vi.* to nod; to raise or
lower the head (pert. to horses);
to incline to one side; (naut., aer.)
to pitch, tilt.—**cabeceo,** *m.* nodding,
nod of the head; (naut., aer.) pitching.

cabecera, *f.* head-board of a bed;
seat of honor; chief city of a district.

cabecilla, *f.* small head.—*m.* ringleader.

cabellera, *f.* head of hair; wig.—
cabello, *m.* a hair; hair of the
head.—*asirse de un c.,* to catch at
trifles.—*traer por los cabellos,* to
drag in irrelevantly.—**cabelludo,** *a.*
hairy.—*cuero c.,* scalp.

caber, *vii.* [7] to fit into, go into; to
be contained; to have enough room
for.—*c. la posibilidad,* to be within
possibility.—*no cabe duda,* there is
no doubt.—*no c. en sí,* to be filled
with conceit.

cabestrillo, *m.* sling (for injured arm).
—**cabestro,** *m.* halter; bullock;
rope, cord.

cabeza, *f.* head; leader; upper part;
intelligence.—*c. de chorlito,* hare-
brained.—*de c.,* headfirst, headlong.
—*de pies a c.,* all over.—*levantar
c.,* to be restored in health or fortune.—*ni pies ni c.,* neither rhyme
nor reason.—**cabezada,** *f.* butt (with
the head); nod; headshake; head-
gear (of a harness); headstall of a
bridle; (naut.) pitching.—**cabezazo,**
m. blow with the head.—**cabezón,
cabezota, cabezudo,** *a.* & *n.* large-
headed (one); headstrong (one).

cabida, *f.* content, capacity; space,
room.—*tener c.,* to be appropiate,
to fit.

cabildo, *m.* chapter of a cathedral or
collegiate church; municipal council;
city hall.

cabilla, *f.* (naut.) dowel; pin;
(mason.) reinforcement pin; iron
rod.

cabina, *f.* (mar.) cabin.

cabizbajo, *a.* crestfallen; thoughtful;
melancholy.

cable, *m.* cable.—**cablegrafiar,** *vt.* to
cable.—**cablegrama,** *m.* cablegram.

cabo, *m.* extreme; tip; bit; cape,
headland; handle; piece of rope;
corporal; end.—*al c.,* at last.—*al c.
de,* at the end of.—*dar c. a,* to
finish.—*de c. a rabo,* from head to
tail, from the beginning to the end.
—*llevar a c.,* to carry out; to accomplish.

cabotaje, *m.* coasting trade; pilotage.

cabra, *f.* goat.—**cabria,** *f.* crane,
winch.—**cabrío,** *m.* herd of goats.
—*a.* goatish.—**cabriola,** *f.* caper,

hop, somersault.—**cabritilla,** *f.* kid, dressed kidskin.—**cabritillo, cabrito,** *m.* kid.—**cabrón,** *m.* buck, he-goat; (fig.) acquiescing cuckold.

cabuya, *f.* (Am.) sisal or hemp cord.

cacahual, *m.* cacao plantation.

cacahuate, cacahué, cacahuete, *m.* peanut.

cacao, *m.* cacao; cacao tree; chocolate.

cacarear, *vi.* to cackle; (coll.) to brag, boast.—**cacareo,** *m.* cackling; boast, brag.

cacatúa, *f.* cockatoo.

cacería, *f.* hunt, hunting.

cacerola, *f.* casserole; saucepan.

cacique, *m.* Indian chief; (coll.) political boss.—**caciquismo,** *m.* caciquism; political bossism.

caco, *m.* pickpocket; thief.

cacumen, *m.* acumen, keen insight.

cacha, *f.* each of the two leaves of a knife or gun (handle).

cachalote, *m.* sperm whale.

cacharrería, *f.* crockery store; collection or stock of earthen pots.—**cacharro,** *m.* coarse earthen pot; (Am.) cheap trinket; (Cuba) jalopy.

cachaza, *f.* first froth on cane juice when boiled; slowness, tardiness.—**cachazudo,** *a.* slow, calm, phlegmatic.

cachemir, *m.* cashmere.

cacheo, *m.* search for hidden arms.

cachetada, *f.* slap on the face.—**cachete,** *m.* cheek; punch in the face or head.—**cachetudo,** *a.* plump-cheeked, fleshy.

cachimba, *f.* smoking pipe.

cachiporra, *f.* cudgel.

cachivache, *m.* piece of junk; (Am.) trinket.

cacho, *m.* slice, piece; (Chile) unsold goods.

cachorro, *n.* cub; puppy; small pistol.

cachucha, *f.* small rowboat; slap.

cada, *a.* every, each.—*c. cual, c. uno,* each; every one.—*c. vez que,* every time; whenever.

cadalso, *m.* gallows; scaffold for capital punishment.

cadáver, *m.* corpse, cadaver.—**cadavérico,** *a.* cadaverous.

cadena, *f.* chain; range (of mountains).—*c. perpetua,* imprisonment for life.—*c. radial,* broadcasting system.

cadencia, *f.* cadence; rhythm; flow of verses or periods; (mus.) cadenza.—**cadencioso,** *a.* rhythmical.

cadeneta, *f.* lace or needlework worked in form of chain.

cadera, *f.* hip.

cadete, *m.* cadet.

caducar, *vii.* [d] to dote; to be worn out by service; to fall into disuse; to become obsolete or extinct; to prescribe; (law) to lapse; to expire.—**caducidad,** *f.* (law) lapse, expiration.—**caduco,** *a.* senile; decrepit; perishable.

caer, *vii.* [8-e] to fall, drop; to fall off; to hang down, droop; to fall due; to befall.—*c. bien,* to create a good impression; to fit; to be becoming.—*c. de la noche,* nightfall.—*c. en cama,* or *enfermo,* to be taken ill.—*c. en gracia,* to please.—*c. en la cuenta,* to understand the situation; to realize.—*c. redondo,* to drop unconscious;—*dejar c.,* to drop; to let fall.—*vri.* to fall down or off; to tumble; to become downcast.—*c. de su peso,* to be self-evident, to be obvious; to fall by itself.—*caérsele a uno la cara de vergüenza,* to be deeply ashamed.

café, *m.* coffee (tree, berry, beverage); coffee house; café.—*c. retinto,* black coffee.—**cafeína,** *f.* caffein.—**cafetal,** *m.* coffee plantation.—**cafetera,** *f.* coffeepot.—**cafetería,** *f.* retail coffee shop; cafeteria.—**cafetero,** *m.* coffee merchant.—**cafetín,** *m.* small café.—**cafeto,** *m.* coffee tree.

caída, *f.* fall; falling; tumble; drop; droop; descent.—*a la c. del sol,* at sunset.—*la c. de la tarde,* at the close of the afternoon.—**caído,** *a.* languid; downfallen.

caimán, *m.* cayman; alligator.

caimito, *m.* star apple.

caja, *f.* box; case; cash box or safe; (com.) cash, funds; cashier's office; printer's case; shell, block (of a pulley).—*c. contadora,* or *registradora,* cash register.—*c. de ahorros,* savings bank.—*c. de caudales, c. fuerte* (Am.), safe, strongbox.—*c. de seguridad,* safe-deposit box.—*con cajas destempladas,* roughly, without ceremony.—*en c.,* cash, cash kept in the safe.—**cajero,** *n.* cashier; box maker.—**cajetilla,** *f.* package (of cigarettes).—**cajista,** *mf.* compositor (in printing).—**cajón,** *m.* large box, case; drawer; locker; mold for casting.—*c. de sastre,* odds and ends.—**cajuela,** *f.* small box; (Am.) automobile trunk.

cal, *f.* lime.—*c. viva,* quicklime.

cala, *f.* cove, small bay; creek; fishing ground; sample slice (of a fruit).

calabacín, *m.* calabash.

calabaza, *f.* pumpkin; (fig.) nincompoop.—*dar calabazas,* to jilt (a suitor); to flunk (a student).

calabozo, *m.* dungeon; prison cell; calaboose.

calado, *m.* open work in metal, stone, wood, or linen; draught of a vessel; lace trimmings.

calafate, calafateador, *m.* calker.—**calafatear,** *vt.* to calk.—**calafateo,** *m.* calking.

calamar, *m.* squid.

calambre, *m.* cramp (of muscles), spasm.

calamidad, *f.* calamity.—**calamitoso,** *a.* calamitous; unfortunate.

calandria, *f.* lark, skylark.

calar, *vt.* to penetrate, soak through, drench; to go through; to make open work in (metal, wood, linen or paper); to fix (the bayonet); to see through (a person); to take or cut out a sample of.—*vi.* (of ships) to draw.—*vr.* to become drenched.

calavera, *f.* skull; madcap; rake, profligate; (Mex.) tail light.—**calaverada,** *f.* foolishness, rash action.

calaña, *f.* sort, kind, quality; (fig.) evil moral character.

calcar, *vti.* [d] to trace; to imitate.

calceta, *f.* hose, stocking.—*hacer c.,* to knit.—**calcetín,** *m.* sock.

calcio, *m.* calcium.

calco, *m.* tracing, transfer; copy, imitation; near image.

calculador, *n.* calculator, computer.—**calcular,** *vt.* to calculate, compute; to estimate.—**calculista,** *mf.* calculator; designer, schemer.—**cálculo,** *m.* calculation; conjecture; calculus (differential, integral, etc.); (med.) calculus, (kidney, etc.) stone.

caldear, *vt.* to heat; to weld.—*vr.* to become warm; to become overheated; to become overexcited.

caldera, *f.* caldron; kettle; boiler.—**calderero,** *m.* coppersmith; boiler maker.—**calderilla,** *f.* any copper coin.—**caldero,** *m.* semispherical caldron or boiler; caldronful.

caldo, *m.* broth; gravy; bouillon.

calefacción, *f.* heating system; heating, warming.

calendario, *m.* calendar, almanac.

caléndula, *f.* marigold.

calentador, *m.* heater.—**calentar,** *vti.* [1] to heat, warm; (fig.) to give a beating.—*vr.* to become hot; to become excited or angry; to be in heat.—**calentura,** *f.* fever.—**calenturiento,** *a.* feverish.

caletre, *m.* (coll.) judgment, acumen.

calibrador, *m.* gauge (instrument); calipers.—**calibrar,** *vt.* to calibrate (a firearm); to gauge.—**calibre,** *m.* caliber; bore (of a cylinder); gauge; diameter (of a wire).

calicanto, *m.* stone masonry.

calidad, *f.* quality; grade; rank; importance.—*pl.* conditions; personal qualifications; parts.

cálido, *a.* warm; hot.

calidoscopio, *m.* kaleidoscope.

caliente, *a.* warm, hot; (Am.) angry.—*en c.* at once.

calificación, *f.* qualification; judgment; mark (in an examination).—**calificar,** *vti.* [d] to qualify; to rate, class; to judge.—**calificativo,** *a.* qualifying; descriptive.

caligrafía, *f.* calligraphy.

calina, *f.* haze, mist, fog.

cáliz, *m.* chalice; communion cup; (bot.) calyx.

calma, *f.* calm; calmness, tranquility; lull, quiet.—*c. chicha,* dead calm.—*con c.,* calmly, quietly.—*en c.,* (of the sea) calm, smooth.—**calmado,** *a.* quiet, calm, still.—**calmante,** *a.* mitigating; quieting, soothing.—*m.* & *a.* sedative; narcotic.—**calmar,** *vt.* to calm, quiet, pacify; to mitigate, soothe.—*vi.* to abate; to be becalmed.—*vr.* to quiet down; to calm oneself, be pacified.—**calmoso,** *a.* calm; slow, phlegmatic.

calor, *m.* heat; warmth, ardor.—*c. de una batalla,* brunt of a battle.—*tener c.* to be, feel warm.—**caloría,** *f.* calorie.—**calórico,** *m.* caloric.—**calorífero,** *m.* heater, radiator.—**caluroso,** *a.* warm, hot; cordial, enthusiastic.

calumnia, *f.* calumny, slander.—**calumniador,** *n.* & *a.* slander(ing).—**calumniar,** *vt.* to slander.

calva, *f.* baldhead; clearing.

calvario, *m.* Calvary; tribulation.

calvicie, *f.* baldness.—**calvo,** *a.* bald; barren.—*m.* baldhead.

calza, *f.* wedge, shoehorn.—*pl.* tights.—**calzada,** *f.* paved road; highway.—**calzado,** *m.* footwear.—**calzador,** *m.* shoehorn.—**calzar,** *vti.* [a] to put on (shoes, etc.); to make steady by wedging.—**calzo,** *m.* wedge.

calzón, *m.,* **calzones,** *m. pl.* breeches; trousers.—*calzón corto,* knee breeches; shorts.—*tener los calzones bién puestos,* to have the heart in the right place.—**calzoncillos,** *m. pl.* drawers, men's shorts.

callandito, *adv.* quietly, stealthily, softly.—**callar,** *vi.* & *vr.* to be silent, keep silent; to stop, cease (talking, singing, etc.); to shut up.—*vt.* & *vr.* to hush, conceal; to suppress, keep secret.—*vr.* to silence; to gag.—*dar la callada por respuesta,* to answer by silence.

calle, *f.* street; passage; lane.—*abrir c.,* to clear the way.—*c. abajo,* down the street.—*dejar en la c.*, to leave penniless.—*echar a la c.*, to put out of the house.—*llevarse de c.*, to sweep away.—**callejear**, *vi.* to saunter, loiter about the streets.—**callejero**, *n.* loiterer; loafer.—**callejón**, *m.* alley.—*c. sin salida*, blind alley; dead end.—**callejuela**, *f.* lane; passage; dingy street.

callista, *mf.* chiropodist.—**callo**, *m.* corn, callus (on foot); callus, hard skin.—*pl.* tripe (food).—**callosidad**, *f.* callousness.—**calloso**, *a.* callous; hard-skinned.

cama, *f.* bed; couch; cot.—*guardar, or hacer c.*, to be confined to bed. —**camada**, *f.* brood, litter; gang.

camafeo, *m.* cameo.

camaleón, *m.* chameleon.

cámara, *f.* chamber; parlor; bedroom; camera.—*c. alta*, senate; House of Lords.—*c. baja*, chamber of deputies; House of Commons.— *c. frigorífica*, icebox; refrigerator.

camarada, *n.* comrade; pal, chum.— **camaradería**, *f.* comradeship; companionship.

camarera, *f.* chambermaid; waitress. —**camarero**, *m.* waiter; valet.

camarilla, *f.* small room; coterie; clique.

camarón, *m.* shrimp, prawn.

camarote, *m.* cabin, berth, stateroom.

cambalache, *m.* (coll.) barter, swap.— **cambalachear**, *vt.* to barter, to swap.—**cambalachero**, *n.* barterer.

cambiante, *a.* bartering, exchanging; changing.—*m. pl.* iridescent sheen or colors.—**cambiar**, *vt.* to change; to barter; to exchange; to alter.— *vi.* to change, shift.—*c. de marcha*, to shift gear.—*c. de opinión*, to change one's mind.—**cambio**, *m.* change; barter; exchange; rate of exchange (of money); alteration.— *en c.* in return; on the other hand. —*en c. de*, in lieu of, instead of.— **cambista**, *mf.* banker, money broker.

camelar, *vt.* to flirt; to court, woo; to seduce.

camelia, *f.* camellia.

camello, *m.* camel.—**camellón**, *m.* ridge turned up by plow.

camilla, *f.* stretcher, litter; couch; cot.—**camillero**, *m.* stretcher-bearer.

caminante, *m.* traveler, walker.— **caminar**, *vi.* to journey, walk, travel, go, move along.—*c. con pies de plomo*, to act cautiously.— **caminata**, *f.* long walk; hike; jaunt. —**camino**, *m.* road; highway; course; passage; way; journey.—*c. de hierro*, railroad.—*de c., en c.*, on the way.—*ponerse en c.*, to set out, start.

camión, *m.* truck; (Mex.) bus.— **camionero**, *m.* truck driver.—**camioneta**, *f.* small or delivery truck; (Am.) bus.

camisa, *f.* shirt, chemise.—*c. de fuerza*, strait jacket.—*c. de vapor*, steam jacket.—**camisería**, *f.* haberdashery.—**camisero**, *n.* shirt maker.

camiseta, *f.* undershirt.—**camisón**, *m.* nightshirt; nightgown; chemise.

camorra, *f.* quarrel.—**camorrista**, *mf.* noisy, quarrelsome person.

camote, *m.* (Am.) sweet potato.

campamento, *m.* encampment; camp.

campana, *f.* bell.—*c. de buzo*, diving bell.—*c. de rebato*, alarm bell.— **campanada**, *f.* stroke of a bell, clang.—**campanario**, *m.* belfry.— **campanear**, *vi.* to ring the bells frequently.—*vt.* to divulge; to noise about.—**campanero**, *m.* bellman; bell founder.—**campanilla**, *f.* small bell; hand bell; uvula; (bot.) bellflower.—**campanillazo**, *m.* violent ringing of a bell.—**campanilleo**, *m.* ringing, tinkling of small bells.

campante, *a.* cheerful; self-satisfied.

campanudo, *a.* high-flown, bombastic.

campar, *vi.* to excel; to encamp.—*c. por sus respetos*, to act as one pleases, to be subject to no control.

campaña, *f.* campaign; countryside, fields, open country.

campear, *vi.* to be in the field; to frisk about; to be prominent.

campechano, *a.* frank; cheerful; hearty; open.

campeón, *m.* champion; defender.— **campeonato**, *m.* championship.

campesino, *a.* rural, rustic.—*n.* countryman (-woman); peasant; farmer. —**campestre**, *a.* rural, bucolic.— **campiña**, *f.* field; country.—**campo**, *m.* country; countryside; field; space, camp; flat land.—*a c. raso*, in the open air.—*a c. traviesa*, across country.—*c. de golf*, golf course.—*c. santo*, or *camposanto*, cemetery.

camuesa, *f.* pippin (apple).

camuflaje, *m.* camouflage.—**camuflar**, *vt.* to camouflage.

cana, *f.* gray hair.—*echar una c. al aire*, to go on a lark.

canadiense, *mf. & a.* Canadian.

canal, *m.* channel; canal; strait; groove.—*abrir en c.*, to cut from top to bottom.—*f.* slot in metal work; drinking trough.

canalete, *m.* bladed paddle for canoeing.

canalizar, *vti.* [a] to construct channels or canals in or for; to channel.

canalla, *f.* rabble, riffraff; mob.—*m.* mean fellow, cur.—**canallada**, *f.*

base, despicable act.—**canallesco,** a. base, churlish.

canana, f. cartridge belt.

canapé, m. couch; lounge; settee.

canario, m. canary.—n. & a. (native) of the Canary Islands.

canasta, f. basket; crate.—**canasto,** m. large basket, crate.—¡**canastos!** interj. gracious! confound it!

cáncamo, m. (Am.) ringbolt.

cancela, f. front door grating or screen.

cancelación, f. cancellation.—**cancelar,** vt. to cancel.

cáncer, m. cancer.—**canceroso,** a. cancerous.

canciller, m. chancellor.—**cancillería,** f. chancellery.

canción, f. song; love poem.—**cancionero,** m. song book; song writer. —**cancionista,** mf. composer or singer of songs, songster.

cancha, f. (tennis, handball, etc.) court; (bowling) alley; game grounds; (Am.) roasted corn or beans.

candado, m. padlock.

candela, f. candle; fire; light.—**candelabro,** m. candelabrum; bracket.— **candelero,** m. candlestick.

candente, a. incandescent, red-hot.

candidato, n. candidate.—**candidatura,** f. candidacy.

candidez, f. ingenuousness; naiveté; candor.—**cándido,** a. candid; simple, innocent; white; unsuspecting.

candil, m. oil lamp; hand lamp.— **candileja,** f. oil receptacle of a lamp.—pl. footlights of a theater.

candor, m. pure whiteness; candor; innocence.—**candoroso,** a. sincere; innocent; pure-minded.

canela, f. cinnamon.

cangrejo, m. crab.

canguro, m. kangaroo.

caníbal, m. cannibal, man-eater.

canica, f. marble; little ball.

canilla, f. tibia; shinbone; (Am.) faucet; spool (for thread).—**canillera,** f. (baseball) shin guard.

canino, a. canine.—tener un hambre canina, to be ravenous.

canje, m. exchange; interchange.— **canjear,** vt. to exchange, interchange.

cano, a. gray-haired.

canoa, f. canoe.

canon, m. canon; rule, precept; catalogue.—**canónigo,** m. (eccl.) canon. —**canonización,** f. canonization.— **canonizar,** vti. [a] to canonize; to consecrate.

canoso, a. gray-haired.

cansado, a. tired; tiring; tiresome; boring.—**cansancio,** m. weariness,

fatigue.—**cansar,** vt. to weary, tire, fatigue; to bore.—vr. to become tired or weary.—vi. to be tiring or tiresome.

cantante, mf. singer, songster, vocalist.—**cantar,** m. song; epic poem.— ese es otro c., that is a horse of another color.—vt. to sing.—cantarlas claras, not to mince words.— vi. to sing; to speak out; (coll.) to squeal.—c. de plano, to make a full confession.

cántaro, m. pitcher; jug.—llover a cántaros, to rain cats and dogs.

cantera, f. (stone) quarry.—**cantero,** m. stone mason.

cántico, m. canticle.

cantidad, f. quantity; amount; large portion; sum of money.

cantimplora, f. canteen; carafe; wine flask.

cantina, f. canteen; bar room, saloon; lunch room; railroad station restaurant; lunch-box.—**cantinero,** n. bartender.

canto, m. singing; song; canto; chant or canticle; end, edge, border; back of a knife; front edge of a book; stone; pebble; quarry stone, block.—de c., on edge.

cantón, m. canton; corner.

cantor, n. singer, songster; minstrel. —a. that sings.

caña, f. cane; reed; reed spear; stem, stalk; walking stick; sugar cane brandy.—c. brava, bamboo.

cañada, f. dell, ravine; cattle path.

cáñamo, m. hemp; cloth made of hemp.—**cañamón,** m. hemp seed; birdseed.

cañaveral, m. cane or reed field.

cañería, f. conduit; pipe line.—**caño,** m. tube, pipe; spout; (Am.) branch of a river, stream.

cañón, m. cannon, gun; barrel of a gun; canyon; flue of a chimney; quill; beard's stubble.—**cañonazo,** m. cannon shot.—**cañonear,** vt. to cannonade, bombard.—vr. to cannonade each other.—**cañoneo,** m. bombardment; cannonade.—**cañonero,** m. cañonera, f. gunboat.

caoba, f. mahogany.

caos, m. chaos.—**caótico,** a. chaotic.

capa, f. cloak, mantle, cape; layer; coat, coating; cover; coat of paint; disguise; pretense.—andar de c. caída, to go downhill.

capacidad, f. capacity; contents; ability.—**capacitación,** f. training.— **capacitar,** vt. & vr. to enable, qualify, prepare; to empower.

capar, vt. (coll.) to castrate.

caparazón, m. shell of crustaceans; caparison.

capataz, *m.* foreman; overseer.

capaz, *a.* capable, able, competent; roomy, large.

capcioso, *a.* captious; insidious; artful.

capellán, *m.* chaplain; clergyman, priest.

caperuza, *f.* pointed hood.

capilar, *a.* capillary.

capilla, *f.* chapel; hood.

capirote, *m.* hood.—*tonto de c.,* dunce.

capital, *m.* capital, funds.—*f.* capital (city).—*a.* capital; main; leading; great.—*pena c.,* death sentence.—**capitalismo,** *m.* capitalism.—**capitalista,** *mf.* & *a.* capitalist(ic).—**capitalización,** *f.* capitalization.—**capitalizar,** *vti.* [a] to capitalize.

capitán, *m.* captain; commander.—*c. de corbeta,* lieutenant commander. —*c. de fragata,* navy commander. —*c. de navío,* navy captain.—*c. general del ejército,* field marshal.—**capitanear,** *vt.* to command; to lead.—**capitanía,** *f.* captainship; captaincy.

capitel, *m.* spire over the dome of a church; capital of a column or pilaster.

capitolio, *m.* capitol.

capítulo, *m.* (book or organization) chapter.

caporal, *m.* ringleader; (Mex.) foreman of a ranch.

capota, *f.* top of convertible vehicles.

capote, *m.* cloak with sleeves; bullfighter's cape.—*dar c.,* to deceive.—*decir para su c.,* to say to oneself.

capricho, *m.* caprice, whim, fancy; (mus.) capriccio.—**caprichoso, caprichudo,** *a.* capricious, whimsical; stubborn.

cápsula, *f.* cartridge shell; capsule.

captar, *vt.* to captivate, attract, win over; to tune in (radio station).—**captura,** *f.* capture, seizure.—**capturar,** *vt.* to arrest; to apprehend.

capucha, *f.* hood.

capullo, *m.* cocoon; flower bud; acorn cup.

caqui, *m.* & *a.* khaki.

cara, *f.* face; countenance; front; facing; surface.—*buena c.,* good appearance.—*c. de pocos amigos,* churlish look.—*c. o cruz,* heads or tails.—*de c.,* facing.—*echar en c.* to reproach, blame.—*sacar la c. por alguien,* to defend another person.

carabina, *f.* carbine.—*la c. de Ambrosio,* a worthless thing.—**carabinero,** *m.* customs armed guard.

caracol, *m.* snail.—*escalera de c.,* winding staircase.—**caracola,** *f.* shell of sea snails.—**caracolear,** *vi.* (of horses) to caracole, to prance.—

caracoleo, *m.* caracoling, prancing about.—¡caracoles! *interj.* good gracious!

carácter, *m.* character; temper; energy.—*caracteres de imprenta,* printing types.—**característica,** *f.* characteristic; feature.—**característico,** *a.* characteristic, distinctive.—*n.* character actor or actress.—**caracterizar,** *vti.* [a] to characterize; (theat.) to act a part.—*vti.* & *vri.* (theat.) to make up, dress up for a part.

¡caramba!, *interj.* (coll.) gracious! great guns!

carámbano, *m.* icicle.

carambola, *f.* carom in billiards.—*por c.,* (coll.) indirectly; by chance.

caramelo, *m.* caramel.

caramillo, *m.* small flute; (mus.) recorder; confused heap of things.

carapacho, *m.* shell (of crabs, lobsters, etc.).

carátula, *f.* title page of a book; mask; (Am.) dial of a watch.

¡caray!, *interj.* good gracious!

carbón, *m.* coal; carbon.—*c. de leña,* charcoal.—**carbonera,** *f.* coal cellar, coal bin.—**carbonería,** *f.* coal yard. —**carbonero,** *a.* pert. to coal or charcoal.—*n.* coal or charcoal seller. —**carbonilla,** *f.* coal dust, cinder.— **carbonizar,** *vti.* [a] & *vri.* to carbonize; to char.—**carbono,** *m.* carbon.

carbunclo, carbunco, *m.* carbuncle; anthrax.

carburador, *m.* carburetor.—**carburante,** *m.* fuel oil.—**carburar,** *vt.* to carburize.—**carburo,** *m.* carbide.

carcaj, *m.* quiver (for arrows).

carcajada, *f.* outburst, or peal, of laughter; guffaw.

cárcel, *f.* jail; prison.—**carcelero,** *n.* jailer, warden.

carcoma, *f.* wood borer.—**carcomido,** *a.* worm-eaten; consumed; decayed.

cardador, *n.* carder, comber.—**cardar,** *vt.* to card or comb wool.

cardenal, *m.* cardinal; cardinal bird; welt, bruise.

cardenillo, *m.* verdigris.—**cárdeno,** *a.* livid; dark purple.

cardíaco, *a.* cardiac.

cardinal, *a.* cardinal (point); main, fundamental.

cardo, *m.* thistle.

carear, *vt.* to confront (criminals).—*vr.* to meet face to face.

carecer, *vii.* [3] (de) to lack, to be wanting in.—**carencia,** *f.* lack; scarcity; deficiency.—**carente,** *a.* lacking, wanting.

carero, *a.* overcharging; profiteering.

—*m.* profiteer.—**carestía,** *f.* scarcity, dearth; famine; high price.

careta, *f.* mask.

carey, *m.* hawksbill; tortoise; hawksbill or tortoise shell.

carga, *f.* charge (all meanings); load; burden; freight; cargo; loading; impost, duty, tax; obligation.—*volver a la c.,* to insist; to harp on a subject.—**cargado,** *a.* full; loaded; fraught; strong, thick.—*c. de espaldas,* stoop-shouldered.—**cargador,** *m.* shipper; carrier; stevedore; porter; ramrod.—**cargamento,** *m.* cargo; shipment.—**cargar,** *vti.* [b] & *vii.* to load; to burden; to carry (a load); to charge (all meanings); to ship; to bore; to be burdensome.—*vii.* to incline, lean towards; to be supported by; (con) to assume responsibility; to bear the blame.—*vri.* (of sky) to become overcast; to be full of; to load oneself (with).—**cargazón,** *f.* cargo; abundance.—*c. de cabeza,* heaviness of the head.—*c. del tiempo,* cloudy, thick weather.—**cargo,** *m.* post, position; duty, responsibility; (com.) debit; charge, custody; accusation.—*c. de conciencia,* remorse, sense of guilt.—*hacerse c. de,* to take charge of; to take into consideration; to realize.—**carguero,** *a.* freight-carrying.—*n.* beast of burden.

cariacontecido, *a.* sad, mournful, downcast.

caribe, *mf.* Carib; savage.

caricatura, *f.* caricature; cartoon.—**caricaturista,** *mf.* caricaturist; cartoonist.—**caricaturizar,** *vti.* [a] to caricature, mock.

caricia, *f.* caress; petting.

caridad, *f.* charity, charitableness.—**caritativo,** *a.* charitable.

caries, *f.* bone decay, tooth decay.

cariño, *m.* love, fondness, affection.—**cariñoso,** *a.* affectionate, loving.

cariz, *m.* aspect.

carlinga, *f.* (aer.) cockpit.

carmelita, *n.* & *a.* Carmelite.—*m.* & *a.* (Cuba, Chile) brown.

carmesí, carmín, *m.* & *a.* crimson, bright red.

carnada, *f.* bait.

carnal, *a.* carnal, sensual.—*primo c.,* first cousin.

carnaval, *m.* carnival; Mardi gras.—**carnavalesco,** *a.* pertaining to a carnival or Mardi gras.

carnaza, *f.* bait.

carne, *f.* flesh; meat; pulp (of fruit).—*c. de cañón,* cannon fodder.—*c. de gallina,* (fig.) goose flesh.—*c. de res,* (Am.) beef.—*c. fiambre,* cold meat.—*c. viva,* quick or raw flesh in a wound.—*c. y hueso,* flesh and blood.—*ni c. ni pescado,* neither fish nor fowl; insipid.—*ser uña y c.,* to be hand and glove, to be one.—**carnero,** *m.* sheep, mutton, ram.—**carnicería,** *f.* meat market, butcher's shop; slaughter.—**carnicero,** *a.* carnivorous; sanguinary, cruel.—*n.* butcher.—**carnívoro,** *n.* carnivore.—*a.* carnivorous.—**carnosidad,** *f.* fleshiness; proud flesh.—**carnoso,** *a.* fleshy; meaty; fat.

caro, *a.* dear, expensive, costly; dear, beloved.—*cara mitad,* better half.—*adv.* dearly, at a high price or cost.

carozo, *m.* core of an apple, pear, etc.; corn cob.

carpa, *f.* (ichth.) carp; canvas tent; circus tent.

carpeta, *f.* table cover; portfolio; desk pad; folder.—**carpetazo,** *m.*—*dar c.,* to lay aside; to pigeonhole.

carpintería, *f.* carpentry; carpenter's shop.—**carpintero,** *m.* carpenter.—*pájaro c.,* woodpecker.

carraspear, *vi.* to clear one's throat; to be hoarse.—**carraspera,** *f.* (coll.) hoarseness; sore throat.

carrera, *f.* run, running race; course; race track; profession, career.—*a la c., de c.,* hastily, hurriedly.

carreta, *f.* wagon, cart.—**carretada,** *f.* cartful.—*pl.* great quantities.—*a carretadas,* (coll.) copiously, in abundance.—**carrete,** *m.* spool, bobbin, reel; coil.—**carretel,** *m.* fishing reel.—**carretera,** *f.* highway; drive.—**carretero,** *m.* cart driver; cartwright.—**carretilla,** *f.* wheelbarrow, handcart; (RR.) gocart.—*de c.,* mechanically; by rote.—**carretón,** *m.* wagon, cart.

carril, *m.* rut; furrow; (RR.) rail.—**carrilera,** *f.* rut (in road).

carrillo, *m.* cheek; small cart.

carro, *m.* car, cart; (Am.) automobile; carriage (of typewriter); cartload.—*c. de combate,* (mil.) tank.—*untar el c.,* (fig.) to grease the palm, to bribe.—**carrocería,** *f.* (auto) body.—**carromato,** *m.* low, strong cart, covered wagon.

carroña, *f.* carrion, putrid carcass.

carroza, *f.* carriage for state occasions.—*c. morturria,* hearse.—**carruaje,** *m.* vehicle; carriage; car.

carta, *f.* letter; map, chart; playing card; charter.—*c. blanca,* carte blanche, full powers.—*c. certificada,* registered letter.—*c. de marear, c. náutica,* sea chart.—*c. de pago,* acquittance, receipt.—*tomar cartas,* to take part; to take sides.

cartabón, *m.* carpenter's square; drawing triangle.

cartapacio, *m.* memorandum book; student's notebook; dossier.

cartear, *vr.* to write to each other, correspond.

cartel, *m.* poster, handbill; placard; cartel.—**cartelera,** *f.* billboard.—**cartelón,** *m.* show bill.

cartera, *f.* brief case; pocketbook; handbag; wallet; portfolio; office and position of a cabinet minister.—**carterista,** *m.* pickpocket.—**cartero,** *m.* letter carrier, postman.

cartílago, *m.* cartilage; parchment.

cartilla, *f.* primer; identity card; passbook.

cartografía, *f.* cartography.—**cartógrafo,** *m.* cartographer.

cartón, *m.* pasteboard; cardboard; cartoon.—**c. piedra,** papier-maché.—**cartulina,** *f.* bristol board, thin cardboard.

cartuchera, *f.* cartridge box or belt; gun holster.—**cartucho,** *m.* paper cone or bag; cartridge.

casa, *f.* house; home; household; firm, concern.—**c. consistorial,** city hall.—**c. de beneficencia,** asylum, poorhouse.—**c. de empeños,** pawnshop.—**c. de huéspedes,** boarding house.—**c. de moneda,** mint.—**c. de socorro,** emergency hospital.—**c. de vecindad,** tenement house.—**c. pública,** brothel.

casaca, *f.* dresscoat.

casado, *a.* & *n.* married (person).—**casamentero,** *n.* matchmaker.—**casamiento,** *m.* marriage; wedding.—**casar,** *vi.* & *vr.* to marry, get married.—*vt.* to marry off; to couple.

cascabel, *m.* jingle bell; snake's rattle; rattlesnake.—**poner el c. al gato,** to bell the cat.—**cascabelero,** *a.* light-witted.

cascada, *f.* cascade, waterfall.

cascado, *a.* broken, burst; decayed.

cascajo, *m.* gravel; fragments; rubbish.

cascanueces, *m.* nutcracker.—**cascar,** *vti.* [d] to crack, break into pieces; to crunch; (coll.) to beat, strike.—*vi.* (coll.) to talk too much.—*vri.* to break open.

cáscara, *f.* peel, shell, rind, hull, husk; bark (of trees).—*pl. interj.* by Jove!—**cascarilla,** *f.* powdered eggshell for cosmetic.—**cascarón,** *m.* eggshell.

cascarrabias, *mf.* crab, irritable person.

cascarudo, *a.* having a thick shell, hull, etc.

casco, *m.* skull; broken fragment of glassware; hull (of a ship); helmet; hoof.—**calentarse los cascos,** to bother one's brain.—**ligero de cascos,** featherbrained.

casera, *f.* housekeeper; landlady; caretaker.—**caserío,** *m.* village, settlement; group of houses.—**casero,** *m.* landlord; caretaker; tenant farmer.—*a.* domestic; home-bred; home-made; homely, homey, informal; household (of articles).—**caseta,** *f.* small house; cabin; booth.

casi, *adv.* almost, nearly.—**c. c.,** very nearly.

casilla, *f.* ticket office; post office box; hut; stall; booth; pigeonhole; square of chessboard.—**sacar a uno de sus casillas,** (coll.) to vex beyond one's patience.—**casillero,** *m.* desk or board with pigeonholes.

casimir, *m.* cashmere.

caso, *m.* case; occurrence, event; matter, question, point.—**c. que,** in case.—**dado el c. que,** supposing that.—**el c. es que,** the fact is that.—**en tal c.,** in such a case.—**en todo c.,** at all events, anyway.—**hacer c.,** to mind, obey, pay attention.—**no venir al c.,** to have nothing to do with the case.—**poner por c.,** to assume, suppose.—**vamos al c.,** let us come to the point.—**verse en el c. de,** to be obliged to, have to.

casorio, *m.* (coll.) wedding.

caspa, *f.* dandruff.

casquillo, *m.* empty cartridge; cap; socket.

casta, *f.* breed, lineage, caste; pedigree; quality.

castaña, *f.* chestnut; (fig.) chignon.

castañetear, *vt.* to rattle the castanets.—*vi.* to chatter (the teeth); to creak (the knees).—**castañeteo,** *m.* sound of castanets; chattering of the teeth.

castaño, *m.* chestnut tree and wood.—*a.* hazel, brown, auburn.

castañuela, *f.* castanet.

castellano, *m.* Spanish language.—*n.* native of Castile.—*a.* Castilian; Spanish (lang., gram., etc.).

castidad, *f.* chastity.

castigar, *vti.* [b] to chastise, punish, castigate.—**castigo,** *m.* chastisement, punishment; penalty.

castillo, *m.* castle.

castizo, *a.* pure, correct (language); of good breed.

casto, *a.* chaste.

castor, *m.* beaver; castor.

castrar, *vt.* to castrate, geld.

castrense, *a.* military.

casual, *a.* accidental, occasional, chance.—**casualidad,** *f.* chance event; accident; coincidence.—*por c.*, by chance.

casucha, *f.* hut, shack, hovel.

cataclismo, *m.* upheaval; catastrophe.

catacumbas, *f.* catacombs.

catador, *m.* taster, sampler.—**catadura,** *f.* act of tasting; (coll.) aspect, looks.—**catar,** *vt.* to sample, try by tasting.

catalán, *n. & a.* Catalan, Catalonian.

catalejo, *m.* telescope.

catalogar, *vti.* [b] to catalogue, list. —**catálogo,** *m.* catalogue, list.

cataplasma, *f.* poultice; (fig.) nuisance, vexer.

catarata, *f.* cataract, cascade, waterfall; cataract of the eye.

catarro, *m.* catarrh; cold, snuffles.

catastro, *m.* census of real property of a county or state.

catástrofe, *f.* catastrophe.

catecismo, *m.* catechism.

cátedra, *f.* subject taught by a professor; professorship; seat or chair of a professor.—**catedrático,** *n.* full professor.

catedral, *f.* cathedral.

categoría, *f.* category; class, condition; rank.—*de c.,* of high rank; prominent.—**categórico,** *a.* categorical; positive.

catequizar, *vti.* [a] to catechize; to proselytize by religious instruction; to persuade, induce.

caterva, *f.* multitude; crowd, throng; herd.

catire, *a. & n.* (Am.) blond, blonde.

católico, *a.* catholic; universal.—*n. & a.* (Roman) Catholic.—*no estar muy c.,* to feel under the weather. —**catolicismo,** *m.* Catholicism.

catre, *m.* small bedstead; cot.—*c. de tijera,* folding cot.

caucásico, *n. & a.* Caucasian.

cauce, *m.* bed of a river; river course.

caución, *f.* caution, precaution; surety, guarantee; bail.

caucho, *m.* rubber (material and tree).

caudal, *m.* volume (of water); abundance; fortune, wealth.—**caudaloso,** *a.* carrying much water; copious, abundant; wealthy.

caudillaje, caudillismo, *m.* leadership; bossism; tyranny.—**caudillo,** *m.* leader, chief; political boss.

causa, *f.* cause; motive, reason; lawsuit, case; trial (at law).—*a* or *por c. de,* on account of, because of, due to.—**causante,** *mf.* originator; (law) the person from whom a right is derived; constituent, principal.—**causar,** *vt.* to cause.

cáustico, *a.* caustic, burning.—*m.* caustic.

cautela, *f.* caution, prudence; cunning.

—**cauteloso,** *a.* cautious, prudent, wary.

cauterizar, *vti.* [a] to cauterize; to blame.

cautivador, cautivante, *a.* captivating, charming.—**cautivar,** *vt.* to captivate, charm; to take prisoner. —**cautiverio,** *m.*, **cautividad,** *f.* captivity.—**cautivo,** *n.* captive.

cauto, *a.* cautious, prudent, wary.

cavar, *vt.* to dig, excavate.—*vi.* to dig; to get to the bottom (of a subject, etc.).

caverna, *f.* cave, cavern.—**cavernoso,** *a.* cavernous; hollow.—*voz cavernosa,* deep-throated voice.

cavidad, *f.* cavity.

cayo, *m.* key, cay, island reef.

cayuco, *m.* (Am.) dugout canoe.

caza, *f.* hunt(ing); wild game.—*dar c.,* to pursue.—**cazador,** *a.* hunting. —*n.* hunter.—**cazar,** *vti.* [a] to chase, hunt; to catch; to pursue.— **cazatorpedero,** *m.* destroyer.

cazo, *m.* dipper; pan; pot.

cazón, *m.* small shark.

cazuela, *f.* cooking pan; stewing pan; stew; crock; (theat.) top gallery.

cazuz, *m.* ivy.

cebada, *f.* barley.—**cebar,** *vt. & vi.* to fatten (animals); to stuff; to feed (a fire, lamp); to prime (a firearm); to excite and cherish (a passion); to bait (a fishhook).—*vr.* to gloat over (a victim).—**cebo,** *m.* bait; incentive; fodder.

cebolla, *f.* onion; onion bulb.— **cebolleta,** *f.* spring onion; scallion.

cebra, *f.* zebra.

cebú, *m.* zebu.

cecear, *vi.* to lisp.—**ceceo,** *m.* lisping, lisp.

cecina, *f.* corned, dried beef.

cedazo, *m.* sieve.

ceder, *vt.* to transfer, cede, yield.— *vi.* to yield, submit; to fail; to slacken; to abate.

cedro, *m.* cedar.

cédula, *f.* scrip; bill; charter; order; decree; warrant; share.—*c. de identidad,* or *c. personal,* official identity document.

céfiro, *m.* zephyr, west wind; breeze.

cegar, *vii.* [1-b] to grow or go blind. —*vti.* to blind; to confuse; to close up, stop up, block up, fill up.—*vri.* to become or be blinded (by passion, etc.).—**cegato,** *a.* (coll.) shortsighted.—**ceguedad, ceguera,** *f.* blindness; ignorance.

ceja, *f.* eyebrow.—*quemarse las cejas,* to burn the midnight oil.—*tener entre c. y c.,* to dislike; to think constantly about.

cejar, *vi.* to give up; to give in, yield; to cede; to relax, slacken.

cejijunto, *a.* frowning, scowling; with knitted eyebrows.

celada, *f.* ambush; artful trick; trap; helmet.—celador, *n.* watchman (-woman); caretaker.—celar, *vt.* to watch over zealously or jealously; to watch, keep under guard; to protect; to conceal.

celda, *f.* cell (in a convent, prison, etc.).—celdilla, *f.* cell in beehives; (bot.) cell.

celebración, *f.* celebration; praise; applause.—celebrar, *vt.* to celebrate; to praise, applaud; to revere; to rejoice at; to say (mass); to hold (formal meeting).—célebre, *a.* famous, renowned.—celebridad, *f.* celebrity; renown, fame.

celeridad, *f.* celerity, quickness.

celeste, *a.* celestial, heavenly.—*azul c.*, sky-blue.—celestial, *a.* celestial, heavenly.

celestina, *f.* procuress; go-between.

celibato, *m.* celibacy.—célibe, *a.* & *mf.* unmarried (person); bachelor.

celo, *m.* zeal; devotion; mating, heat (of animals).—*pl.* jealousy.—*dar celos*, to inspire jealousy.

celofán, *m.* cellophane.

celosía, *f.* lattice work; venetian blind.

celoso, *a.* jealous; zealous, eager; suspicious.

celta, *n.* & *a.* Celt(ic).—céltico, *a.* Celtic.

célula, *f.* (biol.) cell.—celular, *a.* cellular.

celuloide, *m.* celluloid.

celulosa, *f.* cellulose.

cementar, *vt.* to cement.

cementerio, *m.* cemetery, graveyard.

cemento, *m.* cement, concrete.—*c. armado*, reinforced concrete.

cena, *f.* late dinner, supper.

cenagal, *m.* quagmire, slough; arduous, unpleasant affair.

cenagoso, *a.* muddy, miry, marshy.

cenar, *vi.* to sup.—*vt.* to take supper.

cencerrada, *f.*, cencerreo, *m.* serenade with cowbells, pots and pans, etc.—cencerro, *m.* cowbell.

cendal, *m.* gauze, crepe.

cenefa, *f.* border; fringe; valance.

cenicero, *m.* ashtray; ash pan.—cenicienta, *f.* thing or person ill-treated.—*la C.*, Cinderella.—ceniciento, *a.* ash-colored, ashen.

cenit, *m.* zenith.

ceniza, *f.* ash(es), cinder(s).—cenizo, *a.* ash-colored.

censo, *m.* census.

censor, *m.* censor, critic.—censura, *f.* censorship; censure, blame, re-

proach.—censurable, *a.* reprehensible, blameworthy.—censurar, *vt.* to review, criticize; to censure, blame.

centavo, *m.* cent.

centella, *f.* lightning; thunderbolt.—centell(e)ante, *a.* sparkling, flashing.—centellar, centellear, *vi.* to twinkle, sparkle.—centelleo, *m.* sparkling; twinkling.

centena, *f.* a hundred.

centeno, *m.* rye.

centesimal, *a.* (of a number) between one and one hundred.—centésimo, *n.* & *a.* (a) hundredth.

centígrado, *a.* centigrade.—centigramo, *m.* centigram.- centilitro, *m.* centiliter.—centímetro, *m.* centimeter. (See Table of Measures.)

céntimo, *m.* penny.

centinela, *m.* sentry, sentinel.

central, *a.* central.—*f.* main office of a public service; (Am.) sugar mill.—*c. eléctrica*, powerhouse.—centralización, *f.* centralization.- centralizar, *vti.* [a] to centralize.—centrar, *vt.* to center.—céntrico, *a.* central.

centrífugo, *a.* centrifugal.

centrípeto, *a.* centripetal.

centro, *m.* center; middle; midst.—*c. de mesa*, centerpiece (for table).—*estar en su c.*, to be in one's element. -centroamericano, *n.* & *a.* Central American.

centuria, *f.* century (period of time); division of Roman army.

ceñir, *vti.* [9] to gird; to surround, girdle; to fit tight; to hem in.—*vri.* to confine or limit oneself.

ceño, *m.* frown; scowl.—*fruncir el c.*, to frown; to scowl.—ceñudo, *a.* frowning; scowling.

cepa, *f.* stump, stub; vinestock; stock of a family.—*de buena c.*, on good authority; of good stock.

cepillar, *vt.* to brush; to plane; to polish. -cepillo, *m.* brush; (carp.) plane; charity box.

cepo, *m.* stocks, pillory, stock (of an anchor); trap, snare; clamp.

cera, *f.* wax; beeswax; wax tapers.—*pl.* honeycombs.

cerámica, *f.* ceramic art; ceramics.

cerbatana, *f.* pea shooter, blowgun; ear trumpet for the deaf.

cerca, *f.* fence; hedge; enclosure.—*adv.* near, close by, nigh.—*c. de*, closely, close at hand.—cercanía, *f.* nearness; surroundings, neighborhood. cercano, *a.* near, close; neighboring. -cercar, *vti.* [d] to fence in; to circle, gird; to surround; to besiege.

cercenar, *vt.* to clip, trim, pare; to sever, mutilate; to reduce, curtail.

cerciorar, *vt.* to assure, affirm.—*vr.* (de) to ascertain, make sure of.

cerco, *m.* fence; ring; circle; rim, border; blockade, siege.—*levantar el c.,* to raise a blockade.—*poner c. a,* to lay siege to, to blockade.

cerda, *f.* bristle; horse's hair.

cerdo, *m.* hog, pig; pork.

cerdoso, *a.* bristly; hairy.

cereal, *m.* cereal.

cerebro, *m.* brain.

ceremonia, *f.* ceremony; formality.—*guardar c.,* to comply with the formalities.—**ceremonial,** *a. & m.* ceremonial.—**ceremonioso,** *a.* ceremonious, formal.

cereza, *f.* cherry.—**cerezo,** *m.* cherry tree, cherry wood.

cerilla, *f.* wax match; wax taper; ear wax.—**cerillo,** *m.* (Am.) wax match.

cerner, cernir, *vti.* [10] to sift.—*vii.* to drizzle.—*vri.* to soar.

cero, *m.* zero, naught.

cerquillo, *m.* hair bangs.

cerquita, *adv.* very near; at a short distance.

cerrado, *a.* incomprehensible, obscure; close; closed; obstinate; inflexible; cloudy; overcast; stupid.—*a puerta cerrada,* closed (meeting, etc.).—**cerradura,** *f.* lock; closure.—**cerrajería,** *f.* locksmith's shop or forge.—**cerrajero,** *m.* locksmith.—**cerrar,** *vti.* [1] & *vii.* to close, shut, fasten, lock; to fold and seal (a letter).—*vri.* to close; to remain firm in one's opinion; to become cloudy and overcast; to get close to each other. —*cerrársele a uno todas las puertas,* to find all avenues closed.— **cerrazón,** *f.* dark and cloudy weather preceding a storm.

cerrero, *a.* untamed; wild; unbroken (horse).

cerro, *m.* hill.

cerrojo, *m.* bolt, latch.

certamen, *m.* contest; competition.

certero, *a.* well-aimed; accurate; sure; skillful; unfailing.

certeza, *f.* certainty, assurance.—**certidumbre,** *f.* certainty, conviction.

certificación, *f.* certificate, affidavit.—**certificado,** *m.* certificate, attestation; testimonial; piece of registered mail.—**certificar,** *vti.* [d] to certify, attest; to register (a letter); to prove by a public instrument.

cervato, *m.* fawn.

cervecería, *f.* brewery; alehouse; beer tavern.—**cervecero,** *a.* beer.—*n.* brewer; beer seller.—**cerveza,** *f.* beer, ale.

cerviz, *f.* cervix, nape of the neck.—*doblar la c.,* to humble oneself.

cesación, *f.* cessation, discontinuance, stop, pause.—**cesante,** *a.* ceasing.—*mf.* dismissed civil servant.—**cesantía,** *f.* dismissal from a post.—**cesar,** *vi.* to cease, stop; to desist; to retire; to leave a post or employment.—**cese,** *m.* cease; cessation of payment (pension, salary).

cesión, *f.* cession, transfer, conveyance; concession.—**cesionario,** *n.* grantee, assignee, transferee.—**cesionista,** *mf.* transferrer, assigner, grantor.

césped, *m.* lawn; turf; grass; grass plot.

cesta, *f.* basket, pannier; basketful.—**cesto,** *m.* large basket; hutch; hamper.

cetrino, *a.* sallow; jaundiced.

cetro, *m.* scepter; reign.

cibelina, *f.* sable.

cicatería, *f.* niggardliness, stinginess.—**cicatero,** *a.* niggardly, stingy.

cicatriz, *f.* scar.—**cicatrización,** *f.* healing.—**cicatrizar,** *vii.* [a] to heal.

ciclismo, *m.* bicycling.—**ciclista,** *mf.* cyclist.

ciclo, *m.* cycle; period of time.

ciclón, *m.* cyclone; hurricane.

ciclotrón, *m.* cyclotron.

cicuta, *f.* hemlock.

ciego, *a.* blind; blinded.—*n.* blind person; (anat.) blind gut.—*a ciegas,* blindly, in the dark.

cielo, *m.* sky, firmament; heaven(s); ceiling; glory; paradise; roof.—*llovido del c.,* godsend.—*ver el c. abierto,* to find an unforeseen opportunity.

ciempiés, *m.* centipede.

ciénaga, *f.* marsh, moor.

ciencia, *f.* science; knowledge; certainty.—*a c. cierta,* with certainty.

cieno, *m.* mud, mire, slime; slough.

científico, *a.* scientific.—*n.* scientist.

cierre, *m.* act and mode of closing; shutting, locking; fastener; clasp; plug of a valve.

cierto, *a.* sure, positive; certain; true; a certain.—*de c.,* certainly, surely.—*lo c. es que,* the fact is that.—*no por c.,* certainly not.—*por c. que,* indeed; by the way.

cierva, *f.* hind, doe.—**ciervo,** *m.* deer, stag.

cierzo, *m.* cold northerly wind.

cifra, *f.* figure, number; cipher; symbol.—**cifrar,** *vt.* to write in cipher; to abridge.—*c. las esperanzas,* to place one's hopes.

cigarra, *f.* locust.

cigarrera, *f.* cigar cabinet; pocket cigar or cigarette case; woman cigarette maker or dealer.—**cigarrero**, *m.* cigarette maker or dealer.—**cigarrillo**, *m.* cigarette.—**cigarro**, *m.* cigar; cigarette.

cigüeña, *f.* stork; crane; bell-crank; crank.—**cigüeñal**, *m.* crankshaft.

cilíndrico, *a.* cylindrical.—**cilindro**, *m.* cylinder; roller; press roll; chamber.

cima, *f.* summit, peak; top, tiptop.—*dar c.*, to conclude successfully, crown.

címbalo, *m.* cymbal.

cimbrar, *vt.* = CIMBREAR.—**cimbreante**, *a.* willowy.—**cimbrear**, *vt.* to brandish; to shake; to sway; to arch. —*vr.* to bend; to vibrate; to shake. —**cimbreño**, *a.* pliant, flexible.—**cimbreo**, *m.* act of bending, brandishing, swaying, vibrating.

cimentación, *f.* foundation; laying of a foundation.—**cimentar**, *vti.* [1] to lay the foundations of; to found; to ground.—**cimiento**, *m.* foundation; groundwork, bed; base; root.

cinc, *m.* zinc.

cincel, *m.* chisel; engraver.—**cincelar**, *vt.* to chisel, engrave, carve.

cincuentón, *a.* fifty-year old.—*n.* fifty-year-old person.

cincha, *f.* girth, cinch.—**cinchar**, *vt.* to girth, cinch up.

cine, cinema, *m.* moving picture, "movie"; movie theater.—**cinematografía**, *f.* cinematography.—**cinematógrafo**, *m.* cinematograph; moving-picture.

cínico, *a.* cynical; impudent; barefaced.—*n.* cynic.—**cinismo**, *m.* cynicism.

cinta, *f.* ribbon; tape, band, strip, sash; (moving-picture) film, reel.—**cintarazo**, *m.* slap with a belt.—**cintillo**, *m.* hatband; coronet; headline.—**cinto**, *m.* belt, girdle.—**cintura**, *f.* waist, waistline.—*meter en c.*, to control, to discipline.—**cinturón**, *m.* belt; (fig.) girdle.

ciprés, *m.* cypress.—**cipresal**, *m.* cypress grove.

circo, *m.* circus.

circuito, *m.* circuit.

circulación, *f.* circulation; currency; traffic.—**circulante**, *a.* circulatory, circulating.—*biblioteca c.*, lending library.—**circular**, *vi.* to circulate, move.—*vt.* to circulate, pass round. —*a.* circular; circulatory; circling. —*f.* circular letter, notice.—**circulatorio**, *a.* circulatory.—**círculo**, *m.* circle; circumference; ring; social circle, club, association.

circuncidar, *vt.* to circumcise.—**circuncisión**, *f.* circumcision.

circundar, *vt.* to surround, encircle.

circunferencia, *f.* circumference.

circunscribir, *vti.* [49] to circumscribe.

circunspección, *f.* circumspection, prudence.—**circunspecto**, *a.* circumspect, cautious.

circunstancia, *f.* circumstance.—**circunstancial**, *a.* circumstantial.

circunstante, *a.* surrounding; present, attending.—*m. pl.* bystanders; audience.

cirio, *m.* wax taper.

ciruela, *f.* plum.—*c. pasa*, prune.—**ciruelo**, *m.* plum tree.

cirugía, *f.* surgery.—**cirujano**, *n.* surgeon.

cisco, *m.* coal dust; (coll.) bedlam.

cisma, *m.* schism; discord.—**cismático**, *n.* & *a.* schismatic.

cisne, *m.* swan.

cisterna, *f.* cistern; reservoir; underground water tank.

cisura, *f.* incision.

cita, *f.* appointment, engagement, date; quotation.—**citación**, *f.* citation, quotation; summons, judicial notice.—**citar**, *vt.* to make an appointment with; to convoke; to quote; to summon; to give judicial notice.

ciudad, *f.* city.—**ciudadanía**, citizenship.—**ciudadano**, *a.* pertaining to a city.—*n.* citizen.—**ciudadela**, *f.* citadel; tenement house.

cívico, *a.* civic.

civil, *a.* polite.—**civilización**, *f.* civilization.—**civilizador**, *a.* & *n.* civilizing; civilizer.—**civilizar**, *vti.* [a] to civilize.—**civismo**, *m.* good citizenship.

cizaña, *f.* darnel; weed; discord.—**cizañar**, *vi.* to sow discord.—**cizañero**, *n.* troublemaker.

clamar, *vi.* to whine; to clamor, vociferate.—*c. por*, to demand, cry out for.—**clamor**, *m.* clamor, outcry; whine; toll of bells, knell.—**clamorear**, *vi.* to clamor; to toll, knell.—**clamoreo**, *m.* repeated or prolonged clamor; knell.—**clamoroso**, *a.* clamorous, loud, noisy.

clan, *m.* clan; (fam.) clique.

clara, *f.* glair, white of an egg.—*a las claras*, clearly, openly.

claraboya, *f.* skylight; transom; bull's-eye.

clarear, *vt.* to give light to.—*vi.* to dawn; to clear up.—*vr.* to be transparent, translucent.

clarete, *m.* claret.

claridad, *f.* brightness, splendor, light; clearness.—*pl.* plain language, plain truths.—**clarificar**, *vti.* [d] to brighten; to clarify; to purify.

clarín, *m.* bugle, clarion; bugler.—

clarinada, *f.* tart remark.—**clarinete,** *m.* clarinet; clarinet player.

clarividencia, *f.* clairvoyance; clear-sightedness.—**clarividente,** *a.* clairvoyant; clear-sighted.—**claro,** *a.* clear, distinct; bright, cloudless; light (color); transparent; thin; spaced out; frank; outspoken; obvious, evident; open.—*m.* clearing; light spot; clear spot in the sky.—*adv.* clearly.—*¡c. (está)!* of course, naturally.—*pasar la noche en c.,* not to sleep a wink.—*poner en c.,* to make plain.—*sacar en c.,* to conclude, to arrive at a conclusion.

clase, *f.* class, kind, sort; class in school; classroom.—*de c.,* of distinction, of high standing.

clásico, *a.* classic(al).—*n.* classicist.

clasificación, *f.* classification.—**clasificar,** *vti.* [d] to classify; to class.

claudicar, *vii.* [d] to halt, limp; to bungle; to yield.

claustro, *m.* cloister; faculty of a university; monastic state.

cláusula, *f.* period; sentence; clause; article.

clausura, *f.* cloister; inner recess of a convent; closing; clausure, confinement.—**clausurar,** *vt.* to close, conclude, adjourn.

clavar, *vt.* to nail; to fix, fasten; to stick, pin, prick; to pierce; (coll.) to cheat, deceive.—*c. la vista,* or *los ojos,* to stare.

clave, *f.* key of a code; (mus.) key; clef; keystone.

clavel, *m.,* **clavellina,** *f.* pink, carnation.

clavetear, *vt.* to nail; to decorate or stud with nails.

clavícula, *f.* clavicle, collar bone.

clavija, *f.* pin, peg; peg of a string instrument.—*apretar las clavijas,* to put on the thumb screws; to dress down.

clavo, *m.* nail; spike; clove.—*dar en el c.,* to hit the nail on the head.—*un c. saca otro c.,* one grief cures another.

clemencia, *f.* clemency, mercy.—**clemente,** *a.* merciful.

cleptómano, *n. & a.* kleptomaniac.

clerical, *a.* clerical, pert. to the clergy.—**clérigo,** *m.* clergyman.—**clero,** *m.* clergy.

cliente, *mf.* client; customer.—**clientela,** *f.* following, clientele; customers; practice (of lawyers, doctors).

clima, *m.* climate, clime.

clímax, *m.* climax.

clínica, *f.* clinic; private hospital; doctor's or dentist's office; nursing home.

clisé, *m.* cliché; stereotype plate; (phot.) negative.

cloaca, *f.* sewer; cesspool.

cloquear, *vi.* to cluck, cackle.

cloro, *m.* chlorine.—**clorofila,** *f.* chlorophyll.—**cloroformar,** *vt.,* **cloroformizar,** *vti.* [a] to chloroform.—**cloroformo,** *m.* chloroform.

club, *m.* private club.

clueca, *f.* brooding hen.—**clueco,** *a.* broody; (coll.) decrepit.

coacción, *f.* force; coercion.—**coactivo,** *a.* forcible; coercive.

coagular, *vt.* to coagulate; to curdle.—*vr.* to coagulate, clot; to curdle.

coalición, *f.* coalition.

coartada, *f.* alibi.—**coartar,** *vt.* to limit, restrain.

coba, *f.* (coll.) fawning, adulation.—*dar c.,* to flatter.

cobarde, *mf.* coward; poltroon.—*a.* cowardly.—**cobardía,** *f.* cowardice.

cobertizo, *m.* shed, hut; penthouse.—**cobertor,** *m.* bedcover.—**cobertura,** *f.* cover, wrapper, covering, coverlet.

cobija, *f.* cover; (Am.) blanket.—**cobijar,** *vt.* to cover; to shelter; to lodge.—*vr.* to take shelter.

cobrador, *m.* collector; receiving teller.—**cobranza,** *f.* receipt, collection (of money).—**cobrar,** *vt.* to collect (bills, debts); to receive (what is due); to retrieve (shot game); to gain; to charge (price, fee); to cash (check).—*c. ánimo,* to take courage.—*c. fuerzas,* to gather strength.

cobre, *m.* copper; brass kitchen utensils; brass instruments of an orchestra.—*batir el c.,* to hustle.—**cobrizo,** *a.* coppery; copper-colored.

cobro, *m.* receipt, collection (of money); cashing.—*poner en c.,* to put in a safe place.—*ponerse en c.,* to seek a safe place; to withdraw to safety.

coca, *f.* coca; coca leaves.—**cocaína,** *f.* cocaine.

cocal, *m.* coconut plantation.

cocción, *f.* cooking.

cocear, *vt. & vi.* to kick.

cocer, *vti.* [26-a] to boil; to bake; to cook; to calcine (brick, etc.).—*vii.* to boil, cook.—**cocido,** *a.* boiled, baked, cooked.—*m.* a Spanish stew.

cociente, *m.* quotient.

cocimiento, *m.* boiling, concoction.—**cocina,** *f.* kitchen; cuisine, cookery.—**cocinar,** *vt. & vi.* to cook.—**cocinero,** *n.* cook; chef.

coco, *m.* coconut (tree, shell, fruit); bogey.

cocodrilo, *m.* crocodile.

cocotero, *m.* coconut tree.

coctel, *m.* cocktail.—**coctelera,** *f.* cocktail shaker.

cocuyo, *m.* firefly.

cochambre, *m.* (coll.) greasy, dirty thing.—**cochambroso,** *a.* filthy, smelly.

coche, *m.* carriage; coach; car.—*c. cama,* Pullman, sleeping car.—*c. salón,* parlor car.—**cochero,** *m.* coachman.

cochinada, *f.* (coll.) hoggishness; dirty action, dirty trick.—**cochinilla,** *f.* cochineal.—**cochinillo,** *n.* suckling pig.—*c. de Indias,* guinea pig.—**cochino,** *n.* hog (sow), pig.—*a.* & *n.* dirty, vile (person).—**cochiquera,** *f.* (coll.) hog sty, pigpen.

codazo, *m.* blow with the elbow.—**codear,** *vi.* to elbow.—*vt.* to nudge.—*vr.* to rub shoulders, be on intimate terms.—**codeo,** *m.* elbowing; familiarity.

codeína, *f.* codeine.

codiciar, *vt.* & *vi.* to covet.—**codicioso,** *a.* covetous, greedy; ambitious.

codificar, *vti.* [d] to codify.—**código,** *m.* code (of laws).

codo, *m.* elbow; bend.—*alzar el empinar el c.,* to drink too much.—*hablar por los codos,* to talk too much.

codorniz, *f.* quail.

coeducación, *f.* coeducation.

coeficiente, *m.* coefficient.

coerción, *f.* coercion.

coetáneo, *a.* contemporary.

coexistencia, *f.* coexistence.—**coexistir,** *vi.* to coexist.

cofia, *f.* coif; hair net.

cofrade, *mf.* member (of a confraternity, brotherhood, etc.).—**cofradía,** *f.* brotherhood, sisterhood; guild.

cofre, *m.* coffer; trunk; chest.—**cofrecito,** *m.* casket, jewel box.

coger, *vti.* [c] to catch; to seize, grasp; to gather up, collect; to take, receive, hold.—*cogerse una cosa,* to steal something.—**cogida,** *f.* toss or goring by bull; a catch of the ball by a baseball player.

cogollo, *m.* heart of garden plants; shoot of a plant; sugar cane top, used as forage.

cogote, *m.* back of the neck, nape.

cohechar, *vt.* to bribe.—**cohecho,** *m.* bribery.

coherencia, *f.* coherence; connection.—**coherente,** *a.* coherent.—**cohesión,** *f.* cohesion.—**cohesivo,** *a.* cohesive.

cohete, *m.* skyrocket; rocket.

cohibición, *f.* reserve, shyness; restraint.—**cohibido,** *a.* inhibited; embarrassed, uneasy.—**cohibir,** *vt.* to restrain, inhibit.

coincidencia, *f.* coincidence.—**coincidente,** *a.* coincident.—**coincidir,** *vi.* to coincide.

coito, *m.* copulation.

cojear, *vi.* to limp.—*c. del mismo pie,* to have the same weakness.—**cojera,** *f.* limp, lameness.

cojín, *m.* cushion; pad.—**cojinete,** *m.* bearing; pillow block; small cushion.

cojo, *a.* lame, crippled; one-legged; (of table, etc.) unsteady, tilting.—*n.* cripple.

cok, *m.* coke.

col, *f.* cabbage.

cola, *f.* tail; line of people; hind portion of anything; glue.—*estar a la c.,* to be in the last place.—*hacer c.,* to stand in line.—*tener* or *traer c.,* to have serious consequences.

colaboración, *f.* collaboration; contribution (to a periodical, etc.).—**colaborador,** *m.* collaborator; contributor (to a periodical, etc.).—**colaborar,** *vi.* to collaborate.

colación, *f.* collation.—*traer a c,* to bring up for discussion.

coladera, *f.* strainer, sieve.—**colador,** *m.* colander.—**colar,** *vti.* & *vii.* [12] to strain, drain, pass through, percolate.—*vri.* to slip in or out, sneak in.

colapso, *m.* collapse.

colateral, *a.* collateral.

colcha, *f.* coverlet, quilt, bedspread; saddle and trappings.

colchón, *m.* mattress.

colear, *vi.* to wag (the tail).—*vt.* to pull down (cattle) by the tail.

colección, *f.* collection.—**coleccionador, coleccionista,** *n.* collector (of stamps, etc.).—**coleccionar,** *vt.* to form a collection of, collect.—**colecta,** *f.* collection of voluntary contributions, tax assessment.—**colectar,** *vt.* to collect.—**colectividad,** *f.* collectivity; mass of people; community.—**colectivo,** *a.* collective.—**colector,** *m.* collector, gatherer.

colega, *mf.* colleague; fellow worker.

colegial, *a.* collegiate.—*n.* first or secondary school student; (coll.) inexperienced person, greenhorn.—**colegiatura,** *f.* membership in a professional association (bar, medical, engineering, etc.).—**colegio,** *m.* body of professional men; school, academy; elementary or secondary school.

colegir, *vti.* [29-c] to deduce, infer, conclude.

cólera, *f.* anger, rage, fury.—*m.* cholera.—**colérico,** *a.* angry, irascible; choleric.

coleta, *f.* pigtail.—*cortarse la c.,* to

retire, quit the profession (esp. bull-fighters).—**coletilla,** *f.* postscript; small queue (hair).

coleto, *m.* leather jacket; inner self. —*decir para su c.,* to say to oneself. —*echarse al c.,* to drink down; to devour.

colgado, *a.* suspended, hanging; disappointed.—**colgadura,** *f.* tapestry; bunting.—**colgajo,** *m.* tatter or rag hanging from (clothes, etc.).—**colgante,** *m.* drop; pendant; hanger; king post.—*a.* hanging.—**colgar,** *vti.* [12-b] to hang up; to impute, charge with; to kill by hanging; to flunk a student.—*vii.* to be suspended; to dangle; to flag, droop. —*vri.* to hang oneself.

colibrí, *m.* hummingbird.

cólico, *m.* colic.

coliflor, *f.* cauliflower.

coligarse, *vri.* [b] to band together, become allies.

colilla, *f.* cigar stub; cigarette butt.

colina, *f.* hill.

colindante, *a.* contiguous, adjacent, abutting.—**colindar,** *vi.* (con) to be contiguous, or adjacent (to); to abut (on).

coliseo, *m.* theater, opera house; coliseum.

colisión, *f.* collision, clash.

colmado, *a.* (de) abundant; full (of), filled (with).—*m.* specialty eating house (gen. for sea food); grocery store, supermarket.—**colmar,** *vt.* (de) to heap up, fill to the brim (with); to fulfill, make up; to bestow liberally.

colmena, *f.* beehive, (Am.) bee.— **colmenar,** *m.* apiary.

colmillo, *m.* eyetooth; fang; tusk.

colmo, *m.* fill; overflowing; overmeasure; limit; climax, extreme, acme. —*a. c.,* abundantly.—*llegar al c., ser el c.,* to be the limit.

colocación, *f.* situation, position; employment, job; placing, setting, arrangement.—**colocar,** *vti.* [d] to arrange, put in due place or order; to place, provide with employment, take on (in a job).—*vri.* to take (a job); to place oneself.

colombiano, *n.* & *a.* Colombian.

colombino, *a.* pertaining to Columbus; pertaining to pigeons or doves.

colonia, *f.* settlement, colony; plantation; cologne water.—**colonial,** *a.* colonial.—**colonización,** *f.* settlement, colonization.—**colonizador,** *n.* & *a.* colonizer; colonizing.—**colonizar,** *vti.* [a] to colonize, settle.— **colono,** *m.* colonist, settler; tenant farmer.

coloquio, *m.* conversation, dialogue.

color, *m.* color; paint; rouge; coloring tint; pretext.—*sacarle los colores a uno,* to shame, make one blush. —**coloración,** *f.* coloration, coloring, painting.—**colorado,** *a.* red; ruddy; colored.—*ponerse c.,* to blush.— **colorante,** *m.* color, paint; coloring tint.—*a.* coloring.—**colorar, colorear,** *vt.* to color, paint, dye, stain; to make plausible; to palliate.— **coloreado,** *a.* colored.—**colorete,** *m.* rouge.—**colorido,** *m.* coloring or color; pretext, pretense.

colosal, *a.* colossal, huge.

columbrar, *vt.* to perceive faintly, discern at a distance; to conjecture.

columna, *f.* column, pillar.—*c. vertebral,* or *dorsal,* spine.

columpiar, *vt.* & *vr.* to swing.—**columpio,** *m.* swing; seesaw.

collado, *m.* height, hill.

collar, *m.* necklace; collar, collet.— **collarín,** *m.* collar of a coat; (mech.) tube, sleeve; ruff.—**collera,** *f.* horse collar.

coma, *f.* comma (,).—*m.* coma, unconsciousness.

comadre, *f.* mother and godmother with respect to each other; midwife, gossip; go-between.—**comadrear,** *vi.* to gossip, tattle.—**comadreja,** *f.* weasel.—**comadreo,** *m.* gossiping.—**comadrón,** *m.* male midwife, accoucheur.—**comadrona,** *f.* midwife.

comandancia, *f.* command; office of a commander; province or district of a commander.—**comandante,** *m.* commander, commandant.—**comandar,** *vt.* to command.

comandita, *f.* (com.) silent partnership.—**comanditario,** *a.* (com.) pertaining to a silent partnership.

comando, *m.* military command.

comarca, *f.* territory, region.

comba, *f.* curvature, warp, bend.— **combadura,** *f.* bending, bend.— **combar,** to bend, curve.—*vr.* to warp, bulge; to sag.

combate, *m.* combat, fight, battle; struggle.—**combatiente,** *mf.* & *a.* combatant, fighter; fighting.—**combatir,** *vt.* & *vi.* to combat, fight; to attack, oppose; to struggle.

combinación, *f.* combination; connection; compound; plan; slip (underwear).—**combinar,** *vt.* & *vr* to combine, unite.

combustible, *m.* fuel.—*a.* combustible. —**combustión,** *f.* combustion.

comedero, *m.* feeding-trough; (coll.) eating place.—*a.* edible, eatable.

comedia, *f.* comedy; farce; play.— **comediante,** *mf.* actor, actress, comedian; hypocrite.—*a.* (coll.) hypocritical.

comedido, *a.* courteous, polite; prudent, moderate.—comedimiento, *m.* moderation; politeness.—comedirse, *vri.* [29] to govern oneself; to be moderate, polite.

comedor, *m.* dining room.—*n.* & *a.* eater; eating.

comején, *m.* termite.

comensal, *n.* table guest; companion at meals.

comentar, *vt.* to comment; to annotate, expound.—comentario, *m.* commentary.—comentarista, *mf.* commentator.

comenzar, *vti.* [1-a] & *vii.* to commence, begin.

comer, *vt.* to eat; to take (in chess, checkers, etc.).—*vi.* to eat; to lunch, dine.—*vr.* to eat up; to omit, skip. —dar de c., to feed.—ganar para c., to make a living.

comercial, *a.* commercial.—comerciante, *mf.* trader.—comerciar, *vi.* to trade, engage in commerce.—comercio, *m.* commerce, trade,—c. sexual, sexual intercourse.

comestible, *a.* eatable, edible.—*m. pl.* food, provisions, groceries.

cometa, *m.* comet.—*f.* kite.

cometer, *vt.* to commit, perpetrate.—cometido, *m.* commission; charge; task, duty.

comezón, *f.* itch(ing); longing, desire.

comicios, *m. pl.* elections, primaries; district assemblies.

cómico, *m.* player, actor, comedian. —*a.* comic; comical, funny.

comida, *f.* eating; food; luncheon, dinner, supper.

comienzo, *m.* start, beginning.—dar c., to begin, start.

comilón, *m.* great eater, glutton.

comillas, *f. pl.* quotation marks (" ").

comino, *m.* cumin (plant, seed).—no valer un c., not to be worth a bean.

comisaría, *f.* police station; office of the commissary.—comisario, *m.* commissary; police inspector; purser.

comisión, *f.* commission; committee; assignment; perpetration.—comisionado, *m.* commissioner.—*a.* commissional or commissionary; commissioned.—comisionar, *vt.* to commission; to appoint.—comisionista, *mf.* commission merchant; commission agent; commissioner.

comité, *m.* committee; commission.

comitiva, *f.* retinue; group of attendants or followers.

como, *adv.* & *conj.* how; in what manner; to what degree; as; since;

like; as if; about, approximately; if; such as; inasmuch as; as.—*c.* quiera que, although; since.—cómo, *interrog.* what? how? why?—¿a cómo? how much?—¿a cómo estamos? what is the date?—¿cómo? what is it? what did you say?—¿cómo así? how? how so?—¿cómo no? why not? of course.—interj why! is it possible!

cómoda, *f.* chest of drawers, bureau.

comodidad, *f.* comfort, convenience; commodity.—comodín, *m.* something or someone of general utility; joker (at card).—cómodo, *a.* comfortable; cozy; convenient.

comodoro, *m.* commodore.

compacto, *a.* compact.

compadecer, *vti.* [3] to pity, be sorry for.—*vri.* (de) to pity; (con) to conform, agree, tally.

compadraje, compadrazgo, *m.* alliance for mutual protection and advancement (used in a bad sense); clique.—compadre, *m.* godfather and father of a child with respect to each other; friend, pal.

compaginar, *vt.* to arrange in proper order; to unite, join.

compañerismo, *m.* good fellowship, comradeship.—compañero, *m.* companion, pal; fellow member; partner; one of a pair, mate.—compañía, *f.* company; partnership; co-partnership.

comparación, *f.* comparison.—comparar, *vt.* to compare; to confront.—comparativo, *a.* comparative.

comparecencia, *f.* appearance.—comparecer, *vii.* [3] to appear (before a judge, etc.).

comparsa, *f.* (theat.) retinue of persons.—*mf.* (theat.) extra, supernumerary actor.

compartimiento, *m.* division of a whole into parts; compartment; department.—compartir, *vt.* to divide into equal parts; to share.

compás, *m.* compass; measure; beat. —llevar el c., to beat time.

compasión, *f.* compassion, pity.—compasivo, *a.* compassionate, merciful.

compatibilidad, *f.* compatibility.—compatible, *a.* compatible, suitable.

compatriota, *mf.* compatriot, fellow-countryman.

compeler, *vt.* to compel, force.

compendiar, *vt.* to abridge, condense. —compendio, *m.* compendium, abridgment.

compenetración, *f.* intermixture.—compenetrarse, *vr.* to pervade, intermix; to be in full agreement.

compensación, *f.* compensation; recompense, reward.—**compensar,** *vt.* & *vi.* to compensate, recompense; to counterbalance; to balance, equilibrate; to indemnify.

competencia, *f.* competition, rivalry; competence, aptitude; jurisdiction; dispute.—**competente,** *a.* competent, apt; applicable (to); adequate.—**competición,** *f.* competition.—**competidor,** *n.* opponent, competitor.—*a.* competing, vie, rival.—**competir,** *vii.* [29] to compete, vie, rival.

compilación, *f.* compilation.—**compilador,** *n.* & *a.* compiler, compiling.—**compilar,** *vt.* to compile.

compinche, *m.* bosom friend, pal.

complacencia, *f.* pleasure, satisfaction; complacency.—**complacer,** *vti.* [3] to please, accommodate.—*vri.* (en) to be pleased (with or to); to delight (in); to take pleasure (in).—**complaciente,** *a.* pleasing, kind, agreeable.

complejidad, *f.* complexity.—**complejo,** *a.* complex; intricate, arduous.—*m.* complex.

complementario, *a.* complementary.—**complemento,** *m.* complement.

completar, *vt.* to complete, perfect, finish.—**completo,** *a.* complete, unabridged; completed; unqualified.—*por c.,* completely.

complexión, *f.* constitution; temperament, nature.

complicación, *f.* complication, complexity.—**complicar,** *vti.* [d] to complicate; to jumble together.—*vri.* to become difficult, confused.

cómplice, *mf.* accomplice.—**complicidad,** *f.* complicity.

complot, *m.* plot, conspiracy.

componenda, *f.* adjustment, compromise.—**componente,** *mf.* & *a.* component.—**componer,** *vti.* [32] to compose; to compound; to prepare; to repair; to heal, restore; to brace up; to trim, fit up; to reconcile.—*vri.* to prink, (coll.) doll up; to calm oneself.

comportamiento, *m.* behavior.—**comportar,** *vr.* to behave.

composición, *f.* composition; repair.—**compositor,** *n.* composer (of music).—**compostura,** *f.* composure; repair, repairing; cleanliness, neatness of dress.

compota, *f.* compote, stewed fruits; preserves.

compra, *f.* purchase; buying; shopping.—*hacer compras,* to shop.—*ir* or *salir de compras,* to go shopping.—**comprador,** *m.* buyer; purchaser; user.—**comprar,** *vt.* to buy, purchase; to shop.

comprender, *vt.* to understand, comprehend; to comprise, include, cover.—**comprensible,** *a.* comprehensible, understandable.—**comprensión,** *f.* comprehension, understanding, comprehensiveness; act of comprising or containing.—**comprensivo,** *a.* comprehensive; capable of understanding; containing.

compresa, *f.* compress.

compresión, *f.* compression.—**comprimir,** *vt.* to compress.—*vr.* to become compact.

comprobación, *f.* verification, checking; proof, substantiation.—**comprobante,** *m.* proof, evidence; voucher.—**comprobar,** *vti.* [12] to verify, confirm, check.

comprometer, *vt.* to compromise; to endanger; to arbitrate; to engage; to risk; to expose, jeopardize.—*vr.* to commit oneself; to undertake; to expose oneself; to become engaged; to become involved; to expose oneself to risk.—**compromiso,** *m.* compromise; obligation; embarrassment; engagement, appointment.

compuerta, *f.* hatch or half-door; lock, floodgate.

compuesto, *pp.* of COMPONER.—*m.* compound, preparation, mixture.—*a.* compound; composed; repaired; arranged; made up.

compungirse, *vri.* [c] to feel compunction or remorse.

computar, *vt.* to compute, calculate.—**cómputo,** *m.* computation, calculation.

comulgar, *vii.* [b] to take communion; to commune.

común, *a.* common, public; usual, *customary*; current; vulgar.—*por lo c.,* usually.

comunicación, *f.* communication; communiqué, official statement.—*pl.* means of communication.—**comunicado,** *m.* letter to a paper; communiqué.—**comunicar,** *vti.* [d] to communicate; to notify.—*vri.* to communicate; to connect; to be in touch.—**comunicativo,** *a.* communicative, talkative.

comunidad, *f.* the common people; community; corporation; religious group.—**comunión,** *f.* communion; political party.—**comunismo,** *m.* communism.—**comunista,** *mf.* & *a.* communist(ic).

con, *prep.* with; (when followed by infinitive) by; although.—*c. que,* and so, then, so then.—*c. tal que,* provided that.—*c. todo,* nevertheless, notwithstanding.

conato, *m.* endeavor; effort, exertion; attempt, attempted crime.

concavidad, *f.* hollowness, concavity. —**cóncavo,** *a.* hollow, concave.—*m.* concavity.

concebible, *a.* conceivable.—**concebir,** *vti.* [29] & *vii.* to conceive, become pregnant; to imagine; to comprehend.

conceder, *vt.* to concede, admit; to give, grant.

concejal, *m.* councilman.—**concejo,** *m.* municipal council; civic body of a small town; board of aldermen.

concentración, *f.* concentration.—**concentrar,** *vt.* to concentrate.—*vr.* to concentrate (mentally); to come together.—**concéntrico,** *a.* concentric.

concepción, *f.* conception; idea.—**concepto,** *m.* concept, thought; judgment, opinion.—**conceptuar,** *vt.* to judge, think, form an opinion of. —**conceptuoso,** *a.* witty; overelaborate.

concerniente, *a.* (a) concerning, relating (to).—*en lo c. a,* with regard to, as for.—**concernir,** *vii.* [50] to concern, relate to.

concertar, *vti.* [1] to concert, arrange by agreement, adjust, settle. —*vii.* to agree, accord.—*vri.* to come to an agreement; to go hand in hand.

concesión, *f.* concession, grant.—**concesionario,** *m.* concessionary.

conciencia, *f.* conscience; conscientiousness; consciousness.—**concienzudo,** *a.* conscientious.

concierto, *m.* concert; agreement; good order and arrangement.

conciliábulo, *m.* unlawful meeting, or agreement.—**conciliar,** *vt.* to conciliate; to reconcile.—*c. el sueño,* to get to sleep.—**concilio,** *m.* (eccl.) council.

concisión, *f.* conciseness, succinctness. —**conciso,** *a.* concise, succinct.

concitar, *vt.* to excite, stir up, agitate.

conciudadano, *n.* fellow citizen, countryman.

concomitancia, *f.* concomitance.

concubina, *f.* concubine, mistress.—**concubinato,** *m.* concubinage.

concha, *f.* shell; shell-fish; tortoiseshell, conch.

concluir, *vti.* [23-e] to conclude, bring to an end; to decide finally, determine; to infer, deduce.—*vii.* & *vri.* to come to an end, finish.—**conclusión,** *f.* conclusion (all senses).—**concluyente,** *a.* concluding, conclusive.

concordancia, *f.* concordance; harmony; concord, agreement.—**concordar,** *vti.* [12] to reconcile; to make agree; to harmonize.—*vii.* to be in accord; to agree.—**concordia,**

f. concord, harmony; agreement; peace, good will.

concretar, *vt.* to summarize, sum up; to combine, unite.—*vr.* to limit or confine oneself (to a subject).—**concreto,** *a.* concrete (not abstract).—*en c.,* concretely; in brief, in a few words.—*m.* concrete (building material).

conculcar, *vti.* [d] to trample underfoot; to violate, infringe.

concupiscencia, *f.* lust.—**concupiscente,** *a.* sensual.

concurrencia, *f.* attendance; concurrence; audience, gathering, assembly. —**concurrido,** *a.* frequented; (of a meeting, etc.) well-attended.—**concurrir,** *vi.* to concur, agree; to meet in one point, time or place; to attend.

concurso, *m.* competitive contest or examination; concourse; aid, assistance; call for bids (on a piece of work, a service, etc.); gathering.

condado, *m.* earldom; county; dignity of a count.—**conde,** *m.* count, earl.

condecoración, *f.* medal; badge; decoration.—**condecorar,** *vt.* to bestow a medal or insignia on; to decorate.

condena, *f.* penalty; sentence, term of imprisonment.—**condenable,** *a.* condemnable.—**condenación,** *f.* condemnation; punishment; damnation. —**condenado,** *n.* & *a.* damned (in hell); convict; condemned; convicted.—**condenar,** *vt.* to condemn; to damn; to declare guilty; to censure, disapprove; to nail or wall up (a door, etc.); to annoy.—*vr.* to be damned (to hell).

condensación, *f.* condensation.—**condensador,** *a.* condensing.—*m.* (steam, elec., etc.) condenser.—**condensar,** *vt.* to condense, thicken.—*vr.* to be condensed.

condesa, *f.* countess.

condescendencia, *f.* condescension; compliance.—**condescender,** *vii.* [18] to condescend; to yield, comply.

condición, *f.* condition, state; temper; constitution; rank; stipulation. —**condicionado,** *a.* conditioned; conditional.—**condicional,** *a.* conditional.—**condicionar,** *vi.* to impose conditions; to agree, accord.

condimentar, *vt.* to season or dress (foods).—**condimento,** *m.* seasoning, condiment.

condiscípulo, *n.* schoolmate, fellow student.

condolencia, *f.* condolence, expression of sympathy.—**condolerse,** *vri.* [26] (de) to condole (with), be sorry (for), sympathize (with).

condominio, *m.* joint ownership.

cóndor, *m.* condor.

conducción, *f.* conveyance; carriage, transportation; leading, guiding; conducting; driving; conduit.—**conducente,** *a.* conducive, conducent.—**conducir,** *vti.* [11] & *vii.* to convey, carry; to take, accompany; to direct, lead; to manage, conduct; to drive.—*vii.* (a) to conduce, contribute (to); to be suitable (for); to lead, tend (to).—*vri.* to behave, act, conduct oneself.—**conducta,** *f.* conduct, behavior.—**conducto,** *m.* duct, conduit, pipe.—**conductor,** *n.* (Am.) conductor (RR., bus, etc.); leader; driver.—*a.* conducting, conductive (of heat, electricity, etc.).

conectar, *vt.* to connect.

conejo, *m.* rabbit.—*conejillo de Indias,* guinea pig.

conexión, *f.* connection; joint; coherence.

confección, *f.* any handwork; workmanship; fancy work, ready-made article.—**confeccionar,** *vt.* to make, prepare; to compound.

confederación, *f.* confederacy, confederation.—**confederado,** *m.* & *a.* confederate.—**confederar,** *vt.* & *vr.* to confederate, join, form a confederacy.

conferencia, *f.* conference, meeting, interview; lecture.—**conferenciante, conferencista,** *mf.* lecturer.—**conferenciar,** *vi.* to consult together, hold a conference; to lecture.

conferir, *vti.* [39] to confer; to give, bestow.

confesar, *vti.* [1] to confess, hear confession.—*vri.* to confess or make confessions.—**confesión,** *f.* confession.—**confesionario,** *m.* confessional.—**confesor,** *m.* father confessor.

confiable, *a.* trusty, reliable.—**confiado,** *a.* unsuspecting, trusting; confident.—**confianza,** *f.* confidence; familiarity, informality.—**confianzudo,** *a.* (coll.) fresh, over-friendly.—**confiar,** *vii.* (en) to rely (on), to trust (in). —*vt.* to confide; to commit to the care of another.—**confidencia,** *f.* trust, confidence; confidential information.—**confidencial,** *a.* confidential.—**confidente,** *mf.* confidant; police spy.—*m.* love seat.—*a.* faithful, trusty.

confín, *m.* limit, boundary, border.— *a.* bordering; limiting.—**confinamiento,** *m.* confinement.—**confinar,** *vt.* & *vr.* to confine; to banish to a definite place; to border on.

confirmación, *f.* confirmation; corroboration.—**confirmar,** *vt.* to confirm.

confiscación, *f.* confiscation.—**confiscar,** *vti.* [d] to confiscate.

confitar, *vt.* to candy; to preserve (fruit); to sweeten.—**confite,** *m.* candy, bonbon; sweets.—**confitería,** *f.* confectionery; confectioner's shop. —**confitura,** *f.* confection.

conflagración, *f.* conflagration.

conflicto, *m.* conflict.

confluencia, *f.* confluence.—**confluente,** *a.* confluent.—**confluir,** *vii.* [23-e] to join (rivers and sea currents); to assemble in one place.

conformación, *f.* conformation; shape. —**conformar,** *vt.* to conform, adjust, fit.—*vi.* to suit, fit, conform.— *vr.* to comply; to submit; to resign oneself.—**conforme,** *a.* alike, similar; correct, acceptable; compliant; resigned.—*adv.* in due proportion; agreeably, accordingly.—**conformidad,** *f.* likeness; conformity; agreement; resignation, submission.

confortar, *vt.* to comfort; to console; to strengthen.

confrontar, *vt.* to confront; to collate; to compare, check.

confundir, *vt.* to confound; to perplex, confuse; to mystify.—*vr.* to be bewildered, perplexed; to become ashamed and humbled.—**confusión,** *f.* confusion, disorder; perplexity; embarrassment.—**confuso,** *a.* confused, confounded; unintelligible; perplexed.

congelar, *vt.* & *vr.* to congeal, freeze.

congénere, *a.* kindred, of like kind.

congeniar, *vi.* to be congenial; to get along well (with).

congestión, *f.* congestion.—**congestionar,** *vt.* to congest.—*vr.* to get congested.

congoja, *f.* anguish, sorrow, grief.

congraciarse, *vr.* (con) to ingratiate oneself, to win favor.

congratulación, *f.* congratulation.—**congratular,** *vt.* to congratulate.— *vr.* to congratulate oneself, rejoice.

congregación, *f.* congregation; meeting, assembly; religious fraternity, brotherhood.—**congregar,** *vti.* [b] & *vri. to* assemble, congregate.—**congresista,** *mf.* congressman, congresswoman.—**congreso,** *m.* congress; convention, assembly.—*C. de los Diputados,* House of Representatives.

congruencia, *f.* congruence; convenience; fitness.—**congruente,** *a.* congruent, corresponding.

congruencia, *f.* congruence; convenience; fitness.—**congruente,** *a.* congruent, corresponding.

cónico, *a.* conical, conic.

conjetura, *f.* conjecture.—**conjeturar,** *vt.* to conjecture.

conjugación, *f.* conjugation.—**conjugar,** *vti.* [b] to conjugate.

conjunción, *f.* conjunction, union; act of coupling or joining together.

conjunto, *a.* united.—*m.* whole, aggregate.—*en c.,* altogether, as a whole.

conjura, conjuración, *f.* conspiracy, conjuration, plot.—**conjurado,** *m.* conspirator.—**conjurar,** *vi.* to conspire.—*vt.* to exorcise, conjure; to entreat, implore; to avert, ward off. —**conjuro,** *m.* conjuration; exorcism; entreaty.

conllevar, *vt.* to aid; to bear with patience.

conmemoración, *f.* remembrance; commemoration; anniversary.—**conmemorar,** *vt.* to commemorate.

conmensurable, *a.* commensurable.

conmigo, *pron.* with me, with myself.

conmiseración, *f.* commiseration, pity.

conmoción, *f.* commotion, excitement. —**conmovedor,** *a.* touching; sad, pathetic; exciting, thrilling.—**conmover,** *vti.* [26] to touch, move; to appeal to; to disturb, shock; to excite, stir.

conmutación, *f.* commutation, exchange.—**conmutador,** *m.* electric switch; telegraph key.—**conmutar,** *vt.* to exchange, barter.

connivencia, *f.* connivance; plotting.

cono, *m.* cone.

conocedor, *a.* **(de)** familiar (with), expert (in).—*n.* expert, connoisseur. —**conocer,** *vti.* [3] to know; to meet; to experience, comprehend.— *vii.* to know, be competent.—*vri.* to know oneself.—**conocido,** *a.* prominent, well-known.—*n.* acquaintance. —**conocimiento,** *m.* knowledge; skill, ability; acquaintance; bill of lading. —*poner en c. de,* to inform, notify.

conque, *conj.* so then; now then; and so; well then; therefore.

conquista, *f.* conquest, subjugation; conquered territory, thing or person. —**conquistador,** *m.* & *a.* conqueror, conquering; (fig.) Don Juan.—

conquistar, *vt.* to conquer; to win, acquire; to win over, persuade.

consabido, *a.* well-known; in question; before-mentioned, aforesaid.

consagración, *f.* consecration.—**consagrar,** *vt.* to consecrate; to deify; to devote, dedicate.—*vr.* to devote or give oneself to (study, work, etc.).

consanguíneo, *a.* related by blood.— **consanguinidad,** *f.* blood relationship.

consciencia, *f.* consciousness.—**consciente,** *a.* conscious.

consecución, *f.* attainment, obtaining, acquisition.—**consecuencia,** *f.* consequence; consistency; result.—*a c. de,* because of.—*en* or *por c.,* consequently, therefore.—**consecuente,** *m.* effect, issue, consequence.—*a.* consequent, following; logical, consistent. —**consecutivo,** *a.* consecutive, successive.

conseguir, *vti.* [29-b] to attain, get, obtain; to succeed in.

conseja, *f.* story, fairy tale, fable, old wives' tale.

consejero, *m.* counsellor, member of a council; adviser.—**consejo,** *m.* counsel, advice; council, consulting body. —*c. de guerra,* court martial; council of war.—*c. de ministros,* cabinet. —*presidente del c.,* prime minister.

consenso, *m.* general assent; consensus; verdict.

consentido, *a.* & *n.* spoiled (child); cuckold.—**consentidor,** *m.* complier, conniver; coddler.—**consentimiento,** *m.* consent; coddling; acquiescence. —**consentir,** *vti.* [40] to consent, permit; to acquiesce in; to accept, admit; to pamper, spoil.

conserje, *n.* doorman, janitor, porter.

conserva, *f.* canned food, preserve; jam; pickle.—**conservación,** *f.* conservation; preservation; maintenance, upkeep.—**conservador,** *m.* conservator, preserver; curator.—*m.* & *a.* conservative.—**conservar,** *vt.* to conserve, maintain, preserve; to guard; to preserve or pickle (fruit); to can.—*vr.* to keep young, be well preserved; to last, keep well.— **conservatorio,** *m.* (music) conservatory.

considerable, *a.* considerable, important.—**consideración,** *f.* consideration; importance; respect.—**considerado,** *a.* prudent; considerate; thoughtful; esteemed, distinguished. —**considerar,** *vt.* to consider; to treat with consideration.

consigna, *f.* watchword, password; slogan; (RR.) checkroom.—**consignación,** *f.* consignment, shipment.— **consignar,** *vt.* to consign, assign; to deliver; to check (baggage); to set apart.

consigo, *pron.* with oneself (himself, herself, itself, themselves, yourself, yourselves).

consiguiente, *m.* (log.) consequence, result, effect.—*a.* consequent.—*por c.,* therefore.

consistencia, *f.* consistence, consistency.—**consistente,** *a.* consistent, firm, solid.—**consistir,** *vi.* to con-

sist; to be comprised, contained.—
c. en, to consist in, to be a matter
of.

consistorio, *m.* consistory; municipal
council, board of aldermen.

consocio, *n.* partner.

consola, *f.* console; bracket shelf.

consolación, *f.* consolation.—**consolador,** *a.* consoling.—**consolar,** *vti.*
[12] to console, comfort.

consolidación, *f.* consolidation.—
consolidar, *vt.* to consolidate; to
harden, strengthen; to fund (debts).
—*vr.* to consolidate, grow firm; to
unite.

consonante, *m.* rhyming word; (mus.)
consonant or corresponding sound.—
f. & a. (letter) consonant; harmonious.

consorcio, *m.* syndicate, partnership.

consorte, *n.* consort, mate.

conspicuo, *a.* conspicuous; prominent.

conspiración, *f.* conspiracy, plot.—
conspirador, *n.* conspirator.—*a.*
conspiring.—**conspirar,** *vi.* to conspire, plot.

constancia, *f.* written evidence; constancy, perseverance.—**constante,** *a.*
constant; uninterrupted; firm.

constar, *vi.* to be clear, evident, certain; to be recorded, registered;
(de) to be composed (of), consist
(of).

constatar, *vt.* to verify, confirm.

constelación, *f.* constellation.

consternación, *f.* consternation.—
consternar, *vt.* to dismay; to
amaze; to distress, grieve.

constipado, *m.* head cold.—*a.* suffering
from a cold.—**constipar,** *vr.* to catch
cold.—*vt.* to cause a cold.

constitución, *f.* constitution.—**constitucional,** *a.* constitutional.—**constitucionalidad,** *f.* constitutionality.—
constituir, *vti.* [23-e] to constitute.
—*vri.* (en), to set oneself up as.—
constituyente, *mf. & a.* constituent.

constreñir, *vti.* [9] to constrain, compel, force; to contract.

construcción, *f.* construction; act and
art of constructing; structure;
building.—**constructor,** *m.* builder;
maker.—**construir,** *vti.* [23-e] to
construct, build, form.

consuelo, *m.* consolation, relief, solace; joy.

consuetudinario, *a.* customary, generally practiced.

cónsul, *mf.* consul.—**consulado,** *m.*
consulate.

consulta, *f.* consultation, conference;
office hours (of a doctor).—**consultante,** *mf.* consulter.—*a.* consulting.
—**consultar,** *vt.* to consult.—**consul-**

tor, *n.* consulter.—*a.* consulting.—
consultorio, *m.* clinic, doctor's office.

consumación, *f.* consummation; extinction.—**consumar,** *vt.* to consummate, finish, perfect; to commit
(a crime).

consumidor, *n. & a.* consumer, user;
consuming.—**consumir,** *vt.* to consume; to waste away.—*vr.* to be
consumed, exhausted; to run out;
to languish.—**consumo,** *m.* consumption (of provision, fuel, merchandise).

consunción, *f.* consumption, wasting
away.

consustancial, *a.* consubstantial.

contabilidad, *f.* bookkeeping, accounting.—**contable,** *a.* countable.—*mf.*
bookkeeper, accountant.

contacto, *m.* contact.

contado, *a.* scarce, rare.—*al c.*, cash.
—*por de c.*, of course, as a matter
of course.—**contador,** *m.* accountant; auditor; paymaster; purser;
counter; meter (for gas, water,
etc.).—*caja contadora*, or *contadora*,
cash register.—**contaduría,** *f.* office
of a cashier, paymaster or treasurer; box office (in a theater, etc.);
accountant's or auditor's office.

contagiar, *vt.* to infect, contaminate;
to corrupt, pervert.—*vr.* (de) to become infected (with).—**contagio,** *m.*
contagion; corruption of morals.—
contagioso, *a.* contagious; perverting.

contaminación, *f.* contamination, pollution; defilement.—**contaminado,** *a.*
corrupted, contaminated.—**contaminar,** *vt.* to contaminate; to pervert;
to infect by contagion.

contante, *a.* (money) ready.—*m.*
cash.—*dinero c.*, or *dinero c. y
sonante*, cash.—**contar,** *vti.* [12] to
count; to relate, tell.—*vii.* to compute, figure.—*c. con*, to depend on,
rely on; to reckon with, take into
account; to possess, have at one's
disposal.

contemplación, *f.* contemplation,
meditation; complaisance.—**contemplar,** *vt.* to contemplate; to meditate; to be lenient or complaisant
with; to humor.—**contemplativo,** *a.*
contemplative; studious; lenient.—
n. contemplator.

contemporáneo, *n. & a.* contemporary.—**contemporización,** *f.* temporizing, compliance.—**contemporizar,**
vii. [a] to temporize; to comply;
to adapt oneself.

contender, *vii.* [18] to fight, combat;
to contend, debate.—**contendiente,**
mf. fighter, disputant; opponent.—*a.*
fighting.

contener, *vti.* [42] to contain; to include; to curb, stop.—*vri.* to control oneself, to refrain.—**contenido,** *a.* moderate, restrained.—*n.* content(s).

contentar, *vt.* to content, satisfy, make happy.—*vr.* to be contented, satisfied; to become reconciled, make up.—**contento,** *a.* content, contented; satisfied; happy.—*m.* contentment, satisfaction.

contera, *f.* metal tip (of umbrella, cane, etc.).

conterráneo, *n.* = COTERRANEO.

contestación, *f.* answer, reply.—**contestar,** *vt.* to answer, reply.

contexto, *m.* context.—**contextura,** *f.* texture.

contienda, *f.* struggle, fight; debate, dispute.

contigo, *pron.* with you [thee]; with yourself [thyself].

contigüidad, *f.* contiguity, closeness.—**contiguo,** *a.* contiguous, next, adjacent.

continencia, *f.* continence, self-control; abstinence; moderation; chastity.

continente, *m.* continent; container; countenance.—*a.* abstemious, continent; chaste; moderate.

contingencia, *f.* contingency, risk, possibility.—**contingente,** *m.* quota, contingent, share.—*a.* contingent, accidental.

continuación, *f.* continuation, continuance; stay.—*a c.,* immediately, right after; as follows.—**continuar,** *vt. & vi.* to continue; to go on; to pursue; to endure, last, remain; to prolong.—**continuidad,** *f.* continuity.—**continuo,** *a.* continuous, uninterrupted; connected; steady, constant.

contonearse, *vr.* to walk with a waddle; to strut.—**contoneo,** *m.* strut, waddle.

contorn(e)ar, *vt.* to trace the contour or outline of.—**contorno,** m. outline, contour; neighborhood; environs of a place.

contorsión, *f.* contortion, twist; grotesque gesture.

contra, *prep.* against, in opposition to, contrary to, opposite to, versus. —*m.* opposite sense; opposite opinion.—*f.* difficulty, obstacle.—*c. viento y marea,* against all odds.—*el pro y el c.,* the pros and cons.—*en c. (de),* against, in opposition to.—*hacer* or *llevar la c.,* to oppose; to contradict.

contralmirante, *m.* rear admiral.

contraataque, *m.* counterattack.

contrabajo, *m.* bass fiddle.

contrabandear, *vi.* to smuggle.—**contrabandista,** *mf.* smuggler, contrabandist.—**contrabando,** *m.* smuggling, running.

contracción, *f.* contraction, shrinking; corrugation; abbreviation.

contrachap(e)ado, *a.—madera c.,* plywood.

contradecir, *vti.* [14] to contradict.—**contradicción,** *f.* contradiction.—**contradicho,** *pp.* of CONTRADECIR.—**contradictorio,** *a.* contradictory.

contraer, *vti.* [43] & *vii.* to contract; to catch; to reduce.—*vri.* to contract, diminish; to shrink.

contrafuerte, *m.* buttress; spur (of a mountain).

contragolpe, *m.* back or reverse stroke.

contrahacer, *vti.* [22] to counterfeit, forge; to copy, imitate.—**contrahecho,** *pp.* of CONTRAHACER.—*a.* deformed; counterfeit, forged.

contralor, *m.* (Am.) controller, comptroller.

contraluz, *f.* view (of thing) seen against the light.

contramaestre, *m.* overseer, foreman; boatswain.

contramarcha, *f.* countermarch.

contraorden, *f.* countermand.

contraparte, *f.* counterpart.

contrapartida, *f.* emendatory or corrective entry.

contrapelo, *m.—a c.,* against the grain.

contrapesar, *vt.* to counterbalance; to counteract, offset.—**contrapeso,** *m.* counterweight, counterbalance; balancing weight.

contraproducente, *a.* self-defeating, producing the opposite of the desired effect.

contrapuesto, *a.* compared, contrasted (with); opposed (to).

contrapunto, *m.* counterpoint, harmony.

contrariar, *vt.* to contradict, oppose; to disappoint.—**contrariedad,** *f.* disappointment; impediment; setback. —**contrario,** *a.* contrary; adverse.—*m.* opponent.—*al c.,* or *por lo c.,* on the contrary.—*de lo c.,* otherwise.

contrarrestar, *vt.* to oppose, resist; to check, arrest; to counteract.

contrarrevolución, *f.* counterrevolution.

contrasentido, *m.* contradiction in terms; conclusion contrary to premises.

contraseña, *f.* countersign, password; watchword; check for hat, baggage, etc.—*c. de salida,* check to readmit one who went out from theater, etc.

contrastar, *vti.* to contrast; to test (scales, etc.); to assay (metals).—

contraste, *m.* contrast, opposition; inspector (of weights); assayer; assayer's office.

contrata, *f.* contract, agreement.—**contratación,** *f.* contractual transaction.—**contratar,** *vt.* to contract for; to engage, hire; to trade.

contratiempo, *m.* disappointment, setback.

contratista, *mf.* contractor.—**contrato,** *m.* contract.

contraveneno, *m.* antidote.

contravenir, *vti.* [45] to contravene.

contraventana, *f.* window shutter.

contraventor, *n.* transgressor.

contrayente, *mf.* contracting party (to a marriage).—*a.* engaged (to be married).

contribución, *f.* contribution; tax, scot.—**contribuir,** *vii.* [23-e] to contribute.—**contribuyente,** *a.* contributing; contributory.—*mf.* taxpayer.

contrición, *f.* contrition, compunction.

contrincante, *mf.* opponent, competitor, rival.

contrito, *a.* contrite, penitent.

control, *m.* control.—**controlar,** *vt.* to control.

controversia, *f.* controversy, debate.—**controvertible,** *a.* controvertible, disputable.

contubernio, *m.* cohabitation; infamous alliance.

contumacia, *f.* obstinacy; contumacy; persistence in error; (law) contempt of court.—**contumaz,** *a.* obstinate; contumacious.

contundente, *a.* producing contusion; forceful; conclusive, decisive; trenchant.

conturbar, *vt.* to perturb, disturb.—*vr.* to become uneasy, agitated, anxious.

contusión, *f.* contusion, bruise.—**contuso,** *a.* bruised.

conuco, *m.* (Am.) patch of cultivated ground (maize field, etc.).

convalecencia, *f.* convalescence.—**convalecer,** *vii.* [3] to be convalescing.—**convaleciente,** *mf.* & *a.* convalescent.

convalidar, *vt.* to confirm, ratify.

convecino, *m.* neighbor.—*a.* neighboring, near.

convencer, *vti.* [a] to convince.—*vri.* to become convinced.—**convencimiento,** *m.* belief, conviction.

convención, *f.* convention; assembly; pact, agreement.—**convencional,** *a.* conventional.—**convencionalismo,** *m.* conventionalism, conventionality.

convenido, *a.* agreed.—**conveniencia,** *f.* convenience; utility; self-interest; agreement.—**conveniente,** *a.*

useful; advantageous; suitable, befitting.—**convenio,** *m.* convention, agreement.—**convenir,** *vii.* [45] to befit; to agree; to convene, gather; to coincide; to be a good thing to.—*vri.* to agree, make a deal; to suit one's interests.

convento, *m.* convent.

conversación, *f.* conversation, talk.—**conversador,** *n.* talker.—*a.* conversational.—**conversar,** *vi.* to talk, converse; chat.

conversión, *f.* conversion; change.—**convertir,** *vti.* [39] to convert; to change.—*vri.* to become converted; to turn into, become.

convexidad, *f.* convexity.—**convexo,** *a.* convex.

convicción, *f.* conviction.—**convicto,** *a.* convicted, guilty.

convidada, *f.* invitation to drink, treat.—**convidado,** *n.* & *a.* invited (guest).—**convidar,** *vt.* to invite.

convincente, *a.* convincing.

convite, *m.* invitation; treat; banquet.

convocación, *f.* convocation, calling.—**convocar,** *vti.* [d] to convoke, convene, call together.—**convocatoria,** *f.* call, notice of a meeting.

convoy, *m.* convoy.—*c. de mesa,* cruet stand.—**convoyar,** *vt.,* to convoy, escort.

convulsión, *f.* convulsion.—**convulsivo,** *a.* convulsive.—**convulso,** *a.* convulsed; agitated.

conyugal, *a.* conjugal, wedded.—**cónyuge,** *mf.* spouse, consort.—*m. pl.* husband and wife.

coñac, *m.* brandy, cognac.

cooperación, *f.* cooperation.—**cooperador,** *n.* & *a.* cooperator, cooperating, cooperative.—**cooperar,** *vi.* to cooperate.—**cooperativa,** *f.* cooperative (society).—**cooperativo,** *a.* cooperating.

coordinación, *f.* coordination.—**coordinar,** *vt.* to coordinate.

copa, *f.* goblet, wineglass; drink (of liquor); treetop; crown of a hat; (in cards) a card of heart suit.

copar, *vt.* to cut off and capture; to cover (the whole bet); to sweep (all posts in an election); to corner.

copartícipe, *mf.* participant, copartner.

copete, *m.* tuft, bun (hair); forelock; crest; summit.—*de alto c.,* of high rank, aristocratic.—**copetudo,** *a.* tufted, crested; haughty.

copia, *f.* copy, imitation; abundance.—**copiar,** *vt.* to copy.

copiloto, *m.* copilot.

copiosidad, *f.* copiousness, abundance.—**copioso,** *a.* copious, abundant.

copista, *mf.* copyist, transcriber.

copla, *f.* short popular folk song; certain kind of stanza (poetry).

copo, *m.* small bundle of cotton, flax, etc.; snowflake.

cópula, *f.* joining, coupling two things together; connection; copulation.—**copular,** *vi.* to mate (of animals).

coqueluche, *f.* whooping cough.

coqueta, *f.* flirtatious girl.—**coquetear,** *vi.* to flirt.—**coqueteo,** *m.* flirtation.—**coquetería,** *f.* flirtation; affectation.—**coquetón,** *a.* kittenish.—*m.* lady-killer.

coraje, *m.* courage, bravery; anger.

coral, *m.* coral; a white-and-red poisonous snake.—*a.* choral.

coraza, *f.* armor plating; carapace; armor (of a vessel, cable, etc.).

corazón, *m.* heart; core, center; (fig.) courage; love; charity.—*anunciar,* or *decir el c. algo,* to have a presentiment.—*arrancársele a uno el c.,* to be heartbroken.—*de c.,* heartily.—**corazonada,** *f.* premonition, hunch.

corbata, *f.* necktie, cravat.

corbeta, *f.* corvette.—*capitán de c.,* lieutenant commander.

corcel, *m.* war-horse, charger, steed.

corcova, *f.* hump, hunch.—**corcovado,** *a.* & *n.* humpback(ed), hunchback(ed).

corchete, *m.* clasp, hook, hook and eye; snaplock; bracket.

corcho, *m.* cork; cork stopper.

cordaje, *m.* cordage; rigging.

cordal, *m.* wisdom tooth.

cordel, *m.* cord; thin rope; land measure.—*a c.,* in a straight line.—*dar c.,* to banter.

cordero, *m.* lamb; lambskin.

cordial, *a.* hearty, cordial.—*m.* cordial, tonic.—**cordialidad,** *f.* cordiality.

cordillera, *f.* mountain range.

cordobán, *m.* cordovan, goatskin.—**cordobés,** *n.* & *a.* Cordovan; of Córdoba.

cordón, *m.* cord, braid, string; cordon (of soldiers); chord.—**cordoncillo,** *m.* milling on edge of a coin; twisted or small cord; lacing; braid.

cordura, *f.* prudence, practical wisdom, sanity.

coreano, *a.* & *n.* Korean.

corear, *vt.* to chorus, accompany with a chorus; to answer in chorus.—*vi.* to chorus.—**coreografía,** *f.* choreography.—**coreográfico,** *a.* choreographic.—**coreógrafo,** *n.* choreographer.—**corista,** *n.* chorister; member of a chorus.—*f.* chorus girl.

coriza, *f.* head cold.

cornada, *f.* thrust with the horns;

goring.—**cornamenta,** *f.* horns, antlers.—**cornear,** *vt.* to butt; to gore.

corneta, *f.* cornet, bugle.—*m.* bugler.—**cornetín,** *m.* cornet; cornetist.

cornisa, *f.* cornice.

cornudo, *a.* horned.—*m.* (fig.) cuckold.

coro, *m.* choir; chorus.

corola, *f.* corolla.—**corolario,** *m.* corollary.

corona, *f.* crown; wreath; tonsure.—**coronación,** *f.* coronation; crowning.—**coronar,** *vt.* to crown; to top; to complete.

coronel, *m.* colonel.

coronilla, *f.* top of the head.—*estar hasta la c.,* to be fed up.

corpiño, *m.* bodice.

corporación, *f.* corporation; institution.

corporal, *a.* corporal, pertaining to the body.

corporativo, *a.* corporate, pertaining to a corporation.

corpóreo, *a.* corporeal, bodily.

corpúsculo, *m.* corpuscle.

corral, *m.* corral; yard; poultry yard.

correa, *f.* leather strap; leash; belt.—*tener c.,* to be able to endure a lot.—**correaje,** *m.* a set of straps.—**correazo,** *m.* a blow with a strap.

corrección, *f.* correction; correctness.—**correccional,** *a.* corrective.—*m.* reformatory.—**correcto,** *a.* polite, well-bred; proper; correct.—**corrector,** *m.* corrector, amender; proofreader.

corredizo, *a.* running; sliding.—**corredor,** *m.* runner; gallery; corridor; covert way; broker.—*a.* running.

corregir, *vt.* [29-c] to correct; to adjust (an instrument); to remedy; to rebuke, reprove; to punish.—*c. pruebas* (print.) to read proofs.—*vri.* to mend, reform.

correlación, *f.* correlation.—**correlativo,** *a.* correlative.

correntón, *m.* gadder; man about town.

correo, *m.* post, mail; correspondence; courier; letter carrier; post office.—*c. aéreo,* airmail.—*c. certificado,* registered mail.—*echar al c.,* to mail, post.

correr, *vi.* to run; to race; to flow; to extend, expand; to pass, elapse; to go on, continue; to be said, be common talk.—*c. a cargo de,* to be the concern of.—*c. con,* to charge oneself with a matter, take care of.—*c. la voz,* to be said or rumored.—*c. por cuenta de uno,* to be one's affair.—*vt.* to run or move swiftly; to race (a horse, car, etc.); to slide; to pursue, chase; to throw out.—*vr.* to file right or left; to slide, go through easily; to become embarrassed; to run away, to flee.— **correría,** *f.* incursion, foray, raid; excursion.—*pl.* youthful escapades.

correspondencia, *f.* correspondence, relation; interchange; mail, correspondence.—**corresponder,** *vi.* (a) to reciprocate (a favor, etc.); to match, correspond; to respond (to); to fit, suit; to pertain (to); to concern; to agree.—*vr.* to correspond, keep in contact by mail.—**correspondiente,** *a.* corresponding, respective.—*mf.* correspondent.—**corresponsal,** *mf.* correspondent; newspaper correspondent.

corretaje, *m.* brokerage.—**corretear,** *vi.* to walk the streets, ramble; to romp.—**correvedile, correvedidile,** *mf.* tablebearer; gossip.

corrida, *f.* course, run, running, race; career.—*c. de toros,* bullfight.

corrido, *a.* experienced, wise; embarrassed, ashamed; continuous, flowing, unbroken.—*m.* Mexican folk ballad.

corriente, *a.* current; running, fluent, flowing; present, current (month or year); plain, easy; generally received, admitted; ordinary, common; regular, standard.—*f.* current (river, electricity, etc.); tendency; course; trend.—*llevar la c.,* to humor.

corrillo, *m.* group of talkers; clique. —**corro,** *m.* group of gossipers or spectators; circular space.

corroboración, *f.* corroboration.—**corroborar,** *vt.* to corroborate.

corroer, *vt.* to corrode.—*vr.* to corrode, decay.

corromper, *vt.* to corrupt; to vitiate; to debauch.—*vr.* to rot, putrefy; to become corrupt(ed).

corrosivo, *a.* corrosive.

corrugado, *a.* corrugated.

corrupción, *f.* corruption; putrefaction; depravity, immorality.—**corruptela,** *f.* corrupt practice.—**corrupto,** *a.* corrupt, rotten.

corsé, *m.* corset.

cortada, *f.* (Am.) cut, slash, gash.— **cortador,** *m.* (tailoring, bootmaking, etc.) cutter.—**cortadura,** *f.* cut; cutting, incision.—**cortante,** *a.* cutting, sharp, trenchant.—**cortapisa,** *f.* obstacle, restriction.—**cortaplumas,** *m.* pocketknife; penknife.— **cortar,** *vt.* to cut, cut down, cut off, cut out, cut open; to disjoin, separate; to interrupt, stop.—*vr.* to be ashamed, confused.—**corte,** *m.* cutting edge; cutting; cut; material necessary for a garment; style (clothing); sectional view.—*f.* royal

court; (Am.) court of justice.— **cortedad,** *f.* smallness; pusillanimity; timidity.

cortejar, *vt.* to woo, court; to curry favor.—**cortejo,** *m.* courtship; cortege, retinue; procession.

cortés, *a.* polite, courteous; urbane.— **cortesano,** *a.* courtly.—*m.* courtier.— *f.* prostitute.—**cortesía,** *f.* courtesy.

corteza, *f.* bark of a tree; peel, rind, skin; crust of bread, pies, etc.; outward appearance.

cortina, *f.* curtain.—**cortinaje,** *m.* curtains, hangings.

cortisona, *f.* cortisone.

corto, *a.* short; brief; scanty; timid, bashful.—*c. de alcances,* stupid.— *a la corta o a la larga,* sooner or later.—**cortocircuito,** *m.* short circuit.

corva, *f.* back of the knee.—**corvadura,** *f.* curvature.

corvejón, *m.* hock joint of a quadruped.

corveta, *f.* curvet, leap, buck or bound of a horse.

corvo, *a.* bent; arched.

corzo, *n.* roe deer, fallow deer.

cosa, *f.* thing, matter, affair.—*como si tal c.,* as if nothing had happened.—*c. de,* about, approximately. —*no es c.,* it is not worth anything. —*otra c.,* something else.—*poca c.,* matter of slight importance; weak or timid person.

coscorrón, *m.* blow on the head.

cosecha, *f.* harvest, crop, yield; results.—**cosechar,** *vt. & vi.* to reap, gather in; to harvest.—**cosechero,** *m.* owner or reaper of a crop, harvester; grower.

coser, *vt.* to sew (up, on); to stitch.

cosmético, *m. & a.* cosmetic.

cósmico, *a.* cosmic.

cosmopolita, *a. & mf.* cosmopolitan.

coso, *m.* arena, ring.

cosquillas, *f.* tickling.—*buscarle a uno las c.,* to tease.—*hacer c.,* to tickle. —**consquillear,** *vt.* to tickle.—**cosquilleo,** *m.* tickling sensation.— **cosquilloso,** *a.* ticklish; touchy.

costa, *f.* coast, shore; cost, price.— *a c. de,* at the expense of.

costado, *m.* side, flank.

costal, *m.* sack or large bag.—**costalada,** *f.* (a) falling flat on the ground.

costar, *vii.* [12] to cost.—*c. trabajo,* to be difficult.

costarricence, *mf. & a.* Costa Rican.

coste, *m.* cost, price, expense.

costear, *vt.* to pay the cost.—*vi.* to pay, be profitable; to sail along the coast.

costeño, costero, *a.* coastal.

costilla, *f.* rib; chop; cutlet; (fig.) wife.—*medirle a uno las costillas,* to cudgel one.—**costillaje, costillar,** *m.* the ribs, or rib system; frame of a ship.

costo, m. cost, price; expense.—**costoso,** *a.* expensive.

costra, *f.* crust; deposit; scab.—**costroso,** *a.* crusty, scabby.

costumbre, *f.* custom; habit.

costura, *f.* sewing; seam; stitching; needlework; suture.—**costurera,** *f.* seamstress, dressmaker.—**costurero,** *m.* sewing box, table or room.—**costurón,** *m.* large, coarse seam; big scar.

cota, *f.* = CUOTA; coat of mail; coat of arms; number indicating elevation above sea level, etc.—*c. de malla,* coat of mail.

cotarro, *m.*—*alborotar el c.,* to cause disturbance; to produce riot.

cotejar, *vt.* to compare. collate; to confront.—**cotejo,** *m.* comparison, collation.

coterráneo, *a.* fellow citizen.

cotidiano, *a.* daily; quotidian.

cotización, *f.* quotation of prices; current price.—**cotizar,** *vti.* [a] to quote prices; to call out current prices in the stock exchange; to pay (one's share).

coto, *m.* enclosed pasture; preserve; landmark, boundary.—*poner c. a,* to put a stop to.

cotorra, *f.* parrot; (fig.) chatterbox.—**cotorrear,** *vi.* to chatter; to gossip.—**cotorreo,** *m.* chattering; gossiping.

covacha, *f.* small cave or hollow underground; grotto; (fig.) den.

coxis, *m.* coccyx.

coyunda, *f.* strap for yoking oxen; dominion; matrimonial union.

coyuntura, *f.* joint; occasion; nick of time.

coz, *f.* kick; drawback; unprovoked bruskness.

cráneo, *m.* cranium, skull.

cráter, *m.* crater.

creación, *f.* creation.—**creador,** *n.* & *a.* creator, creating, creative.—**crear,** *vt.* to create, establish, found.

crecer, *vii.* [3] to grow; to bud forth; to increase.—*vr.* to swell with pride, authority, etc.—**creces,** *f. pl.* augmentation, excess.—*con c.,* amply. —**crecida,** *f.* swelling of rivers.—**crecido,** *a.* grown, increased.—**creciente,** *a.* growing, increasing; waxing (moon); crescent (moon).—*f.* flood of rivers; crescent (of the moon).—**crecimiento,** *m.* growth; growing; increase.

credencial, *f.* letter or document of appointment to a post.—*pl.* credentials.

crédito, *m.* credit; reputation; credence, belief.—*dar c.,* to believe.

credo, *m.* creed, articles of faith, tenet.—**credulidad,** *f.* credulity.—**crédulo,** *a.* credulous.—**creencia,** *f.* belief; creed; religion.—**creer,** *vti.* [e] to believe; to credit; to think; to assume.—*¡ya lo creo!,* of course.

crema, *f.* cream of milk; custard; select society; cold cream; dieresis.

cremación, *f.* cremation, incineration.

cremallera, *f.* ratchet, rack; toothed bar; zipper fastener.

crematorio, *m.* crematory; incinerator.

crencha, *f.* parting of the hair into two parts; each of these parts.

crepuscular, *a.* crepuscular.—**crepúsculo,** *m.* crepuscule, twilight; dawn; dusk.

crespo, *a.* curly; crispy.—*m.* curl.

crespón, *m.* crepe.

cresta, *f.* comb (of a bird); cockscomb; crest of a helmet; wave crest; top; crest or summit of a mountain.

cretona, *f.* cretonne.

creyente, *mf.* & *a.* believer, believing.

creyón, *m.* crayon; charcoal pencil.

cría, *f.* act of nursing; breeding; bringing up; rearing; brood; litter of animals; suckling; nursing; infant.—**criada,** *f.* female servant, maid.—**criadero,** *m.* breeding place; tree nursery; hatchery.—**criado,** *a.* bred.—*m.* male servant.—**crianza,** *f.* nursing, suckling; secretion of milk; breeding; manners, education, upbringing.—**criar,** *vt.* to breed; to bring up; to nurse; to foster.—**criatura,** *f.* creature; baby; infant; child; tool; puppet.

criba, *f.* sieve, screen.— **cribar,** *vt.* to sift, sieve.

cricquet, *m.* = CRIQUET.

crimen, *m.* crime; murder.—**criminal,** *mf.* & *a.* criminal; murderer.—**criminalidad,** *f.* criminality.—**criminalista,** *m.* criminologist, penologist.

crin, *f.* mane, horsehair.

crío, *m.* (coll.) nursing baby.

criollo, *m.* Spanish-American native; Creole.—*a.* national, traditional (in Spanish America).

cripta, *f.* crypt.

criquet, *m.* (sport) cricket.

crisálida, *f.* pupa, chrysalis.

crisantemo, *m.* chrysanthemum.

crisis, *f.* crisis.

crisma, *m.* chrism.—*f.* (coll.) head.—*romperse la c.,* to break one's neck.

crisol, *m.* crucible, melting pot; hearth of a furnace.

crispar, *vt.* to contract (muscles); to clench (fists).—*vi.* to twitch.

cristal, *m.* crystal; glass; lens; (window) pane.—**cristalería**, *f.* glassware; glass store.—**cristalino**, *a.* crystalline, clear.—*m.* crystalline of the eye.—**cristalización**, *f.* crystalization.—**cristalizar**, *vii.* [a] & *vri.* to crystalize.

cristiandad, *f.* Christendom; Christianity.—**cristianismo**, *m.* Christianity; the body of Christians.—**cristiano**, *a.* & *n.* Christian (person).

criterio, *m.* criterion; judgment, discernment.

crítica, *f.* criticism; critique; censure. —**criticar**, *vti.* [d] to criticize; to judge.—**crítico**, *a.* critical; decisive. —*m.* critic, reviewer.—**criticón**, *m.* & *a.* faultfinder; faultfinding.

croar, *vi.* to croak.

crónica, *f.* chronicle.—**crónico**, *a.* chronic.—**cronista**, *mf.* chronicler, annalist, historian.

cronología, *f.* chronology.—**cronológico**, *a.* chronological, chronologic. —**cronométrico**, *a.* chronometric.— **cronómetro**, *m.* chronometer, timepiece.

croqueta, *f.* croquette, fritter.

croquis, *m.* sketch, rough draft.

cruce, *m.* crossing; crossroads; crossbreeding.—**crucero**, *m.* transept; crossroads; railroad crossing; crosspiece; cruiser; cruise, cruising.— **crucificar**, *vti.* [d] to crucify, torture; to sacrifice; to ruin.—**crucifijo**, *m.* crucifix.—**crucigrama**, *m.* crossword puzzle.

cruda, *f.* (Am.) hangover.—**crudeza**, *f.* crudity, crudeness; rawness.— **crudo**, *a.* raw; crude; uncooked; harsh.

cruel, *a.* cruel, remorseless.—**crueldad**, *f.* cruelty.

crujido, *m.* crack, creak, crackling; creaking; rustle; crunch.—**crujir**, *vi.* to crackle, creak; to rustle.

cruz, *f.* cross; (fig.) affliction; tails (of coin).—*echar a cara e c.*, to toss up.—**cruzada**, *f.* crusade; holy war; campaign.—**cruzamiento**, *m.* crossing.—**cruzar**, *vti.* [a] to cross; to go across, pass; to cruise; to interbreed.

cuadernillo, *m.* quire of paper.— **cuaderno**, *m.* writing book, memorandum book; note or exercises book; booklet.

cuadra, *f.* stable; city block, block of houses; hospital or prison ward.

cuadrado, *a.* square; perfect.—*m.* square; quadrate; (print.) quad, quadrat.—**cuadrante**, *m.* quadrant; sundial.—**cuadrar**, *vt.* & *vi.* to

square; to form into or reduce to a square; to please, suit; to fit in; to correspond.—*vr.* to stand at attention.—**cuadricular**, *vt.* to divide or design into squares.—**cuadriga**, *f.* chariot.—**cuadrilla**, *f.* gang; party; crew; band of armed men; team of bullfighters.—**cuadriplicado**, *a.* quadrupled.—**cuadro**, *m.* square; picture, painting; frame; scene; impressive spectacle; vivid description; (Am.) blackboard.—**cuadrúpedo**, *m.* & *a.* quadruped.—**cuádruple**, **cuádruplo**, *a.* quadruple, fourfold.

cuajada, *f.* curd.—**cuajar**, *vt.* to coagulate; to curd, curdle; to yell; to overdecorate.—*vi.* to succeed, materialize.—*vr.* to coagulate; to curdle; to fill, become full.—**cuajarón**, *m.* clot.—**cuajo**, *m.* rennet; curd; thickening (of a liquid).— *de c.*, radically; by the roots.

cual (*pl.* **cuales**), *rel. pron.* which, such as, as.—*cada c.*, each one.— *c. más c. menos*, some people more, others less.—*el c., la c., los cuales, las cuales,* which, who.—*lo c.* which. —*adv.* as, like.—*c. si,* as if.—*¿cuál? pron. interr.* which one? what?

cualidad, *f.* quality; trait.

cualquier(a), (*pl.* **cualesquier, cualesquiera**), *a.* any.—*pron.* any(one), anybody; someone, somebody; whichsoever, whoever.—*un cualquiera,* a nobody, a person of no account.

cuando (*interr.* ¿cuándo?), *adv.* when; at, or during the time of; in case that, if; though, although, even; sometimes.—*c. más,* at most. —*c. menos,* at the least.—*de c. en c.,* from time to time.

cuantía, *f.* amount, quantity; rank, importance, degree.—**cuantioso**, *a.* numerous, abundant.—**cuanto**, *a.* as much as, all the, whatever.—*pl.* as many as, all the, whatever.—*pron.* all that, everything that.—*pl.* all those, who or which.—**cuánto**, **cuánta**, *a.* & *pron. interr.* how much.—*pl.* how many.—*adv.* as, the more.—*c. antes* as soon as possible. —*c. más que,* all the more so.— *en c.,* as soon as.—*en c. a,* as for, as regards.—*por c.,* therefore, inasmuch.

cuarentena, *f.* forty days; quarantine.—**cuarentón**, *n.* & *a.* (man or woman) in the forties.

cuaresma, *f.* Lent.

cuarta, *f.* fourth; fourth part; span of the hand; short whip.—**cuartazo**, *m.* blow with a whip.—**cuartear**, *vt.* to quarter, divide into four parts; to whip.—*vr.* to split, crack, rive.

cuartel, *m.* quarter, fourth part; barracks; merey; district, ward.—*no dar c.,* to give no quarter.—**cuartelada,** *f.,* **cuartelazo,** *m.* military coup d'état.

cuarteta, *f.* quatrain.—**cuarteto,** *m.* (mus.) quartet.

cuartilla, *f.* sheet of paper; (print.) sheet of copy; fourth part of an *arroba* (about 6 lbs.).—**cuartillo,** *m.* pint. (See Table of Measures).

cuarto, *m. & a.* fourth, fourth part, quarter.—*m.* room, chamber.—*pl.* cash, money.—*no tener un c.,* not to be worth a cent.

cuarzo, *m.* quartz.

cuate, *m.* (Mex.) twin.—*eso no tiene c.,* that has no match.

cuatrero, *m.* horse thief, cattle thief.

cuba, *f.* cask; big-bellied person; drunkard.

cubano, *n. & a.* Cuban.

cubeta, *f.* small barrel or cask.

cubicación, *f.* measurement; volume, capacity; cubing of a number.

cúbico, *a.* cubic.

cubierta, *f.* cover, covering; lid; deck of ship; book wrapper.

cubierto, *pp.* of CUBRIR.—*m.* covert; place for one at the table.

cubil, *m.* lair, den.

cubilete, *m.* dicebox.

cúbito, *m.* ulna, larger bone of forearm.

cubo, *m.* cue; pail, bucket; hub of a wheel; shaft case; millpond; bastion of a castle.

cubrecama, *f.* coverlet, bedspread.—**cubremesa,** *f.* table cover.

cubrir, *vti.* [49] to cover; to coat; to hide; to roof; to meet (a bill or check).—*vri.* to cover oneself; to protect oneself; to hedge; to put on one's hat.

cucaña, *f.* greased pole to climb for a prize; the sport itself.

cucaracha, *f.* cockroach.

cuclillas.—*en c.,* in a crouching or squatting position.

cuclillo, cuco, a. *a.* cunning; prim.—*m.* cuckoo; (Am.) peach, peach tree.

cucurucho, *m.* wrapping in the form of a cone; paper or cardboard cone.

cuchara, *f.* spoon; ladle; scoop.—*meter la c.,* or *su c.,* to meddle, intrude.—**cucharada,** *f.* spoonful.—**cucharadita,** *f.* teaspoonful.—**cucharilla,** *f.* teaspoon, coffee spoon.—**cucharón,** *m.* ladle; large spoon; scoop.

cuchichear, *vi.* to whisper.—**cuchicheo,** *m.* whisper, whispering.

cuchilla, *f.* cleaver; blade of a knife;

any cutting blade; razor blade; penknife.—**cuchillada,** *f.* a cut with a knife; stab; slash; gash.—**cuchillería,** *f.* cutlery, cutler's shop.—**cuchillo,** *m.* knife; gusset.

cuchitril, *m.* narrow hole or corner; very small room; hut; den.

cuchufleta, *f.* joke, jest, fun.

cuelga, *f.* cluster of grapes; string (of garlic, onion, etc.); (Am.) (coll.) birthday present.

cuello, *m.* neck; collar.

cuenca, *f.* wooden bowl; socket of the eye; river basin; deep valley.—**cuenco,** *m.* earthen or wooden bowl.

cuenta, *f.* computation, calculation; account; bill, (coll.) tab; note; bead (of a rosary, etc.).—*a fin de cuentas,* in the end.—*caer en la c.,* (coll.) to catch on, get the point.—*correr de la c. de uno,* to be one's responsibility.—*darse c.,* to realize.—*en resumidas cuentas,* in short.—*no tenerle a uno c.,* to be of no profit to one.—*rendir c.,* to inform, report.—*tener* or *tomar en c.,* to take into account.—*tomar una cosa por su c.,* to take upon oneself.

cuento *m.* tale; story; short story; piece of gossip.—*dejarse de cuentos,* to come to the point.—*sin c.,* numberless.—*traer a c.,* to bring to bear upon the subject; to drag into the subject.—*venir a c.,* to be pertinent.

cuerda, *f.* cord, rope, string; chord; watch spring.—*bajo c.,* or *por debajo de c.,* underhandedly, deceitfully.—*dar c. a,* to wind up (a watch, etc.).

cuerdo, *a.* sane; prudent, wise.

cuerno, *m.* horn; antenna, feeler.—*mandar al c.,* to send to the devil.—*poner cuernos,* to be unfaithful (to a husband).

cuero, *m.* rawhide, skin; leather; wineskin.—*en cueros,* or *en cueros vivos,* or *en el puro c.,* naked.

cuerpo, *m.* body; bulk; corps.—*a. c. descubierto,* without cover or shelter.—*c. a c.,* hand to hand; in single combat.—*en c. y alma,* wholly, sincerely, with pleasure.—*estar de c. presente,* to lie in state.—*tomar c.,* to increase, to grow, to thicken.

cuervo, *m.* crow; raven; (Am.) buzzard.

cuesco, *m.* kernel; stone (of a fruit); the breaking of wind.

cuesta, *f.* hill, slope, grade.—*c. abajo,* downhill.—*c. arriba,* uphill.—*a cuestas,* on one's back.

cuestación, *f.* petition; solicitation or collection for a charitable purpose.

cuestión, *f.* question, dispute, contro-

versy; matter, problem, affair.—
cuestionario, *m.* questionnaire.

cueva, *f.* cave, grotto, cavern; cellar.

cuidado, *m.* care, attention; custody;
carefulness, caution; worry, anxiety.—*no hay c. (de que),* there is
no danger that.—*¡no pase c.!* or
¡pierda c.! don't worry!—*tener c.,*
to be careful; to be worried.—
interj. look out! beware!—**cuida-
doso,** *a.* careful.—**cuidar,** *vt.* to
care for, tend, mind, keep; to execute with care.—*c. de,* to take care
of.—*vr.* to take care of oneself.—
cuidarse de, to look out for, to
guard against; to avoid.

cuita, *f.* care, grief, affliction, trouble.
—**cuitado,** *a.* unfortunate, wretched.

cuje, *m.* withe; pole supported by
two vertical ones for hanging tobacco.—*pl.* hop poles.

culata, *f.* butt, stock (of a firearm);
(Am.) rear (of car, house).—**cula-
tazo,** *m.* blow with the butt; recoil of a firearm.

culebra, *f.* snake; coil.—**culebrear,** *vi.*
to twist, wriggle (as a snake).

culero, *m.* baby's diaper.

culinario, *a.* culinary.

culminación, *f.* culmination.—**culmi-
nar,** *vi.* to culminate.

culo, *m.* buttocks; bottom; anus;
bottom of anything.

culpa, *f.* fault; guilt; blame.—*echar
la c. a,* to blame.—*tener la c. de,*
to be to blame, or responsible for.
—**culpabilidad,** *f.* culpability, guilt.
culpable, *a.* guilty.—**culpar,** *vt.* to
blame, accuse; to condemn.

cultivar, *vt.* to cultivate; to farm,
till, grow.—**cultivo,** *m.* cultivation;
farming.—**culto,** *a.* cultivated; cul-
tured.—*m.* cult, worship.—**cultura,**
f. culture; cultivation.

cumbre, *f.* top, tiptop, summit, crest.

cumpleaños, *m.* birthday.

cumplido, *a.* fulfilled, expired; polite;
faultless; large, ample.—*m.* compliment; courtesy.—**cumplimentar,** *vt.*
to compliment; to show courtesy;
to congratulate.—**cumplimiento,** *m.*
fulfillment, completion, performance; expiration; courtesy, compliment.—**cumplir,** *vt.* to fulfill, carry
out; to reach (age).—*vi.* to fall
due, expire; to do one's duty.—*c.
años,* to have a birthday.—*vr.* to be
realized, come to an end.

cúmulo, *m.* heap, pile; large quantity
or number; cumulus (clouds).

cuna, *f.* cradle; place of birth; lineage, origin.

cundir, *vi.* to spread, propagate; to
yield abundantly; to grow, expand.

cuneta, *f.* road drain; side ditch;
gutter.

cuña, *f.* wedge; splinter.

cuñada, *f.* sister-in-law.—**cuñado,** *m.*
brother-in-law.

cuño, *m.* die (for coining money);
impression made by die; (fig.)
stamp.

cuota, *f.* quota, share; dues, fee.

cuotidiano, *a.* = COTIDIANO.

cupo, *m.* quota; tax rate; contents,
capacity.

cupón, *m.* coupon.

cúpula, *f.* dome, cupola.

cura, *m.* curate, priest.—*f.,* or **cura-
ción,** *f.* healing; cure.—**curador,** *m.*
caretaker.—**curandero,** *n.* quack,
charlatan.—**curar,** *vt. & vi.* to treat,
heal, cure; to season, dry (meats,
woods, etc.).—*vr.* to recover from
sickness; to heal.—**curative,** *a.*
curative, healing.

curiosear, *vi.* to pry, snoop, spy,
peek, peer.—**curiosidad,** *f.* curiosity;
curious thing; rare object or person.—**curioso,** *a.* curious, prying;
careful, diligent, skillful; rare;
neat, clean.

cursar, *vt.* to study; to attend a
course of study; to transmit, expedite.—**curso,** *m.* course, direction,
career; course of study; scholastic
year.

cursi, *a.* ridiculously pretentious in
appearance, behavior or taste.

curtido, *m.* tanning; tanned leather.
—**curtidor,** *m.* tanner.—**curtir,** *vt.*
to tan; to bronze the skin; to
harden; to inure.—*vr.* to become
tanned, sunburned, weather-beaten;
to become hardened or experienced.

curva, *f.* curve; curvature; bend.—
curvatura, *f.* curvature; curving.—
curvo, *a.* curved; bent; arched.

cúspide, *f.* cusp, apex, top, peak,
summit.

custodia, *f.* custody, safe-keeping;
guardian; (eccl.) monstrance.—**cus-
todiar,** *vt.* to guard; to convoy;
to take care of.—**custodio,** *m.* guard,
custodian; watchman.

cutícula, *f.* cuticle.

cutis, *m.* skin, complexion.*

cuyo, cuya (pl. **cuyos, cuyas**), *pron.
poss.* of which, of whom, whose,
whereof.

CH

chabacanería, *f.* coarseness; bad
taste; vulgar expression or action.
—**chabacano,** *a.* coarse, crude, vulgar.—*m.* (Am.) apricot.

chabela, *f.* hut; dugout.

chacal, *m.* jackal.

chacota, *f.* mockery; ridicule.—*hacer ch. de,* to mock at.—**chacotear,** *vi.* to make merry; to joke boisterously.

chacra, *f.* (Am.) small piece of farm land.

cháchara, *f.* chitchat, idle talk.—**chacharear,** *vi.* to chatter.

chafar, *vt.* to flatten, crush; to cut short.

chaflán, *m.* bevel (in buildings).

chal, *m.* shawl.

chalado, *a.* lightwitted, crazy.

chalán, *m.* cattle trader; horsedealer; huckster.

chaleco, *m.* vest.

chalina, *f.* cravat; scarf.

chalupa, *f.* sloop; long boat; small canoe.

chamaco, *m.* (Am.) youngster.

chamarra, *f.* windbreaker; wool jacket; leather jacket.—**chamarreta,** *f.* a short, loose jacket.

chambón, *a.* clumsy, bungling; lucky.—*n.* bungler.

champaña, *m.* champagne.

champú, *m.* shampoo.

chamuscar, *vti.* [d] to singe or scorch.—**chamusquina,** *f.* scorching.

chancear, *vi. & vr.* to jest, joke, fool.—**chancero,** *a.* merry, jolly.

chancla, *f.* old shoe with worn-down heel.—**chancleta,** *f.* slipper.—**chancleteo,** *m.* clatter of slippers.—**chanclo,** *m.* overshoe.

chancho, *n.* (Am.) pig; dirty person.—*a.* dirty, unclean.

chanchullero, *n.* trickster; smuggler.—**chanchullo,** *m.* unlawful conduct; vile trick; (coll.) racket.

changador, *m.* (Am.) carrier, porter; handy man.

chantaje, *m.* blackmail.—**chantajista,** *mf.* blackmailer.

chanza, *f.* joke, jest, fun.

chapa, *f.* veneer; plate, sheet (of metal); rosy spot on the cheek.—**chapado,** *a.* veneered; having red cheeks.—*ch. a la antigua,* old fashioned.

chapapote, *m.* mineral tar, asphalt.

chaparrear, *vi.* to shower; to pour.

chaparreras, *f. pl.* chaps.

chaparro, *a. & n.* short, stocky (person).

chaparrón, *m.* violent shower, downpour.

chapotear, *vi.* to paddle in the water, dabble.—**chapoteo,** *m.* splash, splatter.

chapucear, *vt.* to botch, bungle.—**chapucería,** *f.* bungle; clumsy fib.—**chapucero,** *a.* rough, unpolished, slapdash; clumsy; rude.

chapurrar, chapurrear, *vt.* to jabber

(a language); to speak brokenly; to mix drinks.

chapuzar, *vti.* [a] to duck.—*vii. & vri.* to dive, duck.

chaqueta, *f.* jacket; sack coat; (mech.) casing, jacket.—**chaquetear,** *vi.* to run away in fright.

charanga, *f.* military brass band; fanfare.

charca, *f.* pool, basin, pond.—**charco,** *m.* pool, puddle.

charla, *f.* prattle, chat; informal address.—**charlador,** *n.* prater, talker.—*a.* prating, talking.—**charlar,** *vi.* to chat, prattle, prate.—**charlatán,** *n.* prater, babbler, windbag; charlatan, humbug.—**charlatanería,** *f.* garrulity, verbosity; charlatanism, humbug.—**charlatanismo,** *m.* quackery; verbosity.

charnela, *f.* hinge.

charol, *m.* patent leather.—**charola,** *f.* (Am.) tray.—**charolar,** *vt.* to varnish.

charro, *n.* churl; coarse, ill-bred person; (Mex.) cowboy.—*a.* showy, flashy.

chascarrillo, *m.* joke, spicy anecdote.

chasco, *m.* failure, disappointment; trick, prank.

chasquear, *vt.* to crack or snap (a whip).—*vi.* to crack, snap.—*vt.* to fool; to play a trick on; to disappoint, fail; to cheat.—**chasquido,** *m.* crack of a whip or lash; crack.

chata, *f.* bedpan; barge; (RR.) flatcar.—**chato,** *a.* flat; flat-nosed.

chayote, *m.* vegetable pear; silly fool, dunce.

checo, checo(e)slovaco, *n. & a.* Czechoslovak, Czechoslovakian.

chelín, *m.* shilling.

cheque, *m.* check.—**chequear,** *vt.* (Am.) to check, verify; to check (mark).

chico, *a.* little, small.—*n.* (*f.* chica) child; boy; youngster; fellow; chap.

chicotazo, *m.* blow with a whip; lash.—**chicote,** *m.* whip; cigar; cigar butt.

chicha, *f.* (Am.) a popular fermented beverage (made from maize, pineapple, etc.).

chícharo, *m.* pea.

chicharra, *f.* locust; horse fly; (fig.) talkative woman.

chicharrón, *m.* crackling, fried scrap; overroasted meat.

chichón, *m.* bump; bruise.

chiflado, *a.* flighty, crazy.—**chifladura,** *f.* eccentricity; mania, craziness.—**chiflar,** *vi.* to hiss, whistle.—*vr.* to become mentally unbalanced; to lose one's head.—*vt.* (a) to show noisy disapproval to someone (artist, etc.).—**chiflido**, *m.* shrill whistling sound.

chile, *f.* red pepper.

chileno, *n.* & *a.* Chilean.

chillar, *vi.* to screech, scream; to crackle, creak.—**chillido**, *m.* screech, scream; bawling of a woman or child.—**chillón**, *n.* screamer, bawler; whiner.—*a.* whining; screechy; showy; loud (of colors).

chimenea, *f.* chimney; fireplace.

chimpancé, *m.* chimpanzee.

china, *f.* pebble; Chinese woman; porcelain, chinaware; (Mex.) girl, sweetheart; (Am.) orange.

chinche, *f.* bedbug; thumbtack; tedious, pestering person.

chinchín, *m.* (Am.) drizzle.

chinchorro, *m.* small dragnet; small fishing boat.

chinela, *f.* slipper.

chino, *n.* & *a.* Chinese.—*m.* Chinese language.

chiquero, *m.* pigpen; hut for goats; bullpen.

chiquillada, *f.* childish speech or action.—**chiquillería**, *f.* swarm of children.—**chiquillo**, *n.* child.—**chiquitín**, *n.* baby boy; baby girl; very little child.—**chiquito**, *a.* small, little; very small.—*n.* little boy (girl), little one.

chiribitil, *m.* garret; small room.

chirigota, *f.* jest, joke, fun.

chiripa, *f.* stroke of good luck; chance or unexpected event.—*de ch.*, by chance.

chirivía, *f.* parsnip.

chirle, *a.* insipid, tasteless.—**chirlo**, *m.* wound or scar on the head.

chirona, *f.* (coll.) prison, jail.

chirriar, *vi.* to squeak, creak; to sizzle.—**chirrido**, *m.* squeak; screech.

chisguete, *m.* squirt.

chisme, *m.* gossip, piece of gossip; gadget.—**chismear**, **chismorrear**, *vi.* & *vt.* to gossip, to blab; to tattle.—**chismorreo**, *m.* gossiping, blabber.—**chismoso**, *n.* talebearer, telltale, gossip.—*a.* gossiping.

chispa, *f.* spark; very small diamond; little bit; cleverness, wit; state of drunkenness.—*coger una ch.*, to get drunk.—*echar chispas*, to show anger, to be furious.—**chispeante**, *a.* sparkling, sparking.—**chispear**, *vi.* to spark; to sparkle.—**chisporrotear**, *vi.* to sputter sparks.—**chisporroteo**, *m.* sputtering of sparks.

chistar, *vi.* to mumble, mutter; to open one's lips.

chiste, *m.* joke, jest; witty saying.—**chistoso**, *a.* witty.

chistera, *f.* top hat; fish basket.

¡**chitón**!, *interj.* hush! not a word!

chiva, *f.* she-goat; (Am.) goatee.—**chivato**, *n.* informer, talebearer.—**chivo**, *m.* he-goat.

chocante, *a.* disagreeable; strange, surprising.—**chocar**, *vii.* [d] to strike; to collide; to meet, fight; to happen upon; to irritate; to surprise.

chocarrería, *f.* raillery; coarse jest.—**chocarrero**, *a.* vulgar, scurrilous.

chocolate, *m.* chocolate.

chocha, *f.* (orn.) grouse.

chochear, *vi.* to drivel, act senile; to dote.—**chochera**, **chochez**, *f.* senility; dotage.—**chocho**, *a.* doting, senile.

chofer, **chófer**, *mf.* chauffeur.

cholo, *n.* (Am.) mestizo, half-breed.—*a.* coarse; uncouth; dark-skinned.

chopo, *m.* black poplar.

choque, *m.* impact; collision; clash; dispute, clash.

chorizo, *m.* red pork sausage.

chorlito, *m.* curlew.—*cabeza de c.*, harebrained.

chorrear, *vi.* to spout; to drip; to be dripping wet.—**chorro**, *m.* spurt, jet, gush; stream, flow.—*a chorros*, abundantly.

chotacabras, *f.* (ornith.) nighthawk.

chotear, *vt.* to banter, gibe; to make fun of.—**choteo**, *m.* joking; jeering.

choza, *f.* hut, hovel.

chubasco, *m.* squall, shower.

chuchería, *f.* trifle, trinket.

chucho, *m.* dog; whip; railway switch; electric switch.

chueco, *a.* crooked, bent; (Am.) left-handed.

chuleta, *f.* chop; cutlet; slap.

chulo, *a.* (Am.) pretty, nice, attractive.—*n.* lower-class native of Madrid.—*m.* pimp; bully.

chunga, *f.* jest, joke.

chupar, *vt.* to suck; to absorb; to sip; to sponge on.—**chupete**, *m.* pacifier (for children); teething ring.—**chupón**, *a.* sucking.—*n.* sponger.

churrasco, *m.* piece of broiled meat.—**churrasquear**, *vi.* to barbecue, roast over coals; to prepare (meat) for barbecuing; to eat barbecued meat.

churre, *mf.* filth.—**churriento**, *a.* dirty, greasy.

chuscada, *f.* pleasantry, joke.—**chusco**, *a.* merry, funny.

chusma, *f.* rabble, mob.

chuzo, *m.* (mil.) pike.

D

dable, *a.* possible, practicable; grantable.

dactilógrafo, *n.* typist.

dádiva, *f.* gift, gratification.—**dadivoso,** *a.* bountiful, liberal.

dado, *m.* die; block.—*pl.* dice.

dador, *n.* giver, donor; bearer (of letter).

daga, *f.* dagger.

daltonismo, *m.* color blindness.

dama, *f.* lady; gentlewoman; mistress; (theat.) leading lady.—*juego de damas,* checkers.—**damisela,** *f.* young woman, damsel.

damnificar, *vti.* [d] to hurt, damage, injure.

dandi, *m.* dandy, fop, coxcomb.

danés, *a.* Danish.—*n.* Dane.

danza, *f.* dance.—**danzante,** *mf.* dancer; (coll.) busybody.—**danzar,** *vii.* [a] to dance; to whirl.—**danzarín,** *n.* dancer.

dañado, *a.* spoiled, tinted; dammed.

dañar, *vt.* to hurt, damage; to harm; to spoil; to weaken.—*vr.* to spoil; to be damaged; to hurt oneself.—**dañino,** *a.* destructive, harmful; vicious.—**daño,** *m.* damage, hurt, loss, spoilage; nuisance.—**dañoso,** *a.* injurious.

dar, *vti.* [13] to give; to hand; to grant; to emit; to hit, strike; to yield.—*d. a conocer,* to make known. —*d. a entender,* to insinuate, to suggest.—*d. a luz,* to give birth to. —*d. comienzo,* to begin.—*d. con,* to find, come upon.—*d. cuerda a,* to wind up (clock, watch, etc.).—*d. de baja,* to dismiss.—*d. de comer,* to feed animals.—*d. de sí,* to give, stretch.—*d. fin a,* to complete, finish.—*d. (frente) a,* to face, look out on.—*d. golpes a,* to beat, thrash. —*d. gritos,* to shout.—*d. la razón a,* to say (a person) is right, agree with.—*d. largas a,* to postpone.—*d. las espaldas,* to turn one's back.—*d. darle a uno por,* to take to.—*d. lugar a,* to give rise to.—*d. parte (de),* to report (about), communicate.—*d. pasos,* to take steps.—*d. prestado,* to lend.—*d. que decir,* to give occasion for censure or criticism.—*d. que hacer,* to give trouble. —*d. que pensar,* to give food for thought.—*d. satisfacciones,* to apologize.—*no d. pie con bola,* not to do a thing right, to make a mess of it. —*vri.* to yield, surrender; to devote oneself.—*darse cuenta de,* to realize. —*darse por,* to consider oneself as.—*darse por vencido,* to give up. —*darse prisa,* to hurry.—*darse tono,* to put on airs.

dardo, *m.* dart, arrow.

dársena, *f.* dock; yacht basin, marina.

data, *f.* date; item in an account.—

datar, *vt.* to date; (com.) to credit on account.—*vi.* to take origin, date from.

dátil, *m.* date.—**datilera,** *f.* date palm.

dato, *m.* datum.—*pl.* data.

de, *prep.* of; from; for; by; than; in.

deán, *m.* (ecl.) dean.

debajo, *adv.* beneath, underneath.— *d. de,* under, beneath.—*por d.,* from below; underneath.—*por d. de,* under; below.

debate, *m.* debate; altercation.— **debatir,** *vt.* to argue, discuss, debate.—*vr.* to struggle.

debe, *m.* debit.—**deber,** *vt.* to owe; to have to, be obliged to, must, ought, should.—*d. de,* must have, must be. —*m.* duty, obligation.—**debido,** *a.* fitting, right, just.—*d. a,* owing to, on account of; due to.

débil, *a.* weak, feeble, sickly.—**debilidad,** *f.* weakness, feebleness.— **debilitación,** *f.,* **debilitamiento,** *m.* weakening.—**debilitar,** *vt.* to weaken. —*vr.* to grow weaker.

débito, *m.* debt; debit.

debut, *m.* debut.—**debutar,** *vi.* to make one's debut.

década, *f.* decade; series of ten.

decadencia, *f.* decadence, decay, decline.—**decadente,** *a.* decaying, decadent, declining.—**decaer,** *vii.* [8-e] to decay, fail; to fall off.—**decaimiento,** *m.* decay; weakness.

decano, *n.* dean (of a University); senior member of a group or organization.

decapitación, *f.* beheading.—**decapitar,** *vt.* to behead, decapitate.

decena, *f.* series of ten.—**decenio,** *m.* decade; decennial.

decencia, *f.* decency; modesty; honesty.—**decente,** *a.* decent; honest; modest.

decepción, *f.* disappointment; disillusionment.—**decepcionar,** *vt.* to disappoint.

decidir, *vt.* to decide, determine, resolve.—*vr.* to decide, make up one's mind; to be determined.

decimal, *a.* & *m.* decimal.

decir, *vti.* [14] & *vii.* to say, tell; to speak; to name.—*como quien dice,* as if meaning.—*d. bien,* to be right.—*d. mal,* to be wrong.—*d. para sí or para su capote,* to say oneself.—*d. por d.,* to talk for the sake of talking.—*es d.,* that is to say, that is.—*querer d.,* to mean, signify.—*por decirlo así,* so to speak. —*m.* saying, proverb.—*al d. de,* according to.

decisión, *f.* decision, determination, resolution, issue.—**decisivo,** *a.* decisive, final.

declamación, *f.* declamation, speech; reading, recitation.—**declamador,** *n.* orator; reciter.—**declamar,** *vi.* to declaim; to recite.

declaración, *f.* declaration; statement; manifestation; (law) deposition.—**declarado,** *a.* declared.—**declarante,** *a.* declaring, expounding.—*mf.* declarer; witness.—**declarar,** *vt.* to declare, make known; (law) to testify.—*vr.* to declare one's opinion; (coll.) to make a declaration of love.—**declarativo,** *a.* declarative.

declinación, *f.* declination, fall, decline; (gram.) declension, inflection.—**declinar,** *vi.* to decline; to decay; to diminish.—*vt.* (gram.) to decline.

declive, *m.* declivity; slope, fall; (RR.) grade.—**en d.,** slanting, sloping.

decomisar, *vt.* to confiscate.—**decomiso,** *m.* confiscation.

decoración, *f.* decoration; ornament; (theat.) setting.—**decorado,** *m.* decoration, ornamentation.—**decorador,** *n.* & *a.* decorator; decorating.—**decorar,** *vt.* to decorate; to adorn, embellish.—**decorativo,** *a.* decorative.

decoro, *m.* decency, decorum; honor; propriety.—**decoroso,** *a.* decorous, decent.

decrecer, *vii.* [3] to decrease, diminish.—**decreciente,** *a.* diminishing, decreasing.

decrépito, *a.* decrepit.—**decrepitud,** *f.* decrepitude.

decretar, *vt.* to decree, resolve; to decide.—**decreto,** *m.* decree; decision.

dechado, *m.* model; sample, pattern.

dedal, *m.* thimble.

dedicación, *f.* dedication; consecration.—**dedicar,** *vti.* [d] to dedicate, devote; to autograph (a literary work).—*vri.* (a) to devote oneself (to); to make a specialty (of).—**dedicatoria,** *f.* dedication; dedicatory inscription.

dedillo, *m.*—*saber al d.,* to know perfectly.—**dedo,** *m.* finger; toe; finger's breadth; small bit.—*d. auricular* or *meñique,* little finger.—*d. gordo* or *pulgar,* thumb.

deducción, *f.* deduction, inference, conclusion.—**deducir,** *vti.* [11] to deduce, infer; to draw; to offer as a plea; to deduct.

defecto, *m.* defect, imperfection.—**defectuoso,** *a.* defective, imperfect, unsound.

defender, *vti.* [18] to defend.—

defensa, *f.* defense; protection; shelter; bumper; (football) back.—**defensiva,** *f.* defensive.—**defensivo,** *a.* defensive.—*m.* defense.—**defensor,** *n.* defender; supporter; (law) counsel for the defense, defender.

deferencia, *f.* deference.—**deferir,** *vii.* [2] to yield, submit.—*vti.* to communicate; to delegate.

deficiencia, *f.* deficiency.—**deficiente,** *a.* deficient, faulty.

definición, *f.* definition.—**definible,** *a.* definable.—**definido,** *a.* definite.—**definir,** *vt.* to define; to establish, determine.—**definitivo,** *a.* definitive.—*en definitiva,* in conclusion; in short.

deflación, *f.* deflation.

deformación, *f.* deformation, distortion; deformity.—**deformar,** *vt.* to deform, disfigure.—*vr.* to become deformed, change shape.—**deforme,** *a.* deformed, disfigured; hideous.—**deformidad,** *f.* deformity; ugliness.

defraudación, *f.* defrauding; fraud, deceit.—**defraudador,** *n.* defrauder; defaulter.—**defraudar,** *vt.* to defraud; to rob of.

defunción, *f.* death, demise.

degeneración, *f.* degeneration, degeneracy.—**degenerado,** *n.* & *a.* degenerate.—**degenerar,** *vi.* to degenerate.

deglución, *f.* swallowing.—**deglutir,** *vt.* to swallow.

degollación, *f.* beheading.—**degollar,** *vti.* [12] to behead, decapitate.—**degollina,** *f.* slaughter; butchery.

degradación, *f.* degradation, humiliation, debasement; depravity, degeneracy.—**degradante,** *a.* degrading.—**degradar,** *vt.* to degrade, debase; humiliate, revile.—*vr.* to degrade or lower oneself.

degüello, *m.* beheading, throat-cutting.

dehesa, *f.* pasture ground.

deidad, *f.* deity; goddess.—**deificar,** *vti.* [d] to deify.

dejación, *f.* abandonment, relinquishment.—*d. de bienes,* (law) assignment.—**dejadez,** *f.* slovenliness, neglect.—**dejado,** *pp.* of DEJAR.—*a.* slovenly; indolent, negligent.—**dejar,** *vt.* to leave; to let; to let go, relinquish; to permit, allow; to abandon, quit; to forsake; to yield; to omit.—*d. atrás,* to outdistance.—*d. caer,* to drop.—*d. de,* to stop; to fail to.—*vr.* to be slovenly; to abandon oneself.—**dejo,** *m.* aftertaste; trace; slight accent.

del, *contraction of* DE *and* EL; of the.

delación, *f.* accusation, information.

delantal, *m.* apron.

delante, *adv.* before, ahead, in front.
—**d. de** *prep.* before, in front of,
in the presence of.—**delantera,** *f.*
front, fore end; front seats in
theaters, etc.; lead, advantage.—
delantero, *a.* foremost, first; front.
—*m.* front part; (sport) forward.

delatar, *vt.* to accuse, denounce.—
delator, *n.* informer, accuser, denouncer.

delegación, *f.* delegation; proxy; office of a delegate.—**delegado,** *n.*
delegate, proxy.—**delegar,** *vti.* [b]
to delegate.

deleitable, *a.* delectable, delightful.—
deleitación, *f.* delectation, pleasure,
delight.—**deleitar,** *vt.* to delight,
please.—*vr.* to delight or please.—
deleite, *m.* pleasure, delight; lust.—
deleitoso, *a.* delightful, pleasing.

deletrear, *vt.* to spell.—**deletreo,** *m.*
spelling.

deleznable, *a.* ephemeral; worthless;
negligible; contemptible.

delfín, *m.* porpoise; dolphin.

delgadez, *f.* thinness, slenderness;
leanness.—**delgado,** *a.* thin; lean;
slender, slim.—**delgaducho,** *a.* thin-
nish, lanky.

deliberación, *f.* deliberation.—**deli-
berar,** *vi.* to deliberate, ponder;
to consult or take counsel together.

delicadeza, *f.* delicacy, refinement;
softness; tenderness.—**delicado,** *a.*
delicate; gentle; tender; sickly,
frail; dainty; exquisite.

delicia, *f.* delight, pleasure.—**delicioso,**
a. delicious; delightful.

delincuencia, *f.* delinquency.—**delin-
cuente,** *mf.* delinquent, offender.—*a.*
delinquent, guilty.

delineación, *f.* delineation, draft,
sketch.—**delineante,** *mf.* draftsman,
designer.—**delinear,** *vt.* to delineate,
sketch.

delirante, *a.* delirious.—**delirar,** *vi.* to
be delirious; to talk nonsense; to
rave.—**delirio,** *m.* delirium; frenzied
rapture; nonsense.

delito, *m.* crime; transgression of the
law.

demacrado, *a.* emaciated.—**dema-
crarse,** *vr.* to waste away.

demagogia, *f.* demagogy.

demanda, *f.* (law) claim, complaint;
petition; question, inquiry; (com.)
demand.—*la oferta y la d.,* supply
and demand.—**demandado,** *n.* defendant.—**demandante,** *mf.* plaintiff,
complainant.—**demandar,** *vt.* to demand, ask, solicit; to desire; (law)
to sue.

demás, *a.* other.—*estar d.,* to be useless; to be unwelcome, not wanted.
—*lo d.,* the rest.—*los d., las d.,*

the rest; the others.—*por lo d.,*
aside from this; furthermore.—*todo
lo d.,* everything else.—*y d.,* and
other things, or persons; and so
forth.—*adv.* besides, moreover.—
demasía, *f.* excess, surplus; insolence, outrage.—*en d.,* excessively.—
demasiado, *a.* excessive; too much.
—*pl.* too many.—*adv.* too, excessively; too much.

demencia, *f.* madness, insanity.—
demente, *a.* insane, mad.—*mf.* lunatic.

demérito, *m.* demerit.

democracia, *f.* democracy.—**demó-
crata,** *mf.* democrat.—**democrático,**
a. democratic.

demoledor, *n.* & *a.* demolisher; de-
molishing.—**demoler,** *vti.* [26] to
demolish, destroy, raze.—**demoli-
ción,** *f.* demolition.

demonio, *m.* demon; devil.

demora, *f.* delay.—**demorar,** *vt.* to
delay.—*vi.* to delay, tarry.—*vr.* to
linger, tarry; to be delayed.

demostración, *f.* demonstration;
proof.—**demostrar,** *vti.* [12] to
demonstrate, show; to prove.

demudado, *a.* wan, pale (from illness,
fright, etc.).—**demudarse,** *vr.* to
lose one's calm; to turn pale.

denegación, *f.* denial, refusal.—**dene-
gar,** *vti.* [1-b] to deny, refuse.

dengoso, *a.* fastidious; coy.—**dengue,**
m. fastidiousness; coyness; (med.)
dengue.—*hacer dengues,* to act coy.

denodado, *a.* daring, intrepid.

denominación, *f.* denomination.—
denominador, *m.* denominator.—
denominar, *vt.* & *vr.* to call, give
a name to.

denostar, *vti.* [12] to insult; to revile.

denotar, *vt.* to denote, express.

densidad, *f.* density.—**denso,** *a.* dense,
thick; close, compact.

dentado, *a.* toothed, serrated.—**denta-
dura,** *f.* set of teeth.—*d. postiza,*
false teeth, denture.—**dental,** *a.*
dental.—**dentellada,** *f.* bite; tooth
marks.—**dentera,** *f.* teeth on edge;
(coll.) envy.—**dentición,** *f.* teething.
—**dentífrico,** *m.* toothpaste or tooth-
powder.—**dentista,** *mf.* dentist.

dentro, *adv.* inside, within.—*de d.,*
from inside.—*d. de,* within; inside.
—*d. del año,* in the course of the
year.—*d. de poco,* shortly, soon.—
hacia d., inwards.—*por d.,* inside;
inwardly.

denuedo, *m.* boldness, bravery, courage.

denuesto, *m.* affront, insult.

denuncia, *f.* accusation, arraignment;
denunciation; (min.) claim.—**denun-**

ciante, *mf.* denouncer; accuser.—*a.*
denouncing; accusing.—**denunciar,**
vt. to denounce; to advise, give
notice; to squeal; (min.) to claim.

deparar, *vt.* to offer, afford, furnish,
present.

departamento, *m.* department; compartment, section; apartment.

departir, *vi.* to chat, converse.

dependencia, *f.* dependence, dependency; subordination; branch office;
outbuildings.—**depender,** *vi.* (de) to
depend, rely (on).—**dependiente,** *a.*
dependent, subordinate.—*mf.* clerk,
salesman (-woman); retainer.

deplorable, *a.* deplorable.—**deplorar,**
vt. to deplore, regret.

deponer, *vti.* [32] to depose; to declare; to attest; to lay down.

deportación, *f.* deportation.—**deportar,** *vt.* to deport.

deporte, *m.* sport.—**deportista,** *mf.*
sportsman (-woman).—**deportivo,** *a.*
athletic, sportive.

deposición, *f.* assertion, affirmation;
testimony; removal from office;
bowel movement.

depositar, *vt.* to deposit; to entrust;
to lay aside.—(chem.) to settle.
—**depositario,** *n.* depositary, trustee.
—**depósito,** *m.* deposit, trust; depot,
repository, warehouse; storage;
sediment.—*d. de agua,* reservoir.

depravación, *f.* depravity, viciousness.
—**depravar,** *vt.* to deprave, corrupt.

depreciación, *f.* depreciation.—**depreciar,** *vt. & vr.* to depreciate.

depresión, *f.* depression.—**depresivo,**
deprimente, *a.* depressive, depressing.—**deprimir,** *vt.* to depress; to
belittle.—*vr.* to become depressed or
compressed.

depuesto, *pp.* of **DEPONER.**

depuración, *f.* purifying; purge.—
depurar, *vt.* to purify; to purge.

derecha, *f.* right hand; right side;
(pol.) right wing.—*a derechas,* right;
rightly.—**derechista,** *mf.* rightist.—
derecho, *a.* straight; right (opposite to left); right-handed; vertical; upright.—*adv.* straight ahead,
straightaway.—*m.* right; (D.) the
Law.—*pl.* fees, dues, duties.—*derechos de autor,* copyright; royalties.
—**derechura,** *f.* straightness.

deriva, *f.* ship's course; deviation,
drift.—**derivación,** *f.* derivation.—
derivar, *vi. & vr.* to derive.—*vi.* to
drift.—*vt.* to derive, trace to its
origin.

derogación, *f.* derogation, repeal.—
derogar, *vti.* [b] to derogate; to
annul, revoke, repeal.

derramamiento, *m.* pouring out;
spilling, shedding; overflow; scat-

tering.—*d. de sangre.* bloodshed.—
derramar, *vt.* to pour out; to spill;
to shed; to scatter; to spread.—*vr.*
to overflow, run over; to be scattered or spread.—**derrame,** *m.* overflow; scattering; shedding; leakage;
(med.) discharge.

derredor, *m.* circuit.—*al d.,* or *en d.,*
round about.—*al d. de,* or *en d. de,*
about, around.

derrengado, *a.* crooked; lame, crippled; swaybacked.—**derrengar,** *vti.*
[1-b] to injure the back; to cripple;
to make crooked.

derretir, *vti.* [29] to melt, fuse.—*vr.*
to melt, fuse; to be deeply in love.

derribar, *vt.* to demolish, knock
down; to overthrow.—**derribo,** *m.*
wrecking, demolition; debris.

derrocamiento, *m.* throwing down,
overthrow.—**derrocar,** *vti.* [12-d] to
pull down; to oust; to overthrow.

derrochador, *n.* spendthrift, squanderer.—*a.* extravagant, prodigal.—
derrochar, *vt.* to waste, squander.
—**derroche,** *m.* waste, squandering,
wastefulness.

derrota, *f.* defeat; (naut.) ship's
course.—**derrotar,** *vt.* to defeat;
(naut.) to cause to drift.—**derrotero,** *m.* (naut.) collection of seacharts; ship's course; course of action, way.—**derrotista,** *mf.* defeatist.

derruir, *vti.* [23-e] to demolish, tear
down.

derrumbamiento, *m.* landslide; collapse; downfall.—**derrumbar,** *vt.* to
throw down headlong.—*vr.* to tumble down; to crumble away; to
cave in.—**derrumbe,** *m.* tumbling
down, collapse; landslide.

desabonarse, *vr.* to cancel a subscription.

desabotonar, *vt.* to unbutton.

desabrido, *a.* harsh, sour; ill-humored; tasteless.—**desabrimiento,**
m. ill humor; tastelessness.

desabrigar, *vti.* [b] to uncover; to
strip.—*vri.* to take off outer clothing, expose oneself to cold.

desabrochar, *vt.* to unclasp, unfasten.
—*vr.* to unclasp, or unfasten oneself; to become unclasped or unfastened.

desacatar, *vt.* to treat disrespectfully.
—**desacato,** *m.* disrespect; lack of
reverence.

desacertado, *a.* unwise, mistaken.—
desacierto, *m.* error, mistake, blunder.

desacostumbrado, *a.* unusual; unaccustomed.

desacreditar, *vt.* to discredit.

desacuerdo, *m.* discordance, disagreement.

desafiar, *vt.* to challenge; to defy; to compete with.

desafinación, *f.* discordance, being out of tune.—**desafinar,** *vi.* to be discordant, out of tune.—*vr.* to get out of tune.

desafío, *m.* challenge; duel; struggle, contest, competition.

desaforado, *a.* disorderly; lawless; outrageous.

desafortunado, *a.* unfortunate, unlucky.

desafuero, *m.* excess, outrage.

desagradable, *a.* disagreeable, unpleasant, unattractive.—**desagradar,** *vt.* to displease, offend, miff.

desagradecido, *a.* ungrateful.

desagrado, *m.* discontent, displeasure.

desagraviar, *vt.* to apologize; to make amends for.—**desagravio,** *m.* apology, satisfaction; reparation.

desaguar, *vti.* [b] to drain.—*vii.* to empty (rivers); to urinate.—**desagüe,** *m.* drainage; drain, outlet; waste.

desaguisado, *m.* outrage, wrong.

desahuciado, *a.* despaired of, hopeless; given over; evicted.—**desahuciar,** *vt.* to give over; to evict.—**desahucio,** *m.* eviction.

desahogado, *a.* free, unencumbered; comfortable; well-off; impudent, brazen-faced.—**desahogar,** *vti.* [b] to ease, relieve.—*vri.* to unbosom oneself; to give a piece of one's mind; to relieve oneself.—**desahogo,** *m.* ease, relief; unburdening; relaxation; comfort.

desairar, *vt.* to disregard; to slight; to scorn; to rebuff.—**desaire,** *m.* slight, rebuff, disdain.

desajustar, *vt.* to disarrange, disorder. —*vr.* to get out of order or adjustment.—**desajuste,** *m.* disarrangement, lack of adjustment.

desalentador, *a.* dispiriting, discouraging.—**desalentar,** *vti.* [1] to discourage; to dismay.—*vri.* to jade, become exhausted.—**desaliento,** *m.* dismay, depression of spirits, discouragement; faintness.

desaliñado, *a.* slipshod.—**desaliñar,** *vt. & vr.* to disarrange, disorder, ruffle; to make slovenly.—**desaliño,** *m.* slovenliness, negligence of dress; disarray; neglect.

desalmado, *a.* soulless, merciless, inhuman; impious.

desalojamiento, desalojo, *m.* dislodging; displacement.—**desalojar,** *vt.* to dislodge, oust; to displace.

desalquilado, *a.* unrented, vacant.—vacant.—**desalquilarse,** *vr.* to become vacant.

desamarrar, *vt.* to untie; (naut.) to unmoor; to unbend (a rope).—*vr.* to untie oneself; to get loose.

desamparado, *a.* forsaken; helpless; unsheltered.—**desamparar,** *vt.* to forsake, abandon.—**desamparo,** *m.* abandonment; helplessness.

desamueblado, *a.* unfurnished.—**desamueblar,** *vt.* to strip of furniture.

desandar, *vti.* [4] to retrace one's steps.

desangramiento, *m.* bleeding to excess.—**desangrar,** *vt.* to bleed; to drain.—*vr.* to bleed to death.

desanimación, *f.* lack of enthusiasm; dullness.—**desanimado,** *a.* dull, flat; discouraged.—**desanimar,** *vt.* to discourage, dishearten.—*vr.* to get discouraged; to jade.

desapacible, *a.* disagreeable, unpleasant.

desaparecer, *vii.* [3] & *vri.* to disappear, vanish; to get out of sight.—**desaparición,** *f.* disappearance, vanishing.

desapercibido, *a.* unaware; unprepared, unguarded; unnoticed.

desaplicado, *a.* indolent, careless, neglectful.

desaprensivo, *a.* unscrupulous.

desapretar, *vti.* [1] to slacken, loosen, loose.

desaprobación, *f.* disapproval.—**desaprobar,** *vti.* [12] to disapprove of; to condemn.

desarmado, *a.* unarmed.—**desarmar,** *vt.* to disarm; to dismount; to disassemble.—**desarme,** *m.* disarmament.

desarraigar, *vti.* [b] to eradicate, root out.

desarrapado, *a.* ragged.

desarreglado, *a.* slovenly, disorderly; disarranged; immoderate.—**desarreglar,** *vt.* to disarrange, disorder.—**desarreglo,** *m.* disarrangement, disorder.

desarrollar, *vt.* to develop, unfold; to expound.—*vr.* to develop; to evolve; to unfold.—**desarrollo,** *m.* development; unfolding; expounding.

desarzonar, *vt.* to unseat (from a saddle).

desaseado, *a.* untidy, slovenly.—**desaseo,** *m.* untidiness, slovenliness.

desasir, *vti.* [5] to loosen.—*vri.* (de) to get loose (from); to extricate oneself (from).

desasosiego, *m.* restlessness, uneasiness.

desastrado, *a.* shabby, ragged.—**desastre,** *m.* disaster.—**desastroso,** *a.* disastrous.

desatar, *vt.* to untie, unfasten, loosen. —*vr.* to loosen; to break loose, break out (as a storm).—*d. en,*

to break out into, to pour out
(insults, etc.).

desatascar, *vti.* [d] to pull or draw
out of the mud.

desatención, *f.* inattention; discourtesy.—**desatender,** *vti.* [18] to
pay no attention to; to disregard,
slight, neglect.—**desatento,** *a.* inattentive, careless, discourteous.

desatinado, *a.* nonsensical; foolish.—
desatinar, *vt.* to rattle, bewilder.—
vi. to get rattled or bewildered; to
talk nonsense.—**desatino,** *m.* foolish
act or expression; nonsense.

desatracar, *vti.* [d] to sheer off; to
bear away; to unmoor.

desautorizado, *a.* unauthorized.—**des-
autorizar,** *vti.* [a] to disauthorize.

desavenencia, *f.* discord, disagreement.—**desavenido,** *a.* discordant,
disagreeing.

desayunarse, *vr.* to have breakfast.
—**desayuno,** *m.* breakfast.

desazón, *f.* displeasure; uneasiness;
insipidity.—**desazonar,** *vt.* to displease, annoy.—*vr.* to become indisposed; to become uneasy.

desbancar, *vti.* [d] to break the
bank; to supplant, oust.

desbandada, *f.* disbanding.—*a la d.,*
in disorder.—**desbandarse,** *vr.* to
disband, disperse, scatter.

desbarajuste, *m.* disorder, confusion.

desbaratar, *vt.* to break to pieces,
smash.—*vr.* to fall to pieces.

desbarrar, *vi.* to act foolishly; to
talk nonsense.

desbastar, *vt.* to hew, pare, trim.

desbocado, *a.* runaway (horse); foul-
mouthed, indecent.—**desbocar,** *vti.*
[d] & *vri.* to run away.—*vr.* to use
abusive language, unloosen one's
tongue.

desbordamiento, *m.* overflowing,
flooding.—**desbordar,** *vi.* & *vr.* to
overflow; to lose one's self-control.

descabalgar, *vii.* [b] to dismount
(from a horse).

descabezar, *vti.* [a] to behead; to
cut the upper parts or points of.—
d. el sueño, to take a nap, grab
forty winks.

descabellado, *a.* illogical, absurd.

descalabradura, *f.* wound on the
head.—**descalabrar,** *vt.* to wound on
the head; to injure; to defeat.—*vr.*
to injure one's skull.—**descalabro,** *m.*
calamity; misfortune.

descalificar, *vti.* [d] to disqualify.

descalzar, *vti.* [a] to unshoe, to pull
off the shoes.—*vr.* to take off one's
shoes.—**descalzo,** *a.* barefoot, shoe-
less.

descaminado, *a.* misguided, ill-ad-
vised, mistaken.

descamisado, *a.* shirtless, ragged.—
m. (coll.) ragamuffin.

descampado, *a.* disengaged, open,
clear.—*en d.,* in the open air.

descansar, *vi.* to rest, lean upon; to
depend.—*vt.* to place or set down
on a support or base.—**descanso,** *m.*
rest; relief; landing of stairs;
(mech.) support.

descarado, *a.* impudent, barefaced.

descarga, *f.* unloading, unburdening;
(mil.) volley; (elec.) discharge.—
descargar, *vti.* [b] to unload, un-
burden; to ease, lighten; to empty;
(mil.) to fire; to discharge or unload firearms; (elec.) to discharge;
to acquit.—*vii.* to strike with violence (as a storm).—**descargo,** *m.*
(com.) acquittance, receipt; (law)
plea or answer to an impeachment.

descarnar, *vt.* to remove flesh from;
to eat away.—*vr.* to lose flesh,
become emaciated.

descaro, *m.* impudence, barefaced-
ness; effrontery.

descarriar, *vt.* to lead astray, misguide, mislead; to separate (cattle).
—*vr. to be* separated; to go astray.

descarrilamiento, *m.* derailment.—
descarrilar, *vt.* to derail.—*vi.* &
vr. to run off the track, be derailed.

descartar, *vt.* to discard; to lay
aside.—*vr.* to discard (at cards).

descascar, descascarar, *vt.* to peel,
shell.—*vr.* to peel off, shell off.

descendencia, *f.* descent, origin;
descendants.—**descendente,** *a.* descending.—**descender,** *vii.* [18] to
descend; to get, come or go down;
to drop (of temperature); to derive, come from.—**descendiente,** *a.*
descending.—*mf.* descendant, offspring.—**descendimiento,** *m.* descent,
lowering.—**descenso,** *m.* descent;
lowering; fall.

descifrar, *vt.* to decipher, make out.

descocado, *a.* bold, forward.—**descoco,**
m. impudence, sauciness.

descolgar, *vti.* [12-b] to unhang; to
take down; to lower.—*vri.* to climb
down (a rope, etc.); to turn up
unexpectedly.

descolorar, *vt.* & *vr.* to discolor; to
lose color, fade.—**descolorido,** *a.*
pale, faded.

descollar, *vii.* [12] & *vti.* to tower,
excel, surpass.

descomedido, *a.* excessive, disproportionate; rude, impolite.—**descomedi-
miento,** *m.* rudeness, incivility.

descompasado, *a.* excessive, disproportionate; out of tune or time.

descomponer, *vti.* [32] to disarrange,
upset; to put out of order; (chem.)
to decompose.—*vri.* to decompose,

rot; to get out of order; to lose one's temper.—**descomposición**, *f.* disarrangement; disorder; decomposition, decay.—**descompuesto**, *pp.* of DESCOMPONER.—*a.* insolent; out of temper; immodest; out of order.

descomulgar, *vti.* [b] to excommunicate.

descomunal, *a.* extraordinary; monstrous, enormous.

desconcertante, *a.* disconcerting, baffling.—**desconcertar**, *vti.* [1] to disarrange, disturb, confuse; to disconcert, baffle, mystify; to disjoint.—*vri.* to become perplexed, confused.—**desconcierto**, *m.* discord, disagreement; disorder, confusion.

desconectar, *vt.* to disconnect.

desconfiado, *a.* distrustful; mistrustful.—**desconfianza**, *f.* diffidence; distrust.—**desconfiar**, *vi.* (de) to mistrust; to have no confidence (in); to suspect, doubt.

desconforme, *a.* = DISCONFORME.—**desconformidad**, *f.* = DISCONFORMIDAD.

descongelar, *vt.* to defrost.

desconocer, *vti.* [3] to fail to recognize; to disregard, ignore; to not know; to disown.—**desconocido**, *a.* unknown.—*n.* unknown person, stranger.—**desconocimiento**, *m.* ignorance; disregard.

desconsideración, *f.* inconsiderateness.—**desconsiderado**, *a.* inconsiderate; thoughtless.

desconsolado, *a.* disconsolate, grief-stricken, downhearted.—**desconsolador**, *a.* discouraging; lamentable.—**desconsolar**, *vti.* [12] to afflict.—*vri.* to despair, be disconsolate.—**desconsuelo**, *m.* affliction, disconsolateness.

descontar, *vti.* [12] to discount, deduct; to take for granted.—*vri.* to miscount.

descontentadizo, *a.* hard to please.—**descontentar**, *vt.* to displease.—**descontento**, *a.* discontent, displeased.—*m.* discontent, displeasure.

descontinuar, *vt.* to discontinue, leave off.

descorazonar, *vt.* to dishearten, discourage.

descorchar, *vt.* to uncork; to break open.

descortés, *a.* impolite, discourteous.—**descortesía**, *f.* discourtesy.

descortezar, *vti.* [a] to strip bark; to take off the crust of.

descoser, *vt.* to rip, unstitch, unseam.—*vr.* to rip.

descoyuntar, *vt.* to dislocate or disjoint.—*vr.* to become disjointed.—*d. de risa*, to split one's sides with laughter.

descrédito, *m.* discredit.

descreer, *vti.* [e] to disbelieve; to deny due credit to.—**descreído**, *n.* & *a.* unbeliever; infidel; unbelieving.

describir, *vti.* [49] to describe, depict.—**descripción**, *f.* description; sketch.—**descriptivo**, *a.* descriptive.—**descrito**, *pp.* of DESCRIBIR.—*a.* described.

descuartizamiento, *m.* quartering; breaking or cutting in pieces; carving.—**descuartizar**, *vti.* [a] to quarter; to carve; to cut into pieces.

descubierto, *pp.* of DESCUBRIR.—*a.* discovered; uncovered; unveiled; bareheaded; manifest; exposed.—*m.* deficit; overdraft.—*al d.*, openly; in the open.—*en d.*, overdrawn.—**descubridor**, *n.* discoverer.—**descubrimiento**, *m.* discovery; invention; find.—**descubrir**, *vti.* [49] to discover; to disclose; to uncover; to reveal.—*vri.* to take off one's hat.

descuento, *m.* discount; deduction, allowance.

descuidado, *a.* careless, negligent, slapdash; slovenly; unthinking.—**descuidar**, *vt.* to neglect.—*¡descuide!* don't worry.—*vi.* to lack attention or diligence; to be careless.—*vr.* to be careless, negligent.—**descuido**, *m.* carelessness; oversight, slip; lack of attention.—*al d.*, unobserved, on the sly; carelessly.

desde, *prep.* since, from.—*d. ahora*, from now on.—*a. entonces*, since then, ever since.—*d. luego*, of course.—*d. que*, since, ever since.

desdecir, *vii.* [14] to be unworthy (of); to detract (from).—*vri.* to retract, recant.

desdén, *m.* disdain, slight, scorn.

desdentado, *a.* toothless.

desdeñable, *a.* contemptible, despicable.—**desdeñar**, *vt.* to disdain, scorn.—**desdeñoso**, *a.* disdainful, contemptuous.

desdicha, *f.* misfortune, ill luck.—**desdichado**, *a.* unfortunate; unlucky; wretched.—*n.* wretch; poor devil.

desdoblar, *vt.* to unfold, spread open.

desdoro, *m.* dishonor, blemish, stigma.

deseable, *a.* desirable.—**desear**, *vt.* to desire, wish.

desecar, *vti.* [d] to drain; to dry.

desechar, *vt.* to reject; to exclude; to put or lay aside; to throw away; to cast off.—**desecho**, *m.* surplus, remainder; junk.—*de d.*, cast off, discarded; scrap (iron, etc.).

desembalar, *vt.* to unpack, open.

desembarazar, *vti.* [a] to free, ease.—*vri.* to rid oneself of difficulties.

desembarcar, *vti.* [d] to unload; to

put ashore.—*vii.* to land, disembark, go ashore.

desembocadura, *f.* outlet; mouth (of a river, canal, etc.).—**desembocar,** *vii.* [d] (en) to flow (into); to end (at), lead (to).

desembolsar, *vt.* to pay out, disburse. —**desembolso,** *m.* disbursement, expenditure.

desembragar, *vti.* [b] to disengage the clutch.

desembrollar, *vt.* to unravel, clear, disentangle.

desembuchar, *vt.* to disgorge; to turn out of the maw; (coll.) to tell all.

desempacar, *vti.* [d] to unpack.

desempatar, *vt.* to decide a tie vote; to run, play, or shoot off a tie.

desempedrado, *a.* unpaved.

desempeñar, *vt.* to redeem (from pawn).—*d. un cargo,* to fill a post. —*d. un papel,* to play a part.—*vr.* to extricate oneself from debt.— **desempeño,** *m.* redemption (of a pledge); discharge (of an obligation).

desempleado, *n.* & *a.* unemployed.— **desempleo,** *m.* unemployment.

desempolvar, *vt.* to dust, remove dust or powder from.

desencadenar, *vt.* to unchain; to free, liberate.—*vr.* to break loose, free oneself from chains; to break out with fury (as a storm); to come down in torrents (the rain).

desencajado, *a.* disjointed; ill-looking, emaciated.

desenfado, *m.* freedom, ease, naturalness.

desenfrenado, *a.* ungoverned, unchecked, wanton; riotous.—**desenfreno,** *m.* rashness, wantonness, licentiousness.

desenganchar, *vt.* to unhook, unfasten; to unhitch, unharness.

desengañar, *vt.* to undeceive, set right; to disillusion.—*vr.* to become disillusioned.—**desengaño,** *m.* disillusionment, disappointment.

desengrasar, *vt.* to remove the grease from.

desenlace, *m.* conclusion, end, ending. —**desenlazar,** *vti.* [a] to unlace, untie, loose; to unravel.

desenmarañar, *vt.* to disentangle; to unravel, make clear.

desenmascarar, *vt.* to unmask.

desenredar, *vt.* to untangle, unravel.— *vr.* to extricate oneself.

desenroscar, *vti.* [d] to untwist; to unscrew.

desensillar, *vt.* to unsaddle.

desentenderse, *vri.* [18] (de) to have nothing to do with; to ignore; to pay no attention (to).—*hacerse el*

desentendido, to pretend not to see, notice or understand.

desenterrar, *vti.* [1] to dig up, unearth.

desentonación, *f.* dissonance.—**desentonado,** *a.* out of tune; discordant. —**desentonar,** *vi.* to be off key, out of tune; to clash (in colors); to be out of keeping with.

desentrañar, *vt.* to penetrate or dive into; to bring out, reveal, dig out.

desenvoltura, *f.* sprightliness, ease; impudence.—**desenvolver,** *vti.* [47] to unfold, unwrap, unroll; to unravel; to develop.—*vri.* to behave with self-assurance; to unfold, unroll.—**desenvolvimiento,** *m.* unfolding, development.—**desenvuelto,** *pp.* of DESENVOLVER.—*a.* forward; free, easy.

deseo, *m.* desire, wish.—**deseoso,** *a.* desirous, eager.

desequilibrado, *a.* unbalanced; deranged.—**desequilibrar,** *vt.* to put out of balance.—*vr.* to become deranged.—**desequilibrio,** *m.* lack of balance; derangement.

deserción, *f.* desertion.—**desertar,** *vt.* to desert; to abandon.—*vr.* (de) to desert (from).—**desertor,** *n.* deserter.

desesperación, *f.* despair, desperation; anger.—**desesperado,** *a.* desperate, despairing; hopeless.—**desesperante,** *a.* causing despair; maddening.

desesperanza, *f.* despair.—**desesperanzado,** *a.* discouraged; hopeless, in despair.

desesperar, *vi.* to lose hope, despair. —*vt.* to make one despair; to discourage hope; (coll.) to drive crazy. —*vr.* to despair, despond; to fret.— **desespero,** *m.* despair; vexation.

desestimar, *vt.* to undervalue; to reject, deny.

desfachatado, *a.* impudent, saucy.— **desfachatez,** *f.* effrontery, impudence.

desfalcar, *vti.* [d] to embezzle.— **desfalco,** *m.* embezzlement.

desfallecer, *vii.* [3] to pine; to weaken; to faint.—**desfalleciente,** *a.* pining, languishing.—**desfallecimiento,** *m.* languor; dejection; swoon.

desfavorable, *a.* unfavorable; untoward.

desfigurar, *vt.* to disfigure, deform; to deface; to disguise (as the voice); to distort.

desfiladero, *m.* defile, gorge; road at the side of a precipice.—**desfilar,** *vi.* to file past; to march in review, parade.—**desfile,** *m.* parade, procession.

desflorar, *vt.* to tarnish; to deflower; to violate.

desfogar, *vri.* [b] to vent one's anger. —*vti.* to vent.

desfondar, *vt.* to break or take off the bottom of.

desgaire, *m.* carelessness, indifference. —*al d.*, in an affectedly careless manner; disdainfully.

desgajar, *vt.* to tear, break off (branches).—*vr.* to be torn off; to fall off.

desgañifarse, **desgañitarse**, *vr.* to shriek, scream at the top of one's voice.

desgarbado, *a.* ungraceful, uncouth, gawky.

desgarrador, *a.* tearing; heartbreaking, heart-rending.—**desgarradura**, *f.* laceration, tear, break.—**desgarrar**, *vt.* to rend, tear; to claw; to expectorate.—*vr.* to tear.—**desgarrón**, *m.* large rent or tear (in clothing, etc.).

desgastar, *vt.* to wear away, consume, waste by degrees.—*vr.* to lose strength and vigor; to wear down or away.—**desgaste**, *m.* slow waste; abrasion; wear and tear; erosion.

desgobierno, *m.* mismanagement; misrule.

desgracia, *f.* misfortune, wretchedness; affliction; disgrace.—**desgraciado**, *a. & n.* unfortunate (person), wretched (person).—**desgraciar**, *vt.* to ruin; to maim; to spoil.—*vr.* to disgrace; to lose favor; to become a cripple.

desgranar, *vt.* to remove the grain from; to thrash, thresh (corn, etc.); to shell (peas, etc.).—*vr.* to shed the grains; to scatter about (as beads).

desgreñar, *vt.* to dishevel.

desguarnecer, *vti.* [3] to disarm (an opponent); to unharness; to strip of trimmings and ornaments.

deshabitado, *a.* uninhabited, untenanted, deserted.

deshacer, *vti.* [22] to undo; to destroy; to untie.—*vri.* to be consumed, destroyed; to wear oneself out; to grieve, mourn; to outdo oneself.—*deshacerse de*, to get rid of.

desharrapado, *a.* shabby, ragged, tattered.

deshecho, *pp.* of DESHACER.- *a.* ruined, destroyed, in pieces; undone; worn-out.

deshelar, *vti.* [1] & *vri.* to thaw; to melt.

desherbar, *vti.* [1] to weed.

desheredar, *vt.* to disinherit.

deshermanar, *vt.* to unmatch, spoil a pair.

deshielo, *m.* thaw, thawing.

deshilachar, *vt.* to ravel.—*vr.* to fuzz; to ravel.

deshilar, *vt.* to ravel; to scrape (lint). —*vr.* to fuzz; to grow thin.

deshilvanado, *a.* disconnected, incoherent (of speech).

deshinchar, *vt.* to reduce the swelling of; to deflate.—*vr.* to become deflated; to go down (of anything swollen).

deshojar, *vt.* to strip off the leaves.— *vr.* to shed leaves.

deshollejar, *vt.* to husk, hull; to peel.

deshollinador, *m.* chimney-sweeper.

deshonestidad, *f.* dishonesty; indecency.—**deshonesto**, *a.* dishonest, dishonorable; lewd.

deshonor, *m.* dishonor, disgrace; insult, affront.—**deshonra**, *f.* dishonor; seduction or violation (of a woman).—**deshonrar**, *vt.* to affront, insult, defame; to dishonor, disgrace; to seduce or ruin (a woman). —**deshonroso**, *a.* dishonorable.

deshora, *f.* inconvenient time.—*a d.*, or *a deshoras*, untimely, extemporarily.

deshuesar, *vt.* to bone (an animal); to take the pits out of (fruits).

desidia, *f.* laziness, indolence.—**desidioso**, *a.* lazy, indolent.

desierto, *m.* desert.—*a.* uninhabited, deserted, lonely.

designación, *f.* designation.—**designar**, *vt.* to appoint, designate.—**designio**, *m.* design, purpose, intention.

desigual, *a.* unequal, unlike; uneven, rough; changeable.—**desigualdad**, *f.* inequality, difference; roughness, unevenness.

desilusión, *f.* disappointment, disillusionment.—**desilusionar**, *vt.* to disillusion.—*vr.* to become disillusioned.

desinfección, *f.* disinfection; disinfecting.—**desinfectante**, *m. & a.* disinfectant; disinfecting.—**desinfectar**, *vt.* to disinfect; to sterilize.

desenrollar, *vt.* to unroll, uncoil.

desinflamar, *vt. & vr.* to remove the inflammation of.

desinflar, *vt. & vr.* to deflate.

desintegración, *f.* disintegration.— **desintegrar**, *vt., vi. & vr.* to disintegrate.

desistir, *vi.* (de) to desist (from).

desleal, *a.* disloyal; perfidious.— **deslealtad**, *f.* disloyalty, treachery, unfaithfulness.

desleír, *vti.* [35-e] to dilute; to dissolve.—*vri.* to become diluted.

deslenguado, *a.* impudent; foulmouthed.

desligar, *vti.* [b] to loosen, untie.— *vri.* to get loose; to give way.

deslindar, *vt.* to mark the boundaries of; to clear up, define.—**deslinde**, *m.* demarcation, determination of boundaries.

desliz, *m.* slip, slide; false step.—**deslizamiento**, *m.* slip, slipping; glide; skidding, sliding.—**deslizante**, *a.* gliding, sliding.—**deslizar**, *vii.* [a] & *vri.* to slip; to slide; to skid; to glide; to act or speak carelessly.—*vri.* to shirk, evade.

deslucido, *a.* dull, shabby, shopworn; unsuccessful.—**deslucir**, *vti.* [3] to tarnish, dull; to discredit.—*vri.* to fail, be a failure.

deslumbrador, *a.* dazzling, glaring.—**deslumbramiento**, *m.* glare, dazzling; confusion of sight or mind.—**deslumbrante**, *a.* dazzling.—**deslumbrar**, *vt.* to dazzle.

deslustrar, *vt.* to tarnish; to obscure, dim; to remove the glaze from; to stain (reputation, etc.).

desmadejamiento, *m.* languishment, weakness.—**desmadejar**, *vt.* to enervate.—*vr.* to languish.

desmán, *m.* misbehavior; excess.

desmandar, *vr.* to be impudent; to lose moderation or self-control.

desmantelamiento, *m.* dismantling; dilapidation.—**desmantelar**, *vt.* to dismantle; to abandon.

desmañado, *a.* clumsy, awkward.

desmayar, *vi.* to falter, lose heart.—*vr.* to faint.—**desmaye**, *m.* swoon, faint; discouragement.

desmejorar, *vt.* to debase; to make worse.—*vi.* & *vr.* to decline, become worse; to deteriorate.

desmelenado, *a.* disheveled.

desmemoriado, *a.* forgetful.

desmentir, *vti.* [39] to give the lie to; to contradict.—*vri.* to recant, retract.

desmenuzar, *vti.* [a] to crumble; to shred; to tear into bits; to examine minutely.—*vri.* to crumble, fall into small pieces.

desmerecer, *vti.* [3] to become unworthy of.—*vii.* to deteriorate; to compare unfavorably.—**desmerecimiento**, *m.* demerit, unworthiness.

desmesurado, *a.* disproportionate, excessive.

desmigajar, *vt.* & *vr.* to crumb; to crumble.

desmochar, *vt.* to lop or cut off the top of (a tree, etc.).—**desmoche**, *m.* cutting off.

desmontar, *vt.* to clear (a wood); to uncock (firearms); to take apart (machines).—*vi.* to dismount; to alight (from a horse, mule, etc.).

desmoralización, *f.* demoralization.—**desmoralizar**, *vti.* [a] to demoralize, corrupt.—*vri.* to become demoralized.

desmoronamiento, *m.* crumbling.—**desmoronar**, *vt.* to demolish gradually; to destroy.—*vr.* to fall, crumble.

desmovilizar, *vti.* [a] to demobilize.

desnivel, *m.* unevenness, drop.—**desnivelado**, *a.* unlevel.—**desnivelar**, *vt.* to make uneven.—*vr.* to lose its level.

desnucar, *vti.* [d] to break the neck of.—*vri.* to break one's neck.

desnudar, *vt.* & *vr.* to strip, undress, unclothe.—**desnudez**, *f.* nudity, nakedness.—**desnudismo**, *m.* nudism.—**desnudista**, *mf.* nudist.—**desnudo**, *a.* nude, naked; bare, evident.

desnutrición, *f.* malnutrition.

desobedecer, *vti.* [3] & *vii.* to disobey.—**desobediencia**, *f.* disobedience.—**desobediente**, *a.* disobedient.

desocupación, *f.* leisure; unemployment.—**desocupado**, *a.* idle, without occupation; vacant, unoccupied.—*n.* unemployed person; idler.—**desocupar**, *vt.* to vacate; to evacuate; to empty.—*vr.* to retire (from a business or occupation).

desodorante, *m.* & *a.* deodorant.

desoír, *vti.* [28-e] to pretend not to hear; not to heed.

desolación, *f.* desolation; destruction; affliction.—**desolado**, *a.* desolate; disconsolate.—**desolar**, *vti.* [12] to lay waste.—*vri.* to grieve.

desollar, *vti.* [12] to flay, skin.

desorden, *m.* disorder, confusion; lawlessness; disturbance, riot.—**desordenar**, *vt.* to disorder, disturb, disarrange.

desorientación, *f.* disorientation, loss of bearings; perplexity.—**desorientar**, *vt.* to mislead, confuse.—*vr.* to lose one's bearings.

desosar, *vti.* [15] = DESHUESAR.

desovar, *vii.* [15] to spawn.

despabilado, *a.* vigilant; wakeful; lively, smart.—**despabilar**, *vt.* to trim or snuff (a candle); to rouse; to enliven.—*vr.* to wake up.

despacio, *adv.* slowly; deliberately.—**despacioso**, *a.* slow.—**despacito**, *adv.* very slowly, gently, softly.

despachar, *vt.* to dispatch; to expedite; to attend to; to wait on (as in a shop); to dismiss, discharge.—*vr.* to make haste.—**despacho**, *m.* dispatch; study; office; salesroom; telegram; communiqué; shipment.

despachurrar, *vt.* to squash, smash, crush.

desparpajo, *m.* self-confidence, pertness, cockiness.

desparramar, *vt. & vr.* to scatter, disseminate, spread.

despatarrarse, *vr.* (coll.) to sprawl, go sprawling.

despavorido, *a.* terrified.

despectivo, *a.* contemptuous.

despechar, *vt.* to spite.—*vr.* to be spited.—**despecho,** *m.* spite.—*a despecho de,* in spite (of), despite.

despedazar, *vti.* [a] to tear to pieces, cut up.—*vri.* to break or fall to pieces.

despedida, *f.* leave-taking, farewell; send-off; dismissal.—**despedir,** *vti.* [29] to dismiss; to emit; to see a person off (at a station, airport, etc.).—*vri.* to take leave (of), say goodbye (to); to leave (a post).

despegado, *a.* unglued; unaffectionate, unfeeling.—**despegar,** *vti.* [b] to unglue, disjoin.—*vii.* to rise, take off (of a plane).—*vri.* to come off; to become indifferent.—**despego,** *m.* coolness, indifference; aversion.—**despegue,** *m.* take-off (of a plane).

despeinado, *a.* uncombed.—**despeinar,** *vt. & vr.* to disarrange the hair.

despejado, *a.* smart; clear, cloudless; unobstructed.—**despejar,** *vt.* to remove impediments from, clear; (math.) to find the value of.—*vr.* to become bright and smart; to clear up.

despellejar, *vt.* to flay, skin; to speak ill of.

despensa, *f.* pantry; storeroom (for food); food, provisions.—**despensero,** *n.* butler; (naut.) steward.

despeñadero, *m.* precipice, crag.—**despeñar,** *vt.* to precipitate, to hurl down.—*vr.* to throw oneself headlong.

desperdiciar, *vt.* to squander, waste, misspend.—**desperdicio,** *m.* waste, spoilage; profusion.—*pl.* garbage.

desperdigar, *vti.* [b] to separate, disjoin; to scatter.

desperezarse, *vri.* [a] to stretch one's limbs.

desperfecto, *m.* deterioration; slight injury or damage, imperfection.

despertador, *m.* alarm clock.—**despertar,** *vti.* [1-49] to wake up; to arouse, to stir up.—*vii. & vri.* to wake up.

despiadado, *a.* unmerciful, pitiless.

despido, *m.* discharge, dismissal, lay-off.

despierto, *a.* awake; watchful; diligent; smart.

despilfarrar, *vt.* to waste, squander.—**despilfarro,** *m.* extravagance, squandering; waste.

despintar, *vt.* to take the paint off.—*vr.* to lose color, fade.

despistar, *vt.* to throw off the scent.

desplazamiento, *m.* displacement.—**desplazar,** *vti.* [a] to displace.

desplegar, *vti.* [1-b] to unfold, unfurl; to display.—*vri.* to deploy (as troops).—**despliegue,** *m.* unfurling, unfolding; deployment.

desplomar, *vr.* to tumble down, collapse.—**desplome,** *m.* tumbling down, downfall, collapse.

desplumar, *vt. & vr.* to pluck (a bird); to fleece, skin; to strip of property.

despoblación, *f.* depopulation.—**despoblado,** *m.* uninhabited place, wilderness.—*a.* uninhabited, desolate.—**despoblar,** *vti.* [12] to depopulate; to despoil or desolate.—*vri.* to become depopulated.

despojar, *vt.* to despoil, strip of property; to deprive of; to cut off from.—*vr.* (de) to take off (as a coat).—**despojo,** *m.* spoliation; spoils.—*pl.* leavings, scraps from the table; giblets of fowl; remains.

desposado, *n.* betrothed; bride; bridegroom.—**desposar,** *vt.* to marry (to perform the marriage ceremony for).—*vr.* to be betrothed, or married.

desposeer, *vti.* [e] to dispossess, oust.

déspota, *m.* despot.—**despótico,** *a.* despotic.—**despotismo,** *m.* despotism, tyranny.

despreciable, *a.* contemptible, despicable, insignificant.—**despreciar,** *vt.* to despise, scorn.—**desprecio,** *m.* scorn, contempt.

desprender, *vt.* to unfasten; to separate.—*vr.* to give way; to issue (from), come out (of); to follow, be a consequence (of).—**desprendimiento,** *m.* detachment, landslide; disinterestedness.

despreocupación, *f.* freedom from bias; unconventionality.—**despreocupado,** *a.* unprejudiced; unconventional; carefree.—**despreocuparse,** *vr.* to become unbiased, lose prejudice; (de) to ignore; to pay no attention (to).

desprestigiar, *vt.* to discredit.—*vr.* to lose reputation or prestige.—**desprestigio,** *m.* loss of reputation or prestige.

desprevenido, *a.* unprovided; unprepared.

despropósito, *m.* absurdity, nonsense.

desprovisto, *a.* (de) unprovided (with), lacking (in).

después, *adv.* after, afterward; next, then, later.—*d. de,* after; next to.—*d. de que,* or *d. que,* after.

despuntar, *vt.* to blunt; to crop.—

vi. to sprout or bud; to be outstanding; to excel.

desquiciar, *vt.* to unhinge; to unsettle.—*vr.* to become unhinged; to fall down.

desquitarse, *vr.* (de) to win one's money back, recoup; to get even.—**desquite**, *m.* compensation; recovery of a loss; revenge; return game or bout.

destacamento, *m.* (mil.) detachment. —**destacar**, *vti.* [d] to bring out, make conspicuous; (mil.) to detach.—*vri.* to stand out, be conspicuous; to be outstanding.

destajo, *m.* piece work, task.—*a d.*, by the job, piece work.

destapar, *vt.* to uncover, uncork, take off (cover, lid, cap).—*vr.* to become uncovered.

destartalado, *a.* handled, jumbled; ramshackle, scantily and poorly furnished.

destellar, *vi.* to flash, twinkle, gleam. —**destello**, *m.* flash, sparkle, gleam.

destemplado, *a.* inharmonious; out of tune; out of tone; intemperate; without its temper (of metal).—**destemplanza**, *f.* indisposition.

desteñir, *vti.* [9] & *vri.* to discolor, fade.

desternillarse (de risa), *vr.* to split one's sides with laughter.

desterrar, *vti.* [1] to banish, exile.—**desterrado**, *n.* exile, outcast.

destetar, *vt.* to wean.—**destete**, *m.* weaning.

destiempo, *adv.*—*a d.*, unseasonably, untimely, inopportunely.

destierro, *m.* exile.

destilar, *vt.* to distill; to filter.—*vi.* to distill, to drip, drop; to ooze. —**destilería**, *f.* distillery.

destinar, *vt.* to destine; to appoint; to assign.—**destinatario**, *n.* addressee; consignee.—**destino**, *m.* destiny; destination; employment.—*con d. a*, bound for, going to.

destitución, *f.* dismissal from employment, office or charge.—**destituir**, *vti.* [23-e] to dismiss from office.

destornillador, *m.* screwdriver.—**destornillar**, *vt.* to unscrew.

destrabar, *vt.* to loosen, to unfetter.

destreza, *f.* skill, dexterity, ability; nimbleness.

destripar, *vt.* to disembowel, gut; to smash, crush.

destrozar, *vti.* [a] to break into pieces, smash up.—**destrozo**, *m.* destruction; havoc.

destrucción, *f.* destruction.—**destructivo**, *a.* destructive.—**destructer**, *m.* destroyer.—*a.* destroying.—**destruir**,

vti. [23-e] to destroy; to ruin; to demolish, raze.

desunir, *vt.* to separate, take apart. —*vr.* to become separated.

desusado, *a.* unusual; obsolete, out of date.—**desuso**, *m.* disuse, obsoleteness.

desvalido, *a.* helpless, unprotected, unsheltered.

desvalijar, *vt.* to rob.

desván, *m.* attic; loft; garret.

desvanecer, *vti.* [3] to dispel; to fade; to cause to vanish.—*vri.* to vanish, disappear; to faint.

desvariar, *vi.* to rave, be delirious.—**desvarío**, *m.* delirium, raving; madness; absurdity.

desvelar, *vt.* to keep awake.—*vr.* to go without sleep; to pass a sleepless night; to be watchful or vigilant.—**desvelo**, *m.* insomnia, lack of sleep; watchfulness; anxiety, uneasiness.

desvencijado, *a.* ramshackle, rickety, loose-jointed.

desventaja, *f.* disadvantage.—**desventajoso**, *a.* disadvantageous.

desventura, *f.* misfortune, mishap.—**desventurado**, *a.* unfortunate, unlucky, faint-hearted.

desvergonzado, *a.* impudent; shameless.—**desvergüenza**, *f.* impudence; shamelessness.

desvestir, *vti.* [29] & *vri.* to undress.

desviación, *f.* deviation.—**desviadero**, *m.* (RR.) siding.—**desviar**, *vt.* to deflect; to sway; to dissuade; (fencing) to ward off; (RR.) to switch.—*vr.* to turn aside; to deviate; to swerve; to drift (away from).—**desvío**, *m.* deviation, turning away; coldness, indifference; (RR.) siding, side track.

desvirtuar, *vt.* to impair; to lessen the merit of; to detract from the value of.

desvivirse, *vr.* (por) to have excessive fondness (for); to do one's utmost (in behalf of); to be dying (for, to).

detallar, *vt.* to detail, relate minutely; to specify; to retail.—**detalle**, *m.* detail, particular; (com.) retail.—**detallista**, *mf.* (com.) retailer; one addicted to details (painter, etc.).

detective, *mf.* detective.—**detector**, *m.* (elec., radio) detector.

detención, *f.* delay, stop; arrest.—**detener**, *vti.* [42] to stop, detain; to arrest; to retain, reserve.—*vri.* to tarry, stay; to stop, halt; to pause.—**detenimiento**, *m.* care, thoroughness.

detergente, *a.* & *m.* detergent.

deteriorar, vt. & vr. to deteriorate, spoil, wear out.—**deterioro,** m. deterioration, damage, wear and tear.

determinación, f. determination; resolution; firmness.—**determinado,** a. determined, decided; resolute, purposeful; settled, definite.—**determinar,** vt. to determine, fix; to limit; to specify; to distinguish, discern; to assign (as time and place); to resolve, decide.—vr. to determine, resolve; to make up one's mind.

detestable, a. detestable, hateful.—**detestar,** vt. to detest.

detonación, f. detonation.—**detonante,** a. detonating.—**detonar,** vi. to detonate, explode.

detracción, f. detraction, defamation.—**detractor,** n. & a. detractor, slanderer.—a. detracting.

detrás, adv. behind; back, in the rear.—d. de, behind, in back of.—por d., from the rear, from behind; behind one's back.

detrimento, m. detriment, damage.

deuda, f. debt; indebtedness.—**deudo,** m. relative, kinsman.—**deudor,** n. & a. debtor; indebted.

devanar, vt. to reel, wind.—**devanarse los sesos,** to rack one's brain.

devaneo, m. delirium, giddiness; frenzy; dissipation; love affair.

devastación, f. devastation, destruction.—**devastador,** n. & a. devastator; devastating.—**devastar,** vt. to devastate, ruin, lay waste.

devengar, vti. [b] to earn, draw (as salary, interest, etc.)

devenir, vii. [45] to become; to happen; to befall.

devoción, f. devotion, piety; faithful attachment.—**devocionario,** m. prayer book.

devolución, f. return, restitution; devolution.—**devolver,** vti. [47-49] to return, give back; to restore; to pay back.

devorador, n. devourer.—a. devouring, ravenous.—**devorar,** vt. to devour, swallow up, gobble, wolf.

devoto, a. devout, pious; devoted.

devuelto, pp. of **DEVOLVER.**

día, m. day.—al d., up to date; by the day.—a los pocos días, a few days later.—al otro d., on the following day.—de d., by day.—d. de fiesta or festivo, holiday.—el d. menos pensado, when least expected.—el mejor d., some fine day.—en su d., at the proper time.—hoy (en) d., nowadays.—un d. sí y otro no, every other day.

diablo, m. devil.—**diablura,** f. devil-try, mischief, wild prank.—**diabólico,** a. diabolical, devilish.

diácono, m. deacon.

diafragma, m. diaphragm.

diagnosticar, vti. [d] to diagnose.—**diagnóstico,** m. diagnosis.—a. diagnostic.

diagonal, a. diagonal; oblique.—f. (geom.) diagonal.

diagrama, m. diagram.

dialecto, m. dialect.

dialogar, vii. [b] to dialogize; to chat, converse.—**diálogo,** m. dialogue.

diamante, m. diamond.

diámetro, m. diameter.

diana, f. target, bull's eye; reveille.

diapasón, m. tuning fork.

diapositiva, f. lantern slide; (phot.) plate.

diario, a. daily.—m. journal, diary; daily newspaper; daily expense.—a d., daily, every day.

diarrea, f. diarrhea.

dibujante, mf. designer, draftsman.—**dibujar,** vt. to draw, sketch; to depict.—**dibujo,** m. drawing; sketch; delineation.

dicción, f. diction.—**diccionario,** m. dictionary.

diciembre, m. December.

dictado, m. dictation.—pl. dictates, promptings.—**dictador,** n. dictator.—**dictadura,** f. dictatorship.—**dictamen,** m. judgment, opinion.—**dictaminar,** vi. to express an opinion, pass judgment.—**dictar,** vt. to dictate.

dicterio, m. taunt; insult.

dicha, f. happiness; good luck.

dicharachero, a. witty; wisecracking.—**dicharacho,** m. smart remark; wisecrack.—**dicho,** pp. of **DECIR.**—a. (the) said, mentioned; this.—m. saying, proverb.

dichoso, a. lucky, fortunate; happy.

diente, m. tooth; tusk.—decir or hablar entre dientes, to mumble, to mutter.—de dientes afuera, without sincerity, as mere lip service.

diestra, f. right hand.—**diestro,** m. bullfighter.—a. skillful, able; right.

dieta, f. diet; traveling allowance.

diezmar, vt. to decimate.—**diezmo,** m. tithe.

diferencia, f. difference; disagreement.—**diferenciación,** f. differentiation.—**diferenciar,** vt. to differentiate, distinguish between.—vi. to differ, disagree.—vr. to be different.—**diferente,** a. different.

diferir, vti. [39] to defer, postpone; to procrastinate.—vii. to differ.

difícil, a. difficult, hard.—**dificultad,** f. difficulty.—**dificultar,** vt. to make

difficult; to impede.—dificultoso, *a.*
difficult, hard.

difteria, *f.* diphtheria.

difundir, *vt.* & *vr.* to diffuse, spread
out; to spread (as news); to di-
vulge, publish; to broadcast.

difunto, *a.* defunct, dead.—*n.* corpse.

difusión, *f.* diffusion; diffusiveness,
dispersion; broadcasting.—**difuso,** *a.*
diffuse; wordy; widespread.

digerir, *vti.* [39] to digest.—**digestión,**
f. digestion.

dignarse, *vr.* to condescend.—**digna-
tario,** *n.* dignitary.—**dignidad,** *f.*
dignity; high rank; stateliness.—
digno, *a.* meritorious, worthy; fitting, appropriate.

digresión, *f.* digression.

dije, *m.* trinket; locket; charm.

dilación, *f.* delay.

dilapidación, *f.* dilapidation; squandering.—**dilapidar,** *vt.* to dilapidate;
to squander.

dilatación, *f.* dilatation, expansion;
enlargement.—**dilatado,** *a.* vast, extensive; drawn out.—**dilatar,** *vt.* &
vr. to dilate; to prolong; to retard, delay.

dilema, *m.* dilemma.

diligencia, *f.* diligence; activity;
stagecoach; errand; judicial proceeding.—*hacer d.,* or *la d.,* to try.
—**diligente,** *a.* diligent; prompt,
swift.

diluir, *vti.* & *vri.* [23-e] to dilute.

diluvio, *m.* flood; deluge.

dimanar, *vi.* (de) to spring or flow
(from); to originate (in).

dimensión, *f.* dimension; extent, size.

diminución, *f.* diminution.—**diminu-
tivo,** *a.* diminishing; diminutive.—
m. (gram.) diminutive.—**diminuto,**
a. tiny.

dimisión, *f.* resignation (from post).
—**dimitir,** *vt.* to resign, give up
(post).

dinamarqués, *n.* & *a.* Dane, Danish.

dinámico, *a.* dynamic, energetic.

dinamita, *f.* dynamite.

dinamo, dínamo, *f.* (gen. *m.* in Am.)
dynamo.

dinastía, *f.* dynasty.

dineral, *m.* a lot of money.—**dinero,**
m. money; currency; wealth.—*d.
contante y sonante,* ready money,
cash.—*d. suelto,* small change.

dintel, *m.* lintel, doorhead.

diócesis, *f.* diocese.

dios, *m.* god; (D.) God.—*D. mediante,* God willing.—¡*D. mío*! my
God!—**diosa,** *f.* goddess.

diploma!, *m.* diploma; bull, patent,
license; title.—**diplomacia,** *f.* di-
plomacy.—**diplomático,** *a.* diplo-
matic.—*n.* diplomat.

diptongo, *m.* diphthong.

diputado, *n.* deputy, representative,
delegate; assignee.

dique, *m.* dike; dry dock; check,
restraint.

dirección, *f.* direction, course; management; postal address; office of a
director.—**directivo,** *a.* directive,
managing.—*f.* governing board,
board of directors, management.—*n.*
member of a board of directors; officer of a society, club, etc.—**directo,**
a. direct; straight.—**director,** *n.* &
a. director; directing.—*n.* director,
manager; chief; editor (of a newspaper); principal (of a school);
conductor (of an orchestra).—**direc-
torio,** *a.* directive, directorial.—*m.*
directory; directorate.—**dirigente,** *a.*
directing, leading; ruling.—*mf.*
leader.—**dirigir,** *vti.* [c] to direct;
to address (a letter, etc.); to command; to govern, manage.—*vri.* (a)
to address, speak (to); to apply,
resort (to); to go (to or toward).

dirimir, *vt.* to solve (a difficulty); to
settle (a controversy).

discar, *vti.* [d] (tel.) to dial.

discernimiento, *m.* discernment, judgment.—**discernir,** *vii.* [16] to discern, discriminate.

disciplina, *f.* discipline, training;
obedience; rule of conduct; any art
or science.—*pl.* whip, scourge.—
disciplinar, *vt.* to discipline, educate; to drill.

discípulo, *n.* disciple, follower; pupil.

disco, *m.* disk; phonograph record;
dial of telephone.

díscolo, *a.* ungovernable; undisciplined.

disconforme, *a.* discordant, disagreeing.—**disconformidad,** *f.* non-con-
formity; disparity; disagreement.

discontinuo, *a.* discontinuous.

discordancia, *f.* disagreement, discord; maladjustment.—**discordante,**
a. discordant, dissonant.—**discordar,**
vii. [12] to be in discord, disagree.
—**discorde,** *a.* discordant; dissonant.
—**discordia,** *f.* discord, disagreement.

discreción, *f.* discretion; prudence;
liberty of action and decision.—*a
d.,* at will, unconditionally.

discrepancia, *f.* discrepancy.—**dis-
crepante,** *a.* disagreeing, differing.—
discrepar, *vi.* to differ, disagree.

discreto, *a.* discreet, prudent, unobtrusive; fairly good.

discriminar, *vt.* to discriminate.

disculpa, *f.* apology, excuse.—**dis-
culpable,** *a.* excusable; pardonable.
—**disculpar,** *vt.* & *vr.* to exculpate

(oneself); to excuse (oneself); to apologize.

discurrir, *vi.* to roam, ramble about; to flow (as a river); to reflect, think; to discourse.—*vt.* to invent; to infer.

discurso, *m.* speech; dissertation; space of time; discourse.

discusión, *f.* discussion.—**discutible,** *a.* controvertible, disputable.—**discutidor,** *n.* & *a.* arguer; arguing.—**discutir,** *vt.* & *vi.* to discuss; to argue.

disecación, *f.* = DISECCION.—**disecar,** *vti.* [d] to dissect; to stuff (dead animals).—**disección,** *f.* dissection; anatomy.

diseminación, *f.* scattering, spreading. —**diseminar,** *vt.* to spread, scatter.

disensión, *f.* dissent; contest, strife.

disentería, *f.* dysentery.

disentir, *vii.* [39] to dissent, disagree, differ.

diseñador, *n.* designer, delineator.—**diseñar,** *vt.* to draw; to sketch, outline.—**diseño,** *m.* design, sketch, outline; description.

disertación, *f.* dissertation.—**disertar,** *vi.* (sobre or acerca de) to discourse (on), treat (of), discuss.

disforme, *a.* deformed; hideous; out of proportion.

disfraz, *m.* disguise, mask; costume; dissimulation.—**disfrazar,** *vti.* [a] to disguise; to misrepresent.—*vri.* to disguise oneself; to masquerade.

disfrutar, *vt.* to benefit by; to have the benefit of; to enjoy (good health, etc.).—*vi.* (de) to enjoy; to have.—**disfrute,** *m.* use, benefit.

disgregación, *f.* separation; dissociation.—**disgregar,** *vti.* [b] to separate, disperse.

disgustar, *vt.* to displease; to annoy; to offend.—*vr.* to be, or become displeased, hurt or annoyed; to fall out (with each other).—**disgusto,** *m.* disgust; affliction; displeasure; unpleasantness; quarrel; annoyance; grief.

disimular, *vt.* to dissimulate; to tolerate, overlook; to misrepresent. —**disimulo,** *m.* dissimulation; tolerance.

disipación, *f.* dissipation; waste.—**disipar,** *vt.* & *vr.* to dissipate; to vanish.—*vt.* to squander.

dislocación, *f.* dislocation; sprain.—**dislocar,** *vti.* [d] & *vri.* to dislocate, disjoint; to sprain.

disminución, *f.* diminution; retrenchment.—**disminuir,** *vti.* [23-e] to diminish, lessen; to detract from.—*vii.* to diminish, decrease.

disociación, *f.* separation, dissociation.—**disociar,** *vt.* to dissociate, separate.

disolución, *f.* dissolution; solution.—**disoluto,** *a.* dissolute.—**disolvente,** *m.* solvent.—**disolver,** *vti.* [47] to dissolve; to break up (as a meeting); to separate.—*vri.* to dissolve; to break up.

disonancia, *f.* harsh sound; discord; dissonance.—**disonante,** *a.* dissonant; discordant.

dispar, *a.* unlike; unequal; unmatched.

disparador, *m.* shooter; trigger; ratchet wheel.—**disparar,** *vt.* & *vi.* to shoot, discharge, fire; to throw, hurl.—*vr.* to dart off; to run away (as a horse); to go off (as a gun).

disparatar, *vi.* to talk nonsense; to blunder.—**disparate,** *m.* blunder; absurdity, nonsense.—**disparatero,** *n.* bungler.

disparejo, *a.* uneven.

disparidad, *f.* disparity, inequality.

disparo, *m.* shooting, discharge; shot; sudden dash.

dispendio, *m.* extravagance, prodigality.—**dispendioso,** *a.* costly; extravagant.

dispensa, *f.* exemption, dispensation. —**dispensar,** *vt.* to dispense; to excuse, pardon.—**dispensario,** *m.* dispensary; clinic.

dispersar, *vt.* to disperse, scatter, put to flight.—*vr.* to disperse, disband.—**disperso,** *a.* dispersed; scattered.

displicencia, *f.* disagreeableness; indifference.—**displicente,** *a.* disagreeable, unpleasant; peevish.

disponer, *vti.* [32-49] & *vii.* to dispose; to arrange; to resolve, direct, order.—*d. de,* to have at one's disposal.—*vri.* (para a a) to prepare oneself; to get ready (to); to make one's will.—**disponible,** *a.* available, disposable.—**disposición,** *f.* disposition, arrangement; disposal; aptitude; temper; proportion, order; specification.—**dispositivo,** *m.* device; mechanism; appliance.—**dispuesto,** *pp.* de DISPONER. —*a.* ready, disposed; fit; smart, clever; skillful.

disputa, *f.* dispute, controversy; debate.—**disputar,** *vt.* & *vi.* to dispute, debate, argue; to quarrel.

distancia, *f.* distance; interval; range.—*a d.,* from afar.—**distante,** *a.* distant, far.—**distar,** *vi.* to be distant; to be different.

distender, *vti.* [18] & *vri.* to distend, to expand.—**distensión,** *f.* distention, expansion.

distinción, *f.* distinction; honor, award.—**distinguir,** *vti.* [b] to distinguish, tell apart; to see clearly at a distance, make out, spot; to esteem.—*vri.* to distinguish oneself, to excel; (**de**) to differ, be distinguished.—**distintivo,** *a.* distinctive.—*m.* distinctive mark; badge, insignia.—**distinto,** *a.* distinct; clear; different.

distracción, *f.* absent-mindedness; lack of attention; pastime; oversight.—**distraer,** *vti.* [43] to distract; to amuse; to entertain; to lead astray.—*vri.* to be absentminded; to be inattentive; to amuse oneself.—**distraído,** *a.* inattentive; absent-minded.

distribución, *f.* distribution.—**distribuidor,** *n.* & *a.* distributor; distributing.—**distribuir,** *vti.* [23-e] to distribute, deal out; to sort (as mail).

distrito, *m.* district.

disturbio, *m.* disturbance.

disuelto, *pp.* of DISOLVER.—*a.* dissolved, melted.

disyuntiva, *f.* dilemma; alternative.

diurno, *a.* daily.

divagación, *f.* wandering, digression. —**divagar,** *vii.* [b] to roam, ramble; to digress.

diván, *m.* couch, divan.

divergencia, *f.* divergence, divergency. —**divergente,** *a.* divergent; dissenting.—**divergir,** *vii.* [e] to diverge; to dissent.

diversidad, *f.* diversity, variety.—**diversificar,** *vti.* [d] to diversify, vary.

diversión, *f.* entertainment, amusement.—**divertido,** *a.* amusing.—**divertir,** *vti.* [39] to amuse, entertain.—*vri.* to amuse oneself; to have a good time.

diverso, *a.* diverse, different; various.

dividendo, *m.* dividend.—**dividir,** *vt.* & *vi.* to divide.—*vr.* to divide; to split; to be divided; to separate (from), part company (with).

divinidad, *f.* divinity.—**divinizar,** *vti.* [a] to deify.—**divino,** *a.* divine.

divisa, *f.* badge, emblem.—*pl.* foreign currency.

divisar, *vt.* to sight, make out, perceive.

división, *f.* division; distribution; section; disunity.—**divido,** *a.* divided, disunited.—**divisor,** *n.* divider.—*a.* dividing.

divorciar, *vt.* to divorce; to separate. —*vr.* to get divorced.—**divorcio,** *m.* divorce; breach.

divulgación, *f.* disclosure, divulgation; publication.—**divulgar,** *vti.*

[b] to divulge; to disclose; to publish; to popularize.—*vri.* to become widespread.

dobladillo, *m.* (sewing) hem, border; trousers cuff.—**doblar,** *vt.* to double; to fold; to crease; to bend; to subdue.—*d. la esquina,* to turn the corner.—*vi.* to toll the knell.—*vr.* to bend; to bow, stoop; to submit.—**doble,** *a.* double, twofold, duplicate; thick, heavy; thick-set, strong.—**doblegar,** *vti.* [b] to sway, dominate, force to yield; to fold, bend. —*vr.* to yield, give in; to fold, bend.—**doblez,** *m.* crease, fold.—*f.* double-dealing; hypocrisy.

docena, *f.* dozen.

docente, *a.* educational; teaching.

dócil, *a.* docile; obedient; pliable, malleable.—**docilidad,** *f.* docility, tameness.

docto, *a.* learned, well-informed.—**doctor,** *n.* (academic) doctor.—**doctorado,** *m.* doctorate.—**doctorar,** *vt.* to confer (*vr.* to obtain) the degree of doctor.

doctrina, *f.* doctrine.

documentación, *f.* documentation; documents.—**documentado,** *a.* documented; well-informed; having the necessary documents or vouchers.—**documental,** *a.* documentary.—**documento,** *m.* document.

dogal, *m.* halter; hangman's noose.

dogma, *m.* dogma, tenet.—**dogmático,** *a.* dogmatical or dogmatic.

dolencia, *f.* aching; disease, ailment. —**doler,** *vii.* [26] to pain, ache; to hurt, grieve.—*vri.* to repent; to regret; to be moved, take pity; to complain.—**doliente,** *a.* aching, suffering; sorrowful; sick.—*mf.* mourner; sick person.—**dolor,** *m.* pain, aching, ache; sorrow, affliction. —**dolorido,** *a.* doleful, afflicted; painful.—**doloroso,** *a.* painful; pitiful.

doma, *f.* breaking in (of a horse).—**domador,** *n.* horsebreaker, tamer.—**domar,** *vt.* to tame; to break in; to subdue.—**domeñar,** *vt.* to tame, subdue; to dominate.—**domesticar,** *vti.* [d] to domesticate.—*vri.* to become tame.—**doméstico,** *a.* domestic. —*n.* household servant.

domiciliar, *vt.* to lodge.—*vr.* to take up residence; to dwell, reside.—**domiciliario,** *a.* domiciliary.—**domicilio,** *m.* domicile; home; residence.

dominación, *f.* dominion, domination; rule; power.—**dominante,** *a.* domineering; prevailing; dominant.—**dominar,** *vt.* to dominate; to stand out above (as a hill); to master (a subject, language, etc.); to subdue, repress.—*vr.* to control one-self.

dominio, *m.* domain; dominion; power, authority.

domingo, *m.* Sunday.—**dominguero,** *a.* done on Sunday; pertaining to Sunday.—**dominical,** *a.* pertaining or relative to Sunday.—**dominicano,** *n.* & *a.* Dominican.

don, *m.* gift, present; natural gift, knack; Don (title for a gentleman, equivalent to Mr. or Esq. in English, used only when the given name is mentioned).

donación, *f.* donation; contribution.

donaire, *m.* gracefulness, gentility.—**donairoso,** *a.* graceful, elegant; witty.

donante, *mf.* & *a.* giver; giving.—**donar,** *vt.* to donate, bestow.—**donativo,** *m.* donation, gift.

doncella, *f.* maidservant; maiden.—*a.* virginal.—**doncellez,** *f.* maidenhood.

donde (*interr.* **dónde**), *adv.* where; wherein; in which; wherever.—*a d.,* where, whereto.—*¿de dónde?* where from, whence?—*¿en dónde?* where?—*¿por dónde?* whereabout? by what way or road?—**dondequiera,** *adv.* anywhere; wherever.—*por d.,* everywhere, in every place.

Doña, *f.* title given to a lady, equivalent to the English Mrs. or Miss, used only when the given name is mentioned.

dorado, *a.* gilt, golden.—*m.* gilding.—**dorar,** *vt.* to gild; to palliate.

dormilón, *n.* (coll.) sleepy head.—**dormir,** [17] *vii.* to sleep.—*vri.* to go to sleep, fall asleep.—**dormitar,** *vi.* to doze, nap.—**dormitorio,** *m.* bedroom; dormitory.

dorsal, *a.* dorsal.—**dorso,** *m.* spine; back.

dosel, *m.* canopy; portiere.—**doselera,** *f.* valance.

dosificación, *f.* proportioning; dosage.—**dosificar,** *vti.* [d] to measure out the doses of.—**dosis** *f.* dose; quantity.

dotación, *f.* endowment, foundation; equipment; crew of warship; personnel (of office, etc.).—**dotado,** *a.* endowed with, gifted with.—**dotar,** *vt.* to bestow; to endow; to give a dowry to.—**dote,** *m.* & *f.* dowry.—*f. pl.* gifts, natural talents.

draga, *f.* dredge.—**dragado,** *m.* dredging.—**dragar,** *vti.* [b] to dredge.

drama, *m.* drama; play.—**dramático,** *a.* dramatic.—**dramatizar,** *vti.* [a] & *vii.* to dramatize.—**dramaturgo,** *n.* dramatist; playwright.

drenaje, *m.* drainage.—**drenar,** *vt.* to drain.

dril, *m.* drill, strong cloth.

droga, *f.* drug; medicine; trick.—**droguería,** *f.* drug store; drug trade.—**droguero,** *n.,* **droguista,** *mf.* druggist; impostor.

dúctil, *a.* ductile, malleable.

ducha, *f.* douche, shower bath.

ducho, *a.* skillful, expert.

duda, *f.* doubt.—**dudar,** *vi.* & *vt.* to doubt; to hesitate.—**dudoso,** *a.* doubtful, dubious; hazardous.

duelo, *m.* duel; sorrow, affliction; mourning; mourners; condolence.

duende, *m.* elf, hobgoblin.—**duendecillo,** *m.* pixie, little elf.

dueño, *n.* owner.

dueto, *m.* duet.

dulce, *a.* sweet; fresh (of water); pleasing; ductile (of metals).—*m.* confection, sweetmeat, candy.—**dulcería,** *f.* confectionery shop.—**dulcero,** *n.* confectioner.—**dulcificar,** *vti.* [d] to sweeten.

dulzaina, *f.* (mus.) recorder.

dulzón, *a.* saccharine.—**dulzura,** *f.* sweetness; kindliness.

duna, *f.* dune.

duplicación, *f.* duplication, doubling.—**duplicado,** *m.* copy, duplicate; counterpart.—*por d.,* in duplicate.—**duplicar,** *vti.* [d] to double, duplicate; to repeat.—**duplo,** *m.* double, twice as much.

duque, *m.* duke.—**duquesa,** *f.* duchess.

durabilidad, *f.* durability, permanence.—**durable,** *a.* durable, lasting.—**duración,** *f.* duration.—*ser de d.,* to wear well, last.—**duradero,** *a.* lasting, durable.—**durante,** *prep.* during.—**durar,** *vi.* to last; to endure; to wear well (of clothes).

durazno, *m.* peach; peach tree.

dureza, *f.* hardness, solidity; cruelty, unkindness.—**duro,** *a.* hard, steely; solid, firm; rigorous; rude.—*a duras penas,* with difficulty; scarcely.

durmiente, *a.* sleeping.—*mf.* sleeper.—*f.* (RR.) tie.

E

e, *conj.* and (used only before words that begin with *i* or *hi* not followed by *e*).

ebanista, *mf.* cabinetmaker.—**ebanistería,** *f.* cabinetwork.—**ébano,** *m.* ebony.

ebrio, *a.* intoxicated, drunk.

ebullición, *f.* boiling.

eclesiástico, *a.* ecclesiastical.—*m.* clergyman, priest.

eclipsar, *vt.* to eclipse; to outshine.—*vr.* to be eclipsed.—**eclipse,** *m.* eclipse.

eco, *m.* echo.—*hacer e.*, to become important or famous.

economía, *f.* economy.—*e. política,* economics.—*pl.* savings.—**económico,** *a.* economic(al); saving, thrifty.—**economista,** *mf.* economist.—**economizar,** *vti.* [a] to economize; to save.

ecuación, *f.* equation.

ecuador, *m.* equator.

ecuánime, *a.* equable, calm, serene.—**ecuanimidad,** *f.* equanimity.

ecuatoriano, *n.* & *a.* Ecuadorian.

echar, *vt.* to throw, cast; to expel; to dismiss, fire; to pour (as wine); to put (in, into); to turn (as a key); to give off, emit, eject; to bear (shoots, fruit); to play one's turn (in games).—*e. a,* to start, begin to.—*e. abajo,* to overthrow; to tear down, demolish.—*e. a perder,* to spoil, ruin.—*e. a pique,* to sink a ship.—*e. de menos,* to miss.—*e. de ver,* to notice.—*e. el bofe,* to work very hard.—*e. la cuenta,* to balance the account.—*e. mano,* to seize, grab.—*e. mano de,* to resort to.—*e. suertes,* to draw lots.—*vr.* to lie down; to throw oneself down.—*e. a perder,* to spoil; to become ruined.—*echárselas de,* to fancy oneself as.

edad, *f.* age.—*e. madura,* middle age.—*mayor de e.,* of (legal) age.—*menor de e.,* under age, minor.

edición, *f.* edition, issue; publication.

edicto, *m.* edict, proclamation.

edificación, *f.* edification · construction.—**edificante,** *a.* edifying; erecting.—**edificar,** *vti.* [d] & *vii.* to edify; to build, construct.—**edificio,** *m.* edifice, building, structure.

editar, *vt.* to publish.—**editor,** *n.* & *a.* publisher; publishing.—**editorial,** *mf.* & *a.* editorial.—*f.* publishing house.—*a.* publishing.

edredón, *m.* comforter, quilted blanket.

educación, *f.* education, upbringing; good breeding, politeness.—*e. física,* physical culture.—**educador,** *n.* & *a.* educator; educating.—**educar,** *vti.* [d] to educate, instruct, raise, train.—**educativo,** *a.* educational.

efectivo, *a.* effective; real, actual.—*hacer e.,* to cash (a check, etc.).—*m.* cash, specie.—*en e.,* in cash, in coin.—**efecto,** *m.* effect; impression; end, purpose.—*pl.* assets; goods; drafts.—*efectos públicos,* public securities.—*en e.,* as a matter of fact, actually.—*tener e.,* to become effective.—**efectuar,** *vt.* to effect, carry out, do, make.

eficacia, *f.* efficacy, efficiency.—**eficaz,** *a.* efficacious, effective, telling.—**eficiencia,** *f.* efficiency, effectiveness.—**eficiente,** *a.* efficient, effective.

efigie, *f.* effigy, image.

efusión, *f.* effusion, shedding; warmth of manner.—*e. de sangre,* bloodshed.—**efusivo,** *a.* effusive.

egipcio, *n.* & *a.* Egyptian.

egoísmo, *m.* selfishness.—**egoísta,** *a.* selfish.—*mf.* egoist.—**ególatra,** *mf.* = EGOTISTA.—**egolatría,** *f.* = EGOTISMO.—**egotismo,** *m.* egotism.—**egotista,** *mf.* & *a.* egotist; egotistic.

eje, *m.* axis; axle; (fig.) main point.

ejecución, *f.* execution; carrying out.—**ejecutar,** *vt.* to execute; to perform, carry out; (law) to levy, seize property.—**ejecutivo,** *a.* executive; executory.—*m.* executive (power or person).—**ejecutor,** *n.* executor; executer.—*e. de la justicia,* executioner.—**ejecutoria,** *f.* sentence, judgment; pedigree.

ejemplar, *a.* exemplary.—*m.* specimen, sample; copy.—**ejemplificar,** *vti.* [d] to be an example, typify.—**ejemplo,** *m.* example, instance.—*dar e.,* to set an example.

ejercer, *vti.* [a] to practice (a profession); to perform; to exert.—**ejercicio,** *m.* exercise; practice.—*e. fiscal,* fiscal year.—*hacer e.,* to exercise; (mil.) to drill.—**ejercitar,** *vt.* to exercise, to put into practice; to drill (troops); to train.—*vr.* to practice.—**ejército,** *m.* army.

ejido, *m.* common, public land.

ejote, *m.* (Mex.) stringbean.

el, *art. m. sing. (pl.* los) the.—**él,** *pron. m. sing. (pl.* ellos) he.

elaboración, *f.* elaboration, manufacture.—**elaborar,** *vt.* to elaborate; to manufacture.

elasticidad, *f.* elasticity.—**elástico,** *a.* elastic, springy.—*pl.* suspenders.

elección, *f.* election; choice.—**electivo,** *a.* elective.—**electo,** *ppi.* of ELEGIR; *a.* elect, chosen.—**elector,** *n.* & *a.* elector; electing.—*m.* elector, voter.—**electorado,** *m.* electorate.—**electoral,** *a.* electoral.

electricidad, *f.* electricity.—**electricista,** *mf.* electrician.—**eléctrico,** *a.* electric(al).—**electrificación,** *f.* electrification.—**electrificar,** *vti.* [d] to electrify.—**electrización,** *f.* electrification.—**electrizar,** *vti.* [a] to electrify.—*vri.* to become electrified.—**electrocutar,** *vt.* to electrocute.—**electrón,** *m.* electron.—**electrónica,** *f.* electronics.—**electrotecnia,** *f.* electrical engineering.

elefante, *n.* elephant.

elegancia, *f.* elegance, gracefulness;

neatness.—**elegante,** *a.* elegant, stylish, graceful.

elegible, *a.* eligible.—**elegir,** *vti.* [29-49-c] to elect; to choose.

elemental, *a.* elemental, elementary; fundamental.—**elemento,** *m.* element. —*pl.* elements, rudiments.

elenco, *m.* (theat.) cast; catalogue.

elevación, *f.* elevation; altitude; rise; rapture.—**elevador,** *m.* (Am.) elevator, hoist.—**elevar,** *vt.* to raise, heave; to exalt.—*vr.* to rise, soar.

eliminación, *f.* elimination.—**eliminar,** *vt.* to eliminate.

elocución, *f.* elocution; effective diction, style.—**elocuencia,** *f.* eloquence. —**elocuente,** *a.* eloquent.

elogiar, *vt.* to praise, extol.—**elogio,** *m.* praise, eulogy.

elote, *m.* (Mex., C.A.) ear of green corn; corn on the cob.

eludir, *vt.* to elude, avoid.

ella, *pron. f. sing.* (*pl.* **ellas**) she.— **ello,** *pron. neut. sing.* it.—*e. dirá,* the event will tell.—*e. es que,* the fact is that.—**ellos,** *pron. m. pl.;* **ellas,** *pron. f. pl.* they.

emancipación, *f.* emancipation.— **emancipar,** *vt.* to emancipate.—*vr.* to free oneself; to become free or independent.

embadurnar, *vt.* to smear.

embajada, *f.* embassy; errand, mission.—**embajador,** *n.* ambassador.

embalador, *n.* packer.—**embalaje,** *m.* packing, baling.—**embalar,** *vt.* to bale, pack.

embaldosado, *m.* tile floor.—**embaldosar,** *vt.* to pave with tiles or flagstones.

embalsamamiento, *m.* embalming.— **embalsamar,** *vt.* to embalm; to perfume.

embalse, *m.* dam.

embarazada, *a.* pregnant.—**embarazar,** *vti.* [a] to embarrass, hinder; to make pregnant.—**embarazo,** *m.* impediment; embarrassment, confusion; perplexity; pregnancy.—**embarazoso,** *a.* embarrassing; entangled, cumbersome.

embarcación, *f.* boat, ship; embarkation.—**embarcadero,** *n.* wharf, pier. —**embarcador,** *n.* shipper.—**embarcar,** *vti.* [d] to ship; to embark.— *vri.* to embark; to board (ship or train).

embargar, *vti.* [b] to restrain, suspend; (law) to embargo, to seize.— **embargo,** *m.* embargo, seizure.— *sin e.,* notwithstanding, however, nevertheless.

embarque, *m.* shipment (of goods).

embarrancar, *vii.* [d] & *vri.* to run aground.

embarrar, *vt.* to smear; to daub; to vilify.—*vr.* to be covered with mud; to lose one's self-respect.

embate, *m.* dashing of the waves; sudden impetuous attack.—*embates de la fortuna,* sudden reverses of fortune.

embaucador, *n.* impostor.—**embaucar,** *vti.* [d] to deceive, trick, fool.

embebecimiento, *m.* amazement; rapture; absorption.—**embeber,** *vt.* to imbibe, absorb; to soak.—*vi.* to shrink.—*vr.* to be enraptured; to be absorbed.

embelesamiento, *m.* rapture, ecstasy. —**embelesar,** *vt.* to charm, delight.— *vr.* to be charmed, or delighted.— **embeleso,** *m.* rapture, delight; charm.

embellecer, *vti.* [3] to beautify, embellish.—**embellecimiento,** *m.* embellishment, beautifying.

emberrenchinarse, emberrincharse, *vr.* (coll.) to throw a tantrum.

embestida, *f.* assault, violent attack, onset.—**embestir,** *vti.* [29] to assail, attack; to make a drive on.—*vii.* to attack, rush.

embetunar, *vt.* to blacken; to polish (shoes).

emblema, *m.* emblem, symbol.

embobar, *vt.* to enchant, fascinate.— *vr.* to be struck with astonishment.

embocadura, *f.* entrance by a narrow passage; mouthpiece of a wind instrument; mouth of a river.—**embocar,** *vti.* [d] to enter through a narrow passage.

emborrachar, *vt.* to intoxicate.—*vr.* to become intoxicated, get drunk.

émbolo, *m.* piston; (med.) embolus.

embolsar, *vt.* to put into a purse.— *vr.* to pocket, put into one's pocket.

emborronar, *vt.* to blot.—*vt. & vi.* to scribble.

emboscada, *f.* ambush, ambuscade.— **emboscar,** *vti.* [d] to place in ambush.—*vri.* to lie in ambush.

embotado, *a.* blunt, dull.—**embotamiento,** *m.* blunting; bluntness, dullness.—**embotar,** *vt.* to blunt, to dull (an edge or point); to enervate, debilitate; to dull.—*vr.* to become dull.

embotellar, *vt.* to bottle; to bottle up.

embozado, *a.* muffled, with face covered (with a cloak).—**embozar,** *vti.* [a] to muffle; to cloak; to muzzle.— *vr.* to muffle oneself up.

embragar, *vti.* [b] to throw in the clutch.—**embrague,** *m.* clutch; coupling.

embreado, *a.* tarry.—**embrear,** *vt.* to tar.

embriagador, *a.* spirituous, intoxicating; ravishing.—**embriagar,** *vti.* [b] to intoxicate; to enrapture.—*vri.* to get drunk.—**embriaguez,** *f.* intoxication, drunkenness; rapture.

embrión, *m.* embryo.

embrollar, *vt.* to entangle, mess up; to ensnare, embroil.—**embrollo,** *m.* tangle; trickery, deception; embroilment.

embromar, *vt.* to banter, tease; to vex, annoy; (Am.) to harm.—*vr.* to be annoyed, disgusted.

embrujar, *vt.* to bewitch.—**embruje,** *m.* bewitchment.

embrutecer, *vti.* [3] to brutalize; to stupefy, stultify.—*vri.* to become brutalized; to grow stupid.

embudo, *m.* funnel.

embullar, *vt.* (Am.) to incite to revelry.—*vi.* (Am.) to make noise.—*vr.* (Am.) to revel, make merry.—**embullo,** *m.* (Am.) gaiety, revelry.

embuste, *m.* lie; trick, fraud.—**embustero,** *n.* liar; trickster, cheat.

embutido, *m.* sausage; inlaid work.—**embutir,** *vt.* to inlay, emboss; to insert; to stuff; (coll.) to cram; to eat much.

emergencia, *f.* emergence, emergency.—**emergente,** *a.* emergent, issuing.—**emerger,** *vii.* [c] to emerge, arise.

emigración, *f.* emigration.—**emigrado,** *n.* emigrant; émigré.—**emigrante,** *mf.* & *a.* emigrant.—**emigrar,** *vi.* to emigrate.

eminencia, *f.* eminence; height; outstanding person.—**eminente,** *a.* eminent; high, lofty.

emisario, *m.* emissary.—**emisión,** *f.* emission; issue (of paper money, bonds, etc.); radiation.—*emisiones radiofónicas,* broadcasting.—**emisor,** *a.* emitting; broadcasting.—*m.* radio transmitter.—*f.* broadcasting station.—**emitir,** *vt.* to emit, send forth; to issue (as bonds, etc.); to broadcast.

emoción, *f.* emotion.—**emocional,** *a.* emotional.—**emocionante,** *a.* moving, impressive, thrilling.—**emocionar,** *vt.* to touch, move, shock.—*vr.* to be moved, touched.—**emotivo,** *a.* moving, emotive.

empacador, *n.* packer.—**empacar,** *vti.* [d] to pack; to bale.—*vri.* (Am.) (coll.) to put on airs.

empachar, *vt.* to embarrass; to cram; to cause indigestion.—*vr.* to be embarrassed; to suffer indigestion.—**empacho,** *m.* bashfulness; embarrassment; indigestion.—*sin e.,* without ceremony; unconcernedly.

empadronar, *vt.* to register, take the census of.

empalagar, *vti.* [b] to pall, cloy; to bother.—**empalagoso,** *a.* cloying, too rich or sweet; wearisome, boresome.

empalizada, *f.* palisade, stockade.

empalmar, *vt.* to couple, join; to splice.—*vi.* (RR.) to branch; to join.—**empalme,** *m.* joint, connection; (RR.) junction.

empanada, *f.* meat pie.—**empanadilla,** *f.* small meat pie.—**empanar,** *vt.,* **empanizar,** *vti.* [a] to bread.

empañar, *vt.* to dim, blur, mist; to soil (reputation).

empapar, *vt.* to imbibe; to soak, drench.—*vr.* (en) to imbibe; to be soaked (in); to steep oneself (in).

empapelador, *n.* paperhanger.—**empapelar,** *vt.* to paper; to wrap up in paper.

empaque, *m.* packing; appearance, air; (Am.) boldness, impudence.—**empaquetador,** *n.* packer.—**empaquetadura,** *f.* packing; gasket.—**empaquetar,** *vt.* to pack; to stuff.—*vr.* to dress up.

emparedado, *a.* & *n.* recluse.—*m.* sandwich.—**emparedar,** *vt.* to wall, shut up.

emparejar, *vt.* & *vi.* to level, smooth; to match.

emparentar, *vii.* [1] to become related by marriage.

emparrado, *m.* vine arbor.

empastar, *vt.* to fill a tooth; to paste; to bind books.—**empaste,** *m.* filling (of a tooth); binding.

empatar, *vt.* to equal; to tie (in voting or games); (Am.) to join, tie.—**empate,** *m.* tie (in voting or games); joint.

empecinado, *a.* stubborn.—**empecinarse,** *vr.* (en) to persist (in), be stubborn (about).

empedernido, *a.* hard-hearted; hardened.

empedrado, *m.* stone pavement.—**empedrar,** *vti.* [1] to pave with stones.

empeine, *m.* instep.

empellón, *m.* jostle, shove.—*a empellones,* pushing, by pushing rudely.

empeñado, *a.* determined, persistent.—**empeñar,** *vt.* to pawn; to pledge; to engage.—*vr.* (en) to persist (in); to insist; to begin (a battle); to go into debt.—**empeño,** *m.* pledge, pawn; engagement; earnest desire; persistence; determination.—*casa de empeños,* pawnshop.—*con e.,* eagerly.

empeoramiento, *m.* deterioration.—**empeorar,** *vt.* to impair; to make worse.—*vi.* & *vr.* to grow worse.

empequeñecer, *vti.* [3] to make smaller, diminish; to belittle.

emperador, *m.* emperor.—**emperatriz,** *f.* empress.

emperchar, *vt.* to hang on a perch.—*vr.* (coll.) to dress up.

emperejilar, emperifollar, *vt. & vr.* to dress elaborately, to doll up.

emperramiento, *m.* obstinacy.—**emperrarse,** *vr.* (en) (coll.) to be obstinate or stubborn (about).

empezar, *vti.* [1-a] & *vii.* to begin.

empicotar, *vt.* to pillory; to picket.

empinado, *a.* steep; high, lofty.—**empinar,** *vt.* to raise; to tip, incline.—*e. el codo,* to drink heavily. —*vr.* to stand on tiptoe; to tower, rise high; (aer.) to zoom.

emplasto, *m.* plaster, poultice.

emplazamiento, *m.* (law) summons.—**emplazar,** *vti.* [a] to summon.

empleado, *n.* employee.—**emplear,** *vt.* to employ; to engage, hire.—*vr.* to be employed.—**empleo,** *m.* employ, employment, job; use.

emplomar, *vt.* to lead; to put lead seals on.

emplumar, *vt.* to feather; to tar and feather.

empobrecer, *vti.* [3] to impoverish.—*vri.* to become poor.—**empobrecimiento,** *m.* impoverishment.

empolvar, *vt. & vr.* to cover with dust; to powder.

empollar, *vt.* to hatch, brood.

emponzoñamiento, *m.* poisoning.—**emponzoñar,** *vt.* to poison; to corrupt.

empotrar, *vt.* to embed; to fix in a wall; to splice.

emprendedor, *n. & a.* enterpriser; enterprising.—**emprender,** *vt.* to undertake, engage in.—*e. a,* or *con,* to address, accost.

empreñar, *vt.* to make pregnant.

empresa, *f.* enterprise, undertaking; company, firm; management of a theater.—**empresario,** *n.* promoter; contractor; theatrical manager; impresario.

empréstito, *m.* loan.—*e. público,* government loan.

empujar, *vt.* to push, impel, shove. —**empuje,** *m.* push, shove; energy; (eng.) thrust.—**empujón,** *m.* push, violent shove.—*a empujones,* pushing, jostling.

empuñadura, *f.* hilt (of a sword); handle, grip.—**empuñar,** *vt.* to clinch, grip.

emulsión, *f.* emulsion.—**emulsionar,** *vt.* to emulsify.

en, *prep.* in; at; on, upon; to; into.

enagua(s), *f.* petticoat, slip.

enajenación, *f.,* **enajenamiento,** *m.* alienation (of property); absence of mind; rapture.—*e. mental,* mental derangement.—**enajenar,** *vt.* to alienate; to transfer (property); to transport, enrapture.—*vr.* to be enraptured.

enaltecer, *vti.* [3] to extol, exalt.

enamoradizo, *a.* inclined to fall in love.—**enamorado,** *a.* fond of love-making; in love, enamored.—*n.* lover; sweetheart.—**enamoramiento,** *m.* love, being in love; courting, love-making.—**enamorar,** *vt.* to inspire love in; to make love to, woo. —*vr.* to fall in love.—**enamoriscarse,** *vri.* [d] (coll.) to become infatuated.

enano, *a.* dwarfish, small.—*n.* dwarf.

enarbolar, *vt.* to hoist, raise high, hang out (a flag, etc.).

enardecer, *vti.* [3] to fire with passion, excite, inflame.—*vri.* to be kindled, get excited, inflamed (with passion).—**enardecimiento,** *m.* ardor; passion; inflaming; excitement.

encabezamiento, *m.* headline, heading, title; tax roll.—**encabezar,** *vti.* [a] to draw up (a tax roll); to put a heading or title to; to head, lead.

encabritarse, *vr.* to rear, rise up on the hind legs.

encadenamiento, *m.* chaining; linking.—**encadenar,** *vt.* to chain; to enslave; to link together (as thoughts).

encajar, *vt.* to fit in, insert, adjust; to join.—*vi.* to fit snugly; to fit, suit, be appropriate.—*vr.* to intrude; to squeeze oneself in.—**encaje,** *m.* lace, inlaid work; adjusting, fitting or joining together; socket.

encajonar, *vt.* to box; to case; to narrow.

encallar, *vi.* to run aground.

encallecer, *vti.* [3] & *vii.* to get corns or calluses.—*vri.* to become hardened or callous.

encaminar, *vt.* to guide; to direct.—*vr.* (a) to take the road (to); to be on the way (to).

encandilar, *vt.* to dazzle; to daze, bewilder; (coll.) to stir (the fire).

encanecer, *vii.* [3] to grow gray-haired; to grow old.

encanijamiento, *m.* frailty, lack of development.—**encanijar,** *vt.* to weaken (a baby) by poor nursing.—*vr.* to pine; to become emaciated.

encantado, *a.* enchanted, delighted, charmed; haunted.—**encantador,** *n.* charmer; enchanter.—*a.* charming; delightful.—**encantamiento,** *m.* enchantment.—**encantar,** *vt.* to enchant, charm; to delight; to bewitch.—**encanto,** *m.* enchantment, charm; delight.

encañonar, *vt.* to level a gun at.

encapotamiento, *m.* cloudiness.—**encapotarse,** *vr.* to become cloudy.

encapricharse, *vr.* to indulge in whims; to be stubborn.

encaramar, *vt. & vr.* to raise; to elevate; to extol; to climb; to perch upon.

encarar, *vi.* to face.—*vt.* to aim.—*vr.* (con) to face, be face to face.

encarcelación, *f.*, **encarcelamiento,** *m.* imprisonment.—**encarcelar,** *vt.* to imprison.

encarecer, *vti.*, [3] *vii. & vri.* to raise the price; to extol; to enhance.—**encarecidamente,** *adv.* eagerly, earnestly.—**encarecimiento,** *m.* enhancement.

encargado, *a.* in charge.—*n.* person in charge; agent; foreman; (E.U.) superintendent.—**encargar,** *vti.* [b] to entrust, put under the care (of a person); to order (goods, etc.).—*vri.* to take charge.—**encargo,** *m.* charge, commission; errand; assignment; (com.) order.

encariñamiento, *m.* fondness, attachment.—**encariñarse,** *vr.* (con) to become fond (of).

encarnación, *f.* incarnation; personification.—**encarnado,** *a.* incarnate; flesh-colored; red.—**encarnar,** *vi.* to become incarnate.—*vt.* to incarnate; to embody; to bait (a fishhook).

encarnizado, *a.* bloody; fierce, hard-fought.—**encarnizarse,** *vri.* [a] to become enraged; to fight with fury.—*e. con* or *en,* to be merciless to; to treat inhumanely.

encarrilar, *vt.* to put on the right track; to set right.

encasillar, *vt.* to pigeonhole; to include in a list of (candidates).

encasquetar, *vt. & vr.* to pull down (one's hat) tight.

encasquillar, *vr.* to stick, get stuck (a bullet in a gun).

encastillado, *a.* lofty, haughty.—**encastillarse,** *vr.* to shut oneself up in a castle; to be unyielding or headstrong.

encausar, *vt.* to prosecute, indict.

encauzar, *vti.* [a] to channel; to conduct through channels; to guide, direct.

encenagarse, *vri.* [b] to wallow in dirt, mire, or vice.

encendedor, *m.* (cigarette, etc.) lighter.—**encender,** *vti.* [18] to light, kindle.—*vri.* to take fire; to light up.—**encendido,** *a.* inflamed; red.—*m.* (engine) ignition.

encerado, *a.* waxed; wax-colored.—*m.* oilcloth; tarpaulin; blackboard.—**encerar,** *vt.* to wax.

encerrar, *vti.* [1] to lock or shut up; to confine; to contain, involve.—*vri.* to live in seclusion; to be locked up.—**encerrona,** *f.* allurement.

encía, *f.* gum (of the mouth).

enciclopedia, *f.* encyclopedia.

encierro, *m.* confinement; act of closing or locking up; retreat; prison; fold (of cattle).

encima, *adv.* above; at the top; overhead; over and above, besides; in addition, to boot.—*e. de,* on, upon.—*por e.,* superficially, hastily.—*por e. de,* over, above; regardless of.

encina, *f.* evergreen oak, live oak.

encinta, *a.* pregnant.

encintado, *m.* sidewalk curb.

enclenque, *a.* weak, feeble, sickly.

encoger, *vti.* [c] to contract, shorten, shrink.—*vri.* to shrink; to shrivel.—*encogerse de hombros,* to shrug the shoulders.—**encogimiento,** *m.* contraction, shrinkage; bashfulness.

encolado, *m.*, **encoladura,** *f.* gluing; priming; sizing.—**encolar,** *vt.* to glue; to stick.

encolerizar, *vti.* [a] to anger.—*vri.* to become angry.

encomendar, *vti.* [1] to entrust, commend.—*vri.* to entrust oneself; to pray.

encomiar, *vt.* to praise, eulogize.—**encomio,** *m.* praise, testimonial, eulogy.

encomienda, *f.* commission, charge.—*e. postal,* (Am.) parcel post.

enconar, *vt.* to inflame; to infect.—*vr.* to rankle; to fester, become infected.—**encono,** *m.* rancor, ill-will; soreness; sore spot.

encontrado, *a.* opposite; in front; opposed.—**encontrar,** *vti.* [12] to find; to meet.—*vii.* to meet; to collide.—*vri.* to meet; to collide; to be, find oneself; to feel (app. to health); to be opposed to each other; to conflict; to find; (con) to meet, come across or upon.—**encontronazo,** *m.* collision; bump.

encopetado, *a.* presumptuous; of high social standing.

encordar, *vti.* [12] to string (instruments); to lash or bind with ropes.

encorvar, *vt. & vr.* to bend, curve.

encrespamiento, *m.* curling; fury, roughness (of the sea, etc.).—**encrespar,** *vt.* to curl; to set (the hair) on end; to ruffle (the feathers).—*vr.* to become rough (the sea, the waves).

encrucijada, *f.* crossroads, ambush.

encuadernación, *f.* binding (books); bindery.—**encuadernador,** *n.* bookbinder.—**encuadernar,** *vt.* to bind (books).

encubierto, *ppi.* of ENCUBRIR.—**encubridor,** *n.* & *a.* concealer; concealing; accomplice.—**encubrimiento,** *m.* concealment.—**encubrir,** *vti.* [49] to conceal, hide, cloak.

encuentro, *m.* encounter, meeting; collision, clash; find, finding; (mil.) encounter, fight.—*salir al e. de,* to go to meet; to encounter.

encumbrado, *a.* high, elevated; lofty. **encumbramiento,** *m.* elevation, exaltation; height, eminence.—**encumbrar,** *vt.* to raise, elevate.—*vi.* to ascend.—*vr.* to rise; to be proud, rate oneself high.

encurtido, *m.* pickle.—**encurtir,** *vt.* to pickle.

enchapado, *m.* veneer; plates or sheets forming a cover or lining.—**enchapar,** *vt.* to veneer; to cover with metal plates or sheets.

encharcarse, *vri.* [d] to form puddles.

enchilada, *f.* (Mex.) pancake of maize with chili.

enchufar, *vt.* & *vr.* to plug in; to fit (a tube) into another; to telescope.—**enchufe,** *m.* socket joint; sliding of one thing into another; (elec.) plug; socket; outlet.

endeble, *a.* feeble, weak; flimsy.

endemoniado, *a.* devilish, fiendish, perverse.—**endemoniar,** *vt.* & *vr.* (coll.) to irritate.

endentado, *a.* serrated.—**endentar,** *vti.* [1] & *vii.* to gear, engage.

enderezamiento, *m.* straightening; setting right.—**enderezar,** *vti.* [a] to straighten; to right, set right.—*vri.* to straighten up.

endeudarse, *vr.* to contract debts.

endiablado, *a.* devilish, diabolical; perverse, wicked.

endilgar, *vti.* [b] to spring something on (a person).

endiosar, *vt.* to deify.—*vr.* to be elated with pride.

endosar, *vt.* to indorse (a draft, etc.).—**endosatario,** *n.* indorsee.—**endose, endoso,** *m.* indersement.

endulzar, *vti.* [a] to sweeten; to soften.

endurecer, *vti.* [3] & *vri.* to harden; to inure.—**endurecido,** *a.* hard, hardy; inured.—**endurecimiento,** *m.* hardness; hardening; hard-heartedness.

enema, *m.* enema.

enemigo, *a.* hostile; inimical.—*n.* enemy, foe.—*m.* (mil.) enemy.—*el e. malo,* the devil.—**enemistad,** *f.* enmity, hatred.—**enemistar,** *vt.* to make enemies of.—*vr.* (con) to become an enemy (of); to fall out (with).

energía, *f.* energy; power.—**enérgico,** *a.* energetic, lively.

energúmeno, *n.* violent, impulsive person; person possessed with a devil.

enero, *m.* January.

enervar, *vt.* to enervate, weaken.—*vr.* to become weak.

enfadar, *vt.* to vex, anger.—*vr.* to become angry.—**enfado,** *m.* vexation, anger; trouble, drudgery.—**enfadoso,** *a.* annoying, troublesome.

enfangar, *vti.* [b] & *vri.* to soil with mud; (coll.) to soil one's reputation.—*vr.* to sink (into vice, etc.).

enfardar, *vt.* to pack, bale.

énfasis, *m.* emphasis.—**enfático,** *a.* emphatic; bombastic.

enfermar, *vi.* (Am. *vr.*) to fall ill, be taken ill.—*vt.* to make ill.—**enfermedad,** *f.* illness, sickness.—**enfermera,** *f.* nurse.—**enfermería,** *f.* infirmary, sanitarium.—**enfermero,** *m.* male nurse.—**enfermizo,** *a.* sickly; unhealthful.—**enfermo,** *a.* ill, sick.—*n.* patient.

enfiestarse, *vr.* (Am.) to have a good time; to go on a spree.

enfilar, *vt.* to place in a row or line.

enflaquecer, *vti.* [3] to make thin or lean.—*vii.* & *vri.* to become thin, lose weight; to weaken.—**enflaquecimiento,** *m.* loss of flesh; thinness.

enfocar, *vti.* [d] to focus, focus on.—**enfoque,** *m.* focusing; approach (to a problem, etc.).

enfrascarse, *vri.* [d] to be entangled or involved; to be absorbed, engrossed (in work, affairs, etc.).

enfrentar, *vt.* to confront, put face to face; to face.—*vr.* to confront, face, meet face to face.—*e. con,* to face; to oppose.—**enfrente,** *adv.* opposite, in front.—*de e.,* opposite, across (the street, etc.).

enfriamiento, *m.* refrigeration; cooling; cold, chill (illness).—**enfriar,** *vt.* to cool.—*vr.* to cool; to cool off or down; to become chilled.

enfundar, *vt.* to case, put into a case (as a pillow); to fill up, stuff.

enfurecer, *vti.* [3] to enrage, make furious.—*vri.* to rage; to become furious or stormy.

enfurruñarse, *vr.* (coll.) to become angry; to grumble.

engalanar, *vt.* to adorn, deck; (naut.) to dress.—*vr.* to dress up, doll up.

engallado, *a.* erect, upright; haughty.—**engallarse,** *vr.* to draw oneself up arrogantly.

enganchar, *vt.* to hook, hitch; to ensnare; to press into military service.

—vr. to engage; to enlist in the army.—enganche, m. hooking; enlistment in the army.

engañador, n. & a. deceiver; deceiving.—engañar, vt. to deceive; to cheat; to fool, hoax; to while away (time).—vr. to deceive oneself; to make a mistake, be mistaken.—engaño, m. deceit, fraud; hoax; mistake, misunderstanding.—engañoso, a. deceitful, artful, misleading.

engarce, m. linking; setting (of precious stone).

engarzar, vti. [a] to link; to set (precious stone).

engarrotarse, vr. to become numb with cold; (fig.) to be very cold, frozen.

engastar, vt. to set (jewels).—engaste, m. setting (of stones).

engatusar, vt. (coll.) to inveigle, wheedle, cajole.

engendrar, vt. to father, sire, engender, generate, procreate; to bear.—engendro, m. shapeless embryo; badly-made thing.

englobar, vt. to inclose, embody.

engolfarse, vr. to become engrossed, absorbed into.

engomar, vt. to gum, to size; to glue.

engordar, vt. to fatten.—vi. & (Am.) vr. to become fat.

engorro, m. embarrassment, nuisance.—engorroso, a. troublesome, annoying.

engranaje, m. gear, gearing.—engranar, vi. to gear; to interlock.

engrandecer, vti. [3] to aggrandize; to enlarge; to exalt, extol; to magnify.—engrandecimiento, m. increase, enlargement; exaltation.

engrasador, m. oiler, lubricator.—engrasar, vt. to grease, oil, lubricate.—engrase, m. lubrication, oiling, greasing.

engreído, a. conceited.—engreimiento, m. conceit, presumption, vanity.—engreír, vti. [35] to encourage the conceit of, to make vain; to elate.—vri. to become vain or conceited.

engrifar, vt. & vr. to curl, crisp.

engrosar, vti. [12] to enlarge; to increase; to thicken, broaden.—vii. & (Am.) vri. to become fat; to increase, swell.

engrudo, m. paste, glue.

engullir, vti. [27] to gobble, gorge, wolf.

enhebrar, vt. to thread; to string.

enhiesto, a. erect, upright.

enhorabuena, f. congratulation, felicitation.

enigma, m. enigma, riddle.—enigmático, a. enigmatic.

enjabonadura, f. soaping.—enjabonar, vt. to soap; to wash with soap; (coll.) to soft-soap.

enjaezar, vti. [a] to harness.

enjambre, m. swarm of bees; crowd, agglomeration.

enjaular, vt. to cage; to confine.

enjuagar, vti. [b] & vri. to rinse, rinse the mouth.—enjuagatorio, m. rinsing; mouth wash; finger bowl.—enjuague, m. rinse, rinsing; mouthwash; plot, scheme.

enjugar, vti. [b-49] to dry; to wipe.—vri. to dry oneself.

enjuiciamiento, m. (law) indictment.—enjuiciar, vt. to indict; to carry on (a case); to pass judgment on.

enjundia, f. grease or fat of fowl; substance.

enjuto, ppi. of ENJUGAR.—a. dried; lean, skinny.

enladrillar, vt. to pave with bricks.

enlace, m. connection; tie; link; marriage; (mil.) scout.

enlatar, vt. to can.

enlazar, vti. [a] to lace, bind; to rope, lasso.—vri. to interlock, join; to marry.

enlodar, vt. to soil with mud.—vr. to get muddy.

enloquecer, vti. [3] to madden, drive insane.—vii. & vri. to become insane.—enloquecimiento, m. madness.

enlosado, m. flagstone pavement.—enlosar, vt. to pave with tiles or slabs.

enlutar, vt. to put in mourning; to darken, sadden.—vr. to go into mourning.

enmarañamiento, m. entanglement.—enmarañar, vt. to tangle (as hair, etc.); to entangle, involve in difficulties; to embroil.

enmascarar, vt. to mask.—vr. to masquerade, put on a mask.

enmasillar, vt. to putty, cement.

enmendar, vti. [1] to amend, correct; to repair; to reform.—vri. to mend, reform.—enmienda, f. emendation, correction, amendment.

enmohecer, vti. [3] & vri. to rust; to mold.—enmohecimiento, m. rusting; molding.

enmudecer, vti. [3] hush, silence.—vii. to become dumb; to be silent.

ennegrecer, vti. [3] to blacken; to darken, obscure.—ennegrecimiento, m. blackening.

ennoblecer, vti. [3] to ennoble; to impart dignity to.

enojadizo, a. fretful, peevish, ill-tempered.—enojado, a. angry, cross.—enojar, vt. to make angry, irritate; to annoy.—**enojo**, *m.* anger; annoyance.—**enojoso**, *a.* troublesome; annoying.

enorgullecer, *vti.* [3] to make proud. —*vri.* to be proud; to swell with pride.—**enorgullecimiento**, *m.* pride; haughtiness.

enorme, *a.* enormous.—**enormidad**, *f.* enormousness, great quantity or size; enormity, atrocity.

enraizar, *vii.* [a] & *vri.* to take root.

enramada, *f.* bower, arbor; grove.

enrarecer, *vti.* [3] to thin, rarefy.— *vri.* to become thin or rarefied.— **enrarecimiento**, *m.* rarefaction, rarity.

enredadera, *f.* (bot.) climber; vine.— **enredador**, *n.* entangler; tattler.— **enredar**, *vt.* to entangle, snarl; to puzzle; to mess up, involve in difficulties; to lay, set (snares, nets).— *vr.* to get entangled, snarled; to get involved.—**enredo**, *m.* tangle, entanglement; puzzle; mischievous lie; plot.

enrejado, *m.* railing, grating; lattice. —**enrejar**, *vt.* to fence with railings; to put a trellis or lattice on.

enrevesado, *a.* frisky; difficult.

enriquecer, *vti.* [3] to enrich.—*vri.* to become rich.

enrojecer, *vti.* [3] to redden; to make red-hot.—*vri.* to blush; to turn red.

enrolar, *vt.* to sign on (a crew); to enroll; to enlist.—*vr.* to become a crew member.

enrollar, *vt.* to roll, wind, wrap up.

enronquecer, *vti.* [3] to make hoarse. —*vii.* & *vri.* to get hoarse.—**enronquecimiento**, *m.* hoarseness.

enroscar, *vti.* [d] to twine, to twist. —*vri.* to curl up, roll up.

ensalada, *f.* salad; hodgepodge, medley.—**ensaladera**, *f.* salad dish or bowl.

ensalmo, *m.* enchantment, spell, charm.—*como por e.*, or *por e.*, as if miraculously, suddenly and unexpectedly.

ensalzar, *vti.* [a] to extol, exalt, praise.

ensambladura, *f.*, **ensamble**, *m.* joinery; joint.—**ensamblar**, *vt.* to join, couple, connect.

ensanchamiento, *m.* widening, enlargement, expansion.—**ensanchar**, *vt.* to widen, enlarge.—*e. el corazón*, to cheer up.—*vr.* to expand, enlarge.—**ensanche**, *m.* enlargement, widening, expansion.

ensangrentar, *vti.* [1] & *vri.* to stain with blood.—*vri.* to cover oneself with blood.

ensañamiento, *m.* ferocity, cruelty.—

ensañarse, *vr.* to vent one's fury; to be merciless.

ensartar, *vt.* to string (as beads); to thread; to link.

ensayar, *vt.* to practice, try, rehearse; to test; to assay.—*vr.* to train oneself, practice.—**ensayista**, *mf.* essay writer.—**ensayo**, *m.* test; essay; trial, experiment; rehearsal; preparatory practice.

ensenada, *f.* creek; cove.

enseña, *f.* standard, colors, ensign.

enseñado, *a.* accustomed; trained.— **enseñanza**, *f.* teaching; education. —**enseñar**, *vt.* to teach; to train; to show, point out.

enseñorear, *vt.* to lord, to domineer. —*vr.* to take possession (of a thing).

enseres, *m. pl.* chattels; fixtures, accessories; implements; household goods.

enseriarse, *vr.* (Am.) to become serious; to become angry.

ensillar, *vt.* to saddle.

ensimismarse, *vr.* to become absorbed in thought.

ensoberbecer, *vti.* [3] to make proud. —*vri.* to become proud and haughty.

ensopar, *vt.* to steep, soak; to drench.

ensordecedor, *a.* deafening.—**ensordecer**, *vti.* [3] to deafen.—*vii.* & *vri.* to become deaf.—**ensordecimiento**, *m.* deafness.

ensortijar, *vt.* & *vr.* to curl, form ringlets.

ensuciar, *vt.* to stain, soil, dirty.— *vr.* to soil one's bed, clothes, etc.; to get dirty; (coll.) to be dishonest.

ensueño, *m.* dream; illusion, fantasy.

entablar, *vt.* to cover with boards; to plank; to initiate, start (as a negotiation, etc.); to bring (a suit or action).—**entablillar**, *vt.* (surg.) to splint.

entallar, *vt.* to notch.—*vi.* to fit well or closely (a dress).

entarimado, *m.* parquet floor.—**entarimar**, *vt.* to floor with boards, parquet.

ente, *m.* entity, being; (coll.) guy.

enteco, *a.* sickly; thin, skinny.

entenada, *f.* (Am.) stepdaughter.— **entenado**, *m.* (Am.) stepson.

entendederas, *f. pl.* understanding, brains.—**entender**, *vti.* [18] & *vii.* to understand.—*dar a e.*, to insinuate, hint.—*e. de*, to be an expert in, know.—*vr.* to understand one another; to be understood; to be meant.—*entenderse con*, to have to do with; to deal with.—*m.* understanding, opinion.—*a mi e.*, *según mi e.*, in my opinion, according to my understanding.—**entendido**, *a.*

expert; able; posted.—*tener e.*, to understand.—**entendimiento,** *m.* intellect, mind; understanding; comprehension.

enterado, *a.* posted, informed.—*no darse por e.*, to ignore; to pretend not to understand.—**enterar,** *vt.* to inform, acquaint, advise.—*enterarse de*, to learn, become informed about or familiar with, find out about.

entereza, *f.* entirety; integrity; fortitude, firmness; presence of mind.

enterizo, *a.* of, or in, one piece; whole.

enternecedor, *a.* moving, touching.—**enternecer,** *vti.* [3] to soften; to touch, move to pity.—*vri.* to be moved to pity; to be affected.—**enternecimiento,** *m.* compassion, pity, softening.

entero, *a.* entire, whole; perfect; honest, upright; unqualified, complete; pure; strong, vigorous; uncastrated (animal).—*por e.*, entirely, fully.—*m.* (arith.) integer.

enterrador, *m.* gravedigger.—**enterramiento,** *m.* burial, funeral.—**enterrar,** *vti.* [1] to bury, inter.

entibiar, *vt.* to make lukewarm; to temper.—*vr.* to cool down.

entidad, *f.* entity; value, importance.

entierro, *m.* burial; funeral.

entintar, *vt.* to ink, ink in (a drawing); to tint or dye.

entoldar, *vt.* to cover with an awning; to adorn with hangings.—*vr.* to swell with pride.

entonación, *f.* modulation; intonation.—**entonado,** *a.* haughty, snobbish; (fig.) starchy.—**entonar,** *vt.* to modulate, intone; to sing in tune; to harmonize colors.—*vr.* to put on grand airs.—**entono,** *m.* harmony; snobbishness.

entonces, *adv.* then, at that time; in that case.—*interrog.* then what? and then?—*desde e.*, from then on. *hasta e.*, up to that time.—*por e.*, at the time.

entornar, *vt.* to half-close; to set ajar.

entorpecer, *vti.* [3] to make numb; to stupefy; to obstruct.—**entorpecimiento,** *m.* torpor, numbness, stupefaction; dullness, stupidity.

entrada, *f.* entrance; gate; admission; admittance; entry; arrival; beginning (of a season); familiar access; entrée (course at dinner); (com.) entry (in a book).—*pl.* receding hair at temples; (com.) income.

entrambos, *a. & pron.* both.

entrampar, *vt.* to ensnare; to trick, deceive; to entangle; to encumber

with debts.—*vr.* (coll.) to get into debt; to get into difficulties.

entrante, *a.* entering; coming.—*mes e.*, next month.

entraña, *f.* entrail.—*pl.* entrails; humaneness; (fig.) heart; affection; the inmost recess of anything.—*hijo de mis entrañas*, child of my heart.—*sin entrañas*, heartless.—**entrañable,** *a.* most affectionate; deep (affection).

entrar, *vi.* (a, en, por) to go (in), come (in), enter; to go (into); to flow (into); to be admitted or have free entrance (to); to join; to begin; to fit (of shoes, garment).—*vt.* to introduce, put in.

entre, *prep.* between, among, amongst, amidst; within, in.—*e. manos*, in hand.—*e. tanto*, in the meantime, meanwhile.

entreabierto, *ppi.* of ENTREABRIR.—*a.* half-opened, ajar.—**entreabrir,** *vti.* [49] to half-open; to set ajar.

entreacto, *m.* intermission.

entrecano, *a.* grayish (hair or beard).

entrecejo, *m.* space between inclosures; scowl.

entrecortado, *a.* confused, hesitating; breathless.—**entrecortar,** *vt.* to cut without severing; to interrupt at intervals.

entrecruzar, *vti.* [a] to intercross; to interlace, interweave.

entredicho, *m.* interdiction.

entrega, *f.* delivery, conveyance; installment of a publication; surrender.—**entregar,** *vti.* [b] to deliver; to give up, surrender; to hand (over); (com.) to transfer; to pay.—*a e.*, (com.) to be supplied.—*vri.* to deliver oneself up, surrender, give in.—*entregarse a*, to abandon oneself to or devote oneself to.

entrelazar, *vti.* [a] to interlace, entwine.—**entremés,** *m.* (theat.) one-act farce; side dish.

entremeter, *vt.* to place between.—*vr.* to intrude; to meddle.—**entremetido,** *a.* meddlesome.—*n.* meddler; intruder; busybody.—**entremetimiento,** *m.* intrusion; meddlesomeness.

entremezclar, *vt.* to intermingle, intermix.

entrenador, *n.* trainer, coach.—**entrenamiento,** *m.* training, coaching.—**entrenar,** *vt., vi. & vr.* to train.

entrepaño, *m.* panel; shelf.—**entrepiernas,** *f.* crutch, fork of legs.—**entresacar,** *vti.* [d] to pick out or choose; to select; to sift; to thin out.—**entresuelo,** *m.* mezzanine.—**entretanto,** *adv. & m.* meanwhile.—**entretejer,** *vt.* to intertwine, interweave.—**entretela,** *f.* (sewing) interlining.

entretener, *vti.* [42] to amuse, entertain; to allay (pain); to delay. —*vri.* to amuse oneself; to tarry. —**entretenido,** *a.* entertaining, pleasant, amusing; readable.—**entretenimiento,** *m.* amusement, entertainment, pastime.

entretiempo, *m.* spring or fall (autumn).

entrever, *vti.* [46-49] to glimpse; to see vaguely.

entreverado, *a.* streaky; intermixed. —**entreverar,** *vt.* to intermix, intermingle.

entrevista, *f.* interview, meeting.— **entrevistar,** *vt.* to interview.—**entrevisto,** *ppi.* of ENTREVER.

entristecer, *vti.* [3] to sadden, afflict. —*vri.* to become sad.—**entristecimiento,** *m.* sadness; fretting.

entrometer, *vt. & vr.* = ENTREMETER.— **entrometido,** *a. & n.* = ENTREMETIDO. —**entrometimiento,** *m.* = ENTREMETIMIENTO.

entroncar, *vii.* [d] (RR.) to form a junction.—**entronque,** *m.* connection; (RR.) junction.

entronizar, *vti.* [a] to enthrone; to exalt.

entubar, *vt.* to provide with casing (oil well, etc.).

entumecer, *vti.* [3] to make numb.— *vri.* to become numb (the limbs), go to sleep.—**entumecimiento,** *m.* torpor; deadness; numbness; swelling.—**entumirse,** *vr.* to become numb.

enturbiar, *vt.* to muddle; to make muddy; to dim, confuse.—*vr.* to get muddy.

entusiasmado, *a.* enthusiastic.—**entusiasmar,** *vt.* to make enthusiastic; to enrapture.—*vr.* to become enthusiastic.—**entusiasmo,** *m.* enthusiasm.—**entusiasta,** *mf.* enthusiast.—*a.* enthusiastic.

enumeración, *f.* enumeration.—**enumerar,** *vt.* to enumerate.

enunciación, *f.,* **enunciado,** *m.* statement.—**enunciar,** *vt.* to state.

envainar, *vt.* to sheathe.

envalentonar, *vt.* to encourage; to make bold.—*vr.* to become bold; to brag.

envanecer, *vti.* [3] to make vain.— *vri.* to become vain.—**envanecimiento,** *m.* conceit.

envasador, *n.* filler, packer; funnel. —**envasar,** *vt.* to put into a container; to pack, to can; to sack (grain).—**envase,** *m.* container; filling, bottling; packing.

envejecer, *vti.* [3] to make old; to make look old.—*vii. & vri.* to grow old; to look older.—**envejecimiento,** *m.* oldness, age; aging.

envenenador, *n. & a.* poisoner; poisoning.—**envenenamiento,** *m.* poisoning.—**envenenar,** *vt.* to poison.

envergadura, *f.* breadth of the sails; wingspread of birds; (aer.) span; forcefulness.

envés, *m.* back or wrong side; back; shoulders.

enviado, *n.* envoy; messenger.— **enviar,** *vt.* to send; to ship.

enviciar, *vt.* to corrupt; to vitiate.— *vr.* (en) to acquire bad habits; to take (to) (drinking, etc.).

envidia, *f.* envy.—**envidiar,** *vt.* to envy.—**envidioso,** *a.* envious.

envilecer, *vti.* [3] to vilify, debase.— *vri.* to degrade oneself.—**envilecimiento,** *m.* vilification, debasement.

envío, *m.* remittance; consignment of goods, shipment.

envite, *m.* stake at cards; invitation; push.—*al primer e.,* at once; at the start.

enviudado, *a.* widowed.—**enviudar,** *vi.* to become a widower or widow.

envoltorio, *m.* bundle.—**envoltura,** *f.* cover, wrapper.—**envolver,** *vti.* [47] to wrap; to swaddle; to imply; to contain, carry with it; (mil.) to surround.—*vri.* to be implicated, involved.—**envuelto,** *pp.* of ENVOLVER.

enyesado, *m.* plasterwork; plaster, plastering.—**enyesadura,** *f.* plastering.—**enyesar,** *vt.* to plaster; to chalk; to whitewash.

épica, *f.* epic poetry.—**épico,** *a.* epic.

epidemia, *f.* epidemic.

epifanía, *f.* Epiphany; Twelfth Night.

epigrama, *m.* epigram; witticism.— **epigramático,** *a.* epigrammatic.

epiléptico, *n. & a.* epilectic.

epílogo, *m.* epilogue; summing up.

episcopal, *a.* episcopal; Episcopal.

episodio, *m.* episode; incident.

epístola, *f.* epistle, letter.

epitafio, *m.* epitaph.

epitalamio, *m.* nuptial song.

epíteto, *m.* epithet.

epítome, *m.* epitome.

época, *f.* epoch, era.—*hacer e.,* to be a turning point.

epopeya, *f.* epic poem.

equidad, *f.* equity; justice.

equilibrar, *vt.* to equilibrate; to counterpoise, counterbalance.—**equilibrio,** *m.* equilibrium, balance, counterbalance.—**equilibrista,** *mf.* juggler; acrobat.

equipaje, *m.* baggage; luggage.— **equipar,** *vt.* to fit out, equip, furnish.—**equipo,** *m.* equipment; team; work crew.

equiparación, *f.* comparison, collation.—**equiparar,** *vt.* to compare, collate; to equate.

equitación, *f.* horsemanship; riding.

equitativo, *a.* equitable, fair, just.

equivalencia, *f.* equivalence.—**equivalente,** *a.* equivalent, tantamount.—**equivaler,** *vii.* [44] to be equivalent.

equivocación, *f.* mistake, error; equivocation.—**equivocar,** *vti.* [d] to mistake; to confuse; to equivocate.—*vri.* to be mistaken; to make a mistake.—**equívoco,** *m.* equivocation; quibble; pun.—*a.* equivocal, ambiguous.

era, *f.* era, age; threshing floor.

erario, *m.* public treasury.

erección, *f.* erection; erectness, elevation.

erguir, *vti.* [19] to erect; to set up straight.—*vri.* to straighten up; to stand or sit erect; to swell with pride.

erial, *m.* unimproved land.—*a.* uncultivated.

erigir, *vti.* [c] to erect, raise; to build; to found, establish.—*erigirse en,* to set oneself up as.

erizado, *a.* covered with bristles, spiky.—*e. de,* beset with; covered with; bristling with.—**erizar,** *vti.* [a] to set on end; to bristle.—*vri.* to bristle; to stand on end (of the hair).—**erizo,** *m.* hedgehog; prickly husk.

ermita, *f.* hermitage.—**ermitaño,** *n.* hermit.

erogación, *f.* expense.

erosión, *f.* erosion, wearing away.

erótico, *a.* erotic(al).—**erotismo,** *m.* eroticism.

errado, *a.* mistaken; erroneous.—**errante,** *a.* wandering, nomadic; errant.—**errar,** *vti.* [1-e] to miss (the target, blow, etc.); to fail in (one's duty to).—*vii.* to wander.—*vii. & vri.* to be mistaken; to commit an error.—**errata,** *f.* misprint.—**erróneo,** *a.* erroneous, mistaken; unsound.—**error,** *m.* mistake.—*e. craso,* gross error.

eructar, *vi.* to belch.—**eructe,** *m.* belching.

erupción, *f.* eruption; bursting forth; rash.

esa, V. **ese.**

esbelto, *a.* slender, svelte, willowy.

esbirro, *m.* bailiff; henchman.

esbozar, *vti.* [a] to sketch.—**esbozo,** *m.* sketch, outline; rough draft.

escabechar, *vt.* to pickle; to stab and kill.—**escabeche,** *m.* pickle; pickled fish.

escabel, *m.* footstool.

escabrosidad, *f.* unevenness, rugged-

ness; harshness; wildness.—**escabroso,** *a.* uneven; craggy; rude; off-color.

escabullirse, *vii.* [27] to slip away; to scamper, sneak away.

escafandra, *f.* diver's helmet.

escala, *f.* ladder, stepladder; graduated rule or instrument; port of call; stopover; (mus.) scale.—*hacer e. en,* to touch, or stop at (a place).—**escalafón,** *m.* official personnel roster, or register.—**escalamiento,** *m.* scaling.—**escalar,** *vt.* to scale.

escaldar, *vt.* to burn, scald; to make red-hot.—*vr.* to get scalded.

escalera, *f.* staircase; stairs; stairway; ladder.—*e. de caracol,* winding stair.—*e. de mano,* ladder, stepladder.

escalinata, *f.* flight of stairs (outside of a building).

escalfar, *vt.* to poach (eggs).

escalofrío, *m.* chill.

escalón, *m.* step of a stairway; rung; rank; social position; (mil.) echelon.—**escalonar,** *vt.* (mil.) to form in echelon; to stagger, spread out; to terrace.

escalpelo, *m.* scalpel, dissecting knife.

escama, *f.* fish or reptile scale; suspicion.—**escamar,** *vt.* to scale (fish); to cause suspicion.—**escamoso,** *a.* scaly.

escamoteador, *n.* juggler, prestidigitator; swindler.—**escamotear,** *vt.* (in juggling) to palm; to rob by artful means.

escampar, *vi.* to stop raining.

escandalizar, *vti.* [a] to scandalize, shock.—*vri.* to be shocked, scandalized.—*vii.* to create commotion, to behave noisily.—**escándalo,** *m.* scandal; licentiousness; tumult, commotion.—**escandaloso,** *a.* scandalous, shocking; turbulent.

escandinavo, *n. & a.* Scandinavian.

escaño, *m.* bench (with back).

escapada, *f.* escape, flight, escapade.—*en una e.,* in a minute, a jiffy.—**escapar,** *vi. & vr.* to escape; to run away.—**escapatoria,** *f.* escape, fleeing; excuse, subterfuge; way out (of difficulty, etc.).—**escape,** *m.* escape, flight; subterfuge; exhaust (of steam, etc.).—*a e.,* or *a todo e.,* at full speed, in great haste.

escapulario, *m.* (eccl., med.) scapular.

escarabajo, *m.* black beetle.

escaramuza, *f.* skirmish; dispute.

escarapela, *f.* badge, rosette in lapel; quarrel ending in blows.

escarbar, *vt.* to scrape or scratch (as fowl); to dig; to poke (the fire); to dig into, investigate.

escarcha, *f.* frost, rime; icing.—

escarchar, *vi.* to freeze.—*vt.* to ice, frost (cakes, etc.).

escardillo, *n.* gardener's hoe.

escariar, *vt.* to ream.

escarlata, *f.* & *a.* scarlet, red.—**escarlatina,** *f.* scarlet fever.

escarmentar, *vii.* [1] to learn by experience; to take warning.—*vti.* to inflict an exemplary punishment on. —**escarmiento,** *m.* warning, lesson, punishment.

escarnecer, *vti.* [3] to scoff, mock.— **escarnio,** *m.* scoffing, gibe, mockery.

escarola, *f.* endive; ruff, frill.

escarpa, *f.* slope, bluff; (mil.) scarp. —**escarpado,** *a.* steep, craggy, rugged.

escarpín, *m.* thin-soled shoe; dancing pump; woolen socks.

escasear, *vi.* to be scarce; to diminish. —**escasez,** *f.* scarcity, shortage; niggardliness; want; scantiness.— **escaso,** *a.* small, limited; little; scarce; niggardly.

escatimar, *vt.* to curtail, lessen.

escayola, *f.* stucco, plasterwork.

escena, *f.* stage; scenery; scene; sight, view.—**escenario,** *m.* (theat.) stage.

escepticismo, *m.* skepticism.—**escéptico,** *n.* & *a.* skeptic.

escindir, *vt.* & *vr.* to split (an atom, etc.)

escisión, *f.* division; schism; fission.

esclarecer, *vti.* [3] to lighten, illuminate; to enlighten, elucidate; to ennoble.—**esclarecido,** *a.* illustrious, prominent.—**esclarecimiento,** *m.* enlightening; elucidation; ennoblement.

esclavina, *f.* short cape.

esclavitud, *f.* slavery.—**esclavizar,** *vti.* [a] to enslave, overwork.—**esclavo,** *n.* slave.

esclusa, *f.* lock; sluice, floodgate.

escoba, *f.* broom.—**escobazo,** *m.* blow with a broom.—**escobilla,** *f.* whisk broom; (elec.) brush of a dynamo.

escocer, *vii.* [26-a] to sting, burn; to smart.

escocés, *n.* & *a.* Scotchman; Scottish.

escofina, *f.* rasp, file.—**escofinar,** *vt.* to rasp.

escoger, *vti.* [c] to choose, select; to elect.

escolar, *mf.* pupil, student.—*a.* scholastic.

escolta, *f.* escort, guard.—**escoltar,** *vt.* to escort, guard.

escollo, *m.* reef; difficulty, danger.

escombrar, *vt.* to clear of rubbish.— **escombro,** *m.* rubbish.

esconder, *vt.* to hide, conceal; to include, contain.—*vr.* to hide; to skulk.—**escondidas, escondidillas,** *f.*

pl.—a e., on the sly, secretly.— **escondite, escondrijo,** *m.* lurking place; hiding place.

escopeta, *f.* shotgun, fowling piece.— **escopetazo,** *m.* gunshot; gunshot wound.

escoplo, *m.* chisel.

escorar, *vt.* (naut.) to prop; to shore up.

escorbuto, *m.* scurvy.

escoria, *f.* dross, slag, scum.

escorpión, *m.* scorpion.

escotar, *vt.* to cut a dress low in the neck.—**escote,** *m.* low neck, décolletage; tucker; scot, share, quota. —**escotilla,** *f.* (naut.) hatchway.— **escotillón,** *m.* scuttle, trapdoor; stage trap.

escozor, *m.* burning, smarting.

escriba, *m.* scribe.—**escribano,** *m.* actuary; court clerk.—**escribiente,** *mf.* clerk.—**escribir,** *vti.* [49] to write.—*e. a máquina,* to type.—*vri.* to carry on correspondence with each other.—**escrito,** *ppi.* of ESCRIBIR. —*m.* writing; manuscript; literary composition.—*por e.,* in writing.— **escritor,** *n.* writer, author.—**escritorio,** *m.* writing desk; countinghouse; office.—**escritura,** *f.* writing, handwriting; deed, instrument; (E.) Scripture.

escrófula, *f.* scrofula.

escrúpulo, *m.* scruple, hesitation; squeamishness.—**escrupulosidad,** *f.* scrupulousness; exactness, thoroughness.—**escrupuloso,** *a.* scrupulous, thorough, particular; squeamish.

escrutar, *vt.* to count ballots; to scrutinize.—**escrutinio,** *m.* scrutiny; inquiry.

escuadra, *f.* carpenter's square; drawing triangle; angle iron; knee, angle brace; (mil.) squad; (naut.) squadron, fleet.—**escuadrón,** *m.* (mil.) squadron.

escuálido, *a.* weak; squalid; emaciated.

escuchar, *vt.* to listen to; to mind, heed.—*vi.* to listen.

escudar, *vt.* to shield, protect.— **escudero,** *m.* shield-bearer, squire. —**escudo,** *m.* shield; escutcheon; protection; coin of different values. —*e. de armas,* coat of arms.

escudriñar, *vt.* to scrutinize, search pry into.

escuela, *f.* school; schoolhouse; (art) school, style.

esculpir, *vt.* & *vi.* to sculpture; to engrave.—**escultor,** *n.* sculptor, (*f.*) sculptress.—**escultórico, escultural,** *a.* sculptural.—**escultura,** *f.* sculpture; carved work.

escupidera, *f.* spittoon.—**escupir,** *vt.*

& *vi.* to spit.—**escupitajo,** *m.* spit, spittle, phlegm.

escurridizo, *a.* slippery.—**escurridor,** *m.* colander; dish-draining rack.—**escurriduras,** *f. pl.* rinsings, dregs.—**escurrir,** *vt.* to drain off; to strain off; to wring (as clothes).—*e. el bulto,* to sneak away.—*vr.* to drop, drip; to slip, slide; to escape, sneak away.

ese, *m.* **esa,** *f.* (*pl.* **esos, esas**), *a. dem.* that.—*pl.* those; **ése, ésa** (*pl.* **ésos, ésas**), *pron. dem.* that (one); (*pl.* those); the former.—**eso,** *pron. dem. neut.* that.—*e. es,* that's it.—*e. mismo,* that's right, precisely.—*ni por ésas,* in no way.—*por eso,* so, therefore.

esencia, *f.* essence.—**esencial,** *a.* essential.

eses, *s. pl.,* reeling of a drunken man.—*hacer e.,* to reel.

esfera, *f.* sphere; clock dial.—**esférico,** *a.* spherical.

esfinge, *f.* sphinx.

esforzar, *vti.* [12-a] to strengthen; to encourage.—*vri.* to exert oneself, make efforts, try hard.—**esfuerzo,** *m.* courage, spirit; effort, strong endeavor.

esfumar, *vt.* (art) to shade.—*vr.* to vanish, disappear.

esgrima, *f.* fencing.—**esgrimir,** *vt.* to fence; to wield, brandish (a weapon).

eslabón, *m.* link of a chain; steel for striking fire with a flint.—**eslabonamiento,** *m.* linking, uniting; connection, sequence.—**eslabonar,** *vt.* to link; to join.

eslavo, *n. & a.* Slav.

eslovaco, *n. & a.* Slovak.

esmaltar, *vt.* to enamel; to embellish.—**esmalte,** *m.* enamel; enamel work.

esmerado, *a.* careful; carefully done; painstaking.

esmeralda, *f.* emerald.

esmerarse, *vr.* to do one's best, to take pains (with).

esmeril, *m.* emery.—**esmerilar,** *vt.* to polish with emery.

esmero, *m.* careful attention, nicety.

esnob, *mf.* (neol.) snob.—**esnobismo,** *m.* (neol.) snobbery.

eso, V. **ESE**.

espaciar, *vt.* to space; (printing) to lead.—**espacio,** *m.* space; capacity; interval; blank, empty space.—**espaciosidad,** *f.* spaciousness, capacity.—**espacioso,** *a.* spacious, ample.

espada, *f.* sword; swordsman; (cards) spade; swordfish; matador.—**espadachín,** *m.* dexterous swordsman; bully.

espadaña, *f.* (bot.) gladiolus.

espalda, *f.* (anat.) back.—*pl.* back or back part.—*a espaldas,* treacherously.—*de espaldas,* backwards; from behind.—**espaldar,** *m.* back of a seat.

espantada, *f.* stampede, running away.—**espantadizo,** *a.* timid, skittish.—**espantajo,** *m.* scarecrow; fright.—**espantar,** *vt.* to scare; to chase or drive away.—*vr.* to be astonished.—**espanto,** *m.* fright; horror; threat.—**espantoso,** *a.* frightful; fearful.

español, *n. & a.* Spanish.—*n.* Spaniard (*f.*) Spanish woman.

esparadrapo, *m.* adhesive tape, court plaster.

esparcimiento, *m.* scattering; amusement, relaxation.—**esparcir,** *vti.* [a] to scatter, spread; to divulge.

espárrago, *m.* asparagus.

espasmo, *m.* spasm.—**espasmódico,** *a.* spasmodic, convulsive.

espátula, *f.* spatula; (art) palette knife; putty knife.

especia, *f.* spice.—*pl.* medicinal drugs.

especial, *a.* special.—*en e.,* specially, in particular.—**especialidad,** *f.* specialty; course, subject (of study).—**especialista,** *mf.* specialist.—**especialización,** *f.* specialization; specializing.—**especializar,** *vti.* [a] to specialize.—*vri.* (en) to specialize (in).

especie, *f.* species; kind, sort; piece of news; statement.—*en e.,* in kind.—**especificar,** *vti.* [d] to specify.—**específico,** *a.* specific.—*m.* (med.) specific.—**espécimen,** *m.* specimen, sample.

espectacular, *a.* spectacular.—**espectáculo,** *m.* spectacle, show.—**espectador,** *n.* spectator.—*pl.* audience.

espectro, *m.* specter; spectrum.

especulación, *f.* speculation.—**especulador,** *n. & a.* speculator; speculating.—**especular,** *vt. & vi.* to speculate.—**especulativo,** *a.* speculative.

espejismo, *m.* mirage; illusion.—**espejo,** *m.* mirror.—**espejuelos,** *m. pl.* (Am.) eyeglasses.

espeluznante, *a.* hair-raising.

espera, *f.* waiting; stay, pause.—*en e. de,* waiting for.—*sala de e.,* waiting room.—**esperanza,** *f.* hope; (often *pl.*) prospects.—*dar esperanza(s),* to promise.—**esperanzar,** *vti.* [a] to give hope to.—**esperar,** *vt.* to wait for; to hope.—*vi.* to wait; to hope.—*vr.* to wait, stay.

esperma, *f.* sperm; tallow.

esperpento, *m.* hideous thing or person; absurdity, nonsense.

espesar, *vt.* to thicken, curdle.—*vr.* to thicken; to condense.—**espeso,** *a.*

thick, dense; dull, heavy.—**espesor,** *m.* thickness.—**espesura,** *f.* thicket, close wood; thickness, density.

espetar, *vt.* to skewer, spit; to spring (something) on (one).—**espetera,** *f.* kitchen rack.

espía, *mf.* spy.—**espiar,** *vt.* to spy on; (coll.) to tail.

espiga, *f.* tassel, ear (as of corn, wheat); pin; dowel; spigot.—**espigado,** *a.* tall, grown; (agr.) eared; ripe.—**espigar,** *vii.* [b] to glean; to tenon; to tassel (as corn).—*vri.* to grow tall; to go to seed.

espina, *f.* thorn; fishbone; spine; splinter; suspicion.—*dar mala e.,* to cause suspicion or anxiety.—**espinaca,** *f.* spinach.—**espinazo,** *m.* spine, backbone.—**espinilla,** *f.* shinbone; blackhead.—**espino,** *m.* hawthorn.—**espinoso,** *a.* thorny; arduous; dangerous.

espionaje, *m.* espionage, spying.

espiral, *a.* spiral, winding.

espirar, *vt. & vi.* to breathe, exhale; to emit.

espíritu, *m.* spirit; soul; genius; essence; courage.—*pl.* spirits.—**espiritual,** *a.* spiritual; soulful; ghostly.—**espirituoso,** *a.* spirituous; ardent; spirited.

espita, *f.* faucet, spigot; tap; drunkard.

esplendidez, *f.* splendor; abundance; liberality.—**espléndido,** *a.* splendid, generous; resplendent.—**esplendor,** *m.* splendor; nobleness.—**esplendoroso,** *a.* splendid, radiant.

espliego, *m.* lavender.

espolazo, *m.* violent prick with a spur. —**espolear,** *vt.* to spur; to incite.—**espoleta,** *f.* fuse (of a bomb).—**espolón,** *m.* cock's spur; (naut.) ram; breakwater; buttress.

espolvorear, *vt.* to sprinkle with powder.

esponja, *f.* sponge.—**esponjar,** *vt.* to sponge.—*vr.* to swell.—**esponjoso,** *a.* spongy, porous; springy.

esponsales, *m. pl.* betrothal, engagement.

esposa, *f.* spouse, wife.—*pl.* manacles, handcuffs.—**esposar,** *vt.* to shackle. —**esposo,** *m.* spouse, husband.

espuela, *f.* spur; incitement.

espuerta, *f.* two-handled fruit basket. —*a espuertas,* abundantly.

espulgar, *vti.* [b] to clean lice or fleas from; to examine closely.

espuma, *f.* foam; lather; suds; froth; scum.—**espumadera,** *f.* skimmer, colander.—**espumar,** *vt.* to skim, to scum.—*vi.* to froth, foam. —**espumarajo,** *m.* foam or froth from the mouth.—**espumoso,** *a.* foamy, frothy; sparkling (wine).

esputar, *vt. & vi.* to expectorate, spit. —**esputo,** *m.* spittle, saliva; sputum.

esquela, *f.* billet, note.

esquelético, *a.* thin; skeletal.—**esqueleto,** *m.* skeleton; very thin person.

esquema, *m.* scheme, plan; outline. —**esquemático,** *a.* schematic.—**esquematizar,** *vti.* [a] to sketch, outline.

esquí, *m.* ski.—**esquiador,** *n.* skier.—**esquiar,** *vi.* to ski.

esquife, *m.* skiff, small boat.

esquila, *f.* small bell; cattle bell; sheep shearing.—**esquilador,** *n.* shearer.—**esquilar,** *vt.* to shear, crop, clip.

esquilmar, *vt.* to impoverish; to exploit.

esquilón, *m.* cattle bell.

esquimal, *n. & a.* Eskimo.

esquina, *f.* corner, angle (outside).—**esquinazo,** *m.* corner.—*dar e.,* to evade.

esquirla, *f.* splinter of a bone.

esquivar, *vt.* to elude, avoid; to shun. —*vr.* to disdain, withdraw.—**esquivez,** *f.* disdain; aloofness; coldness. —**esquivo,** *a.* elusive, evasive; cold.

estabilidad, *f.* stability.—**estable,** *a.* stable, steady.

establecer, *vti.* [3] to establish, found; to decree.—*vri.* to establish or settle oneself.—**establecimiento,** *m.* establishment; institution.

establo, *m.* stable; cattle barn.

estaca, *f.* stake, pole; stick, cudgel. —**estacada,** *f.* palisade; paling, fence work.—*dejar (a uno) en la e.,* to leave (one) in the lurch.

estación, *f.* season (of the year); moment, time; (RR., radio, tel., police, etc.) station.—**estacionamiento,** *m.* (auto) parking; stationing, settling.—**estacionar,** *vt.* to park (a car, etc.).—*vr.* to park; to remain stationary; to stagnate.—**estacionario,** *a.* stationary, motionless.

estada, estadía, *f.* stay, sojourn, detention; demurrage; cost of such stay.—**estadio,** *m.* stadium.

estadista, *m.* statesman.

estadística, *f.* statistics.—**estadístico,** *a.* statistical.

estado, *m.* state, condition (of persons or things); estate, class, rank; status; state, commonwealth; state, government; statement, account, report.—*estar en e.,* to be pregnant.— *e. mayor,* (mil.) staff.—*hombre de e.,* statesman.

estadounidense, estadunidense, *mf.* & *a.* of the U.S., North American.

estafa, *f.* swindle.—**estafador,** *n.* swindler, sharper.—**estafar,** *vt.* to swindle.

estafermo, *m.* idle fellow.

estafeta, *f.* post office.

estallar, *vi.* to explode, burst; (of fire, etc.) to break out.—**estallido,** *m.* outburst.

estambre, *m.* worsted, woolen yarn; stamen.

estameña, *f.* serge.

estampa, *f.* print, stamp; image; picture; engraving.—**estampado,** *m.* cotton print, calico; stamping; cloth printing.—**estampar,** *vt.* to print, stamp.

estampida, *f.* stampede.—**estampido,** *m.* report of a gun; outburst.

estampilla, *f.* rubber stamp; seal; (Am.) postage stamp.

estancamiento, *m.* stagnation.—**estancar,** *vti.* [d] to stanch, check, stem.—*vri.* to stagnate, become stagnant.

estancia, *f.* stay; dwelling, habitation; ranch.—**estanciero,** *n.* (Am.) ranch owner, cattle raiser.

estanco, *a.* watertight.—*m.* monopoly; store for monopolized goods; cigar store.

estandarte, *m.* standard, banner, colors.

estanque, *m.* pool, reservoir, pond.—**estanquillo,** *m.* cigar store; small shop.

estante, *m.* shelf; bookcase.—**estantería,** *f.* shelving, shelves.

estaño, *m.* tin.

estar, *vii.* [20] to be.—*¿a cómo estamos? ¿a cuánto estamos?* what day is it? what is the date?—*¿estamos?* is it agreed? do you understand?—*e. bien,* to be well.—*e. con,* to live in company with; to have a (disease), to be ill with; to be in a state of (hurry, anger, etc.).—*e. de más,* to be out of place, in the way.—*e. para,* to be about to; to be in a mood or in condition to or for.—*e. por,* to be in favor of; to feel like.—*e. por ver,* to remain to be seen.—*e. sobre sí,* to be on one's guard.—*vri.* to be, to keep; to stay, to remain.

estarcido, *m.* stencil.—**estarcir,** *vti.* [a] to stencil.

estatal, *a.* pertaining to the state.

estática, *f.* statics.—**estático,** *a.* static, statical.

estatua, *f.* statue.

estatuir, *vti.* [23-e] to establish, ordain, enact.

estatura, *f.* stature, height of a person.

estatuto, *m.* statute, ordinance.

este, *m.* east, orient.

este, *dem. a.* (*f.* **esta**; *pl.* **estos, estas**) this (*pl.* these).—**éste,** *dem. pron* (*f.* **ésta**; *pl.* **éstos, éstas**; *neut.* **esto**) this, this one; the latter (*pl.* these; the latter).—*a todo esto,* meanwhile.—*en esto,* at this juncture, point; herein (to).—*esto es,* that is; that is to say.—*por esto,* for this reason; on this account.

estela, *f.* wake of a ship.

estenografía, *f.* stenography.—**estenógrafo,** *n.* stenographer.

estera, *f.* mat, matting.

estercolero, *m.* dung heap.

estereoscópico, *a.* stereoscopic.—**estereoscopio,** *m.* stereoscope.

estereotipar, *vt.* to stereotype; to print from stereotypes.

estéril, *a.* sterile, barren; unfruitful.—**esterilidad,** *f.* sterility, barrenness, unfruitfulness.—**esterilizar,** *vti.* [a] to sterilize.

esterlina, *a.* sterling.

esternón, *m.* breastbone.

estero, *m.* inlet, estuary.

estertor, *m.* death rattle.

estética, *f.* esthetics.—**estético,** *a.* esthetic.

estetoscopio, *m.* stethoscope.

estiba, *f.* stowage.—**estibador,** *n.* stevedore, longshoreman.—**estibar,** *vt.* to stow.

estiércol, *m.* dung, manure.

estigma, *m.* birthmark; stigma, mark of infamy; (bot.) stigma.—**estigmatizar,** *vti.* [a] to stigmatize.

estilar, *vi.* & *vr.* to be customary.

estilete, *m.* stiletto (dagger); small chisel; (surg.) flexible probe.

estilista, *mf.* stylist.—**estilo,** *m.* style.—*al e. de,* in the style of.—*por el e., or por ese e.,* of that kind, like that.—**estilográfica,** *f.* fountain pen.

estima, *f.* esteem.—**estimable,** *a.* estimable, worthy.—**estimación,** *f.* esteem, regard; estimate.—**estimar,** *vt.* to estimate, value; to esteem; to judge, to think.

estimulante, *a.* stimulating.—*m.* stimulant.—**estimular,** *vt.* to stimulate; to goad, incite, encourage.—**estímulo,** *m.* stimulus; inducement; incitement; stimulation.

estío, *m.* summer.

estipendio, *m.* stipend, fee.

estipulación, *f.* stipulation.—**estipular,** *vt.* to stipulate, specify.

estirpe, *f.* lineage, pedigree.

estirado, *a.* affected, pompous, stuffy; haughty; (fig.) starchy.—**estiramiento,** *m.* stretching.—**estirar,** *vt.*

to stretch, lengthen.—**estirón,** *m.* pull(ing); haul(ing); rapid growth.

estival, *a.* summer.

esto, V. ESTE.

estocada, *f.* stab, sword thrust.

estofa, *f.* quality, class, sort; stuff, cloth.—**estofado,** *m.* stew.—**estofar,** *vt.* to stew; to quilt.

estoicismo, *m.* stoicism.—**estoico,** *n.* & *a.* stoic(al).

estolidez, *f.* stupidity.—**estólido,** *a.* stupid, imbecile.

estómago, *m.* stomach.

estopa, *f.* tow; burlap; oakum.

estoque, *m.* rapier; matador's sword.

estorbar, *vt.* to hinder; to obstruct; to impede.—**estorbo,** *m.* hindrance, obstruction, nuisance.

estornino, *m.* starling.

estornudar, *vi.* to sneeze.—**estornudo,** *m.* sneeze.

estrado, *m.* dais; lecturing platform.

estrafalario, *a.* odd, eccentric.

estragar, *vti.* [b] to deprave, spoil. —**estrago,** *m.* ravage, ruin, havoc; wickedness.

estrambótico, *a.* odd, eccentric.

estrangulación, *f.* strangling; strangulation; throttling.—**estrangular,** *vt.* to strangle, choke, throttle.

estratagema, *f.* stratagem; trick.

estrategia, *f.* strategy.—**estratégico,** *a.* strategic.

estratificar, *vti.* [d] & *vri.* to stratify. —**estrato,** *m.* stratum; layer.

estratosfera, *f.* stratosphere.

estrechar, *vt.* to tighten; to narrow; to take in (a coat, etc.); to constrain.—*e. la mano,* to shake hands; to greet.—*vr.* to narrow; to bind oneself strictly.—**estrechez,** *f.* narrowness; tightness; poverty.—**estrecho,** *a.* narrow, tight.—*m.* strait, channel.

estregar, *vti.* [1-b] to rub; to scour. —**estregón,** *m.* rough rubbing.

estrella, *f.* star.—**estrellar,** *vt.* to dash to pieces, smash up.—*vr.* to fail; to smash; (contra) to crash or dash (against), be shattered (by).

estremecer, *vti.* [3] & *vri.* to shake, tremble, shudder.—**estremecimiento,** *m.* trembling, shaking; shudder(ing).

estrenar, *vt.* to use or to do for the first time.—*vr.* to begin to act in some capacity; to make one's debut; (of a play) to open.—**estreno,** *m.* inauguration; first performance; debut.

estreñimiento, *m.* constipation.—**estreñir,** *vti.* [9] to constipate.

estrépito, *m.* noise, din; crash.—**estrepitoso,** *a.* noisy, deafening; boisterous.

estriar, *vt.* to flute; to gutter.—*vr.* to become grooved, striated.

estribación, *f.* spur of a mountain.—**estribar,** *vi.* (en) to rest (on); to be based (on); to lie (in).

estribillo, *m.* refrain of a song.

estribo, *m.* stirrup; runningboard, step or footboard of a coach; (anat.) stirrup bone; abutment; support.—*perder los estribos,* to talk nonsense; to lose one's head.

estribor, *m.* (naut.) starboard.

estricto, *a.* strict.

estridente, *a.* strident.

estrobo, *m.* loop; oarlock.

estrofa, *f.* (poet.) stanza.

estropajo, *m.* swap; esparto scrubbing pad; worthless thing.

estropear, *vt.* to maim, cripple; to damage, spoil.—*vr.* to get out of order, damaged.—**estropicio,** *m.* breakage, crash.

estructura, *f.* structure.—**estructural,** *a.* structural.

estruendo, *m.* din, clatter; uproar.—**estruendoso,** *a.* obstreperous, noisy.

estrujamiento, *m.* crushing, squeezing.—**estrujar,** *vt.* to squeeze, crush. —**estrujón,** *m.* crush, squeeze.

estuario, *m.* estuary, inlet.

estuco, *m.* stucco; plaster.

estuche, *m.* fancy box or case (as for jewelry, etc.).

estudiante, *mf.* student.—**estudiantil,** *a.* student, pertaining to students.—**estudiar,** *vt.* to study.—**estudio,** *m.* study; reading room; studio.—**estudioso,** *a.* studious.

estufa, *f.* stove; heater; hothouse; drying chamber; small brazier.

estupefacción, *f.* stupefaction, numbness.—**estupefaciente,** *a.* & *m.* narcotic.—**estupefacto,** *a.* motionless; stupefied.

estupidez, *f.* stupidity.—**estúpido,** *a.* & *n.* stupid (person).

estupor, *m.* stupor; amazement.

estupro, *m.* ravishment, rape.

etapa, *f.* stage; station, stop.

éter, *m.* ether.—**etéreo,** *a.* ethereal.

eternidad, *f.* eternity.—**eternizar,** *vti.* [a] to prolong indefinitely.—*vri.* to be everlasting; to be exceedingly slow; to stay forever.—**eterno,** *a.* eternal, everlasting, timeless.

ética, *f.* ethics.—**ético,** *a.* ethical.

etimología, *f.* etymology.—**etimológico,** *a.* etymological.

etíope, *mf.* Ethiopian.—**etiópico,** *a.* Ethiopic, Ethiopian.

etiqueta, *f.* etiquette, formality; formal dress; label.—*de e.,* ceremonious; formal.

étnico, *a.* ethnic.—**etnología,** *f.* ethnology.

eucalipto, *m.* eucalyptus.

eurasiático, eurasio, *n.* & *a.* Eurasian. **—europeo,** *n.* & *a.* European.

eutanasia, *f.* mercy killing.

evacuación, *f.* evacuation; exhaustion. **—evacuar,** *vt.* to evacuate, empty; to quit, leave, vacate.

evadir, *vt.* to evade, elude, avoid.— *vr.* to escape; to sneak away.

evaluación, *m.* appraisal, valuation.— **evaluar,** *vt.* to rate, value, appraise; to price.

evangélico, *a.* evangelical.—**evangelio,** *m.* gospel.—**evangelizar,** *vti.* [a] to evangelize.

evaporación, *f.* evaporation.—**evaporar,** *vt.* & *vr.* to evaporate, vaporize.

evasión, *f.,* **evasiva,** *f.* evasion, dodge, escape.—**evasivo,** *a.* evasive, elusive.

evento, *m.* event, contingency.—**eventual,** *a.* contingent; fortuitous.— **eventualidad,** *f.* contingency.

evidencia, *f.* evidence, proof; obviousness.—**evidenciar,** *vt.* to prove, make evident.—**evidente,** *a.* evident.

evitable, *a.* avoidable.—**evitar,** *vt.* to avoid; to shun; to prevent.

evocación, *f.* evocation, evoking.— **evocar,** *vti.* [d] to evoke.

evolución, *f.* evolution; change.— **evolucionar,** *vi.* to evolve; to change; to develop; to perform evolutions or maneuverings.

exacerbación, *f.* exasperation; exacerbation.—**exacerbar,** *vt.* to irritate, exasperate; to aggravate (disease, etc.).

exactitud, *f.* exactness; punctuality; accuracy.—**exacto,** *a.* exact; accurate; precise; punctual.

exageración, *f.* exaggeration.—**exagerar,** *vt.* to exaggerate, overstate.

exaltación, *f.* exaltation.—**exaltado,** *a.* hot-headed; ultra-radical.—**exaltar,** *vt.* to exalt; to praise.—*vr.* to become excited, upset.

examen, *m.* examination; inquiry.— **examinar,** *vt.* to examine; investigate.—*vr.* to take an examination.

exánime, *a.* spiritless, lifeless.

exasperación, *f.* exasperation.—**exasperar,** *vt.* to exasperate.—*vr.* to become exasperated.

excavación, *f.* excavation.—**excavar,** *vt.* to excavate.

excedente, *a.* exceeding.—*m.* surplus. **—exceder,** *vt.* to exceed, surpass; to overstep.—*vr.* to go too far; to overstep one's authority.

excelencia, *f.* excellence; excellency (title).—**excelente,** *a.* excellent, first-rate, tiptop.—*interj.* good! fine!

excelso, *a.* elevated, sublime, lofty.

excentricidad, *f.* eccentricity.—**excéntrico,** *a.* eccentric(al); odd.

excepción, *f.* exception.—**excepcional,** *a.* exceptional, unusual.—**excepto,** *adv.* excepting, except, with the exception of.—**exceptuar,** *vt.* to except.

excesivo, *a.* excessive.—**exceso,** *m.* excess; atrocity; surplus.

excitable, *a.* excitable.—**excitación,** *f.* excitation, exciting; excitement.— **excitante,** *a.* exciting, stimulating. **—excitar,** *vt.* to excite.—*vr.* to become excited.

exclamación, *f.* exclamation.—**exclamar,** *vi.* to exclaim.

excluir, *vti.* [23-e] to exclude; to bar.—**exclusión,** *f.* exclusion, shutting out, debarring.—**exclusiva,** *f.* refusal; rejection, exclusion; sole right or agency.—**exclusivo,** *a.* exclusive.

excomulgar, *vti.* [b] to excommunicate.—**excomunión,** *f.* excommunication.

excremento, *m.* excrement.

exculpar, *vt.* & *vr.* to exonerate.

excursión, *f.* excursion, trip, tour.— **excursionista,** *mf.* excursionist.

excusa, *f.* excuse.—**excusado,** *a.* unnecessary; reserved, private.—*m.* toilet.—**excusar,** *vt.* to excuse.—*vr.* to excuse oneself; to apologize.

exención, *f.* exemption.—**exento,** *ppi.* of EXIMIR.—*a.* exempt; free.

exequias, *f. pl.* obsequies.

exhalación, *f.* exhalation; bolt of lightning; shooting star; fume, vapor, emanation.—**exhalar,** *vt.* to exhale, breathe forth, emit.

exhausto, *a.* exhausted.

exhibición, *f.* exhibition, exposition. **—exhibir,** *vt.* to exhibit, expose; to show.

exigencia, *f.* demand; requirement; unreasonable request.—**exigente,** *a.* demanding; exacting.—**exigir,** *vti.* [c] to require; to exact, demand.

eximio, *a.* famous, most excellent.

eximir, *vti.* [49] to exempt, excuse, except.

existencia, *f.* existence.—*pl.* (com.) stock in hand.—*en e.,* in stock.— **existente,** *a.* existent, existing; in stock.—**existir,** *vi.* to exist, to be.

éxito, *m.* success; issue, result.

éxodo, *m.* exodus, emigration; **(E.),** Exodus.

exoneración, *f.* exoneration.—**exonerar,** *vt.* to exonerate.

exorbitancia, *f.* exorbitance.—**exorbitante,** *a.* exorbitant, excessive.

exótico, *a.* exotic, foreign.

expansión, *f.* expansion, extension;

recreation.—**expansivo**, *a.* expansive; communicative, sociable.

expatriación, *f.* expatriation.—**expatriar**, *vt.* to expatriate.—*vr.* to emigrate, leave one's country.

expectación, *f.* expectation, expectancy.—**expectante**, *a.* expectant. —**expectativa**, *f.* expectation, expectancy, hope.

expectoración, *f.* expectoration; sputum.—**expectorar**, *vt. & vi.* to expectorate.

expedición, *f.* expedition; dispatch; journey.—**expedicionario**, *a.* expeditionary.—**expediente**, *m.* file of papers bearing on a case; dispatch; (law) action, proceeding; means; pretext.—*cubrir el e.,* to keep up appearances.—**expedienteo**, *m.* (coll.) red tape.—**expedir**, *vti.* [29] to expedite; to issue; to draw out; to ship, send.—**expeditivo**, *a.* expeditious, speedy.

expeler, *vt.* to expel, eject.

expender, *vt.* to spend; to sell.—**expensas**, *f. pl.* expenses, charges, costs.—*a e. de uno,* at one's expense.

experiencia, *f.* experience; experiment.—*e. de la vida,* sophistication. —**experimental**, *a.* experimental.—**experimentar**, *vt.* to experience; to experiment, test.—**experimento**, *m.* experiment, test.—**experto**, *n. & a.* expert.

expiación, *f.* expiation.—**expiar**, *vt.* to expiate, atone for.

expiración, *f.* expiration.—**expirar**, *vi.* to expire; to die.

explanada, *f.* lawn; esplanade.

explayar, *vt.* to extend.—*vr.* to expatriate; to have a good time; to confide (in a person).

explicable, *a.* explainable.—**explicación**, *f.* explanation.—**explicar**, *vti.* [d] to explain.—*vri.* to explain oneself; to understand (the reason, cause, etc.).—**explícito**, *a.* explicit, clear.

exploración, *f.* exploration.—**explorador**, *n. & a.* explorer; exploring; scout.—**explorar**, *vt.* to explore; to scout.

explosión, *f.* explosion.—*hacer e.,* to explode.—**explosivo**, *m. & a.* explosive.—**explotación**, *f.* exploitation; development, working (of a mine, etc.); plant, works; operation, running (of a factory, RR., etc.).—**explotador**, *n. & a.* exploiter; exploiting.—**explotar**, *vt.* to exploit; to work (a mine, etc.); to operate, run (a business, RR., etc.); to exploit (to one's own advantage); (Am.) to explode, detonate.—*vi.* to explode.—*hacer e.,* to explode.

expoliación, *f.* spoliation.—**expoliar**, *vt.* to plunder, despoil.

exponente, *m. & a.* exponent.—**exponer**, *vti.* [32-49] to expose; to show; to jeopardize.—*vri.* to run a risk, lay oneself open to.

exportación, *f.* exportation, export.—**exportar**, *vt.* to export.

exposición, *f.* exposition, statement; risk, jeopardy; exposure; exhibition.

expresar, *vti.* [49] to express.—*vri.* to express oneself; to speak.—**expresión**, *f.* expression; wording; statement; form; phrase, utterance.—**expreso**, *ppi.* of EXPRESAR.—*a.* expressed; express, clear; fast (train, etc.).—*m.* express (train, etc.).

exprimir, *vt.* to squeeze, press out.

expropiar, *vt.* to expropriate.

expuesto, *ppi.* of EXPONER.—*a.* on display; exposed, liable; dangerous; in danger.

expulsar, *vt.* to expel, eject.—**expulsión**, *f.* expulsion, ejection.

exquisito, *a.* exquisite, delicious.

extasiar, *vt. & vr.* to enrapture, delight.—**éxtasis**, *m.* ecstasy.—**extático**, *a.* ecstatic.

extemporáneo, *a.* untimely, inopportune.

extender, *vti.* [18-49] to extend; to unfold; to spread out; to stretch out; to draw up or issue (a document).—*vri.* to extend, last; to spread, become popular.—**extensión**, *f.* extension; extent, length; expanse, spaciousness; stretch; duration.—**extensivo**, *a.* extensive; ample.—**extenso**, *ppi.* of EXTENDER.— *a.* extended, extensive; spacious.

extenuación, *f.* attenuation; exhaustion.—**extenuar**, *vt.* to exhaust, weaken.—*vr.* to languish, waste away.

exterior, *a.* exterior; external, outer; foreign.—*m.* outside; personal appearance; foreign countries.—**exteriorizar**, *vti.* [a] to externalize, make manifest.—*vri.* to unbosom oneself.

exterminador, *n. & a.* exterminator; exterminating.—**exterminar**, *vt.* to exterminate; to raze.—**exterminio**, *m.* extermination, ruin.

externo, *a.* external, outward; exterior.—*n.* day pupil.

extinción, *f.* extinction; extinguishing. —**extinguir**, *vti.* [49-b] & *vri.* to quench, extinguish; to suppress, destroy.—**extinto**, *ppi.* of EXTINGUIR.—*a.* extinct.—**extintor**, *m.* fire-extinguisher.

extirpar, *vt.* to extirpate, root out; eradicate.

extorsión, *f.* extortion.

extracción, *f.* extraction.—**extractar,** *vt.* to epitomize, abstract.—**extracto,** *m.* summary, abstract; extract.

extradición, *f.* extradition.

extraer, *vti.* [43] to extract, draw out, remove.

extralimitarse, *vr.* to overstep one's authority; to take advantage of another's kindness.

extranjero, *a.* foreign, alien.—*n.* foreigner.—*en el e.,* abroad.

extrañar, *vt.* to banish; to estrange; to wonder at, find strange; to miss.—**extrañeza,** *f.* oddity; surprise; estrangement.—**extraño,** *a.* strange; foreign; extraneous; unaccountable.—*n.* stranger, foreigner, outsider.

extraoficial, *a.* unofficial.

extraordinario, *a.* extraordinary.—*m.* extra.—*horas extraordinarias,* overtime.

extravagancia, *f.* oddness; folly; eccentricity.—**extravagante,** *a.* eccentric; unusual, odd.

extraviar, *vt.* to mislead, misguide; to misplace, mislay; to embezzle.—*vr.* to go astray; to lose one's way; to miscarry (as a letter); to deviate; to err.—**extravío,** *m.* deviation; aberration; misconduct; misplacement.

extremar, *vt.* to carry to an extreme.—*vr.* to exert oneself to the utmost, take special pains.—**extremidad,** *f.* extremity; end; edge, border; extreme or remotest part.—**extremo,** *a.* extreme, last; furthest; greatest, utmost.—*m.* extreme, highest degree; apex; furthest end, extremity; greatest care.—*con* or *en e.,* extremely.—*hacer extremos,* to express one's feelings with vehemence, to gush.—**extremoso,** *a.* extreme, vehement.

exudar, *vi. & vt.* to exude; to ooze out.

eyaculación, *f.* ejection; ejaculation.—**eyacular,** *vt.* to eject; to ejaculate.

F

fábrica, *f.* fabrication; structure; factory; mill.—**fabricación,** *f.* manufacturing; manufacture.—**fabricante,** *mf. & a.* maker, manufacturer; making, manufacturing.—**fabricar,** *vti.* [d] to manufacture, make; to build, construct.—**fabril,** *a.* manufacturing.

fábula, *f.* fable, tale, fiction.—**fabuloso,** *a.* fabulous; marvelous; mythical.

facción, *f.* faction, turbulent political party.—*pl.* features, lineaments.—**faccioso,** *a.* factious.—*n.* rebel.

faceta, *f.* oblique side; facet.

facial, *a.* facial.

fácil, *a.* easy; docile, handy; yielding; likely.—**facilidad,** *f.* ease; facility.—*dar facilidades,* to facilitate.—**facilitar,** *vt.* to facilitate, make easy; to provide.

facineroso, *a.* wicked, villainous.

factible, *a.* feasible, practicable.

factor, *m.* factor, element, cause; (com.) agent, commissioner.—**factoría,** *f.* agency; trading post.

factótum, *m.* handyman; busybody.

factura, *f.* invoice, bill; workmanship.—**facturar,** *vt.* (com.) to invoice; to bill; (RR.) to check (baggage).

facultad, *f.* faculty; power; branch, school.—**facultar,** *vt.* to empower, authorize.—**facultativo,** *a.* facultative; optional; pertaining to a faculty.—*m.* physician.

facundia, *f.* eloquence.—**facundo,** *a.* eloquent, fluent.

facha, *f.* (coll.) appearance, look, aspect.—**fachada,** *f.* (arch.) façade; (coll.) outward appearance.

fachenda, *f.* vanity, boastfulness.—**fachendoso,** *a.* vain, boastful.

faena, *f.* work, labor, task.

faisán, *m.* pheasant.

faja, *f.* band; sash; girdle; (geog.) zone; belt.—**fajar,** *vt.* to band, belt, girdle.—*vr.* (Am.) (coll.) to fight.—**fajo,** *m.* sheaf; bundle.

falacia, *f.* fallacy, fraud, deceit.—**falaz,** *a.* deceitful, false, fallacious.

falange, *f.* phalanx.

falda, *f.* skirt, flap; the lap; slope; loin (of beef).—*pl.* (fig.) women.—**faldeta,** *f.* small skirt; covering cloth or canvas, flap.—**faldón,** *m.* coattail, shirttail; flap.

falsario, *n.* forger; liar.—**falsear,** *vt.* to forge; to misrepresent.—*vi.* to slacken.—**falsedad,** *f.* falsehood, lie; deceit.—**falsete,** *m.* (mus.) falsetto.—**falsificación,** *f.* falsification, counterfeit, forgery.—**falsificador,** *n.* counterfeiter, falsifier, forger.—**falsificar,** *vti.* [d] to counterfeit, falsify, forge; to sophisticate.—**falso,** *a.* false, untrue; incorrect; deceitful, untruthful; forged; counterfeit; sham, imitation (as jewels); unsound.

falta, *f.* lack, want, dearth; fault; mistake; defect; offense, misdemeanor; (law) default; (sport) fault.—*a f. de,* for lack of.—*hacer* *f.*, to be necessary.—*sin f.*, without fail.—**faltar**, *vi.* to be wanting, lacking; to be needed; to fall short; to fail in; to commit a fault; to offend; to be absent or missing.—*falta un cuarto para las dos*, it is quarter to two.—*f. a la verdad*, to lie.—*f. al respeto*, to treat disrespectfully.—*¡no faltaba más!* (coll.) of course! that would be the limit! —**falto**, *a.* short; deficient.

faltriquera, *f.* pocket.

falla, *f.* fault, defect; failure; (geol.) fault, slide.—**fallar**, *vt.* to pass sentence, render a verdict on.—*vi.* to fail, be deficient or wanting; to miss, fail to hit; to give way.

falleba, *f.* shutter bolt.

fallecer, *vii.* [3] to die.—**fallecimiento**, *m.* decease, death.

fallido, *a.* disappointed, frustrated.

fallo, *m.* verdict, judgment, decision.

fama, *f.* fame; reputation.

famélico, *a.* hungry, ravenous.

familia, *f.* family.—**familiar**, *a.* familiar; domestic; common, frequent; well-known; homelike; colloquial.—*mf.* relative.—**familiaridad**, *f.* familiarity.—**familiarizar**, *vti.* [a] to acquaint, accustom, familiarize.—*vri.* to accustom, habituate oneself; to become familiar.

famoso, *a.* famous; (coll.) great, excellent.

fanal, *m.* lighthouse; lantern; headlight; bell glass.

fanático, *n.* & *a.* fanatic; (sports) fan.—**fanatismo**, *m.* fanaticism.

fanega, *f.* Spanish grain measure (roughly equivalent to a bushel); land measure.

fanfarrón, *n.* blusterer, swaggerer; boaster.—**fanfarronada**, *f.* boast, bluff, swagger.—**fanfarronear**, *vi.* to brag, swagger.—**fanfarronería**, *f.* bragging.

fangal, *m.* marsh, slough, quagmire.—**fango**, *m.* mire, mud.—**fangoso**, *a.* muddy, miry.

fantasear, *vi.* to fancy; to imagine.—**fantasía**, *f.* fantasy, fancy, whim, imagination.

fantasma, *m.* phantom, ghost.—**fantasmagórico**, *a.* phantasmagoric.—**fantasmón**, *mn.* an inflated, presumptuous person.

fantástico, *a.* fantastic; whimsical.

fantoche, *m.* vain and insignificant person; puppet.

farallón, *m.* headland; cliff.

farándula, *f.* strolling troop of players.—**farandulero**, *n.* comedian, player.

fardo, *m.* bale, bundle; load.

farfullar, *vi.* (coll.) to gabble, jabber.

faringe, *f.* pharynx.

farmacéutico, *a.* pharmaceutical.—*n.* pharmacist, druggist.—**farmacia**, *f.* pharmacy; drugstore.

faro, *m.* lighthouse; beacon; (auto) light, headlight.—**farol**, *m.* lantern, light; street lamp; bluff.—*echar un f.*, to bluff.—**farola**, *f.* street lamp; lighthouse.—**farolear**, *vi.* (coll.) to boast, brag.

farra, *f.* spree.

farsa, *f.* farce; company of players; sham, humbug.—**farsante**, *mf.* & *a.* humbug; fake.

fascinación, *f.* fascination, enchantment.—**fascinador**, *n.* & *a.* fascinator, charmer; fascinating, charming.—**fascinante**, *a.* fascinating, charming.—**fascinar**, *vt.* to fascinate, bewitch, charm.

fase, *f.* phase, aspect.

fastidiar, *vt.* to annoy, bore.—*vr.* to weary; to become vexed, bored or displeased.—**fastidio**, *m.* dislike; weariness; nuisance, annoyance.—**fastidioso**, *a.* annoying; tiresome; displeased, bothersome.

fastuoso, *a.* magnificent, lavish; pompous, ostentatious.

fatal, *a.* fatal; mortal; disastrous; fated.—**fatalidad**, *f.* fatality; fate, destiny; calamity.

fatiga, *f.* fatigue, weariness; hardship; anxiety; hard breathing.—**fatigar**, *vti.* [b] to fatigue, tire.—*vri.* to tire, get tired.—**fatigoso**, *a.* tiring; tiresome, boring; tired, fatigued.

fatuo, *a.* foolish, conceited.—*fuego f.*, will-o'-the-wisp.

fauces, *f. pl.* gullet.

favor, *m.* favor; help, aid; grace; compliment.—*a f. de*, in behalf of; in favor of.—*f. de, hágame el f.* or *por f.*, please.—**favorable**, *a.* favorable.—**favorecer**, *vti.* [3] to favor; to help, befriend; to abet; (of colors, clothes, etc.) to be becoming.—**favoritismo**, *m.* favoritism.—**favorito**, *n.* & *a.* favorite.

faz, *f.* face; outside.

fe, *f.* faith, faithfulness; testimony.—*dar f.*, to attest, certify; to witness.—*f. de bautismo* or *de nacimiento*, baptism or birth certificate.

fealdad, *f.* ugliness, homeliness.

febrero, *m.* February.

febril, *a.* feverish.

fécula, *f.* starch.—**feculento**, starchy.

fecundación, *f.* fecundation, fertilization.—**fecundar**, *vt.* to fertilize, fecundate.—**fecundidad**, *f.* fecundity, fertility, fruitfulness.—**fecundo**, *a.* fecund, fertile; abundant, copious.

fecha, *f.* date; standing.—**fechar,** *vt.* to date.

fechoría, *f.* misdeed, villainy.

federación, *f.* federation, confederation.—**federal,** *a.* federal.

felicidad, *f.* happiness, felicity.—¡*felicidades!* congratulations!—**felicitación,** *f.* congratulation, felicitation.—**felicitar,** *vt.* to congratulate, felicitate.

feligrés, *n.* parishioner.

feliz, *a.* happy, fortunate.

felonía, *f.* felony, treachery.

felpa, *f.* plush.—**felpilla,** *f.* chenille.—**felpudo,** *a.* plushy.—*m.* doormat.

femenino, *a.* feminine.—**feminidad,** *f.* femininity.

fenecer, *vii.* [3] to die; to end.

fenomenal, *a.* phenomenal, extraordinary.—**fenómeno,** *m.* phenomenon; (coll.) freak.

feo, *a.* ugly, homely; improper; offensive.—*m.* slight, affront.—*hacerle un f. a alguien,* to slight someone.

feraz, *a.* fertile, fruitful; abundant, plentiful.

féretro, *m.* bier, coffin.

feria, *f.* fair, market, bazaar.—**feriado,** *a.*—*día f.,* holiday.

fermentación, *f.* fermentation.—**fermentar,** *vi. & vt.* to ferment.—**fermento,** *m.* ferment, leavening; (chem.) enzyme.

ferocidad, *f.* ferocity.—**feroz,** *a.* ferocious, fierce.

férreo, *a.* of or containing iron; harsh, severe.—*vía férrea,* railroad.—**ferretería,** *f.* hardware; hardware shop.—**ferretero,** *n.* hardware dealer.

ferrocarril, *m.* railroad, railway.—*f. de cremallera,* rack railroad.—**ferrocarrilero, ferroviario,** *a.* pertaining to a railroad.—*n.* railroad employee.

fértil, *a.* fertile; plentiful.—**fertilidad,** *f.* fertility; abundance.—**fertilizante,** *m. & a.* fertilizer; fertilizing.—**fertilizar,** *vti.* [a] to fertilize, make fruitful.

ferviente, fervoroso, *a.* fervent; zealous; devout.—**fervor,** *m.* zeal, fervor.

festejar, *vt.* to entertain; to feast; to woo; to celebrate.—**festejo,** *m.* feast, entertainment; courtship.

festín, *m.* banquet, feast.

festival, *m.* festival.—**festividad,** *f.* festivity; gaiety; holiday.—**festivo,** *a.* festive, gay; humorous, witty; festival.—*día f.,* holiday.

fétido, *a.* fetid, stinking.

feto, *m.* fetus.

fiado, *m.—al f.,* on credit, on trust.—**fiador,** *n.* bondsman, guarantor, surety.—*salir f.,* to go surety.

fiambre, *m.* cold food, cold meats; (coll.) old or late news.—**fiambrera,** *f.* lunch basket; dinner pail.

fianza, *f.* surety, bail; caution; security.—*bajo f.,* on bail.—**fiar,** *vt.* to trust; to bail; to sell on trust, give credit for; to entrust, confide.—*vi.* to confide; to sell on trust, give credit.—*ser de f.,* to be trustworthy.—*vr.* **(de)** to have confidence (in), depend (on), trust.

fibra, *f.* fiber, filament; energy, stamina, vigor; (min.) vein of ore.—**fibroso,** *a.* fibrous.

ficción, *f.* fiction; tale, story.—**ficticio,** *a.* fictitious.

ficha, *f.* chip or man (in games); token; personal record; (fig.) rascal, bad person.—**fichar,** *vt.* to file a card of personal record (police, etc.); (coll.) to blacklist.—**fichero,** *m.* card index, catalogue.

fidedigno, *a.* trustworthy; creditable.

fidelidad, *f.* fidelity, faithfulness; accuracy.

fideos, *m. pl.* vermicelli; spaghetti; noodles.

fiebre, *f.* fever; intense excitement.—*f. palúdica,* malaria.

fiel, *a.* faithful, devoted; true, accurate; (pol.) stalwart.—*m.* pointer of a balance or steelyard.—*al f.,* equal weight, even balance.

fieltro, *m.* felt; felt hat.

fiera, *f.* wild beast; vicious animal or person.—**fierabrás,** *m.* (coll.) spitfire, bully; wayward child.—**fiereza,** *f.* fierceness, ferocity.—**fiero,** *a.* fierce, cruel; ferocious; huge; wild, savage.

fierro, *m.* V. HIERRO.

fiesta, *f.* feast, entertainment, party; festivity, holiday.—*aguar la f.,* to mar one's pleasure.—*hacer fiestas,* to caress; to wheedle; to fawn on.—**fiestero,** *a.* gay, jolly.—*n.* jolly person.

figura, *f.* figure; shape; build; image; face card.—**figurado,** *a.* figurative, metaphorical.—**figurar,** *vt.* to shape, fashion; to represent.—*vi.* to figure.—*vr.* to fancy, imagine to occur, come to mind; to seem.—**figurín,** *m.* fashion plate; well-dressed man.

fijador, *n. & a.* fixer; fastener; fixing; fastening;—*m.* hair tonic.—**fijar,** *vti.* [49] to fix, fasten; to determine, establish; to post (bills); to set (a date).—*vri.* **(en)** to settle (in); to fix one's attention (on); to stare at; to take notice (of), pay close attention (to).—**fijeza,** *f.* firmness, stability; steadfastness.—**fijo,** *ppi.* of FIJAR.—*a.* fixed; settled; permanent; (mech.) stationary.—*a punto f.*, exactly; with certitude.—*de f.*, certainly.—*hora fija*, time agreed on.

fila, *f.* row, tier, line; (mil.) rank; hatred.—*en f.*, in a row.

filamento, *m.* filament.

filantropía, *f.* philanthropy.—**filántropo**, *n.* philanthropist.

filarmónico, *a.* philharmonic.

filete, *m.* (arch.) fillet; (sewing) narrow hem; edge, rim; (print.) ornamental line; tenderloin.

filfa, *f.* (coll.) fib, hoax, fake.

filiación, *f.* filiation; personal description.—**filial**, *a.* filial.

filibustero, *m.* filibuster; buccaneer.

filigrana, *f.* filigree; watermark in paper; fanciful thing.

filipino, *n.* & *a.* Filipino.

filmar, *vt.* (neol.) to film (a moving picture).

filo, *m.* cutting edge.

filón, *m.* (geog.) vein, lode.

filoso, *a.* (Am.) sharp.

filosofía, *f.* philosophy.—**filosófico**, *a.* philosophic(al).—**filósofo**, *n.* philosopher.

filtración, *f.* filtration, leak(age).—**filtrar**, *vt.* & *vi.* to filter.—*vi.* to percolate, filter.—*vr.* to leak out; to disappear; to filter through.—**filtro**, *m.* filter.

fin, *m.* end, conclusion; object, purpose.—*a f. de*, in order to, so as to.—*a f. de que*, so that, to the end that.—*al f.*, at last.—*al f. y al cabo*, at last; lastly; after all.—*en f.*, finally, lastly; in short; well.—*poner f.*, to put an end to, stop, get rid of.—*por f.*, at last, finally.—*sin f.*, endless.—**final**, *a.* final; conclusive.—*m.* end, conclusion.—*pl.* (sports) finals.—**finalidad**, *f.* finality; intention.—**finalista**, *mf.* (sports) finalist.—**finalizar**, *vti.* [a] to finish, conclude; (law) to execute (a contract, deed).—*vii.* to end, to be finished or concluded.

financiamiento, *m.* financing.—**financiar**, *vt.* (Am.) to finance.—**financiero**, *a.* financial.—*n.* financier.—**financista**, *mf.* (Am.) financier.—**finanzas**, *f. pl.* public finances.

finca, *f.* real estate, land; country estate, farm, ranch.

finés, *a.* Finnish.—*n.* Finn.

fineza, *f.* fineness; kindness, courtesy; gift, favor.

fingimiento, *m.* simulation, pretense, sham.—**fingir**, [c] *vti.* & *vri.* to feign, dissemble; to affect; to imagine.

finiquitar, *vt.* to settle and close (an account).

finlandés, *a.* Finnish.—*n.* Finn.

fino, *a.* fine; thin, slender; subtle; delicate, nice; affectionate; sharp (as a point); polite, urbane.—**finura**, *f.* fineness; politeness; courtesy.

firma, *f.* signature; hand (as hand and seal); act of signing; (com.) firm, house; firm name.

firmamento, *m.* firmament, sky.

firmante, *mf.* signer, subscriber.—**firmar**, *vt.* to sign; to subscribe, set one's hand.

firme, *a.* firm, stable; hard; unyielding; resolute.—*m.* groundwork, bed; roadbed.—*en f.*, definitive, final, in final form.—*adv.* firmly, strongly.—**firmeza**, *f.* firmness; hardness.

fiscal, *a.* fiscal.—*m.* attorney general; district attorney, public prosecutor.—**fiscalización**, *f.* discharge of a FISCAL'S duties; control.—**fiscalizar**, *vti.* [a] to prosecute; to criticize, censure; to control.

fisgar, *vii.* [b] to snoop; to peep; to pry.—**fisgón**, *n.* snooper; busybody.—*a.* snooping.—**fisgonear**, *vi.* to pry; to snoop.

física, *f.* physics.—**físico**, *a.* physical.—*n.* physicist.—*m.* (coll.) physical appearance, physique.

fisiología, *f.* physiology.—**fisiológico**, *a.* physiological.

fisonomía, *f.* features; face.

fisura, *f.* (geol.) fissure, cleft; (surg.) fissure of bone.

flaco, *a.* thin, lean; feeble; frail.—*m.* weak point, weakness.—**flacura**, *f.* thinness.

flagrante, *a.* flagrant.—*en f.*, in the act.

flama, *f.* V. LLAMA.—**flamante**, *a.* flaming, bright; brand-new.—**flamear**, *vi.* to flame, blaze; to flutter (banners, sails, etc.).

flamenco, *a.* & *n.* Flemish.—*n.* flamingo.—*cante f.*, Andalusian gypsy singing.

flan, *m.* rich custard.

flanco, *m.* side; flank.

flanera, *f.* pudding pan.

flanquear, *vt.* to flank.

flaquear, *vi.* to flag, weaken; to slacken.—**flaqueza**, *f.* leanness, thinness; weakness; frailty.

flatulencia, *f.* belch, wind.

flauta, *f.* flute.—**flautín**, *m.* piccolo.—**flautista**, *mf.* flute player.

fleco, *m.* fringe, purl, flounce.

flecha, *f.* arrow.—**flechar**, *vt.* to shoot an arrow; (fig.) to inspire sudden love.—**flechazo**, *m.* arrow wound; love at first sight.

fleje, *m.* iron hoop or strap.

flema, *f.* phlegm.—**flemático,** *a.* phlegmatic.

flemón, *m.* gumboil.

fletar, *vt.* to charter (a ship); to freight; to hire.—*salir fletado,* to escape fast; to leave on the run.—**flete,** *m.* freight, freightage; hire price (for transporting freight, cargo).

flexibilidad, *f.* flexibility.—**flexible,** *a.* flexible; docile.—**flexión,** *f.* flection, flexure.

flirtear, *vi.* (neol.) to flirt.

flojear, *vi.* to slacken; to grow weak. —**flojedad, flojera,** *f.* weakness, feebleness; laxity, negligence.—**flojo,** *a.* loose, lax; weak; flaccid; lazy; cowardly.

flor, *f.* flower; blossom; prime; compliment.—*decir,* or *echar flores,* to pay compliments, to flatter.—*f. y nata,* flower, elite.—**floreado,** *a.* flowered, figured (goods); made of the finest flour.—**florear,** *vt.* to flower; to bolt (flour); to flourish; to pay compliments to.—**florecer,** *vii.* [3] to flower, bloom; to prosper. —**floreciente,** *a.* flourishing, thriving. —**florecimiento,** *m.* flowering; flourishing.—**floreo,** *m.* idle talk; compliment; (fencing, mus.) flourish. —**florero,** *n.* (Am.) flower vendor. —*m.* flowerpot; flower vase; flower stand.—**floresta,** *f.* wooded field.— **florete,** *m.* fencing foil.—**florido,** *a.* flowery; full of flowers, in bloom; choice, select.—**florista,** *mf.* florist.

flota, *f.* fleet.—**flotación,** *f.* flotation, floating.—*línea de f.,* waterline.— **flotador,** *n. & a.* floater; floating.—*m.* float.—**flotante,** *a.* floating.—**flotar,** *vi.* to float; to waft.

fluctuación, *f.* fluctuation; wavering. —**fluctuar,** *vi.* to fluctuate; waver.

fluente, *a.* fluent, flowing.—**fluidez,** *f.* fluidity; fluency.—**fluido,** *a.* fluid; fluent.—*m.* fluid.—**fluir,** [23-e] *vii.* to flow.—**flujo,** *m.* flux, flow.

fluorescencia, *f.* fluorescence.—**fluorescente,** *a.* fluorescent.

foca, *f.* (zool.) seal.

foco, *m.* focus; center, source; electric-light bulb.

fofo, *a.* spongy, soft.

fogarada, fogata, *f.* bonfire, blaze.— **fogón,** *m.* fireside; cooking place, cooking stove, kitchen range; touchhole of a gun; firebox (of a boiler, locomotive, etc.).—**fogonazo,** *m.* powder flash.—**fogonero,** *n.* fireman, stoker.—**fogosidad,** *f.* fieriness, heat, vehemence.—**fogoso,** *a.* fiery; ardent; impetuous; spirited.

foliar, *vt.* to paginate, number the pages of a book, etc.—**folio,** *m.* folio.

follaje, *m.* foliage; leafage.

folletín, *m.* newspaper serial.—**folleto,** *m.* pamphlet, booklet, brochure.

fomentar, *vt.* to foment; to warm; to promote, encourage.—**fomento,** *m.* fomentation; promotion; development.

fonda, *f.* inn; eating house; second-rate hotel.

fondeadero, *m.* anchoring ground; haven.—**fondear,** *vt.* (naut.) to sound; to search (a ship).—*vi.* to cast anchor.—**fondeo,** *m.* (naut.) search; casting anchor.

fondillo, *m.* seat of trousers; (coll.) bottom, posterior.

fondista, *mf.* innkeeper.

fondo, *m.* bottom; depth; background; nature (of a person); principal or essential part of a thing; fund, capital.—*pl.* funds, resources. —*a f.,* thoroughly.—*andar mal de fondos,* to be short of money.— *en f.,* abreast.

fonética, *f.* phonetics.—**fonético,** *a.* phonetic.—**fónico,** *a.* phonic, acoustic.

fonógrafo, *m.* phonograph.

fontana, *f.* fountain, spring, water jet.—**fontanar,** *m.* water spring.

football, *m.* football.

forajido, *n.* outlaw, fugitive; bandit.

forastero, *a.* foreign.—*n.* stranger; outsider.

forcejar, forcejear, *vi.* to struggle, strive; to contest, contend; to resist; to tussle.

forestal, *a.* pertaining to a forest.— *ingeniería f.,* forestry.

forja, *f.* smelting furnace; smithy; forge; forging.—**forjador,** *n.* blacksmith, forger.—**forjar,** *vt.* to forge; to frame, form.

forma, *f.* form, shape; manner; method, order; pattern, mold; format; block (for hats, etc.).—*pl.* (of persons) figure.—*de f. que,* so as, so that.—*en f.,* in due form; in a thorough and proper manner.— *tomar f.,* to develop, to materialize. —**formación,** *f.* formation, forming. —**formal,** *a.* formal, regular, methodical; proper; serious; truthful, reliable; well-behaved.—**formalidad,** *f.* formality; exactness, punctuality; seriousness, solemnity; requisite; established practice.—**formalismo,** *m.* formalism.—**formalista,** *mf.* formalist.—**formalizar,** *vti.* [a] to put in final form; to legalize.—*vri.* to become serious or earnest.—**formar,** *vt.* to form; to shape.—*f. parte de,* to be a member of.—*vr.* to develop; to take form.—**formativo,** *a.* formative.—**formato,** *m.* format (of a book).

fórmula, *f.* formula; recipe, prescription.—**formular,** *vt.* to formulate.—**formulismo,** *m.* formulism; red tape.

fornido, *a.* robust, husky, stout, stalwart.

foro, *m.* forum; court of justice; bar, the legal profession; back (in stage scenery).

forraje, *m.* forage, fodder; foraging.

forrar, *vt.* to line (as clothes); to cover (as a book, umbrella, etc.); (anat.) to sheathe.—**forro,** *m.* lining, doubling; cover.

fortalecedor, *n.* & *a.* fortifier; fortifying.—**fortalecer,** *vti.* [3] to fortify, strengthen, corroborate.—**fortalecimiento,** *m.* fortifying; fortification, defenses.—**fortaleza,** *f.* fortitude; strength, vigor; fortress, fort.—**fortificación,** fortification; fort; military architecture.—**fortificar,** *vti.* [d] to strengthen; (mil.) to fortify.—**fortín,** *m.* small fort.

fortuna, *f.* fortune; good luck; wealth.—*por f.,* fortunately.

forúnculo, *m.* = FURÚNCULO.

forzar, *vti.* [12-a] to force, break in (as a door); to compel; to subdue by force; to ravish.—**forzoso,** *a.* obligatory, compulsory; unavoidable.—**forzudo,** *a.* strong, vigorous.

fosa, *f.* grave.

fosco, *a.* frowning; cross.

fosfato, *m.* phosphate.

fosforescencia, *f.* phosphorescence.—**fosforecer,** *vii.* [3] to phosphoresce.—**fósforo,** *m.* phosphorous; friction match.

foso, *m.* pit; stage pit; moat.

foto, *f.* photo (photograph).—**fotocopia,** *f.* photostat.—**fotoeléctrico,** *a.* photoelectric.—**fotogénico,** *a.* photogenic.—**fotograbado,** *m.* photoengraving, photogravure.—**fotografía,** *f.* photography; photograph.—**fotografiar,** *vt.* to photograph.—**fotógrafo,** *n.* photographer.

frac, *m.* tail coat.

fracasar, *vi.* to fail.—**fracaso,** *m.* downfall; failure.

fracción, *f.* fragment; fraction.—**fraccionamiento,** *m.* division into fractions.—**fraccionario,** *a.* fractional.

fractura, *f.* fracture; breaking, crack.—**fracturar,** *vt.* & *vi.* to fracture, break.

fragancia, *f.* fragrance, scent.—**fragante,** *a.* fragrant.

frágil, *a.* brittle, breakable, fragile.—**fragilidad,** *f.* fragility; frailty.

fragmentario, *a.* fragmentary.—**fragmento,** *m.* fragment.

fragor, *m.* clamorous noise; blare.

fragosidad, *f.* roughness; impenetrability, thickness, wildness (of a forest); craggedness.—**fragoso,** *a.* craggy, rough; full of brambles and briers; roaring.

fragua, *f.* forge; smithy.—**fraguar,** *vt.* to forge; to hammer out; to plan, plot.—*vi.* (of concrete, etc.) to set.

fraile, *m.* friar, monk.

frambuesa, *f.* (bot.) raspberry.

francachela, *f.* (coll.) lark, spree; gala meal.

francés, *a.* French.—*m.* French language.—*n.* Frenchman (-woman.)

franco, *a.* frank, open; franc; free, clear, disengaged; exempt.—*f. a bordo,* free on board.—*m.* franc.

francotirador, sniper.

franela, *f.* flannel.

franja, *f.* fringe, trimming, band; stripe; strip (of land).

franquear, *vt.* to exempt; to grant immunity to; to enfranchise; to prepay (postage); to open, clear.—*vr.* to unbosom oneself.—**franqueo,** *m.* postage.—**franqueza,** *f.* frankness.—*con f.,* frankly.—**franquicia,** *f.* exemption from taxes; franchise, grant.

frasco, *m.* flask, vial.

frase, *f.* phrase.—**fraseología,** *f.* phraseology; verbosity; wording.

fraternal, *a.* brotherly, fraternal.—**fraternidad,** *f.* fraternity, brotherhood.—**fraternizar,** *vii.* [a] to fraternize.

fraude, *m.,* **fraudulencia,** *f.* fraud.—**fraudulento,** *a.* fraudulent.

frazada, *f.* blanket.

frecuencia, *f.* frequency.—*con f.,* frequently.—**frecuentar,** *vt.* to frequent.—**frecuente,** *a.* frequent.

fregadero, *m.* kitchen sink.—**fregar,** *vti.* [1-b] to rub; to wash; to scrub, scour; (Am.) to annoy, bother.—**fregona,** *f.* kitchenmaid; dishwasher.

freir, *vti.* [35-49] to fry; to pester, irritate.

frenar, *vt.* to brake, apply the brake to; to restrain; to bridle.

frenesí, *m.* frenzy, fury, madness; folly.—**frenético,** *a.* mad, frantic, frenzied.

freno, *m.* brake; bridle or bit of the bridle; curb, restraint, control.

frente, *f.* forehead; countenance.—*m.* front, fore part, façade.—*al f.,* opposite; carried forward.—*al f. de,* in front of; in charge of.—*de f.,* from the front; front; facing;

abreast.—*f. a*, opposite, facing.—*f. a f.*, face to face.—*f. por f.*, directly opposite.—*hacer f.*, to face (a problem, etc.); to meet (a demand, etc.).

fresa, *f.* strawberry; (mech.) drill, bit, milling tool.

fresca, *f.* cool air, fresh air; fresh remark.—**fresco,** *a.* fresh; (of weather, etc.) cool; just made, finished, or gathered.—*m.* cool or fresh air; (art) fresco.—*hacer f.*, to be cool.—*tomar el f.*, to get or go out for some fresh air.—**frescor,** *m.* cool; freshness.—**frescura,** *f.* freshness; impudence; unconcern.

fresno, *m.* ash tree; ash wood.

frialdad, *f.* coldness; unconcern, coolness.

fricasé, *m.* fricassee.

fricción, *f.* friction, rubbing.—**friccionar,** *vt.* to rub.

friega, *f.* friction, rubbing.

frigidez, *f.* frigidity.—**frígido,** *a.* frigid.—**frigorífico,** *a.* refrigerating. —*m.* refrigerator, storage house or room.

frijol, *m.* bean.

frío, *a.* cold; frigid; indifferent, unemotional; dull.—*m.* cold, coldness. —*hacer f.*, to be cold.—*tener f.*, to feel cold.—**friolento,** *a.* chilly; very sensitive to cold.

friolera, *f.* trifle, bauble.

frisar, *vi.* (en) to approach; to be near (to).

frita, *f.* (Am.) hamburger.—**fritada,** *f.* fry; dish of anything fried.— **frito,** *ppi.* of FREÍR.—*estar f.*, to be lost; to be annoyed.—*m.* fry.— **fritura,** *f.* fry, fritter.

frivolidad, *f.* frivolity.—**frívolo,** *a.* frivolous, trifling.

fronda, *f.* leaf; frond.—*pl.* foliage, verdure.—**frondosidad,** *f.* frondage, leafy foliage.—**frondoso,** *a.* leafy, luxuriant.

frontal, *a.* frontal, pertaining to the forehead.—*m.* (eccl.) frontal; (anat.) frontal bone.

frontera, *f.* frontier, border.—**fronterizo,** *a.* frontier; facing, opposite.— **frontero,** *a.* opposite, facing.

frontis, *m.* frontispiece, façade.— **frontispicio,** *m.* frontispiece.

frontón, *m.* main wall of a handball court; Jai-Alai court.

frotación, *f.* rubbing.—**frotamiento,** *m.* rubbing.—**frotar,** *vt.* to rub.

fructífero, *a.* fruit-bearing; fruitful. —**fructificación,** *f.* fructification.— **fructificar,** *vii.* [d] to bear fruit; to yield profit.

frugal, *a.* frugal.—**frugalidad,** *f.* frugality, thrift.

fruición, *f.* fruition, enjoyment.

fruncimiento, *m.* wrinkling; shirring. —**fruncir,** *vti.* [a] to wrinkle; to gather in pleats; to shrivel.—*f. el ceño,* or *f. las cejas,* to frown.—*f. los labios,* to curl or pucker the lips.

fruslería, *f.* trifle, bauble, tidbit.

frustración, *f.* frustration.—**frustrar,** *vt.* to frustrate.—*vr.* to fail.

fruta, *f.* fruit.—**frutal,** *a.* fruit-bearing; fruit.—*m.* fruit tree.—**frutería,** *f.* fruit store.—**frutero,** *n.* fruit seller; fruit basket, fruit dish.— **fruto,** *m.* fruit; fruits, result; benefice, profit.

fuego, *m.* fire; (Am.) skin eruption; firing of firearms; passion.—*f. fatuo,* will-o'-the-wisp.—*juegos artificiales,* fireworks.—*hacer f.*, to fire, shoot. —*romper f.*, to start shooting.

fuelle, *m.* bellows; blower; puckers in clothes.

fuente, *f.* water spring; fountain; source; serving dish, platter.—*beber en buenas fuentes,* to be well-informed.

fuera, *adv.* out, outside.—*de f.*, from the outside.—*f. de,* besides, in addition.—*f. de sí,* beside oneself; aghast.—*hacia f.*, outward.—*por f.*, on the outside.—*interj.* out! away! put him out! get out!

fuero, *m.* statute, law; jurisdiction; privilege or exemption; compilation of laws.

fuerte, *a.* strong; powerful; intense; firm, compact; hard, not malleable. —*m.* fort, fortress; strong point; (mus.) forte.—*adv.* strongly, hard, copiously.—**fuerza,** *f.* force; power; strength; stress; violence; firmness; (mil.) force(s).—*a f. de,* by dint of, by force of.—*a la f.*, *a viva f.*, by main force, forcibly.—*f. mayor,* superior force.

fuetazo, *m.* (Am.) blow with a whip. —**fuete,** *m.* horsewhip, riding whip.

fuga, *f.* flight; escape; runaway; elopement; leak, leakage; fugue.— **fugacidad,** *f.* brevity.—**fugarse,** *vri.* [b] to flee, run away; to escape, leak out.—**fugaz,** *a.* brief.—**fugitivo,** *n. & a.* fugitive, runaway.—*a.* brief, perishable, unstable.

fulano, *n.* (Mr.) so-and-so.

fulgor, *m.* brilliancy.—**fulgurar,** *vi.* to flash, shine with brilliancy.

fullero, *a.* (coll.) shady, dishonest.— *n.* cheat, sharper; card sharp.

fumada, *f.* puff, whiff, (of smoke).— **fumadero,** *m.* smoking room.— **fumador,** *n.* smoker.—*a.* addicted to smoking.—**fumar,** *vt. & vi.* to smoke (cigars, etc.).

fumigación, *f.* fumigation.—**fumigar,** *vti.* [b] to fumigate.

función, *f.* function; duty; functioning; religious ceremony; (theat.) performance, play.—**funcional,** *a.* functional.—**funcionamiento,** *m.* functioning, working, operation, performance.—**funcionar,** *vi.* to function; to work, run.—**funcionario,** *n.* functionary, public official.

funda, *f.* case, sheath, cover, envelope, slip.—*f. de almohada,* pillowcase.

fundación, *f.* foundation; founding; beginning, origin.—**fundador,** *n.* founder.—**fundamental,** *a.* fundamental, basal.—**fundamentar,** *vt.* to establish on a basis; to base; to set firm.—**fundamento,** *m.* basis; reason, fundamental principle; root; good behavior, orderliness.—**fundar,** *vt.* to found; to raise; to establish, institute; to base, ground.—*vr.* (en) to base one's opinion (on).

fundición, *f.* smelting; foundry.—**fundir,** *vt.* to fuse or melt; to merge, blend; to be ruined.

fúnebre, *a.* funereal, mournful; funeral; dark, lugubrious.—**funeral(es),** *m.* funeral.—**funeraria,** *f.* funeral parlor.—**funerario, funeral,** *a.* funeral.—**funesto,** *a.* ill-fated; fatal; mournful; regrettable.

fungir, *vii.* [c] to act in some capacity.

fungosidad, *f.* fungus, fungous growth; spongy morbid growth.

furgón, *m.* wagon; boxcar.

furia, *f.* fury, rage; ill-tempered person.—**furibundo, furioso,** *a.* furious; frantic.—**furor,** *m.* furor, fury, anger; enthusiasm; exaltation of fancy.—*hacer f.,* to be the rage.

furtivo, *a.* furtive, clandestine.

furúnculo, *m.* (med.) boil.

fuselaje, *m.* fuselage.

fusible, *a.* fusible.—*m.* (elec.) fuse.

fusil, *m.* rifle, gun.—**fusilamiento,** *m.* execution by shooting.—**fusilar,** *vt.* to shoot, execute by shooting.—**fusilazo,** *m.* rifle shot.—**fusilería,** *f.* (mil.) guns, rifles.—**fusilero,** *m.* rifleman.

fusión, *f.* fusion, melting; union; merger.—**fusionar,** *vt.* to unite, merge—*vr.* to merge, form a merger.

fusta, *f.* whiplash.—**fustigar,** *vti.* [b] to lash.

fútbol, *m.* soccer.

futesa, *f.* trifle, bagatelle.—**fútil,** *a.* trifling, trivial.

futuro, *a.* future.—*n.* betrothed, future husband (wife); future.—*en lo f.,* in the future, hereafter.

G

gabacho, *a.* (coll.) Frenchlike.—*m.* (coll.) Frenchman.

gabán, *m.* overcoat.

garbardina, *f.* gabardine.

gabinete, *m.* cabinet (of a government); sitting room; private parlor; studio, study; dentist's or doctor's office.

gacela, *f.* gazelle.

gaceta, *f.* official gazette.—**gacetilla,** *f.* personal-news column; gossip; newspaper squib.—**gacetillero,** *n.* gacetista, *mf.* newsmonger, gossip.

gacho, *a.* bent; drooping; turned down.—*a gachas,* (coll.) on all fours.—*con las orejas gachas,* (coll.) crestfallen.

gafas, *f. pl.* spectacles.

gago, *n.* stammerer, stutterer.—**gaguear,** *vi.* to stutter.—**gaguera,** *f.* stuttering.

gaita, *f.* hurdy-gurdy.—*asomar la g.,* to stick out one's neck.—*g. gallega,* bagpipe.—**gaitero,** *n.* piper, bagpipe player.

gaje, *m.*—*pl.* fees.—*gajes del oficio,* fisherman's luck.

gajo, *m.* torn off branch (of a tree); bunch of fruit; segment of fruit.

gala, *f.* full dress; array; gala.—*pl.* trappings.—*galas de novia,* bridal trousseau.—*hacer g. de,* to be proud of, glory in, boast of.

galán, *m.* gallant; lover, wooer; (theat.) leading man.—**galante,** *a.* gallant, polished, attentive to ladies.—**galantear,** *vt.* to court, woo.—**galanteo,** *m.* gallantry, courtship, wooing.—**galantería,** *f.* gallantry, courtesy, politeness; compliment to a lady.

galápago, *m.* fresh-water tortoise.

galardón, *m.* reward, prize.

galeno, *m.* (coll.) physician.

galeote, *m.* galley slave.

galera, *f.* (naut.; print.) galley; wagon, van; prison.—**galerada,** *f.* (print.) galley; galley proof.

galería, *f.* gallery, lobby, corridor; (theat.) gallery; art museum; collection of paintings.

galerna, *f.* (naut.) stormy northwest wind.

galés, *n. & a.* Welshman; Welsh.

galgo, *n.* greyhound.

galillo, *m.* uvula, soft palate.

galocha, *f.* galosh, clog.

galón, *m.* gallon; braid, tape, binding lace; stripe, chevron (on uniforms).—**galonear,** *vt.* (sewing) to bind; to trim with braid.

galopar, *vi.* to gallop.—**galope,** *m.* gallop; haste, speed.—*a g.,* hurriedly, speedily.—**galopín,** m. ragamuffin; rascal; shrewd fellow.

galpón, m. (Am.) shed.

galvanizar, vti. [a] to galvanize; to electroplate.

gallardete, m. pennant, streamer.

gallardía, f. gracefulness; bravery; nobleness.—**gallardo,** a. graceful, elegant; lively; brave.

gallear, vi. to raise the voice in anger; to crow; to bully.

gallegada, f. a Galician dance and its tune.—**gallego,** m. & a. Galician; (Am.) (nickname) Spanish; Spaniard.

galleta, f. cracker, biscuit, hardtack; cookie; slap.—**galletica,** f. small or fine cracker or biscuit.

gallina, f. hen.—g. de Guinea or guineo, guinea hen.—mf. coward.—g. ciega, blindman's buff.—**gallinero,** m. poultry yard, hen coop or house; (coll., theat.) top gallery.—**gallito,** m. small cock; cock of the walk, bully.—**gallo,** m. cock, rooster; false note in singing; bully.—g. de pelea, or inglés, gamecock.—patas de g., wrinkles in the corner of the eye.

gamo, m. buck of the fallow deer.

gamuza, f. chamois; chamois skin.

gana, f. appetite, hunger; desire; mind.—dar g., or ganas de, to arouse desire to.—de buena g., willingly.—de mala g., unwillingly.—no me da la g., I don't want to, I won't.—tener g., or ganas de, to desire; to wish to.

ganadería, f. cattle raising; cattle ranch; cattle brand.—**ganadero,** n. cattleman; cattle dealer; stock farmer.—a. pertaining to cattle.—**ganado,** m. cattle; herd.—g. caballar, horses.—g. de cerda, swine, hogs.—g. lanar, sheep.—g. vacuno, cattle.

ganador, n. & a. winner; winning.—**ganancia,** f. gain, profit.—**ganancioso,** a. lucrative, profitable; gaining.—**ganapán,** m. drudge; common laborer; coarse man.—**ganar,** vt. to win; to gain; to earn.—g. el pan, la vida, or el sustento, to make a living.

gancho, m. hook; crook; crotch.—echar el g., (fig.) to catch; to hook.—g. del pelo, hairpin.—tener g., (coll.) to be attractive.

gandul, n. (coll.) idler, loafer, tramp.—**gandulería,** f. idleness, laziness.

ganga, f. bargain; windfall.

gangoso, a. twangy.

gangrena, f. gangrene.—**gangrenarse,** vr. to become gangrenous.

ganguear, vi. to snuffle; to speak nasally.—**gangueo,** m. snuffle; nasal speech.

gansada, f. (coll.) stupidity.—**ganso,** n. goose, gander; silly person, ninny.

ganzúa, f. picklock, skeleton key; burglar.

gañán, m. farm hand; rustic; (fig.) uncouth, brutal person.

gañote, m. (coll.) throat.

garabateo, m. scribbling, scrawling.—**garabato,** m. scrawl, scribble; hook.

garaje, m. garage.

garantía, f. guarantee; (com. and law) warranty, guaranty, security.—**garantizar,** vti. [a] to guarantee, vouch for.

garañón, m. stallion.

garapiñado, a. candied, sugarcoated.

garbanzo, m. chickpea.

garbo, m. grace, gracefulness, elegant carriage.—**garboso,** a. graceful, sprightly.

garete, m.—al g., (naut.) adrift.

garfio, m. hook; gaff.

garganta, f. throat; gullet; gorge.—**gargantilla,** f. necklace.

gárgara, f., **gargarismo,** m. gargle; gargling.—hacer gárgaras, to gargle.—**gargarizar,** vii. [a] to gargle.

garita, f. sentry box; lodge, hut.

garito, m. gambling house or den.

garlopa, f. (carp.) jack plane, long plane.

garra, f. claw, paw, talon; hook.—echarle g., (coll.) to arrest, grasp.—sacar de las garras de, to free from.

garrafa, f. carafe, decanter.—**garrafal,** a. great, huge.—**garrafón,** m. large carafe.

garrapata, f. (entom.) tick.—**garrapatear,** vi. to scribble, scrawl.

garrocha, f. (sports) pole; goad stick.

garrotazo, m. blow with club or cudgel.—**garrote,** m. club, cudgel; garrote (for capital punishment).—dar g., to garrote.—**garrotero,** n. beater; (coll.) usurer.

garrucha, f. pulley.

garza, f. heron.

garzo, a. blue-eyed.

gas, m. gas; vapor; (coll.) gaslight.

gasa, f. gauze.

gaseosa, f. soda water.—**gaseoso,** a. gaseous.—**gasificar,** vti. [d] to gasify.—**gasolina,** f. gasoline, gas.

gastable, a. expendable.—**gastado,** a. worn-out; shabby; blasé.—**gastador,** a. lavish, prodigal.—n. spender, spendthrift.—**gastar,** vt. to spend, expend; to waste, wear out; to use.—vr. to become old or useless; to waste away, wear out; to fray.—**gasto,** m. expenditure, outlay, expense; consumption; spending, consuming.—*gastos de explotación*, operating or working expenses.—*gastos de representación*, incidental expenses.

gatas, *f. pl.*—*andar a g.*, on all fours.—**gatazo,** *m.* large cat; (coll.) artful trick, cheat.—**gatear,** *vi.* (of children) to creep; to climb up; to go upon all fours.

gatillo, *m.* trigger.

gato, *n.* cat.—*m.* (mech.) jack; (coll.) shrewd fellow.—*cuatro gatos*, (contempt.) just a few people.—*dar or meter g. por liebre*, (coll.) to cheat, to give chalk for cheese.—*aquí hay g. encerrado*, (coll.) there is something fishy here.

gauchada, *f.* artifice; act of a Gaucho.—*hacer una g.*, (Arg.) to do a favor.—**gauchaje,** *m.* (Am.) Gaucho folk, group of Gauchos.—**gaucho,** *n.* Gaucho, pampas cowboy (-girl).

gaveta, *f.* drawer.

gavilán, *m.* sparrow hawk.

gavilla, *f.* bundle or sheaf of grain; gang of thugs.

gaviota, *f.* sea gull, gull.

gaza, *f.* loop of a bow.

gazapo, *m.* young rabbit; (coll.) blunder, mistake.

gazmoñería, *f.* prudery.—**gazmoño,** *a.* prudish, priggish.

gaznápiro, *n.* churl; simpleton.

gaznate, *m.* throttle; windpipe.—**gaznatón,** *m.* (Am.) slap in the face.

gazofia, *f.* = BAZOFIA.

gelatina, *f.* gelatine; jelly.—**gelatinoso,** *a.* gelatinous.

gema, *f.* jewel, gem, precious stone; bud.

gemelo, *n.* twin.—*m.* cufflink.—*pl.* binoculars; opera, field or marine glasses.

gemido, *m.* moan; whine; whimper.—**gemir,** *vii.* [29] to moan; to whine; to whimper.

gendarme, *mf.* (Am.) gendarme, policeman (-woman).

generación, *f.* generation.—**generador,** *n. & a.* generator; generating.—*m.* (mech., elec.) generator.

general, *a.* general; usual.—*por lo g.*, in general, generally.—*m.* (mil.) general.—**generalidad,** *f.* generality.—**generalizar,** *vti.* [a] to generalize.—*vri.* to become general, usual, or popular.

genérico, *a.* generic.—**género,** *m.* genus; class; kind; sort; material, cloth; (gram.) gender.—*pl.* dry goods; (com.) merchandise.—*g. humano*, mankind.

generosidad, *f.* generosity.—**generoso,** *a.* generous.

genial, *a.* genial; pleasant.—**genio,** *m.*

genius; temperament, disposition, temper; character; spirit.—*mal g.*, ill temper.

genital, *a.* genital.—*m.* testicle.

gente, *f.* people, folk, crowd; race, nation; (coll.) folks, family.—*g. baja*, lower classes; mob.—*g. bien*, upper class.—*g. de bien* honest people.—*g. de paz*, friends.—*g. menuda*, children, small fry.

gentil, *a.* graceful, genteel; polite.—*mf.* gentile; pagan.—**gentileza,** *f.* gentility, gracefulness; courtesy.

gentío, *m.* crowd, multitude.—**gentuza,** *f.* rabble, riffraff; mob.

genuino, *a.* genuine; unadulterated.

geografía, *f.* geography.—**geográfico,** *a.* geographical.—**geógrafo,** *n.* geographer.—**geología,** *f.* geology.—**geólogo,** *n.* geologist.—**geometría,** *f.* geometry.—**geométrico,** *a.* geometrical.

geranio, *m.* geranium.

gerencia, *f.* (com.) management, administration.—**gerente,** *mf.* (com.) manager.

germen, *m.* germ; source.—**germinación,** *f.* (bot.) germination.—**germinar,** *vi.* to germinate.

gerundio, *m.* gerund.

gestación, *f.* gestation, pregnancy.

gestión, *f.* management, negotiation; effort.—**gestionar,** *vt.* to manage; to negotiate; to undertake.

gesto, *m.* facial expression; grimace; gesture.—*hacer gestos*, to make faces.

giba, *f.* hump, hunch.—**giboso,** *a.* humpbacked.

gigante, *mf.* giant; giantess.—*a.* gigantic.—**gigantesco,** *a.* gigantic.

gimnasia, *f.* calisthenics.—**gimnasio,** *m.* gymnasium.—**gimnasta,** *mf.* gymnast.—**gimnástica,** *f.* gymnastics.

gimotear, *vi.* (coll.) to whine.—**gimoteo,** *m.* whining.

ginebra, *f.* gin (liquor).

ginecología, *f.* gynecology.

girador, *n.* (com.) drawer of draft.—**girar,** *vi.* to whirl, revolve, rotate; to turn; (com.) to draw (checks, drafts).—*g. contra or a cargo de*, to draw on.—**girasol,** *m.* sunflower.—**giratorio,** *a.* revolving, rotary.—**giro,** *m.* turn; rotation; bend; trend, bias; turn of phrase; (com.) draft; line of business.—*g. postal*, money order.—*tomar otro g.* to take another course.

gitano, *a.* gypsy; gypsylike; honey-mouthed.—*n.* gypsy.

glacial, *a.* glacial.—**glaciar,** *m.* glacier.

gladiolo, *m.* gladiolus.

glándula, *f.* gland.—**glandular,** *a.* glandular.

global, *a.* global, overall.—**globo,** *m.* globe, sphere; balloon.—*en g.,* as a whole; in bulk.—*g. terráqueo* or *terrestre,* (the) globe, (the) earth. —**globular,** *a.* globular.—**glóbulo,** *m.* globule.

gloria, *f.* glory, fame; heavenly state, bliss; splendor.—*saber a g.,* to taste delicious.—**gloriarse,** *vr.* (de or en) to boast (of), to take delight (in).— **glorieta,** *f.* circle or square at intersection of streets; bower, arbor. —**glorificación,** *f.* glorification; praise.—**glorificar,** *vti.* [d] to glorify; to exalt; to praise.—*vri.* = GLORIARSE.—**glorioso,** *a.* glorious.

glosa, *f.* gloss; (mus.) variation of a theme.—**glosar,** *vt.* to gloss, comment; (mus.) to vary (a theme).— **glosario,** *m.* glossary.

glotón, *n. & a.* glutton; gluttonous. —**glotonería,** *f.* gluttony.

gluglú, *m.* gurgle, gurgling sound.

gobernación, *f.* government.—**gobernador,** *n.* governor; ruler.—**gobernante,** *mf.* ruler.—*a.* ruling.—**gobernar,** *vti.* [1] & *vii.* to govern, rule. —*vri.* to manage (one's affairs), carry on.—**gobierno,** *m.* government; management, direction; control (of a business, an automobile, an airplane); helm, rudder.—*para su g.,* for your guidance.

goce, *m.* enjoyment; joy; fruition.

godo, *n. & a.* Goth(ic); (Colombia, pol.) conservative, Spaniard.

gol, *m.* (sports) goal scored.

gola, *f.* ruff; gullet, throat.

goleta, *f.* (naut.) schooner.

golfo, *m.* gulf; sea; bum; ragamuffin.

golondrina, *f.* (ornith.) swallow.

golosear, golosinear, *vi.* to nibble on sweets.—**golosina,** *f.* dainty, delicacy, sweet morsel, tidbit; daintiness; trifle.—**goloso,** *a.* fond of tidbits or sweets.

golpe, *m.* blow; stroke, hit, knock, beat; shock, clash; attack, spell; action.—*de g.,* suddenly.—*g. de vista,* glance; sight.—**golpear,** *vt.* to strike, hit, hammer.—*vi.* to beat; to knock, pound (as a piston).— **golpetear,** *vt. & vi.* to strike or pound continually; to rattle.—**golpeteo,** *m.* knocking, pounding, rattling.

gollería, *f.* dainty; delicious morsel; superfluity, excess.

gollete, *m.* throttle, gullet; neck of a bottle.

goma, *f.* gum; rubber; glue; tire; rubber band; rubber eraser; overshoes, rubbers; (Am.) hangover.— *g. de borrar,* rubber eraser.—*g. de mascar,* chewing gum.—**gomoso,** *a.* gummy; gum-producing.

gonce, *m.* hinge.

góndola, *f.* gondola.—**gondolero,** *n.* gondolier.

gong, *m.* gong.

gonorrea, *f.* gonorrhea.

gordinflón, *a.* (coll.) chubby, flabby, fat.—**gordo,** *a.* fat.—*hacer la vista gorda,* to pretend not to see, wink at.—*m.* fat, suet.—**gordura,** *f.* grease, fat; fatness.

gorgojo, *m.* grub, weevil; (coll.) dwarfish person.

gorgotear, *vi.* to gurgle.—**gorgoteo,** *m.* gurgle, gurgling sound.

gorguera, *f.* ruff.

gorila, *m.* gorilla.

gorjear, *vi.* to warble, trill.—*vr.* to gabble (as a child).—**gorjeo,** *m.* warble, trilling; gabble of a child.

gorra, *f.* cap; (coll.) intrusion at feast without invitation.—*de g.,* at other people's expense.—*ir, comer, andar, etc., de g.,* (coll.) to sponge.

gorrión, *m.* sparrow.

gorrista, *mf.* (coll.) sponger.—**gorro,** *m.* cap, coif.—**gorrón,** *n.* sponger, parasite.

gota, *f.* drop of liquid; gout.—*sudar la g. gorda,* (coll.) to sweat blood.— **gotear,** *vi.* to drop, drip, dribble, leak; to sprinkle, begin to rain.— **gotera,** *f.* leak, leakage; drip, dripping.

gótico, *a.* Gothic.

gotoso, *a.* gouty.

gozar, *vti.* [a] to enjoy; to have possession or result of.—*vii.* (de) to enjoy, have possession (of).—*vri.* to rejoice.

gozne, *m.* hinge.

gozo, *m.* joy, pleasure, gladness.— *saltar de g.,* to be in high spirits, to be very happy.—**gozoso,** *a.* joyful, cheerful, merry.

grabado, *a.* engraved, carved, cut.— *m.* engraving; art of engraving; cut, picture, illustration.—*g. al agua fuerte,* etching.—*g. en madera,* wood engraving, wood carving.—**grabador,** *n.* engraver, carver; cutter, sinker.— **grabar,** *vt.* to engrave; to cut, carve; to impress upon the mind.

gracejo, *m.* graceful, winsome way. —**gracia,** *f.* grace; gracefulness; benefaction; graciousness; pardon, mercy; remission of a debt; witticism, wit; joke, jest; name of a person.—*pl.* thanks; accomplishments.—*caer en g.,* to please, to be liked.—*hacer g.,* to please; to amuse, strike as funny.—*tener g.,* to be witty; to be funny.—**grácil,** *a.*

slender.—**gracioso**, *a.* graceful, pleasing; witty, funny; gracious.

grada, *f.* step of a wide staircase; harrow.—*pl.* stands, seats of bullring or amphitheater.—**gradación**, *f.* (mus.) gradation; graded series of things or events.—**gradería**, *f.* series of steps or seats at bullring or stadium stands.

grado, *m.* degree; step of a staircase; (mil.) rank; grade, class.—*de g.*, or *de buen g.*, willingly, with pleasure.—**graduación**, *f.* graduation; (mil.) rank.—**gradual**, *a.* gradual.—**graduar**, *vt.* to graduate, give a degree or a military rank; to grade; to gauge; to adjust.—*vr.* (en) to graduate (from), to take a degree.

gráfico, *a.* graphic(al); clear, vivid.—*n.* graph, diagram.

grafito, *m.* graphite.

grajo, *m.* jackdaw.

grama, *f.* grama grass; lawn.

gramática, *f.* grammar.—**gramatical**, *a.* grammatical.—**gramático**, *a.* grammatical.—*n.* grammarian.

gramo, *m.* gram (weight). See Table.

gran, *a.* contr. of GRANDE.

grana, *f.* scarlet color; scarlet cloth.

granada, *f.* pomegranate; (mil.) grenade.—**granado**, *a.* remarkable, illustrious; mature; select, choice.—*m.* pomegranate tree.—**granar**, *vi.* to bloom, mature, come to fruition.—**granate**, *m.* garnet.

grande, *a.* large, big; great; grand.—*en g.*, on a large scale.—*mf.* grandee.—**grandeza**, *f.* greatness; grandeur; grandeeship; bigness; size, magnitude.—**grandiosidad**, *f.* greatness; grandeur; abundance.—**grandioso**, *a.* grandiose, grand, magnificent.—**grandullón**, *a.* overgrown.

granear, *vt.* to sow (grain); to stipple; to grain (lithographic stone).—**granel**, *m.* heap of grain.—*a g.*, in a heap; (com.) in bulk.—**granero**, *m.* granary, barn; grange; cornloft.

granito, *m.* granite; small grain; pimple; granule.

granizada, *f.* hailstorm; shower of objects, facts, etc.; water ice.—**granizar**, *vii.* [a-50] to hail.—**granizo**, *m.* hail.

granja, *f.* grange, farm, farmhouse.—**granjear**, *vt.* to gain, earn, profit.—*vt. & vr. to* get, win (as the good will of another).—**granjería**, *f.* gain, profit, advantage.—**granjero**, *n.* farmer.

grano, *m.* grain; cereal; each single seed; pimple.—*pl.* (com.) cereals, corn, breadstuffs.—*ir al g.*, to come to the point.

granuja, *mf.* rogue; waif, urchin.

granulación, *f.* granulation.—**granular**, *vt.* to granulate.—*vr.* to become covered with granules or pimples.—*a.* granular.—**granuloso**, *a.* granulous, granular.

grapa, *f.* staple; paper clip; clamp, clasp.—**grapón**, *m.* brace, hook.

grasa, *f.* grease; fat; suet; oil.—**grasiento**, *a.* greasy; filthy.—**graso**, *a.* fat, unctuous.—**grasoso**, *a.* greasy.

gratificación, *f.* reward; gratuity, tip; fee; gratification.—**gratificar**, *vti.* [d] to reward, recompense; to tip, fee; to gratify, please.—**gratis**, *adv.* gratis, free.—**gratitud**, *f.* gratitude, gratefulness.—**grato**, *a.* pleasing, pleasant; grateful.—**gratuito**, *a.* gratis; gratuitous, uncalled-for; unfounded.

grava, *f.* gravel.

gravamen, *m.* tax, scot; charge, obligation; nuisance; (law) mortgage, lien.—**gravar**, *vt.* to burden; to tax; (law) to encumber.

grave, *a.* weighty, heavy; grave, serious; (mus.) grave; deep (voice).—**gravedad**, *f.* gravity, graveness; seriousness.

gravitación, *f.* gravitation.—**gravitar**, *vi.* to gravitate; to rest, press (on).

gravoso, *a.* costly; onerous; vexatious.

graznar, *vi.* to croak, caw, cackle.—**graznido**, *m.* croak, caw, cackle; croaking.

greda, *f.* clay, chalk, marl, potter's clay.

gremio, *m.* guild; society, brotherhood; trade union.

greña, *f.* entangled or matted mop of hair.—*andar a la g.*, (of women) to pull each other's hair; to argue excitedly.—**greñudo**, *a.* with long, disheveled hair; shy (horse).—*m.* shy horse.

gresca, *f.* wrangle, brawl, row.

griego, *n. & a.* Greek, Grecian.—*m.* the Greek language; unintelligible language.

grieta, *f.* crevice, crack; chink, fissure; scratch in the skin.

grifo, *a.* (print.) script; bristling (hair, fur); kinky, tangled (of hair).—*m.* griffin or griffon; (Am.) child of a negro and an Indian; faucet, spigot, cock.—*pl.* frizzled hair.

grillete, *m.* fetter, shackle.—**grillo**, *m.* (entom.) cricket.—*pl.* fetters.

grima, *f.* fright, horror.—*dar g.*, to set the teeth on edge.—**grimoso**, *a.* horrible; repulsive.

gringo, *n.* (Am.) foreigner (esp. English or American).

gripe, *f.* grippe.

gris, *a.* gray.—*m.* gray color.—
grisáceo, *a.* grayish.

grita, *f.* clamor, outcry; screaming;
hooting.—**gritar,** *vi.* to shout, cry
out, scream; to hoot.—**gritería,** *f.*
outcry, uproar, shouting.—**grito,** *m.*
cry, scream; hoot, whoop.—*a gritos,
a g. pelado, a todo g.,* at the top
of one's voice.—*estar en un g.,* to
be in continual pain.—*poner el g.
en el cielo,* to complain loudly.

grosella, *f.* currant; gooseberry.

grosería, *f.* rudeness, ill-breeding.
discourtesy; clumsiness; vulgarity.—
grosero, *a.* coarse, rough; rude, discourteous; vulgar, uncouth.

grosor, *m.* thickness.

grúa, *f.* crane, derrick.

gruesa, *f.* gross (12 dozen).

grueso, *a.* thick; bulky, corpulent;
fleshy.—*m.* thickness; bulk, corpulence; main part; main body of an
army.

grulla, *f.* (ornith.) crane.

grumete, *m.* apprentice sailor.

grumo, *m.* clot.—**grumoso,** *a.* full of
clots, clotted.

gruñido, *m.* grunt.—**gruñir,** *vii.* [27]
to grunt.—**gruñón,** *n.* & *a.* crank,
irritable.

grupa, *f.* croup, rump of a horse.

grupo, *m.* group; set; clump, cluster.

gruta, *f.* cavern, grotto.

guacamayo, *m.* (ornith.) macaw.

guaco, *m.* (Am.) grouse.

guacho, *a.* & *n.* (Am.) orphan,
foundling; solitary, forlorn; odd
(only one of a pair).

guadaña, *f.* scythe.—**guadañar,** *vt.* to
mow.

guagua, *f.* (Am.) insect that destroys
fruit; trivial thing; omnibus;
baby.—*de g.,* free, gratis.—**gua-
güero,** *n.* (Am.) bus driver; sponger.

guajalote, *m.* (Am.) turkey.

guajiro, *n.* & *a.* Cuban peasant.

guanaco, *m.* (Am.) a kind of llama;
boor, rustic; (coll.) simpleton, idiot.

guanajo, *n.* (Am.) turkey.—*a.* & *n.*
(coll.) fool.

guano, *m.* guano; palm leaves; (coll.,
Cuba) money.

guante, *m.* glove.—*echarle (a uno) el
g.,* (coll.) to seize, grasp; to imprison.—**guantelete,** *m.* gauntlet.

guapear, *vi.* (coll.) to boast of
courage.—**guapetón,** *a.* daring, bold.
—**guapo,** *a.* (coll.) brave, daring;
good-looking or handsome; spruce,
neat; ostentatious; gay, sprightly.
—*m.* gallant, beau; brawler, quarrelsome person.—*ponerse g.,* (Am.)
to get angry.

guaraní, *a.* & *mf.* Guarani.—*m.* Guarani language.

guarapo, *m.* juice of the sugar cane.

guarda, *mf.* guard; keeper.—*f.* custody; trust, wardship, safe-keeping; observance of a law; outside
rib or guard (of a fan, etc.); ward
of a lock or of a key.—**guarda-
barrera,** *n.* (RR.) gatekeeper.—
guardabarro, *m.* fender, splashboard.—**guardabosque,** *m.* forester;
game warden.—**guardacantón,** *m.*
protective stone at corner of buildings.—**guardacostas,** *m.* Coast
Guard; (naut.) revenue cutter.—
guardafango, *m.* = GUARDABARRO.—
guardafrenos, *m.* (RR.) brakeman.
—**guardamonte,** *m.* guard of a gun-
lock; forester, keeper of a forest.
—**guardamuebles,** *m.* warehouse.—
guardar, *vt.* to keep; to guard,
protect, watch over; to store, save,
reserve.—*vr.* (de) to guard (against),
avoid, beware (of), take care not
(to).—**guardarropa,** *m.* wardroom;
wardrobe; cloakroom.—**guardarro-
pía,** *f.* (theat.) wardrobe, properties.
—**guardia,** *f.* guard; defense, protection.—*m.* uniformed policeman.—
guardiamarina, *m.* midshipman.—
guardián, *n.* keeper, watchman.

guarecer, *vti.* [3] to shelter, protect.
—*vri.* to take refuge or shelter.—
guarida, *f.* den, cave; lair of a
wild beast; shelter; lurking place,
cover, haunt.

guarnecer, *vti.* [3] to garnish, adorn,
decorate; (sew.) to trim, bind, line;
(jewelry) to set in gold, silver, etc.;
(mason.) to plaster; (mil.) to garrison.—**guarnición,** *f.* trimming,
etc.; setting; (mech.) packing;
guard of a sword; garrison; adornment.—*pl.* harness; fittings; accessories.

guasa, *f.* joking, jesting; joke, jest.

guaso, *m.* lasso; Chilean cowboy.

guasón, *a.* (coll.) jocose, witty.—*n.*
joker, wag.

guatemalteco, *n.* & *a.* Guatemalan.

guayaba, *f.* guava.—**guayabo,** *m.*
guava tree.

gubernamental, *a.* governmental.—
gubernativo, *a.* administrative, governmental, gubernatorial.

gubia, *f.* (carp.) gouge, centering
chisel.

guedeja, *f.* long lock of hair; forelock; lion's mane.

guerra, *f.* war, warfare.—*dar g.,* to
cause annoyance or trouble.—**gue-
rrear,** *vi.* to war, wage war, fight.—
guerrera, *f.* (mil.) tunic.—**guerrero,**
a. martial, warlike.—*m.* warrior,
fighter.—**guerrilla,** *f.* guerrilla.—
guerrillero, *m.* guerrilla fighter.

guía, *mf.* guide; leader.—*f.* guidebook; (mech.) guide, rule, guide pin, guide screw, etc.—**guiar**, *vt.* to guide, lead; to drive (auto, etc.).—*vr.* (por) to go or be governed (by); to follow.

guija, *f.* pebble; gravel.—*pl.* (coll.) force, vigor.—**guijarro,** *m.* pebble, cobble.—**guijo,** *m.* gravel.

guiñada, *f.* wink; (naut.) yaw; lurch.

guiñapo, *m.* tatter, rag; ragamuffin.

guiñar, *vt.* to wink; (naut.) to yaw; to lurch.—**guiño,** *m.* wink.

guión, *m.* hyphen; dash; (theat., radio, T.V.) script; explanatory text or reference table; cross (carried before a prelate in a procession); leader (among birds and animals); leader in a dance.

guirnalda, *f.* garland, wreath.

güiro, *m.* (Am.) fruit of the calabash tree; bottle gourd; gourd used as a musical instrument.

guisa, *f.* manner, fashion.—*a g. de,* like, in the manner of.

guisante, *m.* pea.—*g. de olor,* sweet pea.

guisar, *vt.* to cook or dress (food); to arrange, prepare.—**guiso,** *m.* cooked dish; seasoning, condiment.

guitarra, *f.* guitar.—**guitarrista,** *mf.* guitarist.

gula, *f.* gluttony, inordinate appetite.

gusano, *m.* worm, grub, caterpillar; meek, dejected person.

gustar, *vt.* to taste, try.—*vi.* to be pleasing; to cause pleasure.—*gustarle a uno una cosa,* to like something.—**gusto,** *m.* taste; tasting; pleasure; liking; choice; discernment.—*a g.,* to one's taste or judgment.—*dar g.,* to please.—**gustoso,** *a.* savory; tasty; cheerful; pleasing; willing.

H

haba, *f.* broad bean; lima bean.

habano, *m.* Havana cigar.

haber, *vti.* [21] to have (used as aux.).—*hay (había, hubo,* etc.), there is, there are (there was, there were).—*hay que,* one must, it is necessary.—*no hay de que,* don't mention it.—*m.* (bookkeeping) credit.—*pl.* property, assets; estate.

habichuela, *f.* kidney bean.—*h. verde,* string bean.

hábil, *a.* capable, skillful.—*día h.,* work day.—**habilidad,** *f.* ability, skill.—*pl.* accomplishments.

habilitación, *f.* habilitation; outfit, equipment.—**habilitar,** *vt.* to qualify, enable; to fit out, equip.

habitable, *a.* habitable.—**habitación,** *f.* room, chamber, suite of rooms; apartment; lodging; (law) caretaking.—**habitante,** *a.* inhabiting.—*mf.* inhabitant.—**habitar,** *vt.* to inhabit, live, reside.

hábito, *m.* habit, custom; dress of ecclesiastics.—*tomar el h.,* to become a nun or a monk.—**habitual,** *a.* habitual, usual, customary.—**habituar,** *vt.* to accustom, habituate.—*vr.* to become accustomed, accustom oneself, get used to.

habla, *f.* speech; language; talk.—*ponerse al h.,* to communicate, get in touch, speak.—**hablador,** *a.* talkative.—*n.* talker, gabber.—**habladuría,** *f.* gossip, empty talk.—**hablar,** *vi.* to speak; to talk.—*h. a tontas y a locas,* to speak recklessly.—*h. claro,* or *en plata,* to speak in plain language, to call a spade a spade.—*h. por h.,* to talk for the sake of talking.—*h. por los codos,* to talk incessantly; to chatter.—*vt.* to speak.—*vr.* to speak to each other; to be on speaking terms.—**hablilla,** *f.* rumor, gossip.

hacedero, *a.* feasible, practicable.—**hacedor,** *m.* maker.—*el Supremo H.,* the Maker, the Creator.

hacendado, *n.* landholder, farmer, rancher.—**hacendoso,** *a.* industrious.

hacer, *vti.* [22] to make; to produce; to do; to gain, earn; to suppose, think; to cause.—*h. alarde,* to boast.—*h. caso,* to mind, pay attention.—*h. daño,* to hurt, harm.—*h. de,* to act as.—*h. juego,* to match.—*h. la vista gorda,* to wink at, to connive at.—*h. una pregunta,* to ask a question.—*no le hace,* never mind, let it go.—*v. impers.*—*¿cuánto (tiempo) hace?* how long ago?—*¿cuánto (tiempo) hace que?* since when?—*hace años,* many years ago.—*hace calor,* it is warm.—*hace tiempo,* a long time ago.—*hace un año,* a year ago, or, it is now one year.—*hace viento,* it is windy.—*vi.* to become, grow; to pretend to be.—*h. a,* to become accustomed.

hacia, *prep.* toward; near, about.—*h. abajo,* downward.—*h. arriba,* upward.—*h. atrás,* backward.

hacienda, *f.* landed property; plantation; ranch; estate, fortune; finance.—*h. pública,* public treasury; public finances.

hacina, *f.* stack; pile.—**hacinamiento,** *m.* accumulation; heaping or stacking.—**hacinar,** *vt.* to stack; to pile; to accumulate.

hacha, *f.* ax; hatchet; torch.—**hachazo,** *m.* blow or stroke with an ax.—**hachuela,** *f.* hatchet.

hada, *f.* fairy.—**hado,** *m.* fate, destiny, doom.

haitiano, *n. & a.* Haitian.

halagador, *a.* flattering; coaxing.—*n.* flatterer, cajoler, coaxer.—**halagar,** *vti.* [b] to cajole; to flatter; to coax, allure; to fondle.—**halago,** *m.* cajolery, allurement, flattery; caress. —**halagüeño,** *a.* flattering; alluring; attractive, promising.

halar, *vt.* to haul, pull, tow.—*vi.* to pull ahead.

halcón, *m.* falcon.

hálito, *m.* breath; vapor.

halo, *m.* halo.

hallar, *vt.* to find; to find out; to discover.—*vr.* to be (in a place or condition); to feel (as to health); to fare.—**hallazgo,** *m.* find, thing found; discovery.

hamaca, *f.* hammock.

hambre, *f.* hunger; appetite; famine. —*h. canina,* inordinate hunger.— *tener h.,* to be hungry.—**hambrear,** *vt.* to starve, famish.—*vi.* to be hungry.—**hambriento,** *a.* hungry; starved; greedy, covetous; longing.

hamburgués, *a.* from or pertaining to Hamburg.—**hamburguesa,** *f.* (Am.) hamburger.

hampa, *m.* underworld.—**hampón,** *m.* gangster, bully, rowdy.

hangar, *m.* (neol.) hangar.

haragán, *n.* idler, loiterer, loafer; lazy person.—*a.* lazy, indolent, idle. —**haraganear,** *vi.* to be lazy; to lounge, idle, loiter.—**haraganería,** *f.* idleness, laziness, sloth.

harapiento, *a.* ragged, tattered.— **harapo,** *m.* tatter, rag.

harina, *f.* flour, meal.—*h. de otro costal,* another matter, a horse of a different color.—**harinoso,** *a.* mealy.

hartar, *vti.* [49] & *vri.* to glut, gorge; to sate, satiate; to satisfy; te fill to excess.—**hartazgo,** *m.* satiety, fill.— **harto,** *ppi.* of HARTAR.—*a.* sufficient, full, complete.—*adv.* enough or sufficiently; very much, abundantly.—**hartura,** *f.* satiety, fill; superabundance.

hasta, *prep.* till, until; up to, down to; as far as; even (emphatic).— *h. después,* or *h. luego,* good-by, so long.—*h. la vista,* (in parting) so long, see you later.—*h. mañana,* (in parting) see you tomorrow.—*conj.* even.—*h. que,* until.

hastiar, *vt.* to disgust; to cloy, sate. —**hastío,** *m.* disgust; boredom.

hatillo, *m.* small bundle; a few clothes.—*coger el h.,* (coll.) to quit, to pack and go.

hato, *m.* herd of cattle; flock of sheep; (Am.) farm or cattle ranch; shepherd's lodge; lot; gang, crowd.

hawaiano, *a. & n.* Hawaiian.

hay, *impers. irreg.* of HABER; there is, there are.

haya, *f.* beech tree.

haz, *m.* fagot, bundle, bunch; (agr.) sheaf.

hazaña, *f.* feat, heroic deed.

hazmerreír, *m.* laughing stock.

hebilla, *f.* buckle, clasp.

hebra, *f.* thread fiber; string; strand.

hebreo, *n. & a.* Hebrew.—*m.* Hebrew language.

hechicería, *f.* witchcraft, enchantment; charm; sorcery, wizardry.— **hechicero,** *n.* witch, wizard; sorcerer; charmer, enchanter.—*a.* charming, bewitching.—**hechizar,** *vti.* [a] to bewitch, enchant; to charm.—**hechizo,** *m.* charm (used to bewitch), enchantment.

hecho, *ppi.* of HACER.—*a.* made; done; ready-made; finished; ripe or developed.—*h. y derecho,* real; complete.—*m.* fact; act, action, deed.— *de h.,* in fact, as a matter of fact. —**hechura,** *f.* making, make; workmanship; form; build (of a person); creature, creation.

heder, *vii.* [18] to stink.—**hediondez,** *f.* stench, stink.—**hediondo,** *a.* stinking, fetid.—**hedor,** *m.* stench, stink.

helada, *f.* frost; nip.—**heladera, heladora,** *f.* refrigerator; ice-cream dish. —**helado,** *a.* icy; freezing, frosty; cold.—*m.* ice cream.—**helar,** *vti.* [1] & *vii.* to freeze; to amaze.—*vri.* to freeze, be frozen.

helecho, *m.* fern.

hélice, *f.* propeller; helix.

helicóptero, *m.* helicopter.

helio, *m.* helium.

hembra, *f.* female; (mech.) nut of a screw.

hemisférico, *a.* hemispherical.—**hemisferio,** *m.* hemisphere.

hemorragia, *f.* hemorrhage.—**hemorrágico,** *a.* hemorrhagic.

hemorroides, *f. pl.* piles, hemorrhoids.

henchir, *vti.* [29] to fill, stuff.—*vri.* to fill or stuff oneself.

hender, *vti.* [19] to crack, split; to cut (as the water).—**hendidura,** *f.* fissure, crack, cut.

heno, *m.* hay.

heráldica, *f.* heraldry.—**heraldo,** *m.* herald; harbinger.

herbazal, *m.* grassy place; pasture ground.

heredad, *f.* improved piece of ground; country estate, farm.—**heredar,** *vt.* to inherit; to deed to another.— **heredero,** *n.* heir; heiress; inheritor; successor.—*h. forzoso,* general or legal heir.—**hereditario, a.** hereditary.

hereje, mf. heretic.—**herejía, f.** heresy; injurious expression.

herencia, f. inheritance, heritage; heredity.

herético, a. heretical.

herida, f. injury, wound.—**herido, a. & n.** wounded (person).—**mal h.,** dangerously wounded.—**herir, vti.** [39] to wound; to hurt, harm; to strike; to offend (the senses).

hermanar, vt. to mate, match, pair; to suit.—**vi.** to fraternize; to match.

hermanastro, n. stepbrother; f. stepsister.—**hermandad, f.** fraternity, brotherhood.—**hermano, n.** brother; (f. sister); twin (app. to objects).—**h. de leche,** foster brother. —**h. político,** brother-in-law.

hermético, a. hermetic, air-proof, airtight; close-mouthed.—**hermetismo, m.** secrecy, complete silence.

hermosear, vt. to beautify, embellish. —**hermoso, a.** beautiful, handsome. —**hermosura, f.** beauty; belle.

hernia, f. hernia.

héroe, m. hero.—**heroicidad, f.** heroism; heroic deed.—**heroico, a.** heroic.—**heroína, f.** heroine.—**heroísmo, m.** heroism.

herradura, f. horseshoe.—**herraje, m.** ironwork; iron or metal fittings or accessories, hardware (gen. pl.).— **herramienta, f.** tool; implement; set of tools.—**herrar, vti.** [1] to shoe (horses); to brand (cattle); to garnish or trim with iron.—**herrería, f.** smithy; forge; ironworks.—**herrero, n.** blacksmith.

herrumbre, f. rust; iron taste.—**herrumbroso, a.** rusty, rusted.

hervidero, m. boiling; small spring whence water bubbles out; multitude, crowd.—**hervir, vti.** [39] & vii. to boil; to seethe.—**vii.** to become choppy (the sea); to bubble.— **hervor, m.** boiling; fervor, heat.— **h. de sangre,** rash.

heterodoxo, a. unorthodox.

heterogéneo, a. heterogenous.

hez, f. sediment, dregs of liquor; scum.—**pl.** dregs; excrement.

híbrido, n. & a. hybrid.

hidráulica, f. hydraulics.—**hidráulico, a.** hydraulic.—**hidroavión, m.** seaplane.—**hidrógeno, m.** hydrogen.— **hidroplano, m.** seaplane.

hiedra, f. ivy.

hiel, f. gall, bile; bitterness.

hielo, m. ice; frost; coolness, indifference.

hiena, f. hyena.

hierba, f. grass; weed; herb; herbage; (Am.) maté.—**mala h.,** weed;

bad character; marijuana.—**hierbabuena, f.** mint.

hierro, m. iron; brand stamped with a hot iron.—**pl.** fetters, shackles, handcuffs.—**h. colado** or **fundido,** cast iron.—**h. forjado,** wrought iron.

hígado, m. liver.—**pl.** courage, bravery.—**echar el h.** or **los hígados,** to work very hard.

higiene, f. hygiene; sanitation.— **higiénico, a.** hygienic, sanitary.— **higienizar, vti.** [a] to make sanitary.

higo, m. fig.—**higuera, f.** fig tree.

hija, f. daughter, child.—**h. política,** daughter-in-law.—**hijastro, n.** stepchild.—**hijo, m.** son, child; (bot.) shoot; fruit, result.—**pl.** children, offspring.—**h. natural,** illegitimate child.—**h. político,** son-in-law.

hila, f. line.—**a la h.,** in a row, single file.—**pl.** (surg.) lint.—**hilacha, f., hilacho, m.** fraying, shred, filament or thread raveled out of cloth.— **pl.** lint.—**hilada, f.** row or line; (mason.) course.—**hilado, m.** spinning; yarn.—**hilandera, f.** woman spinner.—**hilandería, f.** spinning mill.—**hilandero, n. & a.** spinner; spinning.—**m.** spinning room, spinnery.—**hilar, vt. & vi.** to spin.

hilaza, f. yarn; fiber; uneven thread. —**pl.** lint.

hilera, f. row, line, file.

hilo, m. thread; yarn; filament, fiber; linen; wire.—**al h.,** along the thread, with the grain.

hilván, m. (sew.) tacking, basting.— **hilvanar, vt.** to tack, baste; to plan.

himen, m. hymen.—**himeneo, m.** hymen, nuptials.

himno, m. hymn.

hincapié, m. stamping the foot.— **hacer h.,** to emphasize, stress.— **hincar, vti.** [d] to thrust, drive; to plant.—**h. el diente,** to bite; to slander.—**h. la rodilla,** or **hincarse de rodillas,** to kneel down.

hinchar, vt. to swell; to inflate.—**vr.** to swell; to become arrogant, conceited or puffed up.—**hinchazón, m.** swelling; ostentation, vanity, airs; inflation.

hinojo, m. fennel, knee.—**de hinojos,** kneeling.

hipar, vi. to hiccough; to pant.

hipertensión, f. high blood pressure.

hípico, a. equine, pertaining to horses.

hipo, m. hiccough.

hipocresía, f. hypocrisy.—**hipócrita, mf. & a.** hypocrite; hypocritical.

hipódromo, m. race track.

hipoteca, f. mortgage.—**hipotecar, vti.** [d] to mortgage.

hipótesis, *f.* hypothesis.

hiriente, *a.* hurting, cutting, offensive.

hirsuto, *a.* hairy, bristly.

hirviente, *a.* boiling.

hispánico, *a.* Hispanic.—**hispano,** *a.* Hispanic, Spanish.—*n.* Spaniard.—**hispanoamericano,** *n. & a.* Spanish-American.

histérico, *a. & n.* histeric(al); hysterics.—**histerismo,** *m.,* **histeria,** *f.* hysteria.

historia, *f.* history; tale, story.—*dejarse de historias,* to come to the point.—**historiador,** *n.* historian.—**histórico,** *a.* historic(al).—**historieta,** *f.* short story; comics, comic strip.

histrión, *n.* actor, player; buffoon, juggler.

hito, *m.* landmark; guidepost; milestone.—*mirar de h. en h.,* to stare at.

hocicar, *vti.* [d] to root (as hogs).—*vii.* to fall on one's face; to muzzle.—**hocico,** *m.* snout, muzzle, nose (of animal).—*de hocicos,* face downwards.—*meter el h.,* to meddle.

hogar, *m.* home; hearth, fireplace.

hogaza, *f.* large loaf of bread.

hoguera, *f.* bonfire; blaze; pyre.

hoja, *f.* leaf; petal; sheet of paper or metal; blade.—*doblemos la h.,* no more of that.—*h. de lata,* tin plate.—*h. de servicios,* record.—**hojalata,** *f.* tin plate.—**hojalatería,** *f.* tinware; tin shop.—**hojalatero,** *n.* tinsmith.

hojarasca, *f.* dead leaves; excessive foliage; trash, rubbish.

hojear, *vt.* to turn the leaves of; to glance at (a book), look over hastily.

hojuela, *f.* small leaf; flake; thin pancake.

¡hola! *interj.* hello! hi!

holandés, *n. & a.* Dutch.—*m.* Dutch language.

holgado, *a.* loose, wide; large, spacious; at leisure; well-off.—**holganza,** *f.* leisure; idleness.—**holgar,** *vii.* [12-b] to rest; to quit work; to be idle; to be needless or useless.—*vri.* to be glad; to idle; to relax, amuse oneself.—**holgazán,** *a.* idle, lazy.—*n.* idler, loiterer, lounger.—**holgazanear,** *vi.* to idle; to loiter; to lounge.—**holgazanería,** *f.* idleness, laziness.—**holgorio,** *m.* frolic, spree.—**holgura,** *f.* ease, comfort; roominess; (mech.) play.

hollar, *vti.* [12] to tread upon, trample under foot.

hollejo, *m.* skin, peel, pod, husk.

hollín, *m.* soot, lampblack.

hombrada, *f.* manly action; impulse.—**hombre,** *m.* man.

hombrera, *f.* shoulder pad; shoulder armor.

hombría, *f.* manliness.—*h. de bien,* probity, integrity, honesty.

hombro, *m.* shoulder.—*arrimar el h.,* to lend a hand.—*encogerse de hombros,* to shrug one's shoulders.

hombruno, *a.* mannish.

homenaje, *m.* homage, honor.

homicida, *a.* homicidal.—*mf.* murderer, homicide (person).—**homicidio,** *m.* homicide (act).

homogeneidad, *f.* homogeneity.—**homogéneo,** *a.* homogeneous.

homosexual, *a. & mf.* homosexual.

honda, *f.* slingshot.

hondo, *a.* deep, profound.—*m.* depth.—**hondón,** *m.* bottom; depths.—**hondonada,** *f.* dale, glen; gully, ravine.—**hondura,** *f.* depth; profundity.—*meterse en honduras,* (fig.) to go beyond one's depth.—**hondureño,** *a. & n.* Honduran.

honestidad, *f.* decency, decorum; honesty; chastity; modesty.—**honesto,** *a.* honest; decent, decorous; chaste.

hongo, *m.* mushroom; fungus; derby hat.

honor, *m.* honor; dignity; reputation. *pl.* rank, position, honors.—**honorable,** *a.* honorable; illustrious; reputable.—**honorario,** *a.* honorary.—*m. pl.* professional fees.—**honorífico,** *a.* honorary; honorable.

honra, *f.* honor; reputation; chastity.—*pl.* obsequies.—**honradez,** *f.* honesty, probity, integrity.—**honrado,** *a.* honest, honorable, reputable.—**honrar,** *vt.* to honor, do honor to; to respect; to be an honor for.—*vi.* to honor; to be honored.—**honrilla,** *f.* keen sense of honor or duty; punctiliousness.—**honroso,** *a.* honorable; decorous; honoring, honor-giving.

hora, *f.* hour; time.—*altas horas,* small hours.—*dar la h.,* to strike the hour; to tell the time.—*h. de,* time to, or for.—*horas extraordinarias,* overtime.

horadar, *vt.* to perforate, bore; to burrow.

horario, *m.* timetable, schedule; hour hand of a clock or watch.

horca, *f.* gallows; pitchfork; forked prop; rope or string of onions or garlic.

horcajadas, *f. pl.—a h.,* astride or astraddle.

horcón, *m.* forked pole, forked prop; post; (Am.) roof.

horda, *f.* horde.

horizontal, *a. & f.* horizontal.—**hori-**

zontalidad, *f.* horizontality.—**horizonte,** *m.* horizon.

horma, *f.* mold; shoemaker's last; hatter's block; (mason.) dry wall.

hormiga, *f.* ant.—**hormigón,** *m.* (eng.) concrete.—*h. armado,* reinforced concrete.—**hormigonera,** *f.* concrete mixer.—**hormiguear,** *vi.* to itch; to swarm, teem.—**hormigueo,** *m.* itching.—**hormiguero,** *m.* ant hill or hillock; ant hole or nest; swarm of people or little animals.—*oso hormiguero,* anteater.

hormona, *f.* hormone.

hornada, *f.* batch of bread, baking; melt (of a blast furnace).—**hornilla,** *f.* burner; grate (of a stove).—**hornillo,** *m.* portable furnace or stove.—**horno,** *m.* oven; kiln; furnace.

horquilla, *f.* forked pole, bar, pipe, etc.; pitchfork; hairpin; double-pointed tack.

horrendo, *a.* hideous, awful.—**horrible,** *a.* horrid, horrible; hideous, heinous.—**hórrido,** *a.* horrible, hideous.—**horripilante,** a. horrifying, harrowing.—**horripilar,** *vt.* & *vi.* to cause or feel horror.—*vr.* to be horrified.—**horrísono,** *a.* of a terrifying noise.—**horror,** *m.* horror; enormity, frightfulness.—**horrorizar,** *vti.* [a] to horrify, terrify.—*vri.* to be terrified.—**horroroso,** *a.* horrible; hideous, frightful.

hortaliza, *f.* garden produce, vegetables.

hosco, *a.* sullen, gloomy.

hospedaje, *m.* lodging, board.—**hospedar,** *vt.* to lodge, harbor.—*vi.* & *vr.* **(en)** to lodge or take lodging (at); to live (in).

hospicio, *m.* hospice; orphan asylum.

hospital, *m.* hospital.—*h. de sangre,* (mil.) field hospital.—**hospitalario,** *a.* hospitable.—**hospitalidad,** *f.* hospitality.

hosquedad, *f.* sullenness.

hostia, *f.* (eccl.) Host.

hostigamiento, *m.* chastisement; vexation.—**hostigar,** *vti.* [b] to lash, scourge, chastise; to vex, trouble; to gall.

hostil, *a.* hostile.—**hostilidad,** *f.* hostility.—**hostilizar,** *vti.* [a] to commit hostilities against, be hostile to, antagonize.

hotel, *m.* hotel.—**hotelero,** *n.* hotel manager.

hoy, *adv.* today; at the present time. —*de h. a mañana,* before tomorrow; when you least expect it.—*de h. en adelante,* hence forward, in the future.—*h. día,* or *h. en día,* nowadays. —*h. mismo,* this very day.—*h.*

por h., at the present time; this very day.

hoya, *f.* hole, pit; grave; valley, dale, glen; basin (of a river).—**hoyo,** *m.* hole, excavation; dent, hollow; pockmark; grave.

hoz, *f.* sickle; narrow pass.

hozar, *vti.* [a] to root (as hogs).

huacal, *m.* (Am.) crate.

huarache, *m.* (Am.) Mexican leather sandal.

huaso, *m.* (Am.) Chilean cowboy; peasant; halfbreed; lasso.—*a.* rustic, uncouth.

hucha, *f.* money box, bank; savings.

huchear, *vi.* to hoot, shout, cry out, call.

hueco, *a.* hollow; empty; vain, empty-headed; resonant.—*m.* hole; hollow, gap; interval of time or space.

huelga, *f.* labor strike, walkout; rest, repose.—*declararse en h.,* to strike.—**huelguista,** *mf.* striker.

huella, *f.* track, footprint; trace, sign; trail.

huérfano, *n.* & *a.* orphan(ed).

huero, *a.* vain, empty; (Am.) blonde.

huerta, *f.* orchard; vegetable garden; irrigated land.—**huerto,** *m.* small orchard; garden patch.

hueso, *m.* bone; stone, pit; core, center.—*estar en los huesos,* to be very thin.—*la sin h.,* the tongue.—**huesoso,** *a.* = HUESUDO.

huésped, *n.* guest, roomer, lodger; host.—*casa de huéspedes,* boarding house.

hueste, *f.* host, army.

huesudo, *a.* bony, having large bones; rawboned.

hueva, *f.* spawn of fishes, roe.—**huevo,** *m.* egg.—*h. duro,* hard-boiled egg. —*huevos escalfados,* poached eggs. —*huevos fritos,* fried eggs.—*huevos pasados por agua,* soft-boiled eggs. —*huevos revueltos,* scrambled eggs.

huida, *f.* flight, escape.—**huidizo,** *a.* elusive; fugitive, fleeing.—**huir,** *vii.* [23-e] & *vri.* to flee; to escape; to run away; to slip away; **(de)** to keep away (from), shun, avoid.—*h. la cara de,* to avoid, keep away from.

hule, *m.* oilcloth, oilskin; (Am.) India rubber.

hulla, *f.* mineral coal.—*h. blanca,* white coal (water power).

humanidad, *f.* humanity; mankind; humaneness; (coll.) corpulence, fleshiness.—*pl.* humanities.—**humanitario,** *a.* humanitarian.—**humano,** *a.* human; humane.—*m.* man, human being.

humarada, *f.* great deal of smoke.—

humazo, *m.* dense and abundant smoke.—**humeante,** *a.* smoking, steaming, fuming.—**humear,** *vi.* to smoke; emit smoke, fumes, or vapors.

humedad, *f.* humidity, moisture, dampness.—**humedecer,** *vti.* [3] to moisten, dampen.—**húmedo,** *a.* wet, humid, moist, damp.

humildad, *f.* humility, humbleness; meekness.—**humilde,** *a.* humble; meek; lowly.

humillación, *f.* humiliation; humbling.—**humillar,** *vt.* to humiliate; to humble; to subdue.—*vr.* to humble oneself; to lower oneself.

humo, *m.* smoke; fume.—*pl.* airs, conceit.

humor, *m.* humor, wit; disposition, temper, mood.—**humorada,** *f.* pleasant joke, humorous saying.—**humorismo,** *m.* humor; humorism.—**humorístico,** *a.* humorous; amusing; facetious.

hundimiento, *m.* sinking; cave-in; downfall, collapse.—**hundir,** *vt.* to submerge, sink; to stave in, crush; to destroy, ruin.—*vr.* to sink; to cave in, fall down.

húngaro, *n.* & *a.* Hungarian.

huracán, *m.* hurricane.

huraño, *a.* unsociable, shy.

hurgar, *vti.* [b] to stir; to poke; to stir up, excite.

¡hurra!, *interj.* hurrah!

hurtadillas—*a h.,* by stealth, on the sly.—**hurtar,** *vt.* to steal, rob of; to cheat in weight or measure.—*h. el cuerpo,* to flee; to dodge, shy away; to hide.—**hurto,** *m.* theft, robbery, stealing.

husmear, *vt.* to scent, smell; (coll.) to pry, peep.

huso, *m.* spindle; bobbin.

I

ibérico, *a.,* **ibero,** *n.* & *a.* Iberian.—**iberoamericano,** *n.* & *a.* Ibero-American.

ictericia, *f.* jaundice.

ida, *f.* departure; going.—*i. y vuelta,* round trip.

idea, *f.* idea.—**ideal,** *a.* & *m.* ideal.—**idealismo,** *m.* idealism.—**idealista,** *mf.* & *a.* idealist; idealistic.—**idealizar,** *vti.* [a] to idealize.—**idear,** *vt.* to conceive the idea of; to devise.

ídem, *a.* & *pron.* ditto, the same.

idéntico, *a.* (a) identical (with).—**identidad,** *f.* identity.—*de i.,* identification (as *a.*).—**identificación,** *f.* identification.—**identificar,** *vti.* [d]

to identify.—*vri.* to identify oneself.

ideología, *f.* ideology.—**ideológico,** *a.* ideological.

idioma, *m.* language, tongue.—**idiomático,** *a.* idiomatic.

idiota, *mf.* & *a.* idiot; idiotic.—**idiotez,** *f.* idiocy.—**idiotismo,** *m.* expression, idiom; idiotic action.

ido, *ppi.* of IR.

idólatra, *a.* idolatrous; heathen.—*mf.* idolater; (coll.) ardent lover.—**idolatrar,** *vt.* to idolize, worship.—**idolatría,** *f.* idolatry; idolization.—**ídolo,** *m.* idol.

idóneo, *a.* fit, able, suitable.

iglesia, *f.* church.

ignición, *f.* ignition.

ignorancia, *f.* ignorance.—**ignorante,** *a.* ignorant.—**ignorar,** *vt.* to be ignorant of, not to know.

igual, *a.* equal; even, flat; unvarying.—*(me) es i.,* it is all the same (to me).—*m.* equal.—*al i.,* equally.—*sin i.,* unrivaled, matchless; without parallel.—**iguala,** *f.* stipend on agreement.—**igualar,** *vt.* to equalize; to match; to level, smooth; to adjust.—*vi.* to be equal; (sports) to be tied (in score).—*vr.* **(a, con)** to put oneself on the same plane (as).—**igualdad,** *f.* equality.

ijada, *f.,* **ijar,** *m.* flank (of an animal).—*dolor de i.,* pain in the side.

ilación, *f.* inference; connection.

ilegal, *a.* illegal, unlawful.—**ilegalidad,** *f.* illegality, unlawfulness.

ilegible, *a.* illegible.

ilegitimidad, *f.* illegitimacy.—**ilegítimo,** *a.* illegal, unlawful; illegitimate.

ileso, *a.* unhurt; uninjured.

ilícito, *a.* illicit; unlawful.

ilimitado, *a.* unlimited.

ilógico, *a.* illogical; irrational.

iluminación, *f.* illumination, lighting; (art) painting in distemper.—**iluminar,** *vt.* to illuminate, to light; to enlighten.

ilusión, *f.* illusion; delusion; eagerness.—*hacerse ilusiones,* to delude oneself.—**ilusionar,** *vt.* to cause illusion; to delude.—*vr.* **(con)** to have illusions; to get up hopes (of); to bank on.—**iluso,** *a.* deluded, deceived.—*m.* dreamer.

ilustración, *f.* illustration; elucidation, explanation.—**ilustrar,** *vt.* to illustrate.—*vr.* to acquire knowledge, learn.—**ilustrativo,** *a.* illustrative.—**ilustre,** *a.* illustrious, distinguished.

imagen, *f.* image.—**imaginable,** *a.* imaginable.—**imaginación,** *f.* imagination; imagining.—**imaginar,** *vt.*

& *vr.* to imagine; to suspect.—
imaginaria, *f.* (mil.) reserve guard;
(math.) imaginary.—**imaginario,** *a.*
imaginary, imagined; mythical.—
imaginativa, *f.* imagination.—**imagi-
nativo,** *a.* imaginative.
imán, *m.* magnet; magnetism, charm.
imanar, imantar, *vt.* to magnetize.
imantación, *f.* magnetization.
imbécil, *mf.* & *a.* imbecile.—**imbecili-
dad,** *f.* imbecility.
imborrable, *a.* indelible; unforgettable.
imitable, *a.* imitable.—**imitación,** *f.*
imitation.—**imitador,** *n.* & *a.* imitator; imitating.—**imitar,** *vt.* to imitate.
impaciencia, *f.* impatience.—**impa-
cientar,** *vt.* to vex, irritate, make
(one) lose patience.—*vr.* to become
impatient.—**impaciente,** *a.* impat-
tient.
impacto, *m.* impact.
impar, *a.* odd.
imparcial, *a.* impartial.—**imparciali-
dad,** *f.* impartiality.
impartir, *vt.* to impart.
impasibilidad, *f.* impassiveness.—**im-
pasible,** *a.* impassive, unmoved.
impávido, *a.* impassive, stolid; fearless; impudent.
impecable, *a.* impeccable.
impedido, *a.* disabled, crippled.—**im-
pedimento,** *m.* impediment; obstacle, hindrance.—**impedir,** *vti.* [29]
to impede, hinder, prevent.—*i. el
paso,* to block (the way).
impeler, *vt.* to impel; to spur, stimulate.
impenetrable, *a.* impenetrable, impervious.
impenitente, *a.* impenitent, unrepent-
ant.
impensado, *a.* unforeseen, unexpected.
imperante, *a.* commanding, reigning.
—**imperar,** *vi.* to command; to prevail.—**imperativo,** *a.* imperative,
urgent; domineering, bossy.—*m.*
(gram.) imperative.
imperceptible, *a.* imperceptible.
imperdible, *a.* that cannot be lost.—
m. safety pin.
imperdonable, *a.* unpardonable, un-
forgivable.
imperfecto, *a.* imperfect, defective.
imperial, *a.* imperial.—**imperialismo,**
m. imperialism.—**imperialista,** *mf.* &
a. imperialist; imperialistic.
impericia, *f.* unskillfulness, inexpert-
ness.
imperio, *m.* empire; rule; influence;
pride.—**imperioso,** *a.* imperious,
overbearing; pressing, urgent.
impermeable, *a.* waterproof; watertight; impervious.—*m.* raincoat.

impersonal, *a.* impersonal.
impertérrito, *a.* serene; stolid.
impertinencia, *f.* impertinence, folly,
nonsense.—**impertinente,** *a.* not
pertinent; impertinent, meddlesome.
—*m. pl.* lorgnette.
imperturbable, *a.* imperturbable, undisturbed, unruffled.
ímpetu, *m.* impetus, impulse.—**impe-
tuoso,** *a.* impetuous, violent.
impiedad, *f.* impiety; irreligion, infidelity.—**impío,** *a.* impious; god-
less.—*n.* impious person; enemy of
religion.
inplacable, *a.* implacable.
implicar, *vti.* [d] to implicate, involve; to imply.
implícito, *a.* implicit.
implorar, *vt.* to implore, beg, entreat.
imponente, *a.* imposing.—**imponer,**
vti. [32-49] to impose; to command
(respect, fear).—*vri.* to assert oneself, impose one's authority; to
command respect.
impopular, *a.* unpopular.—**impopu-
laridad,** *f.* unpopularity.
importación, *f.* (com.) importation,
imports.—**importador,** *n.* & *a.* im-
porter; importing.
importancia, *f.* importance.—**impor-
tante,** *a.* important.—**importar,** *vi.*
to be important; to concern.—*eso
no importa,* that doesn't matter.—
eso no le importa a Ud., that is
none of your business.—*no importa,*
never mind. —*no me importa,* I
don't care; that makes no difference to me.—*¿qué importa?* what
does it matter? what difference
does it make?.—*vt.* to import; to
amount to; to be worth; to imply.
—**importe,** *m.* amount, price, value.
importunar, *vt.* to importune, pester.
—**importuno,** *a.* inopportune; persistent, annoying.
imposibilidad, *f.* impossibility.—**im-
posibilitado,** *a.* helpless, without
means; disabled, unfit for service.—
imposibilitar, *vt.* to disable, make
unfit for service.—**imposible,** *a.* impossible.
imposición, *f.* imposition (of a duty
etc.); tax, burden.
impostor, *n.* impostor.—**impostura,** *,.*
imposture.
impotencia, *f.* impotence.—**impotente,**
a. impotent, powerless.
impracticable, *a.* impracticable.
impregnación, *f.* impregnation.—**im-
pregnar,** *vt.* to impregnate; to
saturate.—*vr.* to become impreg-
nated.
imprenta, *f.* printing; printing office
or house; press.

imprescindible, *a.* indispensable, essential.

impresión, *f.* impression; print, printing; stamping; footprint.—*i. digital,* fingerprint.—**impresionable,** *a.* impressionable, emotional.—**impresionar,** *vt.* to impress; to affect.—*vr.* to be moved.—**impreso,** *ppi.* of IMPRIMIR.—*a.* printed; stamped.—*m.* publication; printed matter, print; blank.—**impresor,** *n.* printer.

imprevisión, *f.* lack of foresight; improvidence.—**imprevisto,** *a.* unforeseen, unexpected.—*m. pl.* incidental or unforeseen expenses.

imprimir, *vti.* [49] to print, stamp, imprint.

improbable, *a.* improbable, unlikely.

ímprobo, *a.* laborious, painful, arduous.

improcedente, *a.* contrary to law.

improperio, *m.* insult, indignity.

impropio, *a.* inappropriate, unfitting; improper, unbecoming.

improvisación, *f.* improvisation.—**improvisado,** *a.* makeshift, improvised.—**improvisar,** *vt.* to improvise.—**improviso,** *a.* unexpected, unforeseen.—*de i.,* suddenly.

imprudencia, *f.* imprudence, indiscretion.—**imprudente,** *a.* imprudent, indiscreet.

impudicia, *f.* immodesty.—**impúdico,** *a.* immodest; impudent; revealing (of a dress).

impuesto, *ppi.* of IMPONER.—*a.* imposed; informed.—*estar,* or *quedar i. de,* to be informed about.—*m.* tax, duty.

impulsar, *vt.* to impel, move; (mech.) to drive, force.—**impulsión,** *f.* impulsion, impulse, impetus.—**impulsivo,** *a.* impulsive.—**impulso,** *m.* impulsion; impulse.

impureza, *f.* impurity; unchastity.—**impuro,** *a.* impure; defiled.

inacabable, *a.* everlasting, endless.—**inacabado,** *a.* unfinished.

inaccesible, *a.* inaccessible, unapproachable.

inacción, *f.* inaction, inactivity.

inactividad, *f.* inactivity.—**inactivo,** *a.* inactive.

inadecuado, *a.* inadequate.

inadaptable, *a.* unadaptable.—**inadaptación,** *f.* maladjustment.

inadmisible, *a.* inadmissible.

inadvertencia, *f.* inadvertence, oversight.—**inadvertido,** *a.* careless; unseen, unnoticed.

inaguantable, *a.* unbearable.

inalámbrico, *a.* wireless.

inalienable, *a.* inalienable.

inamovible, *a.* immovable.

inanición, *f.* starvation.

inanimado, *a.* inanimate, lifeless.

inapelable, *a.* irrevocable.

inapetencia, *f.* lack of appetite.

inaplazable, *a.* that cannot be deferred.

inaplicable, *a.* irrelevant.

inapreciable, *a.* invaluable; imperceptible.

inasequible, *a.* unattainable, unobtainable, unavailable.

inaudito, *a.* unheard of, most extraordinary.

inauguración, *f.* inauguration.—**inaugurar,** *vt.* to inaugurate; to open (exhibition, etc.); to unveil (statue, monument, etc.).

inca, *mf. & a.* Inca.—**incaico,** *a.* Inca.

incalculable, *a.* incalculable; innumerable.

incalificable, *a.* extremely bad, most reprehensible.

incandescencia, *f.* incandescence.—**incandescente,** *a.* incandescent.

incansable, *a.* indefatigable, tireless.

incapacidad, *f.* incapacity; incompetence.—**incapacitar,** *vt.* to incapacitate, disable.—**incapaz,** *a.* incapable; unable; incompetent.

incauto, *a.* unwary; gullible.

incendiar, *vt.* to set on fire.—*vr.* to catch fire.—**incendiario,** *n.* & *a.* arsonist; incendiary.—**incendio,** *m.* fire, conflagration.

incensar, *vti.* [1] (eccl.) to incense; to bestow excessive praise or adulation.

incentivo, *m.* incentive, inducement; encouragement.

incertidumbre, *f.* uncertainty; quandary.

incesante, *a.* unceasing, incessant.

incidencia, *f.* incident; incidence.—**incidental,** *a.* incidental.—**incidente,** *a.* incidental.—*m.* incident.—**incidir,** *vi.* (en) to fall (into) (as an error).

incienso, *m.* incense.

incierto, *a.* uncertain; untrue; unknown.

incinerar, *vt.* to incinerate, cremate.

incisión, *f.* incision, cut.—**incisivo,** *a.* incisive; keen, sharp.

incitante, *a.* inciting, exciting.—**incitar,** *vt.* to incite, spur, instigate.—**incitativo,** *a.* inciting.—*m.* incitement.

incivil, *a.* uncivil; rude.

inclasificable, *a.* unclassifiable, nondescript.

inclinación, *f.* inclination; tendency, proclivity, bent; pitch; slope; (RR.) grade.—**inclinado,** *a.* inclined; sloping; disposed.—**inclinar,** *vt.* to incline; to bow; to influence.

—*vr.* to incline, slope; to lean; to stoop, bow.

incluir, *vti.* [23-49-e] to include; to enclose.—**inclusión,** *f.* inclusion.—**inclusive,** *adv.* inclusively.—**inclusivo,** *a.* inclusive.—**incluso,** *ppi.* of INCLUIR.—*a.* enclosed; including, included.

incobrable, *a.* (com.) uncollectable.

incógnito, *a.* unknown.—*de i.,* incognito.—*f.* (math.) unknown (quantity).

incoherencia, *f.* incoherence.—**incoherente,** *a.* incoherent.

incoloro, *a.* colorless.

incólume, *a.* sound, safe, unharmed.

incombustible, *a.* fireproof.

incomodar, *vt.* to disturb, inconvenience, trouble.—*vr.* to become vexed or angry.—**incomodidad,** *f.* inconvenience; discomfort; nuisance, annoyance.—**incómodo,** *a.* inconvenient; uncomfortable.

incomparable, *a.* incomparable.

incompetencia, *f.* incompetence.—**incompetente,** *a.* incompetent, unqualified.

incompleto, *a.* incomplete.

incomprensible, *a.* incomprehensible.—**incompresión,** *f.* misunderstanding; lack of understanding.

incomunicado, *a.* isolated; in solitary confinement.—**incomunicar,** *vti.* [d] to isolate, put in solitary confinement.

incondicional, *a.* unconditional; unqualified.

inconexo, *a.* unconnected, not pertinent; incoherent.

inconfundible, *a.* unmistakable.

incongruente, *a.* incongruous, out of place.

inconmensurable, *a.* immeasurable; vast.

inconmovible, *a.* unrelenting, unshakable.

inconsciencia, *f.* unconsciousness; (the) unconscious; unawareness; (coll.) irresponsibility.—**inconsciente,** *a.* unconscious; unaware; (coll.) irresponsible.

inconsecuencia, *f.* inconsistency.—**inconsecuente,** *a.* inconsistent.

inconsistente, *a.* unsubstantial, unstable.

inconstancia, *f.* inconstancy, fickleness, mutability.—**inconstante,** *a.* inconstant, fickle, mutable.

incontable, *a.* countless, innumerable.

incontestable, *a.* unanswerable.

incontrovertible, *a.* unanswerable.

inconveniencia, *f.* inconvenience; discomfort.—**inconveniente,** *a.* inconvenient, uncomfortable.—*m.* difficulty, obstacle.

incorporar, *vt.* to incorporate, embody; to make (someone) sit up.—*vr.* to incorporate; to join (as a mil. unit); to form a corporation; to sit up.

incorpóreo, *a.* bodiless, ethereal, immaterial.

incorrección, *f.* incorrectness: impropriety.—**incorrecto,** *a.* incorrect; improper.

incredulidad, *f.* incredulity.—**incrédulo,** *a.* incredulous.—*n.* unbeliever.—**increíble,** *a.* incredible, unbelievable.

incrementar, *vt.* (neol.) to increase, make bigger.—*vi.* to be increased.—**incremento,** *m.* increment, increase.

increpar, *vt.* to rebuke.

incriminar, *vt.* to incriminate.

incrustar, *vt.* to incrust; to encase; to inlay.

incubación, *f.* incubation; hatching.—**incubadora,** *f.* incubator (apparatus); hatchery.—**incubar,** *vt.* to incubate; to hatch.

inculpar, *vt.* to accuse, blame.

inculto, *a.* uncultured, untutored; uncultivated.—**incultura,** *f.* lack of culture.

incumbencia, *f.* incumbency; concern.—**incumbir,** *vt.* to concern, pertain.

incumplimiento, *m.* nonfulfillment.

incurable, *a.* incurable.

incurrir, *vi.* (en) to incur, become liable (to); to commit (error or crime).

incursión, *f.* (mil.) incursion, raid.

indagación, *f.* investigation, search, inquiry.—**indagar,** *vti.* [b] to investigate, inquire into or about.

indebidamente, *adv.* unduly; improperly; illegally.—**indebido,** *a.* improper; illegal.

indecencia, *f.* indecency; obscenity.—**indecente,** *a.* indecent, obscene.

indecible, *a.* inexpressible, untold.

indecisión, *f.* indecision, irresolution.—**indeciso,** *a.* hesitant, irresolute; undecided.

indecoroso, *a.* indecorous, unbecoming; undignified.

indefectible, *a.* unfailing.

indefendible, *a.* indefensible.—**indefenso,** *a.* defenseless.

indefinible, *a.* undefinable.—**indefinido,** *a.* indefinite; undefined.

indeleble, *a.* indelible.

indemne, *a.* undamaged, unhurt.—**indemnización,** *f.* compensation; indemnity.—**indemnizar,** *vti.* [a] to indemnify, compensate; to recoup.

independencia, *f.* independence.—**independiente,** *a.* independent.—**independizar,** *vti.* [a] to free, emancipate.—*vri.* to become independent, win freedom.

indescifrable, *a.* undecipherable.

indescriptible, *a.* indescribable.

indeseable, *a.* undesirable, unwelcome.

indeterminado, *a.* indeterminate, undetermined.

indiada, *f.* (Am.) crowd or multitude of Indians.— **indiano,** *m.* a Spaniard who returns rich from America.

indicación, *f.* indication; hint.— **indicar,** *vti.* [d] to indicate, suggest, show.—**indicativo,** *a.* indicative, pointing.—*m.* (gram.) indicative.

índice, *m.* index; catalog; pointer; forefinger.—**indicio,** *m.* indication, clue, sign.

indiferencia, *f.* indifference.—**indiferente,** *a.* indifferent.

indígena, *a.* native, indigenous; (Am.) Indian.—*mf.* native; (Am.) Indian.

indigestarse, *vr.* to cause indigestion; to suffer from indigestion; to be unbearable.—**indigestión,** *f.* indigestion.—**indigesto,** *a.* indigestible.

indignación, *f.* indignation.—**indignar,** *vt.* to irritate, anger.—*vr.* to become indignant.—**indignidad,** *f.* indignity; unworthy act.—**indigno, e.** unworthy, undeserving; unbecoming, contemptible; low.

índigo, *m.* indigo.

indio, *n.* & *a.* Indian; Hindu.

indirecta, *f.* innuendo, hint.—*echar indirectas,* to make insinuations.— **indirecto,** *a.* indirect.

indisciplina, *f.* lack of discipline.— **indisciplinado,** *a.* undisciplined; untrained.

indiscreción, *f.* indiscretion.—**indiscreto,** *a.* indiscreet.

indiscutible, *a.* unquestionable, indisputable.

indispensable, *a.* indispensable, vital.

indisponer, *vti.* [32-49] to indispose; to make ill; (**con**) to prejudice (against).—*vri.* to become ill; to fall out (with a person).—**indisposición,** *f.* indisposition, slight ailment; dislike.—**indispuesto,** *ppi.* of INDISPONER.—*a.* indisposed; ill.

indistinto, *a.* indistinct, vague.

individual, *a.* individual.—**individualidad,** *f.* individuality.—**individuo,** *n.* individual, person; fellow.

indivisible, *a.* indivisible.

indócil, *a.* headstrong, unruly.

indocto, *a.* ignorant, untaught, untutored.

indochino, *a.* & *n.* Indo-Chinese.

índole, *f.* class, kind; disposition, nature.

indolencia, *f.* indolence.—**indolente,** *a.* indolent.

indomable, *a.* untamable, indomitable; unmanageable.—**indómito, a.** untamed; unruly.

indostánico, *a.* Hindu.

inducción, *f.* inducement, persuasion; (elec., log.) induction.—**inducir,** *vti.* [11] to induce; to persuade.—**inductor,** *a.* (elec.) inducive.—*m.* magnetic field.

indulgencia, *f.* indulgence; forbearance; forgiveness.—**indulgente, a.** indulgent, forbearing.

indultar, *vt.* to pardon.—**indulto, m.** pardon, amnesty.

indumentaria, *f.* garb, apparel, garments.

industria, *f.* industry.—*caballero de i.,* swindler; confidence man.—**industrial,** *a.* industrial.—*mf.* industrialist.—**industrializar,** *vti.* [a] to industrialize.—**industrioso, a.** industrious.

inédito, *a.* unpublished.

ineficacia, *f.* inefficacy.—**ineficaz, a.** ineffectual, ineffective.

inelegible, *a.* ineligible.

ineludible, *a.* inevitable, unavoidable.

inenarrable *a.* inexplicable; inexpressible, ineffable.

ineptitud, *f.* ineptitude, incompetency. —**inepto,** *a.* inept, incompetent, unqualified.

inequívoco, *a.* unmistakable.

inercia, *f.* inertia; inertness, inactivity.—**inerte,** *a.* inert; slow, sluggish.

inescrutable, *a.* inscrutable; unconfirmable.

inesperado, *a.* unexpected.

inestabilidad, *f.* instability.—**inestable,** *a.* unstable, unsteady.

inestimable, *a.* inestimable, invaluable.

inevitable, *a.* inevitable, unavoidable.

inexactitud, *f.* inexactness; inaccuracy; unfaithfulness.—**inexacto, a.** inexact, inaccurate.

inexistente, *a.* nonexistent.

inexorable, *a.* inexorable, relentless.

inexperiencia, *f.* inexperience.—**inexperto,** *a.* inexperienced, unskillful; unpractical.

inexplicable, *a.* inexplicable, unexplainable, unaccountable.

inexplotado, *a.* undeveloped.

inexpresivo, *a.* inexpressive, wooden.

infalible, *a.* infallible, unerring.

infame, *a.* & *mf.* infamous (person). —**infamia,** *f.* infamy; baseness; dishonor; opprobrium.

infancia, *f.* infancy; childhood.— **infante,** *n.* infante, prince; (*f.* infanta, princess).—**infantería, f.** infantry.—**infantil, a.** infantile, childlike.

infatigable, *a.* untiring, tireless.

infausto, *a.* unlucky; unhappy.

infección, *f.* infection.—**infeccioso,** *a.* infectious.—**infectar,** *vt.* to infect; to corrupt.—*vr.* to become infected.

infecundo, *a.* barren, sterile.

infelicidad, *f.* unhappiness, infelicity. —**infeliz,** *a.* unhappy, unfortunate.— *mf.* poor devil.

inferencia, *f.* inference.

inferior, *a.* inferior; lower; under (part).—*mf.* subordinate.—**inferioridad,** *f.* inferiority.

inferir, *vti.* [39] to infer; to imply; to inflict (as a wound).

infernal, *a.* infernal, hellish.

infestar, *vt.* to infest, plague; to infect.

inficionar, *vt.* to infect; to corrupt.

infidelidad, *f.* infidelity; unfaithfulness.—**infiel,** *a.* unfaithful, faithless; infidel, pagan; inaccurate.— *mf.* infidel.

infiernillo, *m.* spirit lamp.—**infierno,** *m.* hell, inferno.

infiltración, *f.* infiltration.—**infiltrar,** *vt.* & *vr.* to infiltrate, filter through.

ínfimo, *a.* lowest; least.

infinidad, *f.* infinity; infinite number, a lot.—**infinitivo,** *m.* & *a.* infinitive. —**infinito,** *a.* infinite.—*adv.* infinitely, immensely.—*m.* infinity.

inflación, *f.* inflation; conceit, airs.

inflamable, *a.* inflammable.—**inflamación,** *f.* inflammation.—**inflamar,** *vt.* to inflame; to set on fire.—*vr.* to catch fire; to become fiery; (med.) to become inflamed.

inflar, *vt.* to inflate; to exaggerate.— *vr.* to swell; to puff up (with pride, etc.).

inflexibilidad, *f.* inflexibility; stiffness, rigidity.—**inflexible,** *a.* inflexible, rigid, steely; unbending, unyielding.—**inflexión,** *f.* inflection; accent, modulation.

infligir, *vti.* [c] to impose (a penalty), condemn to.

influencia, *f.* influence.—**influenza,** *f.* influenza, grippe.—**influir,** *vti.* [23-e] to influence; to act on.—*vii.* (en) to have influence (on); to contribute (to).—**influjo,** *m.* influence. —**influyente,** *a.* influential.

infolio, *m.* folio.

información, *f.* information; report; inquiry; (law) brief.—**informal,** *a.* informal; unreliable; unconventional.—**informalidad,** *f.* informality; breach of etiquette; unreliability.—**informar,** *vt.* to inform, report to.—*vi.* (law) to plead.—*vr.* (de) to acquaint oneself (with), to inquire (into); to find out (about).

—**informativo,** *a.* instructive, informative.—**informe,** *a.* shapeless.— *m.* information; report; news; account; (law) pleading.

infortunado, *a.* unfortunate, unlucky. —**infortunio,** *m.* misfortune, ill luck; mishap; misery.

infracción, *f.* infraction, infringement, transgression.

infranqueable, *a.* insurmountable.

infrascrito, *a.* undersigned; hereinafter mentioned.

infrecuente, *a.* unusual, infrequent.

infringir, *vti.* [c] to infringe, violate, break.

infructuoso, *a.* fruitless; unsuccessful, unavailing.

ínfulas, *f. pl.* conceit, airs.—*darse í.,* to put on airs.

infundado, *a.* groundless, baseless.

infundio, *m.* (coll.) fib, story.

ingeniería, *f.* engineering.—**ingeniero,** *n.* engineer.—**ingenio,** *m.* talent; wit; cleverness, ingenuity; (Am.) sugar mill; device.—**ingeniosidad,** *f.* ingeniousness, ingenuity.—**ingenioso,** *a.* ingenious; witty, sparkling; resourceful.

ingénito, *a.* inborn, innate.

ingenuidad, *f.* ingenuousness, candor. —**ingenuo,** *a.* ingenuous, candid, unsophisticated.

ingerencia, *f.* interference, meddling. —**ingerir,** *vti.* [39] to insert, introduce.—*vri.* to interfere.

ingle, *f.* groin.

inglés, *a.* English.—*n.* Englishman (-woman).—*m.* English language.

ingratitud, *f.* ingratitude, ungratefulness.—**ingrato,** *a.* ungrateful; thankless; disagreeable.

ingrediente, *m.* ingredient.

ingresar, *vt.* (en) to enter; to deposit (money); to join (a party, group). —**ingreso,** *m.* entrance; entering; joining; (com.) entry, money received.—*pl.* receipts; earnings.

inhábil, *a.* unable; incompetent; unfit, unskillful.—**inhabilitación,** *f.* disabling or disqualifying; disqualification; disability.—**inhabilitar,** *vt.* to disqualify; to disable, render unfit.—*vr.* to lose a right; to become disabled.

inhabitable, *a.* uninhabitable.

inhalación, *f.* inhalation.—**inhalar,** *vt.* to inhale.

inherente, *a.* inherent.

inhibición, *f.* inhibition; prohibition. —**inhibir,** *vt.* to inhibit.—**inhibitorio,** *a.* inhibitory.

inhospitalario, *a.* inhospitable; unsheltering.—**inhóspito,** *a.* inhospitable.

inhumano, *a.* inhuman, cruel.

iniciación, *f.* initiation, introduction. —inicial, *mf.* & *a.* initial.—**iniciar,** *vt.* to initiate; to begin, start.—*vr.* to be initiated.—**iniciativa,** *f.* initiative; resourcefulness.

inicuo, *a.* iniquitous, wicked.

inimaginable, *a.* unimaginable, inconceivable, unthinkable.

inimitable, *a.* inimitable.

ininteligible, *a.* unintelligible.

injerir, *vti.* & [39] *vri.* = INGERIR.

injertar, *vt.* to graft.

injuria, *f.* offense, insult, affront.—**injuriar,** *vt.* to insult, offend.—**injurioso,** *a.* injurious; insulting, offensive.

injusticia, *f.* injustice.—**injustificable,** *a.* unjustifiable.—**injustificado,** *a.* unjustified, unjustifiable.—**injusto,** *a.* unjust, unfair.

inmaculado, *a.* immaculate.

inmanente, *a.* inherent.

inmaterial, *a.* immaterial.

inmaturo, *a.* immature.

inmediación, *f.* contiguity.—*pl.* suburbs; neighborhood.—**inmediato,** *a.* close, adjoining, immediate.

inmejorable, *a.* most excellent.

inmensidad, *f.* immensity, vastness; infinity; great multitude or number. —**inmenso,** *a.* immense; infinite; countless.

inmerecido, *a.* unmerited, undeserved.

inmersión, *f.* immersion.

inmigración, *f.* immigration.—**inmigrante,** *mf.* immigrant.—**inmigrar,** *vi.* to immigrate.—**inmigratorio,** *a.* immigration.

inminencia, *f.* imminence, nearness.— **inminente,** *a.* imminent, near.

inmiscuir, *vti.* [23-e] (fig.) to discuss elements alien to the question.—*vri.* to interfere; to meddle.

inmodestia, *f.* immodesty.—**inmodesto,** *a.* immodest.

inmoral, *a.* immoral.—**inmoralidad,** *f.* immorality.

inmortal, *a.* immortal.—**inmortalidad,** *f.* immortality.—**inmortalizar,** *vti.* [a] to immortalize.—*vri.* to become immortal.

inmovible, *a.* immovable.—**inmóvil,** *a.* motionless; fixed; unshaken.—**inmovilidad,** *f.* immovability, fixedness.—**inmovilizar,** *vti.* [a] to immobilize, fix.

inmueble, *a.* (law) immovable, real (property).—*m.* (law) immovables.

inmundicia, *f.* filth, dirt; garbage; filthiness; uncleanliness; impurity.— **inmundo,** *a.* unclean, filthy.

inmune, *a.* immune; exempt.—**inmunidad,** *f.* immunity; exemption.— **inmunizar,** *vti.* [a] to immunize.

innato, *a.* innate; inborn.

innecesario, *a.* unnecessary.

innegable, *a.* undeniable.

innoble, *a.* ignoble.

innovación, *f.* innovation.—**innovador,** *n.* & *a.* innovator; innovating. **innovar,** *vt.* to innovate.

innumerable, *a.* innumerable, numberless.

inocencia, *f.* innocence.—**inocente,** *a.* innocent.—**inocentón,** *n.* simpleton.

inoculación, *f.* inoculation.—**inocular,** *vt.* to inoculate; to contaminate.

inodoro, *a.* odorless.—*m.* water closet.

inofensivo, *a.* inoffensive, harmless.

inolvidable, *a.* unforgettable.

inopinado, *a.* unexpected, unforeseen.

inoportuno, *a.* inopportune, untimely.

inorgánico, *a.* inorganic.

inoxidable, *a.* nonrusting.

inquebrantable, *a.* unbreakable; unshakable; inflexible.

inquietante, *a.* disquieting, disturbing. —**inquietar,** *vt.* to disquiet, trouble, worry; to vex, harass; to stir up or excite.—*vr.* to become uneasy or restless; to fret, worry.—**inquieto,** *a.* restless; uneasy, worried.—**inquietud,** *f.* restlessness, uneasiness, anxiety.

inquilinato, *m.* occupancy; lease, leasing.—**inquilino,** *n.* tenant, lodger, renter, lessee.

inquina, *f.* (coll.) aversion, hatred, grudge.

inquirir, *vti.* [2] to inquire, search, investigate.

inquisición, *f.* inquest, examination, inquiry; Inquisition, Holy Office.

insalubre, *a.* unhealthful, unsanitary. —**insalubridad,** *f.* unhealthfulness.

insania, *f.* insanity.—**insane,** *a.* insane, crazy.

inscribir, *vti.* [49] to inscribe, register, record, book.—*vri.* to register; to enroll.—**inscripción,** *f.* inscription; record, register, entry; registration; government bond.—**inscrito,** *ppi.* of INSCRIBIR.

insecticida, *m.* & *a.* insecticide; insecticidal.—**insecto,** *m.* insect.

inseguridad, *f.* insecurity; uncertainty.—**inseguro,** *a.* insecure, unsafe; uncertain.

insensatez, *f.* stupidity, folly.—**insensato,** *a.* stupid; mad.

insensibilidad, *f.* insensibility, unconsciousness; hard-heartedness.— **insensibilizar,** *vti.* [a] to make insensible or insensitive.—**insensible,** *a.* insensible, thick-skinned; imperceptible; unfeeling.

inseparable, *a.* inseparable; undetachable.

inserción, *f.* insertion; grafting.— **insertar,** *vti.* [49] to insert.—**inserto,** *ppi.* of INSERTAR.

inservible, *a.* unserviceable, useless.

insidia, *f.* ambush, snare.—**insidioso,** *a.* insidious, sly, guileful.

insigne, *a.* noted, famous, renowned.

insignia, *f.* decoration, medal, badge, standard; (naut.) pennant.—*pl.* insignia.

insignificancia, *f.* insignificance; trifle.—**insignificante,** *a.* insignificant.

insinuación, *f.* insinuation; hint, suggestion.—**insinuar,** *vt.* to insinuate, hint, suggest.—*vr.* to ingratiate oneself; to creep in.

insípido, *a.* insipid, tasteless; unsavory; spiritless, flat; unseasoned.

insistencia, *f.* persistence, insistence, obstinacy.—**insistir,** *vi.* **(en)** to insist (on), persist (in); to dwell (upon), emphasize.

insolación, *f.* sunstroke.

insolencia, *f.* insolence.—**insolentar,** *vt.* to make bold.—*vr.* to become insolent.—**insolente,** *a.* insolent.

insólito, *a.* unusual, unaccustomed.

insomnio, *m.* insomnia, sleeplessness.

insondable, *a.* unfathomable, fathomless; inscrutable.

insoportable, *a.* unbearable, intolerable.

insostenible, *a.* indefensible.

inspección, *f.* inspection; inspector's office.—**inspeccionar,** *vt.* to inspect. —**inspector,** *n.* inspector; supervisor, overseer.

inspiración, *f.* inspiration; inhalation.—**inspirar,** *vt.* to inspire; to inhale.

instalación, *f.* installation.—**instalar,** *vt.* to install.—*vr.* to establish oneself, settle.

instancia, *f.* instance; petition; request.

instantáneo, *a.* instantaneous.—*f.* snapshot.—**instante,** *m.* instant, moment, trice.—*al i.,* immediately.

instar, *vt.* to press, urge.—*vi.* to be urgent.

instaurar, *vt.* to establish; to renovate.

instigador, *n.* instigator, abettor.— **instigar,** *vti.* [b] to instigate, incite.

instintivo, *a.* instinctive.—**instinto,** *m.* instinct.

institución, *f.* institution, establishment.—**instituir,** *vti.* [23-e] to institute, establish, found.—**instituto,** *m.* institute.—**institutriz,** *f.* governess.

instrucción, *f.* instruction; education, learning; tutoring; (law) court proceedings.—*pl.* instructions, orders.— **instructivo,** *a.* instructive.—**instruir,** *vti.* [23-e] to instruct, teach, train; to inform; to put in legal form.

instrumentación, *f.* (mus.) instrumentation, orchestration.—**instrumental,** *a.* (mus.) instrumental; (law) pertaining to legal instruments.—*m.* set of instruments.— **instrumento,** *m.* instrument, implement, apparatus; agent or means.

insubordinación, *f.* insubordination.— **insubordinar,** *vt.* to incite to insubordination.—*vr.* to rebel, mutiny.

insuficiencia, *f.* insufficiency.—**insuficiente,** *a.* insufficient.

insula, *f.* isle, island.—**insular,** *a.* insular.

insulso, *a.* insipid; dull, heavy.

insultar, *vt.* to insult.—**insulto,** *m.* insult, affront.

insuperable, *a.* insuperable, impassable.

insurgente, *mf.* & *a.* insurgent.

insurrección, *f.* insurrection, rebellion. —**insurreccionar,** *vt.* to cause to rebel.—*vr.* to rebel.—**insurrecto,** *n.* & *a.* insurgent, rebel.

insustancial, *a.* unsubstantial.

intacto, *a.* untouched, intact, whole, undisturbed.

intachable, *a.* unexceptionable, irreproachable.

intangible, *a.* intangible, untouchable.

integración, *f.* integration.—**integral,** *a.* integral; whole.—**integrar,** *vt.* to integrate; to compose, make up; (com.) to reimburse.—**integridad,** *f.* wholeness; integrity, honesty; virginity.—**íntegro,** *a.* entire, complete, whole; upright, honest; unabridged.

intelecto, *m.* intellect.—**intelectual,** *a.* & *mf.* intellectual.—**inteligencia,** *f.* intelligence; understanding (between persons).—**inteligente,** *a.* intelligent; smart, clever.

intemperancia, *f.* intemperance, excess.—**intemperante,** *a.* intemperate. —**intemperie,** *f.* rough or bad weather.—*a la i.,* in the open air, outdoors, unsheltered.

intempestivo, *a.* unseasonable, inopportune.

intención, *f.* intention, purpose.—*de primera i.,* provisionally, tentatively.

intendencia, *f.* intendancy; administration; office or district of an intendant.—**intendente,** *n.* intendant; administrator; (mil.) quartermaster.

intensidad, *f.* intensity; vehemence.— **intensivo, intenso,** *a.* intense, intensive, vehement.

intentar, *vt.* to try, attempt, endeavor; to intend; (law) to enter (an action), commence (a lawsuit).— **intento,** *m.* intent, purpose.—*de i.,* purposely, knowingly.—**intentona,** *f.* (coll.) rash attempt.

intercalar, *vt.* to interpolate, place between.

intercambio, *m.* interchange, intercourse.

interceder, *vi.* to intercede.

interceptar, *vt.* to intercept, cut off.

intercesión, *f.* intercession, mediation.

interdicción, *f.* interdiction, prohibition.

interés, *m.* interest.—*pl.* interests.—*intereses creados,* vested interests.—**interesado,** *a.* interested; mercenary, selfish.—*n.* associate; person interested; (law) party in interest.—**interesante,** *a.* interesting.—**interesar,** *vi.* & *vr.* **(en, por, con)** to be concerned (with) or interested (in); to take an interest.—*vt.* to invest; to give an interest; to interest, attract.

interfecto, *n.* (law) murdered person, victim.

interferencia, *f.* interference.—**interferir,** *vi.* to interfere; to meddle.

ínterin, *adv.* meanwhile, interim.—**interino,** *a.* provisional, temporary, acting, interim.

interior, *a.* interior, inner, inside; domestic (as commerce, etc.).—*m.* interior; inside; inner part; mind, soul.—*pl.* entrails, intestines, (coll.) insides.—**interioridades,** *f. pl.* family secrets; inwardness.

interjección, *f.* interjection.

interludio, *m.* (mus.) interlude.

intermediario, *a.* intermediary.—*n.* intermediary; mediator; middleman.—**intermedio,** *a.* intermediate, interposed.—*m.* interval, interim; (theat.) interlude, intermission.

interminable, *a.* interminable, endless.

intermisión, *f.* intermission, interruption.

intermitente, *a.* intermittent.

internacional, *a.* international.

internado, *m.* boarding school; boarding.—**internar,** *vt.* to intern, confine; to place in an institution.—*vi.* to enter.—*vr.* **(en)** to go into the interior (of); to go deeply (into).—**interno,** *a.* interior, internal, inward; boarding.—*n.* boarding student; interne.

interpelar, *vt.* to interrogate, question.

interponer, *vti.* [32-49] to interpose, place between; to appoint as a mediator; (law) to present (a petition) to a court.—*vri.* to go between, to interpose.—**interposición,** *f.* mediation; interjection; interposal; intervention.

interpretación, *f.* interpretation; rendering.—**interpretar,** *vt.* to interpret.—**intérprete,** *mf.* interpreter.

interpuesto, *ppi.* of INTERPONER.—*a.* interposed.

interrogación, *f.* interrogation, question; question mark.—**interrogante,** *a.* interrogative; interrogating.—*mf.* interrogator, questioner.—*m.* question mark.—**interrogar,** *vti.* [b] to question, interrogate.—**interrogatorio,** *m.* interrogatory; (law) cross-examination.

interrumpir, *vt.* to interrupt.—**interrupción,** *f.* interruption.—**interruptor,** *n.* interrupter.—*m.* (elec.) switch; circuit-breaker.

intersección, *f.* intersection.

intervalo, *m.* interval; interlude.

intervención, *f.* intervention; mediation, auditing of accounts; (surg.) operation.—**intervenir,** *vii.* [45] to intervene, mediate, intermediate; to interfere.—*vt.* to supervise; to audit; to control.—**interventor,** *n.* comptroller; supervisor; auditor.

intestino, *a.* intestine, internal; civil, domestic.—*m.* intestine.

intimación, *f.* intimation, hint.—**intimar,** *vt.* to intimate, indicate.—*vr.* to pierce, penetrate.—**intimidad,** *f.* intimacy.

íntimo, *a.* internal, innermost; intimate.

intocable, *a.* untouchable.

intolerable, *a.* intolerable, unbearable.—**intolerancia,** *f.* intolerance.—**intolerante,** *a.* intolerant.

intoxicación, *f.* poisoning.—**intoxicar,** *vti.* [d] to poison.—*vri.* to get poisoned.

intraducible, *a.* untranslatable.

intranquilidad, *f.* restlessness, uneasiness.—**intranquilizar,** *vti.* [a] to worry, make uneasy.—*vri.* to become disquieted, to worry.—**intranquilo,** *a.* uneasy, restless.

intransferible, *a.* not transferable.

intransitable, *a.* impassable; impracticable.

intransitivo, *a.* (gram.) intransitive.

intrepidez, *f.* intrepidity, bravery.—**intrépido,** *a.* intrepid, daring.

intriga, *f.* intrigue.—**intrigante,** *mf.* & *a.* intriguer; intriguing, scheming.—**intrigar,** *vti.* [b] to arouse (one's) interest or curiosity; to mystify.—*vii.* to intrigue.—*vri.* to be interested (in) or curious (about).

intrincado, *a.* intricate, involved.

introducción, *f.* introduction.—**introducir,** *vti.* [11] to introduce; to usher in, put in, insert; to present (a person).—*vri.* **(en)** to gain access (to); to get in; to ingratiate oneself (with); to interfere (in).

intromisión, *f.* influx; interference, meddling.

intrusión, *f.* intrusion, obtrusion.—
intruso, *a.* intrusive, intruding.—*n.*
intruder, outsider.

intuición, *f.* intuition.—**intuir,** *vti.*
[23-e] to know or perceive by intui-
tion.—**intuitivo,** *a.* intuitive.

inundación, *f.* inundation, flood.—
inundar, *vt.* to inundate, flood.

inusitado, *a.* unusual, rare.

inútil, *a.* useless; fruitless, unavailing; needless.—**inutilidad,** *f.* use-
lessness; needlessness.—**inutiliza-
ción,** *f.* spoilage.—**inutilizar,** *vti.*
[a] to render useless; to disable;
to spoil, ruin.—*vri.* to become useless.

invadir, *vt.* to invade; to encroach
upon.

invalidar, *vt.* to invalidate, nullify;
to quash.—**inválido,** *a.* invalid;
crippled; feeble; null, void.—*n.*
invalid.

invariable, *a.* invariable, constant.

invasión, *f.* invasion.—**invasor,** *n.* &
a. invader; invading.

invectiva, *f.* invective.

invencible, *a.* invincible, unconquer-
able.

invención, *f.* invention.

invendible, *a.* unsalable.

inventar, *vt.* to invent; to fib.

inventariar, *vt.* to inventory, take
inventory of.—**inventario,** *m.* inventory.

inventiva, *f.* inventiveness, ingenuity,
resourcefulness.—**invento,** *m.* invention.—**inventor,** *n.* inventor.

invernadero, *m.* winter quarters;
hothouse.—**invernal,** *a.* winter,
wintry.—**invernar,** *vii.* [1] to
winter, pass the winter.

inverosímil, *a.* unlikely, improbable.

inversión, *f.* inversion; (com.) investment.—**inversionista,** *mf.* (neol.)
investor.—**inverso,** *ppi.* of INVERTIR
—*a.* inverse, inverted.—**invertido,** *a.*
& *n.* homosexual.—*a.* inverted.—
invertir, *v'i.* [39-49] to invert; to
reverse; to spend (time) · (com.) to
invest.

investidura, *f.* ceremonial investment.

investigación, *f.* investigation, research; inquest.—**investigador,** *n.* &
a. investigator; investigating.—**in-
vestigar,** *vti.* [b] to investigate,
ascertain, inquire into; to do research work.

investir, *vti.* [29] to invest; to confer
upon.

inveterado, *a.* inveterate, ingrained.

invicto, *a.* invincible, unconquered.

invierno, *m.* winter.

invisible, *a.* invisible.

invitación, *f.* invitation.—**invitado,** *n.*

guest.—**invitar,** *vt.* to invite; to
entice; to treat.

invocación, *f.* invocation.—**invocar,**
vti. [d] to invoke, implore.

involucrar, *vt.* to involve.

involuntario, *a.* involuntary, unin-
tentional.

inyección, *f.* injection.—*poner una i.,*
to give an injection.—**inyectado,** *a.*
bloodshot, inflamed.—**inyectar,** *vt.*
to inject.

iodo, *m.* = YODO.

ir, *vii.* [24] to go; to walk; to be becoming; to fit, suit.—*¿cómo le va?*
how are you?—*i. a,* to go to; to be
going to, to purpose or intend to.—
i. a buscar, to get, fetch.—*i. a
caballo,* to ride, to be riding on
horseback.—*i. a medias,* to go
halves.—*i. a pie,* to walk.—*i. pa-
sando,* to be so-so, to be as usual,
to be getting along.—*no me va ni
me viene,* it does not affect me in
the least.—*¡qué va!* nonsense!—
¡vámonos! let's go!—*¡vamos a ver!*
let's see!—*vri.* to go, go away.—*i.
abajo,* to topple down.—*i. a pique,*
to founder, go to the bottom.

ira, *f.* ire, anger.—**iracundo,** *a.*
wrathful; angry, enraged.—**irascible,** *a.* irascible, irritable, short-
tempered.

iridiscente, *a.* iridescent.

iris, *m.* (anat.) iris.—*arco i.,* rainbow.
—**irisado,** *a.* rainbow-hued.

irlandés, *a.* Irish.—*m.* Irishman; Irish
language.—*f.* Irishwoman.

ironía, *f.* irony.—**irónico,** *a.* ironical,
sarcastic.

irracional, *a.* irrational, unreasoning.

irradiación, *f.* radiation.—**irradiar,**
vt. to radiate.

irrazonable, *a* unreasonable, impracticable.

irreal, *a.* unreal.—**irrealidad,** *f.* un-
reality.—**irrealizable,** *a.* unrealizable.

irrebatible, *a.* indisputable.

irreflexión, *f.* rashness, thoughtlessness.—**irreflexivo,** *a.* thoughtless,
impulsive, unthinking.

irregular, *a.* irreg^ular —**irregularidad,**
f. irregularity.

irreligioso, *a.* irreligious.

irrespetuoso, *a.* disrespectful.

irrespirable, *a.* not fit to be breathed.

irresponsable, *a.* irresponsible.

irreverencia, *f.* irreverence.—**irreve-
rente,** *a.* irreverent.

irrevocable, *a.* irrevocable.

irrigación, *m.* irrigation.—**irrigar,** *vti.*
[b] to irrigate, water.

irrisión, *f.* derision, ridicule.—**irriso-
rio,** *a.* derisive.

irritable, *a.* irritable.—**irritación,** *f.*

irritation.—**irritante**, *a.* irritating; irritant.—**irritar**, *vt.* to irritate.

irrogar, *vti.* [b] to cause (harm or damage).

irrupción, *m.* raid, incursion.

isla, *f.* island.—**islandés, islándico**, *a.* & *n.* Icelandic.—**isleño**, *n.* & *a.* islander; (Cuba) native of the Canary Islands.—**islote**, *m.* small barren island, key.

israelita, *mf.* & *a.* Israelite; Israeli.

istmo, *m.* isthmus.

italiano, *n.* & *a.* Italian.—*m.* Italian language.—**itálico**, *a.* Italic; italic.

ítem, *m.* section, clause, article; addition.—*i.*, or *i. más*, also, likewise, furthermore.

itinerario, *a.* itinerary.—*m.* itinerary; railroad guide, timetable, schedule.

izar, *vti.* [a] to hoist, heave, haul up.

izquierda, *f.* left hand; (pol.) left wing.—*a la i.*, to the left.—**izquierdista**, *mf.* & *a.* (pol.) leftist, radical.—**izquierdo**, *a.* left-handed; left, left-hand side.

J

jaba, *f.* (Am.) basket; crate.

jabalí, *m.* wild boar.—**jabalina**, *f.* sow of a wild boar; javelin.

jabón, *m.* soap; a piece of soap.—*j. de olor*, toilet soap.—**jabonadura**, *f.* washing.—*pl.* suds or soap suds; lather.—**jabonera**, *f.* soap dish.—**jabonería**, *f.* soap factory or shop.

jaca, *f.* pony, cob; gelding.

jacal, *m.* (Mex.) Indian hut.

jacarandoso, *a.* blithe, merry, gay.

jacinto, *m.* hyacinth.

jaco, *m.* sorry nag, jade.

jactancia, *f.* boasting.—**jactancioso**, *a.* boastful, vainglorious.—**jactarse**, *vr.* to boast, vaunt.

jaculatoria, *f.* short prayer.

jade, *m.* (jewel.) jade.

jadeante, *a.* panting, out of breath.—**jadear**, *vi.* to pant.—**jadeo**, *m.* pant, palpitation.

jaez, *m.* harness; trappings; (fig.) manner, kind, quality.—*pl.* trappings.

jaiba, *f.* (Am.) (ichth.) a kind of crab; a cunning, crafty or sneaky person.

jalar, *vt.* = HALAR.—*vr.* (Am.) to get drunk.

jalea, *f.* jelly

jalear, *vt.* to animate dancers by clapping hands.—**jaleo**, *m.* (coll.) carousal; clapping of hands to encourage dancers.

jaletina, *f.* (Am.) calf's foot jelly; gelatine.

jalón, *m.* landmark, stake; (Am.) pull, jerk.—**jalonar**, *vt.* to stake out, mark.—**jalonear**, *vt.* (Am.) to pull, jerk.

jamaiquino, *n.* & *a.* Jamaican.

jamás, *adv.* never.—*nunca j.*, never, nevermore.—*por siempre j.*, forever and ever.

jamelgo, *m.* swaybacked nag.

jamón, *m.* ham.—**jamona**, *f.* (coll.) middle-aged woman; (Am.) spinster.

japonés, *n.* & *a.* Japanese; Japanese language.

jaque, *m.* (chess) check; bully.—*j. mate*, checkmate.

jaqueca, *f.* migraine; headache.

jáquima, *f.* part of a halter which encloses the head.—**jaquimazo**, *m.* (coll.) blow; displeasure; disappointment.

jarabe, *m.* syrup; any sweet mixed drink; (Am.) a Mexican folk dance.—*j. de pico*, empty talk, prattling.

jarana, *f.* (coll.) carousal, revelry.—**jaranear**, *vi.* (coll.) to carouse.—**jaranero**, *a.* jolly.

jarcia, *f.* (naut.) rigging and cordage; shrouds.

jardín, *m.* flower garden.—**jardinería**, *f.* gardening.—**jardinero**, *n.* gardener.—*f.* flowerstand.

jaretón, *m.* (sewing) hem.

jarra, *f.* jar; pitcher.—*en j.*, or *de jarras*, akimbo.

jarrete, *m.* hock (of an animal).

jarro, *m.* pitcher, jug, pot.—**jarrón**, *m.* flower vase; large jar.

jaspe, *m.* (min.) jasper.—**jaspeado**, *a.* mottled, variegated.

jaula, *f.* cage; (Am.) cattle or freight car; cell (in a prison).

jauría, *f.* pack of hounds.

javanés, *a.* & *n.* Javanese.

jazmín, *m.* jasmine.

jefatura, *f.* position or headquarters of a chief.—**jefe**, *n.* chief, head, leader; (fam.) boss; (mil.) commanding officer.

jején, *m.* (Cuba) gnat.

jengibre, *m.* ginger.

jerarquía, *f.* hierarchy.

jerez, *m.* sherry wine.

jerga, *f.* jargon; gibberish; slang.

jergón, *m.* straw bed; mattress, pallet; zircon.

jerigonza, *f.* (coll.) jargon; gibberish; slang.

jeringa, *f.* syringe.—**jeringar**, *vti.* [b] to inject with a syringe; to bother, vex.—**jeringazo**, *m.* injection; squirt.—**jeringuilla**, *f.* syringe.

jeroglífico, *m.* hieroglyph.—*a.* hieroglyphic.

jersey, *m.* sweater, pullover.

jesuíta, *m.* Jesuit.

jeta, *f.* hog's snout; (coll.) person's face.

jíbaro, *a.* (Am.) wild, rustic.—*n.* countryman(-woman).

jibia, *f.* cuttlefish.

jícara, *f.* (Am.) small chocolate or coffee cup; bowl made out of a gourd.

jiga, *f.* jig (dance and tune).

jigote, *m.* hash, minced meat.

jilguero, *m.* linnet.

jinete, *m.* trooper; cavalryman; horseman, rider, equestrian.—**jine-tear,** *vt.* (Am.) to break in (a horse).—*vi.* to ride around on horseback, mainly for show.

jipijapa, *f.* Panama hat.

jira, *f.* picnic, outing; tour.

jirafa, *f.* giraffe.

jirón, *m.* shred, tear; rag; small part (of anything).

jitomate, *m.* (Am.) tomato.

jocoso, *a.* jocose, humorous, facetious.

jofaina, *f.* washbasin, washbowl.

jolgorio, *m.* = HOLGORIO; boisterous frolic.

jornada, *f.* one-day march; working day; stage, journey, travel, trip; (mil.) expedition; act of a play.—**jornal,** *m.* salary; day's wages.—*a j.,* by the day.—**jornalero,** *n.* day laborer.

joroba, *f.* hump; (coll.) importunity, annoyance, nuisance.—**jorobado,** *a.* crooked, humpbacked.—*n.* hunchback.—**jorobar,** *vt.* (coll.) to importune, bother, annoy.

jota, *f.* name of the letter j; jot, tittle, bit; iota; an Aragonese dance and tune.

joven, *a.* young.—*mf.* youth; young man; young woman; young person.

jovial, *a.* jovial, gay, cheerful.—**jovialidad,** *f.* joviality, gaiety.

joya, *f.* jewel, gem; piece of jewelery.—**joyería,** *f.* jeweler's shop.—**joyero,** *n.* jeweler.—*m.* jewel case.

juanete, *m.* bunion.

jubilación, *f.* retirement; pension.—**jubilar,** *vt.* to retire; to pension off.—*vr.* to become a pensioner; to be retired.—**jubileo,** *m.* jubilee.—**júbilo,** *m.* glee, merriment, rejoicing.—**jubiloso,** *a.* joyful, merry, gay.

judaico, *a.* Judaical, Jewish.—**judaísmo,** *m.* Judaism.—**judía,** *f.* Jewess; bean, string bean.

judicatura, *f.* judicature; judgeship.—**judicial,** *a.* judicial, juridical.

judío, *n.* Jew (*f.* Jewess).—*a.* Jewish.

juego, *m.* play, sport, game; gambling; set of cards; movement, work, working (of a mechanism); set; (mech.) play, free space.—*hacer j.,* to match, to fit; to bet (in games of chance).—*j. de manos,* legerdemain.—*j. de palabras,* pun.

juerga, *f.* spree, carousal.

jueves, *m.* Thursday.

juez, *m.* judge, justice; umpire.

jugada, *f.* play, act of playing; a throw, move, stroke; ill turn.—**jugador,** *n.* player; gambler.—**jugar,** *vti.* [25-b] & *vii.* to play; to sport; to gamble; to stake; to move in a game; to take active part in an affair; to intervene; to make game of.—*j. a cara o cruz,* to bet on the toss of a coin.—*j. a la bolsa,* to dabble in stocks.—*vri.* to gamble, to risk (one's salary, one's life).—*jugarse el todo por el todo,* to stake all, to shoot the works.—**jugarreta,** *f.* (coll.) bad play; bad turn, nasty trick.

juglar, *m.* juggler; minstrel.

jugo, *m.* juice, sap; marrow, pith, substance.—**jugosidad,** *f.* succulence, juiciness.—**jugoso,** *a.* juicy, succulent, full of sap.

juguete, *m.* toy.—**juguetear,** *vi.* to play, frolic; trifle, toy.—**juguetería,** *f.* toyshop, toy trade.—**juguetón,** *a.* playful, frolicsome, rollicking, waggish.

juicio, *m.* judgment; decision; prudence, wisdom; thinking; good behavior; (law) trial.—*estar fuera de su j.,* to be crazy.—*perder el j.,* to become insane.—*tener j.,* to be wise; to be cautious; to be well-behaved.—*juicioso,* *a.* judicious, wise; well-behaved.

julio, *m.* July.

juma, *f.* (coll.) spree.

jumento, *m.* donkey; stupid person.

junco, *m.* (bot.) reed, rush; Chinese junk.

jungla, *f.* (Am.) jungle.

junio, *m.* June.

junquillo, *m.* (bot.) jonquil; reed, rattan.

junta, *f.* board, council; meeting, conference; session; joint; coupling.—**juntar,** *vt.* to join, connect, unite; to assemble, congregate; to amass, collect; to pool (resources).—*vr.* to join, meet, assemble; to be closely united; to copulate; (con) to associate (with).—**junto,** *adv.* near, close at hand, near at hand; at the same time.—*j. a,* next to, by, beside.—*j. con,* together with.—*a.* united, joined; together.—**juntura,** *f.* juncture, joining.

jurado, *m.* jury; juryman.—**juramentar,** *vt.* to swear in.—*vr.* to be sworn in, take an oath.—**juramento,** *m.* oath; act of swearing; curse, imprecation.—**jurar,** *vt.* & *vi.* to swear; to take an oath.—*j. en falso*, to commit perjury.—*jurársela(s) a uno*, to threaten one with revenge.—**jurídico,** *a.* legal, juridical.—**jurisconsulto,** *n.* jurist; lawyer.—**jurisdicción,** *f.* jurisdiction; territory.—**jurisprudencia,** *f.* jurisprudence; laws, legislation.—**jurista,** *mf.* jurist; lawyer.

justa, *f.* joust, tournament; contest.

justicia, *f.* justice, rightness.—**justiciero,** *a.* just and strict.—**justificable,** *a.* justifiable.—**justificación,** *f.* justification, defense; production of evidence.—**justificar,** *vti.* [d] to justify; to vindicate.—**justipreciar,** *vt.* to appraise.—**justo,** *a.* just; pious; correct, exact, strict; fit; tight, close.—*m.* just and pious man.—*adv.* tightly.

juvenil, *a.* juvenile, youthful.—**juventud,** *f.* youthfulness, youth; young people.

juzgado, *m.* court of justice.—**juzgar,** *vti.* [b] & *vii.* to judge; to pass or render judgment (on).

K

kaki, *m.* khaki.

kerosén, *m.*, **keroseno,** *m.*, **kerosina,** *f.* keresene.

kilo, *m.* kilo, kilogram.—**kilogramo,** *m.* kilogram.—**kilolitro,** *m.* kiloliter.—**kilométrico,** *a.* kilometric; mileage (ticket); (coll.) very long, interminably long.—**kilómetro,** *m.* kilometer.—**kilovatio,** *m.* kilowatt.

kiosco, *m.* kiosk, small pavilion; newsstand.

L

la, *art. f. sing.* the.—*pron. pers. f. sing.* her, it.—*m.* (mus.) la, A.

laberinto, *m.* labyrinth, maze.

labia, *f.* (coll.) gift of gab, palaver, fluency.—**labial,** *a.* labial; lip.—**labio,** *m.* lip.

labor, *f.* labor, task; work; (sew.) needlework; trimming.—**laborable,** *a.* workable; tillable.—*día l.,* working day.—**laborar,** *vt.* & *vi.* to work; to till.

laboratorio, *m.* laboratory.

laboriosidad, *f.* laboriousness; industry.—**laborioso,** *a.* laborious; industrious.

labrado, *a.* cultivated, tilled; wrought; figured, hewn.—*m.* cultivated land.—**labrador,** *n.* farmer, peasant, tiller.—**labranza,** *f.* cultivation, tillage; farming.—**labrar,** *vt.* to till, cultivate; to carve (stone); to work (metals).—**labriego,** *n.* farmer, peasant; rustic.

laca, *f.* lacquer; shellac.

lacayo, *m.* lackey, footman.

lacio, *a.* straight (as hair); flaccid, languid.

lacónico, *a.* laconic.

lacra, *f.* mark left by illness; fault, defect.

lacrar, *vt.* to seal with sealing wax.—**lacre,** *m.* sealing wax.

lacrimoso, *a.* tearful.

lactancia, *f.* weaning period; nursing (of a baby).—**lactar,** *vt.* to nurse; to feed with milk.—*vi.* to suckle; to feed on milk.—**lácteo,** *a.* milky.—*Via Láctea,* Milky Way.

ladear, *vt.* & *vt.* to tilt, tip, incline to one side.—*vi.* to skirt; to deviate.—*vr.* to lean; to tilt, incline to one side.—**ladeo,** *m.* inclination or motion to one side; tilt.

ladera, *f.* slope, hillside.

ladino, *a.* cunning, crafty.

lado, *m.* side, edge.—*al l.,* just by; near at hand; next door.—*a un l.,* aside.—*hacerse a un l.,* to get out of the way, to move aside.—*l. a l.,* side by side.—*por otro l.,* on the other hand.

ladrador, *n.* & *a.* barker (dog); barking.—**ladrar,** *vi.* to bark.—**ladrido,** *m.* barking, bark.

ladrillazo, *m.* blow with a brick.—**ladrillo,** *m.* brick, tile.

ladrón, *n.* thief; robber.—**ladronzuelo,** *n.* petty thief.

lagaña, *f.* bleariness.—**lagañoso,** *a.* blear-eyed.

lagartija, *f.,* **lagartijo,** *m.* small lizard.—**lagarto,** *m.* lizard; (Am.) alligator; (coll.) sly, artful person.

lago, *m.* lake.

lágrima, *f.* tear.—**lagrimal,** *m.* tearduct.—**lagrimar, lagrimear,** *vi.* to shed tears.—**lagrimeo,** *m.* shedding tears.—**lagrimoso,** *a.* tearful; (of eyes) watery.

laguna, *f.* lagoon; gap.

laico, *a.* lay, laic.

laja, *f.* flagstone; slab.

lamedura, *f.* lick, act of licking.

lamentable, *a.* lamentable, deplorable.—**lamentación,** *f.* lamentation, wail.—**lamentar,** *vt.* to lament, mourn.—*vi.* & *vr.* to lament, grieve, wail; to complain; to moan.—**lamento,** *m.* lament, moan.

lamer, *vt.* to lick; to lap.

lámina, *f.* plate, sheet; print, illustration.—**laminado,** *a.* laminated; (of metals) rolled.—**laminar,** *vt.* to roll or beat (metal) into sheets.

lámpara, *f.* lamp.—**lamparón,** *m.* large grease spot; (med.) scrofula.

lampazo, *m.* mop, swab.

lampiño, *a.* beardless.

lana, *f.* wool.—**lanar,** *a.* wool, woolen.

lance, *m.* cast, throw; incident, episode; event; quarrel; move or turn in a game.—*l. de honor,* duel.

lancear, *vt.* to wound with a lance.—**lancero,** *m.* lancer.—**lanceta,** *f.* (surg.) lancet.

lancha, *f.* boat; launch; flagstone, slab.—*l. cañonera,* gunboat.—**lanchón,** *m.* (naut.) barge, scow.

langaruto, *a.* (coll.) tall and skinny; thin.

langosta, *f.* lobster; locust.—**langostino,** *m.* crayfish.

languidecer, *vii.* [3] to languish.—**languidez,** *f.* languor, pining.—**lánguido,** *a.* languid, faint.

lanilla, *f.* nap (of cloth), down; fine flannel.—**lanudo,** *a.* woolly, fleecy; (Am.) crude; ill-bred; dull.

lanza, *f.* lance, spear.—**lanzada,** *f.* thrust or blow with a lance.

lanzadera, *f.* shuttle.

lanzador, *n.* thrower, ejecter; (baseball) pitcher.—**lanzamiento,** *m.* launching, casting, or throwing; (law) dispossessing, eviction.—**lanzaminas,** *m.* mine layer; minelaying boat.—**lanzar,** *vti.* [a] to throw, fling; to launch; to throw (a ball) up; (law) to evict, dispossess; (baseball) to pitch.—*vr.* to rush or dart; to launch forth; to engage or embark (in).—**lanzatorpedos,** *m.* torpedo boat; torpedo tube.

lanzazo, *m.* thrust or blow with a lance.

lapa, *f.* barnacle.

lapicero, *m.* mechanical pencil.

lápida, *f.* tombstone, gravestone; memorial tablet.

lápiz, *m.* pencil; crayon.—*l. de los labios,* lipstick.

lapón, *n.* Laplander.—*a.* pertaining to Lapland or Laplanders.

lapso, *m.* lapse, slip.

lardo, *m.* lard.

larga, *f.* (gen. in the *pl.*) delay, procrastination.—*a la corta o a la l.,* sooner or later.—*a. la l.,* in the end, in the long run.—*dar largas,* to delay, put off.

largar, *vti.* [b] to loosen; to let go, set free; to expel; to give (as a slap); to heave (as a sigh).—*vri.* (coll.) to get out, quit, leave.—**largo,** *a.* long; generous; shrewd, cunning.—*a lo l.,* lengthwise; at full length.—*traje l.,* evening dress.—*m.* length.—*de l.,* in length, long.—*pasar de l.,* to pass by without stopping.—*adv.* largely, profusely.—*interj.* *¡l.!* or *¡l. de ahí!* get out!—**largor,**

m. length.—**larguero,** *m.* jamb post; stringer.—**largueza,** *f.* liberality, generosity.—**larguirucho,** *a.* (coll.) long and thin.—**largura,** *f.* length.

laringe, *f.* larynx.

larva, *f.* larva.

las, *art. pl.* of LA, the.—*pron. f.* them.

lasca, *f.* slice; chip from a stone.

lascivia, *f.* lasciviousness.—**lascivo,** *a.* lascivious.

lasitud, *f.* lassitude, weariness, faintness.

lástima, *f.* pity; compassion; pitiful object.—*dar l.,* to arouse pity or regret.—*es l.,* it's a pity.—**lastimadura,** *f.* sore, hurt.—**lastimar,** *vt.* to hurt; to injure, damage.—*vr.* to hurt oneself; to get hurt.—**lastimero, lastimoso,** *a.* pitiful, sad, doleful.

lastrar, *vt.* to ballast.—**lastre,** *m.* ballast.

lata, *f.* tin plate or tinned iron plate; tin can; annoyance, nuisance.—*dar (la) l.,* (coll.) to pester.

latente, *a.* latent.

lateral, *a.* lateral, side.

latido, *m.* beat, beating, throb.

latifundio, *m.* large entailed estate.

latigazo, *m.* lash, whipping; crack of a whip.—**látigo,** *m.* whip.

latín, *m.* Latin (language).—**latino,** *a.* Latin.

latir, *vi.* to palpitate, throb, beat.

latitud, *f.* latitude; breadth.

latón, *m.* brass.—**latoso,** *a.* boring, annoying.

latrocinio, *m.* robbery, larceny.

laúd, *m.* (mus.) lute.

laudable, *a.* laudable, praiseworthy.—**laudatorio,** *a.* laudatory, full of praise.—**laudo,** *m.* (law) award; finding (of an arbitrator).

laureado, *a.* laureate.—**laurear,** *vt.* to honor, reward; to crown with laurel.—**laurel,** *m.* laurel; honor.—**lauro,** *m.* glory, honor; laurel.

lava, *f.* lava.

lavabo, *m.* lavatory; washstand; washroom.—**lavadero,** *m.* washing place; laundry.—**lavado,** *m.* wash, washing; laundry work.—**lavadora,** *f.* washing machine.—**lavamanos,** *m.* lavatory; washstand.

lavanda, *f.* lavender.

lavandera, *f.* laundress, washerwoman.—**lavandería,** *f.* laundry.—**lavandero,** *m.* launderer, laundryman.—**lavaplatos,** *mf.* dishwasher.—**lavar,** *vt.* to wash; to launder; (mason.) to whitewash.—**lavativa,** *f.* enema; syringe; nuisance.—**lavatorio,** *m.* washing; lavatory; washstand.

laxante, *m. & a.* laxative.

lazada, *f.* bowknot; (sew.) bow.—
lazar, *vti.* [a] to lasso, capture
with a lasso.

lazareto, *m.* leper hospital.

lazarillo, *m.* blind person's guide.

lazarino, *a.* leprous.—*n.* leper.

lazo, *m.* bow, loop; trap or snare (for
persons); lasso, lariat; slipknot;
tie, bond.

le, *pron.* him; you; to him; to her;
to you.

leal, *a.* loyal; (pol.) stalwart.—
lealtad, *f.* loyalty.

lebrel, *n.* greyhound.

lección, *f.* lesson; lecture; reading.—
dar una l., to say or recite a lesson;
to give a lesson.—**lector,** *n.* reader;
lecturer.—**lectura,** *f.* reading.

lechada, *f.* mixture of water and
plaster; whitewash.

leche, *f.* milk.—**lechera,** *a.* milch (app.
to animals)—*f.* milkmaid, dairy-
maid; milk jug.—**lechería,** *f.* dairy.
—**lechero,** *a.* milky.—*m.* milkman.

lecho, *m.* bed; bed of a river.

lechón, *n.* pig; suckling pig.

lechoso, *a.* milky.—*f.* (Am.) papaya.

lechuga, *f.* (bot.) lettuce.—**lechu-
guino,** *m.* (coll.) dandy, dude.

lechuza, *f.* barn owl.

leer, *vti.* [e] to read.

legación, *f.* legation.—**legado,** *m.*
(law) legacy; legate.

legajo, *m.* docket, file, bundle of
papers.

legal, *a.* legal, lawful; faithful.—
legalidad, *f.* legality, lawfulness.—
legalización, *f.* legalization.—**legali-
zar,** *vti.* [a] to legalize.

legaña, *f.* = LAGAÑA.—**legañoso,** *a.*
= LAGAÑOSO.

legar, *vti.* [b] to send as a legate;
(law) to bequeath.—**legatario,** *n.*
(law) legatee.

legendario, *a.* legendary.

legible, *a.* legible, readable.

legión, *f.* legion.—**legionario,** *n.* & *a.*
legionary.

legislación, *f.* legislation.—**legislador,**
n. & *a.* legislator; legislating, legislative.—**legislar,** *vt.* to legislate.—
legislativo, *a.* legislative.—**legisla-
tura,** *f.* legislature; term of a legislature.

legitimidad, *f.* legitimacy, legality.—
legítimo, *a.* legitimate, lawful,
rightful; genuine.

lego, *a.* lay, laic; ignorant.—*m.* layman.

legua, *f.* league (measure of length).—
a la l., de cien leguas, or *desde
media l.,* very far, at a great distance.

leguleyo, *m.* petty lawyer; shyster.

legumbre, *f.* vegetable, garden stuff.

leído, *a.* well-read, well-informed.—
l. y escribido, (coll. & contempt.)
affecting learning.

lejanía, *f.* distance, remoteness; remote place.—**lejano,** *a.* distant, far.

lejía, *f.* lye; (coll.) severe reprimand.

lejos, *adv.* far away, far off, afar.—
a lo l., in the distance.—*m.* perspective, background.

lelo, *a.* stupid, dull.

lema, *m.* theme; motto; slogan.

lencería, *f.* linen goods; linen-
draper's shop; linen room.

lengua, *f.* (anat.) tongue; language.—
írsele, a uno la l., to give oneself
away.—*morderse la l.,* to hold one's
tongue.

lenguado, *m.* (ichth.) sole, flounder.

lenguaje, *m.* language; speech; style.
—**lenguaraz,** *a.* loquacious.—**len-
güeta,** *f.* tongue (of a shoe); (mus.)
languette; (mec.) feather, wedge;
(coll.) bill, tab.—**lengüetada,** *f.* act
of licking.—**lengüilargo,** *a.* (coll.)
garrulous; scurrilous.

lenidad, *f.* leniency, mildness.

lente, *m.* lens.—*pl.* glasses, spectacles.

lenteja, *f.* lentil.—**lentejuela,** *f.*
spangle, sequin.

lentitud, *f.* slowness, tardiness.—
lento, *a.* slow.

leña, *f.* firewood, kindling wood;
(coll.) beating.—*echar l. al fuego,*
to add fuel to the fire.—**leñador,** *n.*
woodman(-woman), woodcutter.—
leñazo, *m.* cudgeling.—**leño,** *m.* log;
timber.

león, *m.* lion; brave man.—**leona,** *f.*
lioness; undaunted woman.—**leo-
nera,** *f.* cage or den of lions; (coll.)
disorderly room.—**leonino,** *a.* leo-
nine; (law) one-sided, unfair.

leontina, *f.* watch chain.

leopardo, *m.* leopard.

lépero, *n.* (Am.) one of the rabble.

lepra, *f.* leprosy.—**leproso,** *a.* leprous.
—*n.* leper.

lerdo, *a.* slow, heavy· dull, obtuse.

les, *pers. pron.* them; to them; you;
to you.

lesión, *f.* lesion, wound, injury;
damage.—**lesionar,** *vt.* to injure,
wound; to damage, impair.—**lesivo,**
a. prejudicial, injurious.

lesna, *f.* = LEZNA.

letal, *a.* mortal, deadly, lethal.

letanía, *f.* (eccl.) litany.

letargo, *m.* lethargy, drowsiness.

letra, *f.* letter; handwriting; (print.)
type; motto, inscription; literal
meaning; lyrics.—*pl.* letters, learning.—*l. de cambio,* (com.) draft, bill
of exchange.—*l. de molde,* print,
printed letter.—**letrado,** *a.* learned,

erudite.—*n.* lawyer.—**letrero,** *m.* sign, notice; label; legend.

letrina, *f.* privy, latrine.

leucemia, *f.* leukemia.

leva, *f.* (naut.) act of weighing anchor; (mil.) levy, press; (mech.) cam.—**levadura,** *f.* leaven, yeast.—**levantamiento,** *m.* elevation, raising; insurrection, uprising.—**levantar,** *vt.* to raise; to lift, pick up; to erect, build; to rouse; to impute; to stand up.—*vr.* to rise, get up (from bed, chair, etc.); to rise up.—**levante,** *m.* Levant, east coast of Spain.—**levantino,** *a.* & *n.* Levantine.—**levantisco,** *a.* turbulent, restless.—**levar,** *vt.* (naut.) to weigh (anchor).—*vr.* to set sail.

leve, *a.* light, of little weight; trifling; slight.

levita, *f.* frock coat; Levite.

léxico, *m.* lexicon.—**lexicografía,** *f.* lexicography.

ley, *f.* law; rule of action; loyalty.—*de buena l.,* sterling.—*de mala l.,* vicious; crooked; low, base.—*l. del embudo,* oppressive law.—**leyenda,** *f.* reading; legend, inscription; motto.

lezna, *f.* awl.

liar, *vt.* to tie, bind, do up; (coll.) to embroil, draw into an entanglement.—*vr.* to bind oneself; to get tangled up.

libar, *vt.* to suck; to taste.

libelo, *m.* libel.

libélula, *f.* dragon fly.

liberación, *f.* liberation; (law) quittance.—**liberal,** *a.* & *mf.* liberal.—**liberalidad,** *f.* liberality, generosity.—**liberalismo,** *m.* Liberalism.—**libertad,** *f.* liberty, freedom; familiarity; unconventionality; ransom.—**libertador,** *n.* & *a.* liberator, rescuer; liberating.—**libertar,** *vt.* to free, liberate; to exempt; to acquit; to rid, clear.—**libertinaje,** *m.* licentiousness.—**libertino,** *n.* & *a.* libertine, (fam.) wolf; dissolute.

líbico, *a.* & *n.* Libyan.

libidinoso, *a.* lustful.

libio, *a.* & *n.* Libyan.

libra, *f.* pound (weight, coin).

librador, *n.* deliverer; (com.) drawer of a check or draft.—**libramiento,** *m.* delivery, delivering; warrant, order of payment.—**libranza,** *f.* (com.) draft, bill of exchange.—**librar,** *vt.* to free, deliver; to exempt; to pass (sentence); to issue (a decree); (com.) to draw.—*l. batalla* or *combate,* to engage in battle.—*vr.* **(de)** to escape, avoid, be free (from), get rid (of).—**libre,** *a.* free; unencumbered; inde-

pendent; vacant; disengaged; clear, open; exempt; single, unmarried.

librea, *f.* livery, uniform.

librería, *f.* bookstore.—**librero,** *n.* bookseller.—*m.* bookcase.—**libreta,** *f.* notebook, copybook.—**libretista,** *mf.* librettist.—**libreto,** *m.* libretto.—**libro,** *m.* book.

licencia, *f.* permission, license; licentiousness, wantonness; (mil.) furlough; degree of licentiate—**licenciado,** *n.* licentiate; (Am.) lawyer.—**licenciamiento,** *m.* graduation as a licentiate; (mil.) discharge.—**licenciar,** *vt.* to license; to confer a degree on; (mil.) to discharge.—*vr.* to get a master's degree.—**licenciatura,** *f.* degree of licentiate; graduation as a licentiate.—**licencioso,** *a.* licentious, dissolute.

licitar, *vt.* & *vi.* to bid (on, for) at auction or on public works.—**lícito,** *a.* licit, lawful; just.

licor, *m.* liquor; liqueur.

lid, *f.* contest, fight.

líder, *mf.* leader.

lidia, *f.* battle, fight; bullfight.—**lidiar,** *vi.* to fight; to struggle.—*vt.* to run or fight (bulls).

liebre, *f.* hare; coward.

liendre, *f.* nit, egg of a louse.

lienzo, *m.* linen cloth; (art) canvas.

liga, *f.* garter; birdlime; league, alliance; alloy; rubber band.—**ligadura,** *f.* ligature; subjection.—**ligamento,** *m.* bond, tie; ligament.—**ligar,** *vti.* [b] to tie, bind, fasten; to alloy; to join.—*vii.* to combine cards of the same suit.—*vri.* to league, join together; to bind oneself.

ligereza, *f.* lightness; swiftness; inconstancy, fickleness.—**ligero,** *a.* light; fast, nimble; (of cloth) thin; gay; unsteady, giddy; unimportant, trifling; easily disturbed (as sleep).—*a la ligera,* superficially.—*adv.* fast, rapidly.

lija, *f.* sandpaper.—**lijar,** *vt.* to sandpaper.

lila, *f.* lilac tree; lilac flower; lilac color.

liliputiense, *mf.* & *a.* midget; Lilliputian.

lima, *f.* sweet lime; (mech.) file; finish, polishing.—**limar,** *vt.* to file; to polish; to touch up.

limaza, *f.* slug.

limitación, *f.* limitation, limit.—**limitar,** *vt.* to limit; to bound; to restrict; to reduce (expense).—*vr.* to confine oneself to.—**límite,** *m.* limit; boundary.—**limítrofe,** *a.* bounding.

limo, *m.* slime, mud.

limosna, *f.* alms.—**limosnero,** *a.* charitable.—*n.* (Am.) beggar.

limón, *m.* lemon.—**limonada,** *f.* lemonade.—**limonero,** *m.* lemon tree.

limpia, *f.* cleaning; dredging.—**limpiabotas,** *mf.* bootblack.—**limpiador,** *n. & a.* cleaner, scourer; cleaning.—**limpiar,** *vt.* to clean, cleanse; (coll.) to steal; (coll.) to clean out.—**límpido,** *a.* limpid, crystal-clear.—**limpieza,** *f.* cleanness, cleanliness; neatness, tidiness; purity; honesty.—**limpio,** *a.* clean; clear; neat; (coll.) broke.—*poner en l.,* to make a clear copy.—*sacar en l.,* to conclude, infer; to make out, understand.

linaje, *m.* lineage, descent, ancestry.

linaza, *f.* linseed.

lince, *m.* lynx; very keen person.—*a.* keen-sighted, observing.

linchamiento, *m.* lynching.—**linchar,** *vt.* to lynch.

lindar, *vi.* to be contiguous, to border.—**linde,** *m.* landmark; boundary.—**lindero,** *m.* limit, boundary.

lindeza, *f.* neatness, elegance, prettiness.—*pl.* pretty things; (ironic) improprieties, insults.—**lindo,** *a.* pretty.—*de lo l.,* very much; wonderfully; greatly.—**lindura,** *f.* beauty; beautiful thing.

línea, *f.* line; (of persons) lines, figure; boundary, limit; progeny; (mil.) file.—**lineal,** *a.* lineal, linear.—**lineamiento,** *m.* lineament, feature.

lingote, *m.* (foundry) ingot; slug.

lingüista, *mf.* linguist.—**lingüística,** *f.* linguistics.—**lingüístico,** *a.* linguistic.

lino, *m.* flax; linen.

linóleo, *m.* linoleum.

linotipia, *f.* linotype.—**linotipista,** *mf.* linotypist.—**linotipo,** *m.* linotype.

linterna, *f.* lantern; flashlight.

lío, *m.* bundle; (coll.) mess, confusion, scrape.—*armar un l.,* to tangle, mess up, make difficulties.

liquidación, *f.* liquidation, settlement; bargain sale.—**liquidar,** *vt.* to liquefy; (com.) to liquidate, sell out; to settle, pay up; to squander; (coll.) to wipe out; to murder.—*vr.* to liquefy.—**líquido,** *a.* liquid; (econ.) liquid; (com.) net.—*m.* liquid; (com.) balance, net profit.

lira, *f.* (mus.) lyre; lira.—**lírico,** *a.* lyric(al).—*f.* lyric poetry.

lirio, *m.* lily.

lirón, *m.* dormouse; (coll.) sleepy head.

lirondo, *a.* pure, clean, neat.

lis, *f.* (heraldry) lily; iris.

lisiar, *vt.* to cripple.—*vr.* to become crippled.

liso, *a.* smooth, even, flat; plain, unadorned; straight (hair); plaindealing.—*l. y llano,* clear, evident.

lisonja, *f.* flattery.—**lisonjear,** *vt.* to flatter.—**lisonjero,** *n.* flatterer.—*a.* flattering; complimentary.

lista, *f.* list; strip; stripe.—*l. de correos,* Post Office general delivery.—*pasar l.,* to call the roll.—**listado,** *a.* striped, streaky.

listo, *a.* ready; quick, prompt; clever, resourceful.—*estar l.,* to be ready.

listón, *m.* ribbon; tape; (carp.) strip.

lisura, *f.* smoothness, evenness; sincerity, candor.

litera, *f.* litter, stretcher; berth.

literal, *a.* literal.—**literario,** *a.* literary.—**literato,** *n.* writer.—**literatura,** *f.* literature.

litigar, *vti.* [b] *& vii.* to litigate.—**litigio,** *m.* litigation, lawsuit.

litografía, *f.* lithography.

litoral, *a.* coastal.—*m.* coast, shore.

litro, *m.* liter. (See Table.)

liviandad, *f.* lightness; levity, frivolity; lewdness.—**liviano,** *a.* light (not heavy); inconstant, fickle; frivolous; slight; lewd.

lividez, *f.* lividness.—**lívido,** *a.* livid.

lo, *art. neut. the.—pron.* him; you; it; so; that.—*lo de,* that of; that matter of, what.—*lo de siempre,* the same old story.—*lo que,* what, that which.—*sé lo hermosa que es,* I know how beautiful she is.

loable, *a.* laudable, praiseworthy.—**loar,** *vt.* to praise.

lobanillo, *m.* wen, tumor.

lobato, lobezno, *m.* wolf cub.—**lobo,** *n.* wolf.

lóbrego, *a.* murky, obscure; sad, somber.—**lobreguez,** *f.* obscurity, darkness.

local, *a.* local.—*m.* place, site, premises.—**localidad,** *f.* locality, location; (theat., etc.) seat.—**localización,** *f.* localization.—**localizar,** *vti.* [a] to localize; to find out where.

loción, *f.* lotion.

loco, *a.* insane, crazy; excessive.—*n.* insane person, lunatic.

locomoción, *f.* locomotion.—**locomotora,** *f.,. locomotriz,** *a.* locomotive.

locuacidad, *f.* loquacity, talkativeness, volubility.—**locuaz,** *a.* loquacious, talkative.—**locución,** *f.* diction; phrase, locution.

locura, *f.* madness, insanity; folly.

locutor, *n.* radio announcer or speaker.

lodazal, *m.* bog, mire.—**lodo,** *m.* mud, mire.—**lodoso,** *a.* muddy, miry.

lógica, *f.* logic.—**lógico,** *a.* logical.

lograr, *vt.* to get, obtain; to attain.—*vr.* to succeed, be successful.—

logro, *m.* gain, profit, benefit; success, accomplishment; attainment; usury.

loma, *f.* little hill.

lombarda, *f.* red cabbage.

lombriz, *f.* earthworm.—*l. solitaria,* tapeworm.

lomo, *m.* loin; back of an animal; chine of pork; back of a book or cutting tool.

lona, *f.* canvas.

longaniza, *f.* pork sausage.

longevidad, *f.* longevity.

longitud, *f.* length; longitude.—**longitudinal,** *a.* longitudinal.

loncha, *f.* thin slice.

lonja, *f.* (com.) exchange; grocer's shop; warehouse; slice (of meat); strip; leather strap.

lontananza, *f.*—*en l.,* far away, in the distance.

loquero, *n.* attendant in an insane asylum; (Am.) insane asylum.

loro, *m.* parrot.

los, *art. m. pl.* the.—*pron. m. pl.* them.—*l. que,* those who, those which.—*l.* which.

losa, *f.* slab, flagstone; gravestone; grave.—**loseta,** *f.* tile.

lote, *m.* lot; share, part.

lotería, *f.* lottery; raffle; lotto.

loza, *f.* chinaware; porcelain; crockery.

lozanía, *f.* luxuriance; freshness; vigor, lustiness.—**lozano,** *a.* luxuriant; fresh; brisk, spirited.

lubricación, *f.* lubrication.—**lubricante,** *m. & a.* lubricator; lubricating.—**lubricar,** *vti.* [d] to lubricate.

lucero, *m.* bright star; light hole; star on the forehead of horses; brightness, splendor.

lucidez, *f.* brilliancy; brightness; success.—**lucido,** *a.* magnificent, splendid, brilliant; most successful.—**lúcido,** clear, lucid; brilliant, shining.—**luciente,** *a.* shining, luminous, bright.—**luciérnaga,** *f.* glowworm, firefly.—**lucimiento,** *m.* brilliance; success.—**lucir,** *vii.* [3] to shine, glitter, glow; to outshine, exceed; to look, appear.—*vti.* to light, illuminate; to show off, display, exhibit.—*vri.* to shine, be brilliant; to dress to advantage; to be very successful; to do splendidly.

lucrar, *vt. & vr.* to profit.—**lucrativo,** *a.* lucrative, profitable.—**lucro,** *m.* gain, profit.

luctuoso, *a.* sad, mournful.

lucha, *f.* struggle, strife; wrestling, wrestle; dispute, argument.—**luchador,** *n.* wrestler; fighter.—**luchar,** *vi.* to fight, struggle; to wrestle.

luego, *adv.* presently, immediately;

afterwards; next; later.—*desde l.,* of course, naturally.—*hasta l.,* so long, see you later.—*l. que,* after, as soon as.—*conj.* therefore.

lugar, *m.* place, spot, site; town, village; room, space; seat; employment; time, opportunity; cause, reason.—*dar l. a,* to cause, give occasion for.—*en l. de,* instead of.—*hacer l.,* to make room.—*tener l.,* to take place, happen.—**lugarteniente,** *mf.* second in command, deputy, substitute.

lúgubre, *a.* sad, gloomy, dismal.

lujo, *m.* luxury.—**lujoso,** *a.* showy, luxurious; lavish.

lujuria, *f.* lewdness, lechery, lust; excess.—**lujuriante,** *a.* lusting; luxuriant, exuberant.—**lujurioso,** *a.* lustful, lecherous, lewd.

lumbre, *f.* fire (in stove, fireplace, etc.); light (from a match, etc.); splendor.—**lumbrera,** *f.* luminary.

luna, *f.* moon; mirror plate; plate glass.—**lunar,** *a.* lunar.—*m.* mole; beauty spot.—**lunático,** *a. & n.* lunatic.

lunes, *m.* Monday.

luneta, *f.* lens; orchestra chair in a theater.

lupa, *f.* magnifying glass.

lupanar, *m.* brothel.

lúpulo, *m.* hops.

lustrar, *vt.* to polish.—**lustre,** *m.* polish, glaze, sheen; splendor, glory.—**lustroso,** *a.* lustrous, glossy, shining.

luterano, *n. & a.* Lutheran, Protestant.

luto, *m.* mourning; grief.—*pl.* mourning draperies.—*de l.,* in mourning.

luz, *f.* light.—*pl.* culture, enlightenment.—*a todas luces,* evidently.—*dar a l.,* to give birth to; to publish.—*entre dos luces,* by twilight.

LL

llaga, *f* ulcer, sore. **-llagar,** *vti.* [b] & *vri.* to ulcerate.

llama, *f.* flame, blaze; (zool.) llama.

llamada, *f.* call; beckoning; (print.) reference mark to a note.—**llamamiento,** *m.* calling, call; appeal; convocation.—**llamar,** *vt.* to call, summon; to beckon; to invoke; to name.—*ll. la atención,* to attract attention; to call to task.—*ll. por teléfono,* to telephone.—*vi.* to ring; to knock (at the door).—*ll. a capítulo,* to call to account.—*vr.* to be called or named.—*¿cómo se llama Ud.?* what is your name?

llamarada, *f.* sudden blaze; flash; sudden flush.

llamativo, *a.* showy, gaudy, flashy; causing thirst.

llameante, *a.* blazing, flaming.—**llamear,** *vi.* to blaze; to flame.

llanero, *n.* plainsman (-woman).—**llaneza,** *f.* plainness, simplicity; familiarity.—**llano,** *a.* even, level, smooth; plain, unadorned; open, frank.—*de ll.,* openly; clearly.—*m.* plain.

llanta, *f.* rim (of vehicle wheel); (auto) tire.

llanto, *m.* crying, weeping; tears.

llanura, *f.* plain, prairie; flatness.

llave, *f.* key; faucet, spout; (print.) brace; clock winder; key, explanation of anything difficult; switch; (mus.) clef, key.—*bajo ll.,* under lock and key.—*echar ll.,* to lock.—*ll. inglesa,* monkey wrench.—*ll. maestra,* master key, passkey.—**llavero,** *m.* key ring.—**llavín,** *m.* latch key; key.

llegada, *f.* arrival, coming.—**llegar,** *vii.* [b] to arrive; to come; to reach; go as far as; to amount.—*ll. a las manos,* to come to blows.—*ll. a saber,* to find out, get to know.—*ll. a ser,* to become, get to be.—*no ll. a,* not to amount to; not to come up, or be equal, to.—*vri.* (a) to approach; to go up to.

llenar, *vt.* to fill, stuff, pack; to pervade; to satisfy, content.—*vr.* to fill, fill up; (de) to become full (of), or covered (with); (coll.) to lose patience; to get crowded, packed; (of the moon) to be full.—**lleno,** *a.* full, filled, replete; complete; teeming.—*de ll.,* fully, totally.—*m.* fill, fullness; (theat.) full house.

llevadero, *a.* tolerable, bearable.—**llevar,** *vt.* to carry; to bear; to take; to bring; to take off, carry away; to lead (a life); to wear (clothing, etc.); to spend (time); to keep (books).—*ll. a cabo,* to accomplish, carry out.—*ll. a cuestas,* to carry on one's back; to support.—*ll. el compás,* to beat or keep time.—*ll. la contra,* to oppose, antagonize.—*ll. la delantera,* to be ahead.—*lleva un año aquí,* he has been here one year.—*me lleva cinco años,* he is five years older than I.—*vr.* to take or carry away; to get along.—*ll. bien* (or *mal*), to be on good (or bad) terms.—*ll. chasco,* to be disappointed.

llorar, *vi.* to cry, weep.—*vt.* to weep over, bewail, mourn.—**lloriquear,** *vi.* to whimper, whine, snivel, sniffle.—**lloriqueo,** *m.* whining; whimper.—**lloro,** *m.* weeping, crying.—**llorón,**

a. given to weeping.—*n.* weeper, crybaby.—**lloroso,** *a.* mournful, sorrowful, tearful.

llover, *vii.* [26] to rain; to shower.—**llovizna,** *f.* drizzle, sprinkling.—**lloviznar,** *vi.* to drizzle, sprinkle.—**lluvia,** *f.* rain.—**lluvioso,** *a.* rainy.

M

macabro, *a.* macabre; ugly, hideous.

macaco, *m.* monkey.

macana, *f.* (Am.) club, cudgel; (Am.) blunder; fib, joke.

macarela, *f.* (Am.) mackerel.

macarrones, *m. pl.* macaroni.

maceración, *f.,* **maceramiento,** *m.* maceration, steeping.—**macerar,** *vt.* to macerate, steep.

macero, *m.* mace bearer; sergeant-at-arms.

maceta, *f.* flowerpot; mallet; stonecutter's hammer; (Am.) slow person.—**macetero,** *m.* flowerpot stand.

macilento, *a.* pale; emaciated; haggard.

macizo, *a.* solid; massive; firm.—*m.* massiveness; massif; flower bed.

machacar, *vti.* [d] to pound; to crush.—*vii.* to importune; to harp on a subject.—**machacón,** *a.* monotonous; tenacious.

machetazo, *m.* blow with a machete.—**machete,** *m.* machete.—**machetero,** *n.* (Am.) sugar cane cutter.

machihembrar, *vt.* (carp.) to dovetail.

macho, *a.* male; masculine, robust.—*m.* male; he-man; he-mule; hook (of hook and eye); bolt (of a lock); sledge hammer; ignorant fellow; (arch.) buttress; spigot.—*m. cabrío,* he-goat, buck.

machucar, *vti.* [d] to pound; to bruise; to crush.

machuno, *a.* mannish, masculine.

madeja, *f.* hank, skein; lock of hair.

madera, *f.* wood; timber, lumber.—**maderaje, maderamen,** *m.* timber; timber work; woodwork.—**madero,** *m.* beam; timber, piece of lumber; log; blockhead.

madrastra, *f.* stepmother.—**madre,** *f.* mother; origin, source; womb; bed (of a river); dregs.—*m. política,* mother-in-law.—*salirse de m.,* to overflow.—**madreperla,** *f.* mother-of-pearl.—**madreselva,** *f.* (bot.) honeysuckle.

madriguera, *f.* burrow; den, lair, nest.

madrileño, *a. & n.* Madrilenian, native of Madrid.

madrina, *f.* godmother; bridesmaid; protectress, patroness.

madrugada, *f.* dawn; early morning; early rising.—*de m.*, at daybreak. —**madrugador**, *a.* early rising.—*n.* early riser.—**madrugar**, *vii.* [b] to rise early; to anticipate, to be beforehand.—**madrugón**, *m.* (coll.) very early rising.

madurar, *vt. & vi.* to ripen; to mature.—**madurez**, *f.* maturity; ripeness; wisdom.—**maduro**, *a.* ripe; mature; wise, judicious; middle-aged.

maestra, *f.* teacher, schoolmistress; (mason.) guide line.—**maestría**, *f.* mastery; great skill.—**maestro**, *a.* masterly; master.—*obra m.*, masterpiece.—*m.* master, teacher; expert; skilled artisan.—*m. de obras*, builder.

magia, *f.* magic, wizardry.—**mágico**, *a.* magic(al).

magín, *m.* (coll.) imagination.

magisterio, *m.* mastery; mastership; teaching profession.—**magistrado**, *m.* judge, magistrate.—**magistral**, *a.* magisterial, masterly, masterful.— **magistratura**, *f.* judges (as a body).

magnánimo, *a.* magnanimous, generous.

magnate, *m.* magnate; (coll.) tycoon.

magnético, *a.* magnetic.—**magnetismo**, *m.* magnetism.—**magnetizar**, *vti.* [a] to magnetize; to hypnotize.

magnificencia, *f.* magnificence, grandeur, splendor.—**magnífico**, *a.* magnificent; excellent.

magnitud, *f.* magnitude; quantity.— **magno**, *a.* great.

mago, *n.* magician, wizard.—*pl.* magi. —*los Reyes Magos*, The Three Wise Men.

magra, *f.* slice of ham.—**magro**, *a.* meager, lean.

magulladura, *f.* bruise.—**magullar**, *vt.* to bruise; to mangle.

mahometano, *n. & a.* Mohammedan, Mahometan.

maíz, *m.* corn, maize.—**maizal**, *m.* cornfield.

majada, *f.* sheepfold; dung.

majadería, *f.* foolish act, foolishness. —**majadero**, *a.* silly, foolish.—*n.* bore, fool; pestle.—**majar**, *vt.* to pound, bruise, mash; (coll.) to importune, vex, annoy.

majestad, *f.* majesty; stateliness.— **majestuosidad**, *f.* majesty, dignity. —**majestuoso**, *a.* majestic, grand.

majo, *a.* gay, gaudy, handsome, pretty.—*n.* low class dandy or belle.

mal, *a. contr.* of MALO.—*m.* evil; harm; disease, illness.—*adv.* badly; wrongly; deficiently.

malabarista, *mf.* juggler.

malagradecido, *a.* ungrateful.

malandanza, *f.* misfortune, misery.

malanga, *f.* (Am.) (bot.) arum.

malaria, *f.* malaria.

malayo, *n. & a.* Malayan.

malbaratador, *n.* spendthrift, squanderer.—**malbaratar**, *vt.* to squander; to undersell.

malcriado, *a.* ill-bred, rude; spoiled. —**malcriar**, *vt.* to spoil (a child).

maldad, *f.* wickedness, iniquity; badness.

maldecir, *vti.* [14-49] to damn, curse, accurse.—**maldición**, *f.* curse, malediction; damnation.—**maldito**, *ppi.* of MALDECIR.—*a.* damned, accursed; perverse, wicked.—*¡m. lo que me importa!* little do I care!

maleable, *a.* malleable.

maleante, *mf. & a.* rogue; roguish.— **malear**, *vt.* to pervert, corrupt.

malecón, *m.* dike, mole; quay, jetty.

maledicencia, *f.* slander, calumny.

maleficio, *m.* spell; witchcraft, charm. —**maléfico**, *a.* evil-doing; harmful.

malentendido, *m.* misunderstanding.

malestar, *m.* indisposition, slight illness; discomfort.

maleta, *f.* valise, suitcase; (fam.) bungler; (Am.) hump.—*hacer la m.*, to pack.—**maletero**, *m.* porter, (coll.) red cap.—**maletín**, *m.* small valise or case, overnight bag, satchel.

malévolo, *a.* malevolent, malignant, wicked.

maleza, *f.* weeds; underbrush, shrubbery; thicket.

malgastar, *vt.* to waste, squander.

malhablado, *a.* foul-mouthed.

malhadado, *a.* wretched, unfortunate.

malhechor, *n.* evildoer, criminal.

malherir, *vti.* [39] to wound badly.

malhumorado, *a.* ill-humored, peevish.

malicia, *f.* malice, malignity; suspicion; shrewdness.—**maliciar**, *vt.* to suspect.—**malicioso**, *a.* malicious; wicked, knavish; suspicious.

malignidad, *f.* malignity; viciousness. —**maligno**, *a.* malignant; vicious; harmful; baleful.

malintencionado, *a.* ill-intentioned.

malo, *a.* bad, evil, wicked; ill, sick; difficult, hard.—*estar de malas*, to be unlucky; to be ill-disposed.—*por buenas o por malas*, willy-nilly.

malograr, *vt.* to waste, lose.—*vr.* to fail, miscarry.

malparir, *vi.* to miscarry.

malquerencia, *f.* ill-will, hatred.

malquistar, *vt.* to estrange; to create prejudice against.—*m. a uno con*, to set one against.—*vi.* to incur dislike, make oneself unpopular.

malsano, *a.* unhealthy, sickly; noxious.

malta, *f.* malt.

maltratar, *vt.* to ill-treat, abuse; to use roughly, maul.—**maltrato,** *m.* ill-treatment; rough usage.—**maltrecho,** *a.* ill-treated; in bad condition, damaged; badly off, battered.

malvado, *a.* wicked, fiendish.—*n.* wicked man (woman).

malversación, *f.* misuse of funds, embezzlement.—**malversador,** *n.* one who misapplies funds, embezzler.—**malversar,** *vt.* to misapply (funds); to embezzle.

malla, *f.* mesh (of a net); (naut.) network.—*pl.* tights.

mamá, *f.* mamma (mother).—**mama,** *f.* breast.

mamada, *f.* (coll.) act of sucking, suckling.—**mamadera,** *f.* (Am.) nursing bottle.—**mamar,** *vt.* & *vi.* to suck, suckle.—*vr.* (Am.) to get drunk.

mamarracho, *m.* daub; grotesque figure or ornament.

mameluco, *m.* (Am.) child's nightdress; (Am.) overalls; (coll.) dolt.

mamífero, *n.* mammal.—*a.* mammalian.

mamón, *a.* & *n.* suckling.

mamotreto, *m.* bulky book or bundle of papers.

mampara, *f.* screen.

mampostería, *f.* masonry, rubble work.

mamut, *m.* mammoth.

manada, *f.* herd; flock; drove.

manantial, *m.* spring, source; origin.—**manar,** *vi.* to issue, flow out; to ooze; to abound.

manatí, *m.* manatee.

manceba, *f.* mistress.

mancilla, *f.* stain, blemish, smirch.—**mancillar,** *vt.* to stain, smirch, sully.

manco, *n.* armless; handless; one-handed or one-armed person.—*a.* handless; armless; one-handed; one-armed; maimed; faulty.

mancha, *f.* stain, spot, blot; patch of ground or vegetation.—**manchado,** *a.* spotted, speckled.—**manchar,** *vt.* to stain, soil; to tarnish.

mandadero, *n.* messenger, porter; errand boy or girl.—**mandado,** *m.* mandate, order; errand.—**mandamiento,** *m.* order, command; commandment; (law) writ.—**mandar,** *vt.* & *vi.* to command, order; to send.

mandarina, *f.* tangerine.

mandarria, *f.* iron maul, sledge hammer.

mandatario, *n.* proxy; representative;

(law) attorney.—**mandato,** *m.* mandate; command, injunction, order, behest.

mandíbula, *f.* jaw; jawbone.

mando, *m.* command, power; control.—**mandón,** *a.* imperious, domineering.—*n.* imperious, haughty person; (Am.) (min.) boss or foreman.

mandril, *m.* baboon; (mech.) collet.

manducar, *vti.* [d] (coll.) to chew; to eat.

manear, *vt.* to hobble (a horse).

manecilla, *f.* small hand; (print.) fist ( ); hand of a clock or watch.

manejable, *a.* manageable, tractable.—**manejar,** *vt.* to manage, handle; (Am.) to drive (a vehicle, a horse, etc.); to run (an engine, a business).—*vr.* to behave; to get along, manage.—**manejo,** *m.* handling; management, conduct.

manera, *f.* manner, way, mode; fly of trousers; side placket of skirt.—*pl.* ways, customs; manners.—*de mala m.,* blunderingly; roughly; reluctantly.—*de m. que,* so that, so as to.—*de ninguna m.,* in no way; by no means, not at all.—*de otra m.,* otherwise.—*de tal m.,* in such a way; so much.—*de todas maneras,* at any rate.—*sobre m.,* exceedingly.

manga, *f.* sleeve; (water) hose; straining bag; fish trap.—*m. de viento,* whirlwind.—*tener m. ancha,* to be broadminded.

mangana, *f.* lasso, lariat.

manganeso, *m.* manganese.

manglar, *m.* grove of mangrove trees.—**mangle,** *m.* mangrove.

mango, *m.* handle, haft; tiller; (bot.) mango.

mangonear, *vi.* (coll.) to meddle for power, to interfere in order to dominate.—**mangoneo,** *m.* (coll.) domination.

manguera, *f.* (watering) hose; waterspout.

manguito, *m.* muff; wristlet, half-sleeve; oversleeve; (mech.) muff.

maní, *m.* (Am.) peanut.

manía, *f.* mania; whim, fancy.

maniatar, *vt.* to handcuff; to manacle.

maniático, *a.* & *n.* crank; queer, mad (person).—**manicomio,** *m.* insane asylum, madhouse.

manicura, *f.* manicurist; manicure.

manido, *a.* commonplace, trite.

manifestación, *m.* manifestation, statement; (public) demonstration.—**manifestante,** *mf.* (public) demonstrator.—**manifestar,** *vti.* [1-49] to state, declare; to manifest, reveal; to tell, let know.—*vri.* to make a demonstration.—**manifiesto,** *ppi.* of MANIFESTAR.—*a.* manifest, plain. —*m.* manifesto, public declaration; (com.) custom-house manifest.—*poner de m.,* to make evident; to show plainly; to make public.

manigua, *f.* (Am.) thicket, jungle.

manija, *f.* handle, haft; crank; (mech.) brace, clamp.

manilla, *f.* small hand; bracelet; manacle; handcuff.

maniobra, *f.* maneuver; operation, procedure.—**maniobrar,** *vt. & vi.* to maneuver.

manipulación, *f.* manipulation.—**manipular,** *vt.* to manipulate, handle.

maniquí, *m.* manikin; tailor's dummy; puppet.—*f.* model.

manirroto, *n.* squanderer.—*a.* lavish, prodigal, wasteful.

manivela, *f.* (mech.) crank; crank-shaft.

manjar, *m.* food, dish; delicacy, morsel.

mano, *f.* hand; forefoot; hand of a clock or watch; first hand at cards; round of any game; power or means of making or attaining something; coat (of paint, varnish, etc.),—*a la m.,* near, at hand.—*a m.,* by hand; at hand, near by. —*a manos llenas,* liberally, abundantly.—*de la m.,* by the hand; hand in hand.—*de manos a boca,* suddenly, unexpectedly.—*entre manos,* in hand.—*m. a m.,* in friendly cooperation, together; on equal terms.—*¡manos a la obra!* lend a hand! to work!—*m. sobre m.,* idle, doing nothing.—**manojo,** *m.* bunch; handful; bundle.—**manopla,** *f.* gauntlet.—**manosear,** *vt.* to fumble; to touch, feel of.—**manoseo,** *m.* handling, fingering.—**manotazo,** *m.* slap, blow with the hand.—**manotear,** *vi.* to gesticulate.—**manoteo,** *m.* gesturing with the hands.

mansalva, *adv.*—*a m.,* without risk or danger; in a cowardly manner.

mansedumbre, *f.* meekness; tameness.

mansión, *f.* stay, sojourn; mansion, abode; residence.

manso, *a.* tame; gentle, mild; calm; soft, quiet; meek.—*m.* bellwether.

manta, *f.* blanket; (Am.) poncho.—*m. de algodón,* wadding.

manteca, *f.* lard; fat.—**mantecado,** *m.* butter cake; (Am.) ice cream.—**mantecoso,** *a.* greasy, buttery.

mantel, *m.* tablecloth; altar cloth.—**mantelería,** *f.* table linen.—**manteleta,** *f.* lady's shawl.

mantener, *vti.* [42] to support; to maintain; to defend or sustain (an opinion); to keep up (conversation,

correspondence).—*vri.* to support oneself; to remain, continue (in one place).—**mantenimiento,** *m.* maintenance, support; living.

mantequilla, *f.* butter.—**mantequillera,** *f.* butter dish.

mantilla, *f.* mantilla; saddlecloth.—**manto,** *m.* cloak, mantle; robe; (min.) layer, stratum.—**mantón,** *m.* large shawl; (Am.) mantilla.—*m. de Manila,* embroidered silk shawl, Spanish shawl.

manuable, *a.* easy to handle, handy. —**manual,** *a.* manual; handy.—*m.* manual, handbook.

manubrio. *m.* handle; crank.

manufactura, *f.* manufacture.—**manufacturar,** *vt. & vi.* to manufacture. —**manufacturero,** *a.* manufacturing. —*n.* manufacturer.

manuscrito, *m. & a.* manuscript.

manutención, *f.* maintaining; maintenance, support.

manzana, *f.* apple; block (of houses), square.—**manzanilla,** *f.* (bot.) common camomile; dry white sherry wine.—**manzano,** *m.* apple tree.

maña, *f.* skill, cleverness, knack; cunning; evil habit or custom.—*darse m.,* to contrive, manage.

mañana, *f.* morning.—*m.* [the] future. —*de m.,* in the morning; very early. —*por la m.,* in the morning.—*adv.* tomorrow; in the future.—*hasta m.,* until tomorrow, see you tomorrow. —*m. mismo,* tomorrow without fail. —*m. por la m.,* tomorrow morning. —*pasado m.,* day after tomorrow.—**mañanero,** *a.* early rising.

mañoso, *a.* skillful, handy, clever; cunning, shifty, careful; (Am.) lazy.

mapa, *m.* map, chart.

mapache, *m.* raccoon.

mapamundi, *m.* map of the world.

maquillaje, *m.* (neol.) make-up (face).—**maquillar,** *vt. & vr.* (neol.) to make-up, paint.

máquina, *f.* machine, engine.—*a toda m.,* at full speed.—*m. de escribir,* typewriter.—**maquinación,** *f.* machination, plotting; plot.—**maquinal,** *a.* mechanical; unconscious, automatic. —**maquinar,** *vt. & vi.* to machinate, scheme, plot.—**maquinaria,** *f.* machinery.—**maquinista,** *mf.* engineer; machinist.

mar, *m. & f.* sea.—*alta m.,* high seas. —*hacerse a la m.,* to put out to sea.—*la m.,* (coll.) a great deal, a lot, lots.—*m. de fondo,* (sea) swell.

maraña, *f.* tangle, snare; puzzle; intrigue, plot; undergrowth.

maravilla, *f.* wonder, marvel; (bot.) marigold.—*a las mil maravillas,* wonderfully well.—**maravillar,** *vt.*

to surprise, astonish.—*vr.* **(de)** to wonder (at), marvel.—**maravilloso**, *a.* wonderful, marvelous.

marbete, *m.* label, tag; index card; baggage check.

marca, *f.* mark, stamp; sign; make, brand.—*de m.*, excellent, reputed.—*m. de fábrica*, trademark.—**marcador**, *m.* marker; (sports) score board; scorer.—**marcar**, *vti.* [d] to mark, stamp, impress, brand; (sports) to score; to dial (telephone); to note.—*m. el compás*, to beat time, keep time.

marcial, *a.* martial, warlike, soldierly.

marco, *m.* frame; mark (German coin).

marcha, *f.* march; progress; turn, course, run; departure; (naut.) speed; movement of a watch.—*apresurar la m.*, to hurry, speed up.—*¡en marcha!* forward march! go on! let's go!—*poner en m.*, to start, put in motion.—*sobre la m.*, at once, right away.

marchamo, *m.* custom-house mark on goods.

marchante, *mf.* dealer; (Am.) customer, buyer.

marchar, *vi.* to march, parade; to progress, go ahead; to work, run, go (as a machine, engine, clock, etc.).—*vr.* to go; to go away, leave.

marchitar, *vt.* to wither, fade.—*vr.* to wither, fade, decay.—**marchito**, *a.* faded, withered.

marea, *f.* tide.—*contra viento y m.*, against all odds; come what may.—**mareado**, *a.* seasick; dizzy.—**marear**, *vt.* to navigate; (coll.) to vex, annoy, bother.—*vr.* to get dizzy, seasick, carsick.—**marejada**, *f.* swell, surf; tidal wave; commotion, disturbance.—**maremágnum**, *m.* (coll.) confusion, bedlam.—**mareo**, *m.* dizziness, seasickness, carsickness; nausea; (coll.) vexation.

marfil, *m.* ivory.

margarina, *f.* margarine.

margarita, *f.* common daisy.

margen, *mf.* margin; border, edge; bank (of a river).—*dar m.*, to give an opportunity or an occasion.—**marginal**, *a.* marginal.—**marginar**, *vt.* to leave a margin on; to make marginal notes.

marica, *m.* effeminate man, sissy, (coll.) pansy.

marido, *m.* husband.

marimacho, *m.* (coll.) shrew, mannish woman.

marina, *f.* shore, sea coast; seascape; seamanship; navy, fleet, marine.—**marinería**, *f.* seamanship; body of seamen; ship's crew.—**marinero**, *a.*

seaworthy.—*m.* sailor, seaman.—**marino**, *a.* marine, sea.—*m.* seaman, mariner.

mariposa, *f.* butterfly; moth.—**mariposear**, *vi.* to flutter about.

mariscal, *m.* (mil.) marshal.

marisco, *m.* shellfish.

marisma, *f.* marsh, swamp.

marital, *a.* marital.

marítimo, *a.* maritime, marine, sea.

marmita, *f.* kettle, pot, boiler.

mármol, *m.* marble (stone).—**marmóreo**, *a.* marbled, marble.

marmota, *f.* (zool.) marmot; (coll.) sleepy head.

maroma, *f.* rope, cable; (Am.) acrobat's performance.—**maromero**, *n.* (Am.) tight-rope dancer, acrobat.

marqués, *m.* marquis.—**marquesa**, *f.* marchioness, marquise.—**marquesina**, *f.* marquee, awning.

marquetería, *f.* marquetry.

marrana, *f.* sow, female pig; (coll.) dirty woman.—**marranada**, *f.* (coll.) hoggish action; nastiness.—**marrano**, *m.* hog; (coll.) dirty man.

marrón, *a.* maroon; brown.

marroquí, *mf.* & *a.* Moroccan.

marrullería, *f.* wheedling, cajolery.—**marrullero**, *n.* wheedler, coaxer, cajoler.

marsopa, *f.* porpoise.

marta, *f.* sable.

martes, *m.* Tuesday.

martillar, *vt.* to hammer.—**martillazo**, *m.* blow with a hammer.—**martilleo**, *m.* hammering; clatter.—**martillo**, *m.* hammer.

martinete, *m.* drop hammer; pile driver; hammer of a piano.

mártir, *mf.* martyr.—**martirio**, *m.* martyrdom; torture; grief.—**martirizar**, *vti.* [a] to martyr; to torture; to torment.

marzo, *m.* March.

mas, *conj.* but, yet.—**más**, *a.* & *adv.* more; most; (math.) plus.—*a lo m.*, at the most.—*a m.*, besides.—*a m. tardar*, at the latest.—*m. bien*, rather.—*no m. que*, only.—*por m. que*, however much.—*sin m. ni m.*, without more ado.

masa, *f.* dough, mash; (mason.) mortar; (phys.) mass; volume; crowd of people.

masacre, *m.* (neol.) massacre.

masaje, *m.* massage.—**masajista**, *mf.* massagist; masseur, masseuse.

mascada, *f.* chewing; (Am.) chew of tobacco; (Mex.) silk handkerchief.—**mascar**, *vti.* [d] to chew; (coll.) to mumble.

máscara, *f.* mask.—*pl.* masquerade.—*mf.* mask, masquerader.—**masca-**

rada, *f.* masquerade.—**mascarilla,** *f.* death mask; half mask.

mascota, *f.* mascot; (baseball) catcher's mitt.

masculino, *a.* masculine; male.

mascullar, *vt.* to mumble; to munch.

masilla, *f.* putty.

masón, *m.* freemason.—**masonería,** *f.* freemasonry, masonry.

masticación, *f.* chewing.—**masticar,** *vti.* [d] to chew.

mástil, *m.* mast, post; tent-pole.

mastín, *n.* mastiff.

mastuerzo, *m.* dolt, simpleton; (bot.) common cress.

mata, *f.* (bot.) plant; sprig, blade; grove, orchard.—*m. de pelo,* head of hair.

matadero, *m.* slaughterhouse; drudgery.—**matador,** *n. & a.* killer; killing.—*m.* matador.—**matadura,** *f.* sore, gall.—**matanza,** *f.* slaughter, butchery.—**matar,** *vt.* to kill.—*a mata caballo,* in a great hurry.—*m. de hambre,* to starve.—*vr.* to kill oneself; to get killed; to commit suicide.—**matarife,** *m.* slaughterer.—**matasanos,** *m.* (coll.) quack, charlatan, quack doctor.—**matasellos,** *m.* postmark.

mate, *a.* dull, lusterless, mat.—*m.* (chess) checkmate; (bot.) Brazilian holly; maté, Paraguay tea.—*dar m.,* to checkmate.

matemática(s), *f.* (*pl.*) mathematics.—**matemático,** *a.* mathematical.—*n.* mathematician.

materia, *f.* matter; material, stuff; subject, topic; (med.) matter, pus.—*entrar en m.,* to come to the point.—*m. prima,* raw material.—**material,** *a.* material.—*m.* material, stuff; ingredient; (elec. and RR.) equipment.—**materialismo,** *m.* materialism.—**materialista,** *mf. & a.* materialist(ic).—**materializar,** *vti.* [a] to materialize.—*vri.* to become (morally) materialistic.

maternal, *a.* maternal.—**maternidad,** *f.* maternity.—**materno,** *a.* maternal, motherly; mother.

matinal, *a.* of the morning; morning.—**matiné,** *m.* matinée.

matiz, *m.* tint, hue, shade.—**matizado,** *a.* many-hued.—**matizar,** *vti.* [a] to blend (colors); to tint, shade.

matojo, *m.* bush; (bot.) glasswort.

matón, *m.* (coll.) bully.

matorral, *m.* thicket; bush.

matraca, *f.* wooden rattle.—*dar m.,* to banter.

matrero, *a.* cunning, shrewd; (Am.) suspicious.—*n.* trickster, swindler; (Am.) cattle thief.

matrícula, *f.* register, list; matricula-tion; license; car license plate.—**matricular,** *vt. & vr.* to matriculate, register, enroll.

matrimonial, *a.* matrimonial.—**matrimonio,** *m.* marriage, wedlock, matrimony; married couple.

matriz, *a.* first, principal, main.—*f.* womb; mold, form, matrix; screw nut.

matrona, *f.* matron.

matutino, *a.* morning.—*m.* (Am.) morning newspaper.

maula, *f.* rubbish, trash, junk; cunning, craft; deceitful trick.—*mf.* (coll.) malingerer, sluggard; cheat, tricky person.

maullar, *vi.* to mew.—**maullido,** *m.* mew(ing).

máxima, *f.* maxim, proverb; rule.—**máxime,** *adv.* especially, principally.—**máximo,** *m. & a.* maximum.

maya, *mf.* Maya (people and language).—*a.* Mayan.—*f.* daisy.

mayar, *vi.* to mew.

mayo, *m.* May.

mayonesa, *f.* mayonnaise.

mayor, *a.* greater; greatest; larger; largest; older, elder; oldest, eldest; senior; main, principal; major.—*altar m.,* high altar.—*m.* superior; (mil.) major.—*pl.* ancestors, forefathers; superiors; elders.—*al por m.,* (by) wholesale.—*m. de edad,* of age.

mayoral, *m.* foreman, overseer; head shepherd; coach driver.

mayordomo, *m.* butler, steward; major-domo.

mayoría, *f.* majority (in age or number); superiority.

mayorista, *mf.* wholesale merchant or dealer.

mayúscula, *a. & f.* capital (letter).—**mayúsculo,** *a.* large, good-sized; important, prominent.

maza, *f.* mace; drop hammer; war club; roller of a sugar-cane mill.

mazacote, *m.* concrete; dry, tough mass.

mazmorra, *f.* dungeon.

mazo, *m.* mallet, maul, wooden hammer; bundle, bunch.

mazorca, *f.* ear of corn.

me, *pron.* me; to me; for me; myself.

mecanografía, *f.* typewriting.—**mecanógrafo,** *n.* typist, stenographer.

mecate, *m.* (Mex.) maguey rope or cord.

mecedora, *f.* rocking chair.—**mecer,** *vti.* [a] to rock; to swing; to move (a child) gently; to shake.—*vri.* to rock, swing, sway.

mecha, *f.* wick; fuse (of explosive); slice of bacon (for larding); (Am.)

lock of hair.—**mechar**, *vt.* to lard (meat, etc.).—**mechero**, *m.* lamp burner; gas burner; cigarette lighter.—**mechón**, *m.* large lock of hair.

medalla, *f.* medal.—**medallón**, *m.* locket; medallion.

médano, *m.* sand bank; dune.

media, *f.* stocking; hose; (Am.) sock; (math.) mean.—**mediación**, *f.* mediation; intercession.—**mediado**, *a.* half-filled, half-full.—*a mediados de*, (of period of time) about the middle of.—**mediador**, *n.* mediator; intercessor.—**medianamente**, *adv.* middling, so-so, fairly.—**medianería**, *f.* partition wall.—**medianero**, *a.* mediating, interceding; intermediate.—*n.* mediator; adjacent owner.—**medianía**, *f.* halfway; average; mediocrity; moderate means.—**mediano**, *a.* moderate, middling, medium; middle sized; mediocre, tolerable.—**medianoche**, *f.* midnight.—**mediante**, *a.* interceding, intervening.—*adv.* by means of, through.—**mediar**, *vi.* to be at the middle; to intercede, mediate; to intervene.

medicación, *f.* medication.—**medicamento**, *m.* medicine, medicament.—**medicastro**, *m.* quack doctor.—**medicina**, *f.* medicine; remedy.—**medicinal**, *a.* medicinal.—**medicinar**, *vt.* to prescribe or give medicines (to a patient).

medición, *f.* measurement, measuring.

médico, *a.* medical.—*n.* physician.—*m. forense*, coroner.

medida, measure; (shoe, etc.) size, number; gauge; measuring, measurement; rule; moderation, prudence.—*a la m.*, to order, custommade.—*a m. del deseo*, according to one's wishes.—*a m. que*, as, according as, while.—*sin m.*, to excess.—*tomar medidas*, to take measures or steps.—**medidor**, *n.* measurer.

medieval, *a.* medieval.

medio, *a.* half; medium; middle; mean, intermediate.—*media naranja*, (fam.) better half, wife.—*media vuelta*, right about face.—*m.* middle, center; (often *pl.*) means, resources; expedient, measure; environment.—*por m. de*, by means of.—*adv.* half; partially.—*de m. a m.*, completely, entirely.—*de por m.*, between.

mediocre, *a.* mediocre.—**mediocridad**, *f.* mediocrity.

mediodía, *m.* noon, midday; south.

medioeval, *a.* = MEDIEVAL.

medir, *vti.* [29] to measure; to scan (verses).—*vri.* to be moderate; to act with prudence.

meditabundo, *a.* pensive, musing.—

meditación, *f.* meditation.—**meditar**, *vt. & vi.* to meditate, muse.—**meditativo**, *a.* meditative.

mediterráneo, *a.* Mediterranean.

medrar, *vi.* to thrive, prosper.

medroso, *a.* timorous, faint-hearted, cowardly; dreadful, scary.

médula, *f.* marrow; pith; substance, essence.—*m. espinal*, spinal cord.

medusa, *f.* jellyfish.

megáfono, *m.* megaphone.

mejicano, *n. & a.* Mexican.

mejilla, *f.* cheek.

mejillón, *m.* mussel.

mejor, *a.* better, best.—*el m. día*, some fine day.—*lo mejor*, the best thing.—*m. postor*, highest bidder.—*adv.* better; rather.—*a lo m.*, perhaps, maybe.—*m. que*, rather than, instead of.—**mejora**, *f.* improvement, betterment; higher bid.—**mejoramiento**, *m.* improvement.

mejorana, *f.* marjoram.

mejorar, *vt.* to improve, better, enhance; to outbid.—*vi. & vr.* to recover from a disease; to improve; to reform.—**mejoría**, *f.* improvement; betterment; advantage; improvement in health.

mejunje, *m.* concoction.

melado, *m.* cane-juice syrup.

melancolía, *f.* melancholia, gloom, blues.—**melancólico**, *a.* melancholy, gloomy.

melaza, *f.* molasses.—**melcocha**, *f.* (Am.) molasses candy, taffy.

melena, *f.* long hair; mane.—**melenudo**, *a.* bushy-haired.

melifluo, *a.* honeyed (of speech and voice).

melindre, *m.* a sort of fritter; fastidiousness; prudery.—**melindroso**, *a.* prudish, finicky.

melocotón, *m.* peach.—**melocotonero**, *m.* peach tree.

melodía, *f.* melody, tune.—**melodioso**, *a.* melodious.

melón, *m.* melon; muskmelon; cantaloupe.—*m. de agua*, (Am.) watermelon.—**melosidad**, *f.* sweetness; mildness.—**meloso**, *a.* honeyed, sweet, syrupy; soft-voiced; gentle.

mella, *f.* notch, nick, dent; jag in edged tools; gap.—*hacer m.*, to make an impression on the mind; to strike home.—**mellado**, *a.* gaptoothed.—**mellar**, *vt.* to jag, notch; to injure (as honor, credit).

mellizo, *n. & a.* twin (brother, sister).

membrana, *f.* membrane.

membrete, *m.* letterhead; heading.

membrillo, *m.* quince; quince tree.

membrudo, *a.* strong, robust, muscular.

memo, *a.* silly, foolish.

memorable, *a.* memorable.—**memorándum,** *m.* memorandum.—**memoria,** *f.* memory; remembrance, recollection; memoir; report, statement.—*pl.* memoirs; regards, compliments. —*de m.,* by heart.—*hacer m.,* to remember.—**memorial,** *m.* memorial; petition, application; (law) brief.

mención, *f.* mention.—**mencionar,** *vt.* to mention.

mendicidad, *f.* beggary.—**mendigar,** *vti.* [b] & *vii.* to beg; to entreat.—**mendigo,** *n.* beggar.

mendrugo, *m.* crumb of bread.

menear, *vt.* to stir; to shake; to wag, waggle.—*vr.* (coll.) to hustle, be active, get a move on; to waggle. —**meneo,** *m.* shake, shaking; wagging, wriggling; (coll.) drubbing, beating.

menester, *m.* need, want; employment, occupation, office.—*pl.* natural or bodily necessities.—*ser. m.,* to be necessary.—**menesteroso,** *a.* & *n.* needy, indigent (person).

mengano, *n.* (Mr. or Mrs.) so-and-so.

mengua, *f.* diminution, waning, decrease.—**menguar,** *vii.* [b] to diminish, decrease, wane.

menor, *a.* smaller, lesser, younger; smallest, least, youngest; minor.—*mf.* minor.—*m. de edad,* minor, underage.— *por m.,* by retail.—*m.* (mus.) minor.—**menoría,** *f.* inferiority, subordination; underage (person).

menos, *a.* less; least.—*adv.* less; least; except, save.—*al m.* or *a lo m.,* at least.—*a m. que,* unless.—*de m.,* less; wanting, missing.—*echar de m.,* to miss.—*m. mal,* it could be worse, not so bad.—*poco más o m.,* more or less, about.—*por lo m.,* at least.—*venir a m.,* to decline; to become poor.—*prep.* minus, less.—*las ocho m. veinte,* twenty minutes to eight.—**menoscabar,** *vt.* to lessen, diminish; to impair, damage; to discredit.—**menoscabo,** *m.* impairment, damage, detriment. —**menospreciar,** *vt.* to underrate, undervalue; to despise, scorn.—**menosprecio,** *m.* undervaluation; contempt; scorn.

mensaje, *m.* message; errand.—**mensajero,** *n.* messenger; errand boy or girl.

menstruación, *f.* menstruation, period. —**menstruar,** *vi.* to menstruate.—**menstruo,** *m.* menstruation.

mensual, *a.* monthly.—**mensualidad,** *f.* monthly salary or allowance; monthly installment.

ménsula, *f.* bracket; rest for the elbows.

mensurable, *a.* mensurable, measurable.

menta, *f.* mint; peppermint.

mental, *a.* mental.—**mentalidad,** *f.* mentality.

mentar, *vti.* [1] to mention, name.

mente, *f.* mind; intelligence.

mentecatería, mentecatez, *f.* foolishness, silliness.—**mentecato,** *a.* silly, foolish, stupid.—*n.* fool.

mentir, *vti.* [39] & *vii.* to lie.—**mentira,** *f.* lie, falsehood; fib.—*de mentiras,* in jest.—**mentiroso,** *a.* lying, untruthful.

mentón, *m.* chin.

menú, *m.* menu, bill of fare.

menudear, *vt.* to repeat; to do over and over again.—*vi.* to occur frequently; to go into details; to sell by retail.—**menudencia,** *f.* trifle; minuteness.—*pl.* small matters.—**menudeo,** *m.* (com.) retail.—*al m.,* by retail.—**menudo,** *a.* small, little; minute; insignificant.—*m.* small coins, change.—*pl.* entrails of an animal.—*a m.,* often, frequently.

meñique, *a.* little (finger).—*m.* little finger.

meollo, *m.* brain; marrow; judgment; substance.

meple, *m.* (Am.) maple.

mequetrefe, *m.* coxcomb, busybody.

mercachifle, *m.* peddler, hawker, huckster; cheap fellow.—**mercader,** *m.* merchant, dealer.—**mercadería,** *f.* commodity, merchandise; trade. —*pl.* goods, wares, merchandise.—**mercado,** *m.* market; marketplace. —*m. de valores,* stock market.—**mercancía,** *f.* merchandise, goods, wares.—**mercante, mercantil,** *a.* merchant, mercantile, commercial.—**mercar,** *vti.* [d] to buy, purchase.

merced, *f.* favor, grace; mercy.—*estar a m. de,* to be or to live at the mercy of.—*m. a,* thanks to.

mercenario, *a.* mercenary.—*n.* mercenary soldier.

mercería, *f.* small wares, haberdashery, notions.

mercurial, *a.* mercurial.—**mercurio,** *m.* mercury, quicksilver.

merecedor, *a.* deserving, worthy.—**merecer,** *vti.* [3] to deserve, merit. —**merecido,** *m.* fitting punishment.—*a.* deserved.—**merecimiento,** *m.* merit.

merendar, *vti.* [1] to snack on.—*vii.* to have a snack.—**merendero,** *m.* lunchroom; picnic grounds.

merengue, *m.* meringue, sugarplum.

meretriz, *f.* prostitute.

meridiano, *a.* meridian; meridional

(section, cut).—*m*. meridian.—**meridional**, *a*. southern, southerly.—*mf*. southerner.

merienda, *f*. (afternoon) snack; packed meal; picnic.

mérito, *m*. merit; excellence, value.—*hacer méritos*, to make oneself deserving.—**meritorio**, *a*. meritorious, deserving.—*n*. apprentice, unpaid probationer.

merluza, *f*. hake; (coll.) drunkenness.

merma, *f*. decrease; shrinkage.—**mermar**, *vi*. to decrease, wear away.—*vt*. to lessen, reduce, decrease.

mermelada, *f*. marmalade; jam.

merodeador, *n*. marauder.—**merodear**, *vi. to* maraud.—**merodeo**, *m*. marauding.

mes, *m*. month; monthly salary; menstruation.

mesa, *f*. table; desk; executive board; plateau.—*m. de noche*, bedside table.—*poner la m.*, to set the table.

mesada, *f*. monthly wages or allowance.

meseta, *f*. plateau; landing of a staircase.

mesón, *m*. inn, hostel.—**mesonero**, *n*. innkeeper.

mestizaje, *m*. crossing of races.—**mestizo**, *a*. hybrid.—*n. & a.* half-breed, mestizo.

mesura, *f*. civility, politeness; moderation.—**mesurar**, *vr*. to control oneself.

meta, *f*. goal, aim; boundary; finish line.

metáfora, *f*. metaphor.

metal, *m*. metal; (mus.) brass.—*m. de voz*, tone or timbre of the voice.—**metálico**, *a*. metallic.—*m*. cash.—**metalizar**, *vti*. [a] to metallize.—*vri*. to become mercenary.—**metalurgia**, *f*. metallurgy.

metamorfosear, *vt. & vr.* to metamorphose, transform.—**metamorfosis**, *f*. metamorphosis, transformation.

meteórico, *a*. meteoric.—**meteoro**, *m*. meteor.—**meteorología**, *f*. meteorology.—**meteorológico**, *a*. meteorological.—*parte m.*, weather report.

meter, *vt*. to put in(to), insert, introduce; to make (as a noise); to cause (as fear); to induce, get (one into business, etc.).—*vr*. to meddle, intrude; to plunge into. *m. a*, to undertake to; to turn to; to set oneself up as, pretend to be.—*m. con*, to pick a quarrel with.—*m. en*, (coll.) to meddle with, poke one's nose into.

meticuloso, *a*. meticulous, scrupulous.

metódico, *a*. methodical.—**método**, *m*. method; technique.

metralla, *f*. grapeshot; shrapnel.

métrico, *a*. metric(al).—**metro**, *m*. meter; subway.

metrónomo, *m*. metronome.

metrópoli, *f*. metropolis.—**metropolitano**, *a*. metropolitan.—*m*. subway.

mexicano, *n. & a.* V. MEJICANO.

mezcal, *m*. Mexican alcoholic beverage.

mezcla, *f*. mixture; medley; mortar; mixed cloth.—**mezclar**, *vt*. to mix, mingle; blend.—*vr*. to mix; to intermarry; to intermeddle.

mezclilla, *f*. pepper and salt cloth.

mezcolanza, *f*. (coll.) mix-up, hodgepodge.

mezquindad, *f*. niggardliness, stinginess.—**mezquino**, *a*. niggardly, stingy; petty, puny.

mezquita, *f*. mosque.

mi, *pron*. me.—*a*. my.

miaja, *f.* = MIGAJA.

mico, *n*. monkey.

microbio, *m*. microbe.—**micrófono**, *m*. microphone.—**microscopio**, *m*. microscope.

miedo, *m*. fear.—*tener m.*, to be afraid.—**miedoso**, *a*. fearful, afraid.

miel, *f*. honey; molasses.—*m. de abejas*, bee's honey.

miembro, *m*. member; limb; penis.

mientes, *f*. thoughts, ideas.—*parar m. en*, or *poner m. en*, to consider, reflect on.—*traer a las m.*, to remind.

mientras, *adv. & conj.* while; whereas.—*m. más*, the more.—*m. que*, while, as long as, so long as.—*m. tanto*, meanwhile, in the meantime.

miércoles, *m*. Wednesday.

mies, *f*. ripe grain; harvest time.—*pl*. grain fields.

mero, *a*. mere, pure, simple; (Am.) real, true; (Am.) very, very same.—*m*. (ichth.) halibut.

miga, *f*. crumb, soft part of bread; fragment, bit; (coll.) marrow, substance, pith.—*hacer buenas (malas) migas*, (coll.) to get on well (badly) with.—**migaja**, *f*. crumb or bit of bread; fragment, chip or bit; (coll.) little or nothing.—*pl*. leavings; bits of foods.

migración, *f*. migration.

migraña, *f*, migraine, headache.

migratorio, *a*. migrating, migratory.

milagro, *m*. miracle.—**milagroso**, *a*. miraculous.

milicia, *f*. militia; science of war; military profession.—**miliciano**, *n*. militiaman.

militar, *vi*. to serve in the army; to militate.—*m. contra*, to be against.

—*a.* military, soldierly.—*m.* soldier, military man.

milla, *f.* mile.

millar, *m.* thousand.—*pl.* (fig.) a great number.—**millón,** *m.* million; (fig.) a great deal.—*pl.* (fig.) a multitude, a great number.—**millonario,** *n.* & *a.* millionaire.

mimar, *vt.* to pet, fondle; to pamper, spoil (a child); to coax.

mimbre, *m.* osier; willow; wicker.—**mimbrera,** *f.* willow.

mímica, *f.* pantomime, sign language.—**mímico,** *a.* mimic; imitative.

mimo, *m.* caress, petting; pampering; coaxing.—**mimoso,** *a.* soft, spoiled; delicate; fastidious, finicky.

mina, *f.* mine; lead of pencil; (fig.) a gold mine.—**minar,** *vt.* to mine, excavate; to undermine; to consume; to ruin.—**mineral,** *a.* mineral; rich mine.—**mineralogía,** *f.* mineralogy.—**minería,** *f.* mining; force of miners.—**minero,** *a.* pertaining to mines.—*m.* miner; mine operator; source, origin.

mingo, *s.* (billiards) object ball.

miniatura, *f.* miniature.

mínimo, *a.* least, smallest.—*m.* minimum.

ministerio, *m.* ministry; office and term of a cabinet minister; government department and building.—**ministro,** *m.* cabinet minister; minister; judge or justice.

minoría, *f.* minority (in age or in number).—**minoridad,** *f.* minority (in age).

minucia, *f.* minuteness, smallness; mite.—*pl.* minutiae.—**minuciosidad,** *f.* minuteness, thoroughness; trifle; small detail.—**minucioso,** *a.* minutely precise, thorough.

minúsculo, *a.* very small, tiny; of little importance.—*f.* small letter, lower-case letter.

minuta, *f.* first draft; lawyer's bill; memorandum; list.—*pl.* minutes (of a meeting).

minutero, *m.* minute hand.—**minuto,** *m.* minute (in time and geom.).—*al m.,* at once, right away.

mío, mía.—*pl.* míos, mías, *pron.* mine.—*a.* my, of mine.

miope, *a.* near-sighted, myopic; shortsighted.—*mf.* near-sighted person.—**miopía,** *f.* myopia, near-sightedness.

mira, *f.* sight (firearms and instruments); vigilance; design, purpose, intention, view.—*estar a la m.,* to be on the lookout, to be on the watch.—**mirada,** *f.* glance, gaze, look.—*echar una m.,* to glance, cast a glance.—**mirado,** *a.* considerate;

circumspect, prudent; considered, reputed.—*bien m.,* carefully considered; looking well into the matter; in fact.—**mirador,** *m.* veranda; bay window, vantage-point.—**miramiento,** *m.* consideration, reflection; circumspection, prudence; attention, courtesy.—*pl.* fuss, bother, worry.—**mirar,** *vt.* to look, look at; to gaze, gaze upon; to view, survey; to see, regard; to consider, think; to have regard for, esteem; to watch, be careful; to watch, spy; to notice; to concern.—*m. de hito en hito,* to stare at.—*m. de reojo,* to look askance.—*m. por encima,* to examine slightly, glance at.—*vi.* to look.—*m. a,* to face, front on.—*m. por,* to take care of; look after.—*vr.* to look at oneself; to look at each other, one another.

miríada, *f.* myriad, large quantity or number.

mirilla, *f.* peephole; sight (firearms, etc.).

mirlo, *m.* blackbird.

mirón, *n.* spectator, onlooker; kibitzer; busybody, gazer.—*a.* inquisitive, curious.

mirra, *f.* myrrh.

mirto, *m.* myrtle.

misa, *f.* (eccl.) Mass.—*m. mayor,* high Mass.—*no saber de la m. la media,* to know nothing.

miscelánea, *f.* miscellany.—**misceláneo,** *a.* miscellaneous.

miserable, *a.* miserable, wretched, unhappy.—*mf.* wretch, cur, cad.—**miseria,** *f.* misery, wretchedness; need, squalor, poverty; stinginess; trifle, pittance.—**misericordia,** *f.* mercy, mercifulness, pity.—**misericordioso,** *a.* merciful.—**mísero,** *a.* = MISERABLE.

misión, *f.* mission; errand.—**misionero,** *n.* missionary.—**misiva,** *f.* missive, letter.

mismo, *a.* same; similar, like; equal, selfsame.—*ahora m.,* right now.—*el hombre m.,* the man himself.—*el m. hombre,* the same man.—*este m. mes,* this very month.—*lo m.,* the same thing.—*lo m. da,* it is all the same.—*yo m.,* I myself.

misógino, *m.* woman hater.

misterio, *m.* mystery.—**misterioso,** *a.* mysterious.

místico, *n.* & *a.* mystic(al).

mistificador, *n.* = MIXTIFICADOR.—**mistificar,** *vti.* [d] = MIXTIFICAR.

mitad, *f.* half; middle, center.—*cara m.,* better half, spouse.—*por la m.,* in two.

mítico, *a.* mythical.

mitigar, *vti.* [b] to mitigate, alleviate, soothe.

mitin, *m.* political meeting; rally.

mito, *m.* myth.—**mitología**, *f.* mythology.—**mitológico**, *a.* mythological.

mitón, *m.* mitt, mitten.

mitra, *f.* miter; bishopric.

mixtificador, *n.* cheat, deceiver.—**mixtificar**, *vti.* [d] to cheat, deceive.

mixto, *a.* mixed, mingled; composite; halfbreed; assorted.—**mixtura**, *f.* mixture, compound.

mobiliario, moblaje, *m.* household furniture.

mocasín, *m.* moccasin (shoe and snake).—**mocasina**, *f.* moccasin (shoe).

mocedad, *f.* youth; youthfulness.—**mocetón**, *n.* strapping youth; lad.

moción, *f.* motion.

moco, *m.* mucus, snivel, snot.—*llorar a m. tendido*, (coll.) to cry like a child.—**mocoso**, *a.* given to sniveling.—*n.* child; inexperienced youth.

mochar, *vt.* to cut, lop off.

mochila, *f.* knapsack; haversack.

mocho, *a.* cropped, shorn, cut-off; maimed, mutilated.—*m.* butt end.

mochuelo, *m.* red owl.

moda, *f.* fashion, mode, style.—*pasado de m.*, out of style.

modales, *m. pl.* manners.

modelado, *m.* modeling.—**modelar**, *vt.* to model.—**modelo**, *m.* model, pattern, copy.—*mf.* life model.

moderación, *f.* moderation.—**moderador**, *n.* & *a.* moderator, moderating.—**moderar**, *vt.* to moderate, regulate, curb.—*vr.* to calm down, moderate, refrain from excesses.

modernizar, *vti.* [a] & *vri.* to modernize.—**moderno**, *a.* modern.

modestia, *f.* modesty.—**modesto**, *a.* modest, unpretentious; unobtrusive; unassuming.

módico, *a.* reasonable, economical.

modificación, *f.* modification.—**modificar**, *vti.* [d] to modify.

modismo, *m.* idiom, idiomatic expression.

modista, *f.* dressmaker, modiste.—*m.—de sombreros*, milliner.—**modisto**, *m.* couturier, fashion designer.

modo, *m.* mode, way, manner; (gram.) mood.—*a m. de*, like, by way of.—*de buen (mal) m.*, politely (impolitely).—*de m. que*, so that; and so.—*de ningún m.*, by no means, under no circumstances.—*de otro m.*, otherwise.—*de todos modos*, at any rate, anyway.

modorra, *f.* drowsiness.

modoso, *a.* temperate, well-behaved.

modulación, *f.* modulation.—**modular**, *vt.* & *vi.* to modulate.

mofa, *f.* mockery, jeering, ridicule.—**mofar**, *vi.* & *vr.* to jeer, scoff, mock.—*mofarse de*, to mock, sneer at, make fun of.

mofeta, *f.* skunk.

moflete, *m.* fat cheek.—**mofletudo**, *a.* fat-cheeked.

mogol, *a.* & *n.* Mogul, Mongol.

mohín, *m.* grimace, gesture.—**mohíno**, *a.* gloomy, sulky; sad, mournful; (of horses, etc.) black.

moho, *m.* mold, mildew; rust.—**mohoso**, *a.* rusty; moldy, musty, mildewed.

mojadura, *f.* drenching, moistening, wetting.—**mojar**, *vt.* to wet, drench; to moisten, dampen; (coll.) to stab.—*vr.* to get wet.

mojicón, *m.* bun; punch, blow.

mojigatería, mojigatez, *f.* hypocrisy, sanctimoniousness; bigotry; prudery.—**mojigato**, *n.* prude, hypocrite; bigot, fanatic.—*a.* hypocritical, sanctimonious; prudish; bigoted.

mojón, *m.* landmark; milestone; heap, pile; (Am.) solid excrement.

molar, *a.* molar.

molde, *m.* mold, cast; pattern; (eng.) form; (print.) form ready for printing.—**moldear**, *vt.* to mold.—**moldura**, *f.* molding.

mole, *f.* huge mass or bulk.—*m.* (Mex.) chilli gravy.

molécula, *f.* molecule.—**molecular**, *a.* molecular.

moler, *vti.* [26] to grind, mill; to overtire; to vex, bore; to waste, consume.—*m. a palos*, to give a sound beating.

molestar, *vt.* to disturb; to trouble; to annoy, vex; to tease.—*vr.* (en) to bother, put oneself out.—**molestia**, *f.* annoyance, bother; inconvenience, trouble; discomfort; hardship; grievance.—**molesto**, *a.* annoying, vexatious, bothersome; troublesome; uncomfortable.

molicie, *f.* softness; effeminacy.

molienda, *f.* milling, grinding; season for grinding (sugar cane, etc.).—**molimiento**, *m.* grinding, pounding; fatigue, weariness.—**molinero**, *n.* miller, grinder.—**molinete**, *m.* little mill; pinwheel; ventilating wheel; friction roller.—**molinillo**, *m.* hand mill; coffee grinder.—**molino**, *m.* mill.

molusco, *m.* mollusk.

molleja, *f.* gizzard.

mollera, *f.* crown of head; (fig.) intelligence.—*ser duro de m.*, to be dull or obstinate.

momentáneo, *a.* momentary; prompt. **—memento,** *m.* moment, trice; opportunity.—*a cada m.,* continually, every minute.—*al m.,* in a moment, immediately.

momia, *f.* mummy.

mona, *f.* female monkey; (coll.) ludicrous imitator; (coll.) drunkenness. —*dormir la m.,* to sleep off a drunk. **—monada,** *f.* grimace; fawning, flattery; a pretty person or thing.

monaguillo, *m.* (eccl.) acolyte, altar boy.

monarca, *m.* monarch.—**monarquía,** *f.* monarchy; kingdom.—**monárquico,** *a.* monarchical.

monasterio, *m.* monastery.—**monástico,** *a.* monastic.

mondadientes, *m.* toothpick.—**mondadura,** *f.* cleaning, cleansing.—*pl.* paring, peelings.—**mondar,** *vt.* to clean, cleanse; to trim, prune; to hull, peel.—**mondo,** *a.* neat, pure, unmixed.—*m. y lirondo,* (coll.) pure, without adornment.

mondongo, *m.* tripe; intestines.

moneda, *f.* coin; money; specie; coinage.—*m. corriente,* currency.—*m. suelta,* small change.—**monedero,** *m.* coiner.—*m.* purse.

monería, *f.* grimace, mimicry, monkeyshine; cunning action.

monetario, *a.* monetary.

mongol, *n.* Mongol.—**mongólico,** *a.* Mongolian, Mongolic.

monigote, *m.* puppet.

monja, *f.* nun.—**monje,** *m.* monk.

mono, *n.* monkey.—*m.* overalls.—*a.* (coll.) dainty; (coll.) cute.

monograma, *m.* monogram.

monologar, *vii.* [b] to soliloquize.—**monólogo,** *m.* monologue, soliloquy.

monopolio, *m.* monopoly.—**monopolizar,** *vti.* [a] to monopolize.

monosilábico, *a.* monosyllabic.—**monosílabo,** *m. & a.* monosyllable; monosyllabic.

monotonía, *f.* monotony.—**monótono,** *a.* monotonous.

monserga, *f.* (coll.) gabble, gibberish; annoyance.

monstruo, *m.* monster, freak.—**monstruosidad,** *f.* monstrosity; monstrousness.—**monstruoso,** *a.* monstrous; huge; hideous; hateful; shocking.

monta, *f.* act of mounting; amount, sum total.—*poca m.,* little value; little importance.—**montacargas,** *m.* hoist, winch; freight elevator. —**montador,** *n.* mounter; installer (electrician, etc.).—**montaje,** *m.* setting up, installing; assembling.— **montante,** *m.* (carp. & mech.) upright, standard, post, strut, jamb; (arch.) transom; (com.) amount.

montaña, *f.* mountain.—**montañés,** *a.* mountain, of or from the mountains or highlands.—*n.* mountaineer, highlander; native of Santander, Spain. —**montañoso,** *a.* mountainous.

montar, *vi.* to mount, get on top; to ride horseback; to amount; to be of importance.—*m. en cólera,* to fly into a rage.—*vt.* to ride, straddle; to amount (to); to cover (as a horse, etc.); (mech.) to mount, set up; to establish; to assemble; (jewelry) to set; to cock (as a gun); (mil.) to mount (guard).—*vr.* (en) to get into, board (vehicles); to mount (saddle animals).

montaraz, *a.* wild, untamed; uncouth, boorish.—**monte,** *m.* mountain, mount; woods, forest, woodland.— *m. de piedad,* pawnshop.—**montés,** *a.* wild, undomesticated, uncultivated.—**montículo,** *m.* mound.

monto, *m.* sum (of money); amount; sum total.—**montón,** *m.* heap, pile; great number; mass; mound.—*a montones,* abundantly, in heaps.— *del m.,* mediocre, run of the mill.

montuno, *a.* pertaining to the highlands; rustic, boorish.—**montuoso,** *a.* mountainous, hilly.

montura, *f.* riding horse, mount; saddle trappings; (jewelry) frame, setting.

monumental, *a.* monumental.—**monumento,** *m.* monument.

moña, *f.* (Am.) dressmaker's mannequin; doll; (coll.) drunkenness; rosette, ribbon head ornament; elaborate badge on bull's neck when in the arena.

moño, *m.* (of hair) chignon, bun; crest, tuft.

moquear, *vi.* to sniffle, snivel; to run from the nose.—**moquita,** *f.* sniffle, snivel; running from the nose.

mora, *f.* blackberry; mulberry; Moorish woman.

morada, *f.* habitation, residence; stay.—**morado,** *a.* purple.—**morador,** *n.* resident, inhabitant.

moral, *a.* moral.—*f.* morals, morality; morale; mulberry tree.—**moraleja,** *f.* moral, maxim, lesson.—**moralidad,** *f.* morality, morals.—**moralizar,** *vti.* [a] & *vii.* to moralize.

morar, *vi.* to inhabit, dwell, reside.

morbidez, *f.* softness, mellowness; **mórbido,** *a.* morbid; soft, mellow, delicate.—**morbo,** *m.* disease, infirmity.—**morboso,** *a.* diseased, morbid.

morcilla, *f.* blood sausage; (theat., coll.) gag, ad-libbing.

mordacidad, *f.* pungency, sharpness, sarcasm.—**mordaz**, *a.* corrosive, biting; sarcastic, trenchant.

mordaza, *f.* gag; muzzle.

mordedor, *n. & a.* biter; biting.—**mordedura**, *f.* bite; sting.—**morder**, *vti.* [26] to bite; to eat away; to backbite; to nip.—**mordiscar**, *vti.* [d] to nibble.—**mordisco, mordiscón**, *m.* bite; biting; bit, piece bitten off.

moreno, *a.* brown; dark, swarthy; brunette.—*n.* dark-haired person; (Am.) colored person.

morfina, *f.* morphine.—**morfinómano**, *n.* drug addict.

morigeración, *f.* temperance, moderation.

morillos, *m. pl.* andirons.

morir, *vii.* [17-49] & *vri.* to die; to die out (as fire).—*m.* por, to crave for.

moro, *a.* Moorish.—*n.* Moor.

morosidad, *f.* slowness, tardiness.—**moroso**, *a.* slow, tardy; sluggish.

morral, *m.* nose bag; game bag; knapsack.

morralla, *f.* small fry (fish); rubbish; rabble.

morriña, *f.* (coll.) homesickness; sadness, blues.

morro, *m.* muzzle; snout; promontory; thick lip.

morsa, *f.* walrus.

mortaja, *f.* shroud, winding sheet.—**mortal**, *a.* mortal, fatal, deadly.—*mf.* mortal.—**mortalidad**, *f.* mortality; death rate.—**mortandad**, *f.* mortality; slaughter; butchery.—**mortecino**, *a.* dying away or extinguishing; pale, subdued (color).

mortero, *m.* mortar.

mortífero, *a.* death-dealing, fatal.—**mortificación**, *f.* mortification; humiliation.—**mortificar**, *vti.* [d] & *vri.* to mortify; to subdue (passions); to vex; to bother; to humiliate.—**mortuorio**, *a.* mortuary.—*m.* burial, funeral.

moruno, *a.* Moorish.

mosaico, *a.* Mosaic.—*m.* mosaic (work); concrete tile.

mosca, *f.* fly; (coll.) dough, money; nuisance, pest.—*aflojar la m.*, to give or spend money.—*m. muerta*, one who feigns meekness.—*papar moscas*, to gape with astonishment.—**moscardón, moscón**, *m.* bumblebee; (coll.) bore, pest.—**mosquearse**, *vr.* to show resentment.

mosquitero, *m.* mosquito bar or net.—**mosquito**, *m.* gnat; mosquito.

mostacho, *m.* bushy mustache.

mostaza, *f.* mustard.

mosto, *m.* must, grape juice.

mostrador, *m.* counter (in a shop); stand.—**mostrar**, *vti.* [12] to show; to point out.—*vri.* to appear; to show oneself, prove to be.

mostrenco, *a.* (coll.) homeless; unclaimed, unowned; masterless; stray; dull, stupid.

mota, *f.* small knot (in cloth); mote, speck.

mote, *m.* nickname; motto.

motear, *vt.* to speckle, mottle.

motejar, *vt.* to chaff, call offensive names; to censure.—*m. de*, to brand as.

motín, *m.* mutiny, riot.

motivar, *vt.* to give a reason or motive for; to cause; to motivate.—**motivo**, *m.* motive, cause, reason, occasion; (mus.) motif, theme.—*con m. de*, owing to, by reason of; on the occasion of.

moto, motocicleta, *f.* motorcycle.—**motociclista**, *mf.* motorcyclist.—**motor**, *n. & a.* mover; moving.—*m.* motor; engine.—**motorista**, *mf.* motorman (-woman); motorist, driver.—**motorización**, *f.* mechanization.—**motorizar**, *vti.* [a] to mechanize.—**motriz**, *a.* moving.

movedizo, *a.* movable; shaky, unsteady; inconstant, shifting.—**mover**, *vti.* [26] to move; to make move; to drive propel; to persuade, induce; to prompt; to incite, promote; to stir.—*vri.* to move, stir.—**movible**, *a.* movable; mobile; changeable, fickle.—**móvil**, *a.* movable; mobile; unsteady, portable.—*m.* motive, incentive, inducement; mover, motor; moving body.—**movilidad**, *f.* mobility; movableness; fickleness; unsteadiness.—**movilización**, *f.* mobilization.—**movilizar**, *vti.* [a] & *vri.* to mobilize.—**movimiento**, *m.* movement, move, activity; stir, agitation; life, liveliness; animation; motion; (art) distribution of lines, etc., technique; (mus.) tempo, time.

mozalbete, *m.* teenager, youth.—**mozo**, *a.* young, youthful; single, unmarried.—*m.* lad; manservant; waiter; porter.—*f.* lass, maid.—*buen m.*, good-looking.

mu, *m.* lowing of cattle, moo.

mucamo, *n.* (Am.) servant.

mucosidad, *f.* mucosity, mucousness.—**mucoso**, *a.* mucous; slimy, viscous.—*f.* mucous membrane.

muchacha, *f.* girl; maid (servant).—**muchachada**, *f.* boyish act; prank.—**muchachería**, *f.* boyish trick; crowd of boys.—**muchacho**, *m.* boy, lad.

muchedumbre, *f.* multitude; crowd; populace, rabble.

mucho, *a.* much, a great deal of; (of time) long.—*pl.* many.—*adv.* much, very much; a great deal; in a great measure; often; (of time) long; very.—*ni con m.,* not by far; far from it.—*ni m. menos,* nor anything like it.—*no es m.,* it is no wonder. —*no ha m., no hace m.,* not long since.—*por m. que,* no matter how much.

muda, *f.* change, alteration; change of underwear; molt, molting; change of voice in boys; roost of birds of prey.—**mudable,** *a.* changeable; fickle; shifty.—**mudanza,** *f.* change; mutation; removal, moving (residence); inconstancy; fickleness. —**mudar,** *vt.* to change; to remove; to vary, alter; to molt.—*vi.* (de) to change (opinion, mind, etc.).—*vr.* to reform, mend, change; to change one's clothes; to move, change one's place of residence.

mudez, *f.* dumbness.—**mudo,** *a.* & *n.* dumb; silent; mute.

mueblaje, *m.* = MOBILIARIO.—**mueble,** *a.* movable.—*m.* piece of furniture. —*pl.* chattels, furniture, household goods.

mueca, *f.* grimace, wry face, grin.

muela, *f.* molar tooth; millstone, grindstone.—*m. del juicio,* wisdom tooth.

muelle, *m.* (naut.) pier, wharf; (RR.) freight platform; metal spring.—*a.* delicate, soft, voluptuous.

muérdago, *m.* mistletoe.

muerte, *f.* death; murder.—*a la m.,* at the point of death.—*de mala m.,* miserable, of no account.—*de m.,* implacably.—**muerto,** *ppi* of MORIR. —*a.* dead, deceased, killed; languid; slaked.—*estar m. por,* (coll.) to be crazy about.—*m. de,* (fig.) dying with.—*n.* dead person, corpse.— *echarle a uno el m.,* (coll.) to put the blame on one.—*tocar a m.,* to toll.

muesca, *f.* notch, groove, indentation.

muestra, *f.* sample, specimen; shop sign; placard, bill; model, pattern, copy; sign, indication.—**muestrario,** *m.* collection of samples; specimen or sample book.

mugido, *m.* lowing of cattle, moo.— **mugir,** *vii.* [c] to low, bellow.

mugre, *f.* grease, grime, filth; squalor. —**mugriento,** *a.* greasy, grimy, filthy.

mujer, *f.* woman; wife, mate.—**mujeriego,** *a.* fond of women.—*m.* (coll.) wolf.—**mujeril,** *a.* womanish, womanly, feminine.—**mujerío,** *m.* gathering of women.—**mujerzuela,** *f.* woman of no account.

muladar, *m.* dungheap; rubbish heap.

mulato, *n.* & *a.* mulatto.

muleta, *f.* crutch.—**muletilla,** *f.* pet word or phrase often repeated in talking.

mulo, *n.* mule.

multa, *f.* (money) fine.—**multar,** *vt.* to fine.

multicolor, *a.* many-colored, variegated, motley.—**múltiple,** *a.* multiple, complex; (int. combust. eng.) manifold.—**multiplicación,** *f.* multiplication.—**multiplicar,** *vti.* [d] & *vri.* to multiply.—**múltiplo,** *m.* & *a.* multiple.

multitud, *f.* multitude; crowd; the masses.

mullir, *vti.* [27] to fluff, make soft, mollify.

mundanal, *a.* mundane, worldly.— **mundanidad,** *f.* worldliness, sophistication.—**mundano,** *a.* = MUNDANAL. —**mundial,** *a.* world, world-wide.— **mundo,** *m.* world; (coll.) great multitude, great quantity; social life, circle; experience.—*gran m.,* high society.—*medio m.,* many people.— *ser hombre de m.,* to be a man of experience.—*todo el m.,* everybody.

munición, *f.* ammunition; small shot; birdshot; charge of firearms.

municipal, *a.* municipal.—**municipalidad,** *f.* municipality; town hall; municipal government.—**municipio,** *m.* municipality.

munificencia, *f.* munificence, liberality.

muñeca, *f.* wrist; doll; (mech.) puppet; polishing bag.—**muñeco,** *m.* puppet, manikin; boy doll; soft fellow.

muñón, *m.* stump (of mutilated limb).

mural, *a.* mural.—*m.* mural painting. —**muralla,** *f.* rampart; wall (of a city).—**murar,** *vt.* to wall.

murciélago, *m.* (zool.) bat.

murmullo, *m.* whisper, whispering; murmuring, murmur; muttering.

murmuración, *f.* backbiting, gossip.— **murmurar,** *vi.* to purl, ripple; to whisper, murmur; to gossip, backbite.

muro, *m.* wall; (fort.) rampart.

murria, *f.* (coll.) blues; surliness, sullenness.

musa, *f.* Muse, poetic inspiration.— *pl.* (The) Muses.

musaraña, *f.* shrew-mouse; any small animal, insect or vermin.—*mirar a,* or *pensar en las musarañas,* to be absent-minded.

muscular, *a.* muscular.—**músculo,** *m.*

muscle.—**musculoso**, *a.* muscular, brawny.

muselina, *f.* muslin.

museo, *m.* museum.

musgo, *m.* moss.—**musgoso**, *a.* mossy; moss-covered.

música, *f.* music; band; musical composition; sheet music.—**musical**, *a.* musical.—**músico**, *a.* musical.—*n.* musician.

musitar, *vi.* to mumble, mutter, whisper.

muslo, *m.* thigh.

mustio, *a.* withered; sad, languid.

musulmán, *n.* & *a.* Moslem.

mutabilidad, *f.* mutability; fickleness. —**mutación**, *f.* mutation, change; (theat.) change of scene.

mutilación, *f.* mutilation.—**mutilar**, *vt.* to mutilate.

mutis, *m.* (theat.) exit.

mutismo, *m.* muteness, silence.

mutualismo, *m.* system of organized mutual aid.—**mutuo**, *a.* mutual, reciprocal.

muy, *adv.* very; greatly, most.

N

nabo, *m.* turnip (plant and root).

nácar, *m.* mother-of-pearl; pearl color.

nacer, *vii.* [3-49] to be born; to sprout, grow (as branches, plants); to rise (as the sun); to originate, start; to spring (as a stream, a river).—*n. de pies*, to be born lucky. —**naciente**, *a.* rising (sun).—*m.* Orient, East.—**nacimiento**, *m.* birth; beginning; origin; source of a river or spring; model scene of the Nativity at Yuletide.

nación, *f.* nation.—**nacional**, *a.* national.—**nacionalidad**, *f.* nationality; citizenship.—**nacionalización**, *f.* nationalization; naturalization.—**nacionalizar**, *vti.* [a] to nationalize; to naturalize.

nada, *f.* nothing, naught; nothingness.—*indef. pron.* nothing, not anything.—*de n.*, insignificant, good-for-nothing; (after thanks) you are welcome! don't mention it!—*n. de eso*, none of that; not so.—*por n.*, for nothing; under no circumstances; (Am.) you are welcome!— *adv.* not at all, by no means.

nadador, *n.* & *a.* swimmer; swimming. —**nadar**, *vi.* to swim; to float.

nadería, *f.* (coll.) insignificant thing, trifle.

nadie, *indef. pron.* nobody, no one; none; (after negative) anybody, anyone.

nafta, *f.* naphtha.—**naftalina**, *f.* naphthalene.

naipe, *m.* (playing) card.—*pl.* cards; pack or deck of cards.

nalga, *f.* buttock, rump.—**nalgada**, *f.* spanking.—*dar una n.*, to spank.

nana, *f.* (coll.) child's nurse; lullaby.

naranja, *f.* orange.—*media n.*, (coll.) better half (spouse).—**naranjada**, *f.* orangeade.—**naranjal**, *m.* orange grove.—**naranjo**, *m.* orange tree.

narciso, *m.* narcissus; daffodil; coxcomb.

narcótico, *a.* & *m.* narcotic, dope.— **narcotizar**, *vti.* [a] to drug, dope.

nardo, *m.* spikenard.

nariz, *f.* nose; nostril; sense of smell. —*meter la n. en todas partes*, to nose about.

narración, *f.* narration, account.— **narrador**, *n.* narrator; storyteller. —**narrar**, *vt.* to narrate, relate, tell. —**narrativa**, *f.* narrative.—**narrativo**, *a.* narrative.

nata, *f.* cream; prime or choice part; elite.—*pl.* whipped cream with sugar.

natación, *f.* swimming.

natal, *a.* natal, native.—*m.* birthday, birth.—**natalicio**, *m.* birthday.— **natalidad**, *f.* birth rate.

natatorio, *a.* swimming.

natilla, *f.* custard.

natividad, *f.* nativity; Christmas, Yuletide.—**nativo**, *a.* native.

natural, *a.* natural; native; inherent; common, usual; unaffected; plain. —*mf.* native.—*m.* temper, disposition, nature.—*al n.*, without art or affectation.—*del n.*, (art) from life, from nature.—**naturaleza**, *f.* nature; constitution; sort, character, kind; nationality; temperament or disposition.—*n. muerta*, still life.—**naturalidad**, *f.* naturalness; birthright, nationality.—**naturalista**, *mf.* & *a.* naturalist(ic).—**naturalización**, *f.* naturalization.—**naturalizar**, *vti.* [a] to naturalize; to acclimatize.—*vri.* to become naturalized; to get accustomed to.

naufragar, *vii.* [b] to be shipwrecked; to fail.—**naufragio**, *m.* shipwreck; failure.—**náufrago**, *a.* & *n.* shipwrecked (person).

náusea, *f.* nausea, disgust, squeamishness.—**nauseabundo**, *a.* nauseous, sickening, loathsome.

náutica, *f.* navigation.—**náutico**, *a.* nautical.

navaja, *f.* claspknife; jack knife, penknife.—*n. de afeitar*, razor.—**navajazo**, *m.* thrust or gash with a claspknife or razor; stab wound.

naval, *a.* naval.—**nave**, *f.* ship, vessel; (arch.) nave; aisle.—**navegable**, *a.*

navigable.—**navegación**, *f.* navigation; sea voyage.—*n. aérea*, aviation. —**navegante**, *m.* & *a.* navigator; navigating.—**navegar**, *vii.* [b] to navigate, sail, steer.

navidad, *f.* Nativity; Christmas.—*pl.* Christmas season.

naviero, *a.* shipping, ship.—*n.* ship owner.—**navío**, *m.* ship, vessel.

neblina, *f.* fog, mist.—**nebulosa**, *f.* nebula.—**nebulosidad**, *f.* cloudiness; mistiness; nebulousness.—**nebuloso**, *a.* nebulous, hazy, misty.

necedad, *f.* stupidity, foolishness; nonsense; (coll.) tripe.

necesario, *a.* necessary.—**neceser**, *m.* dressing case, toilet case.—*n. de costura*, sewing case.—**necesidad**, *f.* necessity; need, want.—*por n.*, from necessity; necessarily.—**necesitado**, *a.* & *n.* indigent, needy (person).— **necesitar**, *vt.* to need; to necessitate.—*vi.* (de) to be in need (of).

necio, *a* stupid, idiotic, foolish.—*n.* fool.

necrópolis, *f.* cemetery.

nefando, *a.* nefarious, heinous.— **nefasto**, *a.* sad, ominous, unlucky.

negación, *f.* negation; denial; want or total privation; (gram.) negative particle.—**negar**, *vti.* [1-b] to deny; to refuse, withhold; to prohibit; to disown.—*n. el saludo*, to give the cold shoulder to.—*vri.* to decline, refuse.—**negativa**, *f.* negative, refusal.—**negativo**, *a.* negative.—*n.* (photog.) negative.

negligencia, *f.* negligence, neglect, carelessness.—**negligente**, *a.* negligent, careless, neglectful.

negociable, *a.* negotiable.—**negociación**, *f.* negotiation; business transaction, deal.—**negociado**, *m.* bureau, division or section in official departments.—**negociante**, *a.* negotiating, trading.—*mf.* dealer, merchant, trader.—**negociar**, *vi.* to trade; to negotiate.—**negocio**, *m.* business; transaction.—*pl.* business, commercial affairs.—*n. redondo*, good bargain.

negrear, *vi.* to become black; to appear black.—**negro**, *a.* black; gloomy, dark; sad, unfortunate.—*n.* Negro; (Am.) (coll.) dearest, darling, honey.—*m.* black (color).—*n. de humo*, lampblack.—**negrura**, *f.* blackness.—**negruzco**, *a.* blackish, dark brown.

nena, *f.* baby girl; babe.—**nene**, *m.* (coll.) infant, baby boy; dear, darling.

neolatino, *a.* & *m.* Neo-Latin.—*a.* Romance.

neologismo, *m.* neologism.

neozelandés, *n.* New Zealander.—*a.* of or from New Zealand.

nervio, *m.* nerve; energy, stamina, vigor.—**nerviosidad**, *f.*, **nerviosismo**, *m.* nervousness; strength, vigor.— **nervioso**, *a.* nervous.—**nervudo**, *a.* strong, sinewy, vigorous.

neto, *a.* neat, pure; (com.) net (profit, etc.).

neumático, *m.* tire.—*a.* pneumatic.

neumonía, *f.* (med.) pneumonia.— **neumónico**, *a.* pneumonic; pulmonary.

neurastenia, *f.* neurasthenia.—**neurasténico**, *n.* & *a.* neurasthenic.—**neurosis**, *f.* neurosis.—**neurótico**, *n.* & *a.* neurotic.

neutral, *a.* neutral, neuter.—**neutralidad**, *f.* neutrality.—**neutralizar**, *vti.* [a] to counteract; to neutralize.— **neutro**, *a.* (gram.) neuter; neutral.

nevada, *f.* snowfall.—**nevado**, *a.* white as snow.—*m.* snow-covered peak.— **nevar**, *vii.* [1] to snow.—*vti.* to make white as snow.—**nevera**, *f.* icebox, refrigerator.—**nevisca**, *f.* gentle fall of snow.

nexo, *m.* bond, tie, union.

ni, *conj.* neither, nor; not even.—*ni con mucho*, not by a good deal.— *ni siquiera*, not even.

nicaragüense, *mf.* & *a.* Nicaraguan.

nicotina, *f.* nicotine.

nicho, *m.* niche; alcove.

nidada, *f.* nestful of eggs, nest; brood, covey; sitting.—**nidal**, *m.* nest; nest egg; basis, motive; haunt.—**nido**, *m.* nest; haunt; den.

niebla, *f.* fog, mist, haze.

nieto, *n.* grandson (*f.* granddaughter).

nieve, *f.* snow.

nimbo, *m.* halo.

nimiedad, *f.* superfluity, prolixity; excess.—**nimio**, *a.* prolix.

ninfa, *f.* nymph.

ningún, (contr. of) **ninguno**, *a.* no, not one, not any.—*de ningún modo*, *de ninguna manera*, by no means.— *ninguna cosa*, nothing.—**ninguno**, *pron.* nobody, none, no one, not one.—*n. de los dos*, neither of the two.

niñada, *f.* puerility, childishness.— **niñera**, *f.* nurse, nursery-maid.— **niñería**, *f.* puerility, childish action; child's play; plaything; trifle.— **niñez**, *f.* childhood, infancy.—**niño**, *a.* childish, childlike; young; inexperienced.—*n.* child.—*desde n.*, from childhood.—*niña del ojo*, pupil of the eye.—*niñas de los ojos*, (coll.) apple of one's eye; treasure.

nipón, *n.* & *a.* Nipponese, Japanese.

níquel, *m.* nickel.—**niquelar**, *vt.* to plate with nickel.

nitidez, *f.* neatness; brightness, clarity.—**nitido,** *a.* neat; bright, clear.

nitrato, *m.* nitrate.—**nítrico,** *a.* nitric.—**nitro,** *m.* niter, saltpeter.—**nitrógeno,** *m.* nitrogen.

nivel, *m.* level; levelness; watermark.—*a n.,* level, true; on the same level.—*n. de aire* or *de burbuja,* spirit level.—*n. de la vida,* standard of living.—**nivelación,** *f.* leveling; grading.—**nivelar,** *vt.* to level; to grade; to make even.—*vr.* to level off.

no, *adv.* no, not, nay.—*interrog.* isn't it? isn't that so? do you see?—*n. bien,* no sooner.—*n. más,* only; no more.—*n. obstante,* notwithstanding.—*n. sea que,* lest; or else.—*n. tal,* no such thing.—*por sí o por n.,* just in case, anyway.

noble, *a.* noble.—*mf.* nobleman (-woman).—**nobleza,** *f.* nobleness; nobility; noblesse.

noción, *f.* notion, idea; element, rudiment.

nocivo, *a.* noxious, harmful, injurious.

nocturno, *a.* nocturnal, night.—*m.* (mus., lit.) nocturne.

noche, *f.* night; evening (after sunset); (fig.) obscurity, ignorance.—*ayer n.,* last night.—*buenas noches,* good evening; goodnight.—**Nochebuena,** *f.* Christmas eve.

nodo, *m.* (med., astr.) node.

nodriza, *f.* wet nurse.

nódulo, *m.* small node.

nogal, *m.* walnut.

nómada, *mf. & a.* nomad; nomadic.

nombradía, *f.* renown, fame, reputation.—**nombramiento,** *m.* nomination, naming; appointment.—**nombrar,** *vt.* to name; to nominate; to appoint.—**nombre,** *m.* name; fame, reputation; (gram.) noun; watchword.—*n. de pila* or *de bautismo,* Christian name.—*n. y apellidos,* full name.

nómina, *f.* payroll; roster, roll, register.—**nominal,** *a.* nominal.—**nominar,** *vt.* to name.—**nominativo,** *a. & m.* (gram.) nominative.

non, *a.* odd, uneven.—*m.* odd number.—*pl.* refusal.—*estar de n.,* to be unpaired.—*dar* or *echar nones,* to say no.

nonada, *f.* trifle, nothing.

nordeste, *m.* northeast.—**nórdico,** *n. & a.* Nordic.

norma, *f.* standard, norm, rule.—**normal,** *a.* normal; standard.—*f.* normal school; (geom.) normal.—**normalidad,** *f.* normality.—**normalizar,** *vti.* [a] to normalize; to standardize.—*vri.* to become normal, return to normal.

noroeste, *m.* northwest.—**norte,** *m.* north; northwind; rule, guide, clue, direction.—**norteamericano,** *n. & a.* North American, American, from the U. S.—**norteño,** *n. & a.* Northerner; northern.

noruego, *n. & a.* Norwegian.

norueste, *m.* = NOROESTE.

nos, *pron.* us, to us; ourselves.—**nosotros,** *pron.* we; ourselves; us (after preposition).

nostalgia, *f.* nostalgia, longing, homesickness.—**nostálgico,** *a.* nostalgic, homesick.

nota, *f.* note; mark (in exam); annotation; memorandum; (com.) account, bill, check; fame.—**notabilidad,** *f.* notability; a notable (person).—**notable,** *a.* notable, remarkable, telling; distinguished, prominent.—**notación,** *f.* note; notation.—**notar,** *vt.* to note, observe; to notice, take notice of.—**notaría,** *f.* notary's office.—**notario,** *m.* notary public.

noticia, *f.* news item; news; notice, information.—**noticiero,** *m.* newsman, reporter; news sheet or column or bulletin; newsreel (also noticiario).—**noticioso,** *a.* news-giving.—**notificación,** *f.* notification; notice.—**notificar,** *vti.* [d] to notify.

notoriedad, *f.* quality of being well-known; notoriety.—**notorio,** *a.* well-known; evident.

novatada, *f.* hazing (in colleges).—**novato,** *n.* novice, beginner.

novedad, *f.* novelty; newness; surprise, recent occurrence; fad; change.—**novel,** *a.* new, inexperienced.

novela, *f.* novel; story, fiction.—**novelero,** *a.* fond of novels, fads, and novelties; newfangled; fickle.—*n.* newsmonger, gossip.—**novelesco,** *a.* novelistic, fictional; fantastic.—**novelista,** *mf.* novelist.

novia, *f.* bride; fiancée; sweetheart, girl friend.—**noviazgo,** *m.* engagement, betrothal; courtship.

noviciado, *m.* (eccl.) novitiate; apprenticeship; probation.—**novicio,** *a.* new, inexperienced.—*n.* novice, probationer; freshman.

noviembre, *m.* November.

novilla, *f.* young cow, heifer.—**novillada,** *f.* fight with young bulls; drove of young cattle.—**novillero,** *m.* novice fighter; (coll.) truant, idler.—**novillo,** *m.* young bull.—*hacer novillos,* (coll.) to play truant or hooky.

novio, *m.* bridegroom; fiancé; sweetheart, boyfriend.

nubarrón, *m.* large threatening cloud.

—nube, *f.* cloud; film on the eye; shade in precious stones; crowd, multitude.—nublado, *a.* cloudy.—*m.* thundercloud; (fig.) threat of danger.—nublar, *vt.* to cloud, obscure.—*vr.* to become cloudy.

nuca, *f.* nape or scruff of the neck.

nuclear, *a.* nuclear.—núcleo, *m.* nucleus; center.

nudillo, *m.* knuckle; small knot.

nudismo, *m.* nudism.—nudista, *mf.* nudist.

nudo, *m.* knot; tangle; (bot.) node; joint; knotty point, intricacy; crisis of a drama.—nudoso, *a.* knotty, knotted.

nuera, *f.* daughter-in-law.

nuestro, *a.* our, ours.—*pron.* ours.

nueva, *f.* news, tidings.—nuevo, *a.* new.—*de n.*, again, once more.—*¿qué hay de n.?* what's the news? what's new?

nuez, *f.* walnut; nut; Adam's apple.

nulidad, *f.* nullity; inability, incompetency; incompetent person, a nobody.—nulo, *a.* null, void; of no account.

numeración, *f.* numeration; numbering.—numeral, *a. & m.* numeral.—numerar, *vt.* to number; to enumerate.—numerario, *a.* numerary.—*m.* cash, coin, specie.—numérico, *a.* numerical.—número, *m.* number; numeral; size (shirt, etc.); number, issue (magazine, etc.).—numeroso, *a.* numerous.

nunca, *adv.* never.—*n. jamás*, never, never more.

nupcial, *a.* nuptial.—nupcias, *f. pl.* nuptials, wedding.

nutria, *f.* otter.

nutrición, *f.* nutrition, nourishing.—nutrido, *a.* full, abundant, numerous, dense.—nutrir, *vt.* to nourish, feed.—nutritivo, *a.* nutritive, nourishing.

Ñ

ñandú, *m.* (Am.) ostrich.

ñapa, *f.* (Am.) something over or extra.—*de ñ.*, to boot, into the bargain.

ñato, *a.* (Am.) pug-nosed.

ñongo, *n.* (coll.), (Cuba), peasant.—*a.* (Chile) lazy, good-for-nothing; (Colomb.) (of dice) loaded.—*f.* (Chile) laziness.

ñoñería, ñoñez, *f.* dotage, senility; drivel; shyness; silliness.—ñoño, *a.* (coll.) timid, shy; stupid; soft, feeble; flimsy.

O

o, *conj.* or, either.—*o sea*, that is.

oasis, *m.* oasis.

obedecer, *vti.* [3] to obey.—obediencia, *f.* obedience.—obediente, *a.* obedient.

obelisco, *m.* obelisk.

obertura, *f.* (mus.) overture.

obesidad, *f.* obesity, fatness.—obeso, *a.* obese, fat.

óbice, *m.* obstacle, hindrance.

obispado, *m.* bishopric; episcopate.—obispo, *m.* bishop.

obituario, *m.* obituary.

objeción, *f.* objection.—objetar, *vt.* to object to, oppose.

objetivo, *a.* objective.—*m.* (opt.) objective, eyepiece.—objeto, *m.* object; subject matter; thing; purpose; aim.

oblea, *f.* wafer.

oblicuo, *a.* oblique, slanting.

obligación, *f.* obligation, duty; bond, security.—*pl.* engagements; (com.) liabilities.—obligar, *vti.* [b] to obligate, compel, bind; to oblige.—*vri.* to obligate or bind oneself.—obligatorio, *a.* obligatory, compulsory.

óbolo, *m.* donation, alms, contribution; mite.

obra, *f.* work, creation; literary work; manufacture; structure, building; repairs in a house; toil, labor.—*o. maestra*, masterpiece.—*o. muerta*, (naut.) gunwale.—obrar, *vt.* to work; to act; to operate; to perform, execute.—*vi.* to act; to ease nature.—obrero, *n.* worker, workman (-woman), laborer.

obscenidad, *f.* obscenity.—obsceno, *a.* obscene.

obscurecer, = OSCURECER.—obscuridad, *f.* = OSCURIDAD.—obscuro, *a.* = OSCURO.

obsequiar, *vt.* to treat, entertain; to make presents to; to present, make a gift of.—obsequio, *m.* courtesy, attention shown; gift, present.—*en o. de*, for the sake of, out of respect to.—obsequioso, *a.* obsequious; compliant; attentive, obliging.

observación, *f.* observation; remark, note.—*en o.*, under observation.—observador, *n. & a.* observer; observing.—observancia, *f.* observance, fulfillment.—observar, *vt.* to observe; to notice, remark, spot; to watch; to conform to (a rule, etc.).—observatorio, *m.* observatory.

obstaculizar, *vti.* [a] to impede, obstruct.—obstáculo, *m.* obstacle; stumbling block.

obstar, *vi.* to oppose, obstruct, hinder.

—*no obstante*, notwithstanding; nevertheless, however.

obstinación, *f.* obstinacy, stubbornness.—**obstinado,** *a.* obstinate, stubborn, headstrong.—**obstinarse,** *vr.* **(en)** to be obstinate (about), to persist (in); to insist (on).

obstrucción, *f.* obstruction, stoppage. —**obstruccionismo,** *m.* obstructionism.—**obstruccionista,** *mf. & a.* obstructionist(ic).—**obstruir,** *vti.* [23-e] to obstruct, block, stop up. —*vri.* to become obstructed, clogged up.

obtención, *f.* obtainment, attainment. —**obtener,** *vti.* [42] to obtain, get, procure; to attain.

obturador, *m.* (photog.) shutter; throttle; plug, stopper.

obtuso, *a.* obtuse; blunt, dull.

obús, *m.* howitzer, mortar.

obviar, *vt.* to obviate, remove, prevent.—*vi.* to hinder.—**obvio,** *a.* obvious, evident.

ocasión, *f.* occasion; opportunity; cause, motive.—*de o.*, second-hand; at a bargain.—*en ocasiones*, at times. —**ocasional,** *a.* occasional, accidental, casual.—**ocasionar,** *vt.* to cause, occasion.

ocaso, *m.* sunset; setting of any heavenly body; decadence, decline; west.

occidental, *a.* occidental, western.— **occidente,** *m.* occident, west.

oceánico, *a.* oceanic.—**océano,** *m.* ocean.

ocio, *m.* leisure, idleness; pastime, diversion.—*ratos de o.*, spare time. —**ociosidad,** *f.* idleness, leisure.— **ocioso,** *a.* idle; fruitless; useless.

oclusión, *f.* occlusion.

octava, *f.* (mus.) octave.

octubre, *m.* October.

ocular, *a.* ocular.—*testigo o.*, eye witness.—*m.* eyepiece.—**oculista,** *mf.* oculist.

ocultar, *vt.* to hide, conceal.—**oculto,** *a.* hidden, concealed; occult.

ocupación, *f.* occupation; employment, trade, business.—**ocupado,** *a.* occupied, busy, engaged.—**ocupante,** *mf.* occupant.—**ocupar,** *vt.* to occupy; to take possession of; to hold (a job); to employ; to engage the attention.—*vr.* **(en or de)** to busy oneself (with); to be engaged (in), devote oneself (to); to pay attention (to).

ocurrencia, *f.* occurrence, incident; notion; witticism.—**ocurrente,** *a.* occurring; humorous, witty.—**ocurrir,** *vi.* to occur, happen.—*vr.* to occur (to one); to strike one (as an idea).

oda, *f.* ode.

odiar, *vt.* to hate.—**odio,** *m.* hatred. —**odioso,** *a.* odious, hateful, revolting.

odisea, *f.* odyssey.

odre, *m.* wine skin; (coll.) drunkard.

oeste, *m.* west; west wind.

ofender, *vt.* to offend; to make angry. —*vr.* to become angry; to take offense.—**ofensa,** *f.* offense.—**ofensivo,** *a.* offensive; attacking.—*f.* offensive. —**ofensor,** *n. & a.* offender; offending.

oferta, *f.* offer; offering.—*o. y demanda*, supply and demand.

oficial, *a.* official.—*mf.* officer, official; skilled worker; clerk.—**oficialidad,** *f.* (mil.) body of officers.—**oficiar,** *vi.* (eccl.) to officiate, minister; to notify officially.—*o. de*, to act as.— **oficina,** *f.* office; bureau; workshop. —**oficinesco,** *a.* departmental, office. —**oficinista,** *mf.* clerk, employee; office worker.—**oficio,** *m.* employ, work or occupation, vocation; function; official letter; trade or business.—*pl.* (eccl.) office, service.—*de o.*, officially; by trade, by occupation or profession.—**oficioso,** *a.* diligent; officious, meddlesome; useful, fruitful; semi-official, unofficial.

ofrecer, *vti.* [3] to offer; to promise; to show.—*vri.* to offer, occur, present itself; to offer oneself.—*¿se le ofrece algo?* what do you want? may I help you?—**ofrecimiento,** *m.* offer, offering.—**ofrenda,** *f.* offering, gift.—**ofrendar,** *vt.* to present offerings.

oftamólogo, *n.* oculist.

ogro, *m.* ogre, fabulous monster.

oído, *m.* sense of hearing; ear.—*al o.*, whispering, confidentially.—*dar oídos*, to lend an ear.—*de o.*, by ear.—*de oídas*, by hearsay.—**oír,** *vti.* [28] to hear, to listen; to attend (as lectures).—*o. decir*, to hear (it said).—*o. hablar de*, to hear of.

ojal, *m.* buttonhole; loop.

¡ojalá! *interj.* God grant! would to God! I wish.

ojeada, *f.* glance, glimpse.—**ojear,** *vt.* to eye, look at, stare at; to startle, frighten.—**ojera,** *f.* circle under the eye.—**ojeriza,** *f.* spite, grudge, illwill.—**ojeroso,** *a.* haggard, with circles under the eyes.—**ojete,** *m.* (sew.) eyelet.—**ojo,** *m.* eye; eye of a needle; hole; arch of a bridge.— *a los ojos de*, in the presence of.—*a ojos cerrados*, blindly, without reflection.—*costar un o.*, to cost a fortune.—*en un abrir y cerrar de ojos*, in the twinkling of an eye.— *o. avizor*, sharp lookout.—*o. de agua,*

spring (of water).—*o. de la cerradura*, keyhole.—*interj.* take notice!
look out!

ola, *f.* wave, billow.—**oleada,** *f.* big
wave; surge, swell of the sea; surg-
ing of a crowd.

oleaginoso, *a.* oily; unctuous.

oleaje, *m.* continuous movement of
waves.

óleo, *m.* oil; extreme unction; holy oil.
—*al ó.,* in oil colors.—**oleoso,** *a.* oily.

oler, *vti.* [28] to smell, scent.—*vii.* to
smell; to smack of.—**olfatear,** *vt. &
vi.* to smell, scent, sniff.—**olfato,** *m.*
sense of smell.—**oliente,** *a.* smelling.
—*mal o.,* (coll.) smelly.

olimpíada, *f.* Olympic games.—**olím-
pico,** *a.* Olympic.

oliva, *f.* olive; olive tree.—**olivar,** *m.*
olive grove, yard.—**olivo,** *m.* olive
tree.

olmo, *m.* elm tree.

olor, *m.* smell, fragrance; odor; suspicion, smack.—**oloroso,** *a.* fragrant;
(coll.) smelly.

olvidadizo, *a.* forgetful, short of
memory.—**olvidar,** *vt.* to forget.—
vr. to be forgotten, to forget.—
olvido, *m.* forgetfulness; oversight;
oblivion.—*echar al o.* or *en o.,* to
forget; to cast into oblivion.

olla, *f.* pot, kettle.—*o. de grillos*,
great confusion, pandemonium.—*o.
exprés*, pressure cooker.

ombligo, *m.* navel.

ominoso, *a.* ominous, foreboding.

omisión, *f.* omission; carelessness,
neglect.—**omiso,** *ppi.* of OMITIR.—*a.*
neglectful, remiss.—**omitir,** *vti.* [49]
to omit.

ómnibus, *m.* omnibus, stagecoach.

omnipotencia, *f.* omnipotence.—**omni-
potente,** *a.* omnipotent.

onda, *f.* wave; ripple.—**ondear,** *vi.*
to wave, ripple, undulate; to flicker.
—**ondulación,** *f.* wave, or wavy
motion.—**ondulado,** *a.* undulated,
rippled; scalloped, wavy; corrugated.—**ondulante,** *a.* waving, undu-
lating; rolling.—**ondular,** *vt.* to
undulate; to ripple.

oneroso, *a.* burdensome, onerous.

onomástico, *a.* onomastic, nominal.—
m. saint's day, name day

onza, *f.* ounce. See Table.

opaco, *a.* opaque; dark; dull.

ópalo, *m.* opal.

opción, *f.* option, choice; right.—
opcional, *a.* optional.

ópera, *f.* opera.

operación, *f.* operation; process.—
operar, *vt.* to operate; (surg.) to
operate on.—*vi.* to operate, act,
work.—**operario,** *n.* workman
(-woman); operator.

opereta, *f.* operetta, light opera.

opinar, *vi.* to be of the opinion.—
opinión, *f.* opinion.

opio, *m.* opium.

opíparo, *a.* sumptuous (of a meal).

oponente, *mf. & a.* opponent.—**oponer,**
vti. [32-49] to oppose, place against.
—*vri.* to oppose, resist; to act
against; to be opposed to; to compete.

oporto, *m.* port wine.

oportunidad, *f.* opportunity; timeli-
ness.—**oportunismo,** *m.* (pol.) op-
portunism.—**oportunista,** *mf. & a.*
(pol.) opportunist; opportunistic.—
oportuno, *a.* opportune, timely.

oposición, *f.* opposition, clash; competition for official position.—**oposicio-
nista,** *mf. & a.* (pol.) oppositionist.
—**opositor,** *n.* opponent; competitor
(for a position).

opresión, *f.* oppression.—**opresivo,** *a.*
oppressive.—**opresor,** *n.* oppressor.—
oprimir, *vt.* to oppress.

optar, *vi.* (por) to choose, select.—
optativo, *a.* optional.

óptica, *f.* optics.—**óptico,** *a.* optic(al).
—*n.* optician.

optimismo, *m.* optimism.—**optimista,**
mf. & a. optimist; optimistic.

óptimo, *a.* very best.

opuesto, *ppi.* of OPONER.—*a.* opposite.

opulencia, *f.* opulence.—**opulento,** *a.*
opulent, wealthy.

oquedad, *f.* hollow, cavity.

ora, *conj.* whether; either; or.

oración, *f.* (gram.) sentence; speech;
prayer; dusk.

oráculo, *m.* oracle.

orador, *n.* orator, speaker.—**oral,** *a.*
oral, vocal.—**orar,** *vi.* to pray.

orangután, *m.* orang-utan.

orate, *mf.* lunatic, crazy person.

oratoria, *f.* oratory, eloquent speaking.—**oratorio,** *a.* oratorical.—*m.*
oratory, chapel; (mus.) oratorio.

orbe, *m.* orb, sphere; the earth.

órbita, *f.* orbit; eye socket.

orden, *m.* order, orderliness, tidiness;
class, group; proportion, relation.
—*f.* order, command; (com.) order;
religious or honorary order.—*pl.*
orders, instructions. **ordenación,** *f.*
arrangement; disposition; array;
ordination.—**ordenamiento,** *m.* or-
daining, regulating. **ordenanza,** *f.*
method, order; statute, ordinance;
military regulation; ordination.—*m.*
(mil.) orderly.—**ordenar,** *vt.* to arrange, put in order; to order, command; to ordain.—*vr.* (eccl.) to be
ordained.

ordeñar, *vt.* to milk.

ordinal, *m. & a.* ordinal.

ordinariez, f. rough manners, ordinariness.—**ordinario,** a. ordinary, usual; coarse, unrefined.—n. unrefined person.—de o., usually, ordinarily, regularly.

orear, vt. to air, expose to the air.—vr. to take an airing.

oreja, f. ear (external); flap of a shoe; small flap; flange.—aguzar las orejas, to prick up one's ears.—bajar las orejas, to come down from one's high horse.—**orejera,** f. ear muff, earcap.—**orejudo,** a. flap-eared, long-eared.

oreo, m. airing; ventilation.

orfanato, m. orphan asylum, orphanage.—**orfandad,** f. orphanage (the state of being an orphan).

orfebre, mf. goldsmith, silversmith.—**orfebrería,** f. gold or silver work.

orfeón, m. glee club; choral society.

orgánico, a. organic.—**organillo,** m. hand organ, barrel organ.—**organismo,** m. organism; organization, association.—**organista,** mf. (mus.) organist.—**organización,** f. organization; arrangement.—**organizar,** vti. [a] to organize, set up; to arrange.—**órgano,** m. (physiol., & mus.) organ; instrument, agency.

orgasmo, m. orgasm.

orgía, f. orgy.

orgullo, m. pride; haughtiness.—**orgulloso,** a. proud; haughty; conceited.

orientación, f. orientation; bearings.—**oriental,** a. oriental, eastern.—mf. Oriental.—**orientar,** vt. to orientate, orient.—vr. to find one's way about, get one's bearings.—**oriente,** m. east, orient; luster (in pearls).

orificación, f. (dent.) gold filling.

orificio, m. orifice, small hole, opening.

origen, m. origin; source; beginning.—**original,** a. original, new; quaint, odd.—m. original, first copy; (print.) manuscript.—**originalidad,** f. originality.—**originar,** vt. to originate, create; to start.—vr. to originate, arise, spring.—**originario,** a. originating; native; derived.

orilla, f. border, margin; edge; bank (of a river); shore; sidewalk.

orín, m. rust.—pl. urine.—**orina,** f. urine.—**orinal,** m. urinal; chamber pot.—**orinar,** vt. & vi. to urinate.

oriundo, a. native, coming (from).

orla, f. fringe, trimming; matting; ornamental border.—**orlar,** vt. to border with an edging.

ornamentación, f. ornamentation.—**ornamentar,** vt. to adorn, decorate.—**ornamento,** m. ornament; decoration; accomplishment.—**ornar,** vt.

to adorn, embellish, garnish.—**ornato,** m. ornament, decoration, embellishment.

ornitología, f. ornithology.

oro, m. gold; gold color.—pl. diamonds (in Spanish cards).

orondo, a. pompous, showy; hollow.

oropel, m. tinsel; brass foil; glitter.

oropéndola, f. golden oriole.

orquesta, f. orchestra.—**orquestación,** f. orchestration.—**orquestar,** vt. to orchestrate.

orquídea, f. orchid.

ortiga, f. nettle.

ortodoxia, f. orthodoxy.—**ortodoxo,** a. orthodox.

ortografía, f. orthography, spelling.—**ortográfico,** a. orthographical.

oruga, f. (entom.) caterpillar; (bot.) rocket.

orzuelo, m. (med.) sty.

os, pron. you; to you; yourselves.

osadía, f. audacity, daring.—**osado,** a. daring, bold, audacious.—**osar,** vi. to dare, venture; to outdare.

oscilación, f. oscillation.—**oscilar,** vi. to oscillate.—**oscilatorio,** a. oscillatory.

oscuras.—a o., in the dark.—**oscurecer,** vti. [3] to obscure, darken; to dim; to tarnish; (art) to shade.—vii. to grow dark.—vri. to become dark; to cloud over.—**oscurecimiento,** m. darkening; blackout.—**oscuridad,** f. obscurity; darkness; gloominess.—**oscuro,** a. obscure; dark; gloomy; dim.

óseo, a. bone, bony.

osezno, m. whelp or cub of a bear.—**oso,** m. (zool.) bear.—o. blanco, polar bear.—o. gris, grizzly bear.—o. hormiguero, anteater.—o. marino, fur seal, seal.

ostensible, a. ostensible, apparent.—**ostentación,** f. ostentation.—**ostentar,** vt. to make a show of, exhibit.—vi. to boast, brag; to show off.—**ostentoso,** a. sumptuous, magnificent.

ostión, m. large oyster.—**ostra,** f. oyster.—**ostracismo,** m. ostracism.

otear, vt. to observe, examine, pry into.—**otero,** m. hill, knoll.

otoñal, a. autumnal.—**otoño,** m. autumn, fall.

otorgamiento, m. grant, granting; (law) executing an instrument.—**otorgar,** vti. [b] to consent, agree to; (law) to grant.

otro, a. another, other.—pron. other one, another one.

ovación, f. ovation.—**ovacionar,** vt. to give an ovation to; to acclaim.

oval, ovalado, a. oval.—**óvalo,** m. oval.

ovario, m. ovary.

ovas, f. pl. roe.

oveja, f. sheep.—**ovejuno**, a. pertaining to sheep.

overol, m., **overoles**, m. pl. (Am.) overalls.

ovillar, vt to wind (thread) in a ball or skein.—vr. to curl up.—**ovillo**, m. skein, ball of yarn.

oxiacanta, f. hawthorn.

oxidar, vt. & vr. to oxidize; to rust.—**óxido**, m. oxide; rust.

oxígeno, m. oxygen.

oyente, mf. hearer.—pl. audience.

ozono, m. ozone.

P

pabilo, m. wick (of candle); burnt end of wick.

pábulo, m. encouragement; nourishment, food.—dar p., to give basis for (gossip); to stimulate (gossip).

paca, f. bale of goods.

pacana, f. pecan nut; pecan tree.

pacer, vii. [3] to pasture; to graze.

paciencia, f. patience.—**paciente**, a. patient.—mf. patient, sick person.—**pacienzudo**, a. long-suffering.

pacificador, n. pacifier, peacemaker.—**pacificar**, vti. [d] to pacify, appease.—vri. to become calm.—**pacífico**, a. peaceful, pacific.—**pacifismo**, m. pacifism.—**pacifista**, mf. & a. pacifist; pacifistic.

paco, m. alpaca; sniper.

pacotilla, f. (com.) venture.—de p., of poor or inferior quality.

pactar, vt. to make an agreement, contract; to stipulate.—**pacto**, m. agreement, pact; treaty.

pachorra, f. sluggishness, slowness.

padecer, vti. [3] to suffer.—vii. (de) to suffer (from).—**padecimiento**, m. suffering; ailment.

padrastro, m. stepfather.—**padre**, m. father; priest; principal author.—pl. parents, father and mother; ancestors.—P. Eterno, our Father, God Almighty.—**padrenuestro**, m. Lord's Prayer.—**padrino**, m. godfather; second (in a duel); best man; patron, sponsor.

paella, f. dish of rice with meat, chicken and shellfish.

paga, f. payment; wages, salary; pay.—**pagadero**, a. payable.—**pagador**, n. payer; paymaster; paying teller.—**pagaduría**, f. paymaster's office.

paganismo, m. paganism, heathenism.—**pagano**, n. & a. pagan, heathen.—n. sucker, dupe.

pagar, vti. [b] to pay; to pay for; to requite.—p. contra entrega, C.O.D.—p. el pato, to get the blame, be the scapegoat.—p. una visita, to visit, return a call.—vri. (de) to be pleased (with); to boast (of); to be conceited (about).—**pagaré**, m. (com.) promissory note; I.O.U.

página, f. page (of a book); folio.—**paginar**, vt. to page (a book, etc.), paginate.

pago, m. payment; requital.—a. (coll.) paid.

país, m. country, nation; land, region.—del p., domestic, national.—**paisaje**, m. landscape.—**paisano**, a. from the same country.—n. fellow countryman(-woman); civilian; peasant.

paja, f. straw; chaff, trash.—un quitame allá esas pajas, an insignificant reason; a jiffy.—**pajar**, m. barn, straw loft.

pajarera, f. aviary; large bird cage.—**pajarería**, f. bird shop.—**pájaro**, m. bird; shrewd, sly fellow.—p. carpintero, woodpecker.—p. de cuenta, person of importance, big shot; shrewd, sly fellow.—p. mosca, hummingbird.—**pajarraco**, m. large bird; (coll.) shady character.

paje, m. page, valet.

pajizo, a. made of straw; straw-colored.

pajonal, m. (Am.) place abounding in tall grass.

pala, f. shovel; spade; scoop; trowel; blade of an oar; blade of the rudder; artifice; (coll.) fix, thrown game.

palabra, f. word.—interj. honestly! my word of honor!—bajo p., on (one's) word.—de p., by word of mouth.—p. de matrimonio, promise of marriage.—pedir la p., to ask for the floor (at a meeting).—**palabrería**, f. wordiness, palaver, empty talk, verbosity, wind.—**palabrota**, f. coarse expression.

palacio, m. palace.

paladar, m. palate; taste, relish.—**paladear**, vt. to taste with pleasure, to relish.—**paladeo**, m. act of tasting or relishing.

paladín, m. champion.

palafrenero, m. stableboy, groom, ostler.

palanca, f. lever; bar, crowbar; pole for carrying a weight.

palangana, f. washbowl, basin.

palanqueta, f. small lever; (Am.) dumbbell.

palco, m. (theat.) box, loge; stand with seats.

palear, vt. (Am.) to shovel.

palenque, m. palisade; arena.

paleta, f. (cooking) ladle; (anat.) shoulder blade; (mason.) trowel; blade; (art) palette; little shovel.—

paletada, *f.* trowelful.—**paletilla,** *f.* shoulder blade.

palidecer, *vii.* [3] to pale, turn pale. —**palidez,** *f.* paleness, pallor.— **pálido,** *a.* pale, pallid, pasty.

palillo, *m.* toothpick; drumstick; small stick.—*pl.* castanets.

palio, *m.* cloak, mantle; pallium, pall.

palique, *m.* (coll.) chitchat, small talk.

paliza, *f.* beating, thrashing.

palizada, *f.* palisade; (fort.) stock-ade.

palma, *f.* palm tree; leaf of a palm tree; palm of the hand; emblem of victory or martyrdom.—*pl.* applause.—*ganar,* or *llevarse la* p., to carry the day; to win the prize.— **palmada,** *f.* pat; clapping; slap. —**palmar,** *m.* palm grove.

palmario, *a.* clear, obvious, evident.

palmatoria, *f.* small candlestick.

palmear, *vt.* to clap (the hands); to pat.

palmera, *f.* palm tree.—**palmiche,** *m.* fruit of a palm tree.

palmo, *m.* span, measure of length. —*p. a* p., foot by foot.—**palmotear** *vi.* to clap hands.—**palmoteo,** *m.* hand clapping.

palo, *m.* stick; pole; timber, log; wood (material); (Am.) tree; blow with a stick; suit at cards; (Am.) a drink; (naut.) mast.—*pl.* blows, cudgeling.—*dar* (*de*) *palos,* to thrash, club, beat.

paloma, *f.* pigeon; dove; meek, mild person.—*p. mensajera,* carrier pigeon. —*p. torcaz,* wild pigeon.—**palomo,** *m.* cock pigeon.

palpable, *a.* palpable, obvious, evident.—**palpar,** *vt.* to feel (of); to touch; to see as self-evident; (med.) to palpate.—*vi.* to feel by touching; to grope in the dark.

palpitación, *f.* palpitation; throbbing.—**palpitante,** *a.* vibrating, palpitating.—**palpitar,** *vi.* to palpitate, throb, quiver.

palúdico, *a.* malarial.—**paludismo,** *m.* malaria.

pampa, *f.* pampa, prairie.—*estar a la* p., (Am.) to be outdoors.—**pampeano, pampero,** *a.* of or from the pampas —*n.* pampa man (woman).

pamplina *f.* (coll.) trifle, frivolity.

pan, *m.* bread; loaf; wheat; leaf (of gold, silver).—*pl.* breadstuffs.— *p. integral,* whole-wheat bread.— *llamar al* p. p. *y al vino vino,* to call a spade a spade.

pana, *f.* corduroy, plush.

panadería *f.* bakery.—**panadero,** *n.* baker.

panal, *m.* honeycomb; hornet's nest; a sweetmeat.

panameño, *n.* & *a.* Panamanian.

panamericano, *a.* Pan-American.

pandear, *vt., vi.* & *vr.* to bend, warp, bulge out.—**pandeo,** *m.* bulge, bulging.

pandereta, *f.,* **pandero,** *m.* tambourine.

pandilla, *f.* gang, band.—**pandillero,** *n.* (Am.) gangster.

panecillo, *m.* roll (bread).

panel, *m.* (art, elec.) panel.

panetela, *f.* (Am.) sponge cake.

panfleto, *m.* tract, pamphlet; lampoon; libel.

paniaguado, *n.* protégé, henchman.

pánico, *m.* & *a.* panic(ky).

panocha, *f.* ear of grain.

panqué, panqueque, *m.* (Am.) pancake; cupcake.

pantaletas, *f. pl.* (Am.) panties.— **pantalón,** *m.* (gen. *pl.*) trousers; panties; slacks.—*p. corto,* shorts; Bermuda shorts.—**pantaloncitos,** *m. pl.* (Am.) panties.

pantalla, *f.* lamp shade; screen.

pantano, *m.* swamp, marsh, bog.— **pantanoso,** *a.* swampy, marshy, miry; full of difficulties.

pantera, *f.* panther.

pantomima, *f.* pantomime.

pantorrilla, *f.* calf (of leg)

pantufla, *f.* slipper.

panza, *f.* belly, paunch.—**panzada,** *f.* (coll.) bellyful.—**panzón, panzudo,** *a.* & *n.* big-bellied, paunchy (person).

pañal, *m.* diaper.—*estar en pañales,* to have little knowledge or experience.—**paño,** *m.* cloth, woolen material; wash cloth.—*pl.* clothes, garments.—*paños calientes,* half measures.—*paños menores,* underclothes.—**pañoleta,** *f.* triangular shawl.—**pañolón,** *m.* large square shawl.—**pañuelo,** *m.* handkerchief, kerchief.

papa, *m.* pope.—*f.* potato; (Am.) easy job; (coll.) food, grub; lie, fib.

papá, *m.* (coll.) dad, daddy, papa, pop.

papada, *f.* double chin; dewlap.

papagayo, *m.* macaw.

papal, *a.* papal.

papalote, *m.* (Am.) kite.

papamoscas, *m.* flycatcher, flyeater; (coll.) ninny.—**papanatas,** *m.* (coll.) simpleton, dolt, ninny.

paparrucha, *f.* (coll.) fake, humbug; nonsense, silliness.

papaya, *f.* papaya.

papel, *m.* paper; piece of paper; document; (theat.) part, role; character, figure.—**hacer buen** (o **mal**) **p.**, to cut a good (or bad) figure). —**p. de cartas**, stationery.—**p. de estraza;** brown wrapping paper.—**p. de inodoro,** or **p. higiénico,** toilet paper.—**p. de lija,** sandpaper.—**p. de seda,** tissue paper.—**p. secante,** blotting paper.—**papeleo,** m. red tape.—

papelera, f. paper case; paper mill. —**papelería,** f. stationery; stationery shop.—**papelero,** n. paper maker; stationer.—**papeleta,** f. card, ticket, slip.—**papelucho,** m. worthless paper.

papera, f. goiter.—**pl.** mumps.

papilla, f. pap; guile, deceit.— **hacerse p.,** to break into small pieces.

paquete, m. packet, package; bundle of papers; (coll.) dandy, dude.

par, a. even (number).—m. pair, couple; peer; (elec.) cell.—**a la p.,** jointly, equally; (com.) par; at par; (horse racing) in a dead heat. —**de p. en p.,** (of a door, etc.) wide open.—**sin p.,** peerless, incomparable.

para, prep. for, to, in order to, toward, to the end that.—**estar p.,** to be on the point of, about to.— **p. mi capote,** to myself.—**¿p. qué?** what for?—**p. que,** so that, in order that.—**sin qué ni p. qué,** without rhyme or reason.

parabién, m. congratulation, felicitation, greeting.

parábola, f. parable; (geom.) parabola.—**parabólico,** a. parabolic.

parabrisa, m. windshield.

paracaídas, m. parachute.—**paracaidista,** mf. parachutist; (mil.) paratrooper.

parachoques, m. (auto) bumper.

parada, f. stop (as a train, etc.); (mil.) halt, halting; parade; review; stakes, bet; (fencing) parry.—**p. en firme** or **en seco,** dead stop.—**paradero,** m. halting place; (Am.) (RR.) depot, station; whereabouts.

parado, a. unoccupied; (of a clock) stopped; shut down (as a factory); (Am.) standing.—**a. & n.** unemployed.

paradoja, f. paradox.

parafina, f. paraffin.

paraguas, m. umbrella.

paraguayo, n. & a. Paraguayan.

paragüero, n. umbrella maker, repairer or seller; (coll.) Sunday driver.—m. umbrella stand.

paraíso, m. paradise; heaven; (theat., coll.) upper gallery.—**p. terrenal,** Paradise, garden of Eden.

paraje, m. place, spot.

paralela, f. parallel line.—**paralelo,** a. parallel; similar.- m. parallel, resemblance; (geog.) parallel.

parálisis, f. paralysis.—**paralítico,** n. & a. paralytic; paralyzed.—**paralización,** f. paralyzation; (com.) stagnation.—**paralizado,** a. (com.) dull, stagnant.—**paralizar,** vti. [a] to paralyze; to impede, to stop.

páramo, m. bleak plateau, moor; desert.

parangón, m. comparison.—**parangonar,** vt. to compare.

paraninfo, m. assembly hall in a university.

parapeto, m. (mil.) parapet.

parar, vt. to stop, detain; (fencing) to parry; (Am.) to stand, place in upright position.—**p. mientes en,** to consider carefully.—vi. to stop, halt; to come to an end; (**en**) to become, end (in); to stop or stay (at).— **ir a p. a** or **en,** to become, end in, finally to get to.—vr. to stop, halt; (Am.) to stand up.—**sin pararse,** without delay, instantly.—**pararrayos,** m. lightning rod.

parásito, m. & a. parasite; parasitic.

parasol, m. parasol.

parcela, f. parcel of land, lot.— **parcelar,** vt. to divide into lots.

parcial, a. partial.—mf. follower, partisan.—**parcialidad,** f. partiality, bias; party, faction.

parco, a. sparing, scanty; sober, moderate.

parche, m. patch, mending; (pharm.) plaster, sticking plaster; (mil.) drum-head; drum.

pardal, m. (ornith.) sparrow, linnet; crafty fellow.

pardo, a. brown; dark gray.—n. (Am.) mulatto.—**pardusco,** a. grayish, grizzly.

parear, vt. to match, mate, pair.

parecer, vii. [3] to appear, show up; to seem, look like.—**al p.,** apparently.—vri. to look alike, resemble. —m. opinion, thinking; look, mien; appearance.—**parecido,** a. (a) resembling, like, similar (to).—**bien** (**mal**) **p.,** good-(bad-) looking.—m. resemblance, likeness.

pared, f. wall.—**entre cuatro paredes,** confined; imprisoned.—**p. maestra,** main wall.—**p. medianera,** partition wall.

pareja, f. pair, couple; match; dancing partner.—**parejas mixtas,** (games) mixed doubles.—**parejo,** a. equal, even; smooth; (horse racing) neck and neck.

parentela, f. kinsfolk, relatives.— **parentesco,** m. kindred, relationship.

paréntesis, m. parenthesis.—**entre p.,** by the bye, by the way.

pargo, m. red snapper.

paria, m. outcast.

paridad, *f.* parity, equality.

pariente, *n.* relative, relation.

parihuela, *f.* handbarrow; litter; stretcher.

parir, *vt. & vi.* to give birth.—*poner a p.,* to constrain, force (a person).

parlamentar, *vi.* to parley; to converse.—**parlamentario,** *a.* parliamentary, parliamentarian.—*n.* member of parliament; envoy to a parley.—**parlamento,** *m.* parliament; legislative body; parley.

parlanchín, *n. & a.* chatterer, jabberer. talker; chattering, jabbering, talkative.—**parlero,** *a.* loquacious, talkative; chirping (birds); babbling (brooks).—**parlotear,** *vi.* to prattle, prate, chatter.—**parloteo,** *m.* chat, prattle, talk.

paro, *m.* lockout.—*p. forzoso,* unemployment.

parótida, *f.* parotid gland.—*pl.* mumps.

parpadear, *vi.* to wink; to blink, twinkle.—**parpadeo,** *m.* winking; blinking, twinkling.—**párpado,** *m.* eyelid.

parque, *m.* park; (Am.) ammunition. —**parquear,** *vt. & vi.* (Am.) to park (auto).

parra, *f.* grapevine.

párrafo, *m.* paragraph.

parranda, *f.* revel, carousal, spree.— **parrandear,** *vi.* to go on a spree. —**parrandero,** *a.* fond of carousing. —*n.* carouser, reveler.

parricida, *mf.* parricide (person).— **parricidio,** *m.* parricide (act).

parrilla, *f.* grill, broiler; toaster; (furnace) grate.

párroco, *m.* parish priest.—**parroquia,** *f.* parish; parish church; (com.) customers.—**parroquial,** *a.* parochial. —*f.* parochial church.—**parroquiano,** *n.* parishioner; (com.) customer, client.

parsimonia, *f.* moderation, calmness.

parte, *f.* part; portion; share; place; (law) party; (theat.) role.—*pl.* (coll.) the genitals.—*dar p.,* to inform, notify.—*de algún tiempo a esta p.,* for some time past.—*de mi p.,* for my part; on my side; in my name.—*de p. a p.,* from side to side, through.—*de p. de,* from, in the name of; in behalf of.—*en alguna p.,* somewhere.—*en ninguna p.,* nowhere.—*en todas partes,* everywhere.—*la mayor p.,* most.— *la tercera (cuarta, etc.) p.,* one-third (-fourth, etc.).—*p. de la oración,* part of speech.—*por mi p.,* as for me.—*por otra p.,* on the other hand.—*m.* communication, dispatch, report, telegram, telephone message. —*adv.* in part, partly.

partera, *f.* midwife.

partición, *f.* division, partition, distribution.—**participación,** *f.* participation, share; communication; (com.) copartnership.—**participante,** *mf. & a.* participant, sharer; notifier; participating, sharing; notifying.—**participar,** *vt.* to notify, communicate.—*vi.* (de) to share (in); (en) to participate, take part (in). —**partícipe,** *mf.* participator, participant.—**participio,** *m.* participle.

partícula, *f.* particle.

particular, *a.* particular, peculiar, special; personal; private; individual; odd, extraordinary.—*m.* private person, individual; topic, point.—*en p.,* particularly.—**particularidad,** *f.* particularity, peculiarity, detail.

partida, *f.* departure; item in an account; entry; game; band, gang; (com.) shipment, consignment.—*p. de bautismo,* (matrimonio, defunción), certificate of birth (marriage, death).—*p. de campo,* picnic.—**partidario,** *n.* supporter; follower, retainer.—**partido,** *a.* divided; broken. —*m.* (pol.) party; advantage profit; game, contest, match; odds, handicap; territorial division or district.—*sacar p. de,* to turn to advantage.—*tomar p.,* to take sides. —**partir,** *vt.* to split; to divide; to break, crush, crack.—*vi.* to depart, leave.—*a p. de,* starting from.—*vr.* to break; to become divided.

partitura, *f.* (mus.) score.

parto, *m.* childbirth.

parvedad, *f.* smallness, minuteness; light breakfast.

párvulo, *a.* very small; innocent; humble, low.—*n.* child.

pasa, *f.* raisin; (Am.) kinky hair of Negroes; (naut.) narrow channel.

pasable, *a.* passable, able to be traversed, crossed, etc.—**pasada,** *f.* passage, passing; pace, step.—*de p.,* on the way; hastily.—*mala p.,* (coll.) bad turn, mean trick.—**pasadero,** *a.* supportable, sufferable; passable, so-so, tolerably good.—*m.* stepping stone.—**pasadizo,** *m.* passageway, aisle; alley.—**pasado,** *p. a.* past; last (day, week, etc.); stale; (of fruit) spoiled; antiquated, out of date or fashion.—*p. mañana,* day after tomorrow.—*m.* past.—**pasador,** *m.* door bolt; window fastener; pin; woman's brooch.

pasaje, *m.* passage, passageway; fare; number of passengers in a ship; (naut.) strait, narrows.—**pasajero,** *a.*

passing, transient, transitory; provisional.—*n.* traveler, passenger.

pasamano, *m.* handrail, banister.

pasaporte, *m.* passport.

pasar, *vt.* to pass; to take across, carry over; to pass, hand; to go to, in, by, across, over, around, beyond, through; to filter; to surpass; to tolerate; to endure; to pass, spend (as time).—*p. a cuchillo,* to put to the sword.—*p. el rato,* to kill time. —*p. (la) lista,* to call the roll.—*pasarlo bien (mal),* to have a good (bad) time.—*p. por alto,* to overlook.—*p. por las armas,* to shoot, execute.—*¿qué (le) pasa?* what's the matter with (him)?—*vi.* to pass; to live; to get along; to pass, happen, turn out.—*p. de,* to exceed. —*p. de largo,* to pass by without stopping; to skim through.—*p. por,* to be considered as, to be taken for.—*p. sin,* to do without.—*vr.* to become spoiled, tainted or stale; to slip from one's memory; to go too far; to exceed; to be overcooked.

pasarela, *f.* gangplank; (theat.) runway.

pasatiempo, *m.* amusement, pastime.

pascua, *f.* Passover; Easter; Christmas; Twelfth-night; Pentecost.—*estar como una p. or unas pascuas,* to be as merry as a lark.—*felices Pascuas,* Merry Christmas.—*P. de Navidad,* Christmas.—*P. florida,* or *P. de Resurrección,* Easter.

pase, *m.* pass, permit; (fencing) thrust.

paseante, *mf.* walker, stroller.—**pasear,** *vi. & vr.* to take a walk; to ride, drive or sail for pleasure; to walk up and down, pace.—*vt.* to take out to walk (as a child).—**paseo,** *m.* walk; promenade; stroll; drive; ride; boulevard; parade.—*dar un p.,* to take a walk, ride, etc. —*echar or enviar a p.,* to dismiss or reject rudely or without ceremony.

pasillo, *m.* passage, corridor; aisle; short step.

pasión, *f.* passion.

pasivo, *a.* passive; inactive.—*m.* (com.) liabilities.

pasmar, *vt.* to stupefy, stun; to amaze, astound.—*vr.* to wonder, marvel; (of plants) to freeze.—**pasmo,** *m.* astenishment; wonder, awe.—**pasmoso,** *a.* marvelous, wonderful.

paso, *m.* pace, step; pass, passage; passing; gait, walk; footstep.—*apretar el p.,* to hasten.—*de p.,* in passing; on the way.—*p. a nivel,* (RR.) grade crossing.—*p. de tortuga,* snail's pace.—*prohibido el p.,*

no trespassing, keep out.—*salir del p.,* to get out of the difficulty; to get by.—*adv.* softly, gently.

pasquín, *m.* lampoon; anonymous satiric public poster.—**pasquinar,** *vt.* to ridicule, lampoon, satirize.

pasta, *f.* paste; dough; pie crust; noodles; board binding (for books). —*buena p.,* good disposition.

pastadero, *m.* pasture, grazing field. —**pastar,** *vi.* to pasture, graze.—*vt.* to lead (cattle) to graze.

pastel, *m.* pie; combine, plot; (art) pastel.—**pastelear,** *vi.* (coll.) (pol.) make a deal.—**pastelería,** *f.* pastry shop; pastry.—**pastelero,** *n.* pastry cook; (pol.) deal-maker.

pasteurizar, *vti.* [a] to pasteurize.

pastilla, *f.* tablet, lozenge, pastille, drop; cake (of soap).

pastizal, *m.* pasture ground.—**pasto,** *m.* pasture, grazing; grass for feed; pasture ground; food.—*a p.,* abundantly; excessively.—*a todo p.,* freely, abundantly and unrestrictedly.—**pastor,** *n.* shepherd(ess); pastor, clergyman.—**pastoral,** *f.* pastoral; idyl.—*a.* pastoral.—**pastorear,** *vt.* to pasture; to keep, tend (sheep).—**pastoreo,** *m.* pasturing.—**pastoril,** *a.* pastoral.

pastoso, *a.* pasty, soft, mellow, doughy, mushy.

pata, *f.* foot or leg of an animal; leg of a piece of furniture, an instrument, etc.; female duck.—*a or en cuatro patas,* on all fours.—*a la p. la llana,* plainly, unaffectedly. —*a p.,* (coll.) on foot.—*estirar la p.,* (coll.) to kick the bucket.—*meter la p.,* to put one's foot in.—*p. de gallina or de gallo,* crow's-foot wrinkles.—*patas arriba,* topsy-turvy, heels over head; upside down.—**patada,** *f.* kick.—**patalear,** *vi.* to kick about violently.—**pataleo,** *m.* kicking; pattering.—**pataleta,** *f.* (coll.) fainting fit; convulsion; tantrum.

patata, *f.* potato.

patatús, *m.* (coll.) swoon, fainting fit.

pateadura, *f.,* **pateamiento,** *m.* kicking, stamping of the feet.—**patear,** *vt. & vi.* to kick; to stamp the foot; to tramp.

patentar, *vt.* to patent.—**patente,** *a.* patent, manifest, evident.—*f.* patent; privilege, grant.—**patentizar,** *vti.* [a] to make evident.

paternal, *a.* paternal, fatherly.—**paternidad,** *f.* paternity, fatherhood. —**paterno,** *a.* paternal, fatherly.

patético, *a.* pathetic.—**patetismo,** *m.* dramatic quality; pathos.

patibulario, *a.* harrowing; criminal looking.—**patíbulo,** *m.* gallows.

patidifuso, *a.* (coll.) astounded.

patillas, *f. pl.* sideburns; side whiskers.

patín, *m.* skate; (aer.) skid; small patio; (theat.) orchestra.—*p. de ruedas,* roller skate.—**patinador,** *n.* skater.—**patinaje,** *m.* skating.—**patinar,** *vi.* to skate; (of vehicles) to skid.—**patinazo,** *m.* skid.

patio, *m.* yard, patio, courtyard.

patituerto, *a.* crook-legged, knock-kneed.—**patizambo,** *a.* knock-kneed, bowlegged.

pato, *m.* duck.—*pagar el p.,* to get the blame, be the scapegoat.

patochada, *f.* blunder; nonsense.

patología, *f.* pathology.—**patológico,** *a.* pathological.

patoso, *a.* (coll.) boring; awkward.

patraña, *f.* fabulous story; fake, humbug.

patria, *f.* native country, fatherland.

patrio, *a.* native; home.—**patriota,** *mf.* patriot.—**patriótico,** *a.* patriotic. —**patriotismo,** *m.* patriotism.

patrocinar, *vt.* to sponsor; to protect, favor.—**patrocinio,** *m.* sponsorship, auspices; protection, patronage.— **patrón,** *n.* patron(ess); host(ess); landlord (-lady); patron saint.—*m.* master, boss; pattern; standard; (naut.) skipper.—**patronato,** *m.* board of trustees; employers' association; foundation.—**patrono,** *n.* patron, protector; trustee; employer; patron saint.

patrulla, *f.* patrol; gang, squad.— **patrullar,** *vt.* to patrol.

paulatino, *a.* slow, gradual.

pausa, *f.* pause; rest, repose.—**pausado,** *a.* slow, calm, quiet.—*adv.* slowly.

pauta, *f.* guide lines; standard, rule, pattern.

pava, *f.* turkey hen; (Am.) joke, fun.—*pelar la p.,* to carry on a flirtation.

pavesa, *f.* embers, hot cinders.—*pl.* ashes.

pavimentación, *f.* paving; pavement. —**pavimentar,** *vt.* to pave.—**pavimento,** *m.* pavement.

pavo, *m.* turkey; gobbler.—*p. real,* peacock.—*p. silvestre,* wood grouse. —**pavonearse,** *vr.* to strut, show off.

pavor, *m.* fear, fright.—**pavoroso,** *a.* awful, frightful, terrible.

payasada, *f.* clownish joke or action. —**payaso,** *m.* clown.

paz, *f.* peace.—*en p.,* quits, even.

pazguato, *n.* dolt, simpleton.

peaje, *m.* (bridge, road, etc.) toll.

peana, *f.* pedestal stand; (mech.)

ground plate; step before an altar.

peatón, *m.* pedestrian, walker.

peca, *f.* freckle.

pecado, *m.* sin.—*p. capital, grave,* or *mortal,* deadly or mortal sin.— **pecador,** *n. & a.* sinner; sinning.— **pecaminoso,** *a.* sinful.—**pecar,** *vii.* [d] to sin.—*p. de listo,* to be too wise.

pececillo, *m.* minnow, little fish.

pecera, *f.* fishbowl, fish tank; aquarium.

pecoso, *a.* freckled.

peculado, *m.* (law) embezzlement.

peculiar, *a.* peculiar.—**peculiaridad,** *f.* peculiarity.

peculio, *m.* private property.

pechera, *f.* shirt bosom; shirt frill; chest protector; breast strap (of a harness).—**pecho,** *m.* chest, thorax; breast; bosom; teat; courage.— *abrir el p.,* to unbosom oneself.— *dar el p.,* to nurse, suckle; (coll.) to face it out.—*tomar a p.,* to take to heart.—**pechuga,** *f.* breast of a fowl; slope; (coll.) bosom.

pedagogía, *f.* pedagogy.—**pedagógico,** *a.* pedagogical.—**pedagogo,** *n.* pedagogue; teacher; educator.

pedal, *m.* pedal; (mech.) treadle.

pedazo, *m.* piece, fragment, bit.—*a pedazos,* or *en pedazos,* in bits, in fragments.

pedernal, *m.* flint.

pedestal, *m.* pedestal; stand; base.

pedestre, *a.* pedestrian; low, vulgar, common.

pedicuro, *n.* chiropodist.

pedido, *m.* demand, call; (com.) order.—**pedigüeño,** *a.* persistent in begging.—**pedir,** *vti.* [29] to ask for, request, beg, solicit; to demand; to wish, desire; to require; (com.) to order; to ask for in marriage.—*a p. de boca,* just right.—*p. prestado,* to borrow.

pedrada, *f.* throw of a stone; blow or hit with a stone.—**pedrea,** *f.* stone-throwing, stoning; hailstorm.— **pedregal,** *m.* stony ground.—**pedregoso,** *a.* stony, rocky.—**pedrería,** *f.* precious stones; jewelry.—**pedrusco,** *m.* rough piece of stone.

pega, *f.* joining, cementing together; (coll.) jest, practical joke; (ichth.) remora.—**pegajoso,** *a.* sticky; catching, contagious.—**pegar,** *vti.* [b] to stick, glue, cement; to fasten; to post (bills); to sew on; to pin; to patch; to attach; to infect with; to hit, beat, slap.—*no p. los ojos,* not to sleep a wink.—*p. fuego a,* to set fire to.—*p. un tiro,* to shoot.—*vii.* to make an impression on the mind; to join; to be contiguous; to fit, match; to be becoming, fitting, appropriate.—*esa no pega*, (coll.) that won't go.—*vri.* to stick; adhere.—**pegote**, *m.* sticking plaster; coarse patch; sponger.

peina, *f.* = PEINETA.—**peinado**, *m.* hairdo.—**peinador**, *n.* hairdresser.— *m.* dressing gown, wrapper.—**peinar**, *vt.* to comb or dress (the hair); to touch or rub slightly.—**peine**, *m.* comb.—**peineta**, *f.* ornamental shell comb (to wear in the hair).

peladilla, *f.* sugar almond; small pebble.

pelado, *a.* plucked; bared; peeled, stripped; hairless; treeless, bare; penniless, broke.—*n.* penniless person.—*m.* Mexican peasant; haircut. —**peladura**, *f.* paring, peeling.— **pelafustán**, *m.* (coll.) nobody, idler, vagrant.—**pelagatos**, *m.* nincompoop, poor wretch.—**pelaje**, *m.* character or nature of the hair or wool; disposition.—**pelar**, *vt.* to cut the hair of; to pluck; to skin, peel, husk, shell; to cheat, rob; to break the bank.—*duro de p.*, exceedingly difficult, hard to crack.—*vr.* to get one's hair cut; to peel off, flake; to lose the hair (as from illness).

peldaño, *m.* step of a staircase.

pelea, *f.* fight; scuffle, quarrel.—**pelear**, *vi.* to fight; to quarrel; to struggle. —*vr.* to scuffle, come to blows.

pelele, *m.* stuffed figure, dummy; puppet; nincompoop.

peletería, *f.* furrier's trade or shop; (Am.) leather goods or shop; furrier.—**peletero**, *n.* furrier; (Am.) dealer in leather goods; skinner.

peliagudo, *a.* (coll.) arduous, difficult.

pelícano, *m.* pelican.

película, *f.* film; moving picture reel; moving picture.

peligrar, *vi.* to be in danger.—**peligro**, *m.* danger, peril.—*correr p.*, to be in danger.—**peligroso**, *a.* dangerous, perilous, risky.

pelillo, *m.* fine hair; trifle, slight trouble.—*echar pelillos a la mar*, to become reconciled.—**pelirrojo**, *a.* red-haired, red-headed.—**pelirrubio**, *a.* blond, light-haired.

pelmazo, *m.* crushed or flattened mass; undigested food in the stomach; nuisance, sluggard.

pelo, *m.* hair; fiber, filament; nap, pile (of cloth); hairspring (in watches and firearms); grain (in wood).—*de medio p.*, of little account; would-be important.—*de p. en pecho*, brave, daring.—*en p.*, bareback; unsaddled.—*no tener p. de tonto*, to be bright, quick, clever. —*no tener pelos en la lengua*, to

be outspoken.—*tomar el p. a*, to make fun of, pull one's leg.—*venir al p.*, to be to the point, fit the case to a tee.—**pelón**, *a.* hairless, bald.

pelota, *f.* ball; ball game; (Am.) baseball (game).—*en p.*, entirely naked; penniless.—**pelotazo**, *m.* blow or stroke with a ball.—**pelotear**, *vi.* to play ball; to throw (as a ball); to argue, dispute.—**pelotera**, *f.* quarrel, tumult, riot.—**pelotero**, *m.* (Am.) baseball player.—**pelotilla**, *f.* small ball; pellet.—**pelotón**, *m.* large ball; (mil.) platoon.

peluca, *f.* wig, toupee.—**peludo**, *a.* hairy, shaggy.—*m.* shaggy mat.— **peluquería**, *f.* hairdressing shop; barber shop.—**peluquero**, *n.* hairdresser; barber.—**pelusa**, *f.* down; floss, fuzz, nap; (coll.) envy.

pelleja, *f.* skin, hide.—**pellejo**, *m.* skin; rawhide; peel, rind.—*jugarse el p.*, to risk one's life.

pellizcar, *vti.* [d] to pinch; to nip; to clip.—**pellizco**, *m.* pinch, pinching; nip; small bit.

pena, *f.* penalty; punishment; affliction, sorrow, grief; (Am.) embarrassment.—*a duras penas*, with great difficulty, just barely.—*estar con (mucha) p.*, to be (very) sorry. —*merecer la p.*, to be worthwhile.

penacho, *m.* tuft of feathers, plumes, crest.

penado, *n.* convict.—**penal**, *m.* penitentiary, prison.—*a.* penal.—**penalidad**, *f.* trouble, hardship; (law) penalty.—**penalizar**, *vti.* [a] to penalize.—**penar**, *vi.* to suffer; to crave, long for.—*vt.* to impose penalty on.

penco, *m.* swaybacked nag.

pendencia, *f.* quarrel, fight.—**pendenciero**, *a.* quarrelsome, rowdy.

pender, *vi.* to hang, dangle; to be pending or suspended.—**pendiente**, *a.* pendent, hanging; dangling; pending.—*m.* earring, pendant; watch chain.—*f.* slope.

pendón, *m.* standard, banner.

péndulo, *m.* pendulum.

pene, *m.* penis.

penetración, *f.* penetration, penetrating; acuteness, sagacity.—**penetrante**, *a.* penetrating; keen, acute; deep.—**penetrar**, *vt.* to penetrate, pierce; to break or force in; to fathom, comprehend.

penicilina, *f.* penicillin.

península, *f.* peninsula.—**peninsular**, *a.* inhabiting or pert. to a peninsula.

penitencia, *f.* penitence; penance.— **penitenciaría**, *f.* penitentiary.—

penitente, *a.* penitent, repentant.— *mf.* penitent.

penoso, *a.* painful; laborious, arduous; distressing; embarrassing.

pensado, *a.* deliberate, premeditated. —*bien* p., wise, proper.—*mal* p., unwise, foolish.—*tener* p., to have in view, to intend.—**pensador,** *n.* thinker.—**pensamiento,** *m.* mind; thought, idea; thinking; epigram, maxim; (bot.) pansy.—**pensar,** *vii.* [1] to think; to reflect.—*vti.* to think over, or about, consider; to intend, contemplate.—**pensativo,** *a.* pensive, thoughtful.

pensión, *f.* pension; boarding-house; board; fellowship for study abroad. —**pensionado,** *n.* pensioner, pensionary; fellow (study).—**pensionar,** *vt.* to impose or to grant pensions on or to.—**pensionista,** *mf.* boarder, pensioner.

pentagrama, *m.* (mus.) ruled staff.

Pentecostés, *m.* Pentecost.

penúltimo, *a.* next to the last.

penumbra, *f.* dimness.

pabellón, *m.* pavilion; national colors, flag; (anat.) external ear.

penuria, *f.* destitution, indigence.

peña, *f.* rock; boulder.—**peñasco,** *m.* large rock.—**peñascoso,** *a.* rocky.— **peñón,** *m.* large rock; rocky cliff.

peón, *m.* day laborer; foot soldier; spinning top; pawn (in chess); pedestrian.

peonía, *f.* (bot.) peony.

peonza, *f.* top (toy).

peor, *adv.* & *a.* worse; worst.

pepa, *f.* (Am.) seed, stone, pit.

pepino, *m.* cucumber.—*no importarle un* p., not to give a fig.

pepita, *f.* pip or seed of fruit; nugget.

pequeñez, *f.* smallness; childhood; trifle; pettiness; mean act or conduct.—**pequeño,** *a.* little, small; of tender age; lowly, humble.—*n.* child.

pera, *f.* (bot.) pear; goatee.—*pedir peras al olmo,* to expect the impossible.—**peral,** *m.* pear tree.

percal, *m.* percale, calico.

percance, *m.* misfortune; mishap.

percatar, *vi.* & *vr.* to think, consider; to beware.—*p. de,* to notice.

percepción, *f.* perception.—**perceptible,** *a.* perceptible, perceivable.— **percibir,** *vt.* to perceive; to receive, collect.

percudir, *vt.* to tarnish, stain, soil.

percusión, *f.* percussion; collision.

percha, *f.* perch, pole; hat or clothes rack; roost; snare for birds.—**perchero,** *m.* clothes rack or hanger.

perdedor, *n.* loser.—**perder,** *vti.* [18] to lose; to forfeit; to squander

away; to ruin; to miss (train, opportunity, etc.).—*echar a* p., to spoil, ruin.—*p. los estribos,* to lose one's poise; to become reckless.— *¡pierda Ud. cuidado!* don't worry! forget it!—*vii.* to lose.—*vri.* to get lost, lose one's way; to miscarry; to be lost, confounded; to be ruined; to go astray; to be spoiled or damaged (as fruits, crops, etc.); to disappear.—*perderse de vista,* to get out of sight; to be very shrewd. —**pérdida,** *f.* loss; detriment, damage; waste; (com.) leakage.—**perdidamente,** *adv.* desperately; uselessly.—**perdido,** *a.* lost; mislaid; misguided; profligate, dissolute.—*m.* (fig.) black sheep.

perdigón, *m.* young partridge; buckshot; pellet.—**perdigonada,** *f.* peppering of buckshot.—**perdiguero,** *n.* setter, retriever (dog).—**perdiz,** *f.* partridge.

perdón, *m.* pardon, forgiveness; remission.—*interj.* pardon! excuse me! —*con* p., by your leave.—**perdonar,** *vt.* to pardon, forgive; to remit (a debt); to excuse.

perdulario, *a.* reckless, heedless.—*n.* good-for-nothing, ne'er-do-well.

perdurable, *a.* lasting, everlasting.— **perdurar,** *vi.* to last long.

perecedero, *a.* perishable, not lasting. —**perecer,** *vii.* [3] to perish.

peregrinación, *f.,* **peregrinaje,** *m.* traveling; pilgrimage.—**peregrinar,** *vi.* to travel, roam.—**peregrino,** *a.* foreign; traveling, migratory; strange, odd, rare.—*n.* pilgrim.

perejil, *m.* parsley.

perenne, *a.* perennial, perpetual.

perentorio, *a.* urgent, decisive; peremptory.

pereza, *f.* laziness; slowness, idleness. —**perezoso,** *a.* lazy, indolent, idle. —*m.* (zool.) sloth.

perfección, *f.* perfection; perfect thing.—*a la* p., perfectly.—**perfeccionamiento,** *m.* perfecting, improvement, finish.—**perfeccionar,** *vt.* to improve, perfect.—**perfecto,** *a.* perfect.

perfil, *m.* profile, side view; outline.— **perfilar,** *vt.* to outline, profile.—*vr.* to place oneself sideways; to dress carefully.

perforación, *f.* perforation, hole, puncture; drilling, boring.—**perforador,** *a.* & *n.* perforator, driller; perforating, drilling.—**perforadora,** *f.* drill, rock drill.—**perforar,** *vt.* to perforate; to bore, drill.

perfumar, *vt.* to perfume.—**perfume,** *m.* perfume.—**perfumería,** *f.* perfumery; perfumer's shop.—**perfu-mista**, *mf.* perfumer.

pergamino, *m.* parchment, vellum; diploma.

pericia, *f.* skill, expertness.

perico, *n.* parakeet; small parrot.

perifollos, *m. pl.* ribbons, tawdry ornaments of dress.

perilla, *f.* small pear; pear-shaped ornament; knob; pommel of a saddle; goatee; lobe of the ear.—*de p.*, to the purpose.

perillán, *n.* rascal; sly, crafty person.

perimetro, *m.* perimeter.

periódico, *a.* periodic(al).—*m.* newspaper; periodical, journal.—**periodismo**, *m.* journalism.—**periodista**, *mf.* journalist.—**periodístico**, *a.* journalistic.—**período**, *m.* period, age; sentence; menstruation, period; (elec.) cycle; (pol.) term, tenure.

peripecia, *f.* situation, incident, episode.

peripuesto, *a.* dolled up; dressy.

periquete, *m.* (coll.) jiffy, instant.

periquito, *m.* parakeet, lovebird.

periscopio, *m.* periscope.

peritaje, *m.* expertness; appraisal.—**perito**, *a.* skillful, able, experienced.—*n.* expert; appraiser.

perjudicar, *vti.* [d] to damage, impair, harm.—**perjudicial**, *a.* harmful.—**perjuicio**, *m.* damage.

perjurar, *vi.* to commit perjury; to swear.—*vr.* to perjure oneself.—**perjurio**, *m.* perjury.—**perjuro**, *a.* perjured, forsworn.—*n.* forswearer, perjurer.

perla, *f.* pearl; (fig.) jewel.—*de perlas*, perfectly; to a tee.

permanecer, *vii.* [3] to stay, remain.—**permanencia**, *f.* stay, sojourn; duration, permanence.—**permanente**, *a.* permanent.—*f.* permanent (in hair).

permeable, *a.* porous, permeable; not waterproof.

permisible, *a.* permissible.—**permiso**, *m.* permission; permit.—*¡con p.!* excuse me!—**permitir**, *vt.* to permit, allow, let; to grant, admit.

permuta, *f.* barter; exchange.—**permutar**, *vt. & vi.* to exchange, barter.

pernera, *f.* trouser leg.—**perneta**, *f.*—*en pernetas*, barelegged.

pernicioso, *a.* pernicious; harmful.

pernil, *m.* hock (of animals).

perno, *m.* nut and bolt; spike; joint pin.

pernoctar, *vi.* to pass the night.

pero, *conj.* but; except; yet.—*m.* (coll.) fault, defect.—*poner pero(s)*, to find fault.

perogrullada, *f.* (coll.) obvious truth, truism; platitude.

perol, *m.* kettle.

peroración, *f.* peroration.—**perorar**, *vi.* to deliver a speech or oration; to declaim.—**perorata**, *f.* (coll.) harangue, speech.

perpendicular, *f. & a.* perpendicular.

perpetrar, *vt.* to perpetrate, commit (a crime).

perpetuar, *vt. & vr.* to perpetuate.—**perpetuidad**, *f.* perpetuity.—**perpetuo**, *a.* perpetual, everlasting.

perplejidad, *f.* perplexity; quandary.—**perplejo**, *a.* uncertain, perplexed.

perra, *f.* bitch, female dog; slut; drunken state; tantrum.—**perrada**, *f.* mean, base action.—**perrera**, *f.* kennel.—**perrería**, *f.* pack of dogs; angry word; vile action.—**perro**, *m.* dog.—*p. de aguas* or *de lanas*, poodle.—*p. de presa*, or *dogo*, bulldog.—*p. viejo*, (coll.) cautious person; experienced person.—**perruno**, *a.* doggish, canine; currish.

persa, *a. & n.* Persian.

persecución, *f.* persecution; pursuit.—**perseguidor**, *n.* persecutor; pursuer.—**perseguir**, *vti.* [29-b] to pursue; to persecute.

perseverancia, *f.* perseverance.—**perseverante**, *a.* persevering.—**perseverar**, *vi.* to persevere, persist.

persiana, *f.* blind, shutter.

persignarse, *vr.* to cross oneself.

persistencia, *f.* persistence; obstinacy.—**persistente**, *a.* persistent; firm.—**persistir**, *vi.* to persist.

persona, *f.* person.—*en p.*, in person, personally.—**personaje**, *m.* personage; (theat., lit.) character.—**personal**, *a.* personal, private.—*m.* personnel, staff.—**personalidad**, *f.* personality; individuality; (law) person; legal capacity.—**personalizar**, *vti.* [a] to personalize; to become personal.—**personarse**, *vr.* to appear personally; (law) to appear as an interested party.—**personificar**, *vti.* [d] to personify.

perspectiva, *f.* perspective; view; prospect, outlook; appearance.

perspicacia, *f.* perspicacity, sagacity.—**perspicaz**, *a.* acute, sagacious, clear-sighted.

persuadir, *vt.* to persuade.—*vr.* to be persuaded.—**persuasión**, *f.* persuasion.—**persuasivo**, *a.* persuasive.

pertenecer, *vii.* [3] to belong, pertain; to concern.—**perteneciente**, *a.* belonging, pertaining.—**pertenencia**, *f.* possession, holding property.

pértiga, *f.* bar, pole, rod.

pertinente, *a.* pertinent, apt; (law) concerning, pertaining.

pertrechar, *vt.* & *vr.* (mil.) to supply, store, equip; to arrange, prepare.—**pertrechos,** *m. pl.* (mil.) stores; tools.

perturbación, *f.* perturbation, disturbance; agitation.—**perturbar,** *vt.* to perturb, disturb, unsettle; to confuse.

peruano, *n.* & *a.* Peruvian.

perversidad, *f.* perversity, wickedness. —**perversión,** *f.* perversion, perverting; depravity, wickedness.—**perverso,** *a.* perverse, wicked, depraved. —*n.* pervert.—**pervertir,** *vti.* [39] to pervert; to corrupt.—*vri.* to become depraved.

pesa, *f.* weight (in scales, clocks).— *pl.* bar bells.—**pesadez,** *f.* heaviness; slowness; drowsiness; trouble, pain, fatigue.—**pesadilla,** *f.* nightmare.— **pesado,** *a.* heavy; deep, sound (sleep); stuffy (air, atmosphere); cumbersome; tedious, tiresome; dull; slow; clumsy; fat, corpulent; importunate, annoying.—*n.* bore, tease.—**pesadumbre,** *f.* grief, affliction, sorrow; heaviness.—**pésame,** *m.* condolence, sympathy.—**pesantez,** *f.* gravity; heaviness.—**pesar,** *vi.* to weigh, have weight; to be weighty or important; to cause regret, sorrow or repentance; to preponderate. —*vt.* to weigh; to examine, consider.—*m.* sorrow, grief, regret; repentance.—*a p. de,* in spite of, notwithstanding.—*a p. mío,* or *a mi p.,* in spite of me, against my wishes.— **pesaroso,** *a.* sorrowful, regretful; sorry, sad.

pesca, *f.* fishing; fishery; catch, fish caught.—**pescadería,** *f.* fish market. —**pescadero,** *n.* fishmonger.—**pescado,** *m.* fish (caught).—**pescador,** *n.* fisherman, fisher.—**pescar,** *vti.* [d] & *vii.* to fish; to catch fish.— *vti.* to find or pick up; to catch in the act, surprise.

pescozón, *m.* slap on the neck.— **pescuezo,** *m.* neck; throat.

pesebre, *m.* manger; crib, rack.

pesimismo, *m.* pessimism.—**pesimista,** *mf.* & *a.* pessimist(ic).—**pésimo,** *a.* very bad, very worst.

peso, *m.* weight, heaviness; weighing; importance; burden, load; judgment, good sense; peso, monetary unit.—*caerse de su p.,* to be self-evident; to go without saying.—*en p.,* suspended in the air; bodily; totally.

pespunte, *m.* backstitching.

pesquería, *f.* fishing, fishing trip.— **pesquero,** *f.* fishing.

pesquisa, *f.* inquiry, investigation, search.

pestaña, *f.* eyelash; (sewing) fringe, edging; (mech.) flange.—*quemarse las pestañas,* to burn the midnight oil.—**pestañear,** *vi.* to wink; to blink.—**pestañeo,** *m.* winking; blinking.

peste, *f.* pest, plague, pestilence; epidemic; foul smell, stink; (coll.) excess, superabundance.—*pl.* offensive words.—**pestilencia,** *f.* pest, plague, pestilence; foulness, stench. —**pestilente,** *a.* pestilent, foul.

pestillo, *m.* door latch; bolt of a lock.

petaca, *f.* cigar case; (Am.) leather trunk or chest; (Am.) suitcase.

pétalo, *m.* petal.

petardo, *m.* (artil.) petard; bomb.

petate, *m.* (Am.) sleeping mat; (coll.) luggage, baggage.—*liar el p.,* (coll.) to pack up and go.

petición, *f.* petition, request.

petimetre, *m.* fop, coxcomb, beau.

petirrojo, *m.* robin.

pétreo, *a.* rocky; stony, of stone.

petróleo, *m.* crude oil, (fuel, gas or diesel) oil.—**petrolero,** *a.* oil.—*n.* person in the oil industry, oil man; incendiary.—*m.* (naut.) oil tanker.

petulancia, *f.* petulance; insolence; flippancy.—**petulante,** *a.* petulant, insolent, pert.

petunia, *f.* petunia.

pez, *m.* fish (not caught).—*f.* pitch, tar.

pezón, *m.* stem of fruits; leaf stalk; nipple of a teat.

pezuña, *f.* hoof.

piada, *f.* chirping, peeping, peep.

piadoso, *a.* pious, godly; merciful.

piafar, *vi.* (of horses) to paw, to stamp.

pianista, *mf.* pianist.—**piano,** *m.* piano.—*p. de cola,* grand piano.

piar, *vi.* to peep, chirp.

piara, *f.* herd (of swine).

pica, *f.* pike, lance; stonecutter's hammer.—*poner una p. en Flandes,* to achieve a triumph.

picacho, *m.* top, peak, summit.

picada, *f.* pricking, bite; (aer.) dive; diving.—**picadero,** *m.* riding school. —**picadillo,** *m.* hash, minced meat.— **picador,** *m.* horse-breaker; horseman armed with a goad in bull-fights; chopping block; paper pricker.—**picadura,** *f.* pricking; pinking; puncture; bite; sting; pipe tobacco.—**picante,** *a.* pricking, piercing; biting; spicy, racy, highly seasoned.—*m.* piquancy, pungency, acrimony.—**picapleitos,** *m.* shyster, pettifogger; (coll.) litigious person.

picaporte, *m.* spring latch; latchkey; (Am.) door knocker.

picar, *vti.* [d] to prick, pierce, puncture; to sting, bite (as insects); to mince, chop, hash; (of birds) to peck; (of fish) to bite; to nibble, pick at; to spur, goad, incite; to pique, vex.—*vii.* to sting, bite (as insects); (of fish) to bite; to itch, burn; to scorch, burn (as the sun); (aer.) to dive.—*p. alto,* to aim high. —*vri.* to be offended or piqued; to be moth-eaten; to stale, sour (as wine); to begin to rot (as fruit); to begin to decay (of teeth, etc.); (naut.) (of the sea) to get choppy.

picardía, *f.* knavery, roguery; malice, foulness; wanton trick, wantonness; lewdness.—**picaresco,** *a.* roguish, knavish, picaresque.—**pícaro,** *a.* knavish, roguish; vile, low; mischievous; crafty, sly.—*n.* rogue, knave, rascal.—**picarón,** *n.* great rogue, rascal.

picazón, *f.* itching, itch.

pico, *m.* beak or bill of a bird; sharp point; pick, pickaxe; spout; peak, top, summit; small balance of an account; (coll.) mouth; loquaciousness; (coll.) a lot of cash. —*costar un p.,* to be very expensive.—*p. de oro,* man of great eloquence.—*treinta y p.,* thirty odd.

picota, *f.* pillory, stocks; top, peak, point.

picotada, *f.,* **picotazo,** *m.* blow with the beak, peck.—**picotear,** *vt. & vi.* to strike with a beak, to peck; (Am.) to cut into small pieces.

pictórico, *a.* pictorial.

pichón, *m.* young pigeon, squab.—*n.* (coll.) darling, dearest.

pie, *m.* foot; leg, stand, support, base; foot, bottom (of a page); motive, occasion.—*al p.,* near, close to; at the foot.—*al p. de la letra,* literally, exactly.—*a p.,* on foot.— *a p. juntillas,* firmly; most emphatically.—*de p.,* standing.—*en p.* = DE PIE; pending, undecided.—*p. de amigo,* prop, shore.—*p. de imprenta,* imprint, printer's mark.

piedad, *f.* piety; mercy.

piedra, *f.* stone; cobblestone; (med.) gravel; hail.—*no dejar p. sobre p.,* to raze to the ground, to destroy entirely.—*p. angular,* cornerstone.— *p. de amolar* or *de afilar,* whetstone, grinding stone.—*p. falsa,* imitation (precious) stone.—*p. pómez,* pumice.

piel, *f.* skin; hide; leather; fur.

pienso, *m.* fodder.

pierna, *f.* leg.—*dormir a p. suelta,* to sleep soundly.

pieza, *f.* piece; part (of a machine, etc.); bolt or roll of cloth; room

(in a house); (theat.) play.—*de una p.,* solid, in one piece.

pifia, *f.* miscue at billiards; error, blunder.

pigmento, *m.* pigment.

pigmeo, *a.* dwarfish.—*n.* pygmy, dwarf.

pignorar, *vt.* to pledge, give as security.

pijama, *m.* or *f.* pajama.

pila, *f.* sink; (eccl.) font, holy water basin; pile, heap; stone trough or basin; (elec.) battery, cell.—*nombre de p.,* Christian or given name. —**pilar,** *m.* pillar, column, post; basin of a fountain.

píldora, *f.* pill, pellet.

pileta, *f.* (Am.) swimming pool.

pilón, *m.* mortar (for pounding); loaf (of sugar); watering trough; basin of a fountain; rider, sliding weight of a balance).—*de p.,* to boot, in addition.

pilote, *m.* (eng.) pile.

pilot(e)ar, *vt.* to pilot.—**piloto,** *m.* (naut., aer.) pilot, navigator.

piltrafa, *f.* skinny flesh; hide parings.—*pl.* scraps of food.

pillaje, *m.* pillage, plunder, marauding.—**pillar,** *vt.* to pillage, rifle, plunder; (coll.) to catch, grasp.— **pillería,** *f.* gang of rogues; piece of rascality.—**pillo,** *a.* roguish, knavish; shrewd, sly.—*n.* knave, rogue, rascal; petty thief.—**pilluelo,** *n.* little rogue, urchin.

pimentón, *m.* Cayenne or red pepper; paprika.—**pimienta,** *f.* pepper (spice).—**pimiento,** *m.* pepper (vegetable).

pimpollo, *m.* rosebud; spruce, lively youth; sprout, shoot.

pináculo, *m.* pinnacle, summit.

pinar, *m.* pine grove.

pincel, *m.* fine paintbrush.—**pincelada,** *f.* stroke with a brush, touch.

pinchar, *vt.* to prick, puncture, pierce.—**pinchazo,** *m.* prick, puncture, stab.

pinche, *m.* kitchen boy.

pincho, *m.* thorn, prickle; goad; skewer.

pingajo, *m.* (coll.) rag, tatter.— **pingo,** *m.* rag; (Am.) saddle horse. —*pl.* worthless clothes, duds.

pingüe, *a.* plentiful; fat, greasy, oily.

pingüino, *m.* penguin.

pino, *m.* pine.

pin-pón, *m.* ping-pong.

pinta, *f.* spot, mark; appearance, aspect; drop; pint. (See Table.)

pintada, *f.* (Am.) mackerel; guinea hen.

pintar, *vt.* to paint; to picture; to describe, portray; to fancy, imagine.—*vi.* to begin to ripen; to show, give signs of.—*vr.* to make up (one's face).—**pintarrajear,** *vt.* (coll.) to daub.

pintiparado, *a.* perfectly like, closely resembling; pat, fit.

pinto, *a.* (Am.) pinto, spotted.—**pintor,** *n.* painter.—*p. de brocha gorda,* house or sign painter; dauber.—**pintoresco,** *a.* picturesque.—**pintura,** *f.* painting; (art) picture, painting; color, paint, pigment; portrayal, description.

pinzas, *f.* tweezers, pincers; claws (of lobsters, etc.).

piña, *f.* pineapple; pine cone; cluster, gathering; game of pool.—**piñón,** *m.* the edible nut of the nut pine; (mech.) pinion.

pío, *a.* pious; mild, merciful.—*m.* peeping of chickens.

piojo, *m.* louse.—**piojoso,** *a.* lousy.

pionero, *n.* (neol.) pioneer.

pipa, *f.* cask, butt, hogshead; fruit seed; tobacco pipe.—**pipote,** *m.* keg.

pique, *m.* pique, resentment.—*a p. de,* in danger of, on the point of.—*echar a p.,* to sink (a ship).—*irse a p.,* (naut.) to founder, sink; fall.

piqueta, *f.* pickaxe; mason's hammer.

piquete, *m.* pricking; sting; small hole; stake, picket; (mil.) picket.

pira, *f.* pyre, funeral pile.

piragua, *f.* dugout, canoe.

pirámide, *f.* pyramid.

pirata, *m.* pirate.—**piratear,** *vi.* to pirate.—**piratería,** *f.* piracy.

piropear, *vt. & vi.* (coll.) to flatter; to compliment.—**piropo,** *m.* (coll.) flattery; compliment.

pirulí, *m.* lollipop.

pisada, *f.* footstep; footprint; treading.—**pisapapeles,** *m.* paperweight.—**pisar,** *vt.* to tread on, trample, step on; to press; to press on; to stamp on the ground.

pisaverde, *m.* (coll.) fop, oxcomb, dude.

piscina, *f.* swimming pool; fishpond.

piscolabis, *m.* (coll.) snack.

piso, *m.* floor; pavement, flooring; loft, flat, apartment; ground level; story; (Am.) fee for pasturage rights.—*p. bajo,* ground floor.—*p. principal,* second floor, first living floor.—**pisotear,** *vt.* to trample, tread under foot.—**pisotón,** *m.* heavy step or stamp of the foot.

pista, *f.* trail, track, trace, clue; race track, race course; circus ring; dancing floor; tennis court; (aer.) runway; landing strip.

pistilo, *m.* (bot.) pistil.

pistola, *f.* pistol.—**pistolera,** *f.* holster.—**pistoletazo,** *m.* pistol shot.

pistón, *m.* (mech.) piston; (mus.) piston of a brass instrument.

pita, *f.* agave plant, maguey; string, cord.

pitada, *f.* blow of a whistle.

pitanza, *f.* pittance; (coll.) daily food; salary.

pitar, *vi.* to blow a whistle; to hiss.—**pitazo,** *m.* sound or blast of a whistle.

pitillera, *f.* cigarette case.—**pitillo,** *m.* cigarette.

pito, *m.* whistle; (coll.) cigarette.—*no me importa* or *no se me da* or *me importa un p.,* (coll.) I don't care a bit.—*no tocar pitos en,* to have no part in.

pitón, *m.* (of deer, etc.) horn just starting to grow; spout, nozzle.

pivote, *m.* (mech.) king pin; pivot.

piyama, *m.* or *f.* = PIJAMA.

pizarra, *f.* slate; blackboard.—**pizarrín,** *m.* slate pencil.—**pizarrón,** *m.* blackboard.

pizca, *f.* (coll.) mite, speck, sprinkling, crumb, particle.

placa, *f.* plate; badge insignia; plaque, tablet.

pláceme, *m.* congratulation.

placentero, *a.* joyful, pleasant.—**placer,** *vti.* [30] to please.—*m.* pleasure.

placero, *a.* pertaining to the market-place.—*n.* seller at a market; gadder.

plácido, *a.* placid, quiet, calm.

plaga, *f.* plague; calamity; scourge; pest.—**plagar,** *vti.* [b] to plague, infest.—*vri.* (de) to be full of, infested with.

plagiar, *vt.* to plagiarize; (Am.) to kidnap.—**plagiario,** *n. & a.* plagiarist; plagiarizing.—**plagio,** *m.* plagiarism; (Am.) kidnapping.

plan, *m.* plan; design, scheme.—*p. de estudios,* curriculum.

plana, *f.* page; copy; level ground, plain; (mason.) trowel.—*enmendar la p a,* to find fault with, criticize.—*p. mayor,* (mil.) staff.

plancha, *f.* plate, sheet; slab; flat-iron, iron; (coll.) blunder, boner; (naut.) gangplank; photographic plate.—**planchador,** *n.* ironer.—**planchar,** *vt.* to iron, to press.

planeador, *m.* (aer.) glider.—**planear,** *vt. & vi.* to plan, design.—*vi.* (aer.) to glide.

planeta, *m.* planet.—**planetario,** *a.* planetary.—*m.* planetarium.

planicie, *f.* plain.

planilla, *f.* (Am.) list; payroll; (Mex.) list of candidates; ticket; (Cuba) application form, blank.

plano, *a.* plane; level; smooth, even.

—*m.* plan, blueprint; map; flat (of a sword, etc.); (geom.) plane; (aer.) plane, wing.—*de p.*, openly, clearly; flatly.—*primer p.*, foreground.

planta, *f.* sole of the foot; (bot.) plant; (eng.) plan, horizontal projection, top view; plant, works; site of a building.—**plantación**, *f.* plantation; planting.—**plantar**, *vt.* (agr.) to plant; to erect, set up, fix upright; to strike (a blow); to set, put, place; to leave in the lurch, disappoint; to jilt.—*vr.* (coll.) to stand upright; to stop, halt, balk.

plantear, *vt.* to plan, try; to put into action; to state or tackle (a problem); to raise (an issue).

plantel, *m.* nursery, nursery garden; establishment, plant; educational institution.

plantilla, *f.* first sole, insole (shoes); model, pattern; roster, staff; plan, design.

plantío, *m.* planting; plot, bed.

plañidero, *a.* mournful, weeping, moaning.—**plañido**, *m.* moan, lamentation, crying.—**plañir**, *vii.* [41] to lament, grieve; to whimper.

plasma, *m.* plasma.—**plasmar**, *vt.* to mold, shape.

plasta, *f.* soft mass; anything flattened; (coll.) anything poorly wrought.

plasticidad, *f.* plasticity.—**plástico**, *a.* & *m.* plastic.

plata, *f.* silver; silver coin; (Am.) money.—*en p.*, in plain language.

plataforma, *f.* platform.

platal, *m.* great quantity of money, great wealth.

platanal, **platanar**, *m.* banana grove or plantation.—**plátano**, *m.* banana (plant and fruit).

platea, *f.* (theat.) orchestra; pit.

platear, *vt.* to silver, plate with silver.—**platería**, *f.* silversmith's shop or trade.—**platero**, *m.* silversmith; jeweler.

plática, *f.* talk, chat, conversation; address, lecture; sermon.—**platicar**, *vii.* [d] to converse, talk, chat.

platillo, *m.* saucer; pan (of a balance); cymbal.

platino, *m.* platinum.

plato, *m.* dish, plate; dinner course.

platónico, *a.* Platonic.—**platonismo**, *m.* Platonism.

plausible, *a.* plausible.

playa, *f.* beach, shore.

plaza, *f.* plaza, square; marketplace; (com.) emporium, market; room, space; office, position, employment.

—*p. de toros*, bull ring, arena.—*sentar p.*, to enlist.

plazo, *m.* term, time, date, day of payment; credit.—*a plazos*, in installments, on credit.

plazoleta, **plazuela**, *f.* small square.

pleamar, *f.* high water, high tide.

plebe, *f.* common people, populace.—**plebeyo**, *n.* & *a.* plebeian.—**plebiscito**, *m.* (pol.) plebiscite; referendum.

plegable, **plegadizo**, *a.* pliable, folding.—**plegadura**, *f.* plait, fold; plaiting, folding, doubling; crease.—**plegar**, *vti.* [1-b] to fold; to plait; to crease.—*vri.* to fold; to bend; to submit, yield.

plegaria, *f.* prayer, supplication.

pleitear, *vi.* to plead, litigate; to wrangle.—**pleitista**, *mf.* litigious person.—*a.* litigious.—**pleito**, *m.* lawsuit; litigation; proceedings in a case; dispute, contest, debate, strife.—*poner p.* (*a*), to sue, bring suit (against).

plenario, *a.* complete, full; (law) plenary.—**plenilunio**, *m.* full moon.—**plenipotenciario**, *n.* & *a.* plenipotentiary.—**plenitud**, *f.* plenitude, fullness, abundance.—**pleno**, *a.* full, complete; joint (session).

pleuresía, *f.* pleurisy.

pliego, *m.* sheet (of paper).—*p. de condiciones*, specifications; tender, bid.—**pliegue**, *m.* fold, plait; crease.

plisar, *vt.* to pleat, plait.

plomada, *f.* plumb, lead weight, plummet.—**plomería**, *f.* lead roofing; leadware shop; plumbing.—**plomero**, *n.* plumber.—**plomizo**, *a.* leaden; lead-colored.—**plomo**, *m.* lead (metal); piece of lead; plummet; bullet; (coll.) dull person, bore.—*andar con pies de p.*, to proceed with the utmost caution.—*a p.*, true, plumb.—*caer a p.*, to fall down flat.

pluma, *f.* feather; plume; quill; writing pen; penmanship; (fig.) style.—*al correr de la*, or *a vuela p.*, written in haste.—**plumaje**, *m.* plumage; plume, crest.—**plumazo**, *m.* stroke of pen.—**plumero**, *m.* feather duster.—**plumón**, *m.* down, feather bed.—**plumoso**, *a.* feathered.

plural, *m.* & *a.* plural.—**pluralidad**, *f.* plurality.—**pluralizar**, *vti.* [a] to pluralize.

plus, *m.* (mil.) extra pay; bonus; extra.

población, *f.* population; populating; city, town, village.—**poblado**, *a.* populated, inhabited.—*m.* inhabited place, town, settlement.—**poblador**, *n.* settler.—**poblar**, *vti.* [12] & *vii.* to populate, settle; to inhabit; to stock; to breed fast.—*vri.* to bud, leaf.

pobre, *a.* poor; needy; barren; pitiable, unfortunate.—*mf.* poor person; beggar.—**pobrete,** *m.* poor man.—**pobreza,** *f.* poverty; need; scarcity, dearth.

pocilga, *f.* pigsty, pigpen; dirty place.

pocillo, *m.* chocolate cup.

pócima, *f.*, **poción,** *m.* drink, draft; potion.

poco, *a.* little; scanty, limited; small.—*pl.* few, some.—*m.* a little, a bit, a small quantity.— *adv.* little, in a small degree; a short time.—*a p.,* immediately; shortly afterward.—*dentro de p.,* in a short time, soon.—*de p. más o menos,* of little account.—*p. a p.,* little by little, gradually, slowly.—*p. después,* shortly afterward.—*p. más o menos,* more or less.—*por p.,* almost, nearly.

poda, *f.* pruning, lopping; pruning season.—**podar,** *vt.* to prune, lop, trim.

podenco, *m.* hound (dog).

poder, *vti.* & *vii.* [31] to be able; can; may.—*a. más no p.,* or *hasta más no p.,* to the utmost, to the limit.—*no p. con,* not to be able to bear, manage, etc., to be no match for.—*no p. menos de,* to be necessary; cannot but, cannot fail to.—*puede que venga,* (or *que no venga*), he may come (or, he may not come).—*m.* power; faculty, authority; might; proxy; (law) power or letter of attorney.—**poderío,** *m.* power, might; dominion, jurisdiction; wealth.—**poderoso,** *a.* powerful, mighty; wealthy.

podre, *m.* pus; rotten substance.—**podredumbre,** *f.* decay; pus; putrid matter; corruption.—**podridero, podrimento,** *m.* = PUDRIDERO, PUDRIMENTO.—**podrido,** *pp.* of PODRIR, PUDRIR.—**podrir,** *vti.,* [33] *vii.* & *vri.* = PUDRIR.

poema, *m.* poem.—**poesía,** *f.* poetry; poetical composition, poem.—**poeta,** *m.* poet, bard.—**poética,** *f.* poetics.—**poético,** *a.* poetic(al).—**poetisa,** *f.* poetess.

polaco, *a.* Polish.—*m.* Polish language.—*n.* Pole.

polaina, *f.* legging.

polar, *a.* polar.—**polaridad,** *f.* polarity.

polea, *f.* pulley; tackle block, block pulley.

polen, *m.* pollen.

policía, *f.* police.—*mf.* policeman (-woman).—**policíaco, policial,** *a.* pertaining to police, police.

políglota, *a.* & *mf.* multilingual (person).

polígono, *m.* polygon; (artil.) practice ground.

polilla, *f.* moth; clothes moth.

polinesi(an)o, *n.* & *a.* Polynesian.

política, *f.* policy; politics.—**políticastro,** *n.* petty politician.—**político,** *a.* political; polite; suave.—*n.* politician.—*pariente p.,* in-law.—**politiquería,** *f.* (Am.) low politics; political talk and doings, political trash.—**politiquero,** *n.* (Am.) one that indulges in, or is fond of, common politics; political busybody.

póliza, *f.* (com.) policy; scrip; check, draft; voucher, certificate.

polizón, *n.* stowaway; vagrant.

polizonte, *m.* (coll.) cop, policeman.

polo, *m.* (geog. & astr.) pole; (sports) polo.

polonés, *a.* Polish.—*f.* polonaise.

polución, *f.* (med.) ejaculation, pollution.

polvareda, *f.* cloud of dust; (fig.) scandal.—**polvera,** *f.* (cosmetic) powder box.—**polvo,** *m.* dust; powder.—*pl.* toilet powder.—*en p.,* powdered.—**pólvora,** *f.* gunpowder.—**polvorear,** *vt.* to powder, sprinkle powder on.—**polvoriento,** *a.* dusty.—**polvorín,** *m.* (mil.) powder magazine.

polla, *f.* pullet; (cards) pool, (coll.) girl.—**pollada,** *f.* flock of young fowls; hatch, covey.—**pollera,** *f.* chicken roost, chicken coop; gocart; (Am.) skirt; hooped petticoat.—**pollería,** *f.* poultry shop or market.—**pollero,** *m.* poulterer; poultry yard.

pollino, *n.* donkey, ass.

pollo, *m.* chicken; (coll.) young person.—**polluelo,** *n.* little chicken, chick.

pomada, *f.* pomade.

pómez,—*piedra p.,* pumice.

pomo, *m.* small bottle, flask, flagon; pommel; doorknob.

pompa, *f.* pomp, ostentation; bubble.—**pomposidad,** *f.* pomposity, pompousness.—**pomposo,** *a.* pompous, turgid; magnificent, splendid; inflated.

pómulo, *m.* cheek bone.

ponche, *m.* punch.—**ponchera,** *f.* punch bowl.

poncho, *m.* (Am.) poncho; military coat.—*a.* lazy, soft; heedless.

ponderación, *f.* consideration, deliberation; exaggeration.—**ponderar,** *vt.* to weigh, ponder, consider; to exaggerate; to praise highly.

poner, *vti.* [32-49] to put, place, lay; to dispose, arrange, set (as the table); to impose, keep (as order); to oblige, compel; to wager, stake;

to appoint, put in charge; to write, set down; to lay eggs; to cause; to become or turn (red, angry, etc.). —*p. al corriente*, to inform.—*p. al día*, to bring up to date.—*p. como nuevo*, to humiliate, reprimand or treat harshly, dress down.—*p. coto a*, to stop, put a limit to.—*p. de manifiesto*, to make public.—*p. en claro*, to make clear; to clear up.— *p. en duda*, to question, doubt.— *p. en práctica*, to start doing, get (a project, etc.) underway.—*p. en ridículo*, to make ridiculous.—*p. en vigor*, to enforce.—*vri.* to apply oneself to; to set about; to put on (as a garment); to become, get (as wet, angry, dirty); to set (as the sun); to reach, get to, arrive.—*p. a*, to begin to, start to.—*p. a cubierto*, to shelter oneself from danger.— *p. colorado*, to blush.—*p. de acuerdo*, to reach an agreement.—*p. en camino*, to set out, start, take off. —*p. en pie*, to stand up.—*p. en razón*, to become reasonable.

poniente, *m.* west.

pontaje, pontazgo, *m.* bridge toll.

pontifical, *a.* pontifical, papal.— **pontifice,** *m.* pontiff.—*Sumo Pontifice*, Pope.

pontón, *m.* pontoon.

ponzoña, *f.* poison, venom.—**ponzoñoso,** *a.* poisonous.

popa, *f.* (naut.) poop, stern.

popelina, *f.* (neol.) poplin.

populachero, *a.* vulgar, common.— **populacho,** *m.* populace, mob, rabble.—**popular,** *a.* popular.—**popularidad,** *f.* popularity.—**popularizar,** *vti.* [a] to popularize, make popular.—*vri.* to become popular.—**populoso,** *a.* populous.

popurrí, *m.* (mus.) medley; potpourri; mess, confusion.

poquito, *a.* very little; weak of body and mind.—*m.* a wee bit.—*a poquitos*, little by little; a little at a time.

por, *prep.* by; for; through; as; across; about, nearly; per; after, for; for the sake of; in behalf of, on account of; in order to; by way of; in the name of; without, not yet, to be.—*p. cuanto*, inasmuch as, whereas. *p. docena*, by the dozen.—*p. escrito*, in writing.—*p. la mañana (tarde, noche)*, in the morning (afternoon, evening).—*p. más que*, or *p. mucho que*, however much, no matter how much; notwithstanding.—*p. poco*, almost.— *p. qué*, why.—*¿p. qué?* why?— *p. si*, or *p. si acaso*, in case; if by chance. —*p. sí o p. no*, to be sure; to be

on the safe side.—*p. supuesto*, of course.

porcelana, *f.* porcelain; chinaware.

porcentaje, *m.* percentage.

porción, *f.* portion, part; lot.

porche, *m.* porch, portico; covered walk.

pordiosero, *n.* beggar.

porfía, *f.* tussle, dispute, competition, obstinate quarrel.—*a p.*, in competition; insistently.—**porfiado,** *a.* obstinate, stubborn, persistent; importunate.—**porfiar,** *vi.* to contend, wrangle, persist, insist; to importune.

pormenor, *m.* detail, particular.— **pormenorizar,** *vti.* [a] to detail, itemize.

poro, *m.* pore.—**porosidad,** *f.* porosity. —**poroso,** *a.* porous.

porque, *conj.* because, for, as; in order that.—**porqué,** *m.* reason, motive.

porquería, *f.* filth, squalor; vile, dirty act; nasty trick; trifle, worthless thing.—**porquerizo, porquero,** *n.* swineherd.

porra, *f.* bludgeon, club, truncheon; maul.—**porrazo,** *m.* blow, knock; fall; thump.

porta, *f.* porthole.

portaaviones, *m.* airplane carrier.

portada, *f.* portal, porch; frontispiece; cover (of a magazine. etc.); title page.

portador, *n.* bearer, carrier; (com.) holder, bearer.

portaféretro, *m.* pallbearer.

portal, *m.* porch, vestibule; portico.

portalámpara, *m.* (elec.) socket; lamp holder.

portalibros, *m.* book strap.

portalón, *m.* gangway.

portamonedas, *m.* purse.

portapliegos, *m.* large portfolio.

portaplumas, *m.* penholder.

portañuela, *f.* (Am.) fly of trousers.

portar, *vt.* to carry (as arms).—*vr.* to behave, act.—**portátil,** *a.* portable.—**portavoz,** *mf.* spokesman, representative; loudspeaker, megaphone.

portazgo, *m.* toll.

portazo, *m.* slam of a door.

porte, *m.* cost of carriage; freight; postage; bearing (of persons).— **portear,** *vt.* to carry or convey for a price.

portento, *m.* prodigy, wonder; portent.—**portentoso,** *a.* prodigious, marvelous.

porteño, *a. & n.* of or from Buenos Aires.

portería, *f.* porter's lodge or box; janitor's quarters.—**portero,** *n.* gatekeeper, porter; superintendent, janitor.—**portezuela**, *f.* (vehicles) door.

pórtico, *m.* portico; porch.

portilla, *f.* opening, passage; (naut.) porthole.—**portillo**, *m.* opening, gap, breach; wicket, gate; pass between hills.—**portón**, *m.* front door or gate.

portorriqueño, *n. & a.* Porto Rican.

portugués, *n. & a.* Portuguese.—*m.* Portuguese language.

porvenir, *m.* future, time to come.

posada, *f.* inn; lodging house; lodging.—**posadero**, *n.* innkeeper.—*f. pl.* buttocks.

posar, *vi.* (art) to pose.—*vt.* to lay down.—*vr.* to land, alight, sit (on).

posdata, *f.* postscript.

poseedor, *n.* possessor, holder, owner. —**poseer**, *vti.* [e] to possess, own; to hold; to master (an art, language, etc.).—**posesión**, *f.* possession; ownership; property.—**posesionar**, *vt.* to give possession; to install, induct.—*vr.* to take possession.—**posesivo**, *n. & a.* (gram.) possessive.—**poseso**, *ppi.* of POSEER.—*a.* possessed (by evil spirits).

posguerra, *f.* postwar period.

posibilidad, *f.* possibility.—**posibilitar**, *vt.* to render possible, facilitate.— **posible**, *a.* possible.—*m. pl.* personal means.

posición, *f.* position; placing, placement; standing, status.

positivo, *a.* positive, certain; absolute, real; matter-of-fact; (math., elec., photog.) positive.

posma, *f.* (coll.) sluggishness, sloth, dullness.—*n.* (coll.) dull, sluggish person.

poso, *m.* sediment, dregs.

posponer, *vti.* [32-49] (a) to postpone, put off, defer; to subordinate; to put after.—**posposición**, *f.* postponement; subordination.—**pospuesto**, *ppi.* of POSPONER.

postal, *a.* postal.—*giro p.*, money order.—*f.* post card.

postdata, *f.* = POSDATA.

poste, *m.* post, pillar.

postergación, *f.* delaying; leaving behind.—**postergar**, *vti.* [b] to delay, postpone; to disregard someone's rights; to hold back, to pass over.

posteridad, *f.* posterity.—**posterior**, *a.* posterior, rear; later, subsequent.

postguerra, *f.* = POSGUERRA.

postigo, *m.* wicket; peep window; shutter.

postilla, *f.* scab on wounds.

postizo, *a.* artificial, not natural; false (teeth).—*m.* false hair.

postmeridiano, *a.* postmeridian (p.m.).

postración, *f.* prostration, proneness; kneeling; dejection.—**postrar**, *vt.* to prostrate; to weaken, exhaust.—*vr.* to prostrate oneself, kneel down; to be exhausted.

postre, *m.* dessert.—*a la p.*, at last.

postrer(o), *a.* last; hindmost.

postulado, *m.* postulate.—**postular**, *vt.* to postulate; to nominate a candidate.—*vr.* to become a candidate.

postura, *f.* posture, position, stance; bid (auction); wager, bet; egg-laying.

potable, *a.* potable, drinkable.

potaje, *m.* pottage; porridge; medley.

potasa, *f.* potash.

pote, *m.* pot, jar.

potencia, *f.* power; potency; dominion; faculty of the mind; power, strong nation; force, strength.—*en p.*, potentially.—**potencial**, *a. & m.* potential.—**potentado**, *m.* potentate.—**potente**, *a.* powerful.—**potestad**, *f.* power, dominion, jurisdiction; potentate.—**potestativo**, *a.* optional.

potingue, *m.* (coll.) medicinal concoction.

potra, *f.* filly; hernia.—**potranca**, *f.* filly.—**potrero**, *m.* pasture ground; cattle ranch.—**potril**, *m.* pasture for young horses.—**potro**, *m.* colt, foal.

poyo, *m.* stone seat against a wall.

poza, *f.* puddle.—**pozo**, *m.* (water) well.

práctica, *f.* practice; habit; practicing; exercise; manner, method, routine.—**practicable**, *a.* practicable, feasible.—**practicar**, *vti.* [d] to practice; to make; to perform, do, put in execution; to practice, go in for.—**práctico**, *a.* practical; skillful, experienced.—*m.* (naut.) harbor pilot.

pradera, *f.* prairie, meadow.—**prado**, *m.* lawn; field, meadow; pasture.

preámbulo, *m.* preamble; (coll.) evasion.

precario, *a.* precarious.

precaución, *f.* precaution.—**precaver**, *vt.* to prevent, obviate.—*vr.* (de) to guard, be on one's guard (against).

precedencia, *f.* precedence, priority.— **precedente**, *a.* prior, precedent.—*m.* precedent.—**preceder**, *vt.* to precede; to be superior to.

precepto, *m.* precept.—**preceptor**, *n.* teacher, tutor.

preciar, *vt.* to value, price, appraise. —*vr.* (de) to boast, brag (about); to take pride, glory (in).

precintar, *vt.* to strap, hoop, bind; to seal.

precio, *m.* price; importance, worth.— **preciosidad**, *f.* worth, preciousness;

rich or beautiful object, [a] beauty.
—**precioso**, *a.* precious; beautiful.

precipicio, *m.* precipice, chasm; violent fall.

precipitación, *f.* rash haste, unthinking hurry; (chem.) precipitation.—**precipitado**, *a.* headlong; hurried, hasty.—*m.* (chem.) precipitate.—**precipitar**, *vt.* to precipitate; to rush, hasten.—*vr.* to throw oneself headlong; to rush, hurry.

precisar, *vt.* to fix, set, determine; to compel, oblige; to be urgent or necessary.—**precisión**, *f.* necessity; compulsion; preciseness, exactness; precision, accuracy.—**preciso**, *a.* necessary; indispensable; precise, exact, accurate; distinct, clear; concise.

preconizar, *vti.* [a] to praise, eulogize.

predecesor, *n.* predecessor.

predecir, *vti.* [14-49] to foretell, predict, forecast.

predestinación, *f.* predestination.—**predestinar**, *vt.* to predestine, foreordain.

predeterminar, *vt.* to predetermine.

prédica, predicación, *f.* preaching; sermon.—**predicado**, *m.* predicate.—**predicador**, *n.* preacher.—**predicar**, *vti. & vii.* [d] to preach; to praise.

predicción, *f.* prediction.—**predicho**, *ppi.* of PREDECIR.

predilección, *f.* predilection.—**predilecto**, *a.* preferred, favorite.

predisponer, *vti.* [32-49] to prejudice, predispose; to prearrange.—**predisposición**, *f.* predisposition; prejudice.—**predispuesto**, *ppi.* of PREDISPONER.—*a.* predisposed, biased, inclined.

predominante, *a.* predominant, prevailing.—**predominar**, *vt. & vi.* to predominate, prevail; to rise above, overlook, command.—**predominio**, *m.* predominance, superiority.

prefabricado, *a.* prefabricated.

prefacio, *m.* preface, prologue.

preferencia, *f.* preference.—**preferente**, *a.* preferential; preferring; preferable.—**preferible**, *a.* preferable.—**preferir**, *vti.* [39] to prefer.

prefijar, *vt.* to predesignate, set beforehand.—**prefijo**, *a.* prefixed.—*m.* prefix.

pregón, *m.* hawker's cry.—**pregonar**, *vt.* to hawk, proclaim, cry out; to make known.—**pregonero**, *n.* hawker, town crier.

pregunta, *f.* question, query.—**preguntar**, *vt. & vi.* to ask, question, inquire.—*vr.* to wonder.—**preguntón**, *a.* inquisitive.

prejuicio, *m.* prejudice, bias.—**prejuzgar**, *vti.* [b] to prejudge.

prelación, *f.* preference.

prelado, *m.* prelate.

preliminar, *a.* preliminary.—*m.* preliminary; protocol.

preludio, *m.* introduction; (mus.) prelude.

prematuro, *a.* premature; untimely; unripe.

premeditación, *f.* premeditation, willfulness.—**premeditar**, *vt.* to premeditate.

premiar, *vt.* to reward, remunerate; to award a prize.—**premio**, *m.* prize; reward; recompense; (com.) premium, interest.

premisa, *f.* premise.

premura, *f.* urgency, pressure, haste.

prenda, *f.* pledge, token; piece of jewelry; garment; person dearly loved.—*pl.* endowments, natural gifts, talents.—*soltar p.*, to commit oneself.—**prendarse** *vr.* (de), to fall in love with, take a great liking (to).

prendedor, *m.* breastpin; brooch; safety pin; tiepin.—**prender**, *vti.* [49] to seize, grasp, catch, apprehend; to fasten, clasp.—*p. fuego a*, to set on fire.—*p. la luz*, to turn on the light.—*vii.* to take root; to catch or take fire.—**prendería**, *f.* pawnshop.—**prendero**, *m.* pawnbroker.

prensa, *f.* press.—**prensar**, *vt.* to press.

preñada, *a.* pregnant (esp. of animals).—*preñado de*, full of.—**preñez**, *f.* pregnancy.

preocupación, *f.* worry, preoccupation, concern.—**preocupar**, *vt.* to worry, to preoccupy.—*vr.* to worry.

preparación, *f.* preparation; preparing; compound; medicine.—**preparar**, *vt.* to prepare, make ready.—*vr.* to be prepared, get ready, make preparations.—**preparativo**, *a.* preparatory.—*m. pl.* preparations, arrangements.—**preparatorio**, *a.* preparatory.

preponderancia, *f.* preponderance, sway.—**preponderar**, *vi.* to have control; to prevail.

preposición, *f.* preposition.

prepotencia, *f.* predominance.—**prepotente**, *a.* predominant.

prerrogativa, *f.* prerogative.

presa, *f.* capture, seizure; (mil.) booty; quarry, prey; (water) dam; morsel; tusk, fang; claw.

presagiar, *vt.* to presage, foretell.—**presagio**, *m.* presage, omen, prognostication.

presbiteriano, *n. & a.* Presbyterian.—**presbítero**, *m.* priest; presbyter.

prescindir, *vi.* (de) to dispense

(with), do (without); to set aside, ignore, omit.

prescribir, *vti.* [49] to prescribe, specify.—**prescrito,** *ppi.* of PRES-CRIBIR.

presencia, *f.* presence; appearance.—*p. de ánimo,* coolness, presence of mind.—**presenciar,** *vt.* to witness, see; to attend.—**presentación,** *f.* presentation, exhibition; personal introduction.—**presentar,** *vt.* to present; to put on (a program, etc.); to display, show.—*vr.* to appear, present oneself, report; to turn up; to offer one's services.—**presente,** *a.* present, current.—*hacer p.,* to state; to remind of, call attention.—*tener p.,* to bear in mind.—*m.* present, gift; present (time).

presentimiento, *m.* presentiment; misgiving.—**presentir,** *vti.* [39] to have a presentiment of; to forebode, predict.

preservación, *f.* preservation, conservation.—**preservar,** *vt.* to preserve, guard, keep, save.

presidencia, *f.* presidency; presidential chair; chairmanship; presidential term.—**presidencial,** *a.* presidential.—**presidente,** *n.* president; chairman; any presiding officer.

presidiario, *m.* convict.—**presidio,** *m.* penitentiary.

presidir, *vt.* to preside over, or at; to govern, determine.

presilla, *f.* loop, fastener; clip.

presión, *f.* pressure.—**presionar,** *vt.* to press, urge.

preso, *ppi.* of PRENDER.—*a.* arrested, imprisoned.—*n.* prisoner; convict.

prestamista, *mf.* money lender.—**préstamo,** *m.* loan.

prestar, *vt.* to lend, loan.—*p. aten-ción,* to pay attention.—*p. ayuda,* to help.—*p. un servicio,* to do a favor.—*vr.* to offer oneself or itself; to adapt oneself or itself.

presteza, *f.* quickness, promptness.—**prestidigitación,** *f.* legerdemain, sleight of hand; jugglery.—**presti-digitador,** *n.* juggler; magician.

prestigio, *m.* prestige; influence; good name.—**prestigioso,** *a.* renowned; well-reputed.

presto, *a.* quick, swift, prompt; ready, prepared.—*adv.* soon; quickly.

presumible, *a.* presumable.—**presu-mido,** *a.* presumptuous, conceited.—**presumir,** *vti.* [49] to presume, surmise, conjecture.—*vii.* (de) to boast (of being), claim (to be); to be conceited.—**presunción,** *f.* presumption, conjecture; presumptu-ousness, conceit.—**presunto,** *ppi.* of

PRESUMIR.—*a.* presumed.—**presun-tuosidad,** *f.* presumptuousness.—**pre-suntuoso,** *a.* presumptuous, con-ceited.

presuponer, *vti.* [32-49] to presup-pose; to estimate; to budget.—**presuposición,** *f.* presupposition.—**presupuestario,** *a.* budgetary.—**presupuesto,** *ppi.* of PRESUPONER.—*m.* budget, estimate.—*a.* presupposed; estimated.

presuroso, *a.* prompt, quick.

pretender, *vti.* [49] to pretend; to aspire to; to seek, solicit; to try; to intend; to court.—*p. decir,* to mean, be driving at.—**pretensión,** *f.* pretension, claim; presumption.—**pretenso,** *ppi.* of PRETENDER.

preterir, *vti.* [50] to ignore, overlook.—**pretérito,** *m.* & *a.* preterit, past.

pretextar, *vt.* to give as a pretext.—**pretexto,** *m.* pretext, pretense, ex-cuse.

pretil, *m.* railing, battlement.

pretina, *f.* girdle, waistband; belt; fly (of trousers).

prevalecer, *vii.* [3] to prevail.

prevención, *f.* prevention; foresight; warning; prejudice; police station.—**prevenir,** *vti.* [45] to prevent, avoid; to arrange, make ready; to foresee.—*vri.* to be ready, prepared, or on guard; to take precautions.—**preventivo,** *a.* preventive.

prever, *vti.* [46-49] to foresee, antici-pate.—**previo,** *a.* previous, foregoing.—**previsión,** *f.* foresight.—**previsor,** *a.* far-seeing.—**previsto,** *ppi.* of PREVENIR.

prieto, *a.* blackish, very dark; tight.

prima, *f.* female cousin; (mus.) treble; (com.) premium; bounty.—**primacía,** *f.* primacy; superiority; priority.—**primario,** *a.* principal, primary.

primavera, *f.* spring (season); prim-rose.—**primaveral,** *a.* spring.

primer(o), *a.* first; former; leading; principal.—*de buenas a primeras,* suddenly.—*de primera,* of superior quality.—*adv.* first; rather, sooner.

primicia, *f.* first fruit.—*pl.* first pro-duction, maiden effort.

primitivo, *a.* primitive, original.

primo, *n.* cousin; (coll.) simpleton.—*coger a uno de p.,* to deceive some-one easily.—*número p.,* prime num-ber.—*p. carnal,* or *p. hermano,* first cousin.—*a.* first; superior, prime.—**primogénito,** *n.* & *a.* first-born.—**primogenitura,** *f.* state of being the first-born child; seniority.

primor, *m.* beauty; nicety.

primordial, *a.* primal.

primoroso, *a.* neat, fine, exquisite; beautiful; skillful.

princesa, *f.* princess.—**principado**, *m.* princedom.—**principal**, *a.* principal, main; first; famous.—*m.* (com.) principal, capital, stock; chief or head.—**príncipe**, *m.* prince.

principiante, *a.* beginning.—*mf.* beginner.—**principiar**, *vt.* to commence, begin, start.—**principio**, *m.* principle, tenet; beginning; start; original cause; rule of action.—*a principios de*, at the beginning of.—*al p.*, at first.—*en p.*, in principle.

pringoso, *a.* greasy, fatty.—**pringue**, *m.* or *f.* grease, fat; grease stain.

prior, *m.* (eccl.) prior, superior; rector, curate.—**prioridad**, *f.* priority, precedence.

prisa, *f.* haste, promptness; urgency.—*a p.*, quickly.—*darse p.*, to make haste, hurry.—*de p.*, quickly.—*estar de p.*, or *tener p.*, to be in a hurry.

prisión, *f.* seizure, capture; prison; imprisonment.—**prisionero**, *n.* prisoner.

prisma, *m.* prism.

prístino, *a.* pristine.

privación, *f.* privation; lack.—**privado**, *a.* private, secret; personal.—**privar**, *vt.* to deprive.—*vi.* to prevail, be in favor or in vogue.—*vr.* to deprive oneself.—**privativo**, *a.* privative; special, distinctive, particular; exclusive.

privilegiar, *vt.* to favor; to grant a privilege to.—**privilegio**, *m.* privilege grant concession.

pro, *m.* or *f.* profit, benefit, advantage.—*en p. de*, in behalf of, for the benefit of.

proa, *f.* bow, prow.

probabilidad, *f.* probability.—**probable**, *a.* probable.

probar, *vti.* [12] to try, test; to prove; to taste; to sample (as wine); to attempt, try; to try on (as a coat).—*p. fortuna*, to take one's chances.—*vii.* to suit, agree with.—*vri.* to try on (as a coat).

probeta, *f.* pressure gauge; test tube; beaker.

probidad, *f.* probity, honesty, integrity.

problema, *m.* problem.

probo, *a.* upright, honest.

procaz, *a.* impudent, bold, insolent.

procedencia, *f.* origin; source; place of sailing.—**procedente**, *a.* coming or proceeding (from); according to law.—**proceder**, *vi.* to proceed; to go on; to arise; to be the result; to behave; to act; to take action.—*m.* behavior, action.—**procedi-**

miento, *m.* procedure; process; method· (law) proceeding.

prócer, *a.* tall, lofty, elevated.—*mf.* hero, leader, dignitary.

procesado, *a.* (law) related to court proceeding; included in the suit; prosecuted, indicted.—*n.* defendant.—**procesar**, *vt.* to sue; to indict.

procesión, *f.* procession.

proceso, *m.* process; course, development; (law) criminal case; proceedings of a lawsuit, trial.

proclama, *f.* proclamation; publication; banns of marriage.—**proclamación**, *f.* proclamation.—**proclamar**, *vt.* to proclaim; to acclaim.

procrear, *vt.* to father, procreate; to sire.

procuración, *f.* care, diligence; proxy, power or letter of attorney; procurement, procuring; office of an attorney.—**procurador**, *n.* (law) solicitor, attorney.—**procurar**, *vt.* to endeavor, try; to procure; (Am.) to look for.—*vi.* to act as a solicitor.

prodigalidad, *f.* prodigality, wastefulness; abundance.—**prodigar**, *vti.* [b] to lavish; to squander.

prodigio, *m.* prodigy; marvel.—**prodigioso**, *a.* prodigious, marvelous.

pródigo, *a.* prodigal, extravagant, wasteful; liberal, generous.—*n.* spendthrift.

producción, *f.* production; produce.—**producir**, *vti.* [11] to produce; to bring about; to yield.—*vri.* to explain oneself; to be produced; to come about; to break out.—**productivo**, *a.* productive; profitable, fruitful.—**producto**, *m.* product; article (of trade, etc.); production; produce.—**productor**, *a.* productive.—*n.* producer.

proeza, *f.* prowess, feat.

profanación, *f.* profanation, desecration.—**profanar**, *vt.* to profane, desecrate.—**profano**, *a.* profane; secular; irreverent; uninformed, ignorant.—*n.* layman; uninitiated person.

profecía, *f.* prophecy.

proferir, *vti.* [39] to utter, express, speak.

profesar, *vt.* to practice (a profession); to profess, declare; to show, manifest.—*vi.* to take vows.—**profesión**, *f.* profession, vocation.—**profesional**, *a.* professional.—**profesor**, *n.* professor.—**profesorado**, *m.* professorship; faculty; teaching profession.

profeta, *m.* prophet.—**profético**, *a.* prophetic(al).—**profetizar**, *vti.* [a] & *vii.* to prophesy.

proficiente, *a.* proficient, advanced.

profiláctico, *a.* prophylactic, preventive.—*m.* prophylactic.

prófugo, *n.* & *a.* fugitive from justice.

profundidad, *f.* depth; profoundness.—**profundizar**, *vti.* [a] to deepen; to go deep into.—**profundo**, *a.* deep; profound.

profusión, *f.* profusion; lavishness, prodigality.—**profuso**, *a.* profuse, plentiful; lavish.

progenie, *f.* progeny, offspring, issue.

progenitor, *m.* progenitor, ancestor.

programa, *m.* program.

progresar, *vi.* to progress; to advance.—**progresión**, *f.* progression.—**progresista**, *a.* & *mf.* progressive.—**progresivo**, *a.* advancing, progressive.—**progreso**, *m.* progress, civilization; advancement, development.—*pl.* progress, strides (in an undertaking, school, etc.).

prohibición, *f.* prohibition, forbidding.—**prohibir**, *vt.* to prohibit, forbid.—*se prohibe fumar*, no smoking.—**prohibitivo**, *a.* prohibitive, forbidding.

prohijar, *vt.* to adopt.

prójimo, *m.* fellow creature, neighbor.

prole, *f.* progeny, offspring.—**proletariado**, *m.* proletariat.—**proletario**, *a.* proletarian; belonging to the working classes.—*n.* proletarian.

prolífico, *a.* prolific, fruitful.

prólogo, *m.* prologue.

prolongación, *f.* prolongation, lengthening; extension.—**prolongar**, *vti.* & *vri.* [b] to prolong; to extend, continue.

promediar, *vt.* (com.) to average.—*vi.* to mediate. **promedio**, *m.* average.

promesa, *f.* promise, offer; pious offering.—**prometedor**, *a.* promising.—**prometer**, *vt.* to promise; to bid fair.—*vi.* to show promise.—*vr.* to expect with confidence; to become engaged.—**prometido**, *n.* fiancé, fiancée, betrothed.- *m.* promise.

prominencia, *f.* elevation; prominence; protuberance.—**prominente**, *a.* prominent, outstanding; salient.

promiscuidad, *f.* promiscuity.—**promiscuo**, *a.* promiscuous.

promisorio, *a.* promissory.

promoción, *f.* promotion.

promontorio, *m.* promontory; anything bulky and unwieldy.

promotor, *n.* promoter, advancer.—**promover**, *vti.* [26] to promote; to advance.

pronombre, *m.* pronoun.

pronosticar, *vti.* [d] to prognosticate, foretell.—**pronóstico**, *m.* forecast, prediction; omen

prontitud, *f.* promptness; quickness.—**pronto**, *a.* prompt, quick, fast; ready.—*m.* sudden impulse. *adv.* soon; promptly, speedily, quickly.—*de p.*, suddenly, without thinking.—*por lo p.*, for the time being.

pronunciación, *f.* pronunciation.—**pronunciar**, *vt.* to pronounce; to deliver, make (a speech).—*vr.* to declare oneself.

propagación, *f.* propagation; spreading, dissemination.—**propagador**, *n.* & *a.* propagator; propagating.—**propaganda**, *f.* propaganda.—**propagandista**, *mf.* propagandist.—**propagar**, *vti.* [b] to propagate; to spread, disseminate.—*vri.* to spread; to propagate; to multiply.

propalar, *vt.* to publish, divulge.

propasarse, *vr.* to go too far; to go to extremes.

propender, *vii.* [49] to tend, be inclined.

propensión, *f.* tendency, proclivity, proneness.—**propenso**, *ppi.* of PRO-PENDER.—*a.* inclined, disposed.

propiciar, *vt.* to propitiate.—**propicio**, *a.* propitious, favorable.

propiedad, *f.* ownership, proprietorship; property, holding; propriety, fitness; dominion, possession.—**propietario**, *n.* proprietor, owner, landlord.—*a.* proprietary.

propina, *f.* tip, gratuity.—**propinar**, *vt.* to deal (a beating, a kick, etc.).

propio, *a.* one's own; proper, appropriate; characteristic, typical.—*m.* messenger.

proponer, *vti.* [32-49] to propose, propound; to present or name (as candidate).—*vri.* to purpose, plan, intend.

proporción, *f.* proportion; opportunity, chance.—**proporcionado**, *a.* proportioned, fit, relevant.—**proporcional**, *a.* proportional.—**proporcionar**, *vt.* to proportion; to supply, provide, furnish; to adjust, adapt.

proposición, *f.* proposition; proposal; motion (in congress, etc.).

propósito, *m.* purpose, intention; aim, object.—*a p.*, for the purpose; fit; incidentally, by the way.—*a p. de*, in connection with, apropos of.—*de p.*, on purpose, purposely.—*fuera de p.*, irrelevant.

propuesta, *f.* proposal, offer; nomination.—**propuesto**, *ppi.* of PROPONER.

propugnar, *vt.* to advocate, defend strongly, promote.

propulsar, *vt.* to propel.—**propulsión**, *f.* propulsion.—*p. a chorro*, jet propulsion.—**propulsor**, *n.* & *a.* propeller; propelling.

prorrata, *f.* apportionment.—*a p.*, pro rata, in proportion.—**prorratear,** *vt.* to allot in proportion.—**prorrateo,** *m.* pro rata division.

prórroga, *f.* prolongation, extension (of time).—**prorrogable,** *a.* that may be prolonged or extended (in time).—**prorrogar,** *vti.* [b] to prolong, extend (in time).

prorrumpir, *vi.* to break forth, burst out.

prosa, *f.* prose.—**prosaico,** *a.* prosaic. —**prosista,** *mf.* prose writer.

proscribir, *vti.* [49] to proscribe, banish; to outlaw.—**proscripción,** *f.* proscription, banishment.—**poscrito,** *ppi.* of PROSCRIBIR.—*n.* exile; outlaw.

proseguir, *vti.* [29-b] to continue; to carry on with; to resume.—*vii.* to keep going, proceed.

prosodia, *f.* prosody.

prosperar, *vi.* to prosper, thrive.—**prosperidad,** *f.* prosperity, success. —**próspero,** *a.* prosperous; favorable.

prosternarse, *vr.* to prostrate oneself.

prostitución, *f.* prostitution.—**prostituir,** *vti.* [23-49-e] to prostitute, corrupt, debase.—*vri.* to sell one's honor; to turn prostitute.—**prostituto,** *ppi.* of PROSTITUIR.—*n.* prostitute; streetwalker.

protagonista, *mf.* protagonist, hero-(ine).

protección, *f.* protection; favor.—**protector,** *n.* protector.—**proteger,** *vti.* [c] to protect.—**protegido,** *n.* protégé.

proteína, *f.* protein.

protesta, *f.* protestation; protest.—**protestante,** *a.* protesting.—*mf.* & *a.* Protestant.—**protestantismo,** *m.* Protestantism.—**protestar,** *vt.* (com.) to protest; to assure, protest, asseverate; to profess (one's faith). —*p. contra*, to protest, deny the validity of.—*p. de*, to protest against.—**protesto,** *m.* (com.) protest (of a bill).

protocolo, *m.* protocol; registry, judicial record.

protoplasma, *m.* protoplasm.

prototipo, *m.* prototype, original; model.

protuberancia, *f.* protuberance.

provecho, *m.* benefit, advantage; profit, gain; proficiency, progress.—**provechoso,** *a.* profitable; beneficial, good; useful, advantageous.

proveedor, *n.* purveyor, provider; supplier.—**proveer,** *vti.* [49-e] to provide, furnish; to supply with provisions; (law) to decide.—*vri.*

(de) to provide oneself (with), get one's supply (of).

provenir, *vii.* [45] to come, originate, arise; to be due.

proverbial, *a.* proverbial.—**proverbio,** *m.* proverb.

providencia, *f.* providence, foresight; Providence; act of providing; (law) decision, sentence.—**providencial,** *a.* providential.

provincia, *f.* province.—**provincial,** *a.* provincial.—**provinciano,** *n.* & *a.* provincial.

provisión, *f.* provision; supply, stock; measure, means.—**provisional,** *a.* provisional, interim.—**provisorio,** *a.* provisional, temporary.—**provisto,** *ppi.* of PROVEER.—*a.* provided, stocked, supplied.

provocación, *f.* provocation, irritation.—**provocador,** *n.* provoker; inciter.—**provocar,** *vti.* [d] to provoke, excite, incite, anger; to promote; to tempt, arouse desire in.—**provocativo,** *a.* inciting; tempting; provoking, irritating.

proximidad, *f.* proximity.—**próximo,** *a.* next; nearest, neighboring; close.

proyección, *f.* projecting; projection. —**proyectar,** *vt.* to design; to project, plan, devise; to shoot or throw forth; (geom.) to project; to cast (as a shadow); to show (a movie).—*vr.* to be cast, fall (as a shadow).—**proyectil,** *m.* projectile, missile.—**proyectista,** *mf.* planner; designer.—**proyecto,** *m.* project, plan; design.—**proyector,** *m.* projector; searchlight.

prudencia, *f.* prudence; moderation. —**prudente,** *a.* prudent, cautious.

prueba, *f.* proof; evidence; trial, test; probation; sample; testing; temptation; trial, fitting.—*a p.*, on trial; according to the best standard.—*a p. de*, proof against.—*hacer la p.*, to try.—*poner a p.*, to try, put to the test.

prurito, *m.* itching; excessive desire.

prusiano, *n.* & *a.* Prussian.

psicoanálisis, *m.* psychoanalysis.—**psicoanalista,** *mf.* psychoanalist.—**psicoanalizar,** *vti.* [a] to psychoanalyze.—**psicología,** *f.* psychology. —**psicológico,** *a.* psychological.—**psicólogo,** *n.* psychologist.—**psicópata,** *mf.* psychopath.—**psicosis,** *f.* psychosis.—**psicótico,** *n.* & *a.* psychotic.—**psique,** *f.* psyche.—**psiquiatra,** *mf.* psychiatrist.—**psiquiatría,** *f.* psychiatry.—**psíquico,** *a.* psychic(al).

psitacosis, *f.* parrot fever.

púa, *f.* prick, barb; prong; thorn;

spine or quill (of porcupine); (coll.) tricky person.

pubertad, *f.* puberty.

publicación, *f.* publication.—**publicar,** *vti.* [d] to publish.—**publicidad,** *f.* publicity.—**público,** *a.* & *m.* public. —*en p.,* publicly.

puchero, *m.* cooking pot; stew; dinner, food; pouting.—*hacer pucheros,* (coll.) to pout.

pudiente, *a.* powerful; wealthy.

pudín, *m.* pudding.—*p. inglés con pasas,* plum pudding.

pudor, *m.* decorousness, modesty.— **pudoroso,** *a.* modest; bashful, shy.

pudrir, *vti., vii.* & *vri.* [33] to rot, decay.

pueblo, *m.* town, village; people; population; common people; nation.

puente, *m.* bridge.—*p. colgante,* suspension bridge.—*p. giratorio,* swing bridge.—*p. levadizo,* drawbridge.

puerco, *a.* filthy, dirty, foul; low, base, mean.—*n.* pig, hog; (fig.) dirty, base or low person.

pueril, *a.* childish, puerile.

puerta, *f.* door; doorway, gateway; gate; entrance.—*a p. cerrada,* privately, secretly.—*p. falsa,* back door, side door.—*p. franca,* open door, free entrance; free entry.

puerto, *m.* port; mountain pass; harbor; (fig.) shelter, refuge.

puertorriqueño, *n.* & *a.* (Am.) = POR-TORRIQUEÑO.

pues, *conj.* because, for, as; since; then.—*p. bien,* now then, well then. —*p. no,* not at all, not so.—*p. que,* since.—*¿p. qué?* what? what about it? so what?—*p. sí,* yes, indeed, most certainly.—*¿y p.?* so? is that so? how is that?—*adv.* so; certainly; anyhow, just the same.

puesta, *f.* (astr.) set, setting; stake (at cards).—*p. de sol,* sunset.

puesto, *ppi.* of PONER.—*bien (mal) p.,* well (badly) dressed.—*p. que,* since, inasmuch as, as long as.—*m.* place; vendor's booth or stand; position, job; post, dignity, office; military post; blind for hunters; breeding stall.

pugilato, *m.* boxing; boxing bout.— **pugilista,** *mf.* boxer, pugilist, prize fighter.

pugna, *f.* combat, struggle; conflict. —*estar en p.,* to be in conflict, disagree.—**pugnar,** *vi.* to fight, struggle; (con) to conflict (with), be opposed (to); to persist.

puja, *f.* outbidding or overbidding at an auction; higher bid.—**pujante,** *a.* powerful, strong.—**pujanza,** *f.* push, might, strength.—**pujar,** *vi.* to outbid or overbid; to strive,

struggle.—**pujido, pujo,** *m.* grunt· strenuous effort.

pulcritud, *f.* neatness, tidiness.— **pulcro,** *a.* neat, trim.

pulga, *f.* flea.—*ser de* or *tener malas pulgas,* to be ill-tempered.—**pulgada,** *f.* inch.—**pulgar,** *m.* thumb.— **pulgón,** *m.* green fly, plant louse.

pulimentar, *vt.* to burnish, gloss, polish.—**pulimento,** *m.* polish; glossiness.—**pulir,** *vt.* to polish, burnish; to beautify; to render polite.—*vr.* to beautify or deck oneself; to become polished.

pulmón, *m.* lung.—**pulmonar,** *a.* pulmonary.—**pulmonía,** *f.* pneumonia.

pulpa, *f.* pulp, flesh; fruit or wood pulp.—**pulpería,** *f.* (Am.) retail grocery or general store; tavern.— **pulpero,** *n.* (Am.) grocer.

púlpito, *m.* pulpit.

pulpo, *m.* cuttlefish, octopus.

pulsación, *f.* pulsation, throb; pulse, beating.—**pulsar,** *vt.* to feel the pulse of; to finger (a string instrument); to explore, sound, or examine.—*vi.* to pulsate, beat.— **pulsera,** *f.* bracelet; wrist bandage. —*reloj de p.,* wrist watch.—**pulso,** *m.* pulse; beat; firmness or steadiness of hand; (Am.) bracelet.—*a p.,* freehand; with the strength of the hand.—*tomar el p.,* to feel the pulse.

pulular, *vi.* to swarm; to multiply with great rapidity; to bud, sprout.

pulverización, *f.* pulverization.—**pulverizador,** *m.* atomizer, spray; pulverizer.—**pulverizar,** *vti.* [a] to pulverize; to spray.

pulla, *f.* cutting remark, taunt, quip; hint.

puma, *m.* puma, American panther.

puna, *f.* (Am.) cold, desertlike tableland of the Andes; (Am.) desert; (Am.) mountain sickness.

pundonor, *m.* point of honor.

punición, *f.* punishment.

punta, *f.* point, sharp end; end, tip; apex, top; cape, promontory; touch, trace, suggestion; stub of a cigar or cigarette.—*de p.,* point first.—*de p. en blanco,* all dressed up; in full regalia.—*estar de p.,* to be on bad terms.—**puntada,** *f.* stitch; hint.— **puntal,** *m.* prop, support.—**puntapié,** *m.* kick.—**puntear,** *vt.* to play (the guitar); (art) to stipple; (sew.) to stitch.—**puntería,** *f.* aiming or pointing of a weapon; marksmanship.—**puntero,** *m.* pointer; chisel.—**puntiagudo,** *a.* sharp, spiky; pungent.—**puntilla,** *f.* lace edging; tack; joiner's nail.—*de,* or *en puntillas,* softly, gently; on tiptoe.—

puntilloso, a. sensitive, easily offended.—punto, m. point, dot; period in writing; point of a pen; sight in firearms; stitch; mesh; place; instant, moment; stop, rest, recess; end, object, aim.—al p., immediately, at once.—a p. de, on the point of, about to.—a p. fijo, exactly.—dos puntos, colon.—en p., on the dot, (of the hour) sharp.—p. en boca, silence.—p. final, stop; full stop.—p. y coma, semicolon.—puntos suspensivos, leaders.—puntuación, f. punctuation.—puntual, a. prompt, punctual.—puntualidad, f. punctuality.—puntualizar, vti. [a] to give a detailed account of.—puntuar, vt. to punctuate; to point.

punzada, f. prick, puncture; sharp pain.—punzante, a. pricking, sharp; poignant.—punzar, vti. [a] to punch, bore, perforate; to prick, puncture; to cause sharp pain; to grieve.

punzó, a. (Am.) deep scarlet red.

punzón, m. punch; puncher; driver, point, awl.

puñada, f. blow with the fist.—puñado, m. handful; a few.—puñal, m. dagger, poniard.—puñalada, f. stab (with a dagger); sharp pain.—puñetazo, m. = PUÑADA.—puño, m. fist; grasp; handful; cuff, wristband (of garment); hilt of a sword; haft (of a tool); handle (of an umbrella, etc.); head of a staff or cane.

pupila, f. (anat.) pupil.

pupilaje, m. room and board; boarding house.—pupilo, n. ward; boarding-school pupil; boarder.

pupitre, m. writing desk; school desk.

puré, m. thick soup, purée.—p. de papas, mashed potatoes.

pureza, f. purity, chastity; genuineness.

purga, f. physic, cathartic.—purgación, f. purge, purgation; gonorrhea, clap.—purgante, a. purging, purgative.—m. purgative, cathartic, physic.—purgar, vti. [b] to purge, purify; to expiate; to refine, clarify; to drain; to purge.—vri. to take a purgative; to clear oneself of guilt.—purgatorio, m. purgatory.

purificación, f. purification.—purificador, n. & a. purifier; purifying.—purificar, vti. [d] to purify.—vri. to be purified.

puritano, a. & n. Puritan.

puro, a. pure; unadulterated; mere, only, sheer.—m. cigar.

púrpura, f. purple shell; purple; dignity of a cardinal.—purpúreo, purpurino, a. purple.

purulento, a. purulent.—pus, m. pus.

pusilánime, a. faint-hearted, spineless.

pústula, f. pimple.

puta, f. whore, harlot.

puya, f. goad, goad stick.

Q

que, rel. pron. that; which; who, whom.—el q., he who, the one who, the one that.—lo q., what, which.—por más q., no matter how.—conj. that, than; because, for.—más q., more than.—por mucho q., no matter how much.—¿qué? interrog. pron. what? which? how?—¿para q.? what for?—¿por qué? why?—¿q. tal? how goes it?—interj. what a! how!

quebrada, f. ravine; gorge; (Am.) gulch; stream.—quebradizo, a. brittle, fragile; frail, sickly.—quebrado, a. broken; (com.) bankrupt; rough, uneven (ground); (med.) ruptured.—m. (arith.) common fraction.—quebrantar, vt. to break, crush; to burst open; to pound; to transgress; to violate, break (as a contract); to vex; to weaken.—quebranto, m. (com.) loss, damage; breaking, crushing; grief, affliction.—quebrar, vti. [1] to break; to crush.—vii. (com.) to fail, become bankrupt.—vri. to be ruptured; to break (as a plate, a bone, etc.); to be broken.

quechua, mf. & a. Quechua; Quechuan (Indian and language).

quedar, vi. to remain; to stay, stop in a place; to be or be left in a state or condition.—q. bien, (mal), to acquit oneself well (badly); to come out wel" badly).—q. en, to agree to; to have an understanding.—vr. to remain.—quedarse atrás, to get, or be left, behind.—quedarse con, to retain, keep.

quedo, a. quiet, still, noiseless; easy, gentle.—adv. softly, gently; in a low voice.

quehacer, m. occupation, business, work.—pl. chores; duties.

queja, f. complaint; grumbling, moan; grudge.—quejarse, vr. to complain; to grumble; (de) to regret, lament.—quejido, m. moan.—quejoso, a. complaining.—quejumbroso, a. grumbling; plaintive.

quema, f. burning, fire, conflagration.—huir de la q., to get away from trouble, get out.—quemado, a. burnt, crisp; sunburned.—m. burnt down forest or thicket.—quemadura, f. burn, scald.—quemar, vt. to burn; to scald; to scorch; to set on fire; to dispose of at a low price; to annoy.—*vi.* to burn, be too hot.—*vr.* to get burned, burn oneself; to burn, be consumed by fire; to feel very hot.—**quemazón,** *f.* fire, conflagration; (coll.) smarting, burning; (Am.) bargain sale.

querella, *f.* complaint; quarrel; (law) plaint, complaint.—**querellante,** *mf.* & *a.* complainant; complaining.—**querellarse,** *vr.* to complain; (law) to file a complaint, bring suit.

querer, *vti.* [34] to will; to want, desire, wish; to like, love.—*q. decir,* to mean.—*vii.* to be willing.—*como quiera,* in any way.—*como quiera que,* since; however, no matter how.—*como quiera que sea,* in any case.—*como Ud. quiera,* as you like; let it be so.—*cuando quiera,* at any time, whenever.—*donde quiera,* anywhere, wherever.—*sin q.,* unwillingly; unintentionally.—*v. impers.* to look like (rain, etc.), threaten.—*m.* love, affection; will; desire.—**querido,** *a.* dear; beloved.—*n.* lover; mistress.

querosén, *m.* (Am.) kerosene.

querubín, *m.* cherub.

quesería, *f.* dairy.—**quesera,** *f.* cheese dish.—**quesero,** *n.* cheesemaker.—**queso,** *m.* cheese.

quicio, *m.* hinge of a door.—*sacar de q., to* unhinge; to exasperate.

quichua, *mf.* & *a.* = QUECHUA.

quid, *m.* main point, gist.

quidam, *m.* (coll.) person; a nobody.

quiebra, *f.* crack, fracture; gaping fissure; loss, damage; (com.) failure, bankruptcy.

quiebro, *m.* dodge, swerve; (mus.) trill.

quien, *pron.* (pl. QUIENES) who, whom, he who (pl. those who); whose.—**quienquiera,** *pron.* (pl. QUIENES-QUIERA) whoever, whosoever, whomsoever.—**quién,** *interrog. pron.* (pl. QUIENES) who?

quieto, *a.* quiet, still; steady, undisturbed.—**quietud,** *f.* stillness, quietness; tranquility.

quijada, *f.* jaw, jawbone.

quijotesco, *a.* quixotic.

quilate, *m.* (jewelry) carat or karat; degree of excellence.

quilo, *m.* (med.) chyle.—*sudar el q.,* to work hard.

quilla, *f.* (naut.) keel.

quimbombó, *m.* (Am.) okra, gumbo.

quimera, *f.* fancy, absurd idea; quarrel.—**quimérico,** *a.* imaginary; wildly fanciful.

química, *f.* chemistry.—**químico,** *a.* chemical.—*n.* chemist.

quimono, *m.* kimono.

quina, *f.* = QUININA.

quincalla, *f.* (com.) hardware; small wares.—**quincallería,** *f.* hardware trade or store; small wares store.

quincena, *f.* fortnight.—**quincenal,** *a.* fortnightly, semi-monthly.

quinina, *f.* quinine.

quinta, *f.* country seat, villa; manorhouse; (mil.) draft; (mus.) fifth.

quintaesencia, *f.* quintessence.

quintal, *m.* quintal. (See Table.)

quinteto, *m.* (mus.) quintet.

quintuplo, *a.* quintuple, fivefold.

quiosco, *m.* kiosk.

quirófano, *m.* (surg.) operating room.

quiromancia, *f.* palmistry.—**quiromántico,** *n.* palmist.

quirúrgico, *a.* surgical.

quisquilla, *f.* bickering, trifling dispute; shrimp; (coll.) small man.—**quisquilloso,** *a.* fastidious; touchy, peevish.

quitamanchas, *m.* cleaner, spot remover.—*m.* dry cleaner.

quitanieves, *m.* snow plow.

quitar, *vt.* to take away; to subtract; to take off, remove; to separate, take out; to free from; to rob of, deprive of; to forbid, prohibit; (fencing) to parry.—*vr.* to abstain, refrain; to quit, move away, withdraw; to get rid of; to take off (a garment); to come out (as a stain).—**quite,** *m.* parry, dodge.

quitasol, *m.* sunshade, parasol.

quizá, quizás, *adv.* perhaps, maybe.

R

rabadilla, *f.* coccyx; rump.

rábano, *m.* radish.—*r. picante,* horse-radish.—*tomar el r. por las hojas,* (coll.) to be off the track.

rabí, *m.* rabbi.

rabia, *f.* rabies.—*tenerle r. a,* to have a grudge against.—**rabiar,** *vi.* to have rabies; to rage; to rave; to suffer racking pain.—*r. por,* to long eagerly for.—**rabieta,** *f.* tantrum.

rabínico, *a.* rabbinical.—**rabino,** *m.* rabbi.

rabión, *m.* rapids of a river.

rabioso, *a.* rabid; suffering from rabies; enraged.

rabo, *m.* tail; tail end, back, or hind part.—*con el r. entre las piernas,* (coll.) (fig.) with the tail between the legs, crestfallen.—*mirar con el r. del ojo,* to look askance, or out of the corner of the eye.

racial, *a.* racial, race.

racimo, *m.* bunch; cluster.

ración, *f.* ration; supply, allowance.

racional, *a.* rational; reasonable.

racionamiento, *m.* rationing.—**racionar,** *vt.* to ration.

racha, *f.* flaw; gust of wind; streak of luck.

radar, *m.* radar.

radiación, *f.* radiation.—**radiador,** *m.* radiator.—**radial,** *a.* radial; radio. —**radiante,** *a.* radiant, brilliant, beaming.—**radiar,** *vi.* to radiate.— *vt. & vi.* to radio; to broadcast.

radical, *a.* radical.—*mf.* (pol.) radical; (gram. & math.) root.

radicar, *vii.* [d] to take root; to be (in a place).—*vr.* to settle, establish oneself.

radio, *m.* radius; radio set; radiogram; radium; circuit, district.— *mf.* radio.—*r. de acción,* range.— **radioactividad,** *f.* radioactivity.— **radioactivo,** *a.* radioactive.—**radiodifundir,** *vt. & vi.* to broadcast.— **radiodifusión,** *f.* broadcast.—**radiodifusora, radioemisora,** *f.* broadcasting station.—**radioescucha,** *mf.* radio listener.—**radiografía,** *f.* X-ray, radiography.—**radiograma,** *m.* radiogram.—**radiólogo,** *n.* radiologist.—**radiorreceptor,** *m.* radio receiver.—**radiotransmisor,** *m.* radio transmitter.—**radioyente,** *mf.* radio listener.

raer, *vti.* [8] to scrape; to rub off, fray; to erase.

ráfaga, *f.* gust of wind; flash or gleam of light; burst (of an automatic weapon).—*r. de aire,* waft.

raíces, *pl.* of RAÍZ.—*bienes r.,* real estate.

raído, *a.* frayed, worn out, threadbare; shameless.

raigón, *m.* large strong root; root of a tooth.

rail, *m.* (RR.) rail.

raiz, *f.* root; base, foundation; origin. —*a r. de,* immediately, right after. —*de r.,* by the roots, from the root; entirely.—*echar raíces,* to take root, become settled or fixed.

raja, *f.* split, rent, crack; slice (as a fruit).—**rajadura,** *f.* cleft, crack; crevice.—**rajar,** *vt.* to split; to slice (food).—*vr.* to split, crack.—*vi.* (coll.) to chatter.—*a rajatabla(s),* in a great haste.

ralea, *f.* race, breed, stock; kind, quality.—**ralo,** *a.* thin, sparse, not dense.

rallador, *m.* grater.—**rallar,** *vt.* to grate; (coll.) to vex.

rama, *f.* branch, twig, limb, bough.— *andarse por las ramas,* to beat around the bush.—*en r.,* raw.— **ramaje,** *m.* mass of branches; foliage.—**ramal,** *m.* branch, ramification; (RR.) branch road; strand of a rope; halter.—**ramalazo,** *m.* lash, stroke with a rope; mark left by a lash; blow; spot on the face caused by blows or disease.

ramera, *f.* prostitute, whore.

ramillete, *m.* bouquet; cluster.— **ramo,** *m.* bough; branch (of trade, science, art, etc.); branchlet; cluster, bouquet; line of goods.—**ramonear,** *vi.* to lop off twigs; to browse.

rampa, *f.* ramp.

ramplón, *a.* coarse, rude, vulgar, common.

rana, *f.* frog.

rancio, *a.* rank, rancid, stale.—*vino r.,* mellow wine.

ranchería, *f.* settlement; cluster of huts; camp.—**ranchero,** *m.* mess cook; small farmer; (Am.) rancher. —**rancho,** *m.* (mil.) mess, chow; messhall; hut; camp; (Am.) cattle ranch.

rango, *m.* rank, class, position, status.

ranura, *f.* groove, notch; slot.

rapacidad, *f.* rapacity.

rapadura, *f.* shaving; hair cut.— **rapapolvo,** *m.* (coll.) sharp reprimand, dressing down.—**rapar,** *vt.* to shave; to crop the hair); to plunder, snatch, rob.

rapaz, *a.* rapacious, predatory.—*f. pl.* (RAPACES) birds of prey.—*n.* young boy (girl).

rape, *m.* (coll.) hurried shaving or hair cutting.—*al r.,* cropped, clipped, cut close or short.

rapidez, *f.* rapidity, swiftness.— **rápido,** *a.* rapid, swift.—*m.* rapids; express train.

rapiña, *f.* rapine, plundering.—*de r.,* (of birds) of prey.—**rapiñar,** *vt.* (coll.) to plunder; to steal.

raposa, *f.* vixen, fox; (fig.) cunning person.

rapsodia, *f.* rhapsody.

raptar, *vt.* to abduct; to kidnap (a woman).—**rapto,** *m.* kidnapping; abduction, ravishment; rapture, ecstasy.

raqueta, *f.* (sports) racket.

raquítico, *a.* rachitic, rickety; feeble, skinny.

rareza, *f.* rarity, uncommonness; queerness; freak; curiosity; oddness.—*por* or *de r.,* rarely, seldom. —**raro,** *a.* rare; scarce; thin, not dense; queer, odd.—*rara vez,* seldom.

ras, *m.* level, flush.—*al r. con* or *de,* even or flush with.—**rasante,** *a.* leveling, grazing.—*f.* (RR.) grade, grade line.—**rasar,** *vt.* to strike or level with a straight edge; to graze, touch lightly.

rascacielos, *m.* (coll.) skyscraper.—**rascar**, *vti.* [d] to scratch; to rasp; to scrape.—*vri.* to scratch oneself.

rasete, *m.* sateen.

rasgado, *a.* torn, open; generous.—*ojos rasgados*, large eyes.—*m.* tear, rip.—**rasgadura**, *f.* rent, rip.—**rasgar**, *vti.* [b] to tear, rend, rip.—**rasgo**, *m.* stroke, flourish; stroke (of wit, kindness, etc.); feature (of face); characteristic.—*a grandes rasgos*, broadly, in outline.—**rasgón**, *m.* rent, tear.

rasguñar, *vt.* to scratch.—**rasguño**, *m.* scratch.

raso, *a.* clear; plain; flat.—*a campo r.*, in the open air.—*m.* satin.—*soldado r.*, private.

raspadura, *f.* erasure; rasping, scraping; shavings.—**raspar**, *vt.* to scrape, rasp; to erase; to steal.

rastra, sled; dray; (Am.) trailer; (agr.) harrow, rake; anything dragging.—*a rastras*, dragging; by force, unwillingly.—**rastreador**, *n.* tracer; scout.—**rastrear**, *vt.* to trace, scent; to track down, trail; (agr.) to harrow, rake; to follow a clue to.—*vi.* to fly very low.—**rastrero**, *a.* creeping, dragging; trailing; flying low; abject; low.—**rastrillar**, *vt.* to hackle, dress (flax), comb; to rake.—**rastrillo**, *m.* hackle, flax comb; (agr.) rake.—**rastro**, *m.* track, scent, trail; trace; (agr.) rake, harrow; slaughterhouse; sign, token; vestige.—**rastrojo**, *m.* stubble.

rata, *f.* rat.—*m.* (coll.) pickpocket.—**ratería**, *f.* larceny, petty theft; (coll.) meanness, stinginess.—**ratero**, *n.* pickpocket.

ratificación, *f.* ratification, confirmation.—**ratificar**, *vti.* [d] to ratify, confirm.

rato, *m.* short time, while.—*al poco r.*, presently, very soon.—*a ratos*, from time to time, occasionally.—*buen r.*, a great while; a pleasant, good time.—*mal r.*, a hard time.—*pasar el r.*, to pass the time, while away the time.

ratón, *m.* mouse; (Am.) hangover.—**ratonera**, *f.* mousetrap, rat trap.

raudal, *m.* torrent; plenty, abundance.

raudo, *a.* rapid, swift.

raya, *f.* stroke, dash, streak, stripe, line; crease (in trousers); parting in the hair; (print.) dash, rule.—*tener a uno a r.*, to hold one at bay; (ichth.) ray, skate.—**rayado**, *a.* streaky.—**rayano**, *a.* neighboring, contiguous, bordering.—**rayar**, *vt.* to draw lines on; to rule; to scratch, mar; to stripe, streak; to cross out.—*vi.* to excel, surpass; to border (on).—*r. el alba*, to dawn. —**rayo**, *m.* ray, beam; spoke of a wheel; thunderbolt; flash of lightning; lively, ready genius; great power or efficacy of action.

rayón, *m.* (neol.) rayon.

raza, *f.* race, lineage; breed.—*de r.*, pure-breed.

razón, *f.* reason; reasonableness; right; account, explanation; information; (Am.) message; (math.) ratio.—*a r. de*, at the rate of.—*con r. o sin ella*, rightly or wrongly.—*dar la r. a*, to agree with.—*entrar en r.*, to be, or become, reasonable, listen to reason.—*no tener r.*, to be wrong or mistaken.—*perder la r.*, to become insane.—*r. social*, (com.) firm, firm name.—*tener r.*, to be right.—**razonable**, *a.* reasonable; moderate; fair, just.—**razonamiento**, *m.* reasoning.—**razonar**, *vi.* to reason.

reabastecer, *vti. & vri.* [3] to supply again.

reabrir, *vti. & vri.* [49] to reopen.

reacción, *f.* reaction.—**reaccionar**, *vi.* to react.—**reaccionario**, *n. & a.* reactionary.

reacio, *a.* obstinate, stubborn; reluctant.

reacondicionar, *vt.* to recondition.

reactivo, *a.* reactive.—*m.* (chem.) reagent; reactor.

readaptación, *f.* readjustment.—**readaptar**, *vt.* to readjust, adapt again.

reajuste, *m.* readjustment.

real, *a.* real, actual; royal, kingly.—*m.* real, a silver coin; camp, encampment.

realce, *m.* excellence; luster, splendor; raised work, embossment.—*dar r.*, to enhance.

realeza, *f.* royalty, regal dignity.—**realidad**, *f.* reality, fact; truth.—*en r.*, truly; really; in fact.—**realismo**, *m.* realism; royalism.—**realista**, *mf.* realist; royalist.—**realización**, *f.* realization, fulfillment; (com.) sale.—**realizar**, *vti.* [a] to realize, fulfill, carry out, perform; (com.) to sell out.

realzar, *vti.* [a] to raise, elevate; to emboss; to brighten the colors of; to make prominent; to heighten, enhance.

reanimar, *vt.* to cheer, encourage; to revive; reanimate.

reanudación, *f.* renewal; resumption.—**reanudar**, *vt.* to renew, resume.

reaparecer, *vii.* [3] to reappear.—**reaparición**, *f.* reappearance.

rearme, *m.* rearmament.

reasegurar, *vt.* (com.) to reinsure.—**reaseguro,** *m.* (com.) reinsurance.

reasumir, *vt.* to retake; to resume.

reata, *f.* rope, lariat; string of horses.

reavivar, *vt.* & *vr.* to revive, reanimate.

rebaja, *f.* (com.) discount; deduction, diminution.—**rebajar,** *vt.* to abate, lessen, diminish; to reduce, lower, cut down.—*vr.* to be dismissed; to lower oneself.

rebanada, *f.* slice.—**rebanar,** *vt.* to slice; to cut.

rebaño, *m.* herd; flock.

rebasar, *vt.* to exceed; to overflow.

rebatir, *vt.* to beat or drive back, repel; to refute.—**rebato,** *m.* alarm, alarm bell; call to arms; commotion; (mil.) sudden attack.

rebelarse, *vr.* to revolt, rebel.—**rebelde,** *a.* rebellious; stubborn.—*mf.* rebel; (law) defaulter.—**rebeldía,** *f.* rebelliousness, contumacy; stubbornness; (law) default.—**rebelión,** *f.* rebellion, revolt.

rebencazo, *m.* (Am.) blow with a whip.—**rebenque,** *m.* (Am.) whip.

reblandecer, *vti.* & *vri.* [3] to soften.—**reblandecimiento,** *m.* softening.

reborde, *m.* flange, border; rim.—**rebordear,** *vt.* to flange.

rebosar, *vi.* to overflow; (**de**) to abound (in); to teem (with).

rebotar, *vi.* to rebound.—*vt.* to cause to rebound; to repel; to vex.—**rebote,** *m.* rebound, rebounding, bounce, bound.—**de r.,** on the rebound; indirectly.

rebozar, *vti.* [a] to muffle up; to dip (food in flour, etc.).—*vri.* to muffle oneself up.—**rebozo,** *m.* muffler; woman's shawl.—**sin r.,** frankly, openly.

rebullir, *vii.* & *vri.* [27] to stir, begin to move; to boil up.

rebusca, *f.* search; research; searching; gleaning.—**rebuscar,** *vti.* [d] to search carefully; to glean; to dig up.

rebuznar, *vi.* to bray.—**rebuzno,** *m.* braying (of a donkey).

recabar, *vt.* to obtain by entreaty.

recado, *m.* message, errand; present, gift; regards; daily provision or marketing; voucher; equipment; precaution.

recaer, *vii.* [8-e] to fall back, relapse; to fall or devolve; to behoove.—**recaída,** *f.* relapse.

recalar, *vi.* to make, sight, or reach port.—*vt.* to soak, drench, saturate.

recalcar, *vti.* [d] to cram, pack, press; to emphasize, stress.—*vri.* to harp on a subject.

recalentar, *vti.* [1] to reheat; to overheat; to warm over; to superheat.—*vri.* to become overheated or superheated.

recamar, *vt.* to embroider with raised work.

recámara, *f.* dressing room; boudoir; (Mex.) bedroom; (artil.) breech of a gun.

recambiar, *vt.* to exchange or change again; (com.) to refill.

recapacitar, *vi.* to refresh one's memory; to think carefully.

recargar, *vti.* [b] to reload; to overload; to overcharge; to recharge.—*vri.* (**de**) to have in abundance, have an abundance (of).—**recargo,** *m.* overload; overcharge; surtax, additional tax, charge, etc.; extra charge.

recatado, *a.* prudent, circumspect, unobtrusive; shy; modest.—**recatar,** *vt.* to secrete, conceal.—*vr.* to act modestly; to be cautious.—**recato,** *m.* prudence, caution; modesty; bashfulness.

recaudación, *f.* collecting, collection.—**recaudador,** *n.* tax collector.—**recaudar,** *vt.* to gather; to collect (rents or taxes).—**recaudo,** *m.* collection of rents or taxes; precaution, care; (law) bail, bond, security.—*a buen r.,* well guarded, under custody, safe.

recelar, *vt.* to fear, suspect.—*vr.* (**de**) to fear, be afraid or suspicious (of), to beware (of).—**recelo,** *m.* misgiving, fear, suspicion.—**receloso,** *a.* suspicious, fearful, distrustful.

recental, *a.* suckling (lamb or calf).

recepción, *f.* reception, receiving, admission.—**recepcionista,** *mf.* receptionist.

receptáculo, *m.* receptacle.—**receptivo,** *a.* receptive.—**receptor,** *n.* receiver; abettor; (baseball) catcher.—**receptoría,** *f.* receiver or treasurer's office; (law) receivership.

recesar, *vi.* (Am.) to recess, suspend temporarily.—**receso,** *m.* recess; separation, withdrawal.

receta, *f.* prescription; recipe.—**recetar,** *vt.* to prescribe (medicines).

recibidor, *n.* receiver; (com.) receiving teller.—*m.* reception room; vestibule.—**recibimiento,** *m.* reception; greeting, welcome.—**recibir,** *vt.* to receive; to take, accept; to admit; to experience (an injury).—*vr.* (**de**) to graduate (as); to be admitted to practice (as).—**recibo,** *m.* reception; (com.) receipt.—*acusar r.,* (com.) to acknowledge receipt.—*estar de r.,* to be at home to callers.

recién, *adv.* (before *pp.*) recently, lately, newly.—*r. casados,* newlyweds.—*r. llegado,* newcomer.—*r. na-*

cido, newborn.—**reciente,** *a.* recent; new; modern; fresh.

recinto, *m.* enclosure; place (building, hall, etc.); precinct.

recio, *a.* strong, robust, vigorous; loud; rude; hard to bear; severe, rigorous (weather).—*adv.* strongly; rapidly; vigorously; loud.

recipiente, *a.* receiving.—*m.* receptacle; container; recipient.

reciprocar, *vti. & vri.* [d] to correspond.—**reciprocidad,** *f.* reciprocity. —**recíproco,** *a.* reciprocal, mutual.

recitación, *f.* recitation, recital.— **recital,** *m.* (mus.) recital.—**recitar,** *vt.* to recite; to rehearse.

reclamación, *f.* reclamation; (com.) complaint; claim.—**reclamante,** *mf. & a.* complainer; claimer; complaining; claiming.—**reclamar,** *vt.* to claim, demand; to decoy (birds); (law) to reclaim.—*vi.* to complain. —**reclamo,** *m.* decoy bird; lure (of birds); call; claim; complaint; advertisement.

reclinar, *vt.* to incline, recline, lean. —*vr.* to recline, lean back.— **reclinatorio,** *m.* pew; couch, lounge; prayer desk.

recluir, *vti.* [23-e] to shut up; to seclude.—**reclusión,** *f.* seclusion; place of retirement; arrest; jail, prison.—**recluso,** *ppi.* of RECLUIR.

recluta, *f.* (mil.) recruiting.—*m.* recruit.—**reclutamiento,** *m.* (mil.) recruiting.—**reclutar,** *vt.* (mil.) to recruit.

recobrar, *vt. & vr.* to recover, recuperate, regain; to recoup.—**recobro,** *m.* recovery, recuperation; resumption.

recocer, *vti.* [26-a] to boil too much; to boil again; to reheat.—*vri.* to burn with rage.

recodo, *m.* turn, winding, bend, angle.

recoger, *vti.* [c] to gather, pick; to pick up, take up; to take in, collect; to take in, shelter.—*vri.* to take shelter; to retire.—**recogida,** *f.* withdrawal; harvesting; (com.) retiral.—**recogimiento,** *m.* concentration, abstraction.

recolección, *f.* gathering, harvest; compilation; summary.—**recolectar,** *vt.* to gather, collect, harvest.

recomendable, *a.* commendable, laudable.—**recomendación,** *f.* recommendation; request; praise; merit; testimonial.—**recomendar,** *vti.* [1] to recommend; to commend; to entrust; to ask, request.

recompensa, *f.* compensation; recompense, reward.—*en r.,* in return. —**recompensar,** *vt.* to compensate; to recompense, reward.

reconcentrar, *vt.* to concentrate; to dissemble.—*vr.* to concentrate (one's mind).

reconciliación, *f.* reconciliation.—**reconciliar,** *vt.* to reconcile.—*vr.* to become reconciled; to make up; to renew friendship.

reconocer, *vti.* [3] to recognize; to admit; **(por)** to acknowledge (as); to acknowledge; (mil.) to scout, reconnoiter.—**reconocimiento,** *m.* recognition; acknowledgment; gratitude; recognizance; examination, inquiry; (mil.) reconnoitering; (surv.) reconnaissance.

recontar, *vti.* [12] to recount; to relate.

reconvención, *f.* charge, accusation; reproach.—**reconvenir,** *vti.* [45] to accuse, reproach; (law) to countercharge.

recopilación, *f.* summary, compilation; (law) digest.—**recopilar,** *vt.* to compile, digest.

recordación, *f.* remembrance; recollection.—**recordar,** *vti.* [12] to remember, to remind.—*vri.* to remember.—**recordatorio,** *m.* reminder.

recorrer, *vt.* to go over; (mech.) to pass over, travel; to read over; to travel in or over; to overhaul.—*vi.* to resort; to travel.—**recorrido,** *m.* run; space or distance traveled or passed over, course; (auto) mileage.

recortar, *vt.* to cut away, trim, clip; to cut out; to cut to size; to outline (a figure).—**recorte,** *m.* cutting, paring; clipping (from newspaper, etc.); outline.—*pl.* trimmings, parings.

recostar, *vti.* [12] to lean, recline.— *vri.* to go to rest; to repose; to lean back (against); to recline.

recoveco, *m.* turning, winding; nook, cranny; sly approach.

recreación, *f.* recreation.—**recrear,** *vt.* to amuse, delight.—*vr.* to amuse oneself; to be pleased; to divert oneself.—**recreo,** *m.* recreation; place of amusement; (school) recess.

recrudecer, *vii. & vri.* [3] to increase; to recur.

rectángulo, *a.* rectangular; rightangled (triangle, etc.).—*m.* rectangle.

rectificar, *vti.* [d] to rectify; to correct, amend.

rectitud, *f.* straightness; righteousness, rightness, rectitude; accuracy, exactitude.—**recto,** *a.* straight; erect; righteous, just, fair; literal; right.—*m.* rectum.

rector, *n.* rector, curate; president (of a university, college, etc.); principal.—**rectorado,** *m.* rectorship; di-

rectorship; rector's office.—**rectoría,**
f. rectory, curacy; rectorship; rector's or director's office.

recua, *f.* herd of beasts of burden; multitude, pack of things.

recuento, *m.* recount; inventory.

recuerdo, *m.* remembrance; memory; recollection; souvenir; keepsake, memento.—*pl.* compliments, regards.

reculada, *f.* recoil, recoiling.—**recular,** *vi.* to recoil, back up; (coll.) to yield, give up, turn back.

recuperación, *f.* recovery, recuperation.—**recuperar,** *vt. & vr.* to recover, regain, recuperate.

recurrir, *vi.* to resort, apply; to revert.—**recurso,** *m.* recourse; resource, resort; return, reversion; memorial, petition; (law) appeal.—*pl.* resources, means.

recusar, *vt.* to reject, decline; to challenge (a juror).

rechazar, *vti.* [a] to repel, repulse, drive back; to reject; to rebuff.—**rechazo,** *m.* rebound; rebuff; recoil; rejection.

rechifla, *f.* hissing (in derision); hooting; mockery, ridicule.—**rechiflar,** *vt.* to hiss; to mock, ridicule.

rechinar, *vi.* to creak, squeak; to gnash the teeth.

rechoncho, *a.* (coll.) chubby, stocky.

red, *f.* net; network, netting; bag net; snare, trap; system (of RR., tel., etc.).

redacción, *f.* wording; editing; editorial rooms; editorial staff.—**redactar,** *vt.* to edit, be the editor of; to write, word.—**redactor,** *n.* editor.

redada, *f.* casting a net; catch, haul.

redarguir, *vti.* [23-e] to retort; (law) to impugn.

redecilla, *f.* hair net.

rededor, *m.* surroundings, environs.—*al* or *en r.,* around.

redención, *f.* redemption.—**redentor,** *n. & a.* redeemer; redeeming.

redil, *m.* sheepfold.

redimible, *a.* redeemable.—**redimir,** *vt.* to redeem, rescue, ransom; to liberate; (com.) to redeem, pay off.

rédito, *m.* (com.) revenue, interest, yield.

redoblar, *vt.* to double; to clinch; to repeat; (mil.) to roll (a drum).—**redoble,** *m.* (mil. & mus.) roll of a drum.

redoma, *f.* vial, flask.

redomado, *a.* artful, sly, crafty.

redonda, *f.* neighborhood, district.—*a la r.,* roundabout.—**redondamente,** *adv.* clearly, plainly, decidedly.—**redondear,** *vt.* to round, make round; to round off; to perfect.—*vr.* to clear oneself of debts; to

obtain good profits (of a business).—**redondel,** *m.* (coll.) circle; round cloak; bull ring, arena.—**redondez,** *f.* roundness, rotundity.—*r. de la Tierra,* face of the Earth.—**redondilla,** *f.* quatrain.—**redondo,** *a.* round, rotund; clear, straight; (fig.) nice, honest.—*en r.,* all around.—*negocio r.,* (fig.) profitable business.

reducción, *f.* reduction, decrease; discount.—**reducido,** *a.* limited; small; narrow; compact.—**reducir,** *vti.* [11] to reduce; to diminish, decrease; (a) to convert (into); to subdue; to condense, abridge.—*vri.* to adjust oneself, adapt oneself; to be compelled, to decide from necessity.

reducto, *m.* (fort.) redoubt.

redundancia, *f.* redundance.—**redundante,** *a.* redundant, superfluous.—**redundar,** *vi.* to overflow; to be redundant; (en) to redound (to), lead (to).

reduplicar, *vti.* [d] to duplicate again, redouble.

reedificar, *vti.* [d] to rebuild.

reelección, *f.* reëlection.—**reelecto,** *ppi.* of REELEGIR.—**reelegir,** *vti.* [29-49] to reëlect.

reembolsar, *vt.* to reimburse, refund, pay back.—**reembolso,** *m.* reimbursement, refund.

reemplazar, *vti.* [a] to replace; to substitute.—**reemplazo,** *m.* replacement; substitution; (mil.) substitute.

reenvasar, *vt.* (com.) to refill.

reestreno, *m.* (theat.) revival.

reexpedir, *vti.* [29] to forward (mail, etc.).

refacción, *f.* refreshment, luncheon; reparation; (Am.) spare part; financing.

refajo, *m.* underskirt; petticoat.

referencia, *f.* reference; narration.—**referéndum,** *m.* referendum.—**referente,** *a.* referring, relating.—**referir,** *vti.* [39] to refer, relate; to tell, narrate.—*vri.* (a) to refer (to), have relation (to).

refilón.—*de r.,* obliquely, askance.

refinamiento, *m.* refinement; refining.—**refinar,** *vt.* to refine, purify; to make polite or refined.—**refinería,** *f.* refinery.

reflector, *a.* reflecting, reflective.—*m.* searchlight; reflector.—**reflejar,** *vt.* to reflect.—*vr.* to be reflected.—**reflejo,** *a.* reflected; (gram.) reflexive; (physiol.) reflex.—*m.* glare; reflection; light reflected.—**reflexión,** *f.* reflection; thinking.—**reflexionar,**

vi. to think, reflect.—**reflexivo,** *a.* reflexive; reflective; thoughtful.

reflujo, *m.* ebb or ebb tide.

reforma, *f.* reform; reformation; alteration, correction, improvement. —**reformador,** *n.* & *a.* reformer; reforming.—**reformar,** *vt.* to reform; to amend, improve.—*vr.* to reform; to mend.—**reformatorio,** *a.* corrective, reforming.—*m.* reformatory.—**reformista,** *mf.* & *a.* reformer; reforming, reformist.

reforzar, *vti.* [12-a] to strengthen, reinforce.

refrán, *m.* proverb, saying.

refrenar, *vt.* to restrain, check; to rein, curb.

refrendar, *vt* to legalize, authenticate, countersign.

refrescante, *a.* cooling, refreshing.— **refrescar,** *vti.* [d] to refresh; to cool.—*vii.* & *vri.* (of the weather) to get cool; to take the fresh air; to take refreshment; to cool off.— **refresco,** *m.* refreshment.

refriega, *f.* affray, scuffle, fray.

refrigeración, *f.* refrigeration.—**refrigerador,** *a.* refrigerating, freezing, cooling.—*m.* refrigerator, freezer, ice box.—**refrigerar,** *vt.* to cool, refrigerate.—**refrigerio,** *m.* coolness; refreshment, refection.

refuerzo, *m.* reinforcement; strengthening; welt (of shoe); aid, help.

refugiado, *n.* refugee.—**refugiar,** *vt.* to shelter.—*vr.* to take shelter or refuge.—**refugio,** *m.* refuge, shelter.

refundir, *vt.* to remelt or recast; to rearrange, recast, reconstruct.—*vi.* to redound.

refunfuñar, *vt.* to growl, grumble, mutter.—**refunfuño,** *m.* grumbling, growl, snort.

refutar, *vt.* to refute.

regadera, *f.* watering pot, sprinkler. —**regadío,** *a.* & *m.* irrigated (land).

regalar, *vt.* to present, give as a present, make a present of; to regale, entertain; to gladden, cheer, delight.—*vr.* to feast sumptuously.

regalía, *f.* regalia, royal rights; (Am.) advance payment or royalty to owner of patent, etc.; privilege, exemption.

regalo, *m.* present, gift; pleasure; dainty; comfort, luxury.

regañadientes,—*a r.,* reluctantly, grumbling.—**regañar,** *vi.* to growl, grumble; mutter; to quarrel.—*vt.* (coll.) to scold, reprimand.—**regaño,** *m.* scolding, reprimand.—**regañón,** *n.* growler, grumbler; scolder, scold.—*a.* growling, grumbling; scolding.

regar, *vti.* [1-b] to water; to irrigate; to sprinkle; to scatter.

regata, *f.* regatta, boat race.—**regatear,** *vt.* to haggle about, beat down (the price), to resell at retail; to bargain; to dodge, dribble (soccer)—*vi.* to haggle; to wriggle; (naut.) to race.—**regateo,** *m.* chaffer, bargaining, haggling.

regazo, *m.* lap (of body).

regente, *a.* ruling, governing.—*mf.* regent; manager, director.—**regentear,** *vi.* to rule, boss, manage.— **regidor,** *a.* ruling, governing.—*m.* alderman or councilman.

régimen, *m.* regime; management, rule; (gram.) government; (med.) regimen, treatment.—*r. alimenticio,* diet.

regimiento, *m.* (mil.) regiment; administration, government; town council.

regio, *a.* royal, regal; sumptuous, magnificent.

región, *f.* region.—**regional,** *a.* regional, local.

regir, *vti.* [29-c] to rule, govern, direct; to manage.—*vii.* to be in force.

registrador, *n.* register; registrar, recorder, master or clerk of records; searcher, inspector.—*a.* registering. —**registrar,** *vt.* to inspect, examine; to search; to register, record.—*vr.* to register, be registered or matriculated.—**registro,** *m.* search, inspection, examination; census, registry, registration; enrollment; record, entry; enrolling office; certificate of entry; register book; bookmark; (mus.) register, organ stop; regulator (of a timepiece).

regla, *f.* rule, regulation, precept; order, measure, moderation; (drawing) ruler, straight edge; menstruation.—*en r.,* thoroughly, in due form, in order.—**reglamentar,** *vt.* to establish rules; to regulate by rule, law or decree.—**reglamento,** *m.* by-laws; rules and regulations.

regocijado, *a.* merry, joyful, festive.— **regocijar,** *vt.* to gladden, cheer, rejoice.—*vr.* to rejoice, be merry.— **regocijo,** *m.* joy, gladness; merriment; rejoicing.

regodearse, *vr.* to take delight, rejoice.—**regodeo,** *m.* joy, delight.

regordete, *a.* (coll.) chubby, plump.

regresar, *vi.* to return.—**regreso,** *m.* return, coming or going back.

reguero, *m.* trickle, drip; irrigating furrow.

regulación, *f.* regulation; adjustment. —**regulador,** *a.* regulating, governing.—*m.* (mech.) regulator; governor; register; controller (of electric car).—**regular**, *vt.* to regulate; to adjust.—*a.* regular; moderate, sober; ordinary; fairly good, so-so.—*por lo regular*, usually, as a rule.—**regularidad**, *f.* regularity; common usage, custom.—**regularizar**, *vti.* [a] to regularize.

rehacer, *vti.* [22-49] to remodel, make over, remake; do over; to renovate, mend, repair.—*vri.* to regain strength and vigor; (mil.) to rally, reorganize.—**rehecho**, *ppi.* of REHACER.

rehén, *m.* (gen. *pl.*) hostage.

rehuir, *vti., vii. & vri.* [23-e] to shun, avoid; to reject, decline, refuse.

rehusar, *vt.* to refuse, decline, reject, withhold.

reimpresión, *f.* reprint; reissue.—**reimprimir**, *vti.* [49] to reprint.

reina, *f.* queen.—**reinado**, *m.* reign.—**reinante**, *a.* reigning; prevailing.—**reinar**, *vi.* to reign; to prevail, predominate.

reincidir, *vi.* to relapse; to backslide.

reino, *m.* kingdom.

reintegrar, *vt.* to reintegrate, restore; (com.) to reimburse, refund.—*vr.* (de) to recover, recuperate.—**reintegro**, *m.* reimbursement, restitution.

reír, *vii. & vri.* [35] to laugh.—*r. a carcajadas*, to laugh loudly, guffaw.—*reírse de*, to laugh at; to mock.

reiterar, *vt.* to reiterate.

reja, *f.* grate, grating, railing; plowshare; plowing.—**rejilla**, *f.* small lattice or grating; latticed wicket; cane for backs and seats of chairs.

relación, *f.* relation, relationship; dealing; ratio; narration, account; (law) report, brief; (theat.) speech.—*pl.* relations, connections; acquaintance; courting, engagement.—*en* or *con r.* regarding (to or with).—**relacionar**, *vt.* to relate, connect; to make acquainted.—*vr.* to get acquainted, make connections; to be related.

relajación, *f.*, **relajamiento**, *m.* relaxation, laxity; slackening; hernia.—**relajar**, *vt.* to relax, slacken; to release from an obligation; to amuse, divert.—*vr.* to become relaxed, loosened, weakened; to grow vicious; to be ruptured.—**relajo**, *m.* (Am.) disorder, mix-up; (Am.) depravity; diversion.

relamer, *vt.* to lick again.—*vr.* to lick one's lips; to relish; to boast.

relámpago, *m.* lightning; flash; (fig.) quick person or action.—**relampaguear**, *vi.* to lighten; to flash, sparkle.—**relampagueo**, *m.* lightning; flashing.

relatar, *vt.* to relate, narrate.

relatividad, *f.* relativity.—**relativo**, *a.* relative.

relato, *m.* statement; narration; report, account.—**relator**, *n.* narrator.

releer, *vti.* [e] to read over again; to revise.

relegar, *vti.* [b] to relegate, banish; to set aside.

relente, *m.* night dew, night dampness.

relevador, *m.* (elec.) relay.

relevante, *a.* excellent, great, eminent.—**relevar**, *vt.* (mil.) to relieve, substitute; to emboss; to bring into relief; to relieve, release; to forgive, acquit; to exalt, aggrandize.—*vi.* (art) to stand out in relief.—**relevo**, *m.* (mil.) relief.—*carrera de relevos*, relay race.

relicario, *m.* locket; reliquary.

relieve, *m.* relief, raised work, embossment.—*poner de r.*, to bring out, throw into relief, emphasize.—*pl.* (of food) leavings; (fig.) highlights or high points.

religión, *f.* religion.—**religiosidad**, *f.* religiosity; religiousness.—**religioso**, *a.* religious; scrupulous.—*n.* religious, member of a religious order.

relinchar, *vi.* to neigh.—**relincho**, *m.* neigh, neighing.

reliquia, *f.* relic; remains; trace, vestige.

reloj, *m.* clock; watch.—*r. de arena*, hourglass.—*r. de pulsera*, wrist watch.—*r. de sol*, sundial.—*r. despertador*, alarm clock.—*estar como un r.*, (coll.) to be in perfect trim.—**relojero**, *n.* watchmaker.

reluciente, *a.* shining, glittering, bright.—**relucir**, *vii.* [3] to shine, glow, glitter; to be brilliant.

relumbrante, *a.* resplendent.—**relumbrar**, *vi.* to sparkle, shine, glitter.—**relumbrón**, *m.* luster, dazzling brightness; tinsel.—*de r.*, showy, pompous.

rellano, *m.* landing (of a stair).

rellenar, *vt.* to refill; to fill up; (cook.) to stuff; (sewing) to pad; (mason.) to point.—*vr.* to stuff oneself.—**relleno**, *a.* stuffed.—*m.* stuffing; filling; (mech.) packing, gasket; (sewing) padding, wadding.

remachar, *vt.* to clinch; to rivet; to secure, affirm.—**remache**, *m.* rivet; riveting; flattening, clinching.

remanente, *m.* remains, remnant, residue.—*a.* residual.

remangar, *vti.* [b] to tuck up (sleeves, etc.).

remanso, *m.* backwater; dead water; eddy.

remar, *vt. & vi.* to row, paddle.

rematado, *a.* sold (at auction); finished.—*estar r.,* (coll.) to be completely crazy.—**rematar,** *vt.* to end, finish; (com.) to auction; to give the finishing stroke; (sewing) to fasten off (a stitch).—*vr.* to be utterly ruined or destroyed; to become completely crazy.—**remate,** *m.* end, finish, conclusion; (com.) auction, public sale; (arch.) finial, pinnacle. —*de r.,* utterly, completely, hopelessly.—*r. de cuentas,* closing of accounts.

remedar, *vt.* to imitate, copy, mimic.

remediar, *vt.* to remedy; to help; to repair (mischief); to avoid.—*no poder r.,* not to be able to help (prevent).—**remedio,** *m.* remedy; medicine; help; amendment.—*no hay más r. (que),* there's nothing else to do (but).—*no tener r.,* to be unavoidable; to be irremediable; to be no help for.—*sin r.,* inevitable; hopeless.

rememorativo, *a.* reminiscent, reminding, recalling.

remendar, *vti.* [1] to patch, mend, repair; to darn.—**remendón,** *n.* cobbler; botcher, patcher.

remero, *m.* rower, oarsman.

remesa, *f.* (com.) shipment; remittance.—**remesar,** *vt.* (com.) to ship; to send, remit.

remiendo, *m.* patch; mending piece; darning; repair.—*a remiendos,* by patchwork, piecemeal.

remilgado, *a.* affected, prudish, squeamish.—**remilgo,** *m.* affected nicety, prudery, squeamishness.

reminiscencia, *f.* reminiscence.

remirar, *vt.* to review, look at or go over again.—*vr.* (en) to take great pains with; to inspect or consider with pleasure.

remisión, *f.* remission, sending back, remitting, remitment; pardon, forgiveness; remissness, indolence; relaxation, abatement.—**remiso,** *a.* remiss, careless, slack.—**remitente,** *mf. & a.* remitter, sender; remitting, sending.—**remitir,** *vt.* to remit; to forward; to pardon; to refer; (law) to transfer, remit to another court. —*vt., vi. & vr.* to remit, abate.— *vr.* (a) to refer (to); to quote from.

remo, *m.* oar; leg (of quadruped); (coll.) arm or leg (of person).

remoción, *f.* removal, removing; dismissal.

remojar, *vt.* to steep, soak, drench. —**remojo,** *m.* steeping, soaking, soakage.

remolacha, *f.* (bot.) beet.

remolcador, *m.* tug, tugboat, towboat.—**remolcar,** *vti.* [d] to tow, tug, take in tow; to haul.

remolino, *m.* whirl, whirlwind; whirlpool; twisted tuft of hair; crowd, throng; commotion.

remolón, *a.* indolent, lazy, soft.—*n.* malingerer.

remolque, *m.* towing, towage; trackage; towline.—*a r.,* in tow.—*dar r.,* to tow.

remontar, *vt.* (Am.) to go up (river); to repair, resole, revamp (shoes).— *vt. & vr.* to elevate, raise, rise.— *vr.* to soar (as birds); to take to the woods; to go back to, date from.

rémora, *f.* hindrance, obstacle; cause of delay; (ichth.) remora.

remordimiento, *m.* remorse.

remoto, *a.* remote, far off; unlikely.

remover, *vti.* [26] to move, remove, stir, disturb; to dismiss.

rempujar, *vt.* to jostle, shove, push.— **rempujón,** *m.* jostle, push, shove.

remuneración, *f.* remuneration; gratuity, consideration.—**remunerar,** *vt.* to remunerate.

renacer, *vii.* [3] to be born again; to spring up again, grow again.—**renacimiento,** *m.* renaissance, renascence, new birth.

renacuajo, *m.* tadpole; (coll.) little squirt.

rencilla, *f.* grudge; heartburning.

renco, *a.* = RENGO.

rencor, *m.* rancor, animosity, grudge. —**rencoroso,** *a.* rancorous, spiteful.

rendición, *f.* rendition, surrendering, yielding; profit, yield, product.— **rendido,** *a.* obsequious; devoted; fatigued, tired out.

rendija, *f.* crevice, crack, cleft.

rendimiento, *m.* submission; yield; income; output; (mech.) efficiency. —**rendir,** *vti.* [29] to subdue, overcome; to surrender, yield, give up; to render, give back; to do (homage); (com.) to produce, yield; to fatigue, tire out.—*r. las armas,* to throw down the arms, to surrender. —*vri.* to become exhausted, tired, worn out; to yield, submit, give up, surrender.

renegado, *n.* renegade, apostate; wicked person.—**renegar,** *vti.* [1-b] to deny, disown; to detest.—*vii.* to turn renegade, apostatize; to blaspheme, curse; (de) to deny, renounce; to blaspheme, curse.

renegrido, *a.* blackish.

renglón, *m.* written or printed line; (com.) line of business, staple, item.—*a r. seguido,* immediately after; the next moment.—*pl.* lines, writings.

rengo, *a.* lame.—**renguear,** *vi.* to limp, hobble.

reno, *m.* reindeer.

renombrado, *a.* renowned, famous.—**renombre,** *m.* surname, family name; renown.

renovación, *f.* renovation, renewing; change, reform; replacement.—**renovador,** *n. & a.* renovator; renewing.—**renovar,** *vti.* [12] to renew; to renovate; to replace; to repeat.

renquear, *vi.* = RENGUEAR.

renta, *f.* profit; annuity; tax, contribution; revenue.—**rentar,** *vt.* to produce, bring, yield; to rent for.—**rentista,** *mf.* financier; bondholder; one who lives on a fixed income.

renuente, *a.* unwilling, reluctant.

renuevo, *m.* sprout, shoot.

renuncia, *f.* resignation; renunciation; renouncement; waiving.—**renunciamiento,** *m.* renouncement.—**renunciar,** *vt.* to renounce; to resign; to disown; to waive; to reject; to abandon, relinquish.—*vi.* to resign.

reñir, *vti. & vii.* [9] to wrangle, quarrel, fight; to fall out; to scold.

reo, *a.* guilty, criminal.—*mf.* criminal, culprit; (law) defendant.

reojo, *m.*—**mirar de r.,** to look askance.

reorganización, *f.* reorganization.—**reorganizar,** *vti.* [a] to reorganize; to reconstitute.

repantigarse, *vri.* [b] to stretch (oneself) in a chair.

reparación, *f.* reparation, repair, indemnity; atonement.—**reparador,** *n.* repairer; restorer; faultfinder.—**reparar,** *vt.* to repair, recondition; to restore; to observe, notice; to consider, heed; to make up for, indemnify for; to atone for.—**reparo,** *m.* repair, restoration; observation, warning, notice; difficulty; objection.—*poner reparos,* to make objections.

repartidor, *a.* distributing.—*n.* distributor; assessor of taxes.—**repartimiento,** *m.* division, distribution, apportionment; assessment.—**repartir,** *vt.* to divide, distribute, apportion; to assess.—**reparto,** *m.* = REPARTIMIENTO; (theat.) cast of characters; delivery (of goods, mail, etc.).

repasar, *vt.* to pass again; to reëxamine, revise; to glance over; to mend, darn; to review (as a lesson).—**repaso,** *m.* review (of a lesson); revision, reëxamination; final inspection; mending.

repecho, *m.* short, steep incline.

repelar, *vt.* to pull out the hair of.

repeler, *vt.* to repel, repulse; to refute, dispute.

repente, *m.* sudden movement or impulse.—*de r.,* suddenly.—**repentino,** *a.* sudden.

repertorio, *m.* repertory, repertoire.

repetición, *f.* repetition; (theat.) encore.—**repetir,** *vti. & vii.* [29] to repeat.—*vri.* to repeat oneself.

repicar, *vti.* [d] to peal, ring (bells); to mince, chop.—**repique,** *m.* ringing, pealing (bells).—**repiquetear,** *vt.* to ring, peal (bells); to tap (with fingers or shoes).—**repiqueteo,** *m.* ringing of bells; tapping, clicking.

repisa, *f.* mantelpiece; shelf, console; bracket.

replegar, *vti.* [1-b] to fold several times.—*vri.* (mil.) to fall back, retreat in order.

repleto, *a.* replete, very full.

réplica, *f.* reply, answer; retort, rejoinder; objection; exact copy, replica.—**replicar,** *vii.* [d] to reply, answer; to contradict, argue.

repliegue, *m.* doubling, folding; (mil.) orderly retreat.

repollo, *m.* cabbage; round head (of a plant).

reponer, *vti.* [32-49] to replace, put back; to reinstall; to restore.—*vri.* to recover lost health or property.

reportaje, *m.* (journalism) report, reporting.—**reportar,** *vt.* to control, restrain, check; to obtain, get, attain; to carry; to bring.—*vr.* to refrain, forbear, control oneself.—**repórter,** *mf.*, **reportero,** *n.* reporter.

reposado, *a.* quiet, restful.—**reposar,** *vi.* to rest, repose; to stand (on), be supported (by); to take a nap; to lie down; to lie (in the grave).—*vr.* to settle (as liquids).

reposición, *f.* replacement, reinstatement; recovery (in health); (theat.) revival.—**repositorio,** *m.* repository.

reposo, *m.* rest, repose; sleep; tranquillity.

repostería, *f.* confectionery, pastry shop.—**repostero,** *n.* pastry cook.

reprender, *vt.* to scold, reproach.—**reprensión,** *f.* reprimand, reproach.

represa, *f.* dam, dike, sluice; damming; stopping, holding back.

represalia, *f.* reprisal.

representación, *f.* representation; description; (theat.) performance, play; figure, image, idea.—*en r. de,* as a representative of.—**representante,** *a.* representing, representative.—*mf.* representative; agent.—**representar,** *vt.* to represent,

typify; (theat.) to perform, act.—
vr. to image, picture to oneself,
conceive.—**representativo,** *a.* representative.

represión, *f.* repression, check, control.—**represivo,** *a.* repressive, restrictive.

reprimenda, *f.* reprimand.—**reprimir,** *vt.* to repress, check, curb, quash.

reprobable, *a.* blameworthy.—**reprobación,** *f.* reproof.—**reprobado,** *a.* flunked.—**reprobar,** *vti.* [12] to reprove, disapprove, condemn; to damn; to flunk, fail.—**réprobo,** *n.* & *a.* reprobate.

reprochar, *vt.* to reproach, censure; to challenge (witnesses).—**reproche,** *m.* reproach, reproof; repulse, rebuff.

reproducción, *f.* reproduction; (art) copy.—**reproducir,** *vti.* & *vri.* [11] to reproduce.—**reproductor,** *n.* & *a.* reproducer; reproducing.

reptil, *m.* reptile; crawler, creeper.

república, *f.* republic.—**republicano,** *a.* & *n.* republican.

repudiar, *vt.* to repudiate; to reject; to divorce.—**repudio,** *m.* repudiation; rejection; divorce.

repuesto, *ppi.* of REPONER.—*a.* recovered.—*m.* store, stock, supply.—
de r., extra; spare.

repugnancia, *f.* reluctance; aversion; loathing; disgust.—**repugnante,** *a.* loathsome; repulsive, disgusting.—
repugnar, *vt.* to cause disgust; to do with reluctance.

repulgar, *vti.* [b] (sewing) to hem.

repulsa, *f.* refusal, rebuke, repulse.—
repulsión, *f.* repulsion.—**repulsivo,** *a.* repelling.

reputación, *f.* reputation.—**reputar,** *vt.* to repute; to estimate, appreciate.

requebrar, *vti.* [1] to woo, court, make love to; to flatter, wheedle; to break again.

requemar, *vt.* to reburn; to overcook; to inflame (the blood).

requerimiento, *m.* summons; requisition, demand.—**requerir,** *vti.* [39] to summon; to notify; to require, need; to court, woo, make love to.

requesón, *m.* pot cheese, cottage cheese; curd.

requiebro, *m.* flattery, compliment; endearment.

requilorios, *m.* (coll.) useless ceremony; circumlocution.

requisa, *f.* tour of inspection; requisition.—**requisar,** *vt.* to make the rounds of; to requisition.—**requisito,** *m.* requisite, requirement.

res, *f.* head of cattle; beast.

resabio, *m.* unpleasant aftertaste; viciousness; bad habit.

resaca, *f.* surge, surf, undertow; (com.) redraft; (Am.) hangover.

resaltar, *vi.* to stand out; to jut out, project; to rebound; to come off, get loose; to be evident.

resarcimiento, *m.* compensation, reparation, indemnity.—**resarcir,** *vti.* [a] to compensate, indemnify, make amends to; to mend, repair; to recoup.

resbaladizo, *a.* slippery; glib; elusive; tempting, alluring.—**resbalar,** *vt.* & *vr.,* to slip, slide, glide; to skid; to err, go astray.—**resbalón,** *m.* slip, slipping; fault, error, break.
—**resbaloso,** *a.* (Am.) slippery.

rescatar, *vt.* to ransom; to redeem, recover; to rescue; to exchange, barter, commute.—**rescate,** *m.* ransom; redemption; ransom money; exchange, barter.

rescindir, *vt.* to rescind, annul.—
rescisión, *f.* cancellation, annulment.

rescoldo, *m.* embers, hot ashes; scruple, doubt, apprehension.

resecar, *vti.* & *vri.* [d] to dry up; to parch.—**reseco,** *a.* too dry; very lean.

resentimiento, *m.* resentment, grudge; impairment.—**resentirse,** *vri.* [39] to be impaired or weakened; to resent, be offended or hurt.

reseña, *f.* brief description; book review; sketch, summary, outline; (mil.) review.—**reseñar,** *vt.* to review, summarize, outline; (mil.) to review.

reserva, *f.* reserve, reticence; reservation; discretion; (mil.) reserve; salvo—*a r. de,* intending to.—*de r.,* extra, spare.—*en r.,* confidentially. —*guardar r.,* to act with discretion. —*sin r.,* openly, frankly.—**reservación,** *f.* reservation.—**reservar,** *vt.* to reserve, keep; to retain, hold; to postpone; to exempt; to conceal. —*vr.* to bide one's time; to keep for oneself; to beware, be cautious.

resfriado, *m.* cold (illness).—**resfriarse,** *vr.* to catch cold.—**resfrío,** *m.* = RESFRIADO.

resguardar, *vt.* to preserve, defend, protect.—*vr.* to take shelter; **(de)** to guard (against); protect oneself (from).—**resguardo,** *m.* security, safety, safeguard, defense, protection; (com.) guarantee, collateral.

residencia, *f.* residence, domicile.—
residencial, *a.* residential.—**residente,** *a.* residing, resident, residential.—*mf.* dweller, inhabitant.—**residir,** *vi.* to reside, live; dwell; (fig.) to consist.

residuo, *m.* remainder, remnant; residue; (arith.) difference.—*pl.* refuse, leavings.

resignación, *f.* resignation; submission.—**resignar**, *vt.* to resign, give up.—*vr.* to resign oneself, be resigned.

resina, *f.* resin, rosin.—**resinoso**, *a.* resinous.

resistencia, *f.* resistance, endurance.—**resistente**, *a.* resisting; resistant, tough.—**resistir**, *vi.* to resist, offer resistance.—*vt.* to resist; to bear, stand; to endure.—*vr.* to put up a struggle, resist.

resma, *f.* ream (of paper).

resol, *m.* glare of the sun.

resolución, *f.* resolution; resoluteness; determination, courage; solution (of a problem).—*en r.*, in short.—**resolver**, *vti.* [47-49] to resolve, determine; to sum up; to solve (a problem).—*vri.* to resolve, determine; (med.) to resolve, be reduced.

resollar, *vii.* [12] to breathe noisily, pant; (coll.) to breathe; (coll.) to give signs of life.

resonancia, *f.* resonance.—*tener r.*, to cause a stir, attract attention.—**resonante**, *a.* resonant, resounding, sounding.—**resonar**, *vii.* [12] to resound, clatter.

resoplar, *vi.* to puff, breathe audibly; to snort.—**resoplido**, *m.* puff; snort.

resorte, *m.* (mech.) spring; resilience, spring, elasticity; means; motivation.

respaldar, *vt.* to indorse; to back; to answer for, guarantee.—*m.* back of a seat.—**respaldo**, *m.* back of a seat; backing; back of a sheet of paper; indorsement.

respectivo, *a.* respective.—**respecto**, *m.* relation, proportion; relativeness; respect.—*a este r.*, with respect to this.—*al r.*, relatively, respectively.—*con r. a, r. a,* or *r. de,* with respect to, with regard to.

respetabilidad, *f.* respectability.—**respetable**, *a.* respectable, considerable; worthy; honorable, reliable.—**respetar**, *vt.* to respect, revere, honor.—**respeto**, *m.* respect; deference, attention; observance.—*faltar al r. a,* to be disrespectful to.—**respetuoso**, *a.* respectful; respectable.

respingar, *vii.* [b] to kick, wince; to grunt; (coll.) to mutter; to talk back.—**respingo**, *m.* muttering, grumbling; gesture of unwillingness.

respirable, *a.* breathable.—**respiración**, *f.* respiration, breathing.—**respiradero**, *m.* vent, air hole; ventilator.—**respirar**, *vi. & vt.* to rest, take rest or respite; to catch one's breath; to breathe freely; to exhale scents or odors.—**respiratorio**, *a.* respiratory.—**respiro**, *m.* breathing; moment of rest; respite; (com.) extension, time.

resplandecer, *vii.* [3] to glitter, glisten, shine.—**resplandeciente**, *a.* aglow.—**resplandor**, *m.* light, splendor, brilliance, radiance; glare.

responder, *vt. & vi.* to answer, reply; to respond; to acknowledge; to requite; to yield, produce; to have the desired effect; (com.) to correspond.—*vi.* (de) to answer (for), be responsible (for), vouch (for), guarantee.—**respondón**, *a.* saucy, pert, insolent.

responsabilidad, *f.* responsibility; reliability.—**responsable**, *a.* responsible; reliable.

responso, *m.* (eccl.) responsory for the dead.

respuesta, *f.* answer, reply; response, rejoinder; refutation.

resquebra(ja)dura, *f.* crack, cleft, fissure.—**resquebrajar**, *vt. & vr.* to crack, split.

resquicio, *m.* slit, crevice, crack; chance, opportunity.

resta, *f.* (arith.) subtraction; remainder, difference.

restablecer, *vti.* [3] to restore, reestablish, reinstate.—*vri.* to recover (from illness).—**restablecimiento**, *m.* reëstablishment; restoration; recovery.

restallar, *vi.* to crack (a whip); to crackle.

restante, *a.* remaining.—*m.* remainder.

restañar, *vt.* to stanch (wounds); to stop the flow of (blood).

restar, *vt.* to deduct; (arith.) to subtract.—*vi.* to be left, remain; (arith.) to subtract.

restauración, *f.* restoration.—**restaurante**, *m.* restaurant.—**restaurar**, *vt.* to restore; to recondition.

restitución, *f.* restitution.—**restituir**, *vti.* [23-e] to restore; to return, give back.—*vri.* to return, come back

resto, *m.* remainder, balance, rest; limit for stakes at cards.—*pl.* remains.—*echar el r.,* to stake one's all; to do one's best.

restorán, *m.* (Am.) restaurant.

restregar, *vti.* [1-b] to rub, scrub.—**restregón**, *m.* scrubbing, hard rubbing.

restricción, *f.* restriction, limitation.—**restrictivo**, *a.* restrictive, restricting.—**restringir**, *vti.* [c] to restrain, restrict, confine.

resucitar, *vt.* to resuscitate, revive;

to renew.—*vi.* to rise from the dead, return to life.

resuelto, *ppi.* of RESOLVER.—*a.* resolute, determined, quick.

resuello, *m.* breath, breathing; puffing, snorting.

resulta, *f.* result, effect, consequence. —*de resultas,* in consequence.—**resultado,** *m.* result.—**resultar,** *vi.* to result, follow; to turn out; to turn out to be; (coll.) to work (well or badly).

resumen, *m.* summary, résumé.—*en r.,* in brief.—**resumir,** *vt.* to abridge; to summarize, sum up.—*vr.* to be reduced or condensed.

resurrección, *f.* resurrection.

retablo, *m.* series of historical pictures; (eccl.) altarpiece.

retador, *n.* challenger.—*a.* challenging.

retaguardia, *f.* rear, rear guard.

retahíla, *f.* string, series; line.

retar, *vt.* to challenge, dare.

retardado, *a.* retarded.—**retardar,** *vt.* to retard, slow up; to delay, detain.—*vr.* to fall behind, be slow.— **retardo,** *m.* retardation; delay.

retazo, *m.* piece, remnant; cutting; fragment, portion.

retemblar, *vii.* [1] to tremble, shake, quiver.

retención, *f.* retention, keeping or holding back.—**retener,** *vti.* [42] to retain, withhold; to detain.—**retentivo,** *a.* retentive, retaining.—**retentiva,** *f.* retentiveness, memory.

reticencia, *f.* reticence.—**reticente,** *a.* reticent.

retina, *f.* retina of the eye.

retinto, *a.* very black.

retintín, *m.* tinkling, jingle; (coll.) sarcastic undertone.

retirada, *f.* withdrawal; (mil.) retreat; retirement.—**retirado,** *a.* retired; isolated; distant; pensioned. —**retirar,** *vt.* to withdraw; to put aside, reserve; to repel.—*vr.* to withdraw; to retire; to recede; (mil.) to retreat.—**retiro,** *m.* retirement; retreat; secluded place.—*r. obrero,* social security.

reto, *m.* challenge; threat, menace.

retocar, *vti.* [d] to retouch; to touch up, finish.

retoñar, *vi.* to sprout; to reappear.— **retoño,** *m.* sprout, shoot.

retoque, *m.* retouching, finishing touch.

retorcer, *vti.* [26-a] to twist; to contort; to distort, misconstrue.— *vri.* to writhe, squirm.—**retorcimiento,** *m.* twisting; writhing.

retórica, *f.* rhetoric.—*pl.* (coll.) sophistries, quibbles, subtleties.

retornar, *vi. & vr.* to return, come back.—*vt.* to return; to give back. —**retorno,** *m.* return, coming back; repayment, requital.

retorta, *f.* (chem.) retort.—**retortero,** *m.*—*andar al r.,* to hover about.

retortijón, *m.* curling up, twisting up.—*r. de tripas,* cramps, bellyache.

retozar, *vii.* [a] to frisk, romp, frolic. —**retozo,** *m.* romping, frolic; wantonness.—**retozón,** *a.* frolicsome, rollicking.

retractación, *f.* retraction.—**retractar,** *vt. & vr.* to retract, to recant.

retraer, *vti.* [43] to bring again; to dissuade; (law) to redeem.—*vri.* to take refuge or shelter; to withdraw from, shun; to keep aloof, retire. —**retraimiento,** *m.* retirement; refuge; aloofness.

retranca, *f.* (Am.) brake.—**retranquero,** *m.* (Am., RR.) brakeman.

retransmitir, *vt.* to relay (a message, etc.); to broadcast again.

retrasar, *vt.* to defer, postpone; to delay; to set back (timepiece).— *vi.* to go back, decline.—*vr.* to be backward; to be behindhand, late, behind time; (of timepiece) to run slow.—**retraso,** *m.* delay, deferment, lateness.

retratar, *vt.* to portray; to imitate, copy; to photograph.—*vr.* to be reflected; to be depicted; to sit for a portrait or photograph.—**retratista,** *mf.* portrait painter; photographer.—**retrato,** *m.* portrait, picture; photograph; copy, resemblance; description.

retrechero, *a.* (coll.) wily; attractive, winsome.

retreparse, *vr.* to lean back; to recline in a chair.

retrete, *m.* toilet, water closet, privy.

retribución, *f.* retribution; recompense, fee.—**retribuir,** *vti.* [23-e] to remunerate, reward.

retroactividad, *f.* retroactivity.—**retroactivo,** *a.* retroactive.

retroceder, *vi.* to fall back, move backward; (auto) to back up; to recede.—**retroceso,** *m.* backward motion; (med.) relapse.

retrospectivo, *a.* retrospective.

retruécano, *m.* pun.

retumbante, *a.* resonant, resounding; pompous, bombastic.—**retumbar,** *vi.* to resound, rumble.

reuma, *m.,* **reumatismo,** *m.* rheumatism.

reunión, *f.* reunion; meeting; gathering.—**reunir,** *vt.* to unite; to reunite; to gather; to collect, accumulate; to join.—*vr.* to join, to unite; to meet, get together, assemble.

revalidar, *vt.* to ratify, confirm; to renew.

revancha, *f.* revenge.

revelación, *f.* revelation.—**revelador,** *n.* & *a.* revealer; revealing, telltale. —*m.* (photog.) developer.—**revelar,** *vt.* to reveal ; (photog.) to develop.

revendedor, *n.* retailer; ticket speculator.—**revender,** *vt.* to resell; to retail.—**reventa,** *f.* resale.

reventar, *vii.* [1] to blow up, blow out; to burst forth; to explode; to sprout, shoot, blossom.—*vti.* to burst; to break; to crush, smash; to tire, wear out; to vex, annoy. —*vri.* to burst; to blow up, blow out; to break.—**reventón,** *a.* bursting.—*m.* bursting, blowout, explosion.

rever, *vti.* [46] to review, revise, look over again; (law) to try again.

reverdecer, *vii.* [3] to grow green again; to sprout again; to acquire new freshness and vigor.

reverencia, *f.* reverence; curtsy, bow; (eccl.) reverence (title).—**reverenciar,** *vt.* to venerate, revere; to hallow.—**reverendo,** *a.* reverend; worthy of reverence.—**reverente,** *a.* reverent.

reversible, *a.* (law) returnable, revertible; (phys.) reversible.—**reverso,** *m.* reverse (in coins); back, rear side.—*el r. de la medalla,* the opposite in every respect.

revertir, *vii.* [39] to revert.

revés, *m.* reverse, back, wrong side; backhand slap, shot or stroke; counterstroke; misfortune.—*al r.,* on the contrary, contrariwise; in the opposite or wrong way or direction; wrong side out.

revestimiento, *m.* (mason.) covering, facing, coat(ing); finish.—**revestir,** *vti.* [29] to dress, clothe; to cover, face; to line; (fig.) to cloak; (mason.) to coat, cover with a coating.—*vri.* to be invested with.

revisar, *vt.* to revise, review; to reëxamine, check.—**revisión,** *f.* revision, reviewing; reëxamination.—**revisor,** *m.* reviser, corrector; auditor; (R.R.) conductor.—**revista,** *f.* (mil.) review, parade; review, magazine; (theat.) revue.—*pasar r.,* to review; to examine, go over.—**revistero,** *n.* reviewer.

revivir, *vi.* to revive.

revocable, *a.* revocable.—**revocación,** *f.* revocation; abrogation.—*r. de una sentencia,* (law) reversal.—**revocar,** *vti.* [d] to revoke, repeal, reverse; to whitewash, plaster.—**revoco,** *m.* whitewashing, plastering.

revolcar, *vti.* [12-d] to knock down,

tread or trample upon; (coll.) to floor (an opponent).—*vri.* to wallow; to be stubborn.

revolotear, *vi.* to flutter, fly about.—**revoloteo,** *m.* fluttering.

revoltijo, revoltillo, *m.* mess, mass, medley, jumble.—*r. de huevos,* scrambled eggs.—**revoltoso,** *a.* turbulent; rebellious; mischievous.—**revolución,** *f.* revolution.—**revolucionario,** *a.* & *n.* revolutionary; revolutionist.—**revolver,** *vti.* [47-49] to turn over, turn upside down; to stir; to agitate; to wrap up; to mix up.—*vri.* to move to and fro; to rebel; to change (as the weather).—**revólver,** *m.* revolver.

revuelco, *m.* rolling.—**revuelo,** *m.* fluttering; commotion, stir, disturbance.

revuelta, *f.* revolution, revolt; change. —**revuelto,** *ppi.* of REVOLVER.—*a.* mischievous; confused, mixed up; intricate, difficult; topsy-turvy.— *huevos revueltos,* scrambled eggs.

rey, *m.* king.

reyerta, *f.* dispute, wrangle, quarrel.

rezagado, *n.* straggler.—**rezagar,** *vti.* [b] to leave behind; to outstrip; to put off, defer.—*vri.* to fall behind, lag.—**rezago,** *m.* remainder, leftover.

rezar, *vti.* [a] to say, recite (prayers); to say, read, state (of books, etc.).—*vii.* to pray.—*r. con,* to concern, be the business or duty of.—**rezo,** *m.* prayer; praying, devotions.

rezongar, *vii.* [b] to grumble, mutter, growl.—**rezongón,** *n.* grumbler, mutterer, growler.

rezumadero, *m.* dripping place; cesspool.—**rezumar,** *vi.* & *vr.* to ooze, exude, percolate, filter through; (coll.) to transpire; to leak out.

ría, *f.* estuary.—**riachuelo,** *m.* rivulet, rill; small river.

ribazo, *m.* sloping bank; mound, hillock.

ribera, *f.* shore, beach, bank.

ribete, *m.* (sewing) binding; trimming; pretense.—**ribetear,** *vt.* to bind.

ricacho, ricachón, *n.* (coll.) vulgar, rich person.

ricino, *m.* castor-oil plant.

rico, *a.* rich, wealthy, abundant, plentiful; delicious, exquisite; cute (child).

ridiculez, *f.* ridiculous thing or action; ridiculousness.—**ridiculizar,** *vti.* [a] to ridicule.—**ridículo,** *a.* ridiculous.—*ponerse en r.,* or *quedar en r.,* to make oneself ridiculous.— *m.* ridicule.

riego, *m.* irrigation; watering.

riel, *m.* (RR.) rail.—*pl.* tracks.

rienda, *f.* rein of a bridle; (fig.) moderation, restraint.—*pl.* reins, ribbons; government, direction.—*a r. suelta,* with a free rein.—*soltar las riendas,* to act without restraint.

riesgo, *m.* risk.

rifa, *f.* raffle, scuffle, wrangle.—**rifar,** *vt.* to raffle.—*vi.* to quarrel.

rifle, *m.* rifle.

rigidez, *f.* rigidity; sternness.—*r. cadavérica,* rigor mortis.—**rígido,** *a.* rigid, stiff; rigorous, inflexible; puritanical.

rigor, *m.* rigor; sternness.—**rigoroso, riguroso,** *a.* rigorous; exact; absolute; strict, severe, puritanical.—**rigurosidad,** *f.* rigorousness; severity.

rima, *f.* rhyme; heap, pile.—*pl.* poems.—**rimar,** *vi.* to rhyme.

rimbombante, *a.* resounding; bombastic.

rincón, *m.* (inside) corner, nook; cozy corner.—**rinconera,** *f.* corner cupboard, stand, bracket.

ringla, ringlera, *f.* (coll.) row, file, line, tier; swath.

rinoceronte, *m.* rhinoceros.

riña, *f.* quarrel, scuffle, dispute.

riñón, *m.* kidney.—*tener cubierto el r.,* to be rich, to be well off.—**riñonada,** *f.* layer of fat about the kidneys; dish of kidneys.

río, *m.* river.

ripio, *m.* residue, rubbish; padding, useless words.—*no perder r.,* not to miss the least occasion.

riqueza, *f.* riches, wealth; richness; abundance; fertility.

risa, *f.* laugh, laughter.

risco, *m.* crag, cliff.

risible, *a.* laughable, ludicrous.—**risotada,** *f.* outburst of laughter, loud laugh.

ríspido, *a.* harsh, gruff.

ristra, *f.* string (of onions, garlic, etc.).

risueño, *a.* smiling; pleasing, agreeable.

rítmico, *a.* rhythmic.—**ritmo,** *m.* rhythm; rate (of increase, etc.).

rito, *m.* rite, ceremony.—**ritual,** *m.* (eccl.) ritual, ceremonial.—*a.* ritual.

rival, *mf.* rival.—**rivalidad,** *f.* rivalry.—**rivalizar,** *vii.* [a] to rival, compete.

rivera, *f.* brook, creek, stream.

rizar, *vti.* [a] to curl.—*vri.* to curl naturally.—**rizo,** *a.* naturally curled or frizzled.—*m.* curl, ringlet.—*rizar el r.,* (aer.) to loop the loop.

robar, *vt.*, *vi.* & *vr.* to rob, steal; to abduct; to kidnap.

roble, *m.* oak; (fig.) very strong person or thing.

robo, *m.* robbery, theft; plunder, loot.

robustecer, *vti.* [3] to make strong.—**robustez,** *f.* robustness, ruggedness, hardiness.—**robusto,** *a.* robust, vigorous, hale.

roca, *f.* (geol.) rock; cliff.—**rocalloso,** *a.* rocky.

roce, *m.* friction, rubbing; contact, familiarity.

rociada, *f.* sprinkling; reprimand.—**rociar,** *vi.* to fall (of dew).—*vt.* to sprinkle; to spray; to strew about.

rocín, *m.* decrepit nag.

rocío, *m.* dew; spray, sprinkle; light shower.

rocoso, *a.* rocky.

rodada, rodadura, *f.* wheel track, rut, tread.

rodaja, *f.* small wheel or disk; round slice.—**rodante,** *a.* rolling.—**rodapié,** *m.* (arch.) skirting; foot rail; dado.—**rodar,** *vii.* [12] to roll; to rotate, revolve, wheel; to run on wheels; to wander about; to go up and down.—*vt.* to shoot (a film, movie, etc.).

rodear, *vt.* & *vi.* to surround, encircle.—*vi.* to go around; to make a detour.—*vr.* to turn, twist, toss about.—**rodeo,** *m.* turn, winding; roundabout course, method or way; round-up, rodeo; circumlocution, beating around the bush; evasion, subterfuge; corral.

rodilla, *f.* knee.—*de rodillas,* on one's knees.—*doblar* or *hincar las rodillas,* to kneel down.—**rodillazo,** *m.* push or blow with the knee.—**rodillera,** *f.* knee guard; knee patch; bagging of trousers at the knee.

rodillo, *m.* roll, roller; (cook.) rolling pin.

roedor, *n.* & *a.* rodent.—**roer,** *vti.* [36] to gnaw, eat away; to corrode; to harass, annoy.

rogar, *vti.* [12-b] to request, beg, entreat.

rojez, *f.* redness, ruddiness.—**rojizo,** *a.* reddish, sandy; ruddy.—**rojo,** *a.* red; ruddy, reddish.—*m.* red color.

rol, *m.* list, roll, catalogue; muster roll.

roldana, *f.* sheave, pulley wheel; caster.

rollizo, *a.* plump, stocky.—*m.* log.

rollo, *m.* roll; roller, rolling pin.

romadizo, *m.* cold in the head, snuffles; hay fever.

romance, *m.* Romance (language); Spanish vernacular (language); Spanish ballad.—*en buen r.,* in plain language.

romanesco, *a.* Roman; characteristic of novels.—**románico,** *a.* (arch.)

Romanesque; Romance (language).
—romano, n. & a. Roman.

romanticismo, m. romanticism.—romántico, a. romantic.—n. romanticist.—romanza, f. (mus.) romance.

rombo, m. (geom.) rhombus; lozenge, diamond.

romería, f. pilgrimage; picnic.

romero, m. (bot.) rosemary; pilgrim.

romo, a. obtuse; blunt.

rompecabezas, m. puzzle, riddle.—rompehielos, m. ice breaker; ice plow (of a boat).—rompeolas, m. breakwater, jetty.—romper, vti. [49] to break, smash, shatter; to fracture (bone); to tear; to pierce.—vii. to burst; to break; to burst forth; to fall out, quarrel; (of the day) to dawn; to begin, start; to sprout, bloom; to break out, spring out; (of light, sun, etc.) to break through.—vri. to break.—rompiente, a. breaking.—m. reef, shoal.—rompimiento, m. break, breakage, rupture; breach; quarrel.

ron, m. rum.

roncar, vii. [d] to snore; to roar; (coll.) to brag.—ronco, a. hoarse, raucous.

roncha, f. welt; blotch.

ronda, f. night patrol; rounds (by a night watch), beat; round (card game, drinks, cigars); serenade.—rondar, vt. & vi. to patrol, go the rounds; to walk the streets by night; to haunt, hover about; to impend.

ronquedad, ronquera, f. hoarseness.—ronquido, m. snore; raucous sound.

ronronear, vi. to purr.

ronzal, m. halter.

roña, f. filth, grime; scab (in sheep); stinginess; (Am.) ill-will; infection.—roñoso, a. scabby, leprous; dirty, filthy; rusty; (coll.) niggardly, stingy; (Am.) spiteful.

ropa, f. clothes, clothing; garments.—a. quema r., at close range, point-blank; suddenly, unexpectedly.—r. blanca, linen.—ropaje, m. vestments; garb; (art) drapery.—ropero, m. wardrobe, closet.—ropón, m. wide, loose gown.

rorro, m. (coll.) babe in arms.

rosa, f. (bot.) rose; red spot on any part of the body; rose color.—r. náutica, or de los vientos, (naut.) mariner's compass.—rosáceo, a. rose-colored.—rosado, a. rose-colored; rose.—rosal, m. rose plant, rosebush.—rosaleda, f. rosary, rose garden.—rosario, m. rosary.

rosca, f. screw and nut; screw thread; ring-shaped biscuit or bread.

róseo, a. rosy.—roseta, f. small rose; rosette.—rosetón, m. large rosette (arch.) rose window; rosette.

rosquilla, f. ring-shaped fancy cake.

rosillo, a. light red, roan (of horses).

rostro, m. face, countenance; rostrum.

rotación, f. rotation.—rotar, vi. to roll, rotate.—rotativo, a. rotary, revolving.—f. rotary printing press.—rotatorio, a. rotary, rotating.

roto, ppi. of ROMPER.—a. broken, chipped, shattered; torn; ragged; destroyed.—m. tear (in clothes); (Am.) man of the poorer classes; (Am.) hole.

rotonda, f. rotunda.

rótula, f. knee-joint.

rotulación, f. labeling.—rotular, vt. to label, put a title to.—rótulo, m. label, mark; show bill; placard.

rotundidad, f. roundness, rotundity.—rotundo, a. round, rotund; (of voice) full, sonorous; plain.

rotura, f. rupture, fracture; breakage, breach, opening.—roturación, f. breaking up new ground.—roturar, vt. to break up.

rozadura, f. friction; chafing.

rozagante, a. pompous, showy; trailing on the ground (as a gown).

rozamiento, m. friction; rubbing; disagreement, clashing.—rozar, vti. [a] to stub; to nibble; to gall, chafe; to graze, pass lightly over.—vii. to graze, rub.—vri. (con) to have to do with, be on familiar terms with.

rubí, m. ruby; red color.—rubicundez, f. ruddiness; rosiness.—rubicundo, a. reddish, ruddy.

rubio, a. blond(e), golden, fair.

rubor, m. blush, flush; bashfulness.—ruborizarse, vri. [a] to blush, to flush.—ruboroso, a. bashful.

rúbrica, f. mark, flourish; (after signature) rubric; title, heading.—de r., according to rules or custom.—rubricar, vti. [d] to sign with a flourish; to sign and seal.

rucio, a. (of animals) light silver gray.

rudeza, f. roughness, ruggedness, rudeness, coarseness.—rudimentario, a. rudimentary, undeveloped.—rudimento, m. rudiment, embryo; vestige.—pl. rudiments, elements.—rudo, a. rude, rough, unpolished; hard, rigorous; stupid.

rueca, f. distaff (for spinning).

rueda, f. wheel; circle of persons; round slice; turn, time, succession; rack (torture).—hacer la r., to cajole, wheedle; to court.

ruedo, m. bull ring, arena; rotation; circuit; circumference, edge of a

wheel or disk; round mat or rug;
(Am.) (sewing) hem of a skirt.

ruego, m. request, plea, petition,
supplication.

rufián, m. ruffian, rowdy, tough;
pimp, pander.—**rufianismo,** m.
rowdyism.

rufo, a. sandy (haired); curled.

rugido, m. roar; rumbling.—**rugir,**
vii. [c] to roar, bellow, howl.

ruido, m. noise; din; rumor; report.
—hacer or meter r., to attract attention; to create a sensation; to
make a noise.—**ruidoso,** a. noisy,
loud; clamorous.

ruin, a. mean, vile, despicable; puny;
stingy; insidious; (of an animal)
vicious.—m. wicked, mean or vile
man.—**ruina,** f. ruin, downfall;
overthrow, fall.—pl. ruins, debris.
—**ruindad,** f. baseness; avarice;
base action.—**ruinoso,** a. decayed,
ramshackle; ruinous; worthless.

ruiseñor, m. nightingale.

rumano, n. & a. Rumanian.

rumbo, m. bearing, course, direction;
(coll.) pomp, show; generosity.—
con r. a, in the direction of; heading or sailing for.—**rumboso,** a.
pompous, magnificent; liberal, lavish.

rumiante, m. & a. ruminant.—**rumiar,**
vt. to ruminate.

rumor, m. rumor; sound of voices;
murmur.—**rumorarse,** vr. (Am.) to
be said or rumored, be circulating
as a rumor.

runrún, m. (coll.) rumor, report.

ruptura, f. rupture; fracture, breaking.

rural, a. rural.

ruso, n. & a. Russian.—m. Russian
language.

rusticidad, f. rustic nature; rudeness,
clumsiness.—**rústico,** a. rustic, rural;
coarse, clumsy; unmannerly.—en
rústica, (bookbinding) in paper
covers, unbound.—n. peasant.

ruta, f. route, way.

rutilante, a. sparkling, starry.

rutina, f. routine, custom, habit.—
rutinario, a. routine.

S

sábado, m. Saturday.

sábana, f. sheet (for a bed).—pegár-
sele a uno las sábanas, to rise late.

sabana, f. (Am.) savanna, grassy
plain.

sabandija, f. small nasty reptile.—
pl. vermin.

sabañón, m. chilblain.

saber, vti. [37] to know; to be able,
know how to, can; to be aware of,

know about.—vii. to know; to be
very sagacious.—a s., namely, to
wit.—que yo sepa, as far as I know,
to my best knowledge.—¿quién
sabe? perhaps, who knows?—s. a,
to taste of, taste like.—s. de,
to know, be familiar with; to hear of
or from, have news about.—m.
learning, knowledge, lore.—**sabi-
duría,** f. wisdom; learning, knowledge.—**sabiendas.**—a s., knowingly,
consciously.—**sabihondo,** a. know-it-
all.—**sabio,** n. sage, wise person.—
a. wise, learned.

sablazo, m. blow with or wound from
a saber; (coll.) borrowing or spong-
ing.—**sable,** m. saber, cutlass.—
sablear, vt. (coll.) to sponge, borrow.—**sablista,** mf. (coll.) sponger,
one who asks for petty loans.

sabor, m. taste, flavor, savor.—
saborear, vt. to flavor, savor; to
give a relish or zest to.—vt. & vr.
to relish, enjoy; to smack one's
lips.

sabotaje, m. sabotage.—**sabotear,** vt.
& vi. to sabotage.

sabroso, a. savory, tasty, palatable,
delicious; pleasant.

sabueso, m. hound; bloodhound;
(fig.) bloodhound (detective).

sacabocado(s), m. (hollow) punch.—
sacacorchos, m. corkscrew.—**saca-
muelas,** mf. (coll.) tooth extractor,
quack dentist.—**sacapuntas,** m. pencil sharpener.—**sacar,** vti. [d] to
extract, draw out, pull out; to take
out; to put out; to take (a photo);
to bring out; to get, obtain; to
deduce, infer; to draw, win (a
prize); (games) to serve (the ball),
to kick off; to unsheathe (a sword);
to make, take (a copy).—s. a bailar,
to lead out for a dance.—s. a luz, to
print, publish.—s. de quicio, to
make one lose patience.—s. (a uno)
de sus casillas, (fig.) to drive crazy,
to exhaust one's patience.—s. en
claro, or en limpio, to conclude, arrive at the conclusion.—s. la cara,
to stand for, defend.—s. la cuenta,
to figure out.

sacarina, f. saccharin.

sacerdocio, m. priesthood.—**sacerdote,**
m. priest.—**sacerdotisa,** f. priestess.

saco, m. sack, bag; sackful, bagful;
coat, jacket; (mil.) sack, plunder.—
entrar a s., to plunder, loo .—no
echar en s. roto, not to forget, not
to ignore.—s. de noche, hand bag,
satchel.

sacramento, m. sacrament.

sacrificar, vti. [d] to sacrifice.—vri.
to sacrifice oneself, give up one's

life.—**sacrificio**, *m.* sacrifice, offering.

sacrilegio, *m.* sacrilege.—**sacrílego**, *a.* sacrilegious.

sacristán, *m.* sexton, sacristan.—**sacristía**, *f.* sacristy, vestry.

sacro, *a.* holy, sacred.—*m.* (anat.) sacrum.—**sacrosanto**, *a.* very holy, sacrosanct.

sacudida, *f.* shake, shaking, jerk.—**sacudimiento**, *m.* shake, shaking; shock, jerk, jolt.—**sacudir**, *vt.* to shake; jolt, jerk; to beat (to remove dust); to spank, drub; to shake off.—*vr.* to reject, drive away, shake off.

sádico, *a.* sadistic.—**sadismo**, *m.* sadism.

saeta, *f.* arrow, dart.

sagrado, *a.* sacred.

sahumar, *vt.* to perfume; to smoke; to fumigate.—**sahumerio**, *m.* smoke; vapor, steam; fumigation; fuming.

sainete, *m.* (theat.) short farce; flavor sauce; tidbit.

sajón, *n.* & *a.* Saxon.

sal, *f.* salt; wit; grace, winning manners; (Am.) bad luck.

sala, *f.* living room, parlor; hall; courtroom, court of justice (room and judges); tribunal.—*s. de espera*, waiting-room.

salado, *a.* salty, salted; briny; witty; graceful, winsome; (Am.) unlucky; (Am.) expensive.

salamandra, *f.* salamander.

salar, *vt.* to salt; to season or preserve with salt; to cure or corn (meat); to brine; (Am.) to bring bad luck; to spoil, ruin.

salario, *m.* wages, salary.

salcochar, *vt.* (cook.) to boil with water and salt.

salchicha, *f.* sausage.—**salchichón**, *m.* salami.

saldar, *vt.* (com.) to settle, liquidate, balance.—**saldo**, *m.* (com.) balance; settlement; remnants sold at low price; sale.

saledizo, *a.* salient, projecting.—*m.* projection, ledge.

salero, *m.* saltcellar; salt pan; (coll.) gracefulness, winning ways, charm.—**saleroso**, *a.* (coll.) witty; lively, jolly, winsome.

salida, *f.* start, setting or going out, departure; exit; outlet; issue, result; subterfuge, pretext; witty remark; sally; projection; expenditure, outlay.—*sin s.*, dead-end (street).—*s. del sol*, sunrise.—**saliente**, *a.* salient, projecting.—*f.* projection, lug.

salino, *a.* saline.—*f.* salt works, salt mine.

salir, *vii.* [38] to go or come out; to depart, leave; to get out, get off (of a vehicle); to rise (as the sun); to spring; to be issued or published; to come out, do (well, badly); to lead to; to open to; to say or do a thing unexpectedly or unseasonably; (theat.) to enter, appear.—*s. a*, to resemble, look like.—*s. adelante*, to be successful.—*s. al encuentro*, to come out to meet.—*s. de*, to dispose of; to part with; to get rid of.—*s. ganando*, to come out a winner, gain.—*vri.* to leak; to overflow.—*s. con la suya*, to accomplish one's end, to have one's way.

salitre, *m.* saltpeter, niter.

saliva, *f.* saliva, spittle.

salmo, *m.* psalm.

salmón, *m.* salmon.

salmuera, *f.* brine; pickle.

salobre, *a.* brackish, briny, saltish.

salón, *m.* salon, large parlor; living or assembly room.

salpicadura, *f.* splash, spatter, spattering.—**salpicar**, *vti.* [d] to spatter, sprinkle, splash.

salpimentar, *vti.* [1] to season with pepper and salt.

salpullido, *m.* (med.) rash.

salsa, *f.* sauce, dressing, gravy.—**salsera**, *f.* gravy dish, tureen.

saltamontes, *m.* grasshopper.—**saltar**, *vi.* to jump, leap, spring, hop; to skip; to bound; to snap, break in pieces; to come off (as a button).—*s. a la vista*, to be self-evident.—*s. a tierra*, to land, debark.—*vt.* to leap or jump over; to skip.

salteado, *a.* assorted.

salteador, *n.* highwayman(-woman); hold-up man, robber.

saltimbanqui, *mf.* acrobat.—**salto**, *m.* jump, leap; skip, omission; gap.—*a saltos*, leaping, by hops.—*dar un s.*, to jump, leap.—*de un s.*, at one jump; in a flash.—*s. de agua*, waterfall, falls, cataract.—*s. mortal*, somersault.

saltón, *a.* jumping, hopping; protruding.—*ojos saltones*, bulging eyes.—*m.* grasshopper.

salubre, *a.* salubrious, healthful.—**salubridad**, *f.* salubrity, healthfulness.—**salud**, *f.* health; public weal; welfare.—*pl.* compliments, greetings.—*a su s.*, to your health (in drinking).—**saludable**, *a.* healthy; salutary, wholesome.

saludar, *vt.* to greet, bow to, salute, hail.—**saludo**, *m.* bow, salute, salutation, greeting.—**salutación**, *f.* salutation, greeting, salute, bow.

salva, *f.* (artil.) salvo; salver, tray.

salvación, *f.* salvation.

salvado, *m.* bran.

salvador, *n.* savior, rescuer, redeemer.

salvadoreño, *n.* & *a.* Salvadoran.

salvaguardar, *vt.* to safeguard, protect.—**salvaguardia,** *m.* safeguard, security, protection; guard; watchman.—*f.* safe-conduct, passport.

salvajada, *f.* savage word or action. —**salvaje,** *a.* savage, uncivilized; (of plants, animals) wild; rough, wild (country).—*mf.* savage.—**salvajismo,** *m.* savagery.

salvamento, *m.* salvage; safety; rescue.—*bote de s.,* lifeboat.—**salvar,** *vt.* to save, rescue; to avoid (a danger); to jump over, get over (ditch, creek, etc.), clear (an obstacle); to overcome (a difficulty); to excuse, make an exception of.—*s. las apariencias,* to keep up appearances.—*vr.* to be saved; to escape from danger.—**salvavidas,** *m.* life preserver; lifesaver.

¡salve! *interj.* hail!

salvedad, *f.* reservation, exception, qualification; salvo.

salvia, *f.* (bot.) sage.

salvo, *a.* saved, safe; excepted, omitted.—*adv.* save, saving, excepting, barring.—*s. que,* unless.—**salvoconducto,** *m.* safe-conduct; permit, pass.

san, *a. contr.* of SANTO.

sanar, *vt.* to heal, cure.—*vi.* to heal; to recover from sickness.—**sanatorio,** *m.* sanatorium, sanitarium; asylum (for mental illness); nursing home.

sanción, *f.* sanction; ratification.—**sancionar,** *vt.* to sanction; to ratify.

sandalia, *f.* sandal.

sandez, *f.* foolishness, stupidity.

sandía, *f.* watermelon.

sandio, *a.* foolish, stupid.

sandunga, *f.* gracefulness; charm.—**sandunguero,** *a.* (coll.) graceful, charming.

saneamiento, *m.* drainage (of land); sanitation; (law) waiver of lien.—**sanear,** *vt.* to drain, dry up (lands); (law) to indemnify.

sangrar, *vt.* to bleed; to drain.—*vi.* to bleed.—**sangre,** *f.* blood; lineage. —*a s. fría,* in cold blood.—*a s. y fuego,* by fire and sword.—*s. fría,* calmness, presence of mind.—**sangría,** *f.* bleeding; drain, drainage; pilferage.—**sangriento,** *a.* bloody, gory.—**sanguijuela,** *f.* leech.—**sanguinario,** *a.* sanguinary, bloody.—**sanguinolento,** *a.* bloody; bloodstained.

sanidad, *f.* health; healthfulness; health department.—**sanitario,** *a.*

sanitary, hygienic.—*m.* health officer.—**sano,** *a.* healthy, sound; honest.—*s. y salvo,* safe and sound.

sanseacabó, *m.* (coll.) that's all.

santabárbara, *f.* (naut.) magazine; powder room.

santiamén, *m.* (coll.) instant, moment, jiffy.

santidad, *f.* sanctity, sainthood, saintliness, holiness.—**santificar,** *vti.* [d] to sanctify, to consecrate, hallow; to keep.—**santiguar,** *vt.* to bless; to heal by blessing.—*vr.* to cross oneself.—**santo,** *a.* saintly, holy; saint; sacred.—*todo el s. día,* the whole day long.—*n.* saint; saint's day.—*s. y seña,* (mil.) password.—**santuario,** *m.* sanctuary.

saña, *f.* anger, rage, fury.—**sañudo,** *a.* furious, enraged.

sapo, *m.* toad.

saque, *m.* (sports) service; server (in tennis); kick-off (in football).

saqueador, *n.* looter, pillager.—**saquear,** *vt.* to plunder, loot, pillage. —**saqueo,** *m.* pillage, loot, plunder.

sarampión, *m.* measles.

sarao, *m.* dance; evening party.

sarape, *m.* (Am.) serape; blanket.

sarcasmo, *m.* sarcasm.—**sarcástico,** *a.* sarcastic.

sardina, *f.* sardine.

sargento, *m.* (mil.) sergeant.

sarmiento, *m.* vine shoot or branch. —**sarmentoso,** *a.* vinelike, gnarled, knotty.

sarna, *f.* itch, scabies; mange.—**sarnoso,** *a.* itchy; scabbed; mangy.

sarpullido, *m.* = SALPULLIDO.

sarraceno, *n.* Saracen; Moor.—*a.* Saracen; Moorish.

sarro, *m.* tartar on teeth.

sarta, *f.* string, series, row.

sartén, *m.* & *f.* frying pan; skillet.—*tener la s. por el mango,* to have the control or command.

sastre, *m.* tailor.—**sastrería,** *f.* tailor's shop.

satánico, *a.* satanic.

satélite, *m.* satellite; follower, henchman.

satén, *m.* sateen.

sátira, *f.* satire.—**satírico,** *a.* satirical; sarcastic.—**satirizar,** *vti.* [a] to satirize, lampoon.—**sátiro,** *m.* lewd man; satyr.

satisfacción, *f.* satisfaction; apology, excuse.—**satisfacer,** *vti.* [22-49] to satisfy; to pay in full, settle.—*s. una letra,* (com.) to honor a draft. —*vri.* to satisfy oneself; to be satisfied; to take satisfaction; to be convinced.—**satisfecho,** *ppi.* of SATISFACER.—*a.* satisfied, content; arrogant, conceited.

saturación, *f.* saturation.—**saturar,** *vt.* to saturate.—*vr.* to become saturated; to fill, satiate.

sauce, *m.* willow, osier.

saurio, *m.* lizard.

savia, *f.* sap.

saxofón, saxófono, *m.* saxophone.

saya, *f.* skirt.—**sayuela,** *f.* (Am.) petticoat.

sazón, *f.* maturity, ripeness; season; taste, relish, flavor; occasion, opportunity.—*a la s.,* then, at that time.—*en s.,* ripe, in season.—**sazonar,** *vt.* (cook.) to season; to mature.—*vr.* to ripen, mature.

se, *3d. pers. refl. pron.* oneself, herself, itself, himself, themselves, each other, one another.—(*Replaces* le to him, to her, to you (*formal*), to them.

sebo, *m.* tallow, fat.

seca, *f.* drought; dry season.—*a secas,* simply; plain, alone.—**secador,** *a.* drying.—*m.* (Am.) dryer.—*f.* (Am.) clothes dryer.—**secante,** *f.* (geom.) secant.—*a.* drying.—*a. & m.* blotting (paper).—**secar,** *vti.* [d] to dry (out); to parch; to wipe dry; to tease, vex.—*vri.* to dry, dry up; to become lank, lean, or meager; to decay; to wither.

sección, *f.* act of cutting; section; division.—**seccionar,** *vt.* to section.

seco, *a.* dry; dried up; arid; dead (leaves); lean, meager; abrupt, curt; cold; sharp (noise).—*en s.,* high and dry; without cause or reason.—*parar en s.,* to stop suddenly.

secoya, *f.* sequoia.

secreción, *f.* (med.) secretion.—**secretar,** *vt.* (physiol.) to secrete.

secretaría, *f.* secretary's office; secretaryship.—**secretario,** *n.* secretary; actuary.—**secretear,** *vi.* (coll.) to whisper.—**secreteo,** *m.* (coll.) whispering.—**secreto,** *a.* secret; hidden.—*m.* secret; secrecy.—*s. a voces,* open secret.

secuaz, *mf.* follower, supporter, partisan.

secuela, *f.* sequel, result.

secuencia, *f.* sequence.

secuestrador, *n.* kidnapper.—**secuestrar,** *vt.* to kidnap, abduct; (law) to sequestrate.—**secuestro,** *m.* kidnapping, abduction; (law) sequestration.

secular, *a.* centenary; agelong; secular, lay.

secundar, *vt.* to second, aid, favor.—**secundario,** *a.* secondary; subsidiary.—*m.* second hand (of timepiece).

sed, *f.* thirst; longing, desire.—*tener*

s. de, to be thirsty for; to thirst or hunger after.

seda, *f.* silk.—*como una s.,* sweet-tempered; smoothly.

sedal, *m.* fishline.

sedante, sedativo, *m. & a.* sedative.

sede, *f.* see, seat.

sedeño, *a.* silken, silky.—**sedería,** *f.* silks; silk shop.—**sedero,** *a.* silk.—*n.* silk weaver or dealer.

sedición, *f.* sedition.—**sedicioso,** *a.* seditious; mutinous.

sediento, *a.* thirsty; (**de**) eagerly desirous, anxious (for).

sedimento, *m.* sediment, dregs, settling; grouts, grounds.

sedoso, *a.* = SEDEÑO.

seducción, *f.* seduction, deceiving.—**seducir,** *vti.* [11] to seduce; to charm, captivate.—**seductivo,** *a.* seductive; enticing, attractive, tempting.—*n.* seducer; deceiver; delightful person.

segador, *n.* reaper; harvester.—*f.* harvester, mowing machine.—**segar,** *vti.* [1-b] to mow; to harvest; to cut off, mow down.

seglar, *a.* secular, lay.—*mf.* layman (-woman).

segmento, *m.* segment.

segregación, *f.* segregation, separation.—**segregar,** *vti.* [b] to segregate, separate; (med.) to secrete.

segueta, *f.* jig saw, marquetry saw.

seguida, *f.*—*en s.,* at once, immediately.—**seguidamente,** *adv.* right after that, immediately after.—**seguido,** *a.* continued, successive; straight, direct.—**seguidor,** *n.* follower.—**seguimiento,** *m.* pursuit, following; continuation.—**seguir,** *vti.* [29-b] to follow; to pursue; to prosecute; to continue; to keep on.—*vri.* to ensue, follow as a consequence.

según, *prep.* according to.—*s. y como,* or *s. y conforme,* just as; it depends.—*conj.* as; according as.

segundero, *m.* second hand (of watch or clock).—**segundo,** *a. & n.* second.—*segunda intención,* double meaning.—*m.* (time) second.

seguridad, *f.* safety; security; certainty.—**seguro,** *a.* safe; secure; sure, certain, positive; dependable, trustworthy.—*m.* assurance; (mech.) click; safety catch (of a pistol); tumbler of a lock; (com.) insurance, assurance.—*a buen s.,* or *de s.,* certainly, undoubtedly.—*sobre s.,* without risk.

selección, *f.* selection, choice.—**seleccionar,** *vt.* to select, choose.—

selecto, a. select, choice, distinguished.

selva, f. jungle, forest.

sellar, vt. to seal; to stamp; to conclude, finish; to cover, close.—**sello,** m. seal; stamp (sticker, mark or implement); signet.

semana, f. week.—entre s., any weekday except Saturday.—**semanal,** a. weekly.—**semanario,** m. weekly publication.

semblante, m. mien, countenance, look, expression; aspect.—**semblanza,** f. portrait, biographical sketch.

sembrado, m. cultivated field, sown ground.—**sembradura,** f. sowing, seeding.—**sembrar,** vti. [1] to sow, seed; to scatter, spread.

semejante, a. similar, like; such, of that kind.—m. fellow creature, fellow man.—**semejanza,** f. resemblance, similarity, similitude.—a s. de, like.—**semejar,** vi. & vr. to be like; to resemble.

semen, m. semen, sperm; (bot.) seed. —**semental,** a. & m. breeding (horse).

semestre, m. semester.

semicircular, a. semicircular.—**semicírculo,** m. semicircle.

semidiós, m. demigod.—f. demigoddess.

semilla, f. seed.—**semillero,** m. seed bed, seed plot; nursery; hotbed.

seminario, m. seminary.—**seminarista,** m. seminarist.

sempiterno, a. eternal, everlasting.

senado, m. senate.—**senador,** n. senator.

sencillez, f. simplicity; plainness, naturalness; candor.—**sencillo,** a. simple; slight, thin; plain; harmless; natural, unaffected, unsophisticated; unadorned; single.

senda, f. path, footpath, way.—**sendero,** m. path, footpath, byway.

sendos, a. pl. one each, one for each.

senectud, f. old age, senility.—**senil,** a. senile.

seno, m. breast, bosom; womb; lap of a woman; cavity; sinus; bay; innermost recess; (math.) sine.

sensación, f. sensation.—**sensacional,** a. sensational.

sensatez, f. good sense, wisdom.—**sensato,** a. sensible, judicious, wise.

sensibilidad, f. sensibility; sensitiveness.—**sensible,** a. perceptible; sensitive, keen; regrettable; (photog.) sensitive, sensitized.—**sensiblería,** f. false sentimentality.—**sensitivo,** a. sensitive; sensual; appreciable.

sensual, a. sensuous; sensual; sexy.—**sensualidad,** f. sensuality, voluptuousness.

sentar, vti. [1] to seat; to establish, set up (a precedent, etc.).—dar por sentado, to take for granted.—vii. to fit, become, suit; to agree with (of food).—vri. to sit, sit down.

sentencia, f. (law) sentence, verdict, judgment; maxim.—pronunciar s., to pass judgment.—**sentenciar,** vt. (law) to sentence; to pass judgment on.

sentido, a. sensitive, touchy; heartfelt; offended.—m. sense; meaning; direction, course.—en el s. de que, to the effect that; stating that.—perder el s., to lose consciousness; to faint.—sin s., meaningless; unconscious.

sentimental, a. sentimental; emotional, soulful.—**sentimentalismo,** m. sentimentality.—**sentimiento,** m. sentiment, feeling; sensation; grief, sorrow, regret.

sentina, f. (naut.) bilge; sewer.—s. de vicios, place of iniquity.

sentir, vti. [39] to feel, experience; to perceive by the senses; to grieve, regret, mourn; to be sorry for.—vii. to feel; to foresee.—sin s., without noticing, inadvertently.—vri. to complain; to feel (well, bad, sad); to resent.—m. feeling; opinion, judgment.

seña, f. sign, mark, token; nod, gesture; signal.—pl. address; personal description.—**señal,** f. signal; sign, mark; indication; trace, vestige; scar; token.—**señalado,** a. distinguished, noted.—**señalamiento,** m. date, appointment.—**señalar,** vt. to stamp, mark; to point out; to name; to determine; to sign; to assign.—vr. to distinguish oneself, to excel; to call attention to oneself.

señor, m. mister, Mr.; sir; man, gentleman; lord, master.—muy s. mío, Dear Sir (in letters).—**señora,** f. lady; mistress; madam; dame.—**señorear,** vt. to master; to domineer, lord it over; to excel; to control (one's passions).—**señoría,** f. lordship.—**señorial,** a. lordly; manorial.—**señorío,** m. dominion, command; arrogance; lordship; domain, manor.—**señorita,** f. young lady; miss; Miss; (coll.) mistress of the house.—**señorito,** m. Master (title); (coll.) master of the house; (coll.) playboy.

señuelo, m. decoy, lure; bait; enticement.

separable, a. separable, detachable, removable.—**separación,** f. separation.—**separado,** a. separate, apart.—por s., separate, separately.—

separar, *vt.* to separate; to divide; to detach; to remove, take away or off; to lay aside; to dismiss, discharge.—*vr.* to separate; to part company; to withdraw.

sepelio, *m.* burial.

septentrional, *a.* northern, northerly.

septiembre, *m.* September.

sepulcro, *m.* sepulcher, grave, tomb. —**sepultar,** *vt.* to bury, inter; to hide, conceal.—**sepultura,** *f.* burial; tomb, grave, sepulcher.—*dar s.,* to bury.—**sepulturero,** *n.* gravedigger, sexton.

sequedad, *f.* aridity, dryness; gruffness.—**sequía,** *f.* drought.

ser, *vii.* [40] to be; to exist; to happen.—*es tarde,* it is late.—*esto es,* that is to say.—*no sea que,* lest. —*¿qué ha sido de Juan?* what has become of John?—*sea lo que fuere,* sea como fuere, be that as it may; anyhow, anyway.—*son las dos,* it is two o'clock.—*soy yo,* it is I.—*m.* existence; being; essence.

serenar, *vt.* to calm down, pacify.— *vr.* (of weather) to clear up, become calm.

serenata, *f.* serenade.

serenidad, *f.* serenity, calmness; tranquility.—**sereno,** *a.* serene, calm; clear, cloudless.—*m.* night watchman; night dew.

serie, *f.* series; sequence.—*fabricación en s.,* mass production.

seriedad, *f.* seriousness, gravity; earnestness.—**serio,** *a.* serious, grave, dignified; grand, solemn; earnest; sincere.—*en s.,* seriously.

sermón, *m.* sermon; reprimand.— **sermonear,** *vt.* to sermonize; (coll.) to lecture, reprimand.—**sermoneo,** *m.* (coll.) repeated admonition, sermonizing.

serpentear, *vi.* to meander; to wind; to wriggle, squirm.—**serpentín,** *f.* coil (of a heater, etc.).—**serpentina,** *f.* (min.) serpentine; paper streamer. —**serpiente,** *f.* serpent, snake.—*s. de cascabel,* rattlesnake.

serranía, *f.* sierra; mountainous region.—**serrano,** *a.* mountain, highland.—*n.* mountaineer, highlander.

serrar, *vti.* [1] to saw.—**serrín,** *m.* sawdust.—**serrucho,** *m.* handsaw.

servible, *a.* serviceable, adaptable.— **servicial,** *a.* serviceable; obsequious; obliging, kind.—**servicio,** *m.* service; servants; (Am.) toilet, water closet; tea or coffee set.—*s. de mesa,* set of dishes.—**servidor,** *n.* servant.—*s. de Ud.,* at your service.—**servidumbre,** *f.* (staff of) servants or attendants; servitude; (law) right of way.—**servil,** *a.*

servile, slavish, abject; lowly, humble.—**servilismo,** *m.* servility, abjectness.

servilleta, *f.* napkin.

servio, *n.* & *a.* Serb, Serbian.

servir, *vii.* [29] to serve; to be of use.—*no s. para nada,* to be good for nothing.—*para s. a Ud.,* at your service.—*s. de,* to act as, to be used as.—*s. para,* to be for, be used or useful for; to be good for; to do for.—*vti.* to serve; to do a service or a favor to.—*vri.* to please; to help oneself (as at table).—*s. de,* to make use of; to employ.

sesgado, *a.* oblique, slanting, bias.— **sesgar,** *vti.* [b] to slope, slant; to cut on the bias.—*vii.* to take an oblique direction.—**sesgo,** *m.* bias, slope, obliqueness; turn (of an affair).

sesión, *f.* session, meeting; conference, consultation.—*levantar la s.,* to adjourn the meeting.

seso, *m.* brain; brains, intelligence.— *levantarse la tapa de los sesos,* to blow out one's brains.—*perder el s.,* to go crazy; (fig.) to lose one's head. —*sin seso(s),* scatterbrained.

sestear, *vi.* to take a nap.

sesudo, *a.* judicious, discreet, wise.

seta, *f.* mushroom.

seto, *m.* fence, inclosure.—*s. vivo,* hedge.

seudónimo, *m.* pseudonym, pen name.

severidad, *f.* severity, austerity, strictness; seriousness.—**severo,** *a.* severe, rigorous; rigid, strict; serious; puritanical.

sexagenario, *n.* & *a.* sexagenarian.

sex, *m.* sex.—**sexual,** *a.* sexual.

si, *adv.* yes; indeed.—*un s. es no es,* somewhat, a trifle.—*m.* yes, consent. —*3rd. pers. refl. pron.* (after *prep.*) himself, herself, yourself, itself, oneself, themselves, yourselves.—*dar de s.,* to stretch, give.—*metido en s.,* pensive, introspective.—*si,* *conj.* if; whether.—*por s. acaso,* just in case. —*s. bien,* although.

siamés, *n.* & *a.* Siamese, Thai.—*n. pl.* Siamese twins, Siamese.

sibila, *f.* prophetess.

siciliano, *n.* & *a.* Sicilian.

sicoanálisis, sicología, siquiatría, etc., V. PSICOANALISIS, PSICOLOGIA, PSIQUIATRIA, etc.

siderurgia, *f.* iron and steel industry.

sidra, *f.* cider.

siega, *f.* reaping, harvest, mowing.

siembra, *f.* sowing, seeding; seedtime; sown field.

siempre, *adv.* always.—*para* or *por s.* (*jamás*), forever (and ever).—*s. que,* provided; whenever.

sien, f. (anat.) temple.

sierpe, f. serpent, snake.

sierra, f. saw; mountain range.

siesta, f. siesta, afternoon nap; hottest part of the day.—**siestecita,** f. short nap, snooze.

sietemesino, a. & n. prematurely born (baby).—m. puny.

sifón, m. siphon; siphon bottle.

sigilo, m. secrecy, concealment, reserve.—**sigiloso,** a. silent, reserved.

siglo, m. century; age; period; the world, worldly matters.

significación, f. significance; sense, meaning; implication; importance.—**significado,** m. meaning, definition (of a word, etc.).—**significar,** vti. [d] to signify, mean; to indicate; to make known; to import, be worth.—**significativo,** a. significant.

signatario, n. & a. signatory.

signo, m. sign, mark, symbol; signal.

siguiente, a. following, next.

sílaba, f. syllable.—**silabario,** m. primer; reader, speller.

silba, f. (theat.) hiss, hissing (of disapproval).—**silbar,** vi. to whistle.—vt. & vi. (theat.) to hiss, boo.—**silbato,** m. whistle (instrument).—**silbido,** m. whistle, whistling sound; hiss.

silenciador, m. (auto) muffler; silencer (on gun, etc.).—**silencio,** m. silence; noiselessness; taciturnity; secrecy; stillness; quiet; (mus.) rest.—guardar s., to keep quiet.—**silencioso,** a. silent, noiseless; still, quiet.

silueta, f. silhouette; (of person) figure.

silvestre, a. wild; uncultivated; rustic, savage.—**silvicultura,** f. forestry.

silla, f. chair; saddle; (eccl.) see.—s. de montar, riding saddle.—s. de tijera, camp chair.—**silletazo,** m. blow with a chair.—**sillín,** m. light riding saddle; saddle (on bicycle, etc.).—**sillón,** m. armchair; easy chair; sidesaddle.

sima, f. deep cavern; abyss.

simbólico, a. symbolical.—**simbolismo,** m. symbolism.—**simbolizar,** vti. [a] to symbolize, represent, typify.—**símbolo,** m. symbol; mark, device.

simetría, f. symmetry.—**simétrico,** a. symmetrical.

simiente, f. seed; germ; semen, sperm.

símil, m. resemblance, similarity; simile.—**similar,** a. similar, like, alike, resembling.—**similitud,** f. similitude, similarity.

simio, n. simian, ape.

simpatía, f. charm, attractiveness; congeniality; liking, friendly feel-ing; (med.) sympathy.—**simpático,** a. congenial; appealing; charming.—**simpatizar,** vii. [a] to be congenial with; to have a liking for; to be attracted by.

simple, a. simple; mere; foolish; artless, ingenuous; plain, unmixed, unadorned.—mf. simpleton.—**simpleza,** f. silliness, foolishness; silly thing; rusticity, rudeness.—**simplicidad,** f. simplicity.—**simplificación,** f. simplification.—**simplificar,** vti. [d] to simplify.—**simplón,** m. simpleton.

simulación, f. simulation, feigning.—**simulacro,** m. image, idol; show, semblance; pretense; sham battle.—**simulador,** n. simulator; malingerer.—a. simulative.—**simular,** vt. to simulate, pretend, sham.

simultaneidad, f. simultaneity.—**simultáneo,** a. simultaneous.

sin, prep. without; but for; besides, not including.—s. embargo, notwithstanding, nevertheless, however.—s. que, without.

sinagoga, f. synagogue.

sinapismo, m. mustard plaster; (coll.) nuisance, bore.

sincerar, vt. to justify.—vr. to excuse, justify, or vindicate oneself.—**sinceridad,** f. sincerity, good faith.—**sincero,** a. sincere.

síncope, f. (med.) swoon, fainting fit.

sincronizar, vti. [a] to synchronize.

sindéresis, f. common sense, discretion, good judgment.

sindicalismo, m. trade unionism.—**sindicato,** m. labor union.

síndico, m. trustee; (law) assignee, receiver.

sinfín, m. countless number.

sinfonía, f. symphony.—**sinfónico,** a. symphonic.

singular, a. singular; unique; unusual; odd; excellent.—**singularizar,** vti. [a] to single out; to distinguish.—vri. to be conspicuous; to be singled out; to distinguish oneself.

siniestro, a. sinister; left (side); vicious.—m. disaster; catastrophe.—f. left hand; left-hand side.

sino, conj. but; except, besides; solely, only.—m. fate, destiny.

sinónimo, a. synonymous.—m. synonym.

sinopsis, f. synopsis.

sinrazón, f. wrong, injury, injustice.

sinsabor, m. displeasure; trouble, grief, sorrow.

sinsonte, m. (Am.) mockingbird.

sintaxis, f. syntax.

síntesis, f. synthesis.—**sintético,** a. synthetical.—**sintetizar,** vti. [a] to synthesize; to sum up.

síntoma, *m.* symptom; sign.

sinnúmero, *m.* countless number.

sinvergüenza, *mf.* (coll.) scoundrel, rascal; brazen, shameless person.— *a.* shameless.

siquiera, *adv.* even, at least.—*conj.* even if; even.—*ni s.*, not even.

sirena, *f.* siren, mermaid; whistle, foghorn; temptress, vamp.

sirvienta, *f.* servant girl, maid.— **sirviente,** *m.* (domestic) servant; waiter.

sisa, *f.* petty theft; (sewing) dart.— **sisar,** *vt.* to pilfer, filch; (sewing) to take in.

sisear, *vi.* to hiss.—**siseo,** *m.* hiss, hissing.

sísmico, *a.* seismic.—**sismógrafo,** *m.* seismograph.

sistema, *m.* system.—**sistemático,** *a.* systematic.—**sistematización,** *f.* systematization.—**sistematizar,** *vti.* [a] & *vii.* to systematize.

sitial, *m.* seat of honor, presiding chair.

sitiar, *vt.* (mil.) to lay siege to; to surround, hem in, compass.—**sitio,** *m.* place, space, spot, room; stand; seat; location, site; country house, country seat, villa; (Cuba) small farm; (mil.) siege.—*quedar en el s.*, to die on the spot.

sito, *a.* situated, lying, located.— **situación,** *f.* situation; position; site, location; condition, circumstances.—**situar,** *vt.* to place, locate, situate; (com.) to remit or place (funds).—*vr.* to settle in a place; to station oneself.

so, *prep.* under.—*s. capa de,* or *s. color de,* under color of; on pretense of.—*s. pena de,* under penalty of.—*s. pretexto,* under the pretext of.—*interj.* whoa!

sobaco, *m.* armpit; (bot.) axil.

sobado, *a.* shopworn.

sobaquera, *f.* (tailoring) armhole.— **sobaquina,** *f.* bad odor of the armpit.

sobar, *vt.* to knead; to massage, squeeze, soften; to pummel, box; to handle (a person) with too much familiarity.

soberanía, *f.* sovereignty; rule, sway. —**soberano,** *a.* sovereign; supreme, royal; superior.—*n.* sovereign.

soberbia, *f.* excessive pride, haughtiness; presumption; magnificence, pomp; anger.—**soberbio,** *a.* overproud, arrogant, haughty; superb, grand; lofty, eminent.

sobornar, *vt.* to suborn, bribe.— **soborno,** *m.* subornation, bribe; incitement, inducement.

sobra, *f.* surplus, excess; leftover,

leaving.—*de s.,* over and above; more than enough.—*estar de s.,* (coll.) to be one too many; to be superfluous.—**sobrante,** *a.* extra; excess; leftover.—*m.* surplus, remainder.—**sobrar,** *vt.* to surpass; to have in excess.—*vi.* to be in excess; to be intrusive; to remain, be left over.

sobre, *prep.* on, upon; over; above; about, concerning; about, more or less; to, toward, near.—*m.* envelope (for letters).

sobrealimentar, *vt.* to overfeed.

sobrecama, *f.* coverlet, bedspread.

sobrecargar, *vti.* [b] to overload, overburden; (com.) to overcharge.— **sobrecargo,** *m.* (naut.) purser, supercargo.

sobrecoger, *vti.* [c] to surprise, catch unaware; to startle.—*vri.* to become afraid or apprehensive.—**sobrecogimiento,** *m.* fear, apprehension.

sobrecoser, *vt.* (sewing) to fell, sew the edge of a seam flat.

sobreexcitación, *f.* overexcitement.— **sobreexcitar,** *vt.* to overexcite.

sobrehumano, *a.* superhuman.

sobrellevar, *vt.* to ease (another's burden); to carry, bear, endure; to overlook, be lenient about.

sobremanera, *adv.* beyond measure· exceedingly, most.

sobremesa, *f.* tablecloth; after-dinner chat.—*de s.,* during an after-dinner chat.

sobrenadar, *vi.* to float.

sobrenatural, *a.* supernatural.

sobrenombre, *m.* sobriquet; nickname.

sobrentender, *vti.* [18] to understand, deduce, infer.—*vri.* to be understood, go without saying.

sobrepasar, *vt.* to exceed, surpass.

sobrepeso, *m.* overweight.

sobreponer, *vt.* [32-49] to superimpose, overlap.—*vri.* to control oneself.—*s. a,* to master, overcome (difficulties, hardships).

sobreprecio, *m.* extra charge, raise.

sobreprenda, *f.* overdress.

sobrepujar, *vt.* to excel, beat, surpass.

sobresaliente, *a.* outstanding; projecting.—*mf.* substitute, understudy. —**sobresalir,** *vii.* [38] to excel, be prominent, stand out; to project, just out, flange.

sobresaltar, *vt.* to rush upon, assail; to frighten, startle.—*vi.* to stand out.—*vr.* to be startled.—**sobresalto,** *m.* assault; startling surprise; sudden dread or fear.

sobrescrito, *m.* envelope address.

sobreseer, *vi.* [e] to desist from a design; to relinquish a claim; (law) to stay a judgment, etc.

sobrestante, *m.* overseer; foreman; comptroller; inspector; supervisor.

sobresueldo, *m.* extra wages.

sobretodo, *m.* overcoat.

sobrevenir, *vii.* [45] to happen, take place; to follow.

sobreviviente, *mf.* & *a.* survivor; surviving.—**sobrevivir,** *vt.* & *vi.* to survive, outlive.

sobriedad, *f.* sobriety, frugality.

sobrina, *f.* niece.—**sobrino,** *m.* nephew.

sobrio, *a.* sober, temperate, frugal.

socarrón, *a.* cunning, sly, crafty.—**socarronería,** *f.* cunning, artfulness, craftiness.

socavar, *vt.* to excavate, undermine.

sociabilidad, *f.* sociableness, sociability.—**sociable,** *a.* sociable, companionable.—**social,** *a.* social.—**socialismo,** *m.* socialism.—**socialista,** *mf.* & *a.* socialist(ic).—**socialización,** *f.* socialization.—**socializar,** *vti.* [a] to socialize.—**sociedad,** *f.* society; social intercourse; (com.) society, corporation, company.—*s. anónima,* stock company.—**socio,** *n.* partner, copartner; companion; member, fellow.—**sociología,** *f.* sociology.

socorrer, *vt.* to assist, help, succor; to favor.—**socorrido,** *a.* furnished, well-supplied; (coll.) handy; hackneyed, trivial.—**socorro,** *m.* succor, aid, help.—*puesto de s.,* first-aid station.

soda, *f.* (chem.) = **sosa.**

sodio, *m.* sodium.

sodomía, *f.* sodomy.

soez, *a.* mean, vile, base, coarse.

sofá, *m.* sofa.

sofisma, *m.* fallacy; sophism.—**sofisticar,** *vti.* [d] to falsify, pervert or distort by fallacy.

sofocación, *f.* suffocation; smothering, choking.—**sofocante,** *a.* suffocating, stifling.—**sofocar,** *vti.* [d] to choke, suffocate, smother; to quench, extinguish; to stifle; to oppress, harass; to importune, vex; to provoke; to make blush.—**sofoco,** *m.* suffocation; vexation; embarrassment.—**sofocón,** *m.* (coll.) vexation, chagrin.

sofreír, *vti.* [35-49] to fry lightly.

sofrenar, *vt.* to check (a horse) suddenly; to reprimand severely; to check (a passion).

sofrito, *ppi.* of **sofreír.**

soga, *f.* rope, halter, cord.

soja, *f.* soy; soy bean.

sojuzgar, *vti.* [b] to conquer, subjugate, subdue.

sol, *m.* sun; sunlight; (mus.) sol.—*de s. a s.,* from sunrise to sunset.—*hacer s.,* to be sunny.—*tomar el s.,* to bask in the sun, sunbathe;

(naut.) to take the altitude on the sun.—**solana,** *f.* intense sunlight; sunny place.—**solanera,** *f.* sunburn; sunny place.

solapa, *f.* lapel; flap; pretense.—**solapado,** *a.* sly, artful, sneaky.—**solapar,** *vt.* to put lapels on; to overlap, lap; to cloak, conceal.—*vi.* to overlap (as a lapel).

solar, *m.* lot, ground plot; manor house, ancestral mansion.—*a.* solar.—**solariego,** *a.* manorial; of old lineage.

solaz, *m.* solace, consolation; relaxation, comfort; enjoyment.—**solazar,** *vti.* [a] to solace, comfort.—*vri.* to be comforted; to rejoice, have pleasure.

soldada, *f.* wages, salary.—**soldadesca,** *f.* soldiery; undisciplined troops.—**soldadesco,** *a.* soldierly.—**soldado,** *m.* soldier.—*s. raso,* private.

soldador, *m.* solderer; welder; soldering iron.—**soldadura,** *f.* soldering; welding; solder; correction.—**soldar,** *vti.* [12] to solder; to weld; to correct.

soleado, *a.* sunny.—**solear,** *vt.* to sun.

soledad, *f.* solitude, loneliness; lonely place.

solemne, *a.* solemn; imposing; ceremonious; (coll.) great, downright.—**solemnidad,** *f.* solemnity; religious pomp; grand ceremony.—*pl.* formalities.—**solemnizar,** *vti.* [a] to solemnize, celebrate with pomp.

soler, *vii.* [26-50] to be in the habit of, accustomed to, used to.

solera, *f.* vintage wine; lees or mother of wine; crossbeam.

solevantamiento, *m.* upheaval.

solfa, *f.* musical annotation, notes; music, harmony; (coll.) sound beating or flogging.—*estar,* or *poner en s.,* to appear (or present) in a ridiculous light.—**solfeo,** *m.* solfeggio; (coll.) beating, drubbing.

solicitar, *vt.* to solicit; to apply for; to woo, court.—**solícito,** *a.* solicitous, diligent, careful.—**solicitud,** *f.* solicitude; importunity; diligence; petition, application, request; (com.) demand.—*a s.,* on request, at the request (of).—*s. de ingreso,* application for admission.

solidaridad, *f.* solidarity; union.—**solidario,** *a.* solidary; mutually binding.—**solidarizarse,** *vri.* [a] to act together in a common cause.

solideo, *m.* skullcap.

solidez, *f.* solidity; firmness; strength; stability; compactness.—**solidificación,** *f.* solidification.—**solidificar,** *vti.* & *vri.* [d] to solidify.—**sólido,**

a. solid; firm; compact; strong.—*m.* (geom. & phys.), solid.

soliloquio, *m.* soliloquy, monologue.

solista, *mf.* (mus.) soloist.—**solitaria,** *f.* tapeworm.—**solitario,** *a.* solitary, lonely, isolated, secluded.—*m.* recluse, hermit; solitaire.

soliviantar, *vt.* to induce, incite, rouse.

solo, *a.* alone, unaccompanied; only, sole; unaided, unattended; solitary, lonely.—*a solas,* alone; unaided.—*m.* (mus.) solo.—**sólo,** *adv.* = SOLAMENTE.

solomillo, solomo, *m.* sirloin; loin of pork.

soltar, *vti.* [12] to untie, unfasten, loosen; to turn on (the water); to turn loose; to cast off, set free, discharge; to let go, drop; to throw down, throw out; (coll.) to utter, let out (laughter, etc.).—*vri.* to get loose; to come off; to become expert; to lose restraint; to break out (laughing, crying, etc.).—*s. a,* to begin, start.

soltería, *f.* celibacy, bachelorhood.—**soltero,** *a.* single, unmarried.—*m.* bachelor, unmarried man.—*f.* spinster, unmarried woman.—**solterón,** *m.* old bachelor.—**solterona,** *f.* old maid.

soltura, *f.* freedom, abandon, ease; fluency; agility, nimbleness; laxity, licentiousness.

solubilidad, *f.* solubility.—**soluble,** *a.* soluble; solvable.—**solución,** *f.* loosening or untying; climax or denouement in a drama or epic poem; pay, satisfaction; (math., chem.) solution.—**solucionar,** *vt.* to solve; to meet (a difficulty).

solvencia, *f.* (com.) solvency.—**solventar,** *vt.* to settle (accounts); to solve.—**solvente,** *a.* solvent, dissolving; (com.) solvent.

sollozar, *vii.* [a] to sob.—**sollozo,** *m.* sob.

sombra, *f.* shade; shadow; darkness; spirit, ghost; protection; sign, vestige.—*buena s.,* wit; good luck.—**sombrear,** *vt.* to shade.—**sombrería,** *f.* hat factory or shop.—**sombrero,** *m.* hat.—*s. de copa,* or *de copa alta,* silk hat, high (silk) hat.—*s. de jipijapa,* Panama hat.—*s. hongo,* derby.—**sombrilla,** *f.* parasol, sunshade.—**sombrío,** *a.* gloomy, somber; overcast.

somero, *a.* superficial, shallow; concise, summary.

someter, *vt.* to subject; to submit, subdue; to put (to the test, etc.).—*vr.* to humble oneself; to submit; to surrender.—**sometimiento,** *m.* submission, subjection, subduing.

somnolencia, *f.* drowsiness, somnolence.

son, *m.* sound; tune; (Am.) popular song and dance.—*¿a son de qué?* why? for what reason?—*en s. de,* as, like, in the manner of.—*sin ton ni s.,* without rhyme or reason.

sonaja, *f.* jingles; tambourine; rattle.—**sonajero,** *m.* baby's rattle.

sonambulismo, *m.* sleepwalking.—**sonámbulo,** *n.* sleepwalker.

sonante, *a.* sounding, ringing.

sonar, *vti.* [12] to sound, to ring; (mus.) to play.—*vii.* to sound; to ring; (of clock) to strike; to be mentioned, talked about; **(a)** to sound or look (like); to seem; to sound familiar.—*vri.* to blow one's nose.

sonda, *f.* (naut.) sounding (line); lead, sounder, plummet; surgeon's probe.—**sondaje,** *m.* sounding.—**sondar, sondear,** *vt.* (naut.) to sound; to try, sound out (another's intentions); to explore, fathom; to probe.—**sondeo,** *m.* sounding; exploring.

soneto, *m.* sonnet.

sonido, *m.* sound; noise; report.—**sonoridad,** *f.* sonority, sonorousness.—**sonoro,** *a.* sonorous; sounding, clear, loud.

sonreír, *vii.* & *vri.* [35] to smile; to smirk.—**sonriente,** *a.* smiling.—**sonrisa,** *f.* smile; smirk.

sonrojar, *vt.* to make (one) blush.—*vr.* to blush.—**sonrojo,** *m.* blush; blushing.

sonrosado, *a.* pink, rosy.

sonsacar, *vti.* [d] to pilfer; to draw (one) out; to entice, allure; to elicit information.

sonsonete, *m.* singsong (voice).

soñador, *a.* dreamy.—*n.* dreamer.—**soñar,** *vti.* & *vii.* [12] to dream.—*s. con* or *en,* to dream of.—**soñoliento,** *a.* sleepy; somnolent; soporific.

sopa, *f.* soup; sop.—*hecho una s.,* (coll.) drenched, wet through to the skin.

sopapear, *vt.* (coll.) to chuck under the chin; to vilify, to abuse.—**sopapo,** *m.* chuck under the chin; (coll.) box, blow, slap; (mech.) stop valve.

sopera, *f.* soup tureen.

sopesar, *vt.* to test the weight of by lifting.

sopetón, *m.*—*de s.,* suddenly.

soplar, *vi.* to blow; (coll.) to tattle.—*vt.* to blow; to blow out; to fan; to fill with air, inflate; to rob or steal in an artful manner; to prompt, tell what to say.—**soplete,** *m.* blowpipe; blow torch.—**soplido,** *m.* blowing; blast.—**soplo,** *m.* blowing; blast, gust, puff of wind; breath, instant; hint, tip, secret advice or warning; secret accusation. —**soplón,** *n.* talebearer, informer, telltale.

soponcio, *m.* fainting fit, swoon.

sopor, *m.* drowsiness, lethargic sleep. —**soporífero,** *a.* soporific.

soportable, *a.* bearable, endurable.

soportal, *m.* portico.—*pl.* arcades.

soportar, *vt.* to bear, put up with; to support.—**soporte,** *m.* support; rest; bearing.

soprano, *m.* soprano voice.—*f.* soprano singer.

sor, *f.* (eccl.) sister.

sorber, *vt.* to sip, suck; to imbibe, soak, absorb; to swallow.—**sorbete,** *m.* sherbet, water ice.—**sorbo,** *m.* imbibing; absorption; sip, draft, swallow, gulp.

sordera, *f.* deafness.

sordidez, *f.* sordidness.—**sórdido,** *a.* sordid.

sordina, *f.* (mus.) mute; damper (piano).

sordo, *a.* deaf; silent, noiseless, quiet; muffled, stifled; dull; unmoved, insensible.—*n.* deaf person.—**sordomudo,** *a.* & *n.*, deaf and dumb; deaf mute.

sorna, *f.* slyness; ironic undertone, sneer.

sorprendente, *a.* surprising.—**sorprender,** *vt.* to surprise, astonish; to take by surprise.—**sorpresa,** *f.* surprise.—*de s.,* by surprise.

sortear, *vt.* to draw or cast lots for; to raffle; to elude or shun cleverly. —**sorteo,** *m.* casting lots; drawing, raffle.

sortija, *f.* finger ring; curl of hair.

sortilegio, *m.* spell, charm; sorcery, sortilege.

sosa, *f.* (chem.) soda; (bot.) glasswort.

sosegar, *vti.* [1-b] to appease, calm, quiet; to lull.—*vii.* to rest, repose. —*vri.* to become quiet, calm or composed; to quiet down.

sosera, sosería, sosez, *f.* tastelessness; dullness.

sosiego, *m.* tranquillity, calm, quiet.

soslayar, *vt.* to do or place obliquely. —**soslayo,** *m.*—*al s.,* or *de s.,* askance; slanting.

soso, *a.* insipid; dull.

sospecha, *f.* suspicion.—**sospechar,** *vt.* & *vi.* to suspect.—**sospechoso,** *a.* suspicious; suspecting.

sostén, *m.* support (person or thing);

prop; brassiére; upkeep.—**sostener,** *vti.* [42] to support, hold up; to maintain, keep; to assist, help; to encourage; to hold (a conference). —*vri.* to support or maintain oneself.—**sostenido,** *a.* supported; sustained.—*m.* (mus.) sharp.—**sostenimiento,** *m.* sustenance, maintenance; support.

sota, *f.* (cards) jack; hussy, jade.

sotabanco, *m.* garret, attic.

sotana, *f.* cassock.

sótano, *m.* cellar, basement.

sotavento, *m.* leeward, lee.

soterrar, *vti.* [1] to bury, put under ground; to hide.

soto, *m.* grove, thicket.

sóviet, *m.* soviet.—**soviético,** *a.* soviet.

soya, *f.* (Am.) = SOJA.

su, *a. poss.* (*pl.* **sus**), his, her, its, their, your, one's.

suave, *a.* smooth, soft; easy, tranquil; gentle, tractable, docile.— **suavidad,** *f.* softness, smoothness; ease; suavity; gentleness; lenity; forbearance.—**suavizar,** *vti.* [a] to soften, smooth, mitigate; to ease; to temper.

subarrendar, *vti.* [1] to sublet, sublease.

subasta, *f.* auction, auction sale.— *poner en* or *sacar a pública s.,* to sell at auction.—**subastar,** *vt.* to sell at auction.

subconsciencia, *f.* subconscious.—**subconsciente,** *a.* subconscious.

subdirector, *n.* assistant director.

súbdito, *mf.* subject (of a state, etc.).

subdividir, *vt.* to subdivide.

subida, *f.* ascent, going up; climb; taking or carrying up; rise; increase; slope.—**subir,** *vi.* to rise; to come up, go up, climb, mount; to grow; to increase in intensity; (com.) to amount to.—*vt.* to raise, place higher; to take up, bring up; to set up.—*vr.* to go up; to climb; to rise.

súbito, *a.* sudden.—*de s.,* suddenly.

subjetividad, *f.* subjectivity.—**subjetivo,** *a.* subjective.

subjuntivo, *m.* & *a.* (gram.) subjunctive.

sublevación, *f.* insurrection, revolt.— **sublevar,** *vt.* to incite to rebellion, raise in rebellion.—*vr.* to rise in rebellion.

sublimar, *vt.* to heighten, elevate, exalt; (chem.) to sublimate.—**sublime,** *a.* sublime.—**sublimidad,** *f.* sublimity.

submarino, *a.* & *m.* submarine.

subordinación, *f.* subordination; subjection.—**subordinado,** *a.* subordinate, subservient.—*n.* subordinate.—

subordinar, *vt.* to subordinate; to subject.

subproducto, *m.* by-product.

subrayar, *vt.* to underscore, underline; to emphasize.

subsanar, *vt.* to excuse; to mend, correct, repair; to obviate, get over.

subscribir, *vti. & vri.* [49] = SUSCRIBIR.—**subscripción,** *f.* = SUSCRIPCION.—**subscripto,** *ppi.* = SUSCRITO.—**subscriptor,** *n.* = SUSCRITOR.

subsecretaría, *f.* office and employment of an assistant secretary.—**subsecretario,** *n.* assistant secretary.

subsecuente, *a.* subsequent.

subsidiario, *a.* subsidiary; branch; auxiliary.—**subsidio,** *m.* subsidy, monetary aid.

subsiguiente, *a.* subsequent, succeeding.

subsistencia, *f.* livelihood, living; permanence, stability; subsistence.—**subsistir,** *vi.* to subsist, last; to live, exist.

substancia, *f.* = SUSTANCIA.—**substancial,** *a.* = SUSTANCIAL.—**substancioso,** *a.* = SUSTANCIOSO.—**substantivo,** *a. & m.* = SUSTANTIVO.

substitución, *f.* = SUSTITUCION.—**substituir,** *vti.* [23-e] = SUSTITUIR.—**substituto,** *pp.i.* of SUSTITUIR = SUSTITUTO.

substracción, *f.* = SUSTRACCION.—**substraer,** *vti.* [43] = SUSTRAER.

subteniente, *m.* second lieutenant.

subterráneo, *a.* subterranean, underground.—*m.* any place underground; (Arg.) subway.

suburbano, *a. & n.* suburban(ite).

suburbio, *m.* outskirt; suburb.

subvención, *f.* subsidy, money aid.—**subvencionar,** *vt.* to subsidize.—**subvenir,** *vti.* [45] to aid, assist; to provide, supply.

subversión, *f.* subversion, overthrow.—**subversivo,** *a.* subversive, destructive.—**subvertir,** *vti.* [18] to subvert, destroy, ruin.

subyacente, *a.* underlying.

subyugación, *f.* subjugation, subjection.—**subyugador,** *n. & a.* subjugator; subjugating.—**subyugar,** *vti.* [b] to subdue, subjugate.

succión, *f.* suction, suck.

sucedáneo, *a. & m.* substitute.—**suceder,** *vi.* to succeed, follow; to happen.—**sucesión,** *f.* succession.—**sucesivo,** *a.* successive.—*en lo s.,* hereafter, in the future.—**suceso,** *m.* event, happening; issue, outcome.—**sucesor,** *n.* successor.

suciedad, *f.* nastiness, filthiness; dirt, filth.

sucinto, *a.* brief, succinct, concise.

sucio, *a.* dirty, nasty, filthy, squalid; soiled; untidy; low.

sucumbir, *vi.* to succumb; to submit, yield.

sucursal, *a.* subsidiary; branch.—*f.* branch of a commercial house.

sud, *m.* south; south wind.—**sudamericano,** *n. & a.* South American.

sudar, *vi.* to sweat, perspire; to ooze; to toil, labor.—**sudario,** *m.* shroud (for corpse).—**sudor,** *m.* sweat, perspiration.—**sudoroso,** *a.* sweating, perspiring freely.

sueco, *a.* Swedish.—*n.* Swede.—*m.* Swedish language.—*hacerse el s.,* to pretend not to hear.

suegra, *f.* mother-in-law.—**suegro,** *m.* father-in-law.

suela, *f.* sole (of shoe); shoe leather.—*de siete suelas,* downright.

sueldo, *m.* salary, stipend.

suelo, *m.* ground; soil; land, earth; pavement; floor, flooring; bottom.

suelto, *ppi.* of SOLTAR.—*a.* loose; light, expeditious; swift, able; free, bold, daring; fluent; odd, disconnected, unclassified; single (copy); blank (verse).—*s. de lengua,* outspoken.—*m.* editorial paragraph; newspaper item or paragraph; loose change.

sueño, *m.* sleep; sleeping; drowsiness, sleepiness; dream.—*conciliar el s.,* to get to sleep.—*descabezar* or *echar un s.,* to take a nap.—*en sueños,* dreaming; in dreamland.—*tener s.,* to be sleepy.

suero, *m.* whey; serum (of blood).

suerte, *f.* fortune, luck, chance; piece of luck; lot, fate; sort, kind; trick, feat (bullfighting).—*de s. que,* so that; and so.—*echar suertes,* to draw lots.—*tener s.,* to be lucky.—*tocarle a uno la s.,* to fall to one's lot.

suficiencia, *f.* sufficiency; capacity, ability; self-importance.—**suficiente,** *a.* sufficient; fit, competent.

sufijo, *a.* suffixed.—*m.* suffix.

sufragar, *vti.* [b] to defray, pay; to favor; to aid; (Am.) to vote for.—**sufragio,** *m.* suffrage; vote; favor, support, aid.—**sufragista,** *mf.* suffragette.

sufrible, *a.* tolerable, sufferable.—**sufrido,** *a.* patient, long-suffering.—*color s.,* color that does not show dirt.—*mal s.,* rude.—**sufrimiento,** *m.* suffering; sufferance.—**sufrir,** *vt.* to suffer, bear up; to undergo (a change, an operation, etc.); to sustain, resist (an attack); to permit, tolerate.—*vi.* to suffer.

sugerencia, *f.* insinuation, hint.—**sugerir,** *vti.* [39] to suggest, hint, insinuate.—**sugestión,** *f.* suggestion, insinuation, hint.—**sugestionable,** *a.* easily influenced.—**sugestionar,** *vt.* to hypnotize; to influence.—**sugestivo,** *a.* suggestive; revealing (of a dress).

suicida, *a.* suicidal.—*mf.* suicide (person).—**suicidarse,** *vr.* to commit suicide.—**suicidio,** *m.* suicide (crime).

suizo, *n.* & *a.* Swiss.

sujeción, *f.* subjection; control; subordination; submission; connection.—**sujetapapeles,** *m.* paper clip.—**sujetar,** *vti.* [49] to subject, subdue; to hold fast, fasten, grasp.—*vri.* to control oneself; to submit; (a) to abide (by), to observe.—**sujeto,** *ppi.* of SUJETAR.—*a.* subject, liable; amenable.—*m.* subject; person; individual, fellow; (logic & gram.) subject.

sulfato, *m.* sulfate.

sulfurar, *vt.* to irritate, anger.—*vr.* to become furious.

suma, *f.* sum; addition; aggregate; amount; total; summary.—*en s.,* in short.—**sumando,** *m.* (math.) addend.—**sumar,** *vt.* to add; to amount to; to sum up, recapitulate.—*máquina de s.,* adding machine.—**sumario,** *a.* concise; plain, brief; (law) summary.—*m.* summary, abstract; (law) indictment.

sumarísimo, *a.* (law) swift, with dispatch.

sumergible, *a.* submersible.—*m.* submarine.—**sumergir,** *vti.* [c] to immerse; to submerge; to sink.—*vri.* to dive, to plunge; to submerge; to sink.—**sumersión,** *f.* submersion, immersion.—**sumidero,** *m.* sewer, drain, sink, gutter.

suministrar, *vt.* to supply, furnish, provide.—**suministro,** *m.* supply, providing.

sumir, *vt.* & *vr.* to sink; to plunge; to submerge.—**sumisión,** *f.* submission.—**sumiso,** *a.* submissive, humble, meek.

sumo, *a.* high, great, supreme.—*a lo s.,* at most.

suntuosidad, *f.* magnificence, sumptuousness.—**suntuoso,** *a.* sumptuous, magnificent.

supeditación, *f.* subjection; oppression.—**supeditar,** *vt.* to subdue, oppress; to reduce to subjection.

superar, *vt.* to overcome, conquer; to surpass; to exceed.

superávit, *m.* (com.) surplus.

superficial, *a.* superficial, shallow.—**superficialidad,** *f.* superficiality; shallowness.—**superficie,** *f.* surface; area.

superfluo, *a.* superfluous.

superhombre, *m.* superman.

superintendencia, *f.* superintendence, supervision.—**superintendente,** *n.* superintendent, manager; inspector; overseer, supervisor.

superior, *a.* superior; upper; better, finer; higher (algebra, math., studies).—*m.* superior.—*f.* mother superior.—**superioridad,** *f.* superiority.

superlativo, *m.* & *a.* superlative.

superponer, *vti.* [32-49] to superimpose.—**superposición,** *f.* superposition.—**superpuesto,** *ppi.* of SUPERPONER.

superstición, *f.* superstition.—**supersticioso,** *a.* superstitious.

supervisar, *vt.* (neol.) to supervise.—**supervisión,** *s.* (neol.) supervision.—**supervisor,** *m.* (neol.) supervisor.

supervivencia, *f.* survival.—**superviviente,** *mf.* & *a.* survivor; surviving.

suplantación, *f.* supplanting.—**suplantar,** *vt.* to supplant; to forge (as a check).

suplementario, *a.* supplementary.—**suplemento,** *m.* supply, supplying; supplement.

suplente, *a.* & *mf.* supply, substitute; substituting.

súplica, *f.* entreaty; supplication; request.—**suplicar,** *vti.* [d] to entreat; to supplicate; to petition.

suplicio, *m.* torture; execution; gallows; grief, suffering, anguish.

suplir, *vt.* to supply, furnish; to act as a substitute for; to make good, make up for.

suponer, *vti.* [32-49] to suppose, assume; to entail (expense, etc.).—*vii.* to have weight or authority.—**suposición,** *f.* supposition, assumption; imposition, falsehood.

supositorio, *m.* (med.) suppository.

supremacía, *f.* supremacy.—**supremo,** *a.* supreme; last, final.

supresión, *f.* suppression; omission; elimination.—**suprimir,** *vt.* to suppress; to cut out; to omit; to clear of.

supuesto, *ppi.* of SUPONER.—*s. que,* allowing that; granting that; since.—*por s.,* of course.—*m.* supposition; assumption.

supuración, *f.* suppuration.—**supurar,** *vi.* (med.) to suppurate.

sur, *m.* south; south. wind.—**suramericano,** *a.* & *n.* = SUDAMERICANO.

surcar, *vti.* [d] to plow, furrow; to move through.—**surco,** *m.* furrow; rut; wrinkle.

surgir, *vii.* [49-c] to spout; to issue, come forth; to appear, arise; to sprout.

suri, *m.* (Am.) ostrich.

surtido, *a.* (com.) assorted.—*m.* assortment; stock, supply.—**surtidor,** *n.* purveyor, caterer.—*m.* jet, fountain.—**surtir,** *vt.* to supply, furnish, stock.—*s. efecto,* to have the desired effect, to work.—*vi.* to spout, spurt.

suscitar, *vt.* to stir up; to raise; to originate.—*vr.* to rise, start, originate.

suscribir, *vti.* [49] to subscribe; to sign; to endorse; to agree to.—*vri.* to subscribe (periodicals, etc.).—**suscrición,** *f.* subscription.—**suscrito,** *ppi.* of SUSCRIBIR.—**suscritor,** *n.* subscriber.

susodicho, *a.* aforementioned, aforesaid.

suspender, *vti.* [49] to suspend; to hang up; to stop, delay, interrupt; to discontinue; to fail (in exam); to adjourn (a meeting).—**suspensión,** *f.* suspension, interruption; reprieve; discontinuance.—**suspenso,** *ppi.* of SUSPENDER.—*m.* failing mark (in exam).

suspicacia, *f.* suspiciousness.—**suspicaz,** *a.* suspicious, distrustful.

suspirar, *vi.* to sigh.—*s. por,* to crave, long for.—**suspiro,** *m.* sigh; brief pause.

sustancia, *f.* substance; essence; (coll.) judgment, sense.—**sustancial,** *a.* substantial; essential.—**sustancioso,** *a.* juicy; nourishing; substantial.—**sustantivo,** *a.* substantive. —*m.* substantive, noun.

sustentación, *f.* support, sustenance.—**sustentar,** *vt.* to sustain, support, bear; to feed.—**sustento,** *m.* sustenance, maintenance; support.

sustitución, *f.* substitution.—**sustituir,** *vti.* [23-e] to substitute, replace.—**sustituto,** *n.* substitute; supply.—*ppi.* of SUSTITUIR.

susto, *m.* scare, fright, shock.—*dar un s.,* to frighten; to startle.

sustracción, *f.* subtraction.—**sustraer,** *vti.* [43] to subtract, remove, take off, deduct.—*vri.* to withdraw oneself; to elude.

susurrar, *vi.* to whisper; to murmur; to rustle; to hum gently (as the air).—*vr.* to be whispered about.—**susurro,** *m.* whisper, humming, murmur, rustle.

sutil, *a.* thin, slender; subtle, cunning; keen; light, volatile.—**sutileza,** *f.* thinness, slenderness, fineness; sublety, cunning; sagacity; nicety.

sutura, *f.* seam; suture.

suyo, *a.* & *pron. poss.* (*f.* suya.—*pl.* suyos, suyas) his, hers, theirs, one's; his own, its own, one's own, their own.—*de s.* intrinsically; spontaneously.—*salirse con la suya,* to get one's own way.—*una de las suyas,* one of his pranks or tricks.

T

tabacalero, *a.* tobacco.—*n.* tobacco grower or dealer.—**tabaco,** *m.* tobacco; cigar.

tábano, *m.* (entom.) gadfly, horsefly.

tabaquera, *f.* cigar case; tobacco pouch.—**tabaquería,** *f.* cigar store.—**tabaquero,** *n.* cigar maker; tobacconist.

taberna, *f.* tavern, saloon, barroom.

tabernáculo, *m.* tabernacle.

tabernero, *m.* tavern keeper, barkeeper.

tabique, *m.* partition wall, partition.

tabla, *f.* (carp.) board; plank; slab; tablet, plate (of metal); pleat; table, list.—*pl.* (theat.) stage; draw, stalemate (in a game).—*a raja t.,* at any price, ruthlessly.—*hacer t. rasa de,* to ignore entirely; to set at nought.—*salvarse en una t.,* to have a narrow escape.—*t. de salvación,* last resource.—**tablado,** *m.* stage, scaffold, platform; (theat.) stage boards.—**tablero,** *m.* board, panel; sawable timber; drawing board; chessboard, checkerboard; (Am.) blackboard; shop counter; door panel.—*t. de distribución,* (elec.) switchboard.—**tableta,** *f.* tablet; writing pad; (pharm.) tablet, pastille, lozenge.—**tabletear,** *vt.* to rattle clappers.—**tableteo,** *m.* rattling sound of clappers.—**tablilla,** *f.* tablet, slab; bulletin board; (surg.) splint.—**tablón,** *m.* plank, thick board.—**tabloncillo,** *m.* flooring board.

tabú, *m.* taboo.

tabulador, *m.* (neol.) tabulator, computer.—**tabular,** *vt.* (neol.) to tabulate.

taburete, *m.* taboret; stool.

tacañería, *f.* stinginess.—**tacaño,** *a.* stingy, niggardly.

tácito, *a.* tacit, implied; silent. —**taciturno,** *a.* taciturn, reserved; sad, melancholy; silent.

taco, *m.* plug, stopper; (artil.) wad, wadding; billiard cue; (coll.) snack; (Am.) dandy; (Am.) heel (of shoe).—*echar tacos,* (coll.) to swear; to curse.

tacón, *m.* heel (of shoe).—**taconazo,** *m.* blow with a shoe heel.—**taconear,** *vi.* (coll.) to walk or strut loftily on the heels.—**taconeo,** *m.* noise made with the heels.

táctica, *f.* tactics.—**táctico,** *a.* tactical.

tacto, *m.* touch, sense of touch; tact, carefulness.

tacha, *f.* fault, defect, blemish, flaw. —**tachar,** *vt.* to censure, blame, charge; to find fault with; to cut out, cross out.

tachón, *m.* ornamental nail; trimming; crossing out (in writing). —**tachonar,** *vt.* (sew.) to adorn with trimming.

tachuela, *f.* tack, small nail.

tafetán, *m.* taffeta.—*t. inglés,* court plaster, sticking plaster.

tagarnina, *f.* (coll.) bad cigar.

tahalí, *m.* shoulder belt, sword belt.

tahur, *m.* gambler, gamester; sharper, card sharp.

taimado, *a.* sly, cunning, crafty.

taita, *m.* (Am.) (coll.) daddy, dad.

tajada, *f.* slice; (coll.) cut.—**tajar,** *vt.* to cut, cleave, chop.—**tajo,** *m.* cut; incision; cutting edge; steep cliff; chopping block.

tal, *a.* such, such as.—*t. cual,* such as; such as it is.—*pron.* such, such a one, such a thing.—*no hay t.,* there is no such thing.—*t. para cual,* two of a kind.—*t. por cual,* (a) nobody.—*adv.* thus, so, in such manner.—*con t. que, con t. de que,* provided, on condition, that.—*¡qué t.?* hello! how do you do?

talabarte, *m.* sword belt.—**talabartero,** *m.* saddler; harness maker.

taladrar, *vt.* to bore, drill; to pierce (the ears).—**taladro,** *m.* drill, bit, borer, auger; bore, drill hole.

tálamo, *m.* bridal chamber or bed.

talanquera, *f.* picket fence.

talante, *m.* mode or manner; mien; desire, will, disposition.—*de mal t.,* unwillingly, grudgingly.

talar, *vt.* to fell (trees).

talco, *m.* talc; talcum powder.

talega, *f.* bag, sack; money bag; diaper.—**talego,** *m.* bag or sack; clumsy, awkward fellow.

talento, *m.* talent; cleverness.—**talentoso,** *a.* smart, clever, talented.

talión, *m.* retaliation, requital.

talismán, *m.* talisman, charm, amulet.

talón, *m.* (anat., shoe) heel; (com.) check, draft; stub; coupon.—**talonario,** *m.* stub book.—*libro t.,* check book.

talud, *m.* slope, bank.

talla, *f.* carving, wood carving; (jewelry) cut, cutting; height, stature (of person).—*de t.,* (of person) prominent.—**tallar,** *vt.* to carve; to engrave; (jewelry) to cut; to appraise.—*vi.* (card games) to deal.

tallarín, *m.* noodle (for soup).

talle, *m.* form, figure; waist; (tailoring) fit; bodice.

taller, *m.* workshop, factory; atelier; studio.—*t. de reparaciones,* repair shop; (auto) service station.

tallo, *m.* (bot.) stem, stalk; shoot, sprout.

tamal, *m.* (Am.) tamale.

tamaño, *m.* size.—*t. natural,* full size. —*a.* so great; so big, so small; huge.

tambalear, *vi. & vr.* to stagger, totter, reel.—**tambaleo,** *m.* reeling, staggering, tottering.

también, *adv.* also, too; as well; likewise.

tambor, *m.* drum; drummer; band pulley, rope barrel.—**tambora,** *f.* bass drum.—**tamboril,** *m.* tabor, small drum.—**tamborilear,** *vi.* to drum.—*vt.* to praise, extol.—**tamborilero,** *m.* taborer, drummer.

tamiz, *m.* sieve, sifter; bolting cloth. —**tamizar,** *vti.* [a] to sift.

tampoco, *adv.* neither, not either; either (after negative).

tan, *adv. contr.* of TANTO: as so, so much, as well, as much.—*¡qué mujer t. bella!* what a beautiful woman.—*t. solo,* only, merely.

tanda, *f.* turn, rotation; task; gang of workmen, shift; relay; set, batch; each game of billiards.

tangente, *f. & a.* (geom.) tangent.— *salir or salirse por la t.,* to confuse the issue.

tangerina, *f.* tangerine.

tangible, *a.* tangible.

tanque, *m.* tank; (Am.) swimming pool.

tantear, *vt.* to try, test, measure; to feel out; to make an estimate of; to consider carefully; to scrutinize. —*vi.* to keep the score.—**tanteo,** *m.* estimate, calculation; test, trial; points, score (in a game).—*al t.,* by eye; as an estimate; by trial.

tanto, *a. & pron.* so much, as much. —*pl.* as many, so many.—*adv.* so, thus; so much, as much; so long, as long; so hard, so often.—*m.* undetermined sum or quantity; counter, chip; point (in games).—*a las tantas,* in the small hours.— *al t.,* posted about, up to date.—*en t.,* or *entre t.,* in the meantime.— *no ser para t.,* not to be so bad as that.—*otro t.,* as much; the same again.—*por lo t.,* therefore.—*t. así,* so much.—*t. más cuanto,* all the more because.—*t. mejor,* so much the better.—*t. peor,* so much the worse.—*t. que,* so much that.—*treinta y tantos,* thirty odd.

tañer, *vti.* [41] to play (a musical

instrument).—**tañido,** *m.* playing; tune; ringing.

tapa, *f.* lid, cover, cap; cover (of book); heel lift (of shoe).—*t. de los sesos,* top of the skull.—**tapaboca,** *m.* (coll.) slap on the mouth; muffler, scarf.—**tapadera,** *f.* loose lid, cover of a pot.—**tapar,** *vt.* to hide, cover up, veil; to stop up, plug; to close up, obstruct.—**taparrabo,** *m.* loin cloth.

tapete, *m.* cover for a table or chest; small carpet, rug.—*t. verde,* gaming table.

tapia, *f.* wall fence.—*más sordo que una t.,* deaf as a post.—**tapiar,** *vt.* to wall up; to wall in; to close or block up.

tapicería, *f.* tapestry; tapestry making; upholstery; tapestry shop.—**tapicero,** *m.* tapestry maker; upholsterer; carpet layer.

tapioca, *f.* tapioca.

tapiz, *m.* tapestry.—**tapizar,** *vti.* [a] to hang with tapestry; to upholster.

tapón, *m.* cork, stopper; plug; (elec.) fuse; (surg.) tampon.—**taponar,** *vt.* to cork, plug; (surg.) to tampon.

tapujo, *m.* muffle; (coll.) pretext, subterfuge.

taquigrafía, *f.* stenography.—**taquígrafo,** *n.* stenographer.

taquilla, *f.* letter file; booking office; (theat., RR.) ticket office.—**taquillero,** *n.* booking clerk; ticket seller.

tara, *f.* (com.) tare, weight of container; defect.

tarambana, *mf.* giddy person; madcap.

tararear, *vt. & vi.* to hum (a tune). —**tarareo,** *m.* humming.

tarascada, *f.* bite, wound with the teeth; (coll.) pert, rude answer.

tardanza, *f.* delay; slowness, tardiness.—**tardar,** *vi. & vr.* to delay, tarry; to take a long time; to be late.—*a más t.,* at the latest.—**tarde,** *f.* afternoon.—*de t. en t.,* now and then, once in a while.—*adv.* late; too late.—**tardío,** *a.* late, too late; slow, tardy.—**tardo,** *a.* slow, sluggish; tardy; dull, thick.

tarea, *f.* task.

tarifa, *f.* tariff; price list; fare, rate.

tarima, *f.* stand; movable platform; low bench, footstool.

tarjeta, *f.* card.—*t. postal,* post card. —**tarjetero,** *m.* cardcase; index file; wallet.

tarro, *m.* jar; (Am.) horn (of an animal); (Am.) can, pot; (beer) mug.

tarta, *f.* tart; cake.

tartamudear, *vi.* to stutter, stammer. —**tartamudeo,** *m.,* **tartamudez,** *f.*

stuttering, stammering.—**tartamudo,** *n. & a.* stutterer, stammer; stuttering, stammering.

tartera, *f.* baking pan for pastry; dinner pail.

tarugo, *m.* wooden peg or pin; stopper, plug; (fig.) blockhead.

tasa, *f.* measure, rule; standard; rate; scot; valuation, appraisement. —**tasación,** *f.* appraisement, appraisal, valuation.—**tasador,** *n.* appraiser.

tasajo, *m.* jerked beef.

tasar, *vt.* to appraise; to rate; to stint.

tata, *m.* (Am., coll.) dad, daddy; nursemaid; younger sister.

tatarabuelo, *n.* great-great-grandfather(-mother).—**tataranieto,** *n.* great-great-grandson(-daughter).

tatuaje, *m.* tattooing; tattoo.—**tatuar,** *vt. & vr.* to tattoo.

taxi, taxímetro, *m.* taxi, taxicab.

taza, *f.* cup; cupful; bowl; basin of a fountain; cup guard of a sword.—**tazón,** *m.* large bowl; basin.

te, *m.* tea.

te, *pers. & refl. pron.* (*obj. case of* TU) you, to you; yourself; thee.

tea, *f.* torch.

teatral, *a.* theatrical.—**teatro,** *m.* theater; stage; dramatic art; scene.

tecla, *f.* key (of a piano, typewriter, etc.).—*dar en la t.,* to find the way. —**teclado,** *m.* keyboard.

técnica, *f.* technique; technical ability.—**tecnicismo,** *m.* technical term; technology.—**técnico,** *a.* technical.—*n.* technician.—**tecnología,** *f.* technology.

tecolote, *m.* (Mex.) owl.

techado, *m.* roof, roofing; ceiling; shed.—**techar,** *vt.* to roof; to cover with a roof.—**techo,** *m.* = TECHUMBRE; (aer.) absolute ceiling.—**techumbre,** *f.* ceiling; roof, roofing; cover; shed.

tedio, *m.* boredom, tediousness.—**tedioso,** *a.* tedious, boresome, boring, tiresome.

teja, *f.* roof tile; (bot.) linden tree.—**tejado,** *m.* roof; shed.—**tejamanil,** *m.* shingle.—**tejar,** *m.* tile kiln.—*vt.* to tile.

tejedor, *n.* weaver.—**tejemaneje,** *m.* (coll.) skill, cleverness; (Am.) scheming, trick.—**tejer,** *vt.* to weave; (Am.) to knit; to devise.—**tejido,** *m.* texture; weaving; fabric, textile, web; (anat.) tissue.

tejón, *m.* (zool.) badger.

tela, *f.* cloth, fabric; pellicle, film.—*en t. de juicio,* in doubt; under careful consideration.—*t. de cebolla,* onion skin; thin cloth.—*t. metálica,* wire cloth.—**telar,** *m.* loom.—**telaraña,** *f.* cobweb.

telefonear, *vt.* & *vi.* to telephone.—**telefonema,** *m.* telephone message.—**telefónico,** *a.* telephonic.—**telefonista,** *mf.* (telephone) operator.—**teléfono,** *m.* telephone.

telegrafía, *f.* telegraphy.—**telegrafiar,** *vt.* to telegraph; to wire.—**telegráfico,** *a.* telegraphic.—**telegrafista,** *mf.* telegrapher.—**telégrafo,** *m.* telegraph.—**telegrama,** *m.* telegram.

telepatía, *f.* telepathy.

telescópico, *a.* telescopic.—**telescopio,** *m.* telescope.

televisión, *f.* television.—*receptor de t.,* television set.

telón, *m.* (theat.) curtain.—*bajar el t.,* to drop the curtain.—*t. de boca,* drop curtain.

tema, *m.* theme, subject; text, thesis; (mus.) theme, motive.—*f.* mania, obsession.—**temario,** *m.* agenda.

temblar, *vii.* [1] to tremble, shake, quake, quiver; to shiver.—**temblequear,** *vi.* (coll.) to tremble, shake, shiver.—**temblor,** *m.* trembling, tremor, thrill; quake.—*t. de tierra,* earthquake.—**tembloroso,** *a.* trembling, tremulous, shivering, shaking.

temer, *vt.* & *vi.* to fear, dread.—**temerario,** *a.* rash, imprudent; reckless.—**temeridad,** *f.* temerity, rashness, recklessness; foolhardiness.—**temeroso,** *a.* dread; timid; timorous; fearful.—**temible,** *a.* dread, terrible.—**temor,** *m.* dread, fear.

témpano, *m.* kettledrum; drumhead; piece, block.—*t. de hielo,* iceberg.

temperamento, *m.* temperament, constitution; climate.—**temperatura,** *f.* temperature.

tempestad, *f.* tempest, storm.—**tempestuoso,** *a.* tempestuous, stormy.

templado, *a.* moderate (esp. of climate); tempered; lukewarm; fair; brave, firm; (mus.) tuned.—**templanza,** *f.* temperance, moderation; mildness (of temperature or climate).—**templar,** *vt.* to temper, moderate; to temper, quench (metals); (mus.) to tune.—*vr.* to be moderate.—**temple,** *m.* temper (of metals and of persons); courage; disposition; (mus.) temperament.

templo, *m.* temple; church.

temporada, *f.* season; period (of time); spell (of weather).

temporal, *a.* temporal; temporary; secular, worldly.—*m.* tempest, storm; long rainy spell.—**temporero,** *a.* temporary (laborer).

tempranero, *a.* early.—**temprano,** *a.* early.—*adv.* early; in good time.

ten, *m.*—*t. con t.,* tact, wisdom.

tenacidad, *f.* tenacity; tenaciousness, perseverance.—**tenacillas,** *f.* small tongs; pincers; sugar tongs; curling irons.—**tenaz,** *a.* tenacious; strong, firm; stubborn; purposeful, persevering.—**tenaza(s),** *f.* claw (as a lobster's).—*pl.* tongs, nippers, pliers; (dent.) forceps.

tendal, *m.* tent, awning, tilt; piece of canvas.

tendedero, *m.* drying place.—*f.* (Am.) clothesline.—**tendencia,** *f.* tendency, proclivity; trend, drift.—**tendencioso,** *a.* tendentious.—**tender,** *vti.* [18] to stretch, stretch out; to spread out; to hang out (washing); to lay (tablecloth, rails, etc.).—*vii.* to have a tendency, tend.—*vri.* to stretch out, lie full length.

tendero, *n.* retail shopkeeper.

tendido, *a.* lying, spread out.—*m.* washing hung or spread out to dry.—*pl.* uncovered seats in the bullring; bleachers.

tendón, *m.* tendon, sinew.

tenebroso, *a.* dark, gloomy.

tenedor, *m.* (table) fork; keeper; (com.) holder.—*t. de libros,* bookkeeper.—**teneduría,** *f.* position of bookkeeper.—*t. de libros,* bookkeeping.

tenencia, *f.* tenure, occupancy, possession, holding; (mil.) position of a lieutenant.

tener, *vti.* [42] to have, possess; to hold; to contain.—*no tenerlas todas consigo,* to be worried, to be anxious.—*t. a bien,* to please; to find it convenient.—*t. cuatro años,* to be four years old.—*t. cuidado de,* to take care of.—*t. dos metros de ancho,* to be two meters wide.—*t. en cuenta,* to take into account.—*t. gana* or *ganas,* to wish, desire (to); to have in mind (to); to feel like.—*t. gracia,* to be funny.—*t. gusto en,* to be glad to.—*t. hambre (sed, etc.),* to be hungry (thirsty, etc.).—*t. presente,* to bear in mind.—*t. prisa,* to be in a hurry.—*t. razón,* to be right.—*t. suerte,* to be lucky.—*vai.* to have.—*tengo dicho,* I have said.—*tengo entendido,* I understand.—*tengo escritas dos cartas,* I have two letters written.—*tengo pensado,* I intend.—*vri.* to hold fast or steady; to stop, halt.—*t. en pie,* to keep on one's feet, remain standing.

tenería, *f.* tannery.

tenia, *f.* tapeworm.

teniente, *m.* lieutenant.

tenis, *m.* tennis.

tenor, *m.* (mus.) tenor; condition, nature; kind; literal meaning.

tensión, *f.* tension; (mech.) stress; strain; (elec.) voltage, tension.—**tenso,** *a.* tense, tight, taut, stretched.

tentación, *f.* temptation.

tentáculo, *m.* tentacle.

tentador, *n.* & *a.* tempter; tempting, tantalizing.—*el t.,* the devil.—**tentar,** *vti.* [1] to touch, feel with the fingers; to grope; to tempt; to attempt, try; to test; (surg.) to probe.—**tentativa,** *f.* attempt.—**tentativo,** *a.* tentative.

tentempié, *m.* (coll.) light luncheon, snack, refreshment.

tenue, *a.* thin, tenuous; worthless; (art) subdued.

teñir, *vti.* [9–49] to dye, tinge; to stain; (art) to darken (a color).

teologal, *a.* theologic(al).—**teología,** *f.* theology.—**teológico,** *a.* = TEOLOGAL.

teorema, *m.* theorem.

teoría, *f.* theory.—**teórico,** *a.* theoretical.—*mf.* theorist.—**teorizar,** *vii.* [a] to theorize.

terapia, *f.* therapy.

tercer, *a.* third.—**tercería,** *f.* pandering, procuring.—**tercero,** *a.* third.—*n.* mediator; third person; go-between.

terciar, *vt.* to place sidewise; to sling diagonally; to divide into three parts; (mil.) to carry (arms.)—*vi.* to mediate, arbitrate; to go between; to join (in conversation).—**tercio,** *a.* third.—*m.* one-third; (Sp.) Foreign Legion; (Am.) (coll.) fellow, guy.—*hacer mal t.,* to do a bad turn.

terciopelo, *m.* velvet.

terco, *a.* stubborn.

tergiversar, *vt.* to misrepresent, distort.

terminación, *f.* termination; end, ending.—**terminal,** *a.* terminal, final, last.—*m.* (elec.) terminal.—**terminante,** *a.* ending, closing; final, decisive.—**terminar,** *vt.* & *vi.* to end, terminate, conclude.—**término,** *m.* end, ending, completion; term, word; boundary; manner, behavior; outlying district; period, limit; aim, goal; (math., log.) term.—*en buenos términos,* in kind language.—*en último t.,* finally; in the background.—*primer t.,* (art) foreground.—*t. medio,* average.

termita, *f.,* termite, *m.* termite.

termómetro, *m.* thermometer.—**termo(s),** *m.* thermos bottle.—**termóstato,** *m.* thermostat.

ternero, *n.* calf.—*f.* veal.

terneza, *f.* softness; tenderness; affection, caress.—*pl.* sweet nothings.

terno, *m.* set of three, trio; tern (in lottery); bad word; suit of clothes; (jewelry) set.

ternura, *f.* tenderness, softness, fondness.

terquedad, *f.* stubbornness, obstinacy.

terrado, *m.* terrace; flat roof of a house.

terral, *m.* land breeze.

terramicina, *f.* terramycin.

terraplén, *m.* (RR.) embankment; mound; terrace.

terrateniente, *mf.* landowner, landholder.

terraza, *f.* terrace; border in a garden; veranda.

terremoto, *m.* earthquake.—**terrenal,** *a.* worldly, earthly.—**terreno,** *a.* earthly, terrestrial; worldly, mundane.—*m.* land, ground, soil; terrain; piece of land, lot; field, sphere of action.—**terrestre,** *a.* terrestrial.

terrible, *a.* terrible.—**terrífico,** *a.* terrific, frightful.

territorio, *m.* territory; region.

terrón, *m.* clod; lump.

terror, *m.* terror.—**terrorismo,** *m.* terrorism.—**terrorista,** *mf.* & *a.* terrorist; terroristic.

terruño, *m.* native land; piece of ground.

terso, *a.* smooth, polished, glossy.—**tersura,** *f.* smoothness; polish; cleanliness, terseness.

tertulia, *f.* social gathering for entertainment; party; conversation; (Am.) (theat.) gallery.

tesis, *f.* thesis.

tesón, *m.* tenacity, firmness, endurance.—**tesonero,** *a.* (Am.) persistent, tenacious.

tesorería, *f.* treasury; treasurership.—**tesorero,** *n.* treasurer; bursar (of a college, univ.).—**tesoro,** *m.* treasure; treasury.

testa, *f.* (coll.) head; top or crown of the head; front, face; (coll.) brains, cleverness.

testaferro, *m.* man of straw, dummy, figurehead.

testamento, *m.* will, testament.—**testar,** *vi.* to make a will.—*vt.* to scratch out.

testarudez, *f.* hardheadedness, stubbornness, willfulness.—**testarudo,** *a.* stubborn, hardheaded.

testículo, *m.* testicle.

testificar, *vti.* [d] to attest, witness, testify.—**testigo,** *mf.* witness.—*t. de cargo,* witness for the prosecution.—*t. ocular,* eyewitness.—**testimoniar,** *vt.* to attest, bear witness to.—

testimonio, *m.* testimony; affidavit; attestation.

testuz, *m.* nape or forehead (of some animals).

teta, *f.* teat, breast; nipple; udder.

tétano, tétanos, *m.* tetanus, lockjaw.

tetera, *f.* teapot; (Am.) nursing bottle.—**tetilla,** *f.* teat.

tétrico, *a.* sad, sullen; dark, gloomy.

textil, *a.* textile.

texto, *m.* text; quotation; textbook.—**textual,** *a.* textual.

tez, *f.* complexion (of the face).

ti, *pron. 2d. pers. sing.* (after *prep.*) (*obj. case* of TU) you.

tía, *f.* aunt.—*no hay tu t.,* there's no use.

tibia, *f.* tibia, shin bone.

tibieza, *f.* tepidity, lukewarmness; coolness.—**tibio,** *a.* tepid, lukewarm; remiss.

tiburón, *m.* shark.

tibor, *m.* Chinese vase; (Am.) chamberpot.

tictac, *m.* tick, ticking (of a watch, etc.).

tiempo, *m.* time; (mus.) tempo; (gram.) tense; weather.—*andando el t.,* in time, in the long run.—*a su t.,* in due time.—*a t.,* timely, in or on time.—*cuanto t.,* how long.—*fuera de t.,* out of season; inopportunely.—*hace t.,* long ago.—*los buenos tiempos,* the good, old days.

tienda, *f.* shop, store; tent.—*ir de tiendas,* to go shopping.

tienta, *f.* (surg.) probe.—*andar a tientas,* to grope; to feel one's way.—*a tientas,* gropingly.

tiento, *m,* touch, act of feeling; blind man's stick; tact; steady hand; (coll.) blow, cuff; (coll.) swig.—*perder el t.,* to get out of practice, to get rusty.

tierno, *a.* tender, soft; delicate; affectionate; sensitive; young; green, unripe.

tierra, *f.* earth, world; land; soil; ground; native country.—*a t.,* ashore.—*besar la t.,* (coll.) to bite the dust.—*dar en t. con,* or *echar por t.,* to overthrow; to ruin, destroy.—*echar t. a,* to hush up, forget, drop (a matter).—*irse a t.,* to fall down, to topple over.—*t. firme,* mainland; firm, solid ground.—*tomar t.,* to land; to anchor.—*venirse a t.,* = IRSE A TIERRA.

tieso, *a.* stiff; tight, taut; stuck up; too grave or circumspect.

tiesto, *m.* potsherd; flowerpot.

tiesura, *f.* stiffness; rigidity.

tifo, *m.* typhus.—**tifoidea,** *a. & f.* typhoid (fever).

tifón, *m.* whirlwind; typhoon.

tifus, *m.* typhus.

tigre, *m.* tiger.—**tigresa,** *f.* tigress.

tijera, *f.* (usually in *pl.*) scissors; sawbuck.—*cama de t.,* folding bed, cot.—*silla de t.,* folding chair.—**tijeretada,** *f.,* **tijeretazo,** *m.* a cut with scissors, clip, snip.—**tijeretear,** *vt.* to cut with scissors; to snip, clip; to gossip.

tildar, *vt.* to cross or scratch out; to put a tilde over; to criticize.—*t. de,* to accuse of, or charge with being.—**tilde,** *f.* tilde, diacritic (~) of the letter *ñ*; blemish; jot.

timador, *n.* swindler.—**timar,** *vt.* to cheat, swindle.

timba, *f.* gambling party; gambling den; (Am.) guava paste or jelly.

timbrar, *vt.* to stamp.—**timbre,** *m.* seal; postage stamp; call or door bell; timbre, tone; crest (heraldry).—*t. de gloria,* glorious deed.

timidez, *f.* timidity; bashfulness.—**tímido,** *a.* timid, shy, bashful.

timo, *m.* (coll.) cheat, swindle.

timón, *m.* helm, rudder.—*t. de profundidad,* (aer.) elevator.—**timonear,** *vt. & vi.* (naut.) to helm; to steer.—**timonel,** *m.* helmsman, steersman; coxswain.

timorato, *a.* timorous, chicken-hearted.

tímpano, *m.* (anat.) eardrum; kettledrum.

tina, *f.* large earthen jar; vat; tub, wash tub; bathtub.—**tinaco,** *m.* wooden trough, tub, or vat.—**tinaja,** *f.* large earthen jar.—**tinajón,** *m.* very large earthen water jar, or tank.

tinglado, *m.* shed, shed roof; temporary board floor; machination, intrigue.

tiniebla, *f.* (usually in *pl.*) darkness.

tino, *m.* skill; steady and accurate aim; judgment; tact; knack.

tinta, *f.* ink; tint, hue, color.—*de buena t.,* from or on good authority.—*t. china,* India ink.—**tinte,** *m.* dyeing; staining; tint, hue; paint, color, stain; dye; (fig.) guise, color.—**tinterillo,** *m.* (Am.) shyster lawyer.—**tintero,** *m.* inkpot, inkwell.—*dejarse en el t.,* (coll.) to forget to mention.

tintinear, *vi.* to clink, tinkle, jingle.—**tintineo,** *m.* clink, tinkling.

tinto, *ppi.* of TEÑIR.—*a.* tinged; (dark) red; (Am.) black, strong (coffee).—**tintorería,** *f.* cleaner or dyer's shop.—**tintorero,** *n.* cleaner, dyer.—**tintura,** *f.* tincture; tint, color; stain; dye; smattering.

tiña, *f.* (med.) scab; ringworm.—

tiñoso, *a.* scabby, scurvy; stingy, mean.

tío, *m.* uncle; (coll.) good old man; fellow!

tiovivo, *m.* merry-go-round.

típico, *a.* typical, characteristic.

tiple, *m.* (mus.) treble, soprano voice; treble guitar.—*f.* soprano singer.

tipo, *m.* type, pattern; standard, model; (coll.) (of person) figure, physique; (Am.) (com.) rate; (print.) type; (zool.) class; (coll. contempt.) fellow, guy.—**tipografía,** *f.* printing; typography.—**tipógrafo,** *n.* typographer.

tira, *f.* long, narrow strip.

tirabuzón, *m.* corkscrew; corkscrew curl.

tirada, *f.* cast, throw; distance; (print.) edition, issue.—**tirador,** *n.* thrower; drawer; sharpshooter; marksman, good shot.—*m.* handle, knob.—**tirafondo,** *m.* wood screw.

tiranía, *f.* tyranny.—**tiranizar,** *vti.* [a] to tyrannize.—**tirano,** *a.* tyrannical.—*n.* tyrant.

tirante, *a.* drawing, pulling; taut, tense, stretched; strained (as relations).—*m.* trace, gear (of harness); brace, strap.—*pl.* suspenders, braces. —**tirantez,** *f.* tenseness, tightness; stretch; strain; tension.—**tirar,** *vt.* to throw, cast, pitch (as a ball); to cast off, throw away (as a garment); to print; to fire, shoot (as a gun); to draw (a line); to waste, squander.—*t. de,* to pull (on).—*vi.* to draw, pull; (a) to have a shade (of), border (on); to tend, incline (to).—*vr.* to throw oneself; to abandon oneself; to jump (at), spring (upon).

tiritar, *vi.* to shiver.

tiro, *m.* throw, shot; shot, discharge, report (of a firearm); target practice; range; team of draught animals; landing of a stairway; draught of a chimney.—*al t.,* (Am.) right away, immediately.—*a tiros,* with shots, by shooting.—*de t.,* draft (horse).—*de tiros largos,* in full dress, in full regalia.—*errar el t.,* to miss the mark; to be mistaken. —*ni a tiros,* (coll.) not for love or money, absolutely not.—*t. al blanco,* target shooting; shooting gallery.

tirón, *m.* pull, haul, tug; effort.— *de un t.,* at once, at one stroke.

tirotear, *vi. & vr.* to exchange shots, to skirmish.—**tiroteo,** *m.* skirmish; shooting.

tirria, *f.* (coll.) aversion, dislike, grudge.

tísico, *n. & a.* (med.) consumptive. —**tisis,** *f.* consumption, tuberculosis.

tisú, *m.* tissue, gold or silver tissue.

títere, *m.* puppet; whipper-snapper. —*no dejar t. con cabeza,* to upset everything; to leave no one to tell the tale.

titilar, *vi.* to twinkle, flicker.

titiritar, *vi.* to shiver with cold or fear.

titiritero, *n.* juggler, acrobat; puppeteer.

titubear, *vi.* to hesitate; to totter; to toddle (as a child); to stagger.— **titubeo,** *m.* hesitation; tottering.

titular, *vt.* to title, entitle, name, call.—*vr.* to call oneself.—*a.* titular; nominal.—*f.* headline (of a newspaper).—**título,** *m.* title; heading, headline; claim, privilege of right; (law) legal title to property; diploma; professional degree; (com.) certificate, bond.—*a t. (de),* under pretext (of); on the authority (of).

tiza, *f.* chalk; clay.

tiznar, *vt.* to smut, smudge; to stain, tarnish.—**tizne,** *m.* soot, coal smut; stain.

tizón, *m.* firebrand; (agr.) blight, rust; stain; mildew (of plants).

toalla, *f.* towel.—**toallero,** *m.* towel rack.

tobillo, *m.* ankle.

toca, *f.* hood, coif, bonnet, wimple.

tocado, *a.* (fig.) touched (in the head); perturbed; tainted.—*m.* hairdo, hairdress, coiffure.—**tocador,** *m.* dressing table; dressing room, boudoir; dressing case; player (of a musical instrument).—**tocante,** *a.*— *t. a,* respecting, concerning, with regard to.—**tocar,** *vti.* [d] to touch, feel; (mus.) to play; to toll, ring (a bell); to blow (a horn); to knock, rap.—*t. de cerca,* to concern, affect closely.—*t. fondo,* to strike ground.—*vii.* to touch; behoove, concern; to be one's turn; to call at a port; to border on; to be related.

tocayo, *n.* namesake.

tocino, *m.* bacon; salt pork.

tocólogo, *n.* obstetrician.

tocón, *m.* stump of a tree.

todavía, *adv.* still; yet; even.

todo, *a.* all, every, each; whole, entire.—*t. aquello que,* whatever.—*t. aquél que,* whoever.—*t. el mundo,* everybody.—*m.* all; whole; everything.—*pl.* everybody.—*ante t.,* first of all.—*con t.,* nevertheless, however.—*del t.,* entirely, wholly.—*en un t.,* together, in all its parts.— *jugar el t. por el t.,* to stake or risk all.—*sobre t.,* above all.—*adv.* entirely, totally.—*así y t.,* in spite of everything.—**todopoderoso,** *a.* almighty.

toga, *f.* robe or gown (worn by judges, professors, etc.); toga.

toldo, *m.* awning; tarpaulin; (Am.) Indian hut; tent.

tolerable, *a.* tolerable, bearable; permissible.—**tolerancia,** *f.* toleration; tolerance.—**tolerante,** *a.* tolerant.—**tolerar,** *vt.* to tolerate, endure, permit; to be indulgent; to overlook.

tolete, *m.* (Am.) club, cudgel.

toma, *f.* taking, receiving; take; (mil.) capture, seizure; dose (of a medicine); (hydraul.) intake; (elec.) outlet; tap (of a water main or electric wire).—**tomacorriente,** *m.* (Am.) (elec.) socket, plug.

tomaína, *f.* ptomaine.

tomar, *vt.* to take; to drink; to eat.—*t. asiento,* to take a seat, sit down.—*t. el pelo,* (coll.) to banter, make fun of.—*t. en cuenta,* to consider.—*t. la delantera,* to excel; to get ahead.—*vi.* to drink (liquor).—*vr.* to drink; to eat; to rust.

tomate, *m.* tomato.

tomillo, *m.* thyme.

tomo, *m.* volume, tome.—*de t. y lomo,* of weight and bulk; of importance.

ton, *m.*—*sin t. ni son,* without rhyme or reason.

tonada, *f.* tune, song.—**tonalidad,** *f.* tonality.

tonel, *m.* cask, barrel.—**tonelada,** *f.* ton.—**tonelaje,** *m.* tonnage, displacement; (com.) tonnage dues.

tónico, *a.* tonic; (gram.) accented or inflected.—*m.* tonic.—*f.* (mus.) keynote, tonic.—**tonificador, tonificante,** *a.* tonic, strengthening.—**tonificar,** *vti.* [d] (med.) to tone up.—**tono,** *m.* tone; tune; pitch; conceit; manner, social address.—*darse t.,* to put on airs.—*de buen t.,* stylish, fashionable, polite.

tonsila, *f.* (anat.) tonsil.

tontada, tontera, tontería, *f.* foolishness, silliness, nonsense.—**tonto,** *a.* silly, foolish, stupid.—*n.* fool, dunce, dolt.—*a tontas y a locas,* without order, haphazard.—*hacerse el t.,* to play dumb.

topacio, *m.* topaz.

topar, *vt.* to collide with; to meet with by chance; to find.—*vi.* to butt, strike; to stumble upon.—**tope,** *m.* butt, end; top, summit; (mech.) stop; (RR.) buffer; collision, knock.—*hasta el t.* or *los topes,* up to the top, or the brim.—**topetazo, topetón,** *m.* butt, knock, blow, collision.

tópico, *a.* topical.—*m.* commonplace, trite idea; topic.

topo, *m.* (zool.) mole; (coll.) awkward person.

toque, *m.* touch, touching; ringing (of bells); (mil.) bugle call; beat (of a drum).—*t. de diana,* reveille.

tórax, *m.* thorax.

torbellino, *m.* whirlwind; whirlpool; vortex; (fig.) hustling, restless person.

torcaz, torcaza, *f.* wild pigeon.

torcedura, *f.* twisting; sprain.—**torcer,** *vti.* [26-a] to twist, twine, wind (as strands); to sprain; to bend; to distort.—*no dar el brazo a t.,* to be obstinate.—*vii.* to turn (to right or left).—*vri.* to become twisted, bent or sprained; to go crooked or astray.—**torcimiento,** *m.* twist(ing); sprain; winding; bend.

tordillo, *a.* grayish, grizzled.—**tordo,** *a.* dappled (of horses).—*m.* (ornith.) thrush, throstle.

torear, *vi.* to fight bulls in the ring.—*vt.* to fight (bulls); to banter; to provoke.—**toreo,** *m.* bullfighting.—**torero,** *m.* bullfighter.—*a.* pertaining to bullfighters.

tormenta, *f.* storm, tempest; hurricane; misfortune.—**tormento,** *m.* torment, torture.—**tormentoso,** *a.* stormy; boisterous; turbulent.

tornado, *m.* tornado.

tornar, *vt.* to return, restore; to turn; to change, alter.—*vi.* to return, come back; to do again.—*vr.* (en) to change (into), to become.—**tornasol,** *m.* (bot.) sunflower; iridescence, sheen; litmus.—**tornasolado,** *a.* changeable, iridescent.

tornear, *vt. & vi.* to turn (in a lathe); to do lathe work.—**torneo,** *m.* turner.

tornillo, *m.* screw, bolt; vise, clamp.

torniquete, *m.* turnstile; turnbuckle; (surg.) tourniquet.

torno, *m.* lathe; winch, windlass; revolving dumbwaiter; turn; spindle.—*en t.,* round about.

toro, *m.* bull.—*los toros,* bullfighting.

toronja, *f.* grapefruit.

torpe, *a.* slow, heavy, torpid; dull, stupid; bawdy, lewd.

torpedear, *vt.* to torpedo.—**torpedeo,** *m.* torpedoing.—**torpedero,** *m.* torpedo boat.—**torpedo,** *m.* torpedo.

torpeza, *f.* heaviness, dullness; torpor; lewdness.

torre, *f.* tower; turret; steeple; (chess) castle or rook.

torrencial, *a.* torrential; overpowering.—**torrente,** *m.* torrent; rush; plenty.

torreón, *m.* fortified tower.—**torrero,** *m.* lighthouse keeper.

tórrido, *a.* torrid; parched, hot.

torsión, f. twist; twisting.

torso, m. trunk of the body or of a statue.

torta, f. cake, pie; loaf; (coll.) blow, slap.

tortícolis, m. stiff neck.

tortilla, f. omelet; (Am.) cornmeal cake, pancake.—*hacer t.,* to smash to pieces.

tórtola, f. (ornith.) turtledove.

tortuga, f. turtle; tortoise.

tortuoso, a. tortuous, winding; sly, · sneaky.

tortura, f. torture; grief.—**torturar,** vt. to torture.

torvo, a. fierce, stern, severe, grim.

tos, f. cough.—*t. ferina* or *convulsiva,* whooping cough.

tosco, a. coarse, rough; unpolished; slipshod.

toser, vi. to cough.

tosquedad, f. roughness, coarseness; rudeness; clumsiness.

tostada, f. [slice of] toast.—**tostador,** n. toaster; coffee roaster.—**tostadura,** f. toasting.—**tostar,** vti. [12] to toast; to roast; to tan (as the sun).

total, a. total; general.—m. total; totality; result, upshot.—*en t.,* in short, to sum up.—**totalidad,** f. totality; whole.—**totalitario,** a. & n. totalitarian.—**totalitarismo,** m. totalitarianism.—**totalizar,** vti. [a] to sum up; to find the total of.

tóxico, a. toxic.—m. poison.—**toxina,** f. (med.) toxin.

toza, f. log; block of wood; piece of bark.

tozudo, a. stubborn, obstinate.

traba, f. tie, bond, brace, clasp, locking device; anything that binds together; ligament, ligature; hobble, clog; obstacle, hindrance.

trabajador, a. industrious; hard-working.—n. worker; laborer.—**trabajar,** vt. & vi. to work, labor; to shape, form; to endeavor.—**trabajo,** m. work, labor; piece of work; employment; obstacle, hindrance; trouble, hardship.—*pasar trabajos,* to have troubles, to experience hardships or privation.—*trabajos forzados,* hard labor.—**trabajoso,** a. difficult, hard; laborious.

trabalenguas, m. tongue twister.—**trabar,** vt. to seize, fetter, fasten; to impede; to link; to engage in, join in.—vr. to become locked, interlocked; to become confused, rattled.—**trabazón,** f. juncture, union, bond, connection.

tracción, f. traction; cartage; (mech.) tension.—**tractor,** m. tractor.

tradición, f. tradition.—**tradicional,** a. traditional.

traducción, f. translation; rendering.—**traducir,** vti. [11] to translate.—**traductor,** n. translator.

traer, vti. [43] to bring, fetch; to cause; to wear (as a garment); to carry.—*t. a colación,* to bring up for discussion.—*t. a mal t.,* to go hard with one; to disturb, trouble, vex.—*t. entre manos,* to be engaged in, busy with.

tráfago, m. commerce, trade; drudgery; bustle, hustle.

traficar, vii. [d] to traffic, deal, trade; to travel, journey, roam.—**tráfico,** m. trade, business; traffic.

tragaderas, f. gullet.—*tener buenas t.,* to be very gullible.—**tragadero,** m. gullet; pit.—**tragaldabas,** mf. glutton.—**tragaluz,** m. skylight, bull's-eye.—**tragar,** vti. [b] to swallow; to devour; to swallow up, engulf.—vri. to swallow; to dissemble.

tragedia, f. tragedy.—**trágico,** a. tragic.—n. tragedian.

trago, m. gulp, swallow; drink.—*a tragos,* by degrees, slowly.—*echar un t.,* to take a drink.—*mal t.,* calamity, misfortune.—**tragón,** n. & a. glutton(ous).—**tragonería,** f. gluttony.

traición, f. treason; treachery; betrayal.—*a t.,* treacherously.—**traicionar,** vt. to betray.—**traicionero,** a. treacherous.—**traidor,** a. traitorous; treasonable; treacherous.—n. traitor; betrayer.

traílla, f. leash, lash; packthread; (agr.) leveling harrow; road leveler; road scraper.

traje, m. dress; suit; gown; apparel.—*t. de baño,* bathing suit.—*t. de etiqueta,* full dress, evening dress.—*t. de montar,* riding habit.—*t. largo,* evening dress.—*t. sastre,* (woman's) tailored suit.

trajín, m. transport, haulage; traffic; coming and going, bustle, commotion.—**trajinar,** vt. to carry from place to place.—vi. to bustle about; (coll.) to fidget.

trama, f. weft or woof of cloth; intrigue, scheme; (lit.) plot.—**tramar,** vt. to weave; to plot, scheme.

tramitación, f. procedure; transaction, action, carrying out.—**tramitar,** vt. to transact, carry through, conduct.—**trámite,** m. the carrying on (of administration, etc.), the transacting (of business, etc.); step; (law) proceeding.

tramo, m. parcel of ground; flight of stairs; stretch, span, section; panel (of a bridge).

tramoya, *f.* (theat.) stage machinery. —**tramoyista,** *mf.* (theat.) stage machinist; stage carpenter, stage-hand.

trampa, *f.* trap, snare, pitfall; trap-door; falling board of a counter; flap or spring door; cheat, fraud, deceit, trick; bad debt.—*hacer trampa(s),* to cheat.—**trampear,** *vi.* (coll.) to cheat; to swindle; to get along, pull through.—*vt.* to defraud.

trampolín, *m.* springboard.

tramposo, *a.* tricky, deceitful.—*n.* cheater, swindler.

tranca, *f.* crossbar, bolt (for door); club, stick, truncheon; (Am., coll.) drunken spell.—**trancar,** *vti.* [d] to bar (a door).—**trancazo,** *m.* blow with a club; (coll.) influenza.

trance, *m.* plight, predicament; trance, rapture.—*a todo t.,* at all costs, at any price.—*en t. de muerte,* at the point of death.

tranco, *m.* long stride; threshold.— *a trancos,* hurriedly, carelessly.

tranquilidad, *f.* tranquillity, peace, quiet.—**tranquilizador,** *a.* quieting, soothing, reassuring.—**tranquilizar,** *vti.* [a] & *vri.* to calm, quiet down. —**tranquilo,** *a.* tranquil, calm, quiet.

transacción, *f.* transaction, negotiation; compromise; settlement. —**transar,** *vt. & vr.* (Am.) to compromise, adjust, settle.

transatlántico, *a.* transatlantic.—*m.* ocean liner.

transbordador, *a.* transferring.—*m.* transfer boat, car, etc.—**transbordar,** *vt.* to transfer.—**transbordo,** *m.* transfer.

transcribir, *vti.* [49] to transcribe.— **transcripción,** *f.* transcription.— **transcripto,** *ppi.* of TRANSCRIBIR.

transcurrir, *vi.* (of time) to pass, elapse.—**transcurso,** *m.* lapse, course.

transeúnte, *a.* transient; transitory.— *mf.* pedestrian, passer-by.

transferencia, *f.* transference, transfer.—**transferible,** *a.* transferable.— **transferir,** *vti.* [39] to transfer.

transformación, *f.* transformation.— **transformador,** *n. & a.* transformer; transforming.—*m.* (elec.) transformer.—**transformar,** *vt. & vr.* to transform.—*vr.* to be or become transformed.

tránsfuga, *mf.* deserter; fugitive; turncoat.

transfusión, *f.* transfusion.

transición, *f.* transition.

transido, *a.* worn out; famished.

transigencia, *f.* tolerance.—**transigente,** *a.* accommodating, pliable, compromising; tolerant.—**transigir,**

vti. [c] to compromise, settle.—*vii.* to give in, agree.

transitable, *a.* passable, practicable.— **transitar,** *vi.* to go from place to place (as traffic); to flow.—**transitivo,** *a.* transitive.—**tránsito,** *m.* transit; traffic; passing; passage; transition; death.—**transitorio,** *a.* transitory.

translación, etc. = TRASLACION, etc.

transmisible, *a.* transmissible.—**transmisión,** *f.* transmission; (radio) broadcast.—**transmisor,** *a.* transmitting.—*m.* (elec.) transmitter.—*f.* (radio) broadcasting station.—**transmitir,** *vt.* to transmit; to broadcast.

transparencia, *f.* transparency.— **transparentarse,** *vr.* to be transparent; to show through.—**transparente,** *a.* transparent.—*m.* window shade; stained glass window.

transpiración, *f.* perspiration.—**transpirar,** *vi.* to perspire; (fig.) to seep through.

transponer, *vti.* [32-49] to transpose; to transfer; to transplant.—*vri.* (of sun, etc.) to set below the horizon; to go behind; to be rather drowsy.

transportación, *f.* transportation, transport.—**transportar,** *vt.* to transport, carry; (mus.) to transpose.—*vr.* to be in a transport, to be carried away.—**transporte,** *m.* transport(ation), conveyance; cartage; fit; rapture, ecstasy.

transposición, *f.* transposition.— **transpuesto,** *ppi.* of TRANSPONER.

transversal, *a.* transversal.—*sección t.,* cross section.—**transverso,** *a.* transverse.

tranvía, *m.* streetcar, trolley car.

trapacear, *vi.* to cheat, defraud.— **trapacería,** *f.* fraud, cheating.— **trapacero,** *n. & a.,* **trapacista,** *mf.* & *a.* cheat; cheating.

trapecio, *m.* trapezium; trapeze.

trapero, *n.* ragpicker; rag dealer.

trapezoide, *m.* trapezoid.

trapiche, *m.* grinding machine (in sugar mills, etc.).—**trapichear,** *vi.* (coll.) to contrive, shift.—**trapicheo,** *m.* (coll.) contriving, shifting.

trapisonda, *f.* (coll.) bustle, clatter; (coll.) deception, trickery; brawl, scuffle; escapade.

trapo, *m.* rag; tatter; sails of a ship; (coll.) bullfighter's cloak.—*a todo t.,* with all one's might; (naut.) all sails set.--*poner como un t.,* to reprimand severely, to dress down.—*soltar el t.,* (coll.) to burst out (crying or laughing).

tráquea, *f.* trachea, windpipe.

traquetear, *vt. & vi.* to rattle; to shake, jolt; to crack, crackle.—

traqueteo, *m.* shaking, jolting; cracking, creaking; (Am.) confused, noisy movement.—**traquido,** *m.* snapping, rattle; creaking, cracking.

tras, *prep.* after, behind; beyond; besides; in search of.—*t. de,* after, back of; besides, in addition to.

trasanteayer, trasantier, *adv.* three days ago.

trasatlántico, *a.* = TRANSATLÁNTICO.

trasbordador, etc. = TRANSBORDADOR, etc.

trascendencia, *f.* importance, consequence.—**trascendental,** *a.* transcendental; far-reaching; momentous, highly important.—**trascender,** *vii.* [18] to transcend; to spread beyond; to be pervasive; to become known, seep out.

trascribir, trascripción, etc. = TRANSCRIBIR, etc.

trascurrir, trascurso, etc. = TRANSCURRIR, etc.

trasegar, *vti.* [1-b] to upset, overturn; to change the place of; to pour into another vessel.

trasera, *f.* back part, rear.—**trasero,** *a.* hind, back, rear.—*m.* buttock, rump.

trasferencia, etc. = TRANSFERENCIA, etc.

trasfiguración, etc. = TRANSFIGURACIÓN, etc.

trasformación, etc. = TRANSFORMACIÓN, etc.

trásfuga = TRANSFUGA.

trasgo, *m.* goblin, sprite.

trasgredir, etc. = TRANSGREDIR, etc.

trashumante, *a.* (of flocks) nomadic.

trasiego, *m.* upsetting; transfer (of wine, etc.).

traslación, *f.* transfer, removal; translation, change of place.—**trasladar,** *vt.* to move, remove, transfer; to translate; to transcribe, copy.—**traslado,** *m.* transfer; transcription, copy.

trasmisible, etc. = TRANSMISIBLE, etc.

traslúcido, = TRANSLÚCIDO.—**traslucirse,** *vri.* [3] to be translucent.—**trasluz,** *m.* light seen through a transparent body; (art) transverse light.—*al t.,* against the light.

trasnochado, *a.* tired from lack of sleep; haggard; stale, worn-out; trite, hackneyed.—**trasnochador,** *n.* nighthawk; night owl.—**trasnochar,** *vi.* to stay out all night; to spend a sleepless night.

traspapelar, *vt.* to mislay.—*vr.* to become mislaid.

traspasar, *vt.* to pierce; to pass over; to cross over; to go beyond, exceed limits; to transfer (a business); to trespass.

traspié, *m.* slip, stumble.—*dar traspiés,* to stumble; to slip; to err.

trasplantar, *vt.* to transplant.—*vr.* to migrate.—**trasplante,** *m.* transplantation; migration.

trasponer = TRANSPONER.

trasportación, etc. = TRANSPORTACION, etc.

trasposición, etc. = TRANSPOSICION, etc.

traspunte, *mf.* (theat.) prompter.

trasquilar, *vt.* to shear (sheep); to lop; to cut down.

trastada, *f.* (coll.) inconsiderate act; bad turn.

trastazo, *m.* whack, thump, blow.

traste, *m.* fret of a guitar; utensils, implements. —*dar al t. con,* to spoil, ruin, destroy.

trasto, *m.* (pej.) piece of furniture; junk; (coll.) useless person, washout.—*pl.* tools, paraphernalia.

trastornar, *vt.* to upset; to turn upside down; to disorder, disarrange; to excite; to confuse, perplex, unsettle (the mind).—**trastorno,** *m.* upsetting; upheaval; disturbance, disorder, confusion; trouble; disarrangement.

trastrocar, *vti.* [12-d] to change the order of; to disarrange.—**trastrueco, trastrueque,** *m.* disarrangement; transposition; rearrangement.

trasudar, *vt.* to sweat, perspire slightly.

trasunto, *m.* faithful image, likeness; copy.

trasversal, etc. = TRANSVERSAL, etc.

trata, *f.* trade.—*t. de blancas,* white slavery.—**tratable,** *a.* sociable; compliant.—**tratado,** *m.* treaty; treatise. —**tratamiento,** *m.* treatment; manners; title or form of address.—**tratante,** *mf.* dealer, trader.—**tratar,** *vt.* to handle; to treat (a subject, a person, a patient, a substance); to deal with; (con) to have dealings with; to discuss; (de) to try, attempt; to address as, give the title of; to call, charge with being. —*vi.* to treat; to deal, trade.—*t. sobre* or *acerca de,* to treat of, deal with (a subject).—*t. de,* to treat (of a subject).—*t. en,* to deal in.—*vr.* to look after oneself; to be on good terms.—*tratarse de,* to concern, be a question of.—**trato,** *m.* treatment; social behavior; manner; pact, agreement, deal; trade, commerce; friendly intercourse; title or form of address.—*tener buen t.,* (coll.) to be pleasant, nice.—*tener mucho t.,* to be close friends.

traumático, *a.* (med.) traumatic.

través, *m.* bias, inclination; misfortune.—*a(l) t. de*, across, through.—*de t.*, crosswise.—**travesaño**, *m.* crosspiece, crossbar; bolster; rung; (RR.) tie.—**travesía**, *f.* crossing; crossroad, cross passage; sea voyage.

travesura, *f.* prank, frolic; mischief; lively fancy.—**travieso**, *a.* frolicsome, mischievous.

trayecto, *m.* distance between two points; run, stretch, way.—**trayectoria**, *f.* trajectory, path.

traza, *f.* looks, appearance; trick, ruse; sign, indication.—**trazado**, *a.* traced, outlined.—*m.* sketch, outline, plan; (act of) drawing.—**trazar**, *vti.* [a] to design, plan out; sketch, draw up; to trace, mark out; to draw (as a line).—**trazo**, *m.* outline; line, stroke (of a pen or pencil).

trebejo, *m.* implement, tool, utensil.

trébol, *m.* clover, shamrock.

trecho, *m.* space, distance; lapse.—*de t. en t.*, at intervals.

tregua, *f.* truce; reprieve, respite.

tremebundo, *a.* dreadful, frightful, fearful.

tremedal, *m.* quagmire, bog.

tremendo, *a.* tremendous; huge; excessive.

trementina, *f.* turpentine.

tremolar, *vt. & vi.* to wave (as a flag).—**tremolina**, *f.* rustling of the wind; (coll.) uproar.—**trémolo**, *m.* (mus.) tremolo.—**trémulo**, *a.* tremulous, quivering, shaking.

tren, *m.* train; outfit; equipment; following, retinue; show, pomp.—*t. de aterrizaje*, (aer.) landing gear.

trencilla, *f.* braid.—**trenza**, *f.* braid; plait; tress.—**trenzar**, *vti.* [a] to braid; to plait.

trepador, *a.* climbing.—*m.* climber.—*f.* (bot.) climber, creeper.—**trepar**, *vi.* to climb, mount.—*vr.* (Am.) to climb; to perch.

trepidación, *f.* trepidation; vibration, trembling.—**trepidar**, *vi.* to shake, vibrate, jar; to quake.

treta, *f.* trick, wile, craft; (fencing) feint.

triángulo, *m.* triangle.

tribal, *a.* tribal.—**tribu**, *f.* tribe.

tribulación, *f.* tribulation, affliction.

tribuna, *f.* rostrum, platform; tribune; grandstand.—**tribunal**, *m.* tribunal, court of justice.—**tribuno**, *m.* orator; tribune.

tributación, *f.* tribute, contribution; system of taxation.—**tributar**, *vt.* to pay (taxes, etc.); to pay, render (homage, respect).—**tributario**, *a.* tributary.—*n.* taxpayer; tributary river.—**tributo**, *m.* tribute; tax, contribution; gift, offering.

triciclo, *m.* tricycle.

tricornio, *m.* three-cornered hat.

trifulca, *f.* (coll.) squabble, row.

trigal, *m.* wheat field.—**trigo**, *m.* wheat.

trigonometría, *f.* trigonometry.

trigueño, *a.* brunette, swarthy, dark.

trilogía, *f.* trilogy.

trilla, *f.* (agr.) threshing.—**trillado**, *a.* hackneyed, trite, commonplace.—**trillador**, *n.* thresher.—**trilladora**, *f.* thresher, threshing machine.—**trilladura**, *f.* (agr.) threshing.—**trillar**, *vt.* (agr.) to thresh, beat; to frequent; to repeat.—**trillo**, *m.* (Am.) footpath.

trimestral, *a.* quarterly.—**trimestre**, *m.* quarter; quarterly payment.

trinar, *vi.* (mus.) to trill; to quaver; to warble; (coll.) to fume (with fury).

trincar, *vti.* [d] to tie, bind, make fast.

trinchar, *vt.* to carve (food).

trinchera, *f.* (mil.) trench; deep cut, ditch.

trineo, *m.* sleigh, sledge; sled, bobsled.

trinidad, *f.* Trinity, trinity.

trino, *a.* threefold, triple.—*m.* (mus.) trill; warbling.

trío, *m.* trio.

tripa, *f.* gut, intestine; (coll.) belly.—*pl.* insides, entrails.

triple, *a.* triple, treble.—**triplicar**, *vti.* [d] to treble, triple.—**trípode**, *m.* tripod.

tripulación, *f.* crew (or ship, etc.).—**tripulante**, *mf.* one of the crew.—*pl.* crew.—**tripular**, *vt.* to man (ships).

triquina, *f.* trichina.

triquiñuela, *f.* (coll.) trickery, subterfuge.

triquitraque, *m.* crack, clashing; firecracker.

tris.—*en un t.*, almost, coming pretty near.

triscar, *vii.* [d] to romp, frisk, frolic; to walk lively, to hustle.

triste, *a.* sad, sorrowful; dismal.—**tristeza**, *f.* sadness, sorrow, grief.—**tristón**, *a.* rather sad, melancholy.

tritón, *m.* merman.

triturar, *vt.* to crush, grind, pound.

triunfador, *n.* conqueror, victor.—**triunfal**, *a.* triumphal.—**triunfante**, *a.* triumphant.—**triunfar**, *vi.* to conquer; to triumph; to trump (at cards); to win.—**triunfo**, *m.* triumph, victory; trump card.

trivial, *a.* trivial, trifling; trite, banal.—**trivialidad**, *f.* triviality; triteness.

triza, *f.* fragment.—*hacer trizas,* to knock to pieces; to tear to bits.

trocar, *vti.* [12-d] to exchange; to change, alter; to interchange; to distort, pervert.—*vri.* to change; to be changed, transformed or reformed.

trocha, *f.* (Am.) cross path, short cut; rough road, trail; military road.

trofeo, *m.* trophy; spoils of war; memorial.

troj(e), *f.* granary, barn.

trole, *m.* trolley.

tromba, *f.* waterspout.

trombón, *m.* trombone.

trombosis, *f.* (med.) thrombosis.

trompa, *f.* trumpet; (mus.) horn; trunk of an elephant; (Am.) thick lips; (RR.) cowcatcher, pilot (of a locomotive).—**trompada,** *f.,* **trompazo,** *m.* (coll.) heavy blow.—**trompeta,** *f.* trumpet; bugle.—*m.* trumpeter; bugler.—**trompetazo,** *m.* trumpet blast; bugle blast or call.—**trompetear,** *vi.* (coll.) to sound the trumpet.—**trompeteo,** *m.* sounding the bugle or trumpet.—**trompetilla,** *f.* small trumpet; ear trumpet; (Am. coll.) raspberry, Bronx cheer.

trompicón, *m.* stumbling.

trompo, *m.* spinning top.

tronada, *f.* thunderstorm.—**tronar,** *vii.* [12] to thunder, rumble; (coll.) to be ruined, come down in the world.—*por lo que pueda t.,* as a precaution, just in case.

tronco, *m.* trunk; stem, stalk; stock, origin; team of horses; unfeeling person.

tronchar, *vt.* & *vr.* to break off.—**troncho,** *m.* stalk.

tronera, *f.* (fort.) embrasure; loophole; porthole; pocket hole (billiards).—*m.* madcap, man about town.

tronido, *m.* thunder, loud report.

trono, *m.* throne.

tronquista, *m.* (U.S.) teamster; coachman.

tropa, *f.* troops, soldiers; multitude; (Am.) herd of cattle.—*pl.* forces, army.

tropel, *m.* rush, hurry, confusion; huddle; crowd.—*en t.,* tumultuously, in a throng.—**tropelía,** *f.* rush, hurry; injustice, outrage.

tropezar, *vii.* [1-a] to stumble; (con) to strike (against); to stumble, trip (over); to meet (with); to stumble, light (on), happen to find.—**tropezón,** *m.* stumbling; stumble; slip.—*a tropezones,* by fits and starts.

tropical, *a.* tropical.—**trópico,** *m.* tropic.

tropiezo, *m.* stumble; obstacle, hitch, stumbling block; slip, fault; quarrel, dispute.

troquel, *m.* die (as for coining).

trotar, *vt.* & *vi.* to trot.—**trote,** *m.* trot.—*al t.,* trotting, at a trot; (coll.) in haste.—**trotón,** *a.* trotting. —*n.* trotter.—*m.* horse.

trovador, *n.* troubadour, minstrel.

trozo, *m.* piece, fragment, part; selection (of music); passage (from a book, etc.).

truco, *m.* trick.

trucha, *f.* trout.

truchimán, *n.* (coll.) expert buyer; shrewd trader.

trueno, *m.* thunder.

trueque, *m.* exchange, barter.

trufa, *f.* truffle.

truhán, *n.* rascal, scoundrel, knave.—**truhanería,** *f.* rascality.

truncar, *vti.* [49-d] to truncate; to maim; to mutilate (a speech, quotation, etc.).

tú, *pron.* you (*sing.* fam. form); thou.—*tratar de tú,* to be on intimate terms with.—**tu,** *a.* (*pl.* **tus**) your (when on intimate terms); thy.

tubérculo, *m.* (bot.) tuber; (med.) tubercle.—**tuberculosis,** *f.* (med.) tuberculosis.—**tuberculoso,** *a.* & *n.* tubercular; sufferer from tuberculosis.

tubería, *f.* tubing; piping.—**tubo,** *m.* tube; pipe; lamp chimney.—**tubular,** *a.* tubular.

tuerca, *f.* (mech.) nut.

tuerto, *a.* one-eyed.—*n.* one-eyed person.—*m.* tort, wrong, injustice.

tueste, *m.* toast, toasting (by heat).

tuétano, *m.* marrow; pith.—*hasta los tuétanos,* to the marrow.

tufo, *m.* vapor, emanation; (coll.) offensive odor; conceit, airs, snobbishness.

tugurio, *m.* hovel; dive, saloon.

tul, *m.* tulle, net.

tulipán, *m.* (bot.) tulip.

tullir, *vti.* [27] to cripple, maim.—*vri.* to be crippled.

tumba, *f.* tomb, grave.—**tumbar,** *vt.* to fell, throw down; (coll.) to knock down.—*vi.* to tumble, fall down.—*vr.* (coll.) to lie down, tumble into bed.—**tumbo,** *m.* tumble, fall; somersault.

tumefacción, *f.* swelling.

tumor, *m.* tumor.—*t. maligno,* cancer.

túmulo, *m.* tomb.

tumulto, *m.* tumult; mob.—**tumultuario, tumultuoso,** *a.* tumultuous.

tuna, *f.* (bot.) prickly pear, tuna.

tunante, *n.* truant, rake; rascal, rogue.

tunda, *f.* (coll.) trouncing, whipping. —**tundir,** *vt.* tc whip, thrash; to shear.

túnel, *m.* tunnel.

tungsteno, *m.* tungsten.

túnica, *f.* tunic; robe, gown.

tuno, *a.* roguish, cunning.—*m.* truant. rake, rascal.

tuntún, *m.—al buen t.,* (coll.) heedlessly, haphazard.

tupé, *m.* toupee; (coll.) nerve, cheek.

tupir, *vt.* to pack tight; to make thick or compact; to choke, obstruct; to block or stop up.—*vr.* to stuff or glut oneself.

turba, *f.* crowd, rabble, mob; peat.

turbación, *f.* confusion, embarrassment.—**turbador,** *n.* disturber.—*a.* disturbing.—**turbamulta,** *f.* mob.—**turbante,** *a.* disturbing.—*m.* turban. —**turbar,** *vt.* to disturb; to embarrass.—*vr.* to be disturbed, embarrassed.

turbina, *f.* turbine.

turbio, *a.* muddy, turbid; obscure (language).

turbión, *m.* windy shower; sweep, rush.—**turbonada,** *f.* squall, pelting shower.

turco, *a.* Turkish.—*n.* Turk.—*m.* Turkish language.

turgencia, *f.* (med.) swelling.—**turgente,** *a.* turgid, swollen.

turismo, *m.* tourism, touring.—**turista,** *mf.* & *a.* tourist; touring.

turnar, *vi.* & *vr.* to alternate; to take turns.—**turno,** *m.* turn, alternation.—*de t.,* open for service (of a store, etc.); on duty (of a person).

turquesa, *f.* turquoise.

turquí, *a.* deep blue.

turrón, *m.* nougat, almond paste.

turulato, *a.* (coll.) dumbfounded, stupefied.

tutear, *vt.* to use the familiar TU in addressing a person.

tutela, *f.* guardianship, tutelage, protection.

tutiplén.—*a t.,* (coll.) abundantly.

tutor, *n.* tutor.—**tutoría,** *f.* tutelage, guardianship.

tuyo, *a.* & *pron. poss.* (*f.* **tuya.**—*pl.* **tuyos, tuyas**) your(s) (*fam.* form corresp. to TU).

U

u, *conj.* (replaces o when preceding a word beginning with o or ho) or.

ubérrimo, *a.* very fruitful; exceedingly plentiful.

ubicación, *f.* situation, location, position.—**ubicar,** *vti.* & *vii.* [d] to locate; to lie; to be located or situated.—**ubicuidad,** *f.* ubiquity.

ubre, *f.* udder; teat.

ufanarse, *vr.* to boast, pride oneself. —**ufanía,** *f.* pride; conceit; joy, pleasure.—**ufano,** *a.* conceited, proud; gay, cheerful.

ujier, *m.* doorman; usher.

úlcera, *f.* ulcer; open sore.—**ulceración,** *f.* ulceration.—**ulcerar,** *vt.* to ulcerate.—*vr.* to become ulcerated.

ulterior, *a.* ulterior, farther; subsequent.

ultimar, *vt.* to end, finish, close.—**último,** *a.* last, latest; farthest; ultimate; final; latter; most valuable.

ultrajar, *vt.* to outrage, offend, abuse; to despise.—**ultraje,** *m.* outrage, insult; contempt; abuse.

ultramar, *m.* overseas.—**ultramarino,** *a.* oversea.—**ultrarrojo,** *a.* infra-red. —**ultrasónico,** *a.* ultrasonic.—**ultratumba,** *f.—de la u.* or *en u.,* beyond the grave.—**ultraviolado, ultravioleta** *a.* ultraviolet.

ulular, *vi.* to screech, hoot.

umbilical, *a.* umbilical.

umbral, *m.* threshold; (arch.) lintel; beginning, rudiment.

umbrío, *a.* shady.—**umbroso,** *a.* shady.

un (*f.* **una**) *art.* a, an.—*a.* (*abbr.* de UNO) one.

unánime, *a.* unanimous.—**unanimidad,** *f.* unanimity.—*por u.,* unanimously.

unción, *f.* unction; religious fervor.

uncir, *vti.* [a] to yoke.

ungimiento, *m.* unction.—**ungir,** *vti.* [c] to anoint.

ungüento, *m.* unguent, ointment.

único, *a.* only, sole; unique, rare, unmatched, unparalleled.

unidad, *f.* unity; unit.—**unificación,** *f.* unification.—**unificar,** *vti.* [d] to unify.

uniformar, *vt.* to standardize, make uniform; to put into uniform.—**uniforme,** *a.* & *m.* uniform.—**uniformidad,** *f.* uniformity.

unilateral, *a.* unilateral.

unión, *f.* union; harmony; concord; marriage; joining, joint; (com.) consolidation, merger.

unir, *vt.* to join, unite; to connect; to mix; bring together.—*vr.* to join, get together; to wed; (com.) to consolidate, merge.

unisonancia, *f.* state of being unisonal; monotony.—**unísono,** *a.* (mus.) unisonal; unisonous; unanimous.

unitario, *a.* & *n.* (eccl.) Unitarian; (pol.) supporter of centralization.

universal, *a.* universal.—**universidad,** *f.* university.—**universitario,** *a.* university.—**universo,** *m.* universe.

uno, *a.* (*f.* **una**) one; only, sole.—*pl.* some; nearly, about.—*u. que otro,* (only) a few.—*pron.* one, someone.—*pl.* some, a few (people).—*cada u.,* each one.—*u. a otro,* each other, mutually.—*u. y otro,* both.—*unos a otros,* one another.—*unos cuantos,* a few.—*unos y otros,* all, the lot (of them).—*n.* one (number).—*a una,* unanimously, of one accord.—*de u. en u.,* one by one; in single file.—*la una,* (time) one o'clock.—*u. por u.,* one after another; one by one, one at a time.

untar, *vt.* to anoint; to smear; to grease, oil; to bribe.—*u. las manos,* to grease the palm; to bribe.—*vr.* to be greased or smeared; to embezzle.—**unto,** *m.* grease, fat of animals; unguent, ointment.—**untuoso,** *a.* unctuous, greasy.—**untura,** *f.* unction; ointment, liniment.

uña, *f.* fingernail; toenail; hoof, claw; pointed hook of instruments.—*a u. de caballo,* at full gallop, in great haste.—*enseñar* or *mostrar las uñas,* to show one's true nature.—*hincar* or *meter la u.,* to overcharge; to sell at an exorbitant price.—*largo de uñas,* filcher.—*ser u. y carne,* to be hand and glove, to be fast friends.—**uñero,** *m.* ingrowing nail.

uranio, *m.* uranium.

urbanidad, *f.* urbanity, civility, manners.—**urbanización,** *f.* urbanization.—**urbanizar,** *vti.* [a] to lay out (land) for a town; to polish, render polite.—**urbano,** *a.* urban; urbane, courteous.—**urbe,** *f.* large modern city, metropolis.

urdimbre, *f.* warp (of cloth).—**urdir,** *vt.* to warp (cloth); to plot, scheme.

urgencia, *f.* urgency.—**urgir,** *vii.* [c] to be urgent.

urinario, *a.* urinary.—*m.* urinal.

urna, *f.* urn, casket; glass case; ballot box.

urraca, *f.* magpie.

urticaria, *f.* (med.) hives.

uruguayo, *a.* & *n.* Uruguayan.

usanza, *f.* usage, custom.—**usar,** *vt.* to use; to make use of; to wear; to wear out.—*vr.* to be in use or fashion; to be customary.—**uso,** *m.* use; usage, custom; wearing, wear; wear and tear; (com., law) usance.—*a(l) u.,* according to usage.—*en buen u.,* in good condition.—*u. de razón,* discernment, understanding, thinking for oneself (esp. of a child).

usted, *pron.* (usually abbreviated **V.,**

Vd., U., Ud.) you.—*pl.* **ustedes** (abbrev. **VV., Vds., UU., Uds.**) you.—*de Ud.,* your, yours.

usual, *a.* usual, customary.—**usuario,** *n.* user.

usufructo, *m.* (law) usufruct; use, enjoyment; profit.—**usufructuar,** *vt.* to hold in usufruct; to enjoy the use.

usura, *f.* usury.—**usurario,** *a.* usurious.—**usurero,** *n.* usurer; money lender, loan shark.

usurpación, *f.* usurpation.—**usurpador,** *n.* & *a.* usurper; usurping.—**usurpar,** *vt.* to usurp.

utensilio, *m.* utensil; tool, implement.

uterino, *a.* uterine.—**útero,** *m.* (anat.) uterus, womb.

útil, *a.* useful; profitable.—*m. pl.* utensils, tools; outfit, equipment.—**utilidad,** *f.* utility; profit; usefulness.—**utilitario,** *a.* utilitarian.—**utilizable,** *a.* utilizable, available.—**utilizar,** *vti.* [a] to utilize.—*vri.* to be made profitable.

utopia, *f.* utopia.—**utópico,** *a.* utopian.

uva, *f.* grape.—*hecho una u.,* dead drunk.—*u. pasa,* raisin.

úvula, *f.* uvula.

uxoricida, *m.* uxoricide. (person).—*a.* uxoricidal.—**uxoricidio,** *m.* uxoricide (act).

V

vaca, *f.* cow.—*carne de v.,* beef.—*hacer una v.,* or *ir en una v.,* to pool money (two or more gamblers).—*v. lechera,* milch cow.

vacación, *f.* vacation.—*pl.* holidays, summer recess.—*de vacaciones,* on holidays.

vacada, *f.* herd of cows.

vacante, *a.* vacant; unoccupied.—*f.* vacancy.—**vacar,** *vii.* [d] to give up work or employment temporarily; to be vacant.

vaciado, *m.* plaster cast.—**vaciar,** *vt.* to empty; to pour out; to cast, mold; to hone, grind.—*vi.* to flow (into) (as rivers).—*vr.* to spill; to be drained; to become empty or vacant.—**vaciedad,** *f.* nonsense, silly remark.

vacilación, *f.* hesitation; vacillation; wavering.—**vacilante,** *a.* hesitating, irresolute; unstable.—**vacilar,** *vi.* to vacillate, fluctuate; to hesitate; to reel.

vacío, *a.* empty; hollow; vain, presumptuous; vacant, unoccupied.—*m.* void, empty space; vacuum; opening; hollowness; blank; gap.—*en el v.,* in vacuo.

vacuna, *f.* vaccine; vaccination; cow-pox.—**vacunación,** *f.* vaccination.—**vacunar,** *vt.* to vaccinate.—**vacuno,** *a.* bovine.—*ganado v.,* (bovine) cattle.

vadear, *vt.* to wade through, ford.—**vado,** *m.* ford of a river; expedient.

vagabundear, *vi.* (coll.) to wander, rove or loiter about.—**vagabundo,** *n.* vagabond, vagrant, rover; roamer, tramp.—*a.* roving, roaming, tramping, vagrant.—**vagancia,** *f.* vagrancy.—**vagar,** *vii.* [b] to rove, roam, loiter about; wander; to be idle.—*m.* leisure, idleness, loitering. —**vago,** *a.* roving, roaming; vagrant; vague; wavering; loose; (art) hazy; indistinct.—*n.* vagabond, loafer, vagrant, tramp.

vagón, *m.* (RR.) car; wagon.—*v. de cola,* caboose.—**vagoneta,** *f.* (RR.) small open car; (Am.) open delivery cart.

vaguear, *vi.* = VAGAR.

vaguedad, *f.* vagueness; vague statement.

vahido, *m.* vertigo, dizziness.

vaho, *m.* vapor, fume, steam; odor.

vaina, *f.* scabbard, sheath, case; (bot.) pod, capsule; (Am.) nuisance, annoyance.

vainilla, *f.* vanilla.

vaivén, *m.* fluctuation, oscillation, sway; unsteadiness, inconstancy; giddiness; rocking; (mech.) swing, seesaw.—*pl.* ups and downs.—*sierra de v.,* jig saw.

vajilla, *f.* table service, tableware, dinner set; crockery.—*v. de plata,* silverware.

vale, *m.* (com.) bond, promissory note, IOU; voucher; sales slip; bonus given to schoolboys.—**valedero,** *a.* valid, efficacious, binding. —**valedor** *n.* protector, defender; (Am.) chum, pal.

valenciano, *n.* & *a.* Valencian.

valentía, *f.* valor, courage, bravery; heroic exploit; brag, boast.—**valentón,** *a.* blustering, arrogant.—*m.* hector, bully.

valer, *vti.* [44] to protect, favor; to cost; to cause, bring upon or to (one) (discredit, fame); to amount to; to be worth, be valued at; to be equal to.—*hacer v.,* to assert (one's rights); to avail oneself of. —*ni cosa que lo valga,* nor anything of the kind, or like it.—*v. la pena,* to be worth while.—*vii.* to be valuable; to be worthy; to possess merit or value; to prevail, avail, (of coins) to be legal and current; to be valid or binding; to be important or useful; to be or serve

as a protection; to be equivalent to; to mean.—*hacer v.,* to turn to account.— (*impers.*) *más vale, más valiera,* it is better, it would be better.—*más vale tarde que nunca,* better late than never.—*v. por,* to be equal to, to be worth.—*¡válgame Dios!* good Heavens! bless me!—*vri.* to help oneself, take care of oneself.—*no poderse v.,* to be helpless.—*v. de,* to make use of, have recourse to.—*m.* value; merit, worth. —**valeroso,** *a.* brave, courageous.—**valía,** *f.* value, worth; favor, influence.— **validar,** *vt.* to validate.—**validez,** *f.* validity; soundness; vigor, strength.—**válido,** *a.* valid.

valiente, *a.* valiant, brave, courageous. —*mf.* brave person.

valija, *f.* valise, suitcase; mail bag; mail.

valimiento, *m.* benefit, advantage; favor, support; favoritism.—**valioso,** *a.* valuable; highly esteemed, of great influence; wealthy.—**valor,** *m.* value; price; worth; activity, power; valor, bravery; (fig.) cheek, nerve.—**valoración,** *f.* appraisement, valuation.—**valorar,** *vt.* **valorizar,** *vti.* [a] to appraise, value, price.

vals, *m.* waltz.

valuación, *f.* appraisement, valuation. —**valuar,** *vt.* to rate, price, value, appraise.

valva, *f.* valve (of a mollusk).—**válvula,** *f.* valve.

valla, *f.* fence, stockade; barrier, barricade; obstacle, impediment.—**valladar,** *m.* = VALLADO; obstacle.—**vallado,** *m.* stockade; inclosure; stone wall.

valle, *m.* valley; vale, dell.

¡vamos!, *interj.* well! come, now! go on! let's go!

vampiro, *m.* ghoul; vampire; (fig.) bloodsucker.

vanagloria, *f.* vainglory, boast, conceit.—**vanagloriarse,** *vr.* to be vainglorious; to glory; to boast.

vanguardia, *f.* vanguard.

vanidad, *f.* vanity; nonsense; shallowness.—**vanidoso,** *a.* vain, conceited.—**vano,** *a.* vain; hollow; inane, empty, shallow, insubstantial; unavailing.—*m.* opening in a wall (as for a door).

vapor, *m.* vapor, steam; mist; steamer, steamship.—**vaporización,** *f.* vaporization.—**vaporizador,** *m.* vaporizer.—**vaporoso,** *a,* vaporous, misty, cloudy.

vapulear, *vt.* (coll.) to whip, flog, beat.—**vapuleo,** *m.* (coll.) whipping, flogging, beating.

vaquería, *f.* dairy; stable for cows.—

vaquero, *n.* cowherd.—*m.* cowboy. —*a.* pertaining to a cowherd.— **vaqueta,** *f.* sole leather.

vara, *f.* twig; pole, staff; stick, rod, wand; yard, yardstick.—*v. alta,* sway, high hand.

varadero, *m.* shipyard.—**varar,** *vt.* to beach (a boat).—*vi. & vr.* (naut.) to run aground, be stranded; to be at a standstill.

variable, *a.* variable, changeable.—*f.* variable.—**variación,** *f.* variation.— **variado,** *a.* varying, varied; variegated.—**variante,** *a.* varying; deviating.—*f.* difference, discrepancy (in texts).—**variar,** *vt.* to vary, change; to shift; to variegate.—*vi.* to vary, change; to differ.

várice, varice, *f.* varicose vein.

varicela, *f.* (med.) chicken pox.

variedad, *f.* variety; change, variation.—*pl.* miscellany of things or items; variety show.

varilla, *f.* rod; spindle, pivot; wand; rib (of an umbrella, a fan, etc,); whalebone, stay.

vario, *a.* various, different; inconstant, changeable.—*pl.* various; some, several.

varón, *m.* male, man.—*santo v.,* (coll.) good but simple fellow.— **varonil,** *a.* manly; virile; vigorous.

vasco, vascongado, *n. & a.* Basque.

vaselina, *f.* vaseline.

vasija, *f.* vessel, container, receptacle (for liquids).—**vaso,** *m.* (drinking) glass; vessel, reeceptacle; glassful; vase.

vástago, *m.* stem, sapling, shoot; scion, offspring.

vasto, *a.* vast, huge, immense.

vate, *m.* bard, poet.—**vaticinar,** *vt.* to divine, predict, foretell.—**vaticinio,** *m.* prediction.

vatio, *m.* (elec.) watt.

¡vaya!, *interj.* go! come! indeed! certainly! well!

vecinal, *a.* neighboring, adjacent.— **vecindad,** *f.* neighborhood, vicinity. —*casa de v.,* tenement.—**vecindario,** *m.* population of a district, ward, etc.; neighborhood, vicinity.— **vecino,** *a.* neighboring, next, near by.—*n.* neighbor; resident; citizen.

veda, *f.* prohibition, interdiction by law; closed season (hunting, etc.). —**vedar,** *vt.* to prohibit, forbid; to impede.

vega, *f.* flat lowland; (Am.) tobacco plantation.

vegetación, *f.* vegetation.—**vegetal,** *a. & m.* vegetable, vegetal, plant.— **vegetar,** *vi.* to vegetate.

vehemencia, *f.* vehemence.—**vehe-** **mente,** *a.* vehement; persuasive; vivid; keen.

vehículo, *m.* vehicle.

veintena, *f.* score (twenty).

vejación, *f.,* **vejamen,** *m.* vexation, annoyance; oppression.—**vejar,** *vt.* to vex, tease, annoy; to oppress.

vejestorio, *m.* (coll.) valueless finery; shriveled old person.—**vejete,** *m.* (coll.) ridiculous old man.—**vejez,** *f.* old age.

vejiga, *f.* bladder; blister.

vela, *f.* candle; (naut.) sail; vigil, wakefulness; wake; watch, watchfulness.—*a toda v.,* with all sails up and full of wind; in full swing. —*en v.,* vigilantly, without sleep.— *hacerse a la v.,* to set sail.—**velada,** *f.* evening party or celebration.— **velador,** *n.* watchman(-woman), nightguard.—*m.* small round table. —**velamen,** *m.* (naut.) canvas; set of sails.—**velar,** *vi.* to watch; to be awake; to observe; to be vigilant; (por) to watch (over), protect.— *vt.* to veil; to cover, hide.

veleidad, *f.* fickleness; versatility.— **veleidoso,** *a.* fickle, inconstant.

velero, *a.* (naut.) swift-sailing.—*m.* sailboat, bark.

veleta, *f.* weathercock, vane.—*mf.* fickle person.

velo, *m.* veil; curtain.—*v. del paladar,* (anat.) soft palate, velum.

velocidad, *f.* velocity.—*a toda v.,* at full speed.—**velocímetro,** *m.* speedometer.

velorio, *m.* wake, watch (over a dead person); (Am.) boring party.

veloz, *a.* fast, quick, swift, rapid.

vello, *m.* down; nap; fuzz.

vellón, *m.* fleece, wool of one sheep; lock of wool; ancient copper coin.

velloso, *a.* downy, hairy, fuzzy.— **velludo,** *a.* = velloso.—*m.* shag, velvet.

vena, *f.* vein; (min.) vein, seam, lode. —*estar en v.,* to be in the mood; to be inspired.—*v. de loco,* fickle disposition.

venablo, *m.* javelin, dart.

venado, *m.* deer, stag; venison.

venático, *a.* (coll.) cranky, erratic, daft.

vencedor, *a.* winning, victorious; conquering.—*n.* winner, victor; conqueror.—**vencer,** *vti.* [a] to conquer, subdue, defeat, vanquish; to surpass; to surmount, overcome; to win.—*vii.* to conquer; to win; (com.) to fall due, mature; to expire.—*vri.* to control oneself.—**vencido,** *a.* (com.) due; payable; conquered; defeated.—**vencimiento,** *m.* defeat; (com.) maturity, expiration.

venda, *f.* bandage.—**vendaje,** *m.* bandage; bandaging.—**vendar,** *vt.* to bandage.

vendaval, *m.* gale wind.

vendedor, *n.* seller, salesman (-woman); vendor.—**vender,** *vt.* & *vi.* to sell.—*v. al por mayor,* to sell at wholesale.—*v. al por menor,* or *v. al detalle,* to sell at retail.—*v. a plazos,* to sell on credit.—*vr.* to sell out, accept a bribe; to expose oneself to danger.—*v. caro,* to sell (be sold) dear.—**vendido,** *a.* sold; betrayed.—*estar v.,* to be duped; to be exposed to great risks.

vendimia, *f.* vintage.

venduta, *f.* (Am.) small vegetable store; (Am.) auction.

veneno, *m.* poison, venom.—**venenoso,** *a.* poisonous, venomous.

venerable, *a.* venerable.—**veneración,** *f.* veneration; worship.—**venerar,** *vt.* to venerate, revere; to worship.

venéreo, *a.* venereal.

venero, *m.* water spring; (min.) bed, lode; origin, source.

venezolano, *n.* & *a.* Venezuelan.

vengador, *n.* avenger; revenger.—*a.* avenging; revenging.—**venganza,** *f.* vengeance; revenge.—**vengar,** *vti.* [b] to avenge.—*vri.* (de) to take revenge (on).—**vengativo,** *a.* revengeful, vindictive, vengeful.

venia, *f.* pardon, forgiveness; leave, permission; bow with the head.

venial, *a.* venial; pardonable.

venida, *f.* arrival, return; flood, freshet; rashness, rush.—**venidero,** *a.* future, coming.—**venir,** *vii.* [45] to come; to arrive; to fit, suit; to occur (to one's mind).—*¿a qué viene eso?* what has that to do with the case?—*la semana que viene,* next week.—*si a mano viene,* perhaps.—*v. a buscar,* to come for, or to get.—*v. a las manos,* to come to blows.—*v. a menos,* to decay, to decline.—*v. a ser,* to get to be, become; to turn out to be.—*v. bien,* to suit, to be becoming.— *v. como anillo al dedo,* or *v. de perilla,* to come in the nick of time; to fit the case, be to the point.

venoso, *a.* venous; veined.

venta, *f.* sale; selling; roadside inn.—*de v.* or *en v.,* for sale.—*v. (al) por mayor,* wholesale.—*v. (al) por menor,* retail sale; retailing.—*v. pública,* public auction sale.

ventaja, *f.* advantage; gain, profit; handicap (in races, sports, etc.).—**ventajoso,** *a.* advantageous; profitable; advisable.

ventalla, *f.* valve; (bot.) pod.

ventana, *f.* window; (carp.) window frame.—*echar la casa por la v.,* to go to a lot of expense.—*v. de la nariz,* nostril.—**ventanilla,** *f.* window (vehicles, banks, theaters, etc.).—**ventanillo,** *m.* small window shutter; peephole.

ventarrón, *m.* stiff wind, gust.—**ventear,** *vt.* to smell; to scent, sniff (as dogs); to investigate, inquire; to air.

ventilación, *f.* ventilation.—**ventilador,** *m.* ventilator; (ventilating) fan.—**ventilar,** *vt.* to ventilate, air; to discuss.

ventisca, *f.* snowstorm, blizzard.—**ventisquero,** *m.* snowstorm, snowdrift; glacier; snow-capped mountain.

ventolera, *f.* gust of wind; whim, notion; scurry.

ventorrillo, *m.* poor inn or tavern.

ventosear, *vi.* to break wind.—**ventosidad,** *f.* flatulence, windiness.—**ventoso,** *a.* windy; flatulent.

ventrílocuo, *m.* ventriloquist.

ventura, *f.* happiness; luck, fortune; chance, hazard; risk.—*buena v.,* fortune told by cards, etc.—*por v.,* by chance; fortunately.—**venturoso,** *a.* lucky; successful, prosperous.

ver, *vti.* & *vii.* [46] to see; to look into, examine; to look; to look at.—*¡a v.!* let's see!—*no poder v. a,* to abhor or detest (can't bear).—*no tener que v. con,* to have nothing to do with.—*v. de,* to try to.—*v. el cielo abierto,* to see a great opportunity.—*vri.* to be seen; to be conspicuous; to find oneself (in a situation), be; to meet, have an interview; to see oneself or look at oneself (in a mirror); to see each other, one another; to meet one another.—*ya se vé,* it is obvious.—*m.* sense of sight, seeing.—*a mi modo de v.,* in my opinion, to my way of thinking.

vera, *f.* edge, border.—*a la v. de,* close, by the side of.

veracidad, *f.* veracity, truthfulness.

veraneante, *mf.* summer resident or vacationer.—**veranear,** *vi.* to summer.—**veraneo,** *m.* summering, summer vacation.—**veraniego,** *a.* summer.—**verano,** *m.* summer.

veras, *f. pl.* reality, truth.—*de v.,* really, in truth, in earnest.—**veraz,** *a.* veracious, truthful.

verbal, *a.* verbal; oral.

verbena, *f.* (bot.) verbena, vervain; night carnival (on a saint's day eve).

verbigracia, *adv.* for example, for instance.

verbo, *m.* verb.—*el Verbo,* the Word, second person of the Trinity.

verdad, *f.* truth, verity.—*a decir v.*, to tell the truth; in reality, in fact. —*a la v.*, truly, really, in truth.— *bien es v. que*, it is true that.—*decir cuatro verdades*, to speak one's mind freely.—*de v.* or *a la v.*, in earnest; real.—*en v.*, truly, really.—¿*no es v.?* isn't it? isn't that so?—*ser v.*, to be true.—¿*v.?* isn't it? isn't that so? is that so?—**verdadero**, *a.* true; real, actual; truthful.

verde, *a.* green; verdant; unripe; young, blooming; unseasoned (wood); off-color.—*están verdes*, sour grapes.—*m.* green (color); verdure; vert.—**verdear**, *vi.* to grow green; to look green.—**verdín**, *m.* mildew; verdigris.—**verdinegro**, *a.* dark green.—**verdor**, *m.* greenness; verdure, verdancy.—**verdoso**, *a.* greenish.

verdugo, *m.* executioner; shoot of a tree; lash, scourge; wale, welt; torturer, very cruel person.—**verdugón**, *m.* large wale or welt.

verdulera, *f.* market woman; (coll.) coarse, low woman.—**verdura**, *f.* verdure, verdancy; greenness.—*pl.* greens, vegetables.—**verdusco**, *a.* dark greenish.

vereda, *f.* path, trail; (Am.) sidewalk.

veredicto, *m.* verdict.

vergel, *f.* flower garden.

vergonzoso, *a.* bashful, shy; shameful, disgraceful.—**vergüenza**, *f.* shame; bashfulness, shyness; modesty; disgrace.—*pl.* private parts. —*tener v.*, to be ashamed; to be shy; to have shame.

vericueto, *m.* rough and pathless place.

verídico, *a.* truthful.—**verificación**, *f.* verification, confirmation.—**verificar**, *vti.* [d] to verify, confirm; to test, adjust (an instrument); to fulfil, accomplish, carry out.—*vri.* to be verified; to take place, occur.

verja, *f.* grate, grating; iron railing.

vernáculo, *a.* vernacular, native.

verosímil, *a.* credible, probable; true to life.—**verosimilitud**, *f.* verisimilitude, probability.

verraco, *m.* male hog or boar.

verruga, *f.* wart.

versado, *a.* versed, conversant.— **versar**, *vi.*—*v. acerca de* or *sobre*, to treat of, deal with.—*vr.* to become versed or conversant.

versátil, *a.* changeable, fickle, shifty. —**versatilidad**, *f.* versatility.

versículo, *m.* (eccl.) versicle.

versificación, *f.* versification.—**versificador**, *n.* versifier, verse maker.— **versificar**, *vti. & vii.* [d] to versify.

versión, *f.* version; translation.

verso, *m.* line (of poetry).—*pl.* poems.

vértebra, *f.* (anat.) vertebra.—**vertebrado**, *n. & a.* vertebrate.

vertedero, *m.* sink, dumping place; small dam; spillway.—**verter**, *vti.* [18] to pour, spill, shed, cast; to empty; to dump; to translate; to construe, interpret.—*vii.* to run, flow.

vertical, *a.* vertical.—*f.* vertical line. —**verticalidad**, *f.* verticality.

vértice, *m.* vertex; apex, top.

vertiente, *f.* watershed; slope.

vertiginoso, *a.* giddy.—**vértigo**, *m.* giddiness, dizziness, vertigo.

vesania, *f.* insanity.—**vesánico**, *a.* mentally deranged.

vesícula, *f.* blister, vesicle.—*v. biliar*, gall bladder.

vespertino, *a.* evening.—*m.* evening paper.

vestíbulo, *m.* vestibule, hall, lobby.

vestido, *m.* dress; apparel, clothing.— **vestidura**, *f.* vesture.—*pl.* (eccl.) vestments.

vestigio, *m.* vestige, trace; relic.— *pl.* remains.

vestimenta, *f.* clothes, garments.— **vestir**, *vti.* [29] to clothe, dress; to deck, adorn; to don, put on; to wear; to cover.—*vii.* to dress; to be dressy.—*vri.* to dress oneself; to be covered; to be clothed.—**vestuario**, *m.* apparel, wardrobe, clothes, clothing, dress; (eccl.) vestry; (theat.) wardrobe, dressing room.

veta, *f.* (min.) vein; grain (in wood).

vetar, *vt.* to veto.

veteado, *a.* striped, veined, grained, mottled.—**vetear**, *vt.* to grain, mottle.

veterano, *a.* (mil.) veteran; having had long experience.—*n.* veteran, old hand.

veterinario, *m.* veterinarian.

veto, *m.* veto; prohibition, interdict.

vetusto, *a.* very ancient.

vez, *f.* turn, time, occasion.—*a la v.*, at a time; at the same time; at one time.—*a la v. que*, while.— *alguna v.* (in a question) ever.— *alguna que otra v.*, once in a while, occasionally.—*algunas veces*, sometimes; some times.—*a su v.*, in his (one's) turn; on his (one's) part.— *a veces*, sometimes, occasionally.— *cada v.*, each time, every time.— *cada v. más*, more and more.—*cada v. que*, every time that, whenever. —*de una v.*, all at once; at one time.—*de v. en cuando*, occasionally, from time to time.—*en v. de*, instead of.—*otra v.*, again, once more; some other time.—*pocas* or *raras veces*, seldom, rarely; only a few

times.—*tal v.*, perhaps, maybe, perchance.—*todas las veces que*, whenever, as often as.—*una que otra v.*, once in a while, a few times.—*una v. que*, since, inasmuch as; after.

vía, *f.* way, road; route; carriage track; (RR.) track, line; gauge; manner, method; duct, conduit; passage.—*en v. de*, in the process of.—*por v. de*, by way of, as.—*v. muerta*, siding.—**viable,** *a.* viable; feasible, practicable.—**viaducto,** *m.* viaduct.

viajante, *a.* traveling.—*mf.* traveler.—*m.* traveling salesman.—**viajar,** *vi.* to travel, journey.—**viaje,** *m.* journey, voyage, travel, trip.—*v. de ida y vuelta*, round trip.—**viajero,** *n.* traveler, voyager; passenger.

vianda, *f.* food, viands.—*pl.* (Am.) vegetables for a stew.

viandante, *mf.* walker, pedestrian; tramp, vagabond.

víbora, *f.* viper; (fig.) perfidious person.

vibración, *f.* vibration.—**vibrar,** *vt.* to vibrate; to brandish; to throw, dart.—*vi.* to vibrate.—**vibratorio,** *a.* vibratory.

vicepresidente, *n.* vice president.—**vicesecretario,** *n.* assistant secretary.—**vicetesorero,** *n.* assistant treasurer.

viciar, *vt.* to vitiate, spoil; to adulterate; to pervert, corrupt; to falsify; to misconstrue.—*vr.* to become corrupt.—**vicio,** *m.* vice; (bad) habit; defect; craving.—*de v.*, by habit or custom.—**vicioso,** *a.* vicious; defective; licentious.

vicisitud, *f.* vicissitude.—*pl.* ups and downs.

víctima, *f.* victim.

victoria, *f.* victory, win, triumph.—**victorioso,** *a.* victorious, triumphant.

vid, *f.* (bot.) vine, grapevine.

vida, *f.* life; living, livelihood; activity, animation.—*darse buena v.*, to live comfortably.—*de por v.*, for life, during life.—*en v.*, while living, during life.—*ganarse la v.*, to earn one's living.—*v. airada*, licentious life, gay life.—*v. mía*, dearest, darling.

vidente, *a.* seeing.—*mf.* seer, prophet.

vidriar, *vt.* to glaze (earthenware).—**vidriera,** *f.* glass window or partition; (Am.) glass case, show case, show window.—**vidriero,** *n.* glazier; glassblower; glass dealer.—**vidrio,** *m.* glass; any article made of glass.—**vidrioso,** *a.* glassy; brittle; slippery (from sleet); peevish, touchy.

viejo, *a.* old, aged; ancient, anti-

quated; stale; worn-out; old-fashioned.—*n.* old man (woman).—*v. verde*, lecherous old man; girlish old woman.

viento, *m.* wind; bracing rope; scent of dogs; vanity.—*a los cuatro vientos*, in all directions.—*beber los vientos por*, to be crazy about.

vientre, *m.* abdomen; belly; bowels; womb; pregnancy.

viernes, *m.* Friday.—*V. Santo*, Good Friday.

viga, *f.* beam, girder; rafter.—*v. maestra*, chief supporting beam.

vigencia, *f.* currency; operation (of a law); life (of a ruling body, etc.).—**vigente,** *a.* (law) in force; standing.

vigía, *f.* watchtower; watch; watching; (naut.) shoal, rock.—*m.* watchman, lookout.—**vigilancia,** *f.* vigilance, watchfulness.—**vigilante,** *a.* vigilant, watchful.—*m.* watchman.—**vigilar,** *vt. & vi.* to watch (over); to keep guard; to look out (for); (coll.) to tail.—**vigilia,** *f.* vigil, wakefulness; (eccl.) vigil, fast.

vigor, *m.* vigor, stamina; validity.—*en v.*, in force, in effect.—**vigorizar,** *vti.* [a] to strengthen, invigorate; to encourage.—**vigoroso,** *a.* vigorous; substantial; trenchant.

viguería, *f.* set of girders or beams; timberwork.—**vigueta,** *f.* small beam; joist; beam.

vihuela, *f.* guitar.

vil, *a.* vile, low, despicable, soulless.—**vileza,** *f.* baseness, meanness, vileness; base act or conduct.—**vilipendiar,** *vt.* to scorn, revile, vilify.—**vilipendio,** *m.* contempt; reviling.

vilo, *m.*—*en v.*, in the air; insecurely; in suspense.

villa, *f.* village; villa, country house.

villancico, *m.* Christmas carol.

villanía, *f.* meanness; villainy, villainousness; vile, base deed.—**villano,** *a.* villainous; rustic, boorish.—*n.* villain.

villorrio, *m.* small village or hamlet.

vinagre, *m.* vinegar; acidity, sourness.—**vinagrera,** *f.* vinegar cruet.—**vinajera,** *f.* (eccl.) wine vessel for the Mass.—**vinatero,** *a.* pertaining to wine.—*n.* vintner, wine merchant.

vinculación, *f.* entail; binding; grounding.—**vincular,** *vt.* to entail; to tie, bond, unite; to ground or found upon.—**vínculo,** *m.* tie, bond; entail.

vindicar, *vti.* [d] to vindicate; to avenge; to assert (as rights), defend; (law) to reclaim.

vinícola, *a.* wine-growing.—**vino,** *m.*

wine.—*v. de Jerez*, sherry wine.—
v. tinto, red table wine.
viña, *f.*, **viñedo**, *m.* vineyard.
viñeta, *f.* (print. & photog.) vignette.
violáceo, *a.* violet-colored.
violación, *f.* violation; ravishment.
—**violado**, *pp.* of VIOLAR.—*a.* violet
(color).—**violador**, *m.* violator;
rapist.—**violar**, *vt.* to violate; to
rape; to desecrate; to tarnish.—
violencia, *f.* violence; compulsion,
force; rape, outrage.—**violentar**, *vt.*
to do violence to; to break into;
to distort.—*vr.* to force oneself (to
do something distasteful); to control one's unwillingness.—**violento**,
a. violent; impulsive; irascible;
forced, unnatural; exceedingly intense or severe.
violeta, *f.* (bot.) violet.
violín, *m.* violin; violinist.—**vio-
linista**, *mf.* violinist.—**violón**, *m.*
bass viol, double bass; bass-viol
player.—*tocar el v.*, to do or say
something absurd or nonsensical; to
talk through one's hat.—**violonce-
lista**, *mf.* (violon)cellist.—**violen-
celo**, *m.* (violon)cello.
viperino, *a.* viperish.
virago, *f.* mannish woman; shrew,
harpy.
virar, *vt.* to turn, turn around, change
direction; (naut.) to tack.—**virazón**,
f. sea breeze.
virgen, *f.* & *a.* virgin.—**virginal**,
virgíneo, *a.* virginal, virgin.—
virginidad, *f.* virginity.—**virgo**, *m.*
(anat.) hymen; (V.) (astr.) Virgo,
Virgin; virginity.
viril, *a.* virile, manly.—**virilidad**, *f.*
virility, manhood; vigor, strength.
virreinato, **virreino**, *m.* viceroyalty.—
virrey, *m.* viceroy.
virtual, *a.* apparent; virtual; potential.
virtud, *f.* virtue; power.—**virtuoso**, *a.*
virtuous, righteous; chaste.—*a.* & *n.*
(mus.) virtuoso.
viruela, *f.* (med.) pock; smallpox.
virulencia, *f.* virulence.—**virulento**, *a.*
virulent.—**virus**, *m.* (med.) virus.
viruta, *f.* wood shaving.
visa, *f.*, **visado**, *m.* visa.
visaje, *m.* grimace, grin, smirk.—
hacer visajes, to make wry faces.
visar, *vt.* to issue a visa; to countersign; to O.K.
víscera, *f.* vital organ.—*pl.* viscera.—
visceral, *a.* visceral.
viscosidad, *f.* viscosity, stickiness.—
viscoso, *a.* viscous, sticky.
visera, *f.* visor of a cap or helmet;
eyeshade.
visibilidad, *f.* visibility.—**visible**, *a.*
visible; evident; conspicuous.

visillo, *m.* window curtain or shade.
—**visión**, *f.* sight; vision; fantasy;
phantom, apparition; revelation;
(coll.) grotesque person, sight.—
visionario, *a.* & *n.* visionary.
visita, *f.* visit; call; visitor(s); visi-
tation, inspection.—*pagar una v.*, to
return or make a call.—*v. de cumplido* or *de cumplimiento*, formal
call.—**visitante**, *mf.* visitor; inspector.—**visitar**, *vt.* to visit; to call
on; to inspect, search, examine.—
vr. to visit one another, call on one
another.—**visiteo**, *m.* frequent visit-
ing or calling.
vislumbrar, *vt.* to glimpse, have a
glimmer of; to see imperfectly at
a distance; to know imperfectly;
to suspect, surmise.—**vislumbre**, *f.*
glimpse, glimmer; glimmering; conjecture, surmise; appearance, semblance.
viso, *m.* gloss, sheen (of fabric);
glass curtain; lady's slip.—*pl.*
aspect, appearance.
visón, *m.* mink.
víspera, *f.* eve, day before; fore-
runner; time just before.—*pl.*
vespers.
vista, *f.* sight, seeing, vision; view,
vista; eye, eyesight; glance, look;
aspect, looks; (law) trial.—*a la v.*,
at sight; in sight; before one's
eyes.—*a la v. de*, in the presence
of.—*a simple v.*, at first sight; with
the naked eye.—*estar a la v.*, to be
obvious.—*hacer la v. gorda*, to wink
at, overlook.—*hasta la v.*, good-by.
—*perder de v.*, to lose sight of.—
tener v. a, to face, look out on.—
v. cansada, farsightedness.—*m.* customs officer.—**vistazo**, *m.* glance.—
dar un v. a, to glance at, to look
over.—**visto**, *pp.* of VER.—*a.* obvious,
evident, clear; (law) whereas.—
bien v., proper or approved, good
form.—*mal v.*, improper or disap-
proved, bad form.—*v. bueno*
(*V°.B°.*), correct, approved, O.K.—*v.
que*, considering that, since.—**vistoso**,
a. showy; beautiful; flaring, loud.—
visual, *a.* visual; of sight.—*f.* line
of sight.
vital, *a.* vital; essential, necessary.—
vitalicio, *a.* lasting for life; during
life.—**vitalidad**, *f.* vitality.
vitamina, *f.* vitamin.
vitela, *f.* vellum, parchment.
vítor, *m.* cheer, applause.—*interj.*
hurrah!—**vitorear**, *vt.* to cheer,
acclaim.
vítreo, *a.* vitreous, glassy.—**vitrina**, *f.*
show case; (Am.) show window.
vitriolo, *m.* vitriol.

vituallas, *f. pl.* victuals, provisions, food.

viuda, *f.* widow.—**viudez,** *f.* widowhood.—**viudo,** *m.* widower.

vivac, vivaque, *m.* (mil.) bivouac; (Am.) police headquarters.

vivacidad, *f.* vivacity, liveliness; brilliance.—**vivaracho,** *a.* lively, frisky. —**vivaz,** *a.* lively, active; ingenious; bright, witty.

víveres, *m. pl.* provisions, foodstuffs.

vivero, *m.* hatchery; (bot.) nursery.

viveza, *f.* liveliness; vivacity; quickness; witticism; perspicacity.— **vívido,** *a.* vivid, bright.—**vivienda,** *f.* dwelling; housing; domicile.— **viviente,** *a.* living.—**vivificar,** *vti.* [d] to animate, enliven.—**vivir,** *vi.* to live, be alive; to last, endure. —*vt.* to live, experience; to dwell. —*¡viva!,* hurrah! long live!.— *¿quién vive?* (mil.) who goes there? —*m.* life, living, existence.—*mal v.,* riotous living.—**vivo,** *a.* alive, live; lively; intense; (of color) vivid; acute, ingenious; quick, bright, smart; lasting, enduring.—*a lo v., al v.,* vividly.—*de viva voz,* by word of mouth.—*en v.,* living, alive.— *tocar en lo v.,* to cut or hurt to the quick.—*m.* (sewing) edging, piping.

vizcaíno, *a. & n.* Biscayan, Basque.

vizconde, *m.* viscount.—**vizcondesa,** *f.* viscountess.

vocablo, *m.* word, term.—**vocabulario,** *m.* vocabulary, lexicon.

vocación, *f.* vocation, calling; occupation.

vocal, *a.* vocal, oral; (gram.) vowel. —*f.* vowel.—*mf.* voting member of a governing body.—**vocalizar,** *vii.* [a] to vocalize.

vocear, *vi.* to cry out, shout.—*vt.* to cry, publish, proclaim; to call, hail. —**vocería,** *f.,* **vocerío,** *m.* clamor, outcry, shouting.—**vocero,** *n.* spokesman (for another).—**vociferar,** *vi.* to vociferate, shout.—**vocinglero,** *a.* vociferous; prattling, chattering.— *n.* loud babbler.

volador, *a.* flying.—*m.* skyrocket.— **voladora,** *f.* flywheel of a steam engine.—**voladura,** *f.* blast, explosion; blasting.—**volante,** *a.* flying, fluttering, unsettled.—*m.* steering wheel; balance wheel; handbill, circular; ruffle, frill; escapement (of a watch).—**volar,** *vii.* [12] to fly; to flutter, hover (as insects); to run or move swiftly; to vanish, disappear; to make rapid progress; to explode, burst.—*vti.* to blow up; to blast.— **volátil,** *a.* volatile; fickle; mercurial. —**volatinero,** *n.* tightrope walker; acrobat.

volcán, *m.* volcano.—**volcánico,** *a.* volcanic.

velcar, vti. [12-d] to upset, overturn; to tilt.—*vri.* to overturn.

velición, *f.* volition.—**volitivo,** *a.* volitional.

volt, *m.* volt.—**voltaje,** *m.* voltage.

voltear, *vt.* to turn; to revolve; to overturn; (arch.) to arch; to vault. —*vi.* to turn; to revolve; to roll over; to tumble (as an acrobat).— *vr.* to turn over; to upset; (coll.) to change one's party or creed.— **volteo,** *m.* whirl; whirling; turn; turning; overturning; felling; tumbling.—**veltereta,** *f.* tumble, somersault.

veltio, *m.* volt.

volubilidad, *f.* volubility.—**voluble,** *a.* easily moved about; voluble; fickle; versatile.

velumen, *m.* tome; volume, size, bulk; corpulence.—**voluminoso,** *a.* voluminous; bulky.

veluntad, *f.* will; goodwill, benevolence; desire; disposition; consent. —*a v.,* optional, at will.—*de (buena) v.,* with pleasure, willingly.—*de mala v.,* unwillingly.—**voluntariedad,** *f.* voluntariness; willfulness.—**voluntario,** *a. & n.* voluntary; volunteer.— **voluntarioso,** *a.* willful, self-willed.

veluta, *f.* (arch.) volute; spiral.

volver, vti. [47] to turn; to turn up, over, upside down, inside out; to return; to repay; to give back, restore; to send back.—*v. loco,* to drive crazy.—*vii.* to return, come, or go back; to come again; to turn (to the right, etc.).—*v. a cantar,* to sing again.—*v. atrás,* to come, or go, back.—*v. en sí,* to recover consciousness, come to.—*v. por,* to stand up for, to defend.— *vri.* to turn, become; to turn about, turn around; to change one's views. —*v. atrás,* to flinch; to back out.— *v. loco,* to lose one's mind.

vemitar, vt. to vomit, puke.—**vomitivo,** *m. & a.* emetic.—**vómito,** *m.* vomiting; vomit.

verágine, *f.* vortex, whirlpool.

veraz, *a.* voracious, greedy; fierce (as fire).

vórtice, *m.* vortex, whirlpool, whirlwind; center of a cyclone.

vesotros, *pron. pl.* (*f.* **vesotras**) (fam.) you.

vetación, *f.* voting, vote, balloting.— **votar,** *vi. & vt.* to vote; to vow. —*¡voto a tal!* goodness!—**voto,** *m.* vote; vow; votive offering; oath, curse.—*hacer votos por,* to pray for; to wish.

vez, *f.* voice; sound; clamor, outcry;

word, term; rumor, report.—*a media v.*, in a whisper.—*a una v.*, unanimously.—*a v. en cuello*, at the top of one's voice.—*a voces*, clamorously.—*correr la v.*, to be said, to be rumored; to spread the rumor.—*dar voces*, to scream, shout. —*secreto a voces*, open secret.—*ser v. común*, to be a common rumor.

vuelco, *m.* tumble, overturning, upset.

vuelo, *m.* flight; flying; sweep, space flown through; fullness of clothes; ruffle or frill; (arch.) projection, jut.—*al v.*, on the fly; quickly, in a moment; in passing.—*alzar* or *levantar v.*, to fly; to take off, depart.—*tomar v.*, to progress; to grow.

vuelta, *f.* turn; revolution (of a wheel, etc.); turning; return; reverse side; returning, giving back; (money) change; stroll, walk.—*a la v.*, on returning; round the corner; (turn) over (the page); (bookkeeping) carried over, carried forward. —*a la v. de*, within (time).— *dar la v. a*, to turn; to go around. —*dar una v.*, to take a stroll.—*dar vueltas*, to turn; to walk to and fro; to fuss about; to hang around. —*de la v.*, brought forward.—*de v.*, on returning.—*estar de v.*, to be back; to be knowing.—*no tener v. de hoja*, to be self-evident.—*poner de v. y media*, (coll.) to give a dressing down, or a going over, to. —*vuelto*, *ppi.* of VOLVER.—*m.* (Am.) (money) change.

vuestro, *pron. & a.* (coll.) your, yours.

vulcanización, *f.* vulcanization; mending (a tire, etc.).—**vulcanizar**, *vti.* [a] to vulcanize; to mend (a tire, etc.).

vulgar, *a.* vulgar, coarse; common, in general use.—**vulgaridad**, *f.* vulgarity; triteness.—**vulgarización**, *f.* vulgarization.—**vulgarizar**, *vti.* [a] to vulgarize, popularize.—*vri.* to become vulgar.—**vulgo**, *m.* common people; populace.

vulnerable, *a.* vulnerable.—**vulnerar**, *vt.* to harm, injure, damage.

X

xilófono, *m.* xylophone.

Y

y, *conj.* and.—*¿y bien?* *¿y qué?* and then? so what?

ya, *adv.* already; now; at once; presently; in time; once, formerly. —*interj.* oh yes! I see.—*ya lo creo,*

naturally, of course.—*ya no*, no longer.— *ya que*, since, seeing that. —*ya se ve*, yes, indeed! it is clear, it is so.

yacaré, *m.* (Am.) alligator.

yacer, *vii.* [48] to lie in the grave; to lie, be located; to be lying down.— **yacimiento**, *m.* (geol.) bed; deposit, field.

yanqui, *n. & a.* American (of U.S.).

yarda, *f.* yard (measure).

yatagán, *m.* saber dagger.

yate, *m.* yacht.

yedra, *f.* = HIEDRA.

yegua, *f.* mare.—**yeguada**, *f.* herd of mares.

yelmo, *m.* helm, helmet.

yema, *f.* yolk (of an egg); bud; candied egg yolk; heart, center.— *dar en la y.*, to hit the nail on the head.—*y. del dedo*, fleshy tip of the finger.

yerba, *f.* = HIERBA.—**yerbabuena**, *f.* = HIERBABUENA.

yermo, *a.* barren, sterile.—*m.* wasteland, desert.

yerno, *m.* son-in-law.

yerro, *m.* error, mistake; fault.

yerto, *a.* stiff, motionless; rigid, tight.

yesca, *f.* tinder, touchwood, (fig.) fuel, incentive.—*pl.* tinderbox.

yeso, *m.* gypsum; plaster; plaster cast; chalk.

yo, *pron.* I.—*y. mismo*, I myself.— *m.* ego.

yodado, *a.* iodic.—**yodo**, *m.* iodine.

yugo, *m.* yoke; marriage tie.—*sacudir el y.*, to throw off the yoke.

yuguero, *m.* plowman.

yugular, *a.* jugular.

yunque, *m.* anvil; (anat.) incus.

yunta, *f.* couple, pair, yoke of draft animals.

yute, *m.* jute (fiber).

yuxtaponer, *vti.* [32-49] to juxtapose; to place next to each other.— **yuxtaposición**, *f.* juxtaposition.— **yuxtapuesto**, *ppi.* of YUXTAPONER.

Z

zafarrancho, *m.* turmoil, confusion.— *z. de combate*, (naut.) clearing for battle.

zafio, *a.* coarse, uncivil, ignorant, uncouth.

zafir(o), *m.* sapphire.

zafra, *f.* sugar crop; sugar making; sugar-making season.

zaga, *f.* rear, back.—*a la z.* or *en z.*, behind.—*no ir en z. a*, to be equal to.

zagal, *m.* shepherd boy; country lad. —**zagala**, *f.* shepherdess; lass, maiden.—**zagalón**, *n.* overgrown boy or girl.

zaguán, *m.* entrance hall, vestibule.

zaguero, *a.* laggard, loitering.—*m.* back-stop (at the game of pelota).

zaherir, *vti.* [39] to censure, blame, reproach, upbraid.

zahorí, *mf.* seer, clairvoyant.

zahurda, *f.* pigsty, hogsty.

zaino, *a.* chestnut-colored (horse); vicious (animal); treacherous, wicked.

zalamería, *f.* flattery, wheedling.—**zalamero**, *n.* flatterer.—*a.* flattering.—**zalema**, *f.* bow, curtsy.—*pl.* flattery.

zamarra, *f.* sheepskin jacket.

zambo, *a.* knock-kneed; half-breed (Indian and Negro).

zambullida, *f.* dive, plunge.—**zambullir**, *vti.* [27] to plunge, immerse; to give a ducking to.—*vri.* to plunge, dip, dive.

zambullo, *m.* chamber pot; toilet.

zampar, *vt.* to stuff away; to conceal hurriedly; to devour eagerly.—*vr.* to rush in; to thrust oneself in or into; to scoff; to devour.

zanahoria, *f.* (bot.) carrot.

zanca, *f.* long shank or leg; large pin.—**zancada**, *f.* long stride.—**zancadilla**, *f.* sudden catch to trip one; trick, deceit.—**zancajear**, *vi.* & *vt.* to run, rush about.—**zanco**, *m.* stilt.—**zancudo**, *a.* long-legged. —*m.* (Am.) mosquito.

zanfona, *f.* hurdy-gurdy.

zanganada, *f.* impertinence.—**zanganear**, *vi.* to idle.—**zángano**, *m.* drone; (coll.) idler, sponger; (Am.) rascal; wag.

zangolotear, *vi.* (coll.) to shake violently; to fuss, fidget.—*vr.* to rattle, swing or slam.—**zangoloteo**, *m.* fuss, bustle; swinging, rattling.

zanguango, *a.* (coll.) lazy, sluggish; silly.—*m.* dunce, fool.—*f.* (coll.) feigned illness, malingering; wheedling, fawning.

zanja, *f.* ditch, trench.—**zanjar**, *vt.* to cut ditches in; to excavate; to settle amicably; to obviate, surmount.—**zanjón**, *m.* deep ditch; large drain.

zapa, *f.* spade; (fort.) sap.—**zapador**, *m.* mining engineer; miner.—**zapapico**, *m.* pickaxe.—**zapar**, *vt.* (fort.) to sap, mine; (fig.) to undermine.

zapateado, *m.* tap dance.—**zapatear**, *vt.* to strike with the shoe.—*vi.* to tap-dance.—**zapatería**, *f.* trade of shoemaker; shoemaker's shop.—**zapatero**, *m.* shoemaker; shoe dealer.—**zapateta**, *f.* caper, leap.—

zapatilla, *f.* slipper, pump.—**zapato**, *m.* shoe.

zafado, *a.* (Am.) brazen, shameless; (Am.) alert, wide-awake; (Am.) crazy, crackbrained.—**zafar**, *vt.* to loosen, untie.—*vr.* to loosen oneself or itself; to run away; to keep out of the way; to dodge; to slip away. —*z. de*, to get rid of; to avoid.

zaquizamí, *m.* garret; small wretched room.

zarabanda, *f.* saraband; bustle, noise.

zaragata, *f.* turmoil; scuffle, quarrel.

zaranda, *f.* sieve, sifter.

zarandajas, *f. pl.* trifles, odds and ends.

zarandear, *vt.* to winnow; to sift; to shake (coll.) to stir and move nimbly.—*vr.* to be in motion; to move to and fro; to stalk, strut.—**zarandeo**, *m.* sifting or winnowing; shaking; stalking, strut.

zarcillo, *m.* eardrop.

zarco, *a.* light blue (of eyes).

zarpa, *f.* claw, paw of an animal.—*echar la z.*, to grasp, grip.—**zarpar**, *vi.* (naut.) to weigh anchor; to sail. —**zarpazo**, *m.* blow with a paw; bang, thud, whack.

zarrapastroso, *a.* ragged, slovenly, shabby.—*n.* ragamuffin.

zarza, *f.* bramble; blackberry bush.—**zarzal**, *m.* bramble thicket.—**zarzamora**, *f.* blackberry.—**zarzaparrilla**, *f.* sarsaparilla.

zarzuela, *f.* Spanish musical comedy.

zascandil, *m.* (coll.) busybody.

zinc, *m.* zinc.

zipizape, *m.* (coll.) row, rumpus, scuffle.

zócalo, *m.* base of a pedestal; baseboard.

zocato, *a.* (of fruits) overripe.

zoco, *m.* market; market place.

zodíaco, *m.* zodiac.

zoilo, *m.* malicious critic.

zona, *f.* zone, belt; district, area, region.

zonzo, *a.* dull.—*n.* (Am.) simpleton, dunce.

zoología, *f.* zoology.—**zoológico**, *a.* zoologic(al).

zopenco, *a.* (coll.) doltish, dull.—*n.* dolt, blockhead, fool.

zopilote, *m.* (Am.) buzzard.

zoquetada, *f.* foolishness, foolish words or acts.—**zoquete**, *m.* (carp.) chump, chunk; bit of stale bread; (coll.) dolt, dunce; (Am.) slap.

zorra, *f.* (zool.) fox; foxy person; truck.—**zorro**, *a.* cunning, foxy.—*n.* fox; foxy person.

zorzal, *m.* (ornith.) thrush.

zote, *a.* dull and ignorant.—*m.* dolt.

zozobra, *f.* worry, anxiety; (naut.) foundering, sinking.—**zozobrar,** *vi.* (naut.) to sink. founder; to capsize; to be in great danger.

zueco, *m.* sabot, wooden soled shoe.

zumba, *f.* mule bell; banter, raillery; sarcasm.—**zumbar,** *vi.* to buzz, hum; to whiz; (of the ears) to ring.—**zumbido,** *m.* humming, buzzing, whiz; ringing in the ears.—**zumbón,** *a.* waggish; sarcastic.—*n.* wag, joker.

zumo, *m.* sap, juice.

zuncho, *m.* metal band or hoop.

zurcido, *m.* (sewing) darning.—**zurcir,** *vti.* [a] to darn, mend; (coll.) to concoct (lies).

zurdo, *a.* left-handed.—*n.* left-handed person.

zurra, *f.* beating, thrashing.—**zurrar,** *vt.* to thrash, flog.

zurrapa, *f.* sediment, dregs; rubbish, trash.

zurrón, *m.* shepherd's pouch; game bag; leather bag.

Zutano, *n.* (coll.) Mr. So-and-So.— *Fulano, Z. y Mengano,* Tom, Dick and Harry.

GEOGRAPHICAL NAMES THAT DIFFER IN ENGLISH AND SPANISH

A

Abisinia, Abyssinia.
Adriático, Adriatic.
Afganistán, Afghanistan.
Alejandría, Alexandria.
Alemania, Germany.
Alpes, Alps.
Alsacia y Lorena, Alsace-Lorraine.
Alto Volta, Upper Volta.
Amazonas, Amazon.
Amberes, Antwerp.
América del Norte, North America.
América del Sur, South America.
América Española, Spanish America.
América Meridional, South America.
Andalucía, Andalusia.
Antillas, Antilles, West Indies.
Apeninos, Apennines.
Arabia Saudita, Saudi Arabia.
Aragón, Arragon.
Argel, Algiers.
Argelia, Algeria.
Argentina, Argentine.
Asia Menor, Asia Minor.
Asiria, Assyria.
Atenas, Athens.
Atlántico, Atlantic.

B

Babilonia, Babylon.
Baja California, Lower California.
Báltico, Baltic.
Basilea, Basel.
Baviera, Bavaria.
Belén, Bethlehem.
Bélgica, Belgium.
Belgrado, Belgrade.
Belice, Beliza, Belize; British Honduras.
Berbería, Barbary.
Berlín, Berlin.
Berna, Bern.
Birmania, Burma.
Bizancio, Byzantium.
Bolonia, Bologna.
Bona, Bonn.
Borgoña, Burgundy.
Bósforo, Bosporus.
Brasil, Brazil.
Bretaña, Bretagne, Brittany.

Bruselas, Brussels.
Bucarest, Bucharest.
Burdeos, Bordeaux.

C

Cabo de Buena Esperanza, Cape of Good Hope.
Cabo de Hornos, Cape Horn.
Cachemira, Kashmir.
Calcuta, Calcutta.
Caldea, Chaldea.
Cambrige, Cambridge.
Camerón, Cameroons.
Canadá, Canada.
Canal de la Mancha, English Channel.
Canarias, Canary (Islands).
Caribe, Caribbean.
Carolina del Norte, North Carolina.
Carolina del Sur, South Carolina.
Cartagena, Carthagena.
Cartago, Carthage.
Caspio, Caspian (Sea).
Castilla (la Nueva, la Vieja), Castile (New C., Old C.).
Cataluña, Catalonia.
Cáucaso, Caucasus.
Cayena, Cayenne.
Cayo Hueso, Key West.
Ceilán, Ceylon.
Cerdeña, Sardinia.
Colonia, Cologne.
Columbia Británica, British Columbia.
Constantinopla, Constantinople.
Copen(h)ague, Copenhagen.
Córcega, Corsica.
Córdoba, Cordova.
Corea, Korea.
Corinto, Corinth.
Costa del Marfil, Ivory Coast.
Costa de Oro, Gold Coast.
Creta, Crete.
Croacia, Croatia.
Curasao, Curazao, Curaçao.

CH

Champaña, Champagne.

Checoslovaquia, Czechoslovakia.
Chile, Chili, Chile.
Chipre, Cyprus.

D

Dakota del Norte, North Dakota.
Dakota del Sur, South Dakota.
Dalmacia, Dalmatia.
Damasco, Damascus.
Danubio, Danube.
Dardanelos, Dardanelles.
Delfos, Delphi.
Dinamarca, Denmark.
Dresde, Dresden.
Duero (Río), Douro (River).
Dunquerque, Dunkirk.
Duvres, Dover.

E

Edimburgo, Edinburgh.
Egeo, Ægean.
Egipto, Egypt.
Elba, Elbe.
Escandinavia, Scandinavia.
Escocia, Scotland.
Escorial, Escurial.
Eslavonia, Slavonia.
Eslovaquia, Slovakia.
Eslovenia, Slovenia.
Esmirna, Izmir, Smyrna.
España, Spain.
Española, Hispaniola; Santo Domingo, Haiti.
Esparta, Sparta.
Espoleto, Spoleto.
Estados Federados de Malaya, Malay Federated States.
Estados Unidos de América, United States of America.
Estambul, Istanbul.
Estocolmo, Stockholm.
Estonia, Esthonia.
Estrasburgo, Strasbourg.
Estrecho de Magallanes, Strait of Magellan.
Etiopía, Ethiopia.
Eufrates, Euphrates.
Europa, Europe.

F

Fenicia, Phoenicia.
Filadelfia, Philadelphia.
Filipinas, Philippines.

237

Finlandia, Finland.
Flandes, Flanders.
Florencia, Florence.
Francfort del Mein, Frankfort-on-the-Main.
Francia, France.

G

Gales, Wales.
Galia, Gaul.
Galilea, Galilee.
Gante, Ghent.
Gascuña, Gascony.
Génova, Genoa.
Ginebra, Geneva.
Golfo Pérsico, Persian Gulf.
Gran Bretaña, Great Britain.
Grecia, Greece.
Groenlandia, Greenland.
Guadalupe, Guadeloupe.
Guaján, Guam, Guam.
Guayana, Guiana.

H

Habana, Havana.
Haití, Haiti.
Hamburgo, Hamburg.
Hauai, Hawai, Hawaii.
Haya (La), Hague.
Hébridas, Hebrides.
Hispano-América, Hispanoamérica, Spanish America.
Holanda, Holland.
Honduras Británicas, British Honduras.
Hungría, Hungary.

I

Indias (Occidentales, Orientales), Indies (West I., East I.).
Indostán, Hindustan, India.
Inglaterra, England.
Irlanda, Ireland.
Isla de San Salvador, Watling Island.
Islandia, Iceland.
Islas Baleares, Balearic Islands.
Islas Británicas, British Isles.
Islas Filipinas, Philippine Islands.
Islas Vírgenes, Virgin Islands.
Italia, Italy.

J

Japón, Japan.
Jericó, Jericho.
Jerusalén, Jerusalem.
Jonia, Ionia.
Jutlandia, Jutland.

K

Kartum, Khartoum.
Kenia, Kenya.
Kurdistán, Kurdistan.

L

Laponia, Lapland.
Lasa, Lhasa.
Lausana, Lausanne.
Leningrado, Leningrad.
Letonia, Latvia.
Líbano, Lebanon.
Libia, Libya.
Lieja, Liége.
Liorna, Leghorn.
Lisboa, Lisbon.
Lituania, Lithuania.
Lombardía, Lombardy.
Londres, London.
Lorena, Lorraine.
Lucerna, Lucerne.
Luisiana, Louisiana.
Luxemburgo, Luxemburg.

M

Madera, Madeira.
Malaca, Malay.
Mallorca, Majorca.
Mar de las Indias, Indian Ocean.
Mar del Norte, North Sea.
Mar Muerto, Dead Sea.
Mar Negro, Black Sea.
Mar Rojo, Red Sea.
Marañón, (upper reaches of the) Amazon.
Marruecos, Morocco.
Marsella, Marseilles.
Martinica, Martinique.
Meca, Mecca.
Mediterráneo, Mediterranean.
Méjico, Mexico.
Menfis, Memphis.
Menorca, Minorca.
Misisipí, Mississippi.
Misuri, Missouri.
Mobila, Mobile.
Mompeller, Montpellier.
Montañas Rocosas (o Rocallosas), Rocky Mountains.
Montes Apalaches, Appalachian Mountains.
Moscú, Moscow.
Mosela, Moselle.

N

Nápoles, Naples.
Navarra, Navarre.
Nazaret, Nazareth.
Niasalandia, Nyasaland.
Nilo, Nile.
Niza, Nice.
Normandía, Normandy.
Noruega, Norway.
Nueva Escocia, Nova Scotia.
Nueva Gales del Sur, New South Wales.
Nueva Inglaterra, New England.
Nueva Orleáns, New Orleans.
Nueva York, New York.
Nueva Zelandia, New Zealand.

Nuevo Brúnswick (Brúnsvick), New Brunswick.
Nuevo México (or Méjico), New Mexico.
Nuremberga, Nuremberg.

O

Oceanía, Oceania, Oceanica.
Océano Índico, Indian Ocean.
Olimpo, Olympus.
Omán, Masqat.
Ostende, Ostend.

P

Pacífico, Pacific.
Países Bajos, Low Countries, Netherlands.
Palestina, Palestine.
Panamá, Panama.
París, Paris.
Parnaso, Parnassus.
Paso de Calais, English Channel.
Pekín, Peking.
Peloponeso, Peloponnesus.
Pensilvania, Pennsylvania.
Perú, Peru.
Pirineos, Pyrenees.
Polinesia, Polynesia.
Polonia, Poland.
Pompeya, Pompeii.
Praga, Prague.
Provenza, Provence.
Providencia, Providence.
Provincias Vascas (or Vascongadas), Basque Provinces.
Prusia, Prussia.
Puerto (de) España, Port of Spain.
Puerto Príncipe, Port-au-Prince.
Puerto Rico, Porto Rico, Puerto Rico.

R

Reino Unido, United Kingdom.
Renania, Rhineland.
Rhin, Rin, Rhine.
Rocallosas, Rocosas, Rocky (Mountains).
Ródano, Rhone.
Rodas, Rhodes.
Rodesia, Rhodesia.
Roma, Rome.
Ruán, Rouen.
Rusia, Russia.

S

Saboya, Savoy.
Sajonia, Saxony.
Sena, Seine.
Servia, Serbia.
Seúl, Seoul.
Sevilla, Seville.
Sicilia, Sicily.
Sierra Leona, Sierra Leone.

Sión, Zion.
Siracusa, Syracuse.
Siria, Syria.
Somalia, Somaliland.
Sud-África, Sudáfrica, South Africa.
Sud-América, Sudamérica, South America.
Sudán, Sudan.
Suecia, Sweden.
Suiza, Switzerland.
Sur-América, Suramérica, South America.

T
Tabago, Tobago.
Tahití, Tahiti.
Tajo, Tagus.
Támesis, Thames.
Tanganica, Tanganyika.
Tánger, Tangier.
Tebas, Thebes.
Tejas, Texas.
Terranova, Newfoundland.

Thailandia, Thailand.
Tierra del Labrador, Labrador.
Tierra Santa, Holy Land.
Tirol, Tyrol.
Tokío, Tokyo.
Tolosa, Toulouse.
Toscana, Tuscany.
Tracia, Thrace.
Trento, Trent.
Troya, Troy.
Túnez, Tunis (City), Tunisia (Country).
Turquestán, Turkestan.
Turquía, Turkey.

U
Ucrania, Ukraine.
Unión Soviética, Soviet Union.
Unión Sudafricana, Union of South Africa.
URSS (Unión de Repúblicas Socialistas Soviéticas), USSR (Union of Soviet Socialist Republics).

V
Varsovia, Warsaw.
Venecia, Venice.
Versalles, Versailles.
Vesuvio, Vesuvius.
Viena, Vienna.
Virginia Occidental, West Virginia.
Vizcaya, Biscay.

Y
Yugoeslavia, Yugoslavia, Jugoslavia.

Z
Zanzíbar, Zanzibar.
Zaragoza, Saragossa.
Zelandia, Zealand.
Zululandia, Zululand.

PROPER NAMES OF PERSONS, INCLUDING THOSE OF HISTORICAL, LITERARY, AND MYTHOLOGICAL PERSONAGES

(Only those which differ in English and Spanish are included)

A
Abelardo, Abelard.
Abrahán, Abraham.
Adán, Adam.
Adela, Adele.
Adelaida, Adelaide.
Adolfo, Adolf, Adolph.
Adriano, Hadrian.
Ágata, Águeda, Agatha.
Agustín, Augustine.
Alano, Allan, Allen.
Alberto, Albert.
Alejandro, Alexander.
Alfonso, Alphonso.
Alfredo, Alfred.
Alicia, Alice.
Alonso, Alphonso.
Ana, Ann(e), Anna, Hannah.
Andrés, Andrew.
Ángel, Angel.
Aníbal, Hannibal.
Antonio, Anthony.
Aquiles, Achilles.
Aristófanes, Aristophanes.
Aristóteles, Aristotle.
Arminio, Herman.
Arnaldo, Arnold.
Arquimedes, Archimedes.
Arturo, Arthur.

Atila, Attila.
Augusto, Augustus.

B
Baco, Bacchus.
Bartolomé, Bartholomew.
Basilio, Basil.
Beatricz, Beatrice.
Benita, Benedicta.
Benito, Benedicto.
Benjamín, Benjamin.
Bernardo, Bernard.
Berta, Bertha.
Bibiana, Vivian.
Bruto, Brutus.
Buda, Buddha.
Buenaventura, Bonaventura.

C
Calvino, Calvin.
Camila, Camille.
Camilo, Camillus.
Carlomagno, Charlemagne.
Carlos, Charles.
Carlota, Charlotte.
Carolina, Caroline, Carolyn.
Casandra, Cassandra.

Catalina, Catharine, Catherine, Katharine, Katherine.
Catón, Cato.
Catulo, Catullus.
Cecilia, Cecile.
Cenón, Zeno.
César, Caesar.
Cicerón, Cicero.
Ciro, Cyrus.
Claudio, Claude.
Clemente, Clement.
Clodoveo, Clovis.
Colón, Columbus.
Confucio, Confucius.
Constancia, Constance.
Constantino, Constantine.
Constanza, Constance.
Cristina, Christine.
Cristo, Christ.
Cristóbal, Christopher.

D
Dalila, Delilah.
Demóstenes, Demosthenes.
Diego, James.
Diógenes, Diogenes.
Dionisio, Dennis, Dionysius.

239

Domingo, Dominic.
Dorotea, Dorothy.

E

Edita, Edith.
Edmundo, Edmund.
Eduardo, Edward.
Elena, Ellen, Helen.
Elisa, Eliza.
Eloísa, Eloise.
Ema, Emma.
Emilia, Emily.
Emilio, Emil.
Eneas, Æneas.
Engracia, Grace.
Enrique, Henry.
Enriqueta, Henrietta.
Epicuro, Epicurus.
Erasmo, Erasmus.
Ernestina, Ernestine.
Ernesto, Ernest.
Escipión, Scipio.
Esopo, Æsop.
Esquilo, Æschylus.
Esteban, Stephen, Steven.
Ester, Esther, Hester.
Estrabón, Strabo.
Estradivario, Stradivarius.
Euclides, Euclid.
Eugenia, Eugénie.
Eugenio, Eugene.
Eva, Eve.
Ezequías, Hezekiah.
Ezequiel, Ezekiel.

F

Federica, Frederica.
Federico, Frederick.
Fedra, Phaedra.
Felicia, Felicia.
Felipa, Philippa.
Felipe, Filipo (de Macedonia), Philip.
Felisa, Felicia.
Fernando, Ferdinand.
Florencia, Florence.
Francisca, Frances.
Francisco, Francis.

G

Galeno, Galen.
Gaspar, Jasper.
Geofredo, Jeffrey, Geoffrey.
Gerarda, Geraldine.
Gerardo, Gerard, Gerald.
Gerónimo, Jerome.
Gertrudis, Gertrude.
Gilberto, Gilbert.
Godofredo, Godfrey.
Graco, Gracchus.
Gregorio, Gregory.
Gualterio, Walter.
Guillermina, Wilhelmina.
Guillermo, William.
Gustavo, Gustave, Gustavus.

H

Haroldo, Harold.
Heriberto, Herbert.
Herodes, Herod.

Herodoto, Herodotus.
Hipócrates, Hippocrates.
Hipólito, Hippolytus.
Homero, Homer.
Horacio, Horace, Horatio.
Hortensia, Hortense.
Huberto, Hubert.
Humberto, Humbert.
Hunfredo, Humphrey.

I

Ignacio, Ignatius.
Ildefonso, Alphonso.
Inés, Inez, Agnes.
Inocencio, Innocent.
Isabel, Isabella, Elizabeth.
Isidoro, Isidro, Isidor(e).

J

Jacobo, Jaime, James.
Javier, Xavier.
Jehová, Jehovah.
Jenofonte, Xenophon.
Jerjes, Xerxes.
Jerónimo, Jerome.
Jesucristo, Jesus Christ.
Joaquín, Joachim.
Jonás, Jonah.
Jonatán, Jonatás, Jonathan.
Jorge, George.
José, Joseph.
Josefa, Josefina, Josephine.
Juan, John.
Juana, Jane, Joan:
Juana de Arco, Joan of Arc.
Judit, Judith.
Julia, Juliet.
Julián, Juliano (el Emperador), Julian.
Julieta, Juliet.
Julio, Julius.
Justiniano, Justinian.

L

Lázaro, Lazarus.
Leandro, Leander.
Lenora, Lenore, Leonora.
León, Leo, Leon.
Leonardo, Leonard.
Leonor, Eleanor, Elinor.
Leopoldo, Leopold.
Licurgo, Lycurgus.
Livio, Livy.
Lorenzo, Laurence, Lawrence.
Lucano, Lucan.
Lucas, Luke.
Lucía, Lucy.
Luciano, Lucian.
Lucrecia, Lucretia.
Lucrecio, Lucretius.
Luis, Lewis, Louis, Aloysius.
Luisa, Louise.
Lutero, Luther.

M

Magallanes, Magellan.
Magdalena, Magdalen.

Mahoma, Mohammed, Mahomet.
Manuel, Em(m)anuel.
Manuela, Emma.
Marcial, Martial.
Marco, Marcos, Mark.
Margarita, Margaret, Marjorie, Daisy.
María, Mary, Miriam.
Mariana, Marian, Marion.
Marta, Martha.
Marte, Mars.
Mateo, Matthew.
Mauricio, Maurice, Morris.
Mercurio, Mercury.
Mesías, Messiah.
Miguel, Michael.
Miguel Angel, Michelangelo.
Moisés, Moses.

N

Nabucodonosor, Nebuchadnezzar.
Natán, Nathan.
Nataniel, Nathaniel.
Neptuno, Neptune.
Nerón, Nero.
Nicolás, Nicholas.
Noé, Noah.

O

Octavio, Octavius.
Oliverio, Oliver.
Orlando, Roland.
Otón, Otto.
Ovidio, Ovid.

P

Pablo, Paul.
Patricio, Patrick.
Paulina, Pauline.
Pedro, Peter.
Perseo, Perseus.
Pilatos, Pilate.
Píndaro, Pindar.
Pío, Pius.
Pitágoras, Pythagoras.
Platón, Plato.
Plauto, Plautus.
Plinio, Pliny.
Plutarco, Plutarch.
Pompeyo, Pompey.
Poncio, Pontius.
Prometeo, Prometheus.

Q

Quintiliano, Quintilian.
Quintín, Quentin.

R

Rafael, Raphael.
Raimundo, Raymond.
Ramón, Raymond.
Randolfo, Randolph.
Raquel, Rachel.
Rebeca, Rebecca.
Reinaldo, Reginald.
Renaldo, Ronald.
Renato, René.
Ricardo, Richard.

Roberto, Robert.
Rodolfo, Ralph, Rudolph.
Rodrigo, Roderick.
Rogelio, Rogerio, Roger.
Rolando, Roland.
Rómulo, Romulus.
Rosa, Rose.
Rosalía, Rosalie.
Rosario, Rosary.
Rubén, Reuben, Rubin.
Ruperto, Rupert.

S

Saladino, Saladin.
Salomé, Salome.
Salomón, Solomon.
Salustio, Sallust.
Sansón, Samson.
Santiago, James.
Sara, Sarah.
Satanás, Satan.
Saturno, Saturn.
Sila, Sulla.
Silvestre, Sylvester.
Sofía, Sophia.

Sófocles, Sophocles.
Solimán, Suleiman.
Suetonio, Suetonius.
Susana, Susan.

T

Tácito, Tacitus.
Tadeo, Thaddeus.
Tamerlán, Tamerlane.
Teócrito, Theocritus.
Teodoro, Theodore.
Teófilo, Theophilus.
Terencio, Terence.
Teresa, Theresa.
Tertuliano, Tertullian.
Tiberio, Tiberius.
Ticiano (el Ticiano), Titian.
Timoteo, Timothy.
Tito, Titus.
Tolomeo, Ptolemy.
Tomás, Thomas.
Trajano, Trajan.
Tristán, Tristram, Tristan.
Tucídides, Thucydides.

U

Ulises, Ulysses.
Urano, Uranus.
Urbano, Urban.
Urías, Uriah.

V

Valentina, Valentine.
Valeriano, Valerian.
Ventura, Bonaventura.
Veronés, Veronese.
Vespasiano, Vespasian.
Vespucio, Vespucci.
Vicente, Vincent.
Virgilio, Vergil, Virgil.

Y

Yugurta, Jugurtha.

Z

Zacarías, Zachary.
Zenón, Zeno.
Zoroastro, Zoroaster.
Zuinglio, Zwingli.

ABBREVIATIONS MOST COMMONLY USED IN SPANISH

A

a., área.
(a), alias.
@, arroba.
ab., abril.
A.C., antes de Cristo.
admón., administración.
admor., administrador.
afmo., afectísimo.
afto., afecto.
ag., agosto.
ap., aparte.
atto., atento.
Av., Avenida.

B

B.L.M., besa la mano.
bto., bulto; bruto.

C

c/, cargo; contra.
C.A., corriente alterna.
cap., capítulo.
C.C., corriente continua.
c. de., en casa de.
cg., centigramo(s).
Cía., Compañía.
cl., centilitro(s).
cm., centímetro(s).
Co., Compañía.
Const., Constitución.
corrte., corriente.
cta., cuenta.
cta. cte., cuenta corriente.

cts., céntimos.
c/u, cada uno.

D

D., don.
Da., doña.
D.C., después de Cristo.
dcha., derecha.
descto., descuento.
d/f, días fecha.
dg., decigramo(s).
Dg., decagramo(s).
dic., diciembre.
dl., decilitro(s).
Dl., decalitro(s).
dls., dólares ($).
dm., decímetro(s).
Dm., decámetro(s).
dna(s)., docena(s).
dom., domingo.
d/p, días plazo.
Dr., Doctor.
dup., duplicado.
d/v, días vista.

E

E., Este, oriente.
EE. UU., Estados Unidos.
E.M., Estado Mayor.
en., enero.
E.P.D., en paz descanse.
E.P.M., en propia mano.
etc., etcétera.
E.U., Estados Unidos.

E.U.A., Estados Unidos de América.
Exc., Excelencia.
Excmo., Excelentísimo.

F

f/, fardo(s).
fact., factura.
F.C., f.c., ferrocarril.
feb., febrero.
fol., folio.
Fr., Fray.
fra., fractura.

G

g., gramo(s).
gnte., gerente.
gob., gobierno.
gobr., gobernador.
gral., general.
gte., gerente.

H

hect., hectáreas.
Hg., hectogramo(s).
Hl., hectolitro(s).
Hm., hectómetro(s).
H.P., caballo(s) de fuerza.
id., ídem.
Ilmo., Ilustrísimo.
Ing., Ingeniero.
izda., izdo., izquierda, -do.

241

J

J.C., Jesucristo.
juev., jueves.
jul., julio.
jun., junio.

K

Kg., kg., kilogramo(s).
Kl., kl., kilolitro(s).
Km., km., kilómetro(s).
k.w., kilovatio.

L

L/, letra.
Ldo., Licenciado.
l., litro(s).
lb(s)., libra(s).
lun., lunes.

M

m., minuto(s); metro (s); mañana (A.M.).
M., Madre.
m/, mes; mi(s); mío(s).
Ma., María.
mar., marzo.
mart., martes.
m/f, mi favor.
mg., miligramo(s).
mierc., miércoles.
M/L, mi letra.
ml., mililitro(s).
mm., m/m, milímetro (s).
m/o, mi orden.
m/ o m/, más o menos.
Mons., Monseñor.

N

n., noche (P.M.)
N., Norte.
n/, nuestro.
Nª Sª, Nuestra Señora.
N.B., Nota bene.
n/cta., nuestra cuenta.
no., nro., número.
nov., noviembre.
N.S.J.C., Nuestro Señor Jesucristo.
nto., neto.

O

O., Oeste.

o/, orden.
ob., obpo., obispo.
oct., octubre.
O.E.A., Organización de Estados Americanos.
O.N.U., Organización de las Naciones Unidas.
onz., onza.
orn., orden.

P

P., Padre; pregunta.
pág., págs., página(s).
Part., Partida.
P.D., Posdata.
p.ej., por ejemplo.
P.O., por orden.
P.P., Porte pagado; por poder.
ppdo., próximo pasado.
pral., principal.
prof., profesor.
prov., provincia.
próx., próximo.
ps., pesos.
ptas., pesetas.
pte., parte.
pza., pieza.

Q

4., que.
Q.B.S.M., que besa su mano.
Q.D.G., que Dios guarde.
q.e.g.e., que en gloria esté.
q.e.p.d., que en paz descanse.
q.e.s.m., que estrecha su mano.
qq., quintales.

R

R., Reverendo.
Rbí., Recibí.
Rda. M., Reverenda Madre.
Rdo. P., Reverendo Padre.
R.I.P., Requiescat in pace.
r.p.m., revoluciones por minuto.

rust., rústica.

S

S., San(to); Sur.
s/, su(s); sobre.
sáb., sábado.
S.A.R., Su Alteza Real.
S.C., s.c., su casa.
s/c, su cuenta.
s/cta., su cuenta.
sept., septiembre.
set., septiembre.
S.E. u O., salvo error u omisión.
S.M., Su Majestad.
S.N., Servicio Nacional.
Sr., Señor.
Sra(s)., Señora(s).
Sres., Señores.
Sría., Secretaría.
Srta., Señorita.
S.S., Su Santidad.
S.S.S., s.s.s., Su seguro servidor.
Sta., Santa; Señorita.
Sto., Santo.

T

t., tarde
tít., título.
tpo., tiempo.
trib., tribunal.
tom., tomo.

U

U., Ud., usted.
Uds., UU., ustedes.

V

V., usted; venerable; véase.
Vers., Versículo.
Vd., usted.
Vds., ustedes.
V.E., Vuestra Excelencia.
vg., verbigracia.
v.gr., verbigracia.
vier., viernes.
Vto. Bno., Visto Bueno.
Vol., volumen; voluntad.
vols., volúmenes.
vta., vto., vuelta, vuelto.